Haynes

THE BOOK ®

Peugeot 307
Service and Repair Manual

Martynn Randall

Models covered

(4147 - 6AN1 - 384)

Petrol: 1.4 litre SOHC & DOHC (1360cc), 1.6 litre (1587cc) & 2.0 litre (1997cc)
Turbo-Diesel: 1.4 litre SOHC (1398cc), 1.6 litre DOHC (1560cc) & 2.0 litre SOHC & DOHC (1997cc)

Does NOT cover 307CC, Coupe models or 180bhp 2.0 litre petrol engine

© Haynes Publishing 2009

ABCDE
FGHIJ
KLMNO

A book in the **Haynes Service and Repair Manual Series**

ISBN **978 1 84425 800 0**

British Library Cataloguing in Publication Data
A catalogue record for this book is available from the British Library.

Printed in the USA

Haynes Publishing
Sparkford, Yeovil, Somerset BA22 7JJ, England

Haynes North America, Inc
861 Lawrence Drive, Newbury Park, California 91320, USA

Haynes Publishing Nordiska AB
Box 1504, 751 45 UPPSALA, Sverige

Contents

LIVING WITH YOUR PEUGEOT 307

MAINTENANCE

Routine maintenance and servicing

Contents

REPAIRS & OVERHAUL

Engine and associated systems

Transmission

Brakes and suspension

Body equipment

Wiring diagrams

REFERENCE

Index

The Peugeot 307 was introduced into the UK in early 2001. At its launch, the 307 was offered with a choice of 1.4 (1360cc), 1.6 (1587cc) and 2.0 litre (1997cc) petrol engines or 1.4 litre (1398cc), 1.6 litre (1560cc) and 2.0 litre (1997cc) turbo-diesel engines. It was available in two body styles – a 3/5-door Hatchback, or a 5-door Estate. In March 2002 the SW (Sports Wagon) model was released, with three rows of passenger seats, and a full-length glass panel roof as the main distinguishing features.

The engines fitted to the 307 range are all versions of the well-proven units which have appeared in many Peugeot/Citroën vehicles over the years, with the exception of the 1.4 and 1.6 litre HDI engine, newly developed in a joint venture with the Ford Motor Co.

The engine is mounted transversely at the front of vehicle, with the transmission mounted on its left-hand end. All engines are fitted with a manual transmission as standard (an automatic transmission is available on certain engines).

All models have fully-independent front suspension, incorporating shock absorbers, coil springs and an anti-roll bar. The rear beam axle has a built-in anti-roll bar, with separate shock absorbers and coil spring.

A wide range of standard and optional equipment is available within the range to suit most tastes, including central locking, electric windows and front, side and curtain airbags. An air conditioning system is available on all models.

Provided that regular servicing is carried out in accordance with the manufacturer's recommendations, the vehicle should prove reliable and very economical. The engine

compartment is well-designed, and most of the items requiring frequent attention are easily accessible.

Your Peugeot 307 manual

The aim of this manual is to help you get the best value from your vehicle. It can do so in several ways. It can help you decide what work must be done (even should you choose to get it done by a garage). It will also provide information on routine maintenance and servicing, and give a logical course of action and diagnosis when random faults occur. However, it is hoped that you will use the manual by tackling the work yourself. On

simpler jobs it may even be quicker than booking the car into a garage and going there twice, to leave and collect it. Perhaps most important, a lot of money can be saved by avoiding the costs a garage must charge to cover its labour and overheads.

The manual has drawings and descriptions to show the function of the various components so that their layout can be understood. Tasks are described and photographed in a clear step-by-step sequence.

References to the 'left' and 'right' of the vehicle are in the sense of a person in the driver's seat facing forward.

Acknowledgements

Thanks are due to Draper tools Limited, who provided some of the workshop tools, and to all those people at Sparkford who helped in the production of this manual.

We take great pride in the accuracy of information given in this manual, but vehicle manufacturers make alterations and design changes during the production run of a particular vehicle of which they do not inform us. No liability can be accepted by the authors or publishers for loss, damage or injury caused by any errors in, or omissions from, the information given.

Working on your car can be dangerous. This page shows just some of the potential risks and hazards, with the aim of creating a safety-conscious attitude.

General hazards

Scalding

• Don't remove the radiator or expansion tank cap while the engine is hot.
• Engine oil, automatic transmission fluid or power steering fluid may also be dangerously hot if the engine has recently been running.

Burning

• Beware of burns from the exhaust system and from any part of the engine. Brake discs and drums can also be extremely hot immediately after use.

Crushing

• When working under or near a raised vehicle, always supplement the jack with axle stands, or use drive-on ramps. *Never venture under a car which is only supported by a jack.*
• Take care if loosening or tightening high-torque nuts when the vehicle is on stands. Initial loosening and final tightening should be done with the wheels on the ground.

Fire

• Fuel is highly flammable; fuel vapour is explosive.
• Don't let fuel spill onto a hot engine.
• Do not smoke or allow naked lights (including pilot lights) anywhere near a vehicle being worked on. Also beware of creating sparks (electrically or by use of tools).
• Fuel vapour is heavier than air, so don't work on the fuel system with the vehicle over an inspection pit.
• Another cause of fire is an electrical overload or short-circuit. Take care when repairing or modifying the vehicle wiring.
• Keep a fire extinguisher handy, of a type suitable for use on fuel and electrical fires.

Electric shock

• Ignition HT voltage can be dangerous, especially to people with heart problems or a pacemaker. Don't work on or near the ignition system with the engine running or the ignition switched on.

• Mains voltage is also dangerous. Make sure that any mains-operated equipment is correctly earthed. Mains power points should be protected by a residual current device (RCD) circuit breaker.

Fume or gas intoxication

• Exhaust fumes are poisonous; they often contain carbon monoxide, which is rapidly fatal if inhaled. Never run the engine in a confined space such as a garage with the doors shut.
• Fuel vapour is also poisonous, as are the vapours from some cleaning solvents and paint thinners.

Poisonous or irritant substances

• Avoid skin contact with battery acid and with any fuel, fluid or lubricant, especially antifreeze, brake hydraulic fluid and Diesel fuel. Don't syphon them by mouth. If such a substance is swallowed or gets into the eyes, seek medical advice.
• Prolonged contact with used engine oil can cause skin cancer. Wear gloves or use a barrier cream if necessary. Change out of oil-soaked clothes and do not keep oily rags in your pocket.
• Air conditioning refrigerant forms a poisonous gas if exposed to a naked flame (including a cigarette). It can also cause skin burns on contact.

Asbestos

• Asbestos dust can cause cancer if inhaled or swallowed. Asbestos may be found in gaskets and in brake and clutch linings. When dealing with such components it is safest to assume that they contain asbestos.

Special hazards

Hydrofluoric acid

• This extremely corrosive acid is formed when certain types of synthetic rubber, found in some O-rings, oil seals, fuel hoses etc, are exposed to temperatures above 400ºC. The rubber changes into a charred or sticky substance containing the acid. *Once formed, the acid remains dangerous for years. If it gets onto the skin, it may be necessary to amputate the limb concerned.*
• When dealing with a vehicle which has suffered a fire, or with components salvaged from such a vehicle, wear protective gloves and discard them after use.

The battery

• Batteries contain sulphuric acid, which attacks clothing, eyes and skin. Take care when topping-up or carrying the battery.
• The hydrogen gas given off by the battery is highly explosive. Never cause a spark or allow a naked light nearby. Be careful when connecting and disconnecting battery chargers or jump leads.

Air bags

• Air bags can cause injury if they go off accidentally. Take care when removing the steering wheel and/or facia. Special storage instructions may apply.

Diesel injection equipment

• Diesel injection pumps supply fuel at very high pressure. Take care when working on the fuel injectors and fuel pipes.

⚠️ *Warning: Never expose the hands, face or any other part of the body to injector spray; the fuel can penetrate the skin with potentially fatal results.*

Remember...

DO

• Do use eye protection when using power tools, and when working under the vehicle.

• Do wear gloves or use barrier cream to protect your hands when necessary.

• Do get someone to check periodically that all is well when working alone on the vehicle.

• Do keep loose clothing and long hair well out of the way of moving mechanical parts.

• Do remove rings, wristwatch etc, before working on the vehicle – especially the electrical system.

• Do ensure that any lifting or jacking equipment has a safe working load rating adequate for the job.

DON'T

• Don't attempt to lift a heavy component which may be beyond your capability – get assistance.

• Don't rush to finish a job, or take unverified short cuts.

• Don't use ill-fitting tools which may slip and cause injury.

• Don't leave tools or parts lying around where someone can trip over them. Mop up oil and fuel spills at once.

• Don't allow children or pets to play in or near a vehicle being worked on.

The following pages are intended to help in dealing with common roadside emergencies and breakdowns. You will find more detailed fault finding information at the back of the manual, and repair information in the main chapters.

If your car won't start and the starter motor doesn't turn

- [ ] If it's a model with automatic transmission, make sure the selector is in the P or N position.
- [ ] Open the bonnet and make sure that the battery terminals are clean and tight.
- [ ] Switch on the headlights and try to start the engine. If the headlights go very dim when you're trying to start, the battery is probably flat. Try jump starting (see next page) using another car.

If your car won't start even though the starter motor turns as normal

- [ ] Is there fuel in the tank?
- [ ] Is there moisture on electrical components under the bonnet? Switch off the ignition, then wipe off any obvious dampness with a dry cloth. Spray a water-repellent aerosol product (WD-40 or equivalent) on ignition and fuel system electrical connectors like those shown in the photos. Pay special attention to the ignition coils wiring connector. (Note that diesel engines don't normally suffer from damp.)

A Remove the plastic cover and check the condition and security of the battery connections.

B Check that the fuel/ignition system (as applicable) wiring connectors are securely connected (1.6 litre petrol model shown).

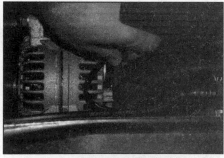

C Check that the alternator wiring connectors are securely connected.

Check that electrical connections are secure (with the ignition switched off) and spray them with a water dispersant spray like WD-40 if you suspect a problem due to damp.

D Check that all fuses are still in good condition and none have blown.

Jump starting

When jump-starting a car using a booster battery, observe the following precautions:

✔ Before connecting the booster battery, make sure that the ignition is switched off.

✔ Ensure that all electrical equipment (lights, heater, wipers, etc) is switched off.

✔ Take note of any special precautions printed on the battery case.

✔ Make sure that the booster battery is the same voltage as the discharged one in the vehicle.

✔ If the battery is being jump-started from the battery in another vehicle, the two vehicles MUST NOT TOUCH each other.

✔ Make sure that the transmission is in neutral (or PARK, in the case of automatic transmission).

 HAYNES HiNT *Jump starting will get you out of trouble, but you must correct whatever made the battery go flat in the first place. There are three possibilities:*

1 The battery has been drained by repeated attempts to start, or by leaving the lights on.

2 The charging system is not working properly (alternator drivebelt slack or broken, alternator wiring fault or alternator itself faulty).

3 The battery itself is at fault (electrolyte low, or battery worn out).

1 Connect one end of the red jump lead to the positive (+) terminal of the flat battery

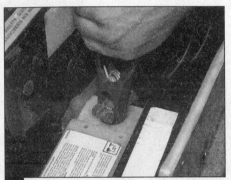

2 Connect the other end of the red lead to the positive (+) terminal of the booster battery.

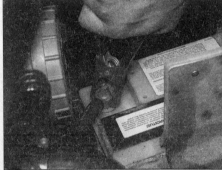

3 Connect one end of the black jump lead to the negative (-) terminal of the booster battery

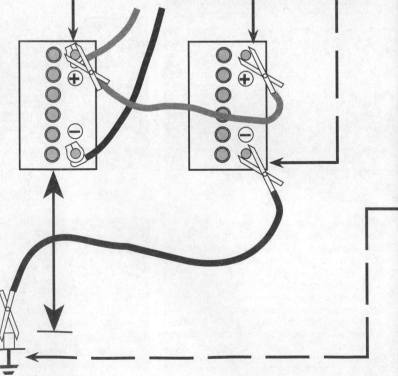

4 Connect the other end of the black jump lead to a bolt or bracket on the engine block, well away from the battery, on the vehicle to be started.

5 Make sure that the jump leads will not come into contact with the fan, drive-belts or other moving parts of the engine.

6 Start the engine using the booster battery and run it at idle speed. Switch on the lights, rear window demister and heater blower motor, then disconnect the jump leads in the reverse order of connection. Turn off the lights etc.

Identifying leaks

Puddles on the garage floor or drive, or obvious wetness under the bonnet or underneath the car, suggest a leak that needs investigating. It can sometimes be difficult to decide where the leak is coming from, especially if the engine bay is very dirty already. Leaking oil or fluid can also be blown rearwards by the passage of air under the car, giving a false impression of where the problem lies.

 Warning: Most automotive oils and fluids are poisonous. Wash them off skin, and change out of contaminated clothing, without delay.

HAYNES HINT *The smell of a fluid leaking from the car may provide a clue to what's leaking. Some fluids are distinctively coloured. It may help to clean the car carefully and to park it over some clean paper overnight as an aid to locating the source of the leak. Remember that some leaks may only occur while the engine is running.*

Sump oil

Engine oil may leak from the drain plug...

Oil from filter
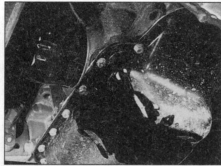
...or from the base of the oil filter.

Gearbox oil
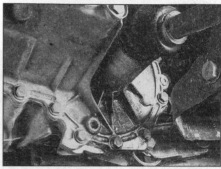
Gearbox oil can leak from the seals at the inboard ends of the driveshafts.

Antifreeze

Leaking antifreeze often leaves a crystalline deposit like this.

Brake fluid

A leak occurring at a wheel is almost certainly brake fluid.

Power steering fluid
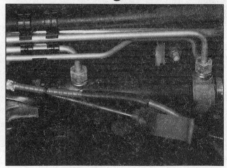
Power steering fluid may leak from the pipe connectors on the steering rack.

Towing

When all else fails, you may find yourself having to get a tow home – or of course you may be helping somebody else. Long-distance recovery should only be done by a garage or breakdown service. For shorter distances, DIY towing using another car is easy enough, but observe the following points:

☐ Use a proper tow-rope – they are not expensive. The vehicle being towed must display an ON TOW sign in its rear window.
☐ Always turn the ignition key to the 'on' position when the vehicle is being towed, so that the steering lock is released, and that the direction indicator and brake lights work.

☐ The towing eye is kept inside the spare wheel (see *Wheel changing*) on Hatchback models, and behind the right-hand side luggage compartment trim panel on Estates. To fit the eye, unclip the access cover from the relevant bumper and screw the eye firmly into position.
☐ Before being towed, release the handbrake and select neutral on the transmission.
Caution: On models with automatic transmission, do not tow the car at speeds in excess of 30 mph (50 kph) or for a distance greater than 30 miles (50 km). If towing speeds/distances are to exceed these limits, then the car must be towed with its front wheels off the ground.

☐ Note that greater-than-usual pedal pressure will be required to operate the brakes, since the vacuum servo unit is only operational with the engine running.
☐ The driver of the car being towed must keep the tow-rope taut at all times to avoid snatching.
☐ Make sure that both drivers know the route before setting off.
☐ Only drive at moderate speeds and keep the distance towed to a minimum. Drive smoothly and allow plenty of time for slowing down at junctions.

Wheel changing

 Warning: Do not change a wheel in a situation where you risk being hit by another vehicle. On busy roads, try to stop in a lay-by or a gateway. Be wary of passing traffic while changing the wheel - it is easy to become distracted by the job in hand.

Preparation

☐ When a puncture occurs, stop as soon as it is safe to do so.
☐ Park on firm level ground, if possible, and well out of the way of other traffic.
☐ Use hazard warning lights if necessary.

☐ If you have one, use a warning triangle to alert other drivers of your presence.
☐ Apply the handbrake and engage first or reverse gear (or Park on models with automatic transmission).

☐ If the ground is soft, use a flat piece of wood to spread the load under the foot of the jack.

Changing the wheel

1 The spare wheel and tools are stored in the luggage compartment on Hatchback models. Lift up the carpet/rear family seat (as applicable), release the retaining strap and remove the tool kit and jack from the centre of the spare wheel. Remove the spare wheel.

2 On Estate models, the spare wheel and some tools are stored beneath the rear of the vehicle, whilst the remaining tools are stored behind the right-hand plastic trim in the luggage compartment. Pull up the cover in the luggage compartment floor, swivel the cover around and, using the tool supplied in the tool kit behind the plastic trim, rotate the winch bolt anti-clockwise to lower the spare wheel and jack/tool box.

3 Remove the wheel trim/hub cap (as applicable).

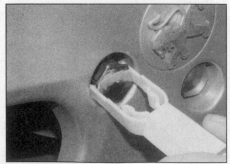

4 On models where anti-theft wheel bolts are fitted, pull off the plastic cover using the yellow plastic tool in the tool kit . . .

5 . . . then unscrew the anti-theft bolt using the special tool provided – normally stored in the passenger glovebox or toolkit.

6 Place the chock (arrowed) provided in the vehicle tool kit against the wheel diagonally opposite the wheel to be removed, or use a stone to stop the car rolling.

7 Using the tool provided, slacken each wheel bolt by half a turn. On models with alloy wheels, use the special tool to undo the locking wheel nuts.

8 Make sure the jack is located on firm ground, and engage the jack head correctly with the sill. Then raise the jack until the wheel is raised clear of the ground.

9 Unscrew the wheel bolts and remove the wheel. Place the wheel under the vehicle sill in case the jack fails. Fit the spare wheel and screw in the bolts. Lightly tighten the bolts with the wheelbrace then lower the car to the ground.

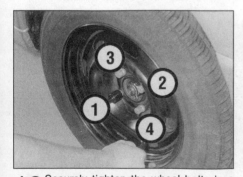

10 Securely tighten the wheel bolts in a diagonal sequence then refit the wheel trim/hub cap/wheel bolt covers (as applicable). Stow the punctured wheel and tools back in the boot, and secure them in position (Hatchback models) . . .

11 . . . on Estate models feed the winch cable through the wheel, locate the cable end in the lid of the tool/jack box, and use the brace to retract the winch cable.

Finally...

☐ Remove the wheel chock.

☐ Check the tyre pressure on the wheel just fitted. If it is low, or if you don't have a pressure gauge with you, drive slowly to the next garage and inflate the tyre to the correct pressure.

☐ The wheel bolts should be slackened and retightened to the specified torque at the earliest possible opportunity (see Chapter 1A or 1B).

☐ Have the damaged tyre or wheel repaired as soon as possible, or another puncture will leave you stranded.

Introduction

There are some very simple checks which need only take a few minutes to carry out, but which could save you a lot of inconvenience and expense.

These *Weekly checks* require no great skill or special tools, and the small amount of time they take to perform could prove to be very well spent, for example;

☐ Keeping an eye on tyre condition and pressures, will not only help to stop them wearing out prematurely, but could also save your life.

☐ Many breakdowns are caused by electrical problems. Battery-related faults are particularly common, and a quick check on a regular basis will often prevent the majority of these.

☐ If your car develops a brake fluid leak, the first time you might know about it is when your brakes don't work properly. Checking the level regularly will give advance warning of this kind of problem.

☐ If the oil or coolant levels run low, the cost of repairing any engine damage will be far greater than fixing the leak, for example.

Underbonnet check points

◀ 1.6 litre petrol (1.4 and 2.0 similar)

A *Engine oil level dipstick*

B *Engine oil filler cap*

C *Coolant expansion tank*

D *Brake (and clutch) fluid reservoir*

E *Screen washer fluid reservoir*

F *Power steering fluid reservoir*

G *Battery*

◀ 1.4 litre diesel (1.6 and 2.0 similar)

A *Engine oil level dipstick*

B *Engine oil filler cap*

C *Coolant expansion tank*

D *Brake (and clutch) fluid reservoir*

E *Screen washer fluid reservoir*

F *Power steering fluid reservoir*

G *Battery*

Engine oil level

Before you start

✔ Make sure that your car is on level ground.
✔ Check the oil level before the car is driven, or at least 5 minutes after the engine has been switched off.

HAYNES HiNT *If the oil is checked immediately after driving the vehicle, some of the oil will remain in the upper engine components, resulting in an inaccurate reading on the dipstick.*

The correct oil

Modern engines place great demands on their oil. It is very important that the correct oil for your car is used (See *'Lubricants and fluids'*).

Car Care

● If you have to add oil frequently, you should check whether you have any oil leaks. Place some clean paper under the car overnight, and check for stains in the morning. If there are no leaks, the engine may be burning oil.

● Always maintain the level between the upper and lower dipstick marks (see photo 3). If the level is too low severe engine damage may occur. Oil seal failure may result if the engine is overfilled by adding too much oil.

1 The dipstick is located at the front of the engine (see *Underbonnet check points* on page 0•12); The dipstick is often brightly-coloured or has a picture of an oil can on the top for identification. Withdraw the dipstick.

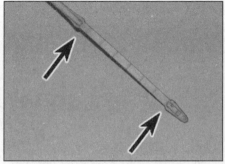

3 Note the oil level on the end of the dipstick, which should be between the upper (MAX) mark and lower (MIN) mark. Approximately 1.0 litre of oil will raise the level from the lower mark to the upper mark.

2 Using a clean rag or paper towel remove all oil from the dipstick. Insert the clean dipstick into the tube as far as it will go, then withdraw it again.

4 Oil is added through the filler cap. Unscrew the cap and top-up the level; a funnel may help to reduce spillage. Add the oil slowly, checking the level on the dipstick often. Don't overfill (see *Car care*).

Coolant level

Warning:
DO NOT attempt to remove the expansion tank pressure cap when the engine is hot, as there is a very great risk of scalding. Do not leave open containers of coolant about, as it is poisonous.

Car Care

● Adding coolant should not be necessary on a regular basis. If frequent topping-up is required, it is likely there is a leak. Check the radiator, all hoses and joint faces for signs of staining or wetness, and rectify as necessary.

● It is important that antifreeze is used in the cooling system all year round, not just during the winter months. Don't top-up with water alone, as the antifreeze will become too diluted.

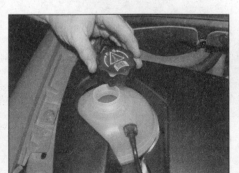

1 The coolant level must be checked with the engine cold. Remove the pressure cap (see *Warning*) from the expansion tank which is located on the right-hand side of the engine compartment.

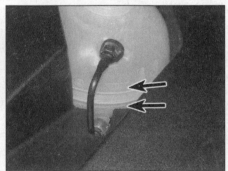

2 The coolant level should be between the MAX and MIN marks on the expansion tank.

3 If topping-up is necessary, add a mixture of water and antifreeze to the expansion tank until the coolant level is between the level marks. Once the level is correct, securely refit the cap.

Tyre condition and pressure

It is very important that tyres are in good condition, and at the correct pressure - having a tyre failure at any speed is highly dangerous. Tyre wear is influenced by driving style - harsh braking and acceleration, or fast cornering, will all produce more rapid tyre wear. As a general rule, the front tyres wear out faster than the rears. Interchanging the tyres from front to rear ("rotating" the tyres) may result in more even wear. However, if this is completely effective, you may have the expense of replacing all four tyres at once!

Remove any nails or stones embedded in the tread before they penetrate the tyre to cause deflation. If removal of a nail does reveal that the tyre has been punctured, refit the nail so that its point of penetration is marked. Then immediately change the wheel, and have the tyre repaired by a tyre dealer.

Regularly check the tyres for damage in the form of cuts or bulges, especially in the sidewalls. Periodically remove the wheels, and clean any dirt or mud from the inside and outside surfaces. Examine the wheel rims for signs of rusting, corrosion or other damage. Light alloy wheels are easily damaged by "kerbing" whilst parking; steel wheels may also become dented or buckled. A new wheel is very often the only way to overcome severe damage.

New tyres should be balanced when they are fitted, but it may become necessary to re-balance them as they wear, or if the balance weights fitted to the wheel rim should fall off. Unbalanced tyres will wear more quickly, as will the steering and suspension components. Wheel imbalance is normally signified by vibration, particularly at a certain speed (typically around 50 mph). If this vibration is felt only through the steering, then it is likely that just the front wheels need balancing. If, however, the vibration is felt through the whole car, the rear wheels could be out of balance. Wheel balancing should be carried out by a tyre dealer or garage.

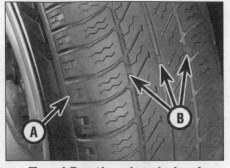

1 Tread Depth - visual check
The original tyres have tread wear safety bands (B), which will appear when the tread depth reaches approximately 1.6 mm. The band positions are indicated by a triangular mark on the tyre sidewall (A).

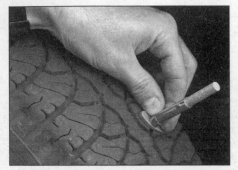

2 Tread Depth - manual check
Alternatively, tread wear can be monitored with a simple, inexpensive device known as a tread depth indicator gauge.

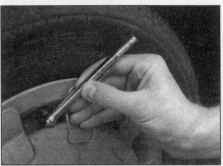

3 Tyre Pressure Check
Check the tyre pressures regularly with the tyres cold. Do not adjust the tyre pressures immediately after the vehicle has been used, or an inaccurate setting will result.

Tyre tread wear patterns

Shoulder Wear

Underinflation (wear on both sides)
Under-inflation will cause overheating of the tyre, because the tyre will flex too much, and the tread will not sit correctly on the road surface. This will cause a loss of grip and excessive wear, not to mention the danger of sudden tyre failure due to heat build-up.
Check and adjust pressures
Incorrect wheel camber (wear on one side)
Repair or renew suspension parts
Hard cornering
Reduce speed!

Centre Wear

Overinflation
Over-inflation will cause rapid wear of the centre part of the tyre tread, coupled with reduced grip, harsher ride, and the danger of shock damage occurring in the tyre casing.
Check and adjust pressures

If you sometimes have to inflate your car's tyres to the higher pressures specified for maximum load or sustained high speed, don't forget to reduce the pressures to normal afterwards.

Uneven Wear

Front tyres may wear unevenly as a result of wheel misalignment. Most tyre dealers and garages can check and adjust the wheel alignment (or "tracking") for a modest charge.
Incorrect camber or castor
Repair or renew suspension parts
Malfunctioning suspension
Repair or renew suspension parts
Unbalanced wheel
Balance tyres
Incorrect toe setting
Adjust front wheel alignment
Note: *The feathered edge of the tread which typifies toe wear is best checked by feel.*

Brake and clutch fluid level

Warning:
- Brake fluid can harm your eyes and damage painted surfaces, so use extreme caution when handling and pouring it.
- Do not use fluid that has been standing open for some time, as it absorbs moisture from the air, which can cause a dangerous loss of braking effectiveness.

HAYNES HiNT *The fluid level in the reservoir will drop slightly as the brake pads wear down, but the fluid level must never be allowed to drop below the MIN mark.*

Before you start

✔ Make sure that your car is on level ground.

Safety First!

- If the reservoir requires repeated topping-up this is an indication of a fluid leak somewhere in the system, which should be investigated immediately.

- If a leak is suspected, the car should not be driven until the braking system has been checked. Never take any risks where brakes are concerned.

1 The upper (MAX) fluid level marking is on the side of the reservoir, which is located in the left-hand rear corner of the engine compartment.

2 If topping-up is necessary, first wipe clean the area around the filler cap with a clean cloth, then unscrew the cap and remove it along with the rubber diaphragm.

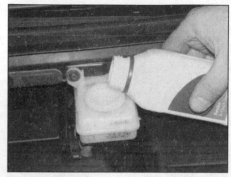

3 Carefully add fluid, avoiding spilling it on the surrounding paintwork. Use only the specified hydraulic fluid. After filling to the correct level, refit the cap and diaphragm and tighten it securely. Wipe off any spilt fluid.

Power steering fluid level

Before you start

✔ Park the vehicle on level ground.
✔ Set the steering wheel straight ahead.
✔ The engine should be at ambient temperature and turned off.

Safety First!

- The need for frequent topping-up indicates a leak, which should be investigated immediately.

1 The fluid reservoir is on the right-hand side of the engine compartment. Push down the centre pins a little, prise out the complete plastic expanding rivets, release the side clip, and remove the plastic cover from the coolant and washer fluid reservoirs. Clean the area around the reservoir cap (arrowed).

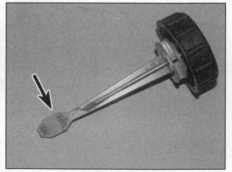

2 Unscrew the reservoir cap, and check the fluid level is up to the upper (MAX) level indicator on the dipstick.

3 Top-up the reservoir with the specified type of the fluid, using a funnel. Once the level is between the level marks, securely refit the reservoir cap. Do not overfill the reservoir.

Screen washer fluid level

● Screenwash additives not only keep the windscreen clean during foul weather, they also prevent the washer system freezing in cold weather - which is when you are likely to need it most. Don't top up using plain water as the screenwash will become too diluted, and will freeze during cold weather.

On no account use coolant antifreeze in the washer system - this could discolour or damage paintwork.

1 The washer fluid reservoir is located in the right-hand front corner of the engine compartment. To check the fluid level, open the cap and look down the filler neck.

2 If topping-up is necessary, add water and a screenwash additive in the quantities recommended on the bottle.

Wiper blades

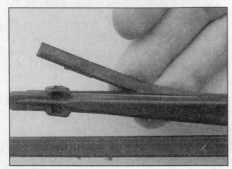

1 Check the condition of the wiper blades: if they are cracked or show signs of deterioration, or if the glass swept area is smeared, renew them. For maximum clarity of vision, wiper blades should be renewed annually.

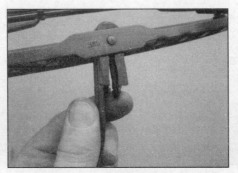

2 To remove an early windscreen wiper blade, turn the ignition on, then turn the ignition off, and press the wiper switch stalk down once. This places the arms in the 'service' position. Lift the wiper arm, rotate the blade on the arm and squeeze together the ends of the plastic insert.

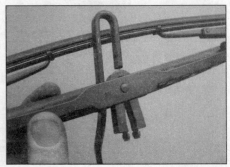

3 Disengage the blade from the wiper arm and remove it from the vehicle, taking care not to allow the arm to damage the windscreen. To return the blades to the park position, press the wiper switch stalk again.

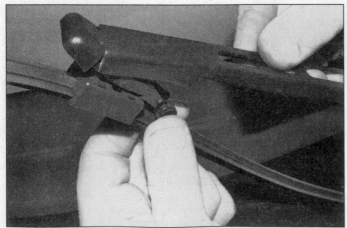

4 To remove a later windscreen wiper blade, turn the ignition on, then turn the ignition off, and press the wiper switch stalk down once. This places the arms in the 'service' position. Lift the wiper arm and squeeze together the side clips to lower the blade from the arm.

5 Tilt the wiper blade and unhook it from the end of the arm, taking care not to allow the arm to damage the windscreen. To return the blades to the park position, press the wiper switch stalk again.

Battery

Caution: Before carrying out any work on the vehicle battery, read the precautions given in 'Safety first!' at the start of this manual.

✔ Make sure that the battery tray is in good condition, and that the clamp is tight. Corrosion on the tray, retaining clamp and the battery itself can be removed with a solution of water and baking soda. Thoroughly rinse all cleaned areas with water. Any metal parts damaged by corrosion should be covered with a zinc-based primer, then painted.

✔ Periodically (approximately every three months), check the charge condition of the battery, as described in Chapter 5A.

✔ If the battery is flat, and you need to jump start your vehicle, see *Roadside Repairs*.

1 Lift the plastic cover to gain access to the battery positive terminal, which is located on the left-hand side of the engine compartment. The exterior of the battery should be inspected periodically for damage such as a cracked case or cover.

2 Check the battery lead clamps for tightness to ensure good electrical connections, and check the leads for signs of damage.

HAYNES HiNT

Battery corrosion can be kept to a minimum by applying a layer of petroleum jelly to the clamps and terminals after they are reconnected.

3 If corrosion (white, fluffy deposits) is evident, remove the cables from the battery terminals, clean them with a small wire brush, then refit them. Automotive stores sell a tool for cleaning the battery post . . .

4 . . . as well as the battery cable clamps.

Bulbs and fuses

✔ Check all external lights and the horn. Refer to the appropriate Sections of Chapter 12 for details if any of the circuits are found to be inoperative.

✔ Visually check all accessible wiring connectors, harnesses and retaining clips for security, and for signs of chafing or damage.

HAYNES HiNT

If you need to check your brake lights and indicators unaided, back up to a wall or garage door and operate the lights. The reflected light should show if they are working properly.

1 If a single indicator light, stop-light, sidelight or headlight has failed, it is likely that a bulb has blown, and will need to be renewed. Refer to Chapter 12 for details. If both stop-lights have failed, it is possible that the switch has failed (see Chapter 9).

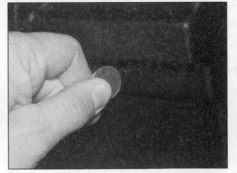

2 If more than one indicator or tail light has failed, it is likely that either a fuse has blown or that there is a fault in the circuit. Fuses are located behind a cover in the glovebox. Open the glovebox, rotate the screw fastener anti-clockwise to lower the cover. Additional fuses and relays are located in the left-hand side of the engine compartment fusebox.

3 To renew a blown fuse, simply pull it out and fit a new fuse of the correct rating (see Chapter 12). If the fuse blows again, it is important that you find out why – a complete checking procedure is given in Chapter 12.

Lubricants and fluids

Engine (petrol)	Multigrade engine oil 5W30 to 10W40 to ACEA A3 or API SH/SJ specification: Total Quartz or Esso Ultra/Ultron
Engine (diesel)	Fully-synthetic multigrade engine oil 5W30 to 10W40 to ACEA B3 or API CFB3 specification: Esso Ultron diesel or Total Activa/Quartz 9000
Cooling system	Gurit Essex Revko Gel2000 or BASF Glysantin G33-23F
Manual transmission	SAE 75W-80W to API GL5 specification: ESSO gear oil BV or Total Transmission BV
Automatic transmission	ESSO 4HP20-AL4 Automatic Transmission Fluid
Braking and clutch system	Hydraulic fluid to DOT 4
Power steering	Total Fluide DA

Choosing your engine oil

Engines need oil, not only to lubricate moving parts and minimise wear, but also to maximise power output and to improve fuel economy.

HOW ENGINE OIL WORKS

• *Beating friction*

Without oil, the moving surfaces inside your engine will rub together, heat up and melt, quickly causing the engine to seize. Engine oil creates a film which separates these moving parts, preventing wear and heat build-up.

• *Cooling hot-spots*

Temperatures inside the engine can exceed 1000° C. The engine oil circulates and acts as a coolant, transferring heat from the hot-spots to the sump.

• *Cleaning the engine internally*

Good quality engine oils clean the inside of your engine, collecting and dispersing combustion deposits and controlling them until they are trapped by the oil filter or flushed out at oil change.

OIL CARE - FOLLOW THE CODE

To handle and dispose of used engine oil safely, always:

* *Avoid skin contact with used engine oil. Repeated or prolonged contact can be harmful.*
* *Dispose of used oil and empty packs in a responsible manner in an authorised disposal site. Call 0800 663366 to find the one nearest to you. Never tip oil down drains or onto the ground.*

Tyre pressures (cold)

Note 1: *The make of tyres, the sizes and the pressures for each specific vehicle are given on a label attached to the driver's door A-pillar. On models with a space-saver spare wheel (family Estates), a separate pressure is given for the spare tyre, and care must be taken not to misread the sticker; the space-saver wheel is inflated to a lot higher pressure than the standard tyres (typically 60 psi). On models with a space-saver spare wheel, note that the spare is for temporary use only; whilst the spare is fitted, the vehicle should not be driven at speeds in excess of 50 mph (80 kmh).*
Note 2: *Pressures on the label apply to original-equipment tyres listed, and may vary if any other make or type of tyre is fitted; check with the tyre manufacturer or supplier for correct pressures if necessary.*
Note 3: *Tyre pressures must always be checked with the tyres cold to ensure accuracy.*

Hatchback models (typical)	Front (psi)	Rear (psi)
195/65 R15 tyres	33	33
205/55 R16 tyres	35	35

Estate models (typical)		
195/65 R15 tyres	33	35
205/55 R16 tyres	35	35

SW (Sports Wagon) models (typical)		
195/65 R15 tyres	33	35
205/55 R16 tyres	35	35

Chapter 1 Part A:
Routine maintenance and servicing – petrol models

Contents

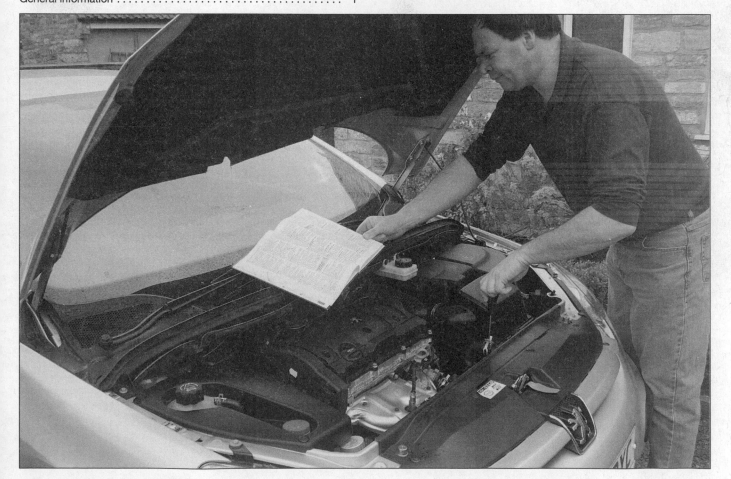

Degrees of difficulty

| Easy, suitable for novice with little experience | Fairly easy, suitable for beginner with some experience | Fairly difficult, suitable for competent DIY mechanic | Difficult, suitable for experienced DIY mechanic | Very difficult, suitable for expert DIY or professional |

Lubricants and fluids................................. Refer to end of *Weekly checks* on page 0•18

Capacities

Engine oil

Including filter:
1.4 litre engine	3.00 litres
1.6 litre engine	3.25 litres
2.0 litre engine	4.00 litres
Difference between MAX and MIN dipstick marks	1.5 litres

Cooling system (approximate)
1.4 litre engine	6.0 litres
1.6 litre engine	6.2 litres
2.0 litre engine	6.4 litres

Transmission

Manual:
1.4 and 1.6 litre engine	2.0 litres
2.0 litre engine	1.9 litres

Automatic:
Refilling after draining	4.5 litres
From dry	6.0 litres

Power-assisted steering (approximate) .... 0.8 litres

Fuel tank .... 60 litres

Engine

Auxiliary drivebelt tensions (for use with belt tensioning tool – see text):

1.4 litre models:
New belt	120 SEEM units
Used belt	60 to 80 SEEM units

1.6 litre models:

Without air conditioning:
New belt	87 SEEM units
Used belt	61 SEEM units

With air conditioning:
New belt	120 SEEM units
Used belt	58 SEEM units
2.0 litre models	Automatic adjustment

Cooling system

Frost and corrosion protection............................. Refer to antifreeze manufacturer's concentration recommendations

Ignition system

Spark plugs:
1.4 litre engine	Bosch FR7DE
1.6 litre engine	Bosch FR7ME
2.0 litre engines	Bosch FR8ME
Electrode gap	0.9 mm

Brakes

Brake pad friction material minimum thickness................... 2.0 mm

Tyre pressures .... See end of *Weekly checks* on page 0•18

Torque wrench settings	Nm	lbf ft
Alternator mounting bolts	37	27
Automatic transmission:		
Filler plug	24	18
Level plug	24	18
Auxiliary drivebelt tensioner pulley nut	45	33
Manual transmission filler/level plug:		
1.4 and 1.6 litre models	25	18
2.0 litre models	20	15
Oil filter cover (1.4 and 1.6 litre models)	25	18
Roadwheel bolts	85	63
Spark plugs	25	18
Sump drain plug	30	22

Note: *This maintenance schedule is a guide recommended by Haynes, for servicing your own vehicle. For the manufacturer's mainten-ance schedule, check with your local dealer.*

1 The maintenance intervals in this manual are provided with the assumption that you, not the dealer, will be carrying out the work. These are the minimum maintenance intervals recommended by us for vehicles driven daily. If you wish to keep your vehicle in peak condition at all times, you may wish to perform some of these procedures more often. We encourage frequent maintenance, because it enhances the efficiency, performance and resale value of your vehicle.

2 If the vehicle is driven in dusty areas, used to tow a trailer, or driven frequently at slow speeds (idling in traffic) or on short journeys, more frequent maintenance intervals are recommended.

3 When the vehicle is new, it should be serviced by a dealer service department (or other workshop recognised by the vehicle manufacturer as providing the same standard of service) in order to preserve the warranty. The vehicle manufacturer may reject warranty claims if you are unable to prove that servicing has been carried out as and when specified, using only original equipment parts or parts certified to be of equivalent quality.

4 Valve clearance checking on 1.4 litre engines (Chapter 2A, Section 9) is no longer specified as part of the routine maintenance schedule (the 1.6 and 2.0 litre engines have hydraulic adjusters). Check the valve clearances if there is any tapping or rattling from the top of the engine, or in the event of an unexplained lack of performance. The prudent owner may wish to check the clear-ances, perhaps at 40 000 mile (60 000 km) or four-yearly intervals.

Every 250 miles (400 km) or weekly

- [ ] Refer to *Weekly checks*

Every 10 000 miles (15 000 km) or 12 months – whichever comes sooner

- [ ] Renew the engine oil and filter* (Section 3).
- [ ] Check all underbonnet components or fluid leaks (Section 4).
- [ ] Check the condition of the driveshaft rubber gaiters and CV joints (Section 5).
- [ ] Lubricate all hinges and locks (Section 6).
- [ ] Carry out a road test (Section 7).

***Note:** Peugeot recommend the engine oil and filter are changed every 20 000 miles or two years. However, oil and filter changes are good for the engine and we recommend changing the oil more frequently, especially if the vehicle is used on a lot of short journeys.*

Every 20 000 miles (30 000 km) or two years – whichever comes sooner

- [ ] Reset the service interval indicator (Section 8).
- [ ] Check the pollen filter (Section 9).
- [ ] Check the condition of the auxiliary drivebelt (Section 10).
- [ ] Check the condition of the brake pads (Section 11).
- [ ] Check the operation of the handbrake (Section 12).
- [ ] Check the steering and suspension components (Section 13).

Every 40 000 miles (60 000 km)

- [ ] Renew the timing belt (Section 14).

Note: *Although the normal interval for timing belt renewal is 80 000 miles (120 000 km), it is strongly recommended that the interval is reduced to 40 000 miles (60 000 km), especially on vehicles which are subjected to intensive use, ie, mainly short journeys or a lot of stop-start driving. The actual belt renewal interval is therefore very much up to the individual owner, but bear in mind that severe engine damage will result if the belt breaks.*

Every 40 000 miles (60 000 km) or two years – whichever comes sooner

- [ ] Renew the brake fluid (Section 15).

Note: *A hydraulic clutch shares its fluid reservoir with the braking system, and may also need to be bled.*

Every 40 000 miles (60 000 km) or four years – whichever comes sooner

- [ ] Renew the spark plugs (Section 16).
- [ ] Renew the fuel filter* (Section 17).
- [ ] Renew the air cleaner filter element (Section 18).
- [ ] Check the manual transmission oil level (Section 19).
- [ ] Check the automatic transmission fluid level (Section 20).
- [ ] Check the exhaust emissions (Section 21).
- [ ] Renew the coolant (Section 22).

***Note:** Only fitted to markets where inferior quality fuel is sold.*

Every ten years

- [ ] Renew the airbags and seat belt pretensioners (Section 23).

Underbonnet view of a 1.6 litre model

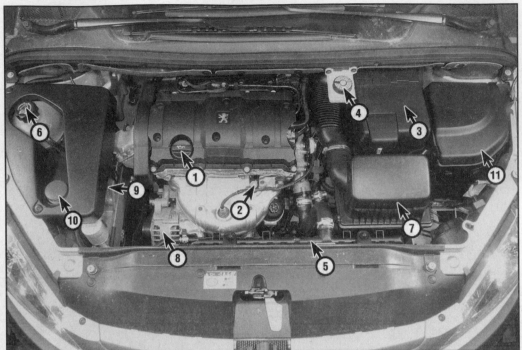

1   Engine oil filler cap
2   Engine oil level dipstick
3   Battery
4   Brake/clutch fluid reservoir
5   Radiator
6   Coolant expansion tank
7   Air filter housing
8   Alternator
9   Power steering fluid
     reservoir
10 Washer fluid reservoir
11 Fuse/electrical box

Front underbody view

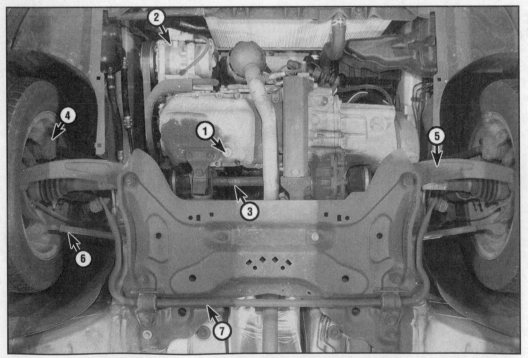

1   Engine oil drain plug
2   Air conditioning
     compressor
3   Driveshaft
4   Brake caliper
5   Suspension lower arm
6   Track rod
7   Anti-roll bar

1 Fuel tank
2 Beam axle
3 Handbrake cable
4 Brake caliper
5 Coil spring

Maintenance procedures

1 General information

1 This Chapter is designed to help the home mechanic maintain his/her vehicle for safety, economy, long life and peak performance.
2 The Chapter contains a master maintenance schedule, followed by Sections dealing specifically with each task in the schedule. Visual checks, adjustments, component renewal and other helpful items are included. Refer to the accompanying illustrations of the engine compartment and the underside of the vehicle for the locations of the various components.
3 Servicing your vehicle in accordance with the mileage/time maintenance schedule and the following Sections will provide a planned maintenance programme, which should result in a long and reliable service life. This is a comprehensive plan, so maintaining some items but not others at the specified service intervals will not produce the same results.
4 As you service your vehicle, you will discover that many of the procedures can – and should – be grouped together, because of the particular procedure being performed, or because of the close proximity of two otherwise-unrelated components to one another. For example, if the vehicle is raised for any reason, the exhaust can be inspected at the same time as the suspension and steering components.

5 The first step in this maintenance programme is to prepare yourself before the actual work begins. Read through all the Sections relevant to the work to be carried out, then make a list and gather together all the parts and tools required. If a problem is encountered, seek advice from a parts specialist, or a dealer service department.

2 Routine maintenance

1 If, from the time the vehicle is new, the routine maintenance schedule is followed closely, and frequent checks are made of fluid levels and high-wear items, as suggested throughout this manual, the engine will be kept in relatively good running condition, and the need for additional work will be minimised.
2 It is possible that there will be times when the engine is running poorly due to the lack of regular maintenance. This is even more likely if a used vehicle, which has not received regular and frequent maintenance checks, is purchased. In such cases, additional work may need to be carried out, outside of the regular maintenance intervals.
3 If engine wear is suspected, a compression test (refer to Chapter 2A) will provide valuable information regarding the overall performance of the main internal components. Such a test can be used as a basis to decide on the extent

of the work to be carried out. If, for example, a compression test indicates serious internal engine wear, conventional maintenance as described in this Chapter will not greatly improve the performance of the engine, and may prove a waste of time and money, unless extensive overhaul work (Chapter 2F) is carried out first.
4 The following series of operations are those often required to improve the performance of a generally poor-running engine:

Primary operations

a) Clean, inspect and test the battery (See 'Weekly checks').
b) Check all the engine-related fluids (See 'Weekly checks').
c) Check the condition and tension of the auxiliary drivebelt (Section 10).
d) Renew the spark plugs (Section 16).
e) Check the condition of the air cleaner filter element, and renew if necessary (Section 18).
f) Renew the fuel filter (Section 17).
g) Check the condition of all hoses, and check for fluid leaks (Section 4).

5 If the above operations do not prove fully effective, carry out the following operations:

Secondary operations

All items listed under Primary operations, plus the following:
a) Check the charging system (Chapter 5A).
b) Check the ignition system (Chapter 5B).
c) Check the fuel system (Chapter 4A).

3.3a Remove the screws . . .

3.3b . . . securing the engine undershield (right-hand side arrowed)

Every 10 000 miles (15 000 km) or 12 months

3 Engine oil and filter renewal

Note: *A suitable square-section wrench may be required to undo the sump drain plug. These wrenches can be obtained from most motor factors or your Peugeot dealer.*

3.4 Slacken the sump drain plug

HAYNES HiNT

As the drain plug releases from the sump threads, move it away sharply, so the stream of oil issuing from the sump runs into the container, not up your sleeve.

1 Frequent oil and filter changes are the most important preventative maintenance procedures which can be undertaken by the DIY owner. As engine oil ages, it becomes diluted and contaminated, which leads to premature engine wear.

2 Before starting this procedure, gather together all the necessary tools and materials. Also make sure that you have plenty of clean rags and newspapers handy, to mop-up any spills. Ideally, the engine oil should be warm, as it will drain better, and more built-up sludge will be removed with it. Take care, however, not to touch the exhaust or any other hot parts of the engine when working under the vehicle. To avoid any possibility of scalding, and to protect yourself from possible skin irritants and other harmful contaminants in used engine oils, it is advisable to wear gloves when carrying out this work. Access to the underside of the vehicle will be greatly improved if it can be raised on a lift, driven onto ramps, or jacked up and supported on axle stands (see *Jacking and vehicle support*). Whichever method is chosen, make sure that the vehicle remains level, or if it is at an angle, that the drain plug is at the lowest point.

3 Undo the screws and remove the engine undershield – where fitted **(see illustrations)**.
4 Slacken the drain plug about half a turn **(see illustration)**. Position the draining container under the drain plug, then remove the plug completely. If possible, try to keep the plug pressed into the sump while unscrewing it by hand the last couple of turns **(see Haynes Hint)**. Recover the sealing ring from the drain plug.
5 Allow some time for the old oil to drain, noting that it may be necessary to reposition the container as the oil flow slows to a trickle.
6 After all the oil has drained, wipe off the drain plug with a clean rag, and fit a new sealing washer. Clean the area around the drain plug opening, and refit the plug, tightening it to the specified torque.
7 Move the container into position under the oil filter, which is located on the front of the cylinder block.

1.4 and 1.6 litre engines

8 On these engines, the filter element is contained within a filter cover. Using a socket or spanner, slacken and remove the filter cover from above **(see illustrations)**. Be prepared for fluid spillage, and recover the O-ring seal from the cover.

3.8a Slacken the filter cover . . .

3.8b . . . and recover the O-ring seal

3.11a Fit the new element into the cover . . .

3.11b . . . and apply a little clean engine oil to the O-ring seal

3.13 Use an oil filter removal tool to slacken the canister type oil filter

9 Pull the filter element from the filter cover.
10 Use a clean rag to remove all oil, dirt and sludge from the inside and outside of the filter cover.
11 Insert the new filter element in to the cover, then apply a little clean engine oil to the new O-ring seal, and fit it to the filter cover **(see illustrations)**.
12 Refit the filter/cover to the housing and tighten the cover to the specified torque.

2.0 litre engines

13 Using an oil filter removal tool if necessary, slacken the filter initially, then unscrew it by hand the rest of the way **(see illustration)**. Empty the oil in the old filter into the container.
14 Use a clean rag to remove all oil, dirt and sludge from the filter sealing area on the engine. Check the old filter to make sure that the rubber sealing ring hasn't stuck to the engine. If it has, carefully remove it.
15 Apply a light coating of clean engine oil to the sealing ring on the new filter, then screw it into position on the engine **(see illustrations)**. Tighten the filter firmly by hand only – **do not use any tools.**

All engines

16 Remove the old oil and all tools from under the car, then lower the car to the ground (if applicable).
17 Remove the dipstick, then unscrew the oil filler cap from the cylinder head cover. Fill the engine, using the correct grade and type of oil (see *Lubricants and fluids*). An oil can spout or funnel may help to reduce spillage. Pour in half the specified quantity of oil first, then wait a few minutes for the oil to run to the sump. Continue adding oil a small quantity at a time until the level is up to the lower mark on the dipstick. Refit the filler cap.
18 Start the engine and run it for a few minutes; check for leaks around the oil filter seal and the sump drain plug. Note that there may be a delay of a few seconds before the oil pressure warning light goes out when the engine is first started, as the oil circulates through the engine oil galleries and the new oil filter before the pressure builds-up.
19 Refit the engine undershield (where

3.15a Lubricate the sealing ring of the new filter with clean engine oil . . .

applicable), and secure it in place with the screw fasteners.
20 Switch off the engine, and wait a few minutes for the oil to settle in the sump once more. With the new oil circulated and the filter completely full, recheck the level on the dipstick, and add more oil as necessary.
21 Dispose of the used engine oil safely, with reference to *General repair procedures*.

4	Hose and fluid leak check

1 Visually inspect the engine joint faces, gaskets and seals for any signs of water or oil leaks. Pay particular attention to the areas around the cylinder head cover, cylinder head, oil filter and sump joint faces. Bear in mind that, over a period of time, some very slight seepage from these areas is to be expected – what you are really looking for is any indication of a serious leak. Should a leak be found, renew the offending gasket or oil seal by referring to the appropriate Chapters in this manual.
2 Also check the security and condition of all the engine-related pipes and hoses. Ensure that all cable ties or securing clips are in place, and in good condition. Clips which are broken or missing can lead to chafing of the hoses, pipes or wiring, which could cause more serious problems in the future.
3 Carefully check the radiator hoses and heater hoses along their entire length.

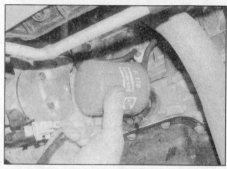

3.15b . . . then screw the filter onto the engine and tighten firmly by hand

Renew any hose which is cracked, swollen or deteriorated. Cracks will show up better if the hose is squeezed. Pay close attention to the hose clips that secure the hoses to the cooling system components. Hose clips can pinch and puncture hoses, resulting in cooling system leaks. If crimped-type hose clips are used, it may be a good idea to replace them with standard worm-drive clips.
4 Inspect all the cooling system components (hoses, joint faces, etc) for leaks **(see Haynes Hint)**.
5 Where any problems are found on system components, renew the component or gasket with reference to Chapter 3.
6 Where applicable, inspect the automatic transmission fluid cooler hoses for leaks or deterioration.

A leak in the cooling system will usually show up as white- or rust-coloured deposits on the area adjoining the leak.

5.1 Check the driveshaft gaiters for signs of damage or deterioration

7 With the vehicle raised, inspect the petrol tank and filler neck for punctures, cracks and other damage. The connection between the filler neck and tank is especially critical. Sometimes a rubber filler neck or connecting hose will leak due to loose retaining clamps or deteriorated rubber.

8 Carefully check all rubber hoses and fuel pipes leading away from the petrol tank. Check for loose connections, deteriorated hoses, crimped lines, and other damage. Pay particular attention to the vent pipes and hoses, which often loop up around the filler neck and can become blocked or crimped. Follow the pipes to the front of the vehicle, carefully inspecting them all the way. Renew damaged sections as necessary.

9 From within the engine compartment, check the security of all fuel pipe attachments and unions, and inspect the fuel pipes and vacuum hoses for kinks, chafing and deterioration.

10 Where applicable, check the condition of the power steering fluid hoses and pipes.

5 Driveshaft gaiter and CV joints check

1 With the vehicle raised and securely supported on stands (see *Jacking and vehicle support*), turn the steering onto full lock, then slowly rotate the roadwheel. Inspect the condition of the outer constant velocity (CV) joint gaiters, squeezing the gaiters to open out the folds **(see illustration)**. Check for signs of cracking, splits or deterioration of the gaiter, which may allow the grease to escape, and lead to water and grit entry into the joint. Also check the security and condition of the retaining clips.

Repeat these checks on the inner CV joints. If any damage or deterioration is found, the gaiters should be renewed (see Chapter 8).

2 At the same time, check the general condition of the CV joints themselves by first holding the driveshaft and attempting to rotate the wheel. Repeat this check by holding the inner joint and attempting to rotate the driveshaft. Any appreciable movement indicates wear in the joints, wear in the driveshaft splines, or a loose driveshaft retaining nut.

6 Hinge and lock lubrication

1 Work around the vehicle, and lubricate the hinges of the bonnet, doors and tailgate with a small amount of general-purpose oil.

2 Lightly lubricate the bonnet release mechanism and exposed section of inner cable with a smear of grease.

3 Check carefully the security and operation of all hinges, latches and locks, adjusting them where required. Check the operation of the central locking system (if fitted).

4 Check the condition and operation of the tailgate struts, renewing them if either is leaking or no longer able to support the tailgate securely when raised.

7 Road test

Instruments and electrical equipment

1 Check the operation of all instruments and electrical equipment.

2 Make sure that all instruments read correctly, and switch on all electrical equipment in turn to check it functions properly.

Steering and suspension

3 Check for any abnormalities in the steering, suspension, handling or road 'feel'.

4 Drive the vehicle, and check that there are no unusual vibrations or noises.

5 Check that the steering feels positive, with no excessive 'sloppiness', or roughness, and check for any suspension noises when cornering, or when driving over bumps.

Drivetrain

6 Check the performance of the engine, clutch, transmission and driveshafts.

7 Listen for any unusual noises from the engine, clutch and transmission.

8 Make sure the engine idles smoothly, and that there is no hesitation when accelerating.

9 Check that the clutch action is smooth and progressive, that the drive is taken up smoothly, and that the pedal travel is not excessive. Also listen for any noises when the clutch pedal is depressed.

10 Check that all gears can be engaged smoothly, without noise, and that the gear lever action is smooth and not vague or 'notchy'.

11 On automatic transmission models, make sure that all gearchanges occur smoothly, without snatching, and without an increase in engine speed between changes. Check that all the gear positions can be selected with the vehicle at rest. If any problems are found, they should be referred to a Peugeot dealer.

12 Listen for a metallic clicking sound from the front of the vehicle, as the vehicle is driven slowly in a circle with the steering on full lock. Carry out this check in both directions. If a clicking noise is heard, this indicates wear in a driveshaft joint, in which case, the complete driveshaft must be renewed (see Chapter 8).

Braking system

13 Make sure that the vehicle does not pull to one side when braking, and that the wheels do not lock when braking hard.

14 Check that there is no vibration through the steering when braking.

15 Check that the handbrake operates correctly, without excessive movement of the lever, and that it holds the vehicle on a slope.

16 Test the operation of the brake servo unit as follows. With the engine off, depress the footbrake four or five times to exhaust the vacuum. Start the engine, holding the brake pedal depressed. As the engine starts, there should be a noticeable 'give' in the brake pedal as vacuum builds-up. Allow the engine to run for at least two minutes, and then switch it off. If the brake pedal is depressed now, it should be possible to detect a hiss from the servo as the pedal is depressed. After about four or five applications, no further hissing should be heard, and the pedal should feel considerably firmer.

Every 20 000 miles (30 000 km) or two years

8 Resetting the service indicator

1 On completion of the service, reset the service interval indicator as follows.

2 With the ignition switched off, press and hold trip meter button.

3 Turn on the ignition switch, and the display begins a countdown. When the countdown reaches 0, release the trip meter button, and the spanner service symbol in the display will disappear.

4 Turn off the ignition switch.

5 Turn on the ignition switch and check the correct mileage to the next service interval is displayed on the indicator.

Note: *If you need to disconnect the battery after carrying out this procedure, lock the vehicle and wait at least 5 minutes. Otherwise the display reset may not register.*

9.2a Prise up the centre pins, and lever out the plastic expanding rivets (arrowed) . . .

9.2b . . . then remove the sound insulation material

9.3 Pull the filter cover (arrowed) from the bulkhead

9 Pollen filter check

1 Open the bonnet.
2 Prise up the centre pins, lever out the complete plastic expanding rivets, then remove the sound insulation trim covering the pollen filter cover **(see illustrations)**.
3 Grasp the filter cover and pull it from the bulkhead **(see illustration)**.
4 Slide the filter out **(see illustration)**.
5 Check the condition of the filter, and renew it if dirty.
6 Wipe clean the inside of the housing and fit the pollen filter element, making sure that it is correctly seated.
7 Refit the pollen filter cover.
8 Refit the sound insulation trim, and secure it place with the plastic rivets.
9 Close the bonnet.

10 Auxiliary drivebelt check and renewal

Note: *On models without power steering and air conditioning, Peugeot specify the use of a special electronic tool (SEEM C.TRONIC type 105.5 belt tension measuring tool) to correctly set the auxiliary drivebelt tension. If access to this equipment cannot be obtained, an approximate setting can be achieved using the method described below. If this method is used, the tension should be checked using the special electronic tool at the earliest opportunity.*

Check

1 Apply the handbrake, slacken the front right-hand roadwheel bolts, then jack up the front of the car and support it on axle stands (see *Jacking and vehicle support*). Remove the right-hand front roadwheel.
2 Remove the plastic expanding rivets (pull out the centre pin then remove the complete rivet) securing the wheel arch liner to the body then manoeuvre the liner out from underneath the wing.
3 Using a suitable socket and extension bar fitted to the crankshaft sprocket bolt, rotate

the crankshaft so that the entire length of the drivebelt can be examined. Examine the drivebelt for cracks, splitting, fraying or damage. Check also for signs of glazing (shiny patches) and for separation of the belt plies. Renew the belt if worn or damaged.
4 If the condition of the belt is satisfactory, on 1.4 and 1.6 litre models, check the drivebelt tension as described below. **Note:** *On 2.0 litre models, there is no need to check the drivebelt tension (an automatic tensioner is fitted).*
5 Refit the wheel arch liner, securing it in position with the plastic expanding rivets.
6 Refit the roadwheel then lower the vehicle to the ground and tighten the wheel bolts to the specified torque.

1.4 and 1.6 litre without air conditioning

Renewal

7 If not already done, proceed as described in paragraphs 1 and 2.
8 On 1.4 litre models, slacken both the alternator upper and lower mounting bolts, whilst on 1.6 litre models it is only necessary to slacken the lower mounting bolt.
9 Back off the adjuster bolt to relieve the tension in the drivebelt, then slip the drivebelt

9.4 Slide the pollen filter out

from the pulleys. **Note:** *If the belt is going to be re-used, mark the direction of rotation on the belt prior to removal. This will ensure it is refitted the correct way around.*
10 If the belt is being renewed, ensure that the correct type is used. If the original belt is being refitted, use the mark made on removal to ensure it is fitted the correct way around.
11 Fit the belt around the pulleys, and take up the slack in the belt by tightening the adjuster bolt **(see illustrations)**. Tension the drivebelt as described in the following paragraphs.

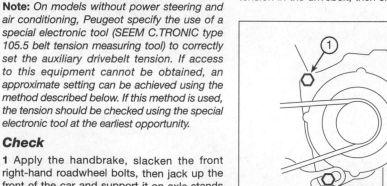

H44694

10.11a Auxiliary belt routing and adjustment (1.4 litre models without air conditioning)

1 *Alternator pivot bolt*
2 *Adjuster bolt*

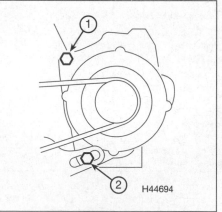

H44693

10.11b Auxiliary belt routing and adjustment (1.6 litre models without air conditioning)

1 *Alternator pivot bolt*
2 *Adjuster bolt*

Tensioning

12 If not already done, proceed as described in paragraphs 1 and 2.

13 If the special measuring tool is available, fit the measuring equipment to the 'lower run' of the belt, approximately midway between the crankshaft and alternator pulleys. The belt tension should be set to the figure given in the Specifications at the start of this Chapter.

14 If the measuring tool is not available, the belt should be tensioned so that, under firm thumb pressure, there is about 5.0 mm of free movement at the mid-point between the pulleys on the lower belt run.

Caution: Correct tensioning of the drivebelt will ensure it has a long life. A belt which is too slack will slip and squeal. Beware of overtightening, as this can cause wear in the alternator bearings.

15 To adjust the belt tension, with the mounting bolt(s) just slackened, turn the adjuster bolt until the correct tension is achieved.

16 Rotate the crankshaft a couple of times, recheck the tension, then tighten the alternator mounting bolt(s) to the specified torque.

17 Refit the wheel arch liner, securing it in position with the plastic expanding rivets.

18 Refit the roadwheel then lower the vehicle to the ground and tighten the wheel bolts to the specified torque. Reconnect the battery.

1.4 and 1.6 litre with air conditioning

Renewal

19 If not already done, proceed as described in paragraphs 1 and 2.

20 Slacken the tensioner pulley bracket bolts and rotate the adjuster bolt to release the tension in the belt, then remove the belt from the pulleys. **Note:** *If the belt is to be re-used, mark the direction of rotation on the belt prior to removal. This will ensure it is refitted the correct way around.*

21 If the belt is being renewed, ensure that the correct type is used. If the original belt is being refitted, use the mark made on removal to ensure it is fitted the correct way around. Fit the drivebelt around the pulleys in the following order **(see illustration)**:

a) Air conditioning compressor.
b) Crankshaft.
c) Alternator.
d) Idler roller
e) Tensioner pulley.

22 Ensure that the ribs on the belt are correctly engaged with the grooves in the pulleys, and that the drivebelt is correctly routed. Tension the belt as follows.

Tensioning

23 If not already done, proceed as described in paragraphs 1 and 2.

24 If the special measuring tool is available, fit the measuring equipment to the belt, approximately midway between the crankshaft and air conditioning compressor pulleys. Check the belt tension is as given in the Specifications at the start of this Chapter.

25 If the measuring tool is not available, the belt should be tensioned so that, under firm thumb pressure, there is about 5.0 mm of free movement at the mid-point between the crankshaft and air conditioning compressor pulleys.

Caution: Correct tensioning of the drivebelt will ensure it has a long life. A belt which is too slack will slip and squeal. Beware of overtightening, as this can cause wear in the alternator bearings.

26 To adjust the tension, rotate the adjuster bolt until the correct tension is achieved. Once the belt is correctly tensioned, tighten the tensioner pulley bracket bolts to the specified torque. Rotate the crankshaft a couple of times and recheck the tension.

27 When the belt is correctly tensioned, refit the wheel arch liner, securing it in position with the plastic expanding rivets.

28 Refit the roadwheel then lower the vehicle to the ground and tighten the wheel bolts to the specified torque. Reconnect the battery.

2.0 litre

Removal

29 If not already done, proceed as described in paragraphs 1 and 2.

30 Move the tensioner pulley away from the drivebelt, using a spanner on the tensioner pulley retaining nut. Rotate the tensioner pulley anti-clockwise away from the belt. **Note:** *The tensioner pulley has a **left-hand** thread, so it will not slacken when releasing the tension on the belt.*

31 Once the tension is released, disengage the belt from all the pulleys, noting its correct routing. Remove the drivebelt from the engine. **Note:** *If the belt is going to be re-used, mark the direction of rotation on the belt prior to removal. This will ensure it is refitted the correct way around.*

Refitting and tensioning

32 If the belt is being renewed, ensure that the correct type is used. If the original belt is being refitted, use the mark made on removal to ensure it is fitted the correct way around. Fit the drivebelt around the pulleys in the following order **(see illustration)**:

a) Alternator.
b) Idler pulleys
c) Air conditioning compressor (where applicable).
d) Crankshaft.
e) Automatic tensioner pulley.

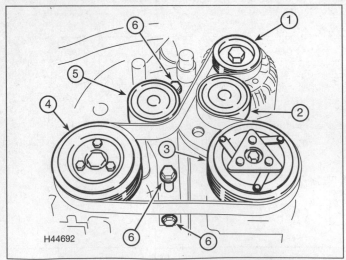

**10.21 Auxiliary belt routing and adjustment
(1.4 and 1.6 litre models with air conditioning)**

1 Alternator pulley   3 Compressor pulley   5 Tensioner pulley
2 Idler pulley   4 Crankshaft pulley   6 Tensioner bolts

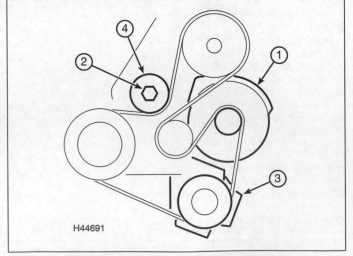

**10.32 Auxiliary belt routing and adjustment
(2.0 litre models with air conditioning)**

1 Alternator   3 Compressor
2 Tensioner pulley bolt   4 Tensioner pulley

33 Ensure that the ribs on the belt are correctly engaged with the grooves in the pulleys
Caution: Do not allow the tensioner pulley to spring forcefully onto the belt as this could result in damage.
34 Refit the wheel arch liner, securing it in position with the retaining plastic expanding rivets.
35 Refit the roadwheel then lower the vehicle to the ground and tighten the wheel bolts to the specified torque.

11 Brake pad check

1 Slacken the front roadwheel bolts. Firmly apply the handbrake, then jack up the front of the car and support it securely on axle stands (see *Jacking and vehicle support*). Remove the front roadwheels.
2 For a quick check, the pad thickness can be carried out via the inspection hole on the front caliper **(see Haynes Hint)**. Using a steel rule, measure the thickness of the pad friction material. This must not be less than the specified minimum given in the Specifications.
3 For a comprehensive check, the brake pads should be removed and cleaned. The operation of the caliper can then be checked, and the brake disc itself can be fully examined on both sides. Refer to Chapter 9 for details.
4 If any pad's friction material is worn to the specified minimum thickness or less, all four pads must be renewed as a set. Refer to Chapter 9 for details.
5 On completion, refit the roadwheels then lower the vehicle to the ground and tighten the wheel bolts to the specified torque.

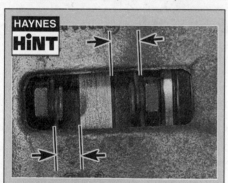

For a quick check, the thickness of the friction material on each brake pad can be measured through the aperture in the caliper body.

6 Slacken the rear roadwheel bolts. Jack up the rear of the car and support it securely on axle stands. Remove the rear roadwheels. Repeat the procedure described in Paragraphs 2 to 5 on the rear brake pads.

12 Handbrake check and adjustment

1 The handbrake should be fully applied before 8 clicks can be heard from the lever ratchet mechanism. Check and, if necessary, adjust the handbrake as described in Chapter 9.

13 Steering and suspension check

Front suspension and steering

1 Raise the front of the vehicle, and securely support it on axle stands (see *Jacking and vehicle support*).
2 Visually inspect the balljoint dust covers and the steering gear gaiters for splits, chafing or deterioration. Any wear of these components will cause loss of lubricant, together with dirt and water entry, resulting in rapid deterioration of the balljoints or steering gear.
3 Check the power steering fluid pipes/hoses for chafing or deterioration, and the pipe and hose unions for fluid leaks. Also check for signs of fluid leakage under pressure from the steering gear rubber gaiters, which would indicate failed fluid seals within the steering gear.
4 Grasp the roadwheel at the 12 o'clock and 6 o'clock positions, and try to rock it **(see illustration)**. Very slight free play may be felt, but if the movement is appreciable, further investigation is necessary to determine the source. Continue rocking the wheel while an assistant depresses the footbrake. If the movement is now eliminated or significantly reduced, it is likely that the hub bearings are at fault. If the free play is still evident with the footbrake depressed, then there is wear in the suspension joints or mountings.
5 Now grasp the wheel at the 9 o'clock and 3 o'clock positions, and try to rock it as before. Any movement felt now may again be caused by wear in the hub bearings or the steering track rod balljoints. If the inner or outer balljoint is worn, the visual movement will be obvious.

6 Using a large screwdriver or flat bar, check for wear in the suspension mounting bushes by levering between the relevant suspension component and its attachment point. Some movement is to be expected as the mountings are made of rubber, but excessive wear should be obvious. Also check the condition of any visible rubber bushes, looking for splits, cracks or contamination of the rubber.
7 With the car standing on its wheels, have an assistant turn the steering wheel back-and-forth about an eighth of a turn each way. There should be very little, if any, lost movement between the steering wheel and roadwheels. If this is not the case, closely observe the joints and mountings previously described, but in addition, check the steering column universal joints for wear, and the steering gear itself.

Suspension strut/ shock absorber

8 Check for any signs of fluid leakage around the suspension strut/shock absorber body, or from the rubber gaiter around the piston rod. Should any fluid be noticed, the suspension strut/shock absorber is defective internally, and should be renewed. **Note:** *Suspension struts/shock absorbers should always be renewed in pairs on the same axle, or the handling of the vehicle will be adversely affected.*
9 The efficiency of the suspension strut/shock absorber may be checked by bouncing the vehicle at each corner. Generally speaking, the body will return to its normal position and stop after being depressed. If it rises and returns on a rebound, the suspension strut/shock absorber is probably suspect. Examine also the suspension strut/shock absorber upper and lower mountings for any signs of wear.

13.4 Check for wear in the hub bearings by grasping the wheel and trying to rock it

Every 40 000 miles (60 000 km)

14 Timing belt renewal

1 Refer to Chapter 2A or 2B, as applicable.

Every 40 000 miles (60 000 km) or two years

15 Brake fluid renewal

⚠️ **Warning: Brake hydraulic fluid can harm your eyes and damage painted surfaces, so use extreme caution when handling and pouring it. Do not use fluid that has been standing open for some time, as it absorbs moisture from the air. Excess moisture can cause a dangerous loss of braking effectiveness.**

Note: *A hydraulic clutch shares its fluid reservoir with the braking system, and may also need to be bled (see Chapter 6).*

1 The procedure is similar to that for the bleeding of the hydraulic system as described in Chapter 9, except that the brake fluid reservoir should be emptied by syphoning, using a clean ladle or similar before starting, and allowance should be made for the old fluid to be expelled when bleeding a section of the circuit.

2 Working as described in Chapter 9, open the first bleed screw in the sequence, and pump the brake pedal gently until nearly all the old fluid has been emptied from the master cylinder reservoir.

HAYNES HiNT *Old hydraulic fluid is in-variably much darker in colour than the new, making it easy to distinguish the two.*

3 Top-up to the MAX level with new fluid, and continue pumping until only the new fluid remains in the reservoir, and new fluid can be seen emerging from the bleed screw. Tighten the screw, and top the reservoir level up to the MAX level line.

4 Work through all the remaining bleed screws in the sequence until new fluid can be seen at all of them. Be careful to keep the master cylinder reservoir topped-up to above the DANGER level at all times, or air may enter the system and increase the length of the task.

5 When the operation is complete, check that all bleed screws are securely tightened, and that their dust caps are refitted. Wash off all traces of spilt fluid, and recheck the master cylinder reservoir fluid level.

6 Check the operation of the brakes before taking the car on the road.

Every 40 000 miles (60 000 km) or four years

16 Spark plug renewal

1 The correct functioning of the spark plugs is vital for the correct running and efficiency of the engine. It is essential that the plugs fitted are appropriate for the engine (see Specifications). If this type is used and the engine is in good condition, the spark plugs should not need attention between scheduled renewal intervals. Spark plug cleaning is rarely necessary, and should not be attempted unless specialised equipment is available, as damage can easily be caused to the firing ends.

2 To gain access to the spark plugs, remove the ignition HT coil as described in Chapter 5B.

3 Unscrew the plugs using a spark plug spanner, suitable box spanner or a deep socket and extension bar **(see illustration)**. Keep the socket aligned with the spark plug – if it is forcibly moved to one side, the ceramic insulator may be broken off. As each plug is removed, examine it as follows.

4 Examination of the spark plugs will give a good indication of the condition of the engine **(see illustration)**. If the insulator nose of the spark plug is clean and white, with no deposits, this is indicative of a weak mixture or too hot a plug (a hot plug transfers heat away from the electrode slowly, a cold plug transfers heat away quickly).

5 If the tip and insulator nose are covered with hard black-looking deposits, then this is indicative that the mixture is too rich. Should the plug be black and oily, then it is likely that the engine is fairly worn, as well as the mixture being too rich.

6 If the insulator nose is covered with light tan to greyish-brown deposits, then the mixture is correct and it is likely that the engine is in good condition.

7 The spark plug electrode gap is of considerable importance as, if it is too large or too small, the size of the spark and its efficiency will be seriously impaired. The gap should be set to the value given in the Specifications at the beginning of this Chapter.
Note: *The electrode gap on multi-electrode spark plugs cannot be adjusted.*

8 To set the gap on single-electrode plugs, measure the gap with a feeler blade, and then bend open, or closed, the outer plug electrode until the correct gap is achieved **(see illustration)**. The centre electrode should never be bent, as this may crack the insulator and cause plug failure, if nothing worse. If using feeler blades, the gap is correct when the appropriate-size blade is a firm sliding fit.

9 Special spark plug electrode gap adjusting tools are available from most motor accessory shops, or from spark plug manufacturers.

10 Before fitting the spark plugs, check that the threaded connector sleeves are tight, and that the plug exterior and threads are clean **(see Haynes Hint opposite).**

16.3 Unscrew the spark plugs

16.4 Examine the spark plugs to check the condition of the engine – see text

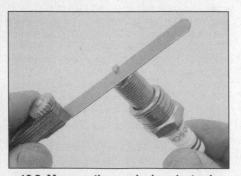
16.8 Measure the spark plug electrode gap with a feeler gauge

11 Remove the rubber hose (if used), and tighten the plug to the specified torque using the spark plug socket and a torque wrench. Refit the remaining spark plugs in the same manner.

12 Refit the ignition HT coil as described in Chapter 5B.

17 Fuel filter renewal

⚠ **Warning: Before carrying out the following operation, refer to the precautions given in 'Safety first!' at the beginning of this manual, and follow them implicitly. Petrol is a highly-dangerous and volatile liquid, and the precautions necessary when handling it cannot be overstressed.**

Note: *Only fitted to vehicles available in countries where inferior quality fuel is sold.*

Note: *Before disconnecting any fuel lines, depressurise the fuel system, as described in Chapter 4A.*

1 The fuel filter is situated underneath the rear of the vehicle, on the right-hand side of the front of the fuel tank. To improve access to the filter, chock the front wheels, then jack up the rear of the vehicle and support it on axle stands (see *Jacking and vehicle support*).

2 Undo the nuts, prise up the centre pins a little, then prise out the complete plastic rivets and remove the plastic tray from the underside of the fuel tank. Place a container beneath the fuel filter to catch all spilt fuel.

3 Position a large rag around the fuel pipe union, to catch any fuel spray which may be expelled as the fuel pressure is released, then depress the retaining clips and slowly disconnect the fuel pipe. Disconnect the other pipe from the opposite end of the filter and allow the filter contents to drain into the container.

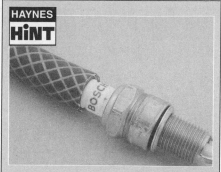

It is very often difficult to insert spark plugs into their holes without cross-threading them. To avoid this possibility, fit a short length of 8 mm internal diameter rubber hose over the end of the spark plug. The flexible hose acts as a universal joint to help align the plug with the plug hole. Should the plug begin to cross-thread, the hose will slip on the spark plug, preventing thread damage to the cylinder head.

4 Release the retaining clips and slide the fuel filter out of its holder, noting which way around it is fitted. Dispose of the old filter safely; it will be highly inflammable, and may explode if thrown on a fire.

5 Slide the new filter into position, ensuring it is fitted the correct way around; the filter will either have an arrow on its body (indicating the correct direction of fuel flow) or be stamped OUT on one end (indicating the fuel outlet end of the filter).

6 Ensure the filter is clipped securely in its holder then reconnect both fuel pipes. Ensure the pipes 'click' into position on the filter and are securely retained by their quick-release fittings.

7 Start the engine and check the fuel filter for signs leaks.

18 Air cleaner filter element renewal

1 Undo the retaining screws securing the lid to the air cleaner housing **(see illustration)**.

2 Lift the lid and remove the air filter element from the housing, noting which way up it is fitted **(see illustration)**. If necessary, slacken the retaining clip securing the intake duct to the air cleaner housing lid then remove the lid to improve access.

3 Wipe clean the inside of the housing then fit the new element, ensuring it is correctly located.

4 Locate the lid correctly on the housing and securely tighten the retaining screws. Where necessary, reconnect the intake duct and securely tighten the retaining clip.

19 Manual transmission oil level check

Note: *A suitable square-section wrench may be required to undo the transmission filler/ level plug on some models. These wrenches can be obtained from most motor factors or your Peugeot dealer.*

1 Park the car on a level surface. The oil level must be checked before the car is driven, or at least 5 minutes after the engine has been switched off. If the oil is checked immediately after driving the car, some of the oil will remain distributed around the transmission, resulting in an inaccurate level reading.

2 Push in the centre pins a little, then prise out the complete expanding plastic rivets, and remove the left-hand wheel arch liner **(see illustration)**.

3 Wipe clean the area around the filler/level plug, which is on the left-hand end of the

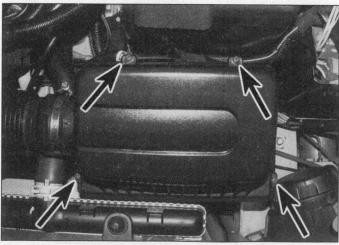

18.1 Undo the air cleaner housing lid screws

18.2 Note which way around the filter element is fitted

19.2 Push in the centre pin, then lever out the complete plastic rivet

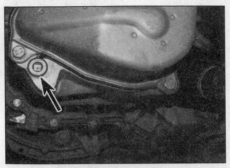

19.3a Oil level/filler plug (MA5 transmission)

19.3b Oil level/filler plug (BE4 transmission)

transmission. Unscrew the plug and clean it; discard the sealing washer **(see illustrations)**.

4 The oil level should reach the lower edge of the filler/level hole. A certain amount of oil will have gathered behind the filler/level plug, and will trickle out when it is removed; this does **not** necessarily indicate that the level is correct. To ensure that a true level is established, wait until the initial trickle has stopped, then add oil as necessary until a trickle of new oil can be seen emerging. The level will be correct when the flow ceases; use only good-quality oil of the specified type (see *Lubricants and fluids*).

5 Filling the transmission with oil is an extremely awkward operation; above all, allow plenty of time for the oil level to settle properly before checking it. If a large amount is added

to the transmission, and a large amount flows out on checking the level, refit the filler/level plug and take the vehicle on a short journey so that the new oil is distributed fully around the transmission components, then recheck the level when it has settled again.

6 If the transmission has been overfilled so that oil flows out as soon as the filler/level plug is removed, check that the car is completely level (front-to-rear and side-to-side), and allow the surplus to drain off into a container.

7 When the level is correct, fit a new sealing washer to the filler/level plug. Refit the plug, tightening it to the specified torque setting. Wash off any spilt oil then refit the wheel arch liner, securing it in position with the screws and fasteners.

20 Automatic transmission fluid level check

Note: *The transmission unit is equipped with a fluid wear sensor to inform the driver when the fluid needs renewing (the ECU flashes the Sport and Snow mode indicator lights when fluid renewal is necessary). Every time the transmission unit is topped-up, this sensor should be adjusted to compensate for the new fluid being added, however this can only be done using the Peugeot diagnostic test box. Adding fluid without adjusting the sensor will not cause any problems but will mean the sensor is giving an inaccurate reading, resulting in fluid renewal being recommended earlier than is actually necessary.*

1 Take the vehicle on a short journey, to warm the transmission up to normal operating temperature, then park the vehicle on level ground. Firmly apply the handbrake and place the selector lever in the P position.

2 Wipe clean the area around the filler plug, which is situated on the top of the transmission, directly beneath the battery. Remove the battery and battery tray/box as described in Chapter 5A, then unscrew the filler plug from the transmission and recover the sealing washer **(see illustration)**.

3 Carefully add 0.5 litre of the specified type of fluid to the transmission via the filler plug aperture. Fit a new sealing washer to the filler plug then refit the plug, tightening it to the specified torque.

4 Undo the screws and remove the engine undershield – where fitted **(see illustrations 3.3a and 3.3b)**.

5 Position a suitable container under the drain/filler plug arrangement, situated on the base of the transmission. The level plug is the smaller plug fitted to the centre of the larger drain plug **(see illustration)**.

Caution: Do not remove the drain plug by mistake.

6 Start the engine and allow it to idle. With the engine running, retain the drain plug then slacken and remove the level plug and sealing washer.

 Warning: The fluid will be hot, take precautions against scalding.

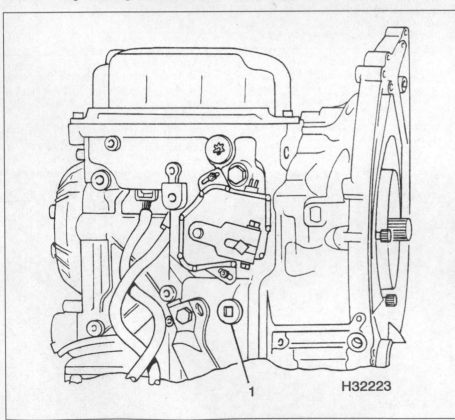

20.2 Unscrew the automatic transmission filler plug (1)

H32223

7 If there is sufficient fluid in the transmission unit, fluid should trickle out the centre of the drain plug before slowing to a drip. **Note:** *If no fluid trickles out, or just a few drips appear when the plug is removed, the fluid level is too low. Refit the level plug then switch off the engine. Add a further 0.5 litre of fluid to the transmission then refit the filler plug and repeat the check (see paragraphs 3 to 5).*

8 Once the flow of fluid stops, the level is correct. Fit a new sealing washer to the level plug then refit the plug and tighten it to the specified torque. Switch off the engine.

21 Emissions control systems check

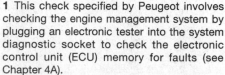

1 This check specified by Peugeot involves checking the engine management system by plugging an electronic tester into the system diagnostic socket to check the electronic control unit (ECU) memory for faults (see Chapter 4A).

2 In reality, if the vehicle is running correctly and the engine management warning light on the instrument panel is functioning normally, then this check need not be carried out.

22 Coolant renewal

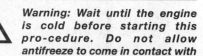

⚠️ *Warning: Wait until the engine is cold before starting this pro-cedure. Do not allow antifreeze to come in contact with your skin, or with the painted surfaces of the vehicle. Rinse off spills immediately with plenty of water. Never leave antifreeze lying around in an open container, or in a puddle in the driveway or on the garage floor. Children and pets are attracted by its sweet smell, but antifreeze can be fatal if ingested.*

Cooling system draining

1 With the engine completely cold, unscrew the expansion tank filler cap.

2 Remove the engine undershield (where

20.5 The level plug is the smaller plug (arrowed)

fitted). The undershield is secured by several screw type fasteners. Rotate the fasteners 90 degrees anti-clockwise to remove them.

3 Position a suitable container beneath the coolant drain outlet at the lower left-hand side of the radiator.

4 Release the retaining clamp and disconnect the lower hose from the radiator, then allow the coolant to drain into the container **(see illustration)**.

5 To assist draining, remove the cooling system bleed cap/screw (as applicable) from the heater matrix outlet hose union on the engine compartment bulkhead and, on some models, the bleed screw and sealing washer from the top of the coolant housing on the left-hand end of the cylinder head **(see illustration)**. In order to improve access to the bleed screw on the heater union, remove the battery as described in Chapter 5A.

6 If the coolant has been drained for a reason other than renewal, then provided it is clean and less than four years old, it can be re-used, though this is not recommended.

7 Refit the radiator hose and secure it with the hose clamp.

Cooling system flushing

8 If coolant renewal has been neglected, or if the antifreeze mixture has become diluted, then in time, the cooling system may gradually lose efficiency, as the coolant passages become restricted due to rust, scale deposits, and other sediment. The cooling system efficiency can be restored by flushing the system clean.

9 The radiator should be flushed separately from the engine, to avoid excess contamination.

Radiator flushing

10 Disconnect the top and bottom hoses and any other relevant hoses from the radiator (see Chapter 3).

11 Insert a garden hose into the radiator top inlet. Direct a flow of clean water through the radiator, and continue flushing until clean water emerges from the radiator bottom outlet.

12 If after a reasonable period, the water still does not run clear, the radiator can be flushed with a good proprietary cleaning agent. It is important that their manufacturer's instructions are followed carefully. If the contamination is particularly bad, insert the hose in the radiator bottom outlet, and reverse-flush the radiator.

Engine flushing

13 To flush the engine, remove the thermostat (see Chapter 3).

14 With the bottom hose disconnected from the radiator, insert a garden hose into the coolant housing. Direct a clean flow of water through the engine, and continue flushing until clean water emerges from the radiator bottom hose.

15 When flushing is complete, refit the thermostat and reconnect the hoses (see Chapter 3).

Cooling system filling

16 Before attempting to fill the cooling system, make sure that all hoses and clips are in good condition, and that the clips are tight. Note that an antifreeze mixture must be used all year round, to prevent corrosion of the engine components (see following sub-Section).

17 Remove the expansion tank filler cap.

18 Remove the cooling system bleed screws (see paragraph 5).

19 Peugeot recommend the use of a 'header tank' when refilling the cooling system, to reduce the possibility of air being trapped in the system. Although Peugeot dealers use a special header tank which screws onto the expansion tank, the same effect can be achieved by using a suitable 1.0 litre bottle, with a seal between the bottle and the expansion tank **(see illustration)**.

22.4 Squeeze together the tabs to release the hose clamp

22.5 Undo the bleed screw from the heater outlet hose union (arrowed)

22.19 Use a 1.0 litre plastic bottle as a header tank

20 Fit the header tank to the expansion tank and slowly fill the system whilst observing the bleed holes. Coolant will emerge from each of the bleed holes in turn, starting with the heater matrix hose. As soon as coolant free from air bubbles emerges from the heater matrix hose outlet, securely refit the cap/screw (as applicable) then watch the bleed hole on the coolant housing. Once coolant free from air bubbles emerges from the housing hole, refit the bleed screw and sealing washer and tighten securely.

21 Continue to fill the cooling system until bubbles stop appearing in the expansion tank. Help to bleed the air from the system by repeatedly squeezing the radiator bottom hose.

22 When no more bubbles appear, ensure the header tank is full (at least 1.0 litre of coolant) then start the engine. Run the engine at a fast idle speed (do not exceed 2000 rpm) until the cooling fan cuts in and out TWICE, then when the fan has stopped for the second time, switch the engine off.

Caution: The coolant will be hot. Take great care not to scald yourself.

23 Allow the engine to cool, then remove the header tank. Wash off any spilt coolant with cold water.

24 When the engine has cooled, check the coolant level with reference to *Weekly checks*. Top-up the level if necessary, and refit the expansion tank cap.

Antifreeze mixture

25 The antifreeze should always be renewed at the specified intervals. This is necessary not only to maintain the antifreeze properties, but also to prevent corrosion which would otherwise occur as the corrosion inhibitors become progressively less effective.

26 Always use an ethylene-glycol based antifreeze which is suitable for use in mixed-metal cooling systems.

27 Before adding antifreeze, the cooling system should be completely drained, preferably flushed, and all hoses checked for condition and security.

28 After filling with antifreeze, a label should be attached to the expansion tank, stating the type and concentration of antifreeze used, and the date installed. Any subsequent topping-up should be made with the same type and concentration of antifreeze.

29 Do not use engine antifreeze in the windscreen/tailgate washer system, as it will damage the vehicle paintwork. A screenwash additive should be added to the washer system in the quantities stated on the bottle.

Every ten years

23 Airbags and seat belt pretensioners renewal

1 Peugeot recommend that the airbags and seat belt pretensioners are renewed regardless of their condition every ten years. Refer to Chapter 12 for airbag renewal, and Chapter 11 for seat belt pretensioner renewal.

Chapter 1 Part B:
Routine maintenance and servicing – diesel models

Contents

Degrees of difficulty

Easy, suitable for novice with little experience

Fairly easy, suitable for beginner with some experience

Fairly difficult, suitable for competent DIY mechanic

Difficult, suitable for experienced DIY mechanic

Very difficult, suitable for expert DIY or professional

Lubricants and fluids
Refer to *Weekly checks* on page 0•18

Capacities

Engine oil (including oil filter)
1.4 litre engines . . . . 3.75 litres
1.6 litre engines . . . . 3.75 litres
2.0 litre engines:
   SOHC . . . . 4.50 litres
   DOHC . . . . 5.25 litres

Cooling system
1.4 litre engines (approximate) . . . . 6.0 litres
1.6 litre engines (approximate) . . . . 6.5 litres
2.0 litre engines (approximate) . . . . 8.2 litres

Transmission
Manual transmission (approximate):
   MA5 . . . . 2.0 litres
   BE4/5 . . . . 1.9 litres
   ML6CL:
      Without cooling fins on the gearbox casing . . . . 2.6 litres
      With cooling fins on the gearbox casing . . . . 1.9 litres
Automatic transmissions:
   Drain and refill . . . . 4.5 litres
   Total capacity (including torque converter) . . . . 6.0 litres

Power-assisted steering (approximate) . . . . 0.8 litres

Fuel tank . . . . 60 litres

Cooling system
Antifreeze mixture:
   50% antifreeze . . . . Protection down to –37°C
   55% antifreeze . . . . Protection down to –45°C
Note: *Refer to antifreeze manufacturer for latest recommendations.*

Brakes
Brake pad friction material minimum thickness . . . . 2.0 mm

Tyre pressures
See end of *Weekly checks* on page 0•18

Torque wrench settings

	Nm	lbf ft
Automatic transmission:		
Filler plug	24	18
Level plug	24	18
Engine oil filter cover (1.4 and 1.6 litre engine)	25	18
Engine sump drain plug	16	12
Manual transmission filler/level plug	20	15
Roadwheel bolts	90	66

The maintenance intervals in this manual are provided with the assumption that you, not the dealer, will be carrying out the work. These are the minimum maintenance intervals recommended by us for vehicles driven daily. If you wish to keep your vehicle in peak condition at all times, you may wish to perform some of these procedures more often. We encourage frequent maintenance, because it enhances the efficiency, performance and resale value of your vehicle.

After completion of any of the following services, re-set the service indicator with reference to Section 8 of Part 1A of this Chapter.

When the vehicle is new, it should be serviced by a dealer service department (or other workshop recognised by the vehicle manufacturer as providing the same standard of service) in order to preserve the warranty. The vehicle manufacturer may reject warranty claims if you are unable to prove that servicing has been carried out as and when specified, using only original equipment parts or parts certified to be of equivalent quality.

Weekly, or every 250 miles (400 km)

☐ Refer to *Weekly checks*

Every 6000 miles (10 000 km) or 12 months – whichever comes sooner

☐ Renew the engine oil and filter* (Section 3)
☐ Drain any water from the fuel filter (Section 4)
☐ Check all underbonnet components and hoses for fluid leaks (Section 5)
☐ Check the steering and suspension (Section 6)
☐ Check driveshaft rubber gaiters and CV joints (Section 7)
☐ Lubricate all hinges and locks (Section 8)

* **Note:** *Peugeot recommend that the engine oil and filter are changed every 10 000 miles (16 000 km) or 2 years. However, oil and filter changes are good for the engine and we recommend that the oil and filter are renewed more frequently, especially if the vehicle is used on a lot of short journeys.*

Every 12 000 miles (20 000 km)

☐ Check the pollen filter (Section 9)
☐ Check the condition of the brake pads, and renew if necessary (Section 10)
☐ Check the operation of the handbrake (Section 11)
☐ Carry out a road test (Section 12)
☐ Check the condition of the auxiliary drivebelt, and renew if necessary (Section 13)

Every 24 000 miles (40 000 km)

☐ Renew the air filter (Section 14)
☐ Renew the fuel filter (Section 15)
☐ Check the manual transmission oil level, and top-up if necessary (Section 16)
☐ Check the automatic transmission fluid level, and top up if necessary (Section 17)

Every 36 000 miles (60 000 km)

☐ Renew the timing belt – (Section 18)

Note: *Although the Peugeot interval for timing belt renewal is 96 000 miles (160 000 km) for normal use, and 80 000 miles (130 000 km) for use in adverse conditions, it is strongly recommended that the timing belt renewal interval is reduced to 36 000 miles (60 000 km) on vehicles which are subjected to intensive use, ie, mainly short journeys or a lot of stop-start driving. The actual belt renewal interval is therefore very much up to the individual owner, but bear in mind that severe engine damage will result if the belt breaks.*

Every 36 000 miles (60 000 km) or 2 years, whichever comes sooner

☐ Renew the brake fluid (Section 19)

Note: *A hydraulic clutch shares its fluid reservoir with the braking system, and may also need to be bled.*

Every 48 000 miles (80 000 km)

☐ Check the particulate emission system (where fitted on models manufactured up to November 2002) (Section 20)

Every 72 000 miles (120 000 km) or 5 years, whichever comes sooner

☐ Check the particulate emission system (where fitted on models manufactured from November 2002 – build code 9492) (Section 20)
☐ Renew the coolant (Section 21)

Every 10 years

☐ Renew the airbags and seat belt pretensioners (Section 22)

Underbonnet view of a 1.4 litre model

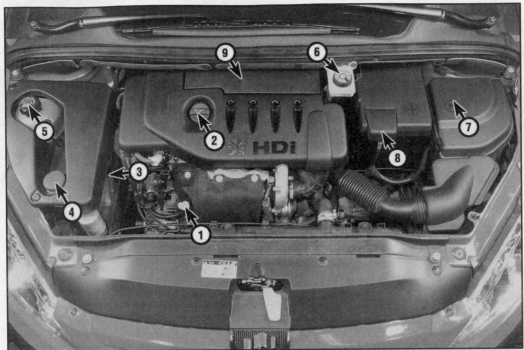

1 Engine oil dipstick
2 Engine oil filler cap
3 Power steering reservoir filler cap
4 Washer fluid reservoir
5 Coolant expansion tank filler cap
6 Brake/clutch cylinders fluid reservoir
7 Engine compartment electrical box
8 Battery positive terminal cover
9 Air cleaner housing

Front underbody view

1 Engine oil drain plug
2 Air conditioning compressor
3 Driveshaft
4 Brake caliper
5 Lower suspension arm
6 Track rod
7 Anti-roll bar

Rear underbody view (Estate model shown)

1 Fuel tank
2 Beam axle
3 Handbrake cable
4 Brake caliper
5 Coil spring
6 Tool kit

Maintenace procedures

1 General information

This Chapter is designed to help the home mechanic maintain his/her vehicle for safety, economy, long life and peak performance.

The Chapter contains a master maintenance schedule, followed by Sections dealing specifically with each task in the schedule. Visual checks, adjustments, component renewal and other helpful items are included. Refer to the accompanying illustrations of the engine compartment and the underside of the vehicle for the locations of the various components.

Servicing your vehicle in accordance with the mileage/time maintenance schedule and the following Sections will provide a planned maintenance programme, which should result in a long and reliable service life. This is a comprehensive plan, so maintaining some items but not others at the specified service intervals, will not produce the same results.

As you service your vehicle, you will discover that many of the procedures can – and should – be grouped together, because of the particular procedure being performed, or because of the proximity of two otherwise-unrelated components to one another. For example, if the vehicle is raised for any reason, the exhaust can be inspected at the same time as the suspension and steering components.

The first step in this maintenance programme is to prepare yourself before the actual work begins. Read through all the Sections relevant to the work to be carried out, then make a list and gather all the parts and tools required. If a problem is encountered, seek advice from a parts specialist, or a dealer service department.

2 Regular maintenance

1 If, from the time the vehicle is new, the routine maintenance schedule is followed closely, and frequent checks are made of fluid levels and high-wear items, as suggested throughout this manual, the engine will be kept in relatively good running condition, and the need for additional work will be minimised.
2 It is possible that there will be times when the engine is running poorly due to the lack of regular maintenance. This is even more likely if a used vehicle, which has not received regular and frequent maintenance checks, is purchased. In such cases, additional work may need to be carried out, outside of the regular maintenance intervals.
3 If engine wear is suspected, a compression test (refer to Chapter 2C) will provide valuable information regarding the overall performance of the main internal components. Such a test can be used as a basis to decide on the extent of the work to be carried out. If, for example,

a compression test indicates serious internal engine wear, conventional maintenance as described in this Chapter will not greatly improve the performance of the engine, and may prove a waste of time and money, unless extensive overhaul work is carried out first.
4 The following series of operations are those most often required to improve the perfor-mance of a generally poor-running engine:

Primary operations

a) Clean, inspect and test the battery (refer to 'Weekly checks').
b) Check all the engine-related fluids (refer to 'Weekly checks').
c) Check the condition and tension of the auxiliary drivebelt (Section 13).
d) Check the condition of the air filter, and renew if necessary (Section 14).
e) Check the condition of all hoses, and check for fluid leaks (Section 5).
f) Renew the fuel filter (Section 15).
5 If the above operations do not prove fully effective, carry out the following secondary operations:

Secondary operations

All items listed under *Primary operations*, plus the following:
a) Check the charging system (refer to Chapter 5A).
b) Check the preheating system (refer to Chapter 5C).
c) Check the fuel system (refer to Chapter 4B).

3.2 Undo the engine undershield screws

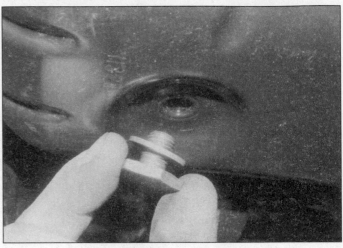

3.3 Unscrew the sump plug

Every 6 000 miles (10 000 km) or 12 months

3 Engine oil and filter renewal

1 Frequent oil and filter changes are the most important preventative maintenance procedures which can be undertaken by the DIY owner. As engine oil ages, it becomes

HAYNES HINT

As the drain plug releases from the threads, move it away sharply so the stream of oil issuing from the sump runs into the container, not up your sleeve.

3.7 Engine oil filter cover (arrowed)

diluted and contaminated, which leads to premature engine wear.

2 Before starting this procedure, gather together all the necessary tools and materials. Also make sure that you have plenty of clean rags and newspapers handy, to mop-up any spills. Ideally, the engine oil should be warm, as it will drain better, and more built-up sludge will be removed with it. Take care, however, not to touch the exhaust or any other hot parts of the engine when working under the vehicle. To avoid any possibility of scalding, and to protect yourself from possible skin irritants and other harmful contaminants in used engine oils, it is advisable to wear gloves when carrying out this work. Access to the underside of the vehicle will be greatly improved if it can be raised on a lift, driven onto ramps, or jacked up and supported on axle stands. Whichever method is chosen, make sure that the vehicle remains level, or if it is at an angle, that the drain plug is at the lowest point. Release the screws and remove the engine undershield **(see illustration)**.

3 Slacken the drain plug about half a turn, position the draining container under the drain plug, then remove the plug completely **(see illustration)**. If possible, try to keep the plug

3.10a Fit the new O-ring to the cover

pressed into the sump while unscrewing it by hand the last couple of turns **(see Haynes Hint)**. Recover the sealing ring from the drain plug.

4 Allow some time for the old oil to drain, noting that it may be necessary to reposition the container as the oil flow slows to a trickle.

5 After all the oil has drained, wipe off the drain plug with a clean rag, and fit a new sealing washer. Clean the area around the drain plug opening, and refit the plug. Tighten the plug securely.

6 If the filter is also to be renewed, move the container into position under the oil filter, which is located on the front side of the cylinder block.

1.4 and 1.6 litre engines

7 On these engines, the filter element is contained within a filter cover. Using a socket or spanner, slacken and remove the filter cover from above **(see illustration)**. Be prepared for fluid spillage, and recover the O-ring seal from the cover.

8 Pull the filter element from the filter housing.

9 Use a clean rag to remove all oil, dirt and sludge from the inside and outside of the filter cover.

10 Fit the new O-ring to the filter cover, then insert the new filter element into the housing, ensuring that the element locating peg engages correctly with the corresponding hole in the housing **(see illustrations)**.

11 Apply a little clean engine oil to the O-ring seal, then refit the filter/cover to the housing and tighten the cover to the specified torque.

2.0 litre engines

12 Using an oil filter removal tool if necessary, slacken the filter initially, then unscrew it by hand the rest of the way **(see illustration)**. Empty the oil in the old filter into the container.

3.10b Ensure the filter locating peg (arrowed) locates into the corresponding hole in the housing (arrowed)

3.12 Use a filter removal tool to slacken the oil filter

5 Hose and fluid leak check

Cooling system

⚠️ **Warning: Refer to the safety information given in 'Safety first!' and Chapter 3 before disturbing any of the cooling system components.**

1 Carefully check the radiator and heater coolant hoses along their entire length. Renew any hose which is cracked, swollen or which shows signs of deterioration. Cracks will show up better if the hose is squeezed. Pay close attention to the clips that secure the hoses to the cooling system components. Hose clips that have been overtightened can pinch and puncture hoses, resulting in cooling system leaks.

2 Inspect all the cooling system components (hoses, joint faces, etc) for leaks. Where any problems of this nature are found on system components, renew the component or gasket with reference to Chapter 3.

3 A leak from the cooling system will usually show up as white or rust-coloured deposits, on the area surrounding the leak **(see Haynes Hint)**.

13 Use a clean rag to remove all oil, dirt and sludge from the filter sealing area on the engine. Check the old filter to make sure that the rubber sealing ring hasn't stuck to the engine. If it has, carefully remove it.

14 Apply a light coating of clean engine oil to the sealing ring on the new filter, then screw it into position on the engine. Tighten the filter firmly by hand only – **do not** use any tools. Where necessary, refit the splash guard under the engine.

All engines

15 Remove the old oil and all tools from under the car, then lower the car to the ground (if applicable).

16 Remove the dipstick, then unscrew the oil filler cap from the top of the filler tube on the front side of the cylinder block. Fill the engine, using the correct grade and type of oil (*see Lubricants and fluids*). An oil can spout or funnel may help to reduce spillage. Pour in half the specified quantity of oil first, then wait a few minutes for the oil to fall to the sump. Continue adding oil a small quantity at a time until the level is up to the lower mark on the dipstick. Adding approximately 1.0 litre will bring the level up to the upper mark on the dipstick. Refit the filler cap.

17 Start the engine and run it for a few minutes; check for leaks around the oil filter seal and the sump drain plug. Note that there may be a delay of a few seconds before the oil pressure warning light goes out when the engine is first started, as the oil circulates through the engine oil galleries and the new

oil filter (where fitted) before the pressure builds-up.

18 Switch off the engine, and wait a few minutes for the oil to settle in the sump once more. With the new oil circulated and the filter completely full, recheck the level on the dipstick, and add more oil as necessary.

19 Dispose of the used engine oil safely, with reference to *General Repair Procedures*.

4 Fuel filter water draining

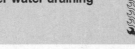

1 Remove the battery as described in Chapter 5A on 1.4 litre models. On 2.0 litre models, unscrew the four fasteners and remove the plastic cover from the top of the engine.

2 Where fitted, a water drain plug and tube are provided at the base of the fuel filter housing **(see illustrations)**. *Note: A water drain facility is not provided on later models – if an air purge screw is located on top of the fuel filter, there is no water drain facility.*

3 Place a suitable container beneath the drain tube, and cover the surrounding area with rags.

4 Open the drain plug, and allow fuel and water to drain until fuel which is free from water, emerges from the end of the tube. Close the drain plug.

5 Dispose of the drained fuel safely.

6 Start the engine. If difficulty is experienced, bleed the fuel system (Chapter 4B).

Fuel

⚠️ **Warning: Refer to the safety information given in 'Safety first!' and Chapter 4B before disturbing any of the fuel system components.**

4 Check all fuel lines at their connections to the injection pump, injectors and fuel filter housing.

5 Examine each fuel hose/pipe along its length for splits or cracks. Check for leakage from the union nuts and examine the unions between the metal fuel lines and the fuel filter housing. Also check the area around the fuel injectors for signs of leakage.

6 To identify fuel leaks between the fuel tank and the engine bay, the vehicle should raised and securely supported on axle stands. Inspect the fuel tank and filler neck

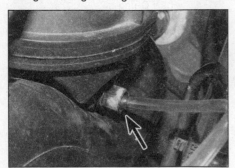

4.2a Fuel filter water drain plug (arrowed) – 1.4 litre engine . . .

4.2b . . . and 2.0 litre engine (arrowed)

HAYNES HiNT

A leak in the cooling system will usually show up as white- or rust-coloured deposits on the area adjoining the leak.

6.2 Check the steering rack gaiters for damage

for punctures, cracks and other damage. The connection between the filler neck and tank is especially critical. Sometimes a rubber filler neck or connecting hose will leak due to loose retaining clamps or deteriorated rubber.

7 Carefully check all rubber hoses and metal fuel lines leading away from the fuel tank. Check for loose connections, deteriorated hoses, kinked lines, and other damage. Pay particular attention to the vent pipes and hoses, which often loop up around the filler neck and can become blocked or kinked, making tank filling difficult. Follow the fuel supply and return lines to the front of the vehicle, carefully inspecting them all the way for signs of damage or corrosion. Renew damaged sections as necessary.

Engine oil

8 Inspect the area around the camshaft cover, cylinder head, oil filter and sump joint faces. Bear in mind that, over a period of time, some very slight seepage from these areas is to be expected – what you are really looking for is any indication of a serious leak caused by gasket failure. Engine oil seeping from the base of the timing belt cover or the transmission bellhousing may be an indication of crankshaft or input shaft oil seal failure. Should a leak be found, renew the failed gasket or oil seal by referring to the appropriate Chapters in this manual.

Power-assisted steering fluid

9 Examine the hose running between the fluid reservoir and the power steering pump, and the return hose running from the steering rack

6.3 Check for wear in the hub bearings by grasping the wheel and trying to rock it

to the fluid reservoir. Also examine the high pressure supply hose between the pump and the steering rack.

10 Where applicable, check the hoses leading to the PAS fluid cooler at the front of the engine bay. Look for deterioration caused by corrosion and damage from grounding, or debris thrown up from the road surface.

11 Pay particular attention to crimped unions, and the area surrounding the hoses that are secured with adjustable worm-drive clips.

Air conditioning refrigerant

 Warning: Refer to the safety information given in 'Safety first!' and Chapter 3, regarding the dangers of disturbing any of the air conditioning system components.

12 The air conditioning system is filled with a liquid refrigerant, which is retained under high pressure. If the air conditioning system is opened and depressurised without the aid of specialised equipment, the refrigerant will immediately turn into gas and escape into the atmosphere. If the liquid comes into contact with your skin, it can cause severe frostbite. In addition, the refrigerant contains substances which are environmentally damaging; for this reason, it should not be allowed to escape into the atmosphere.

13 Any suspected air conditioning system leaks should be immediately referred to a Peugeot dealer or air conditioning specialist. Leakage will be shown up as a steady drop in the level of refrigerant in the system.

14 Note that water may drip from the condenser drain pipe, underneath the car, immediately after the air conditioning system has been in use. This is normal, and should not be cause for concern.

Brake (and clutch) fluid

 Warning: Refer to the safety information given in 'Safety first!' and Chapter 9, regarding the dangers of handling brake fluid.

15 With reference to Chapter 9, examine the area surrounding the brake pipe unions at the master cylinder for signs of leakage. Check the area around the base of fluid reservoir, for signs of leakage caused by seal failure. Also examine the brake pipe unions at the ABS hydraulic unit.

16 If fluid loss is evident, but the leak cannot be pinpointed in the engine bay, the brake calipers and underbody brake lines and should be carefully checked with the vehicle raised and supported on axle stands. Leakage of fluid from the braking system is serious fault that must be rectified immediately.

17 Refer to Chapter 6 and check for leakage around the hydraulic fluid line connections to the clutch master cylinder at the bulkhead, and to the clutch slave cylinder, bolted to the side of the transmission bellhousing.

18 Brake/clutch hydraulic fluid is a toxic substance with a watery consistency. New

fluid is almost colourless, but it becomes darker with age and use.

Unidentified fluid leaks

19 If there are signs that a fluid of some description is leaking from the vehicle, but you cannot identify the type of fluid or its exact origin, park the vehicle overnight and slide a large piece of card underneath it. Providing that the card is positioned in roughly in the right location, even the smallest leak will show up on the card. Not only will this help you to pinpoint the exact location of the leak, it should be easier to identify the fluid from its colour. Bear in mind, though, that the leak may only be occurring when the engine is running!

Vacuum hoses

20 Although the braking system is hydraulically-operated, the brake servo unit amplifies the effort you apply at the brake pedal, by making use of the vacuum created by the pump (see Chapter 9). Vacuum is ported to the servo by means of a large-bore hose. Any leaks that develop in this hose will reduce the effectiveness of the braking system.

21 In addition, many of the underbonnet components, particularly the emission control components, are driven by vacuum supplied from the vacuum pump via narrow-bore hoses. A leak in a vacuum hose means that air is being drawn into the hose (rather than escaping from it) and this makes leakage very difficult to detect. One method is to use an old length of vacuum hose as a kind of stethoscope – hold one end close to (but not in) your ear and use the other end to probe the area around the suspected leak. When the end of the hose is directly over a vacuum leak, a hissing sound will be heard clearly through the hose. Care must be taken to avoid contacting hot or moving components, as the engine must be running, when testing in this manner. Renew any vacuum hoses that are found to be defective.

---

6 Steering and suspension check

Front suspension and steering

1 Raise the front of the vehicle, and securely support it on axle stands.

2 Visually inspect the balljoint dust covers and the steering rack-and-pinion gaiters for splits, chafing or deterioration **(see illustration)**. Any wear of these components will cause loss of lubricant, together with dirt and water entry, resulting in rapid deterioration of the balljoints or steering gear.

3 Grasp the roadwheel at the 12 o'clock and 6 o'clock positions, and try to rock it **(see illustration)**. Very slight free play may be felt, but if the movement is appreciable, further

investigation is necessary to determine the source. Continue rocking the wheel while an assistant depresses the footbrake. If the movement is now eliminated or significantly reduced, it is likely that the hub bearings are at fault. If the free play is still evident with the footbrake depressed, then there is wear in the suspension joints or mountings.

4 Now grasp the wheel at the 9 o'clock and 3 o'clock positions, and try to rock it as before. Any movement felt now may again be caused by wear in the hub bearings or the steering track rod balljoints. If the inner or outer balljoint is worn, the visual movement will be obvious.

5 Using a large screwdriver or flat bar, check for wear in the suspension mounting bushes by levering between the relevant suspension component and its attachment point. Some movement is to be expected as the mountings are made of rubber, but excessive wear should be obvious. Also check the condition of any visible rubber bushes, looking for splits, cracks or contamination of the rubber.

6 With the car standing on its wheels, have an assistant turn the steering wheel back-and-forth about an eighth of a turn each way. There should be very little, if any, lost movement between the steering wheel and roadwheels. If this is not the case, closely observe the joints and mountings previously described, but in addition, check the steering column universal joints for wear, and the rack-and-pinion steering gear itself.

Suspension strut/ shock absorber

7 Check for any signs of fluid leakage around the suspension strut/shock absorber body, or from the rubber gaiter around the piston rod. Should any fluid be noticed, the suspension strut/shock absorber is defective internally, and should be renewed. **Note:** *Suspension struts/shock absorbers should always be renewed in pairs on the same axle.*

8 The efficiency of the suspension strut/shock absorber may be checked by bouncing the vehicle at each corner. Generally speaking, the body will return to its normal position and stop after being depressed. If it rises and returns on a rebound, the suspension strut/shock absorber is probably suspect. Examine also the suspension strut/shock absorber upper and lower mountings for any signs of wear.

7 Driveshaft gaiter and CV joints check

1 With the vehicle raised and securely supported on axle stands, turn the steering to full left or right lock, then slowly rotate the roadwheel. Inspect the outer constant velocity (CV) joint rubber gaiters, squeezing the gaiters to open out the folds **(see illustration)**. Check for signs of cracking, splits or deterioration of the rubber, which may allow the grease to escape, or water and grit to enter. Also check the security and condition of the retaining clips. Repeat these checks on the inner CV joints. If any damage or deterioration is found, the gaiters should be renewed (see Chapter 8).

2 At the same time, check the general condition of the CV joints themselves by

7.1 Check the driveshaft gaiter for damage

first holding the driveshaft and attempting to rotate the wheel. Repeat this check whilst holding the inner joint and attempting to rotate the driveshaft. Any appreciable movement indicates wear in the CV joints, wear in the driveshaft splines, or a loose driveshaft retaining nut.

8 Hinge and lock lubrication

1 Lubricate the hinges of the bonnet, doors and tailgate with a light general-purpose oil. Similarly, lubricate all latches, locks and lock strikers – don't overdo it, or it will get on your clothes as you get in! At the same time, check the security and operation of all the locks, adjusting them if necessary (see Chapter 11).

2 Lightly lubricate the bonnet release mechanism and cable with a suitable grease.

Every 12 000 miles (20 000 km)

9 Pollen filter check

1 Open the bonnet.

2 Prise up the centre pins, lever out the complete plastic expanding rivets, then remove the sound insulation trim covering the pollen filter cover **(see illustrations)**.

3 Grasp the filter cover and pull it from the bulkhead **(see illustration)**.

4 Slide the filter out **(see illustration)**.

5 Check the condition of the filter, and renew it if dirty.

6 Wipe clean the inside of the housing and fit the pollen filter element, making sure that it is correctly seated.

9.2a Prise up the centre pins, then lever out the complete plastic rivets (arrowed) . . .

9.2b . . . then remove the sound insulation material

9.3 Pull the filter cover (arrowed) from the bulkhead

9.4 Slide the pollen filter out

7 Refit the pollen filter cover.
8 Refit the sound insulation trim, and secure it place with the plastic rivets.
9 Close the bonnet.

10 Brake pad check

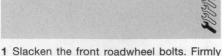

1 Slacken the front roadwheel bolts. Firmly apply the handbrake, then jack up the front of the car and support it securely on axle stands (see *Jacking and vehicle support*). Remove the front roadwheels.
2 For a quick check, the pad thickness can be carried out via the inspection hole on the front caliper (**see Haynes Hint**). Using a steel rule, measure the thickness of the pad friction material. This must not be less than the minimum given in the Specifications.
3 For a comprehensive check, the brake pads should be removed and cleaned. The operation of the caliper can then be checked, and the brake disc itself can be fully examined on both sides. Refer to Chapter 9 for details.
4 If any pad's friction material is worn to the specified minimum thickness or less, all four pads must be renewed as a set. Refer to Chapter 9 for details.
5 On completion, refit the roadwheels then lower the vehicle to the ground and tighten the wheel bolts to the specified torque.
6 Slacken the rear roadwheel bolts. Jack up the rear of the car and support it securely on

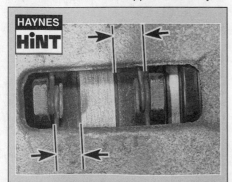

For a quick check, the thickness of the friction material remaining on each brake pad can be measured through the aperture in the caliper body.

axle stands. Remove the rear roadwheels. Repeat the procedure described in Paragraphs 2 to 5 on the rear brake pads.

11 Handbrake check

1 The handbrake should be fully applied before 8 clicks can be heard from the lever ratchet mechanism. Check and, if necessary, adjust the handbrake as described in Chapter 9.

12 Road test

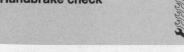

Instruments and electrical equipment

1 Check the operation of all instruments and electrical equipment.
2 Make sure that all instruments read correctly, and switch on all electrical equipment in turn, to check that it functions properly.

Steering and suspension

3 Check for any abnormalities in the steering, suspension, handling or road 'feel'.
4 Drive the vehicle, and check that there are no unusual vibrations or noises.
5 Check that the steering feels positive, with no excessive 'sloppiness', or roughness, and check for any suspension noises when cornering and driving over bumps.

Drivetrain

6 Check the performance of the engine, clutch, transmission and driveshafts.
7 Listen for any unusual noises from the engine, clutch and transmission.
8 Make sure that the engine runs smoothly when idling, and that there is no hesitation when accelerating.
9 Check that the clutch action is smooth and progressive, that the drive is taken up smoothly, and that the pedal travel is not excessive. Also listen for any noises when the clutch pedal is depressed.
10 Check that all gears can be engaged smoothly without noise, and that the gear lever action is smooth and not abnormally vague or 'notchy'.
11 On automatic transmission models, make sure that all gearchanges occur smoothly, without snatching, and without an increase in engine speed between changes. Check that all the gear positions can be selected with the vehicle at rest. If any problems are found, they should be referred to a Peugeot dealer.
12 Listen for a metallic clicking sound from the front of the vehicle, as the vehicle is driven slowly in a circle with the steering on full lock. Carry out this check in both directions. If a clicking noise is heard, this indicates wear in a driveshaft joint, in which case, the complete driveshaft must be renewed (see Chapter 8).

Braking system

13 Make sure that the vehicle does not pull to one side when braking, and that the wheels do not lock when braking hard.
14 Check that there is no vibration through the steering when braking.
15 Check that the handbrake operates correctly without excessive movement of the lever, and that it holds the vehicle stationary on a slope.
16 Test the operation of the brake servo unit as follows. With the engine off, depress the footbrake four or five times to exhaust the vacuum. Hold the brake pedal depressed, then start the engine. As the engine starts, there should be a noticeable 'give' in the brake pedal as vacuum builds-up. Allow the engine to run for at least two minutes, and then switch it off. If the brake pedal is depressed now, it should be possible to detect a hiss from the servo as the pedal is depressed. After about four or five applications, no further hissing should be heard, and the pedal should feel considerably harder.

13 Auxiliary drivebelt check and renewal

1 All models are equipped with a single poly-V type, multi-ribbed auxiliary drivebelt. The belt tension is adjusted automatically by means of a spring-loaded tensioner.

Checking condition

2 Slacken the right-hand front roadwheel bolts. Apply the handbrake, then jack up the front of the car and support it securely on axle stands (see *Jacking and vehicle support*). Remove the right-hand front roadwheel.
3 Remove the plastic expanding rivets (push in the centre pin a little, then prise out the rivet) and remove the wheel arch liner from under the right-hand front wing for access to the crankshaft pulley bolt.
4 Using a suitable socket and bar fitted to the crankshaft pulley bolt, rotate the crankshaft so that the entire length of the drivebelt can be examined. Examine the drivebelt for cracks, splitting, fraying or damage. Check also for signs of glazing (shiny patches) and for separation of the belt plies. Renew the belt if worn or damaged.
5 On 1.6 and 2.0 litre models, the automatic tensioner has markings which align with each other when the belt is in need of renewal. On 1.6 litre models, the small square lug aligns with the large square on the front of the tensioner body. On 2.0 litre models, a groove aligns with a mark on the mounting bracket (**see illustration**).

Removal

6 If not already done, proceed as described in paragraphs 2 and 3.
7 Remove the plastic cover from the top of

13.5 When the groove (A) lines up with the mark (B) on the mounting bracket, the belt requires renewal

13.7 Push in the centre pin a little, then prise out the complete plastic expanding rivet

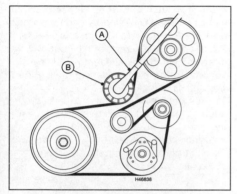

13.8 Use an open-ended spanner to rotate the tensioner arm clockwise, then lock it in place by inserting a 4 mm drill into the hole in the tensioner body (arrowed)

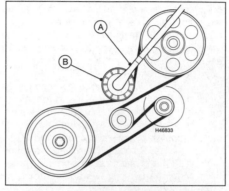

13.10a Move the spanner (A) anti-clockwise to release the tension roller (B) from the drivebelt – early 2.0 litre SOHC models with air conditioning

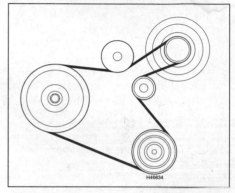

13.10b Auxiliary drivebelt routing on early 2.0 litre SOHC models without air conditioning

A Spanner   B Tensioner roller

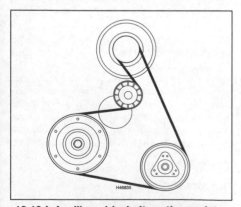

13.10c Auxiliary drivebelt routing on later 2.0 litre SOHC models with air conditioning

the coolant and windscreen washer reservoirs. The cover is secured by two expanding plastic rivets. Push the centre pins in a little, then prise the complete rivets from place (**see illustration**).

1.4 and 1.6 litre engines

8 Using an open-ended spanner, reach down and rotate the tensioner arm clockwise to release the belt tension. Insert a 4 mm drill bit or rod into the hole in the tensioner body, so that the tensioner arm rests against it, and locks it in this position (**see illustration**). It is useful to have a small mirror available to enable

the alignment of the locking holes to be more easily seen in the limited space available.
9 Remove the belt from the pulleys. Note that if the belt is to be re-used, mark the direction of rotation. The belt must be refitted the same way around.

2.0 litre engines

10 Using a suitable spanner engaged with the hexagonal stud in the centre of the automatic tensioner pulley, move the pulley towards the rear of the car to release the tension on the drivebelt. Note that considerable effort will be needed to move the pulley against spring

tension. Insert a 4 mm drill bit or rod into lock the tensioner in this position (**see illustrations**). Slip the belt off the pulleys. If the belt is to be re-used, mark the direction of rotation. The belt must be refitted the same way around.

Refitting and tensioning

1.4 and 1.6 litre engines

11 Fit the belt around the pulleys, ensuring that the ribs on the belt are correctly engaged with the grooves in the pulleys, and the drivebelt is correctly routed (**see illustrations**). If refitting a used belt, use the mark made on removal to ensure it's fitted the correct way around.

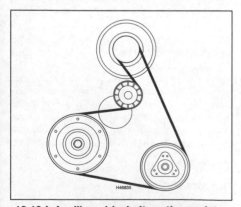

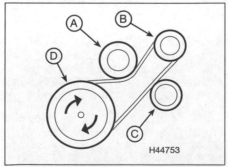

13.11a Auxiliary drivebelt routing (1.4 and 1.6 litre engine without air conditioning)

A Tensioner   C Idler pulley
B Alternator   D Crankshaft

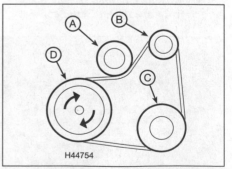

13.11b Auxiliary drivebelt routing (1.4 and 1.6 litre with air conditioning)

A Tensioner   C Compressor
B Alternator   D Crankshaft

13.10d Auxiliary drivebelt routing on later 2.0 litre DOHC models with air conditioning

12 Using an open-ended spanner, hold the tensioner arm so that the locking drill bit/rod can be removed, then release the pressure on the spanner so that the automatic tensioner takes up the slack in the drivebelt.

13 Refit the plastic cover over the coolant and windscreen washer reservoirs, and refit the wheel arch liner.

2.0 litre engines

14 Fit the belt around the pulleys, ensuring that the ribs on the belt are correctly engaged with the grooves in the pulleys, and the drivebelt is correctly routed. If refitting a used belt, use the mark made on removal to ensure it's fitted the correct way around.

15 Using a suitable spanner, hold the tensioner pulley so that the locking drill bit/rod can be removed, then release the pressure on the spanner so that the automatic tensioner takes up the slack in the drivebelt.

16 On completion, refit the wheel arch liner. Refit the roadwheel, and lower the vehicle to the ground.

Every 24 000 miles (40 000 km)

14 Air filter element renewal

1.4 litre engines

1 Remove the plastic cover from the top of the engine. The cover is retained by rubber grommets, and pulls upwards to release.

2 Undo the three screws at the front of the filter cover, then lift the cover and withdrawn the filter element. Note which way up the element was fitted **(see illustrations)**.

3 Position the new element in the filter housing and refit the filter cover. Note the three lugs at the rear of the cover which engage with the housing. Tighten the retaining screws securely.

4 Refit the plastic cover to the top of the engine.

1.6 litre engines

5 Remove the engine top cover. Remove the wiper arms (Chapter 12), then release the clips and remove the plastic scuttle trim panel. The trim is secured by a plastic expanding rivet at each end. Push the centre pins in a little, then prise out the complete rivets. Pull up the ends of the trim to release it from the windscreen clips, then pull the trim down and forward to release it from the centre of the windscreen. Undo the two screws securing the brake/clutch master cylinder reservoir and move it to one side. Release the sound insulation material from the plastic scuttle crossmember, then undo the two screws and remove the crossmember.

6 Remove the primary air inlet duct from the front of the engine compartment, then remove the turbocharger inlet duct, and the air cleaner inlet duct.

7 Remove the fuel priming pump and support from the top of the air cleaner.

8 Disconnect the wiring then remove the air mass meter with reference to Chapter 4B.

9 Undo the three screws at the front of the air cleaner, then unhook and remove the cover.

10 Withdraw the filter element, noting which way up it is fitted.

11 Position the new element in the air cleaner housing and refit the cover, making sure the rear lugs engage properly. Tighten the retaining screws securely.

12 Refit the remaining parts using a reversal of the removal procedure.

2.0 litre engines

13 Undo the screws securing the top to the air filter housing body, lift the top up, disengage the lugs at the rear of the cover, and withdraw the filter element **(see illustrations)**.

14 If required, slacken the clip and disconnect the intake duct from the filter housing top to give better access to the filter housing body.

15 Where applicable, release any wiring or coolant hoses from their retaining clips on the air filter housing top.

16 Wipe clean the housing body and top.

17 Place the new element in position in the housing body. Refit the filter housing top, securing it in position with its retaining screws.

18 Refit any wiring or coolant hoses (where applicable) to their locating clips in the air filter housing, then reconnect the intake duct and securely tighten its retaining clip.

15 Fuel filter renewal

Note: Check with your dealer for the availability of fuel filter/housing before removal. On some models the fuel filter/ housing may come as a complete assembly.

Removal

1.4 litre engines

1 Remove the battery as described in Chapter 5A.

2 Undo the two screws and move aside the

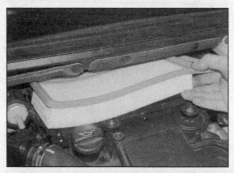

14.2b . . . and remove the filter element

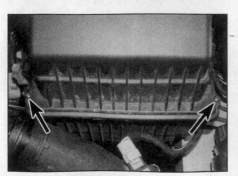

14.2a Undo the three air filter cover screws (arrowed), lift off the cover . . .

14.13a Undo the air filter cover screws (arrowed), lift off the cover . . .

14.13b . . . and remove the filter element

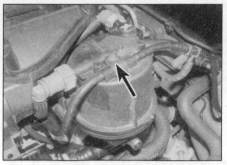

15.2 Brake/clutch fluid upper reservoir screws (arrowed)

15.3 Undo the vacuum pipe bracket screw (arrowed)

15.6 Depress the button (arrowed) and disconnect the fuel feed and return pipes

brake fluid upper reservoir (**see illustration**). Do not disconnect any fluid pipes/hoses.

3 Undo the screw, release the retaining bracket, and position the brake servo vacuum pipe to one side (**see illustration**).

4 Place a suitable container beneath the drain screw, and cover the surrounding area with rags. Take care not to allow fuel to enter the transmission bellhousing which is just below. If available, fit a length of hose over the drain screw (**see illustration 4.2a**).

5 Open the drain plug by turning it anti-clockwise. Allow fuel and water to drain. Close the drain plug.

6 Release the retaining clips and disconnect the fuel feed and return pipes from the filter (**see illustration**). Plug the pipes to prevent dirt ingress and fuel loss.

7 Undo the single filter retaining screw, and manoeuvre the filter from the bracket. Disconnect the fuel heater and water detector wiring plugs (where fitted) as the filter is withdrawn (**see illustrations**).

15.7a Undo the filter retaining screw (arrowed) . . .

15.7b . . . then disengage the filter lug from the bracket

8 Unscrew the fuel heater and water detector (where fitted) from the filter. Discard the O-ring seals, new ones must be fitted.

1.6 litre engines

9 Remove the battery cover and the battery as described in Chapter 5A (**see illustrations**).
10 Remove the engine top cover.

11 Remove the primary air inlet duct from the front of the engine compartment, then remove the turbocharger inlet duct, and the air cleaner inlet duct (**see illustrations**).

12 Undo the two screws and move aside the brake fluid upper reservoir (**see illustration**). Do not disconnect any fluid pipes/hoses.

15.9a Remove the battery cover . . .

15.9b . . . and the battery

15.11a Remove the primary air inlet duct . . .

15.11b . . . the turbocharger inlet duct . . .

15.11c . . . and the air cleaner inlet duct

15.12 Move the brake/clutch fluid reservoir to one side

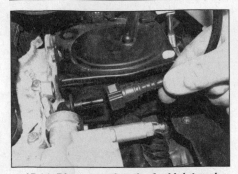

15.14 Disconnecting the fuel inlet and outlet pipes

15.15a Release the clip . . .

15.15b . . . and remove the fuel filter housing complete

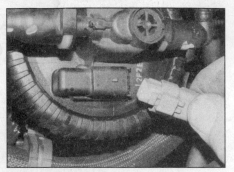

15.19 Disconnect the filter wiring plug

13 Disconnect the wiring from the fuel heater.

14 Place cloth rags beneath the filter, then disconnect the fuel inlet and outlet pipes **(see illustration)**.

15 Release the clip and remove the fuel filter housing from the engine compartment **(see illustrations)**.

16 The new filter is supplied as one complete housing. As applicable, remove the water detector and fuel heater from the old filter housing and transfer them to the new unit.

2.0 litre engines

17 Undo the four fasteners and remove the plastic cover from the top of the engine.

18 Position a suitable container under the end of the fuel filter drain hose. Open the drain screw on the base of the filter housing and allow the fuel to drain completely **(see illustration 4.2b)**.

19 Where applicable, disconnect the wiring connector from the top of the fuel filter **(see illustration)**.

20 Disconnect the fuel lines from the top of the fuel filter housing by releasing the quick-release fittings using a small screwdriver. Move them to one side, covering the ends of the fuel lines to prevent dirt entry.

21 Unscrew the top of the fuel filter and lift the filter from the housing **(see illustrations)**. **Note:** *Although in theory the collar on top of the filter unscrews, in practice we have found it impossible to unscrew the filter without damaging the housing, necessitating the renewal of the complete filter housing. The housing is secured to the engine by two bolts.*

Refitting

1.4 litre engines

22 Renew the water detector and fuel heater O-ring seals, and refit them to the new filter, tightening them securely.

23 Manoeuvre the filter into position and secure it in place with the fixing screw.

24 Reconnect the fuel feed/return pipes and the wiring plugs.

25 Refit the retaining bracket – tighten the screw securely.

26 Close the fuel drain plug and prime the fuel system as described in Chapter 4B. The remainder of refitting is a reversal of removal.

1.6 litre engines

27 Fit the new filter using a reversal of the removal procedure, then prime the fuel system as described in Chapter 4B.

2.0 litre engines

28 Refitting is a reversal of removal. Place the new filter in the housing, making sure that

a new seal is fitted before refitting the top to the filter housing. If the complete assembly is being replaced, refit the filter to the engine and tighten the bolts securely.

29 Refit the filter housing assembly, close the fuel filter drain screw and prime the fuel system (see Chapter 4B).

16 Manual transmission oil level check

Note: *A new sealing washer will be required for the transmission filler/level plug, when refitting.*

1 Slacken the left-hand front roadwheels bolts. Jack up the front and rear of the car and securely support it on axle stands so that it remains level (see *Jacking and vehicle support*). If the car has been recently driven, wait at least 5 minutes after the engine has been switched off. If the oil level is checked immediately after driving the car, some of the oil will remain distributed around the transmission components, resulting in an inaccurate level reading.

2 Remove the left-hand front roadwheel then push in the centre pins a little, prise out the complete plastic expanding rivet, and remove the wheel arch liner from under the wing for access to the filler/level plug.

3 Wipe clean the area around the filler/level plug. The filler/level plug is the largest bolt among those securing the end cover to the transmission. Unscrew the plug and clean it; discard the sealing washer **(see illustration)**.

15.21a Unscrew the top of the filter

15.21b Depress the clip to disconnect the fuel pipe

16.3 Manual transmission oil filler/level plug

16.4 Add oil until a trickle emerges

4 The oil level should reach the lower edge of the filler/level hole. A certain amount of oil will have gathered behind the filler/level plug, and will trickle out when it is removed; this does *not* necessarily indicate that the level is correct. To ensure that a true level is established, wait until the initial trickle has stopped, then add oil as necessary until a trickle of new oil can be seen emerging **(see illustration)**. The level will be correct when the flow ceases; use only good-quality oil of the specified type.

5 Refilling the transmission is an awkward operation; above all, allow plenty of time for the oil level to settle properly before checking it. If a large amount had to be added to the transmission, or if a large amount flowed out on checking the level, refit the filler/level plug and take the vehicle on a short journey. With the new oil distributed fully around the transmission components, recheck the level after allowing time for it to settle again.

6 If the transmission has been overfilled so that oil flows out as soon as the filler/level plug is removed, first check that the car is completely level (front-to-rear and side-to-side). Allow any surplus oil to drain off into a suitable container.

7 When the level is correct, fit a new sealing washer to the filler/level plug. Tighten the plug to the specified torque wrench setting. Wash off any spilt oil. Refit the wheel arch liner, and secure it in position with its plastic rivets. Refit the roadwheel then lower the car to the ground.

8 Frequent need for topping-up indicates a leak, which should be found and corrected before it becomes serious.

17 Automatic transmission fluid level check

Note: *The transmission unit is equipped with a fluid wear sensor to inform the driver when the fluid needs renewing (the ECU flashes the Sport and Snow mode indicator lights when fluid renewal is necessary). Every time the transmission unit is topped-up, this sensor should be adjusted to compensate for the new fluid being added, however this can only be done using the Peugeot diagnostic test box. Adding fluid without adjusting the sensor will not cause any problems but will mean the sensor is giving an inaccurate reading, resulting in fluid renewal being recommended earlier than is actually necessary.*

1 Take the vehicle on a short journey, to warm the transmission up to normal operating temperature, then park the vehicle on level ground. Firmly apply the handbrake and place the selector lever in the P position. Undo the screws and remove the engine undershield **(see illustration 3.2)**.

2 Wipe clean the area around the filler plug, which is situated on the top of the transmission, directly beneath the battery. Unscrew the filler plug from the transmission and recover the sealing washer **(see illustration)**.

3 Carefully add 0.5 litre of the specified type of fluid to the transmission via the filler plug aperture. Fit a new sealing washer to the filler plug then refit the plug, tightening it to the specified torque.

4 Position a suitable container under the drain/filler plug arrangement, situated on the base of the transmission. The level plug is the smaller plug fitted to the centre of the larger drain plug **(see illustration)**.
Caution: Do not remove the drain plug by mistake.

5 Start the engine and allow it to idle. With the engine running, retain the drain plug then slacken and remove the level plug and sealing washer.

⚠ *Warning: The fluid will be hot, take precautions against scalding.*

6 If there is sufficient fluid in the transmission unit, fluid should trickle out the centre of the drain plug before slowing to a drip. **Note:** *If no fluid trickles out, or just a few drips appear when the plug is removed, the fluid level is too low. Refit the level plug then switch off the engine. Add a further 0.5 litre of fluid to the transmission then refit the filler plug and repeat the check (see paragraphs 3 to 5).*

7 Once the flow of fluid stops, the level is correct. Fit a new sealing washer to the level plug then refit the plug and tighten it to the specified torque. Switch off the engine.

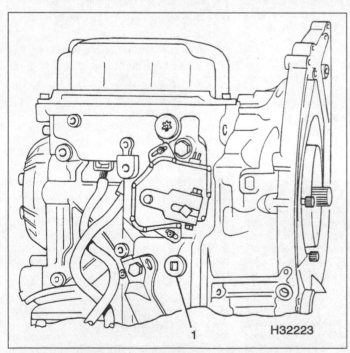

17.2 Transmission oil filler plug (1) as viewed from above

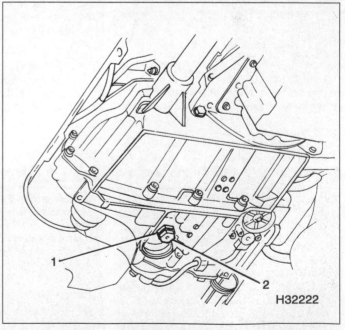

17.4 Transmission oil drain plug (1) and oil level plug (2), inside the drain plug

Every 36 000 miles (60 000 km)

18 Timing belt renewal

Note: *See note in 'Maintenance schedule'*
Refer to Chapter 2C, 2D or 2E.

Every 36 000 miles (60 000 km) or 2 years

19 Brake fluid renewal

Warning: Brake hydraulic fluid can harm your eyes and damage painted surfaces, so use extreme caution when handling and pouring it. Do not use fluid that has been standing open for some time, as it absorbs moisture from the air. Excess moisture can cause a dangerous loss of braking effectiveness.

Note: *A hydraulic clutch shares its fluid reservoir with the braking system, and may also need to be bled (see Chapter 6).*

1 The procedure is similar to that for the bleeding of the hydraulic system as described in Chapter 9, except that the brake fluid reservoir should be emptied by syphoning, using a clean ladle or similar before starting, and allowance should be made for the old fluid to be expelled when bleeding a section of the circuit.

2 Working as described in Chapter 9, open the first bleed screw in the sequence, and pump the brake pedal gently until nearly all the old fluid has been emptied from the master cylinder reservoir.

HAYNES HINT *Old hydraulic fluid is in-variably much darker in colour than the new, making it easy to distinguish the two.*

3 Top-up to the MAX level with new fluid, and continue pumping until only the new fluid remains in the reservoir, and new fluid can be seen emerging from the bleed screw. Tighten the screw, and top the reservoir level up to the MAX level line.

4 Work through all the remaining bleed screws in the sequence until new fluid can be seen at all of them. Be careful to keep the master cylinder reservoir topped-up to above the DANGER level at all times, or air may enter the system and increase the length of the task.

5 When the operation is complete, check that all bleed screws are securely tightened, and that their dust caps are refitted. Wash off all traces of spilt fluid, and recheck the master cylinder reservoir fluid level.

6 Check the operation of the brakes before taking the car on the road.

Every 48 000 miles (80 000 km)

20 Particulate emission system check

1 A particulate filter is fitted to some 1.6 and 2.0 litre models. This filter is combined with the catalytic converter in the exhaust pipe. An additive is used to help clean the filter element.

This additive is stored in a separate reservoir adjacent to the fuel tank. However, checking the filter and refilling the reservoir should be entrusted to a Peugeot dealer or specialist, as parameters of the engine management ECU must be re-initialised, and special equipment/tools must be used due to the hazardous nature of the additive.

2 Depending the date of manufacture, the additive requires topping-up at:

48 000 miles (80 000 km) for vehicles manufactured before November 2002 – additive: EOLYS DPX 42.

72 000 miles (120 000 km) for vehicles manufactured from November 2002 (build code 9492) – additive: EOLYS 176.

Note that these two products are not mixable or interchangeable.

Every 72 000 miles (120 000km) or 5 years

21 Coolant renewal

Cooling system draining

Warning: Wait until the engine is cold before starting this pro-cedure. Do not allow antifreeze to come in contact with your skin, or with the painted surfaces of the vehicle. Rinse off spills immediately with plenty of water. Never leave antifreeze lying around in an open container, or in a puddle in the driveway or on the garage floor. Children and pets are attracted by its sweet smell, but antifreeze can be fatal if ingested.

1 Remove the battery and battery tray/box as described in Chapter 5A.

1.4 and 1.6 litre engine

2 With the engine completely cold, unscrew and remove the expansion tank cap, then undo the screws and remove the engine undershield.

3 Position a suitable container beneath the radiator lower hose outlet at the lower left-hand side of the radiator.

4 Release the retaining clip and disconnect the radiator lower hose **(see illustration)**. Be prepared for coolant spillage.

5 With the engine completely cold, reach under the scuttle and unscrew the bleed screw located in the heater hose at the bulkhead connection **(see illustration)**.

6 To drain the engine, pull out the clip and remove the plug located in the coolant manifold at the rear of the cylinder head **(see**

21.4 Squeeze together the tabs to release the hose retaining clip

21.5 Undo the heater outlet hose union bleed screw cap (arrowed)

21.6 Prise out the retaining clip (arrowed) and pull out the drain plug

illustration). The plug must be refitted with a new clip and O-ring.

2.0 litre engines

7 With the engine completely cold, unscrew and remove the expansion tank cap.

8 Position a suitable container beneath the radiator lower hose outlet.

9 Slacken the bleed screw at the heater hose bulkhead connection, and the screw at the coolant outlet housing. On some engines, a third bleed screw is located at the top of the heater matrix outlet fitted to the base of the air cleaner housing **(see illustrations)**.

10 Release the radiator lower hose retaining clip, and pull the hose from the fitting. Be prepared for coolant spillage.

11 When the flow of coolant stops, reposition the container below the cylinder block drain plug, located at the rear of the cylinder block.

12 Remove the drain plug, and allow the coolant to drain into the container.

13 If the coolant has been drained for a reason other than renewal, then provided it is clean and less than five years old, it can be re-used, though this is not recommended.

14 Refit the cylinder block drain plug on completion of draining.

Cooling system flushing

15 If coolant renewal has been neglected, or if the antifreeze mixture has become diluted, then in time, the cooling system may gradually lose efficiency, as the coolant passages become restricted due to rust, scale deposits, and other sediment. The cooling system

efficiency can be restored by flushing the system clean.

16 The radiator should be flushed independently of the engine, to avoid unnecessary contamination.

Radiator flushing

17 To flush the radiator, first tighten the radiator bleed screw, where applicable.

18 Disconnect the top hose and any other relevant hoses from the radiator, with reference to Chapter 3.

19 Insert a garden hose into the radiator top inlet. Direct a flow of clean water through the radiator, and continue flushing until clean water emerges from the radiator bottom outlet.

20 If after a reasonable period, the water still does not run clear, the radiator can be flushed with a good proprietary cleaning agent. It is important that their manufacturer's instructions are followed carefully. If the contamination is particularly bad, insert the hose in the radiator bottom outlet, and reverse-flush the radiator.

Engine flushing

21 To flush the engine, first refit the cylinder block drain plug, and tighten the cooling system bleed screws.

22 Remove the thermostat as described in Chapter 3, then temporarily refit the thermo-stat cover.

23 With the top and bottom hoses disconnected from the radiator, insert a garden hose into the radiator top hose. Direct a clean flow of water through the engine, and

continue flushing until clean water emerges from the radiator bottom hose.

24 On completion of flushing, refit the thermostat and reconnect the hoses with reference to Chapter 3.

Cooling system filling

25 Before attempting to fill the cooling system, make sure that all hoses and clips are in good condition, and that the clips are tight. Note that an antifreeze mixture must be used all year round, to prevent corrosion of the engine components (see following sub-Section). Also check that the radiator and cylinder block drain plugs are in place and tight.

26 Remove the expansion tank filler cap.

27 Open all the cooling system bleed screws (see paragraphs 5 and 9).

28 Some of the cooling system hoses are positioned at a higher level than the top of the radiator expansion tank. It is therefore necessary to use a 'header tank' when refilling the cooling system, to reduce the possibility of air being trapped in the system. Although Peugeot dealers use a special header tank, the same effect can be achieved by using a suitable 1.0 litre bottle, with a seal between the bottle and the expansion tank **(see Haynes Hint)**.

21.9a Coolant outlet housing bleed screw (arrowed) . . .

21.9b . . . and air cleaner heater matrix bleed screw (DW10ATED)

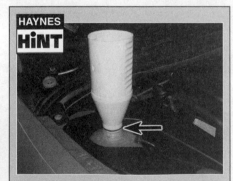

HAYNES HiNT

Cut the bottom off an old anti-freeze container to make a 'header tank' for use when refilling the cooling system. The seal at the point arrowed should be as tight as possible – use an O-ring if available, or seal the joint by some other means.

29 Fit the header tank to the expansion tank and slowly fill the system. Coolant will emerge from the bleed screw. As soon as coolant free from air bubbles emerges from the screw, tighten the screw.

30 Ensure that the header tank is full (at least 1.0 litre of coolant). Refit the battery, start the engine, and run it at a fast idle speed (do not exceed 2000 rpm) until the cooling fan cuts in, and then cuts out. Stop the engine. **Note:** *Take great care not to scald yourself with the hot coolant during this operation.*

31 Allow the engine to cool, then remove the header tank.

32 When the engine has cooled, check the coolant level as described in *Weekly checks*.

Top-up the level if necessary, and refit the expansion tank cap.

Antifreeze mixture

33 The antifreeze should always be renewed at the specified intervals. This is necessary not only to maintain the antifreeze properties, but also to prevent corrosion which would otherwise occur as the corrosion inhibitors become progressively less effective.

34 Always use an ethylene-glycol based antifreeze which is suitable for use in mixed-metal cooling systems. The quantity of antifreeze and levels of protection are indicated in the Specifications.

35 Before adding antifreeze, the cooling system should be completely drained, preferably flushed, and all hoses checked for condition and security.

36 After filling with antifreeze, a label should be attached to the expansion tank, stating the type and concentration of antifreeze used, and the date installed. Any subsequent topping-up should be made with the same type and concentration of antifreeze.

37 Do not use engine antifreeze in the washer system, as it will cause damage to the vehicle paintwork. A screen wash additive should be added to the washer system in the quantities stated on the bottle.

Every 10 years

22 Airbags and seat belt pretensioners renewal

1 Peugeot recommend that the airbags and seat belt pretensioners are renewed regardless of their condition every ten years. Refer to Chapter 12 for airbag renewal, and Chapter 11 for seat belt pretensioner renewal.

Chapter 2 Part A:
1.4 and 1.6 litre petrol engines in-car repair procedures

Contents

Degrees of difficulty

Easy, suitable for novice with little experience	**Fairly easy,** suitable for beginner with some experience	**Fairly difficult,** suitable for competent DIY mechanic	**Difficult,** suitable for experienced DIY mechanic 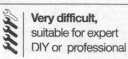	**Very difficult,** suitable for expert DIY or professional

Specifications

Engine (general)

Capacity:
- 1.4 litre engine 1360cc
- 1.6 litre engine 1587cc

Designation:
- 1.4 litre SOHC engine................................... TU3JP
- 1.4 litre DOHC engine.................................. ET3JP4
- 1.6 litre DOHC engine.................................. TU5JP4

Engine codes*:
- 1.4 litre SOHC engine................................... KFW
- 1.4 litre DOHC engine.................................. KFU
- 1.6 litre DOHC engine.................................. NFU

Bore:
- 1.4 litre engine .... 75.00 mm
- 1.6 litre engine .... 78.50 mm

Stroke:
- 1.4 litre engine .... 77.00 mm
- 1.6 litre engine .... 82.00 mm

Direction of crankshaft rotation .... Clockwise (viewed from right-hand side of vehicle)

No 1 cylinder location...................................... At transmission end of the block

Compression ratio:
- 1.4 litre SOHC engine.................................. 10.2 : 1
- 1.4 litre DOHC engine.................................. 11.1 : 1
- 1.6 litre DOHC engine.................................. 10.8 : 1

Maximum power output:
- 1.4 litre SOHC engine.................................. 55 kW @ 5500 rpm
- 1.4 litre DOHC engine.................................. 65 kW @ 5250 rpm
- 1.6 litre DOHC engine.................................. 80 kW @ 5500 rpm

Maximum torque output:
- 1.4 litre SOHC engine.................................. 120 Nm @ 3000 rpm
- 1.4 litre DOHC engine.................................. 135 Nm @ 3250 rpm
- 1.6 litre DOHC engine.................................. 150 Nm @ 4500 rpm

The engine code is situated on front, left-hand end of the cylinder block.

Camshaft(s)

Drive . . . .   Toothed belt

Valve clearances (engine cold)

1.4 litre SOHC engine:
  Intake . . . .   0.20 mm
  Exhaust. . . . .   0.40 mm
1.4 and 1.6 litre DOHC engines . . . .   Hydraulic adjusters

Lubrication system

Oil pump type. . . . .   Gear type, chain-driven off the crankshaft
Minimum oil pressure at 80°C . . . .   4 bars @ 4000 rpm
Oil pressure warning switch operating pressure . . . .   0.8 bars

Torque wrench settings

	Nm	lbf ft
Big-end bearing cap nuts*:		
1.4 litre SOHC and 1.6 litre DOHC engines	40	30
1.4 litre DOHC engine:		
Stage 1	30	22
Stage 2	Angle-tighten a further 45°	
Camshaft bearing housing to cylinder head		
(1.4 and 1.6 litre DOHC engines)	10	7
Camshaft sprocket retaining bolt(s):		
1.4 litre SOHC and 1.6 litre DOHC engines	45	33
1.4 litre DOHC engine:		
Camshaft thrust fork retaining bolt (1.4 litre SOHC engine).	16	12
Crankshaft oil seal housing bolts.	8	6
Crankshaft pulley retaining bolts	25	18
Crankshaft sprocket retaining bolt*:		
Stage 1	40	30
Stage 2	Angle-tighten a further 45°	
Cylinder head bolts:		
1.4 litre SOHC engine:		
Stage 1	20	15
Stage 2	Angle-tighten a further 240°	
1.4 litre DOHC engine:		
Stage 1	15	11
Stage 2	25	18
Stage 3	Angle-tighten a further 200°	
1.6 litre engine:		
Stage 1	20	15
Stage 2	Angle-tighten a further 260°	
Cylinder head cover screws/nuts (1.4 litre SOHC engine)	8	6
Cylinder head cover bolts (1.4 and 1.6 litre DOHC engines)	10	7
Driveplate bolts	67	49
Engine-to-transmission bolts:		
Manual transmission models	40	30
Automatic transmission models	35	26
Engine/transmission left-hand mounting:		
Mounting centre nut	65	48
Mounting-to-bracket bolts	30	22
Mounting bracket-to-body bolts	19	14
Mounting bracket-to-manual transmission nuts	25	18
Mounting bracket-to-automatic transmission bolts.	45	33
Mounting stud/nut (automatic transmission)	40	30
Engine/transmission rear mounting:		
Mounting-to-cylinder block bolts.	40	30
Mounting link-to-mounting bolt	55	41
Mounting link-to-subframe bolt	39	29
Engine/transmission right-hand mounting:		
Mounting bracket nuts.	45	33
Support bracket:		
Bracket to cylinder head	45	33
Bracket to mounting bracket	60	44
Bracket to engine	26	19
Mounting bolts to body	60	44
Mounting vibration damper	32	24

Torque wrench settings (continued)

	Nm	lbf ft
Exhaust sprocket retaining bolt	45	33
Flywheel bolts*	70	52
Inlet sprocket retaining bolt cover	40	30
Inlet sprocket retaining bolt:		
Stage 1	20	15
Stage 2	60	44
Main bearing cap bolts (1.6 litre engine):		
Stage 1	20	15
Stage 2	Angle-tighten a further 49°	
Main bearing ladder casting (1.4 litre engine):		
M11 bolts:		
Stage 1	20	15
Stage 2	Angle-tighten a further 44°	
M6 bolts	8	6
Oil filter	25	18
Oil filter housing to engine block (1.6 litre engine)	10	7
Oil pressure switch:		
1.4 litre SOHC engine	30	22
1.4 and 1.6 litre DOHC engines	20	15
Oil pump retaining bolts	9	7
Piston oil jet spray tube bolts	10	7
Roadwheel bolts	90	66
Sump drain plug	30	22
Sump retaining nuts and bolts	8	6
Timing belt cover bolts	8	6
Timing belt tensioner pulley nut:		
1.4 litre engine	20	15
1.6 litre engine	22	16

Do not re-use

1 General information

How to use this Chapter

1 This Part of Chapter 2 describes those repair procedures that can reasonably be carried out on the petrol engine while it remains in the car. If the engine has been removed from the car and is being dismantled, as described in Part F, any preliminary dismantling procedures can be ignored.

2 Note that, while it may be possible physically to overhaul items such as the piston/ connecting rod assemblies while the engine is in the car, such tasks are not normally carried out as separate operations. Usually, several additional procedures (not to mention the cleaning of components and of oilways) have to be carried out. For this reason, all such tasks are classed as major overhaul procedures, and are described in Part F of this Chapter.

3 Part F describes the removal of the engine/ transmission from the vehicle, and the full over-haul procedures that can then be carried out.

Petrol engine description

4 The petrol engines in this Part of Chapter 2 are from the TU and ET series, and are well-proven engines which have been fitted to many previous Peugeot and Citroën vehicles. 1.4 litre single overhead camshaft (SOHC) 8-valve or 1.4 and 1.6 litre double overhead camshaft (DOHC) 16-valve, in-line four cylinder engines are fitted, being mounted transversely at the front of the car with the transmission attached to the left-hand end. The 1.4 litre SOHC and DOHC engines share the same block incorporating wet liners. Both 1.4 and 1.6 litre DOHC engines have similar cylinder heads and repair procedures are identical, except in the area of the hydraulic lifters. On the 1.6 litre, the camshaft operates directly on the hydraulic lifters which are located in the cylinder head beneath the camshaft. On the 1.4 litre, the valves are operated by roller rocker arms between the camshaft and the tops of the valves – one end of the rocker arm is clipped to the hydraulic lifter and the other end rests on top of the valve stem.

5 The crankshaft runs in five main bearings. Thrustwashers are fitted to No 2 main bearing (upper half) to control crankshaft endfloat.

6 The connecting rods rotate on horizontally-split bearing shells at their big-ends. The pistons are attached to the connecting rods by gudgeon pins, which are an interference fit in the connecting rod small-end eyes. The aluminium-alloy pistons are fitted with three piston rings – two compression rings and an oil control ring.

7 On 1.4 litre engines, the cylinder block is made of aluminium, and wet liners are fitted to the cylinder bores. Sealing O-rings are fitted at the base of each liner, to prevent the escape of coolant into the sump.

8 On 1.6 litre engines, the cylinder block is made from cast-iron, and the cylinder bores are an integral part of the cylinder block. On this type of engine, the cylinder bores are sometimes referred to as having dry liners.

9 The intake and exhaust valves are each closed by coil springs, and operate in guides pressed into the cylinder head; the valve seat inserts are also pressed into the cylinder head, and can be renewed separately if worn.

10 On SOHC engines, the camshaft is driven by a toothed timing belt, and operates the eight valves via rocker arms. Valve clearances are adjusted by a screw-and-locknut arrangement. The camshaft rotates directly in the cylinder head. The timing belt also drives the coolant pump.

11 On DOHC engines, the camshafts are driven by a timing belt, and operate the 16 valves via followers incorporating hydraulic clearance adjusters. The camshafts rotate directly in the cylinder head and are retained by a one-piece bearing housing. The belt also drives the coolant pump.

12 Lubrication is by means of an oil pump, which is driven (via a chain and sprocket) off the right-hand end of the crankshaft. It draws oil through a strainer located in the sump, and then forces it through an externally-mounted filter into galleries in the cylinder block/ crankcase. From there, the oil is distributed to

the crankshaft (main bearings) and camshaft. The big-end bearings are supplied with oil via internal drillings in the crankshaft, while the camshaft bearings also receive a pressurised supply. On 1.6 litre engines, piston cooling oil spray jets are fitted to spray oil on the underside of each piston. The camshaft lobes and valves are lubricated by splash, as are all other engine components.

Operations with engine in car

13 The following work can be carried out with the engine in the car:
a) *Compression pressure – testing.*
b) *Cylinder head cover – removal and refitting.*
c) *Timing belt covers – removal and refitting.*
d) *Timing belt – removal, refitting and adjustment.*
e) *Timing belt tensioner and sprockets – removal and refitting.*
f) *Camshaft oil seal(s) – renewal.*
g) *Camshaft(s) and rocker arms/followers – removal, inspection and refitting.*
h) *Cylinder head – removal and refitting.*
i) *Cylinder head and pistons – decarbonising.*
j) *Sump – removal and refitting.*
k) *Oil pump – removal, overhaul and refitting.*
l) *Crankshaft oil seals – renewal.*
m) *Engine/transmission mountings – inspection and renewal.*
n) *Flywheel/driveplate – removal, inspection and refitting.*

2 Compression test – description and interpretation

1 When engine performance is down, or if misfiring occurs which cannot be attributed to the ignition or fuel systems, a compression test can provide diagnostic clues as to the engine's condition. If the test is performed regularly, it can give warning of trouble before any other symptoms become apparent.
2 The engine must be fully warmed-up to normal operating temperature, the battery must be fully charged. The aid of an assistant will also be required.
3 Remove the ignition HT coil assembly (see

Chapter 5B) then remove the spark plugs (see Chapter 1A).
4 Fit a compression tester to the No 1 cylinder spark plug hole – the type of tester which screws into the plug thread is to be preferred.
5 Have the assistant hold the throttle wide open, and crank the engine on the starter motor; after one or two revolutions, the compression pressure should build-up to a maximum figure, and then stabilise. Record the highest reading obtained.
6 Repeat the test on the remaining cylinders, recording the pressure in each.
7 All cylinders should produce very similar pressures; a difference of more than 2 bars between any two cylinders indicates a fault. Note that the compression should build-up quickly in a healthy engine; low compression on the first stroke, followed by gradually-increasing pressure on successive strokes, indicates worn piston rings. A low compression reading on the first stroke, which does not build-up during successive strokes, indicates leaking valves or a blown head gasket (a cracked head could also be the cause). Deposits on the undersides of the valve heads can also cause low compression.
8 Although Peugeot do not specify exact compression pressures, as a guide, any cylinder pressure of below 10 bars can be considered as less than healthy. Refer to a Peugeot dealer or other specialist if in doubt as to whether a particular pressure reading is acceptable.
9 If the pressure in any cylinder is low, carry out the following test to isolate the cause. Introduce a teaspoonful of clean oil into that cylinder through its spark plug hole, and repeat the test.
10 If the addition of oil temporarily improves the compression pressure, this indicates that bore or piston wear is responsible for the pressure loss. No improvement suggests that leaking or burnt valves, or a blown head gasket, may be to blame.
11 A low reading from two adjacent cylinders is almost certainly due to the head gasket having blown between them; the presence of coolant in the engine oil will confirm this.
12 If one cylinder is about 20 percent lower than the others and the engine has a slightly rough idle, a worn camshaft lobe could be the cause.

13 If the compression reading is unusually high, the combustion chambers are probably coated with carbon deposits. If this is the case, the cylinder head should be removed and decarbonised.
14 On completion of the test, refit the spark plugs and ignition HT coil (see Chapters 1A and 5B).

3 Engine assembly/ valve timing holes – general information and usage

Note: *Do not attempt to rotate the engine whilst the crankshaft/camshaft are locked in position. If the engine is to be left in this state for a long period of time, it is a good idea to place warning notices inside the vehicle, and in the engine compartment. This will reduce the possibility of the engine being accidentally cranked on the starter motor, which is likely to cause damage with the locking pins in place.*

1 On all models, timing holes are drilled in the camshaft sprocket(s) and in the rear of the flywheel/driveplate. The holes are used to ensure that the crankshaft and camshaft(s) are correctly positioned when assembling the engine (to prevent the possibility of the valves contacting the pistons when refitting the cylinder head), or refitting the timing belt. When the timing holes are aligned with access holes in the cylinder head and the front of the cylinder block, suitable diameter bolts/pins can be inserted to lock both the camshaft and crankshaft in position, preventing them from rotating. Proceed as follows.
2 Remove the timing belt upper cover as described in Section 5.

1.4 litre SOHC engines

3 The crankshaft must now be turned until the timing hole in the camshaft sprocket is aligned with the corresponding hole in the cylinder head. The holes are aligned when the camshaft sprocket hole is in the 2 o'clock position, when viewed from the right-hand end of the engine. The crankshaft can be turned by using a spanner on the crankshaft sprocket bolt, noting that it should always be rotated in a clockwise direction (viewed from the right-hand end of the engine).
4 With the camshaft sprocket hole correctly positioned, insert a 6 mm diameter stud or pin, 90 mm long, welded to a length of weld rod bent to the appropriate shape, through the hole in the front left-hand flange of the cylinder block, and locate it in the timing hole in the rear of the flywheel **(see illustration)**. A purpose-made Peugeot tool No 0132-QY is available from dealers. Note that it may be necessary to rotate the crankshaft slightly to get the holes to align.
5 With the flywheel correctly positioned, insert a 10 mm diameter bolt or a pin through the timing hole in the camshaft sprocket, and locate it in the hole in the cylinder head **(see illustration)**.

3.4 Insert a 6 mm diameter bolt/pin (arrowed) into the hole in the cylinder block flange and into the flywheel hole

3.5 Lock the camshaft sprocket in position with a 10 mm diameter bolt/pin (arrowed) (1.4 litre SOHC engine)

1.4 and 1.6 litre DOHC engines

6 Turn the crankshaft until the holes in the camshaft sprockets align with the corresponding holes in the cylinder head. The crankshaft can be turned by using a spanner on the crankshaft sprocket bolt, noting that it should always be rotated in a clockwise direction (viewed from the right-hand end of the engine).

7 With the camshaft sprocket holes correctly positioned, insert a 6 mm diameter stud or pin, 80 mm long, welded to a length of weld rod bent to the appropriate shape, through the hole in the front left-hand flange of the cylinder block, and locate it in the timing hole in the rear of the flywheel/driveplate (see illustrations). A purpose-made Peugeot tool No 0132-QY is available from dealers. Note that it may be necessary to rotate the crankshaft slightly to get the holes to align.

8 With the crankshaft correctly positioned, insert 8 mm diameter bolts or pins through the timing holes in the camshaft sprockets, and locate them in the holes in the cylinder head (see illustration). Note: On 1.4 litre engines, the hole in the inlet camshaft sprocket is 5 mm diameter, however the exhaust camshaft sprocket on all engines has a 8 mm diameter hole.

All models

9 The crankshaft and camshaft are now locked in position, preventing unnecessary rotation.

4 Cylinder head cover – removal and refitting

1.4 litre SOHC engine

Removal

1 Disconnect the battery (see Chapter 5A).

2 Depress the clip and disconnect the breather hose from the cylinder head cover (see illustration).

3 Remove the ignition HT coil as described in Chapter 5B.

4 Undo the two retaining nuts and sealing washers (where fitted) then lift off the cylinder head cover, complete with its rubber seal.

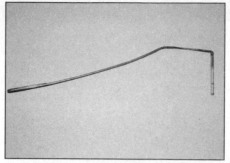

3.7a Weld a 90 mm length of 6 mm rod/stud to a length of weld rod . . .

3.8a Use suitable bolts/pins (arrowed) to lock the camshaft sprockets in position (1.6 litre DOHC engine)

Examine the seal for signs of damage and deterioration, and if necessary, renew it.

5 Remove the spacer from each cover stud then lift off the oil baffle plate (see illustrations).

Refitting

6 Carefully clean the cylinder head and cover mating surfaces, and remove all traces of oil.

7 Fit the rubber seal over the edge of the cylinder head cover, ensuring that it is correctly located along its entire length (see illustration).

8 Refit the oil baffle plate then fit the spacers to the cover studs.

9 Carefully refit the cylinder head cover to the engine, taking great care not to displace the rubber seal.

10 Fit the sealing washers (where fitted) and cover retaining nuts, tightening them to the specified torque.

3.7b . . . and insert it into the hole in the cylinder block flange (arrowed)

3.8b Lock the camshaft sprockets in position using 5 mm and 8 mm diameter drill bits/bolts (1.4 litre DOHC engine)

11 Refit the ignition HT coil (see Chapter 5B) then reconnect the breather hose securely to the cylinder head cover. On completion reconnect the battery.

4.2 Disconnect the breather hose from the cylinder head cover

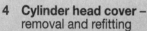
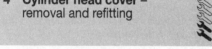

4.5a Remove the spacers (arrowed) from the studs . . .

4.5b . . . then lift off the baffle plate

4.7 Ensure the rubber seal is correctly located on the cylinder head cover

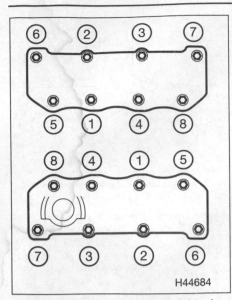

4.16 Cylinder head cover bolts tightening sequence

1.4 and 1.6 litre DOHC engines

Removal

12 Disconnect the battery (see Chapter 5A), and remove the ignition coil as described in Chapter 5B.
13 Working in a spiral pattern, progressively and evenly slack the cylinder head cover bolts, and remove the covers. Recover the gaskets.

Refitting

14 Carefully clean the cylinder head and cover mating surfaces, and remove all traces of oil.
15 Check the condition of the cover's composite gasket, and re-use it if undamaged. If it is damaged, a repair may be effected using silicone sealing compound.
16 Refit the cover(s) and tighten the bolts in sequence (see illustration).
17 Refit the ignition coils (Chapter 5B).
18 Reconnect the battery.

5.1a Unscrew the retaining bolts (arrowed) . . .

5.3a Undo the bolts (arrowed) securing the mounting and bracket . . .

5 Timing belt covers – removal and refitting

Upper cover removal

1.4 litre engines

1 Slacken and remove the two retaining bolts (one at the front and one at the rear), and remove the upper timing cover from the cylinder head (see illustrations).

1.6 litre engines

2 Position a trolley jack under the engine, with a block of wood between the jack head

5.1b . . . and remove the timing belt upper cover – SOHC engine shown

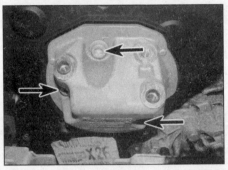

5.3b . . . and the bolts (arrowed) securing the bracket to the engine

and the sump to prevent damage. Raise the jack to take the weight of the engine.
3 Slacken the right-hand engine mounting bolts, then remove the mounting and brackets from the end of the engine (see illustrations).
4 Slacken the two lower bolts, the undo the five upper bolts and remove the upper timing belt cover (see illustration).

Lower cover removal

5 Remove the upper cover as described previously.
6 Remove the auxiliary drivebelt as described in Chapter 1A.
7 Undo the three crankshaft pulley retaining bolts and remove the pulley, noting which way round it is fitted (see illustrations).

5.4 Undo the screws (arrowed) and remove the upper timing belt cover

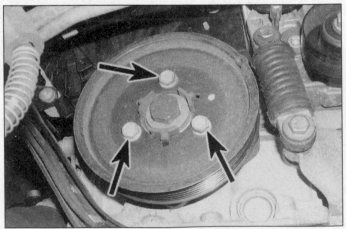

5.7a Undo the retaining bolts (arrowed) . . .

5.7b . . . and remove the crankshaft pulley

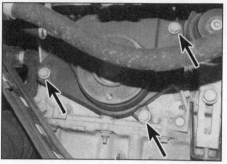

5.8 Unscrew the bolts (arrowed) and remove the timing belt lower cover

6.7 Slacken the nut then pivot the tensioner pulley clockwise to relieve the timing belt tension

8 Slacken and remove the retaining bolts then remove the lower cover from the engine **(see illustration)**.

Inner cover removal

9 Remove the camshaft sprocket(s) and tensioner pulley as described in Section 7.
10 Undo the bolts and remove the inner cover.

Refitting

Upper cover

11 Refitting is the reverse of removal.

Lower cover

12 Locate the lower cover over the timing belt sprocket, and tighten its retaining bolts.
13 Fit the pulley to the end of the crankshaft, ensuring it is fitted the correct way round, and tighten its bolts to the specified torque.
14 Refit the upper cover as described above.
15 Refit and tension the auxiliary drivebelt as described in Chapter 1A.

Inner cover

16 Refitting is a reversal of removal.

6 Timing belt – general information, removal and refitting

Note: *With early 1.4 litre engines (up to engine number 3666765) Peugeot specify the use of a special electronic tool (SEEM C.TRONIC type 105.5 belt tensioning measuring tool) and the rocker arm contact plate (0132-AE) to correctly set the timing belt tension. If access to this equipment cannot be obtained, an approximate setting can be achieved using the method described below. If this method is used, the tension must be checked using the special electronic tool at the earliest possible opportunity. Do not drive the vehicle over large distances, or use high engine speeds, until the belt tension is known to be correct. Refer to a Peugeot dealer for advice.*
Note: *Timing belts, tensioners and sprockets are not interchangeable between early (up to engine number 3666765) and late 1.4 litre engines.*

General information

1 The timing belt drives the camshaft(s) and coolant pump from a toothed sprocket on

the front of the crankshaft. If the belt breaks or slips in service, the pistons are likely to hit the valve heads, resulting in extensive (and expensive) damage.
2 The timing belt should be renewed at the specified intervals (see Chapter 1A), or earlier if it is contaminated with oil or if it is at all noisy in operation (a 'scraping' noise due to uneven wear).
3 If the timing belt is being removed, it is a wise precaution to check the condition of the coolant pump at the same time (check for signs of coolant leakage). This may avoid the need to remove the timing belt again at a later stage, should the coolant pump fail.

Removal

4 Disconnect the battery (see Chapter 5A).
5 Align the engine assembly/valve timing holes as described in Section 3, and lock both the camshaft sprocket(s) and the flywheel/driveplate in position.
Caution: Do not attempt to rotate the engine whilst the locking tools are in position.
6 Remove the timing belt lower cover as described in Section 5.

1.4 litre SOHC engines

7 Loosen the timing belt tensioner pulley retaining nut **(see illustration)**. Pivot the

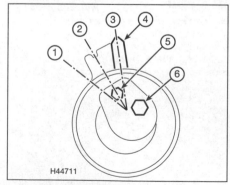

6.8 Timing belt tensioner (1.4 and 1.6 litre DOHC engines)

1 Minimum tension position
2 Normal tension position
3 Maximum tension position
4 Index arm
5 Hole for hexagonal key
6 Tensioner pulley bolt

pulley approximately 60° in a clockwise direction, using a key fitted in the hole in the pulley hub, then retighten the retaining nut. On early engines (up to engine number 3666765), an 8 mm square section key will be required, and a hexagonal key on later engines.

1.4 and 1.6 litre DOHC engines

8 Slacken the timing belt tensioner pulley retaining nut and, using a hexagonal key, rotate the pulley clockwise until the index arm is in the minimum tension position **(see illustration)**. Temporarily tighten the tensioner pulley nut in this position.

All models

9 If the timing belt is to be re-used, use white paint or similar to mark the direction of rotation on the belt (if markings do not already exist). Slip the belt off the sprockets.
10 Check the timing belt carefully for any signs of uneven wear, splitting, or oil contamination. Pay particular attention to the roots of the teeth. Renew the belt if there is the slightest doubt about its condition. If the engine is undergoing an overhaul, and has covered more than 40 000 miles (60 000 km) with the existing belt fitted, renew the belt as a matter of course, regardless of its apparent condition. The cost of a new belt is nothing when compared to the cost of repairs, should the belt break in service. If signs of oil contamination are found, trace the source of the oil leak, and rectify it. Wash down the engine timing belt area and all related components, to remove all traces of oil.
11 Prior to refitting, thoroughly clean the timing belt sprockets. Check that the tensioner

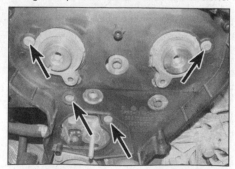

6.10 Undo the bolts (arrowed) and remove the inner cover (1.6 litre DOHC engine)

pulley rotates freely, without any sign of roughness. If necessary, renew the tensioner pulley as described in Section 7. Make sure that the locking tools are still in place, as described in Section 3.

Refitting – early 1.4 litre SOHC engine*

* Up to engine number 3666765

12 Manoeuvre the timing belt into position, ensuring that the arrows on the belt are pointing in the direction of rotation (clockwise, when viewed from the right-hand end of the engine).

13 Do not twist the timing belt sharply while refitting it. Fit the belt over the crankshaft and camshaft sprockets. Make sure that the 'front run' of the belt is taut – ie, ensure that any slack is on the tensioner pulley side of the belt. Fit the belt over the coolant pump sprocket and tensioner pulley. Ensure that the belt teeth are seated centrally in the sprockets.

14 Loosen the tensioner pulley retaining nut. Pivot the pulley anti-clockwise to remove all freeplay from the timing belt, then retighten the nut (see illustration 6.7). Tension the timing belt as described under the relevant sub-heading.

Tensioning without the electronic tool

Note: If this method is used, ensure that the belt tension is checked by a Peugeot dealer at the earliest possible opportunity.

15 If the special tool is not available, an approximate setting may be achieved by pivoting the tensioner pulley anti-clockwise until it is just possible to twist the timing belt through 90° by finger and thumb (without using excessive force), midway between the crankshaft and camshaft sprockets. The deflection of the belt at the mid-point between the sprockets should be approximately 6.0 mm.

16 Remove the locking tools from the camshaft sprocket and flywheel.

17 Using a suitable socket and extension bar on the crankshaft sprocket bolt, rotate the crankshaft through four complete rotations in a clockwise direction (viewed from the right-hand end of the engine). Refit the flywheel locking tool and check that the camshaft timing hole is correctly aligned with the cylinder head hole.

Caution: Do not at any time rotate the crankshaft anti-clockwise.

18 Slacken the tensioner pulley nut, retension the belt as described in paragraph 15, then tighten the tensioner pulley nut to the specified torque.

19 Remove the flywheel locking tool then rotate the crankshaft through a further two turns clockwise.

20 Check that both the camshaft sprocket and flywheel timing holes are still correctly aligned.

21 If all is well, refit the timing belt covers as described in Section 5.

22 Clip the wiring harness back into position then reconnect the battery.

Tensioning with the electronic tool

23 Fit the special belt tensioning measuring equipment to the 'front run' of the timing belt, approximately midway between the camshaft and crankshaft sprockets. Position the tensioner pulley so that the belt is tensioned to a setting of 44 SEEM units, then retighten its retaining nut.

24 Remove the locking tools from the camshaft sprocket and flywheel, and remove the measuring tool from the belt.

25 Using a suitable socket and extension bar on the crankshaft sprocket bolt, rotate the crankshaft through four complete rotations in a clockwise direction (viewed from the right-hand end of the engine). Refit the flywheel locking tool and check that the camshaft timing hole is correctly aligned with the cylinder head hole.

Caution: Do not at any time rotate the crankshaft anti-clockwise.

26 To ensure an accurate reading, it is necessary to remove the valve spring load from the camshaft by fitting the rocker arm plate (0132-AE). Remove the cylinder head cover (see Section 4) then back off all the rocker arm contact bolts on the plate (0132-AE). Fit the plate to the cylinder head cover studs, ensuring it is fitted the correct way around then secure it in position with the cylinder head cover nuts. Tighten each rocker arm contact bolt until all rockers are lifted clear of the camshaft lobes. If the rocker arm plate is not available, obtain clearance between the rocker arms and camshaft by slackening the locknut and backing off the adjusting screws on all the necessary rocker arms. It will be found that two of the rocker arms remain in contact with the camshaft, even with the adjusting screws backed fully off. To hold these arms clear of the camshaft, use an arrangement similar to that shown (see Tool Tip).

Caution: Do not overtighten the contact bolts any more than is necessary to obtain a small amount of clearance between the rocker arm roller and cam lobe. If the bolts are overtightened, there is a risk of the valves being forced into contact with the pistons, resulting in serious engine damage.

27 Refit the tensioning measuring equipment to the front run of the belt.

28 Slacken the tensioner pulley retaining nut whilst holding the pulley stationary. Gradually

TOOL TiP

To hold their arms clear of the camshaft, fix a stout metal bar to the cylinder head cover studs with the nuts, and lift the arms using shorter lengths of metal bar pivoted on large sockets.

release the tensioner pulley until a tension setting of between 29 and 33 SEEM units is indicated on the measuring equipment. With the belt correctly tensioned, hold the pulley stationary and tighten its retaining nut to the specified torque.

29 Remove the measuring tool from the belt then unscrew the nuts and remove the rocker arm contact plate (or home-made alternative) from the cylinder head.

30 Remove the flywheel locking tool, then rotate the crankshaft through another four complete rotations in a clockwise direction. Refit the flywheel locking tool and check that the camshaft timing hole is correctly aligned with the cylinder head hole.

31 If all is well, refit the timing belt covers and cylinder head cover as described in Sections 4 and 5. **Note:** *If the rocker arm adjusting screws were moved, adjust the valve clearances before refitting the cylinder head cover.*

Refitting – later SOHC 1.4 litre engine*

* From engine number 3666766

32 These engines are equipped with a spring-loaded tensioner, so access to the belt tensioning gauge is unnecessary.

33 Manoeuvre the timing belt into position, ensuring that the arrows on the belt are pointing in the direction of rotation (clockwise, when viewed from the right-hand end of the engine).

34 Do not twist the timing belt sharply while refitting it. Fit the belt over the crankshaft and camshaft sprockets. Make sure that the 'front run' of the belt is taut – ie, ensure that any slack is on the tensioner pulley side of the belt. Fit the belt over the coolant pump sprocket and tensioner pulley. Ensure that the belt teeth are seated centrally in the sprockets.

35 Remove the crankshaft and camshaft locking tools, then slacken the tensioner pulley nut and, using a hexagonal key, rotate the pulley anti-clockwise until the index arm is in the maximum tension position (see illustration). Tighten the pulley retaining nut.

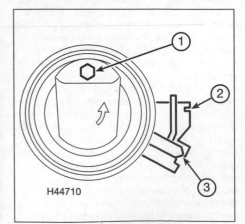

H44710

6.35 Timing belt tensioner (later 1.4 litre engine)

1 *Hole for hexagonal key*
2 *Normal tension position*
3 *Maximum tension position*

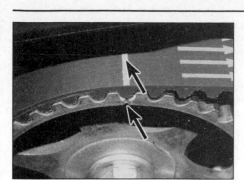

6.42 Note the timing belt marks which correspond to the camshaft sprockets and crankshaft sprocket

36 Using a socket on the crankshaft pulley bolt, rotate the crankshaft clockwise 10 complete revolutions, and refit the crankshaft locking tool as described in Section 3.

37 Check the timing is correct by inserting the camshaft sprocket locking tool (Section 3). If the tool cannot be inserted, slacken the tensioner, remove the belt, refit the locking tools, and start again from Paragraph 33.

38 Remove the crankshaft and camshaft locking tools.

39 Hold the hexagonal key in the tensioner pulley to maintain the tension, then slacken the pulley nut, and rotate the tensioner to bring the index arm to the normal tension position **(see illustration 6.35)**. Tighten the pulley nut to the specified torque.

40 Rotate the crankshaft two complete revolutions, and check that the crankshaft and camshaft locking tools can still be inserted.

41 The remainder of refitting is a reversal of removal.

Refitting –
1.4 and 1.6 litre DOHC engines

42 Manoeuvre the timing belt into position, ensuring that the arrows on the belt are pointing in the direction of rotation (clockwise, when viewed from the right-hand end of the engine). Note that there are three marks on a new belt which correspond to marks on the crankshaft and camshaft sprockets **(see illustration)**.

43 Do not twist the timing belt sharply while refitting it. Fit the belt over the crankshaft and camshaft sprockets aligning the marks on the belt with those on the crankshaft and camshaft sprockets. Make sure that the 'front run' of the belt is taut – ie, ensure that any slack is on the tensioner pulley side of the belt. Fit the belt over the coolant pump sprocket and tensioner pulley. Ensure that the belt teeth are seated centrally in the sprockets.

44 Insert the hexagonal key on the tensioner pulley, slacken the pulley nut and rotate the key to bring the index arm to the maximum tension position **(see illustration 6.8)**. Tighten the tensioner roller nut securely.

45 Remove the camshaft and crankshaft locking tools, and rotate the crankshaft 4 complete revolutions clockwise, and refit the crankshaft locking tool.

46 Insert the hexagon key in the tensioner, slacken the nut and rotate the tensioner using the key, until the index arm is in the normal tension position **(see illustration 6.8)**. Tighten the tensioner nut to the specified torque.

47 Remove the crankshaft locking tool, and rotate the crankshaft two complete revolutions clockwise. Check the position of the tensioner index arm – it should be no more than 2.0 mm away from the normal tension position. If it is not, repeat the belt fitting procedure from Paragraph 42.

48 The remainder of refitting is a reversal of removal.

7 Timing belt tensioner and sprockets – removal, inspection and refitting

Removal

Camshaft sprocket – 1.4 litre SOHC engine

1 Remove the timing belt as described in Section 6.

2 Withdraw the crankshaft and camshaft locking tools, and using a spanner or socket on the crankshaft pulley bolt, rotate the crankshaft backwards (anti-clockwise) 90°. This is to prevent any accidental contact between the pistons and valves.

3 Slacken the camshaft sprocket retaining bolt and remove it, along with its washer. To prevent the camshaft rotating as the bolt is slackened, a sprocket-holding tool will be required. In the absence of the special Peugeot tool, an acceptable substitute can be fabricated as follows. Use two lengths of steel strip (one long, the other short), and three nuts and bolts; one nut and bolt forms the pivot of a forked tool, with the remaining two nuts and bolts at the tips of the 'forks' to engage with the sprocket spokes **(see Tool Tip)**.

Caution: Do not attempt to use the sprocket locking pin to prevent the sprocket from rotating whilst the bolt is slackened.

4 With the retaining bolt removed, slide the sprocket off the end of the camshaft. If the sprocket locating pin is a loose fit, remove it for safe-keeping. Examine the camshaft oil seal for signs of oil leakage and, if necessary, renew it as described in Section 8.

Camshaft sprockets – 1.4 and 1.6 litre DOHC engines

5 Remove the cylinder head covers as described in Section 4.

6 Remove the timing belt as described in Section 6.

7 Withdraw the crankshaft and camshaft locking tools, and using a spanner or socket on the crankshaft pulley bolt, rotate the crankshaft backwards (anti-clockwise) 90°. This is to prevent any accidental contact between the pistons and valves.

Using a home-made tool to hold the camshaft sprocket stationary whilst the bolt is tightened (shown with the cylinder head removed).

8 Using an open-ended spanner on the square section to counterhold the camshaft, undo the sprocket retaining bolt **(see illustration)**.

Caution: Do not attempt to use the sprocket locking pin to prevent the sprocket from rotating whilst the bolt is slackened.

9 With the retaining bolt removed, slide the sprocket off the end of the camshaft. Note that the key is integral with the sprocket. Examine the camshaft oil seals for signs of oil leakage and, if necessary, renew it as described in Section 8.

Crankshaft sprocket

10 Remove the timing belt as described in Section 6.

11 Slacken the crankshaft sprocket bolt. To prevent crankshaft rotation on manual transmission models, select top gear, and have an assistant apply the brakes firmly. If the engine has been removed from the vehicle or the vehicle is equipped with an automatic transmission unit, it will be necessary to lock the flywheel/driveplate (see Section 15).

Caution: Do not be tempted to use the flywheel/driveplate locking pin to prevent the crankshaft from rotating; temporarily remove the locking pin prior to slackening the pulley bolt, then refit it once the bolt has been slackened.

12 Unscrew the retaining bolt and washer,

7.8 Use an open-ended spanner to counter-hold the camshaft whilst slackening the bolt

7.12a Remove the retaining bolt and washer . . .

7.12b . . . then slide off the crankshaft sprocket

7.13 Remove the Woodruff key and flanged spacer (where fitted) from the crankshaft

then slide the sprocket off the end of the crankshaft **(see illustrations)**.

13 If the Woodruff key is a loose fit in the crankshaft, remove it and store it with the sprocket for safe-keeping. If necessary, also slide the flanged spacer (where fitted) off the end of the crankshaft **(see illustration)**. Examine the crankshaft oil seal for signs oil leakage and, if necessary, renew as described in Section 14.

Tensioner pulley

14 Remove the lower timing belt cover (see Section 5).

15 Lock the camshaft and crankshaft at TDC on No 1 cylinder as described in Section 3.

16 Slacken and remove the timing belt tensioner pulley retaining nut, and slide the pulley off its mounting stud. Examine the mounting stud for signs of damage and, if necessary, renew it.

Inspection

17 Clean the sprockets thoroughly, and renew any that show signs of wear, damage or cracks.

18 Clean the tensioner assembly, but do not use any strong solvent which may enter the pulley bearing. Check that the pulley rotates freely about its hub, with no sign of stiffness or of free play. Renew the tensioner pulley if there is any doubt about its condition, or if there are any obvious signs of wear or damage.

19 Inspect the timing belt (see Section 6). Renew the belt is there is any doubt about its condition.

Refitting

Camshaft sprocket

20 Refit the locating pin (where removed) then locate the sprocket on the end of the camshaft. Ensure that the locating pin is correctly engaged with the sprocket and the cut-out in the camshaft end. Note that on 1.6 litre engines, the exhaust sprocket is marked E and the inlet sprocket marked A **(see illustrations)**.

21 Refit the sprocket retaining bolt and washer. Tighten the bolt to the specified torque, whilst retaining the sprocket/camshaft with the method used on removal.

22 Realign the timing hole in the camshaft sprocket (see Section 3) with the corresponding hole in the cylinder head, and refit the locking pin.

23 Rotate the crankshaft 90° in the normal direction of rotation (clockwise), until the crankshaft locking pin can be inserted.

24 Refit the timing belt as described in Section 6. Refit the cylinder head covers as described in Section 4.

Crankshaft sprocket

25 Locate the Woodruff key in the crankshaft end, then slide on the flanged spacer (where fitted) aligning its slot with the Woodruff key.

26 Align the crankshaft sprocket slot with the Woodruff key, and slide it onto the end of the crankshaft.

27 Temporarily remove the locking pin from the rear of the flywheel/driveplate, then refit the crankshaft sprocket retaining bolt and washer. Tighten the bolt to the specified torque, whilst preventing crankshaft rotation using the

method employed on removal. Refit the locking pin to the rear of the flywheel/driveplate.

28 Refit the timing belt as described in Section 6.

Tensioner pulley

29 Refit the tensioner pulley to its mounting stud, ensuring the cut-out aligns with the pin **(see illustration)**, and fit the retaining nut.

30 Ensure that the 'front run' of the belt is taut – ie, ensure that any slack is on the pulley side of the belt. Check that the belt is centrally located on all its sprockets. Rotate the pulley anti-clockwise to remove all free play from the timing belt, then tighten the pulley retaining nut securely.

31 Tension the timing belt as described in Section 6.

32 Once the belt is correctly tensioned, refit the timing belt covers as described in Section 5.

8 Camshaft oil seal(s) – renewal

Note: *If the camshaft oil seal has been leaking, check the timing belt for signs of oil contamination; the belt must be renewed if signs of oil contamination are found. Ensure that all traces of oil are removed from the sprockets and surrounding area before the new belt is fitted.*

1 Remove the camshaft sprocket as described in Section 7.

2 Punch or drill two small holes opposite each other in the oil seal. Screw a self-tapping screw into each, and pull on the screws

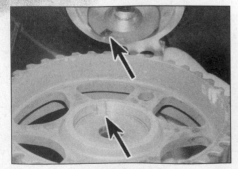

7.20a The locating pin must engage with the slot (arrowed)

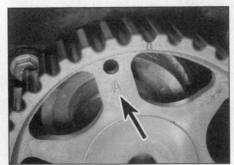

7.20b On 1.6 litre engines, the inlet sprocket is marked A (arrowed) and the exhaust E

7.29 The cut-out aligns the locating pin (arrowed)

with pliers to extract the seal. Alternatively, carefully prise the seal out using a flat-bladed screwdriver **(see illustration)**.

3 Clean the seal housing, and polish off any burrs or raised edges, which may have caused the seal to fail in the first place.

4 Lubricate the lips of the new seal with clean engine oil, and drive it into position until it seats on its locating shoulder. Use a suitable tubular drift, such as a socket, which bears only on the hard outer edge of the seal. Take care not to damage the seal lips during fitting. Note that the seal lips should face inwards.

5 Refit the camshaft sprocket as described in Section 7.

8.2 Carefully prise the camshaft oil seal out with a flat-bladed screwdriver

9.5 Check the valve clearances using feeler gauges

9 Valve clearances – checking and adjustment

Note: *The valve clearances must be checked and adjusted only when the engine is cold.*

Note: *This procedure applies only to the 1.4 litre SOHC 8V engine – the valve clearances on DOHC engines are maintained by hydraulic compensator units built into the cam followers.*

1 The importance of having the valve clearances correctly adjusted cannot be overstressed, as they vitally affect the performance of the engine. If the clearances are too big, the engine will be noisy (characteristic rattling or tapping noises) and engine efficiency will be reduced, as the valves open too late and close too early. A more serious problem arises if the clearances are too small, however. If this is the case, the valves may not close fully when the engine is hot, resulting in serious damage to the engine (eg, burnt valve seats and/or cylinder head warping/cracking). The clearances are checked and adjusted as follows.

2 Remove the cylinder head cover as described in Section 4.

3 The engine can now be turned using a suitable socket and extension bar fitted to the crankshaft sprocket bolt.

4 It is important that the clearance of each valve is checked and adjusted only when the valve is fully closed, with the rocker arm resting on the heel of the cam (directly opposite the peak). This can be ensured by carrying out the adjustments in the following sequence, noting that No 1 cylinder is at the transmission end of the engine. The correct valve clearances are given in the Specifications at the start of this Chapter. The valve locations can be determined from the position of the manifolds.

Valve fully open	Adjust valves
No 1 exhaust	No 3 intake / No 4 exhaust
No 3 exhaust	No 4 intake / No 2 exhaust
No 4 exhaust	No 2 intake / No 1 exhaust
No 2 exhaust	No 1 intake / No 3 exhaust

5 With the relevant valve fully open, check the clearances of the two valves specified. The clearances are checked by inserting a feeler blade of the correct thickness between the valve stem and the rocker arm adjusting screw. The feeler blade should be a light, sliding fit. If adjustment is necessary, slacken the adjusting screw locknut, and turn the screw as necessary **(see illustration)**. Once the correct clearance is obtained, hold the adjusting screw and tighten the locknut securely. Once the locknut has been tightened, recheck the valve clearance, and adjust again if necessary.

6 Rotate the crankshaft until the next valve in the sequence is fully open, and check the clearances of the next two specified valves.

7 Repeat the procedure until all eight valve clearances have been checked (and if necessary, adjusted), then refit the cylinder head cover as described in Section 4.

10 Camshaft(s) and rocker arms/followers – removal, inspection and refitting

General information

1 The valves are operated by followers incorporating hydraulic compensator units, between the camshafts and the top of the valves on DOHC engines. On SOHC engines, the valves are operated by rockers arms between the camshaft and the top of the valves. The rocker arm assembly is secured to the top of the cylinder head by the cylinder head bolts. Although in theory it is possible to undo the head bolts and remove the rocker arm assembly without removing the head, in practice, this is not recommended. Once the bolts have been removed, the head gasket will be disturbed, and

the gasket will almost certainly leak or blow after refitting. For this reason, removal of the rocker arm assembly cannot be done without removing the cylinder head and renewing the head gasket.

2 On DOHC engines, the camshafts cam be removed upwards from the cylinder head. On SOHC engines, the camshaft is slid out of the right-hand end of the cylinder head, and it therefore cannot be removed without first removing the cylinder head, due to a lack of clearance.

Removal

Rocker arms – SOHC engine

3 Remove the cylinder head as described in Section 11.

4 To dismantle the rocker arm assembly, carefully prise off the circlip from the right-hand end of the rocker shaft; retain the rocker pedestal, to prevent it being sprung off the end of the shaft. Slide the various components off the end of the shaft, keeping all components in their correct fitted order **(see illustration)**. Make a note of each component's correct fitted position and orientation as it is removed, to ensure it is fitted correctly on reassembly. **Note:** *Avoid touching the rocker arm roller bearing surfaces with your fingers.*

5 To separate the left-hand pedestal and shaft, first unscrew the cylinder head cover retaining stud from the top of the pedestal; this can be achieved using a stud extractor, or two nuts locked together **(see illustration)**. With the stud removed, unscrew the grub screw from the top of the pedestal, and withdraw the rocker shaft.

10.4 Remove the circlip and slide the components from the rocker shaft

10.5 Lock two nuts together to enable the stud to be unscrewed from the left-hand end pedestal

10.9 Undo the bolt and slide out the camshaft thrust fork (arrowed)

10.10a Prise out the oil seal . . .

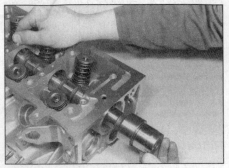

10.10b . . . then slide out the camshaft from the cylinder head

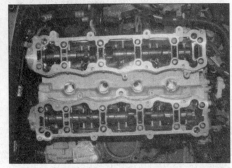

10.12 Evenly and progressively slacken the camshaft housing retaining bolts

Camshaft – SOHC engine

6 Remove the cylinder head as described in Section 11.

7 With the head on a bench, remove the locking pin, then remove the camshaft sprocket as described in paragraphs 5 and 6 of Section 7.

8 Unbolt the coolant housing from the left-hand end of the cylinder head.

9 Undo the retaining bolt and slide out the camshaft thrust fork (see illustration).

10 Using a large flat-bladed screwdriver, carefully prise the oil seal out of the right-hand end of the cylinder head, then slide out the camshaft (see illustrations).

Camshafts/followers – DOHC engine

11 Remove the camshaft sprockets as described in Section 7. Undo the screws and securing the inner timing cover to the cylinder head.

12 Starting from the outside, working in a spiral pattern, progressively and evenly slacken the camshaft bearing housing retaining bolts, and lift the housing from the cylinder head (see illustration).

13 Identify each camshaft for position – the intake camshaft is at the rear and the exhaust camshaft is at the front of the cylinder head. Also note the TDC position of each camshaft for correct refitting.

14 Remove the camshafts by pressing on the transmission ends to release the opposite ends from their bearings. Withdrawn the camshafts from the cylinder head and slide the oil seals from the ends.

15 Obtain 16 small, clean plastic containers, and number them intake 1 to 8 and exhaust 1 to 8; alternatively divide a large container into 16 compartments and number each compartment accordingly. On 1.6 litre engines, use a rubber sucker to withdraw each follower in turn, and place it in its respective container. On 1.4 litre engines, withdraw each rocker arm complete with hydraulic lifter, and place it in its respective container (see illustrations). Don't interchange the followers since the wear rate will be much increased.

Inspection

Rocker arm assembly

16 Examine the rocker arm surfaces which contact the camshaft lobes for wear ridges and scoring. Renew any rocker arms on which the rollers show signs of damage. If a rocker arm roller surface is badly scored, also examine the corresponding lobe on the camshaft for wear, as both will likely be worn. Renew worn components as necessary. The rocker arm assembly can be dismantled as described in paragraphs 4 and 5.

17 Inspect the ends of the (valve clearance) adjusting screws for signs of wear or damage, and renew as required.

18 If the rocker arm assembly has been dismantled, examine the rocker arm and shaft bearing surfaces for wear ridges and scoring. If there are obvious signs of wear, the relevant rocker arm(s) and/or the shaft must be renewed.

Camshaft(s)

19 Examine the camshaft bearing surfaces and cam lobes for signs of wear ridges and scoring. Renew the camshaft if any of these conditions are apparent. Examine the condition of the bearing surfaces, both on the camshaft journals and in the cylinder head/bearing housing. If the head bearing surfaces are worn excessively, the cylinder head will need to be renewed. If the necessary measuring equipment is available, camshaft bearing journal wear can be checked by direct measurement, noting that No 1 journal is at the transmission end of the head.

20 On SOHC engines, examine the thrust fork for signs of wear or scoring, and renew as necessary.

21 On DOHC engines, examine the hydraulic follower surfaces which contact the camshaft lobes for wear ridges and scoring. Renew any follower where these conditions are apparent. If a follower bearing surface is badly scored, also examine the corresponding lobe on the camshaft for wear, as it is likely that both will be worn (see illustration). Renew any components as necessary.

10.15a Remove the rocker arms complete with hydraulic lifter . . .

10.15b . . . and keep them in a clean container

10.21 Check the roller surface (arrowed) on the rocker arm

10.32 Position the intake camshaft locking notch at the 7 o'clock position and the exhaust camshaft at 8 o'clock (arrowed)

Refitting

Rocker arms – 1.4 litre SOHC engine

22 If the rocker arm assembly was dismantled, refit the rocker shaft to the left-hand pedestal, aligning its locating hole with the pedestal threaded hole. Refit the grub screw, and tighten it securely. With the grub screw in position, refit the cylinder head cover mounting stud to the pedestal, and tighten it securely. Apply a smear of clean engine oil to the shaft, then slide on all removed components, ensuring each is correctly fitted in its original position. **Note:** *Avoid touching the rocker arm roller bearing surfaces with your fingers.* Once all components are in position on the shaft, compress the right-hand pedestal and refit the circlip. Ensure that the circlip is correctly located in its groove on the shaft.

23 Refit the cylinder head and rocker arm assembly as described in Section 11.

Camshaft – 1.4 litre SOHC engine

24 Ensure that the cylinder head and camshaft bearing surfaces are clean, then liberally oil the camshaft bearings and lobes. Slide the camshaft back into position in the cylinder head.

25 Locate the thrust fork with the left-hand end of the camshaft. Refit the fork retaining bolt, tightening it to the specified torque setting.

26 Ensure that the coolant housing and cylinder head mating surfaces are clean and dry, then apply a smear of sealant to the housing mating surface. Refit the housing to the left-hand end of the head, and securely tighten its retaining bolts.

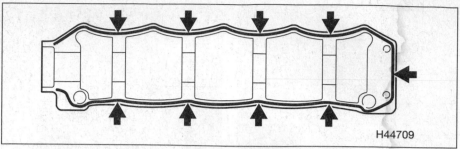

10.33 Apply a bead of silicone sealant to the cylinder head mating surface (arrowed)

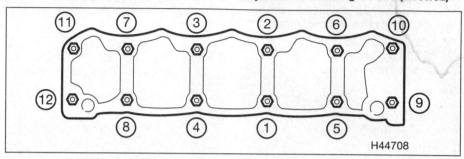

10.34 Camshaft bearing housing bolts tightening sequence

27 Lubricate the lips of the new seal with clean engine oil, then drive it into position until it seats on its locating shoulder. Use a suitable tubular drift, such as a socket, which bears only on the hard outer edge of the seal. Take care not to damage the seal lips during fitting. Note that the seal lips should face inwards.

28 Refit the camshaft sprocket as described in paragraphs 20 to 24 of Section 7.

29 Refit the cylinder head as described in Section 11.

Camshafts/followers – 1.4 and 1.6 litre DOHC engines

30 Before commencing refitting, remove all traces of oil from the bearing housing retaining bolts holes in the cylinder head, using a clean rag. Also ensure that both the cylinder head and bearing housing mating faces are clean and free from oil.

31 Liberally oil the cylinder head hydraulic follower bores and the followers. Carefully refit the followers to the cylinder head, ensuring that each follower is refitted to its original bore. Some care will be required to enter the followers squarely into their bores.

Check that each follower rotates freely. On the 1.4 litre engine, make sure the rocker arms are clipped to the hydraulic lifter securely (**see illustrations**).

32 Liberally oil the camshaft bearings in the cylinder head and the camshaft lobes, then refit the camshafts to the cylinder head in the previously noted positions. The locating notch in the right-hand end of the camshafts should be positioned at the 7 o'clock position on the intake camshaft, and the 8 o'clock position on the exhaust camshaft (**see illustration**).

33 Apply a bead of silicone-based jointing compound around the perimeter of the mating faces and around the retaining bolt hole locations (**see illustration**).

34 Refit the bearing housing, and tighten the bolts progressively, in sequence, to the specified torque (**see illustration**).

35 Fit new oil seals with reference to Section 8.

36 Ensure that the lower edge of the inner timing belt cover engages correctly with the upper edge of the crankshaft oil seal housing (**see illustration**).

37 Refit the camshaft sprockets as described in Section 7.

10.31a Refit the rocker arm and hydraulic lifter . . .

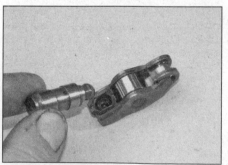

10.31b . . . making sure the hydraulic lifter is clipped into the rocker arm securely

10.36 Ensure the lower edge of the inner timing belt cover engages correctly (arrowed)

11.11 Slacken and remove the cylinder head bolts

11.13 Lift off the rocker arm assembly

11.14 Use two stout screwdrivers to rock the cylinder head free from the block

11 Cylinder head – removal and refitting

Note: *Ensure the engine is cold before removing the cylinder head.*

Removal

1 Disconnect the battery (see Chapter 5A).
2 Drain the cooling system as described in Chapter 1A.
3 Remove the ignition HT coil assembly (see Chapter 5B) then remove the spark plugs (see Chapter 1A).
4 Remove the cylinder head cover(s) as described in Section 4.
5 Align the engine assembly/valve timing holes as described in Section 3, and lock both the camshaft sprocket(s) and flywheel/driveplate in position.
Caution: Do not attempt to rotate the engine whilst the tools are in position.
6 Note that the following text assumes that the cylinder head will be removed with both intake and exhaust manifolds attached; this is easier, but makes it a bulky and heavy assembly to handle. If it is wished to remove the manifolds first, proceed as described in Chapter 4A.
7 Carry out the following operations as described in Chapter 4A:
a) *Disconnect the exhaust system front pipe from the manifold. Disconnect or release the oxygen sensor wiring.*
b) *Remove the air cleaner housing and intake duct assembly.*
c) *Disconnect the fuel feed and return hoses from the fuel rail (plug all openings, to prevent loss of fuel and entry of dirt into the fuel system).*
d) *Note their fitted positions, then disconnect the relevant electrical connectors and vacuum/breather hoses from the intake manifold.*
e) *Where necessary unbolt the support bracket from the intake manifold.*
f) *Disconnect the accelerator cable (where fitted).*
8 Remove the timing belt inner cover as described in Section 5.
9 Undo the mounting bolt and remove the

upper section of the oil dipstick guide tube. Note their fitted positions, then slacken the retaining clips, and disconnect the coolant hoses from the cylinder head. Likewise, note the routing, then disconnect all electrical connectors from the cylinder head.
10 On DOHC engines, remove the camshafts as described in Section 10.
11 Working in the *reverse* of the tightening sequence **(see illustration 11.30a or 11.30b)**, progressively slacken the cylinder head bolts by half a turn at a time, until all bolts can be unscrewed by hand **(see illustration)**.
12 On DOHC engines, lift the cylinder head away; seek assistance if possible, as it is a heavy assembly, especially if it is being removed complete with the manifolds.
13 On SOHC engines, with all the cylinder head bolts removed, lift the rocker arm assembly off the cylinder head **(see illustration)**. **Note:** *Avoid touching the rocker arm roller bearing surfaces with your fingers.* Note the locating pins which are fitted to the base of each rocker arm pedestal. If any pin is a loose fit in the head or pedestal, remove it for safe-keeping.
14 On 1.4 litre engines, the joint between the cylinder head and gasket, and the cylinder block/crankcase must now be broken without disturbing the wet liners. To break the joint, obtain two stout screwdrivers which fit into the cylinder head bolt holes. Gently 'rock' the cylinder head free towards the front of the car **(see illustration)**. Do not try to swivel the head on the cylinder block/crankcase; it is located by dowels, as well as by the tops of the liners. **Note:** *If care is not taken and the liners are moved, there is also a possibility of the bottom seals being disturbed, causing leakage after refitting the head.* When the joint is broken, lift the cylinder head away; seek assistance if possible, as it is a heavy assembly, especially if it is being removed complete with the manifolds.
15 On all models, remove the gasket from the top of the block, noting the two locating dowels. If the locating dowels are a loose fit, remove them and store them with the head for safe-keeping. Do not discard the gasket – on some models it will be needed for identification purposes (see paragraphs 20 and 21). Operations that require

the rotation of the crankshaft (eg, cleaning the piston crowns), should only be carried out on 1.4 litre engines once the cylinder liners are firmly clamped in position **(see illustration)**. In the absence of the special Peugeot liner clamps, the liners can be clamped in position using large flat washers positioned underneath suitable-length bolts. Alternatively, the original head bolts could be temporarily refitted, with suitable spacers fitted to their shanks.
Caution: On 1.4 litre engines, do not attempt to rotate the crankshaft with the cylinder head removed, otherwise the wet liners may be displaced.
16 If the cylinder head is to be dismantled for overhaul, refer to Part F of this Chapter.

Preparation for refitting

17 The mating faces of the cylinder head and cylinder block/crankcase must be perfectly clean before refitting the head. Use a hard plastic or wood scraper to remove all traces of gasket and carbon; also clean the piston crowns. **Note:** *On 1.4 litre engines, clamp the liners in position before turning the crankshaft (see paragraph 15).* Take particular care during the cleaning operations, as aluminium alloy is easily damaged. Also, make sure that the carbon is not allowed to enter the oil and water passages – this is particularly important for the lubrication system, as carbon could block the oil supply to the engine's components. Using adhesive tape and paper, seal the water, oil and bolt holes in the cylinder block/crankcase. To prevent carbon entering the gap between the pistons and bores, smear a little grease in the gap. After cleaning each

11.15 On 1.4 litre engines, clamp the cylinder liners in position before rotating the crankshaft (clamps arrowed)

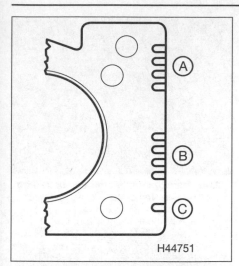

11.21 Cylinder head gasket identification markings

A *Engine type identification cut-out locations*
B *Gasket manufacturer identification cut-out locations*
C *Gasket thickness identification cut-out locations*

piston, use a small brush to remove all traces of grease and carbon from the gap, then wipe away the remainder with a clean rag. Clean all the pistons in the same way.

18 Check the mating surfaces of the cylinder block/crankcase and the cylinder head for nicks, deep scratches and other damage. If slight, they may be removed carefully with a file, but if excessive, machining may be the only alternative to renewal.

19 If warpage of the cylinder head gasket surface is suspected, use a straight-edge to check it for distortion. Refer to Part F of this Chapter if necessary.

20 When purchasing a new cylinder head gasket, it is essential that a gasket of the correct thickness is obtained. On some models only one thickness of gasket is available, so this is not a problem. On other models, there are two different thicknesses available – the standard gasket, and a slightly thicker 'repair' gasket (+ 0.2 mm). The gaskets can be identified as described in the following paragraph, using the cut-outs on the left-hand end of the gasket.

11.30a Cylinder head bolt tightening sequence (SOHC engine)

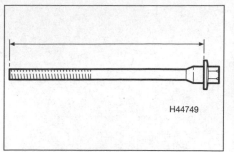

11.22 Measure the bolt length from the underside of the bolt head to the end of the bolt

21 With the gasket fitted the correct way up on the cylinder block, there will be a single or double cut-out at the rear of the left-hand side of the gasket identifying the engine type (eg, TU3JP engine). In the centre of the gasket there will likely be another series of between 0 and 4 cut-outs, identifying the manufacturer of the gasket and whether or not it contains asbestos (these cut-outs are of little importance). The important cut-out location is at the front of the gasket; on the standard gasket there will be no cut-out in this position, whereas on the thicker 'repair' gasket there will be a single cut-out **(see illustration)**. Identify the gasket type, and ensure that the new gasket obtained is of the correct thickness. If there is any doubt as to which gasket is fitted, take the old gasket along to your Peugeot dealer, and have him confirm the gasket type.

22 Check the condition of the cylinder head bolts, and particularly their threads, whenever they are removed. Wash the bolts in suitable solvent, and wipe them dry. Check each for any sign of visible wear or damage, renewing any bolt if necessary. Measure the length of each bolt, from the underside of its head to the bolt end, to check for stretching **(see illustration)**. The bolts for the 1.4 litre SOHC engine are 175.5 mm in length when new; if any bolt has stretched to more than 176.5 mm, renew all the cylinder head bolts as a set. On the 1.4 litre DOHC engine, the maximum length for the bolts is 118.6 mm and they can only be re-used 2 times. On 1.6 litre DOHC engines, the maximum length for the bolts is 122.6 mm. Although Peugeot

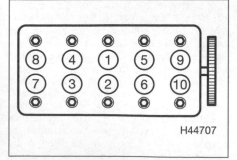

11.30b Cylinder head bolt tightening sequence (DOHC engine)

11.24 Ensure the locating dowels (arrowed) are in position then fit the new head gasket

do not actually specify that the bolts must be renewed, it is strongly recommended that the bolts should be renewed as a complete set, regardless of their apparent condition, whenever they are disturbed.

23 On 1.4 litre engines, prior to refitting the cylinder head, check the cylinder liner protrusion as described Chapter 2F, Section 11.

Refitting

24 Wipe clean the mating surfaces of the cylinder head and cylinder block/crankcase. Check that the two locating dowels are in position at each end of the cylinder block/ crankcase surface and, if necessary, remove the cylinder liner clamps **(see illustration)**.

25 Position a new gasket on the cylinder block/crankcase surface, ensuring that its identification cut-outs are at the left-hand end of the gasket, and the side marked TOP is uppermost.

26 Check that the flywheel/driveplate and camshaft sprocket(s) are still correctly locked in position with their respective tools then, with the aid of an assistant, carefully refit the cylinder head assembly to the block, aligning it with the locating dowels. On DOHC engines, ensure that the inner timing cover lower edge engages correctly with the upper edge of the crankshaft oil seal housing.

27 On SOHC engines, ensure that the locating pins are in position in the base of each rocker pedestal, then refit the rocker arm assembly to the cylinder head.

28 On all engines, lubricate the threads and underside of the heads of the cylinder head bolts lightly with clean engine oil.

29 Carefully enter each bolt into its relevant hole (*do not drop them in*) and screw in, by hand only, until finger-tight.

30 Working progressively and in the sequence shown, tighten the cylinder head bolts to their Stage 1 torque setting, using a torque wrench and suitable socket **(see illustrations)**.

31 Once all the bolts have been tightened to their Stage 1 setting, working again in the given sequence, angle-tighten the bolts through the specified Stage 2 angle, using a socket and extension bar. It is recommended that an angle-measuring gauge is used during this stage of the tightening, to ensure accuracy. If a gauge is not available, use white paint to make alignment marks between the bolt head and cylinder head prior to tightening; the marks can then be used to check that the bolt has been rotated through the correct angle during tightening.

32 Refit the timing belt inner cover as described in Section 5. Reconnect the all wiring plugs to the cylinder head and manifold.

33 On DOHC engines, refit the camshafts with reference to Section 10.

34 Working as described in the Chapter 4A, carry out the following tasks:

a) *Refit all disturbed wiring, hoses and control cable(s) to the intake manifold and fuel system components.*

b) *Reconnect and adjust the accelerator cable (where fitted).*

c) *Reconnect the exhaust system front pipe to the manifold and reconnect the oxygen sensor wiring connector.*

d) *Refit the air cleaner and intake duct.*

35 On SOHC engines, check and, if necessary, adjust the valve clearances as described in Section 9.

36 Refit the cylinder head cover(s) as described in Section 4.

37 Refit the spark plugs and install the ignition HT coil (see Chapters 1A and 5B).

38 On completion, reconnect the battery (Chapter 5A), and refill the cooling system as described in Chapter 1A.

12 Sump – removal and refitting

Removal

1 Firmly apply the handbrake, then jack up the front of the vehicle and support it on axle stands (see *Jacking and vehicle support*). Undo the screws and remove the engine undershield.

2 Drain the engine oil, then clean and refit the engine oil drain plug, tightening it to the specified torque. If the engine is nearing its service interval when the oil and filter are due for renewal, it is recommended that the filter is also removed, and a new one fitted. After reassembly, the engine can then be refilled with fresh oil. Refer to Chapter 1A for further information.

3 Remove the exhaust system front pipe as described in Chapter 4A.

4 Progressively slacken and remove all the sump nuts and bolts/nuts and position the wiring harness guide clear of the sump **(see illustrations)**.

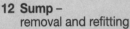

5 Break the joint by striking the sump with the palm of your hand, then lower and withdraw the sump from under the car. On 1.6 litre engines, recover the gasket

6 While the sump is removed, take the opportunity to check the oil pump pick-up/strainer for signs of clogging or splitting. If necessary, remove the pump as described in Section 13, and clean or renew the strainer.

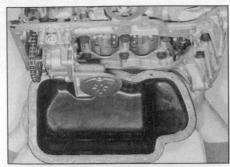

12.4a Undo the nuts and bolts, then remove the sump from the engine (1.4 litre engine)

Refitting

7 Clean all traces of sealant from the mating surfaces of the cylinder block/crankcase and sump, then use a clean rag to wipe out the sump and the engine's interior.

8 Ensure that the sump and cylinder block/crankcase mating surfaces are clean and dry then, on 1.4 litre engines, apply a coating of suitable sealant to the sump mating surface. On 1.6 litre engines, if the gasket is undamaged, refit it to the sump, otherwise fit a new gasket.

9 Offer up the sump and locate it on its studs. Locate the wiring harness guide back in position then refit the sump retaining nuts and bolts. Tighten the nuts and bolts evenly and progressively to the specified torque.

10 Refit the exhaust front pipe as described in Chapter 4A, and refit the engine undershield.

11 Replenish the engine oil (see Chapter 1A).

13 Oil pump – removal, inspection and refitting

Removal

1 Remove the sump (see Section 12).

2 Slacken and remove the three bolts securing the oil pump in position **(see illustration)**. Disengage the pump sprocket from the chain, and remove the oil pump. If the pump locating dowel is a loose fit, remove and store it with the bolts for safe-keeping.

Inspection

3 Examine the oil pump sprocket for signs of damage and wear, such as chipped or missing teeth. If the sprocket is worn, the pump assembly must be renewed, as the sprocket is not available separately. It is also recommended that the chain and drive sprocket, fitted to the crankshaft, are renewed at the same time. On 1.4 litre engines, renewal of the chain and drive sprocket is an involved operation requiring the removal of the main bearing ladder, and therefore cannot be carried out with the engine still fitted to the vehicle. On 1.6 litre engines, the oil pump drive sprocket and chain can be removed with the engine *in situ*, once the crankshaft sprocket

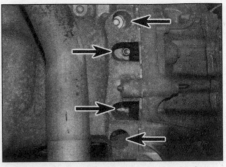

12.4b Access to the sump end bolts/nuts is through holes in the casing (arrowed) (1.6 litre engine)

has been removed and the crankshaft oil seal housing has been unbolted.

4 Slacken and remove the bolts securing the strainer cover to the pump body, then lift off the strainer cover. Remove the relief valve piston and spring (and guide pin – 1.6 litre engines only), noting which way round they are fitted.

5 Examine the pump rotors and body for signs of wear ridges and scoring. If worn, the complete pump assembly must be renewed.

6 Examine the relief valve piston for signs of wear or damage, and renew if necessary. The condition of the relief valve spring can only be measured by comparing it with a new one; if there is any doubt about its condition, it should also be renewed. Both the piston and spring are available individually.

7 Thoroughly clean the oil pump strainer with a suitable solvent, and check it for signs of clogging or splitting. If the strainer is damaged, the strainer and cover assembly must be renewed.

8 Locate the relief valve spring, piston and (where fitted) the guide pin in the strainer cover, then refit the cover to the pump body. Align the relief valve piston with its bore in the pump. Refit the cover retaining bolts, tightening them securely.

Refitting

9 Ensure that the locating dowel is in position, then engage the pump sprocket with its drive chain. Locate the pump on its dowel, and refit the pump retaining bolts, tightening them to the specified torque setting.

10 Refit the sump as described in Section 12.

13.2 Unscrew the three bolts securing the oil pump is position

14 Crankshaft oil seals – renewal

Right-hand oil seal

1 Remove the crankshaft sprocket and flanged spacer (where fitted) as described in Section 7.

2 Make a note of the correct fitted depth of the seal in its housing then carefully punch or drill two small holes opposite each other in the seal. Screw a self-tapping screw into each, and pull on the screws with pliers to extract the seal. Alternatively, the seal can be levered out of position using a suitable flat-bladed screwdriver, taking great care not to damage the crankshaft/oil pump drive gear shoulder or seal housing **(see illustration)**.

3 Clean the seal housing, and polish off any burrs or raised edges, which may have caused the seal to fail in the first place.

4 Lubricate the lips of the new seal with clean engine oil, and carefully locate the seal on the end of crankshaft. Note that its sealing lip must face inwards. Take care not to damage the seal lips during fitting.

5 Using a suitable tubular drift (such as a socket) which bears only on the hard outer edge of the seal, tap the seal into position, to the same depth in the housing as the original was prior to removal. The inner face of the seal must be flush with the inner wall of the crankcase.

6 Wash off any traces of oil, then refit the crankshaft sprocket as described in Section 7.

Left-hand oil seal

7 Remove the flywheel/driveplate (see Section 15).

8 Make a note of the correct fitted depth of the seal in its housing. Punch or drill two small holes opposite each other in the seal. Screw a self-tapping screw into each, and pull on the screws with pliers to extract the seal.

9 Clean the seal housing, and polish off any burrs or raised edges, which may have caused the seal to fail in the first place.

10 Lubricate the lips of the new seal with

clean engine oil, and carefully locate the seal on the end of the crankshaft.

11 Using a suitable tubular drift, which bears only on the hard outer edge of the seal, drive the seal into position, to the same depth in the housing as the original was prior to removal.

12 Wash off any traces of oil, then refit the flywheel/driveplate as described in Section 15.

15 Flywheel/driveplate – removal, inspection and refitting

Flywheel

Removal

1 Remove the transmission as described in Chapter 7A, then remove the clutch assembly as described in Chapter 6.

2 Prevent the flywheel from turning by locking the ring gear teeth **(see illustration)**. Alternatively, bolt a strap between the flywheel and the cylinder block/crankcase.

Caution: Do not attempt to lock the flywheel in position using the locking pin described in Section 3.

3 Slacken and remove the flywheel retaining bolts.

4 Remove the flywheel. Do not drop it, as it is very heavy. If the locating dowel is a loose fit in the crankshaft end, remove and store it with the flywheel for safe-keeping.

Inspection

5 If the flywheel's clutch mating surface is deeply scored, cracked or otherwise damaged, the flywheel must be renewed. However, it may be possible to have it surface-ground; seek the advice of a Peugeot dealer or engine reconditioning specialist.

6 If the ring gear is badly worn or has missing teeth, it must be renewed. This job is best left to a Peugeot dealer or engine reconditioning specialist. The temperature to which the new ring gear must be heated for installation is critical and, if not done accurately, the hardness of the teeth will be destroyed.

Refitting

7 Clean the mating surfaces of the flywheel and crankshaft.

8 If the new flywheel retaining bolts are not supplied with their threads already precoated, apply a suitable thread-locking compound to the threads of each bolt.

9 Ensure that the locating dowel is in position. Offer up the flywheel, locating it on the dowel, and fit the retaining bolts.

10 Lock the flywheel using the method employed on dismantling, and tighten the retaining bolts evenly and progressively to the specified torque.

11 Refit the clutch as described in Chapter 6. Remove the locking tool, and refit the transmission as described in Chapter 7A.

Driveplate

Removal

12 Remove the transmission as described in Chapter 7B.

13 Prevent the driveplate from turning by locking the ring gear teeth with a similar arrangement to that for the flywheel **(see illustration 15.2)**. Alternatively, bolt a strap between the driveplate and the cylinder block/crankcase.

Caution: Do not attempt to lock the driveplate in position using the locking pin described in Section 3.

14 Slacken and remove the driveplate retaining bolts and remove the outer spacer plate and torque converter mounting plate.

15 Remove the driveplate and inner spacer plate from the end of the crankshaft. If the locating dowel is a loose fit in the crankshaft end, remove and store it with the driveplate for safe-keeping. **Note:** *The inner and outer spacer plates are different and are not interchangeable.*

Inspection

16 Inspect the driveplate and torque converter mounting plate for signs of wear or damage. If damage is found, the worn component must be renewed (it is not possible to renew the driveplate ring gear separately).

Refitting

17 Ensure all mating surfaces are clean and dry.

18 Remove any traces of locking compound from the threads of the driveplate bolts and apply a small amount of fresh locking compound (Peugeot recommend Loctite Frenbloc) to the bolt threads.

19 Ensure that the locating dowel is in position then refit the inner spacer plate, driveplate, torque converter mounting plate and outer spacer plate. Ensure all components are correctly located on the dowel then fit the retaining bolts.

20 Lock the driveplate using the method employed on dismantling, and tighten the retaining bolts evenly and progressively to the specified torque.

21 Refit the transmission as described in Chapter 7B.

14.2 Use a screwdriver to lever out the crankshaft right-hand oil seal

15.2 Use a tool to lock the flywheel ring gear and prevent rotation

16 Engine/transmission mountings – inspection and renewal

Inspection

1 If improved access is required, raise the front of the car and support it on axle stands (see *Jacking and vehicle support*).

2 Check the mounting rubber to see if it is cracked, hardened or separated from the metal at any point; renew the mounting if any such damage or deterioration is evident.

3 Check that all the mounting's fasteners are securely tightened; use a torque wrench to check if possible.

4 Using a large screwdriver or a crowbar, check for wear in the mounting by carefully levering against it to check for free play. Where this is not possible, enlist the aid of an assistant to move the engine/transmission back-and-forth, or from side-to-side, while you watch the mounting. While some free play is to be expected even from new components, excessive wear should be obvious. If excessive free play is found, check first that the fasteners are secure, then renew any worn components as described below.

Renewal

Right-hand mounting

5 Place a jack beneath the engine, with a block of wood on the jack head. Raise the jack until it is supporting the weight of the engine.

6 Slacken and remove the bolts securing the mounting to the body, and the mounting bracket to the bracket bolted to the cylinder head **(see illustrations)**.

7 If required, undo the three bolts and remove the bracket from the cylinder head **(see illustration)**.

8 Check for signs of wear or damage on all components, and renew as necessary.

9 On reassembly, refit the bracket to the cylinder head, tightening the screws/nuts to the specified torque.

10 Install the mounting and mounting bracket and tighten its retaining bolts to the specified torque setting.

11 Remove the jack from under the engine.

Left-hand mounting

12 Remove the battery, and battery tray/box as described in Chapter 5A.

13 Place a jack beneath the transmission, with a block of wood on the jack head. Raise the jack until it is supporting the weight of the transmission.

14 Slacken and remove the mounting rubber's centre nut and two retaining bolts and remove the mounting from the engine compartment **(see illustration)**.

15 If necessary, undo the retaining bolts and remove the mounting bracket from the body **(see illustration)**.

16 Check carefully for signs of wear or

16.6a Right-hand engine mounting and bracket bolts (arrowed) (1.4 litre engine)

damage on all components, and renew them where necessary.

17 Refit the mounting bracket to the vehicle body and tighten its bolts to the specified torque.

18 Fit the mounting rubber to the bracket and tighten its retaining bolts to the specified torque. Refit the mounting centre nut, and tighten it to the specified torque.

19 Remove the jack from underneath the transmission, then refit the battery as described in Chapter 5A.

Rear mounting

20 If not already done, firmly apply the handbrake, then jack up the front of the vehicle and support it securely on axle stands (see *Jacking and vehicle support*).

21 Unscrew and remove the bolt securing the rear mounting link to the mounting on the rear of the cylinder block **(see illustration)**.

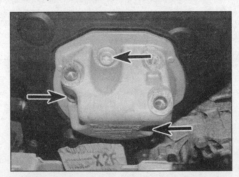

16.7 Engine mounting bracket-to-cylinder head bolts (arrowed) (1.6 litre engine)

16.15 Undo the nut/bolts (arrowed) and remove the mounting bracket

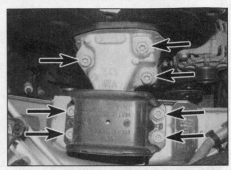

16.6b Right-hand engine mounting and bracket bolts (arrowed) (1.6 litre engine)

22 Remove the bolt securing the rear mounting link to the subframe and remove the mounting link.

23 To remove the mounting assembly it will first be necessary to remove the right-hand driveshaft as described in Chapter 8.

24 With the driveshaft removed, undo the retaining bolts and remove the mounting from the rear of the cylinder block.

25 Check carefully for signs of wear or damage on all components, and renew them where necessary.

26 On reassembly, fit the rear mounting assembly to the rear of the cylinder block, and tighten its retaining bolts to the specified torque. Refit the driveshaft as described in Chapter 8.

27 Refit the rear mounting link, and tighten both its bolts to their specified torque settings.

28 Lower the vehicle to the ground.

16.14 Undo the left-hand mounting centre nut and two retaining nuts (arrowed)

16.21 Undo the link-to-engine block bracket bolt (A) and the link-to-subframe bolt (B)

Chapter 2 Part B:
2.0 litre petrol engine in-car repair procedures

Contents

Degrees of difficulty

| **Easy,** suitable for novice with little experience | | **Fairly easy,** suitable for beginner with some experience | | **Fairly difficult,** suitable for competent DIY mechanic | 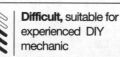 | **Difficult,** suitable for experienced DIY mechanic | | **Very difficult,** suitable for expert DIY or professional | |

Specifications

Engine (general)

Type . . . . 2.0 litre (1997cc) DOHC 16V
Designation . . . . EW10J4 and EW10A
Engine codes*:
  EW10J4 . . . . RFN
  EW10A . . . . RFJ
Bore . . . . 85.00 mm
Stroke. . . . . 88.00 mm
Direction of crankshaft rotation . . . . Clockwise (viewed from the right-hand side of vehicle)
No 1 cylinder location. . . . . At the transmission end of the block
Compression ratio:
  EW10J4 . . . . 10.8 : 1
  EW10A . . . . 11.0 : 1
Maximum power output:
  EW10J4 . . . . 100 kW @ 6000 rpm
  EW10A . . . . 103 kW @ 6000 rpm
Maximum torque output:
  EW10J4 . . . . 190 Nm @ 4100 rpm
  EW10A . . . . 200 Nm @ 4000 rpm

* The engine code is stamped on a plate attached to the front right-hand end of the cylinder block, below the right-hand branch of the exhaust manifold. The code is the first 3-digits on the first line, and this is the code most often used by Peugeot.

Camshafts

Drive. . . . . Toothed belt
No of bearings 5

Lubrication system

Oil pump type	Crescent-type driven directly from crankshaft
Minimum oil pressure at 80°C:	
1000 rpm	1.5 bars
3000 rpm	5.0 bars
Oil pressure warning switch operating pressure	0.5 bars

Torque wrench settings

	Nm	lbf ft
Big-end bearing bolts*:		
Stage 1	10	7
Stage 2	Slacken each bolt 180°	
Stage 3	25	18
Stage 4	Angle-tighten a further 46° ± 5°	
Camshaft bearing housings:		
Stage 1	5	4
Stage 2	10	7
Camshaft sprocket/hub-to-camshaft retaining bolts	75	55
Crankshaft pulley to sprocket endplate	21	15
Crankshaft sprocket centre bolt (with gold washer):		
Stage 1	40	30
Stage 2	Angle-tighten a further 53°	
Crankshaft sprocket centre bolt (with metallic washer):		
Stage 1	40	30
Stage 2	Angle-tighten a further 40°	
Cylinder head bolts:		
Stage 1	15	11
Stage 2	50	37
Stage 3	Slacken fully	
Stage 4	20	15
Stage 5	Angle-tighten a further 285° (maximum of two steps)	
Cylinder head cover bolts	11	8
Engine-to-transmission fixing bolts	45	33
Flywheel/driveplate retaining bolts*:		
Stage 1	25	18
Stage 2	Slacken fully	
Stage 3	20	15
Stage 4	Angle-tighten a further 22°	
Left-hand engine/transmission mounting:		
Mounting bracket-to-body bolts	22	16
Mounting stud to transmission bracket	50	37
Rubber mounting centre nut	65	48
Rubber mounting-to-bracket nuts	30	22
Main bearing cap housing:		
Stage 1 – 11.0 mm diameter bolts	10	7
Stage 2 – 6.0 mm diameter bolts	5	4
Stage 3 – 11.0 mm diameter bolts	Slacken fully	
Stage 4 – 11.0 mm diameter bolts	20	15
Stage 5 – 11.0 mm diameter bolts	Angle-tighten a further 70° ± 5°	
Stage 6 – 6.0 mm diameter bolts	10	7
Oil pressure switch	30	22
Oil pump-to-engine bolts	9	7
Rear engine/transmission mounting:		
Connecting link-to-mounting bracket bolt	40	30
Connecting link-to-subframe bolt	55	41
Mounting bracket-to-cylinder block bolts	45	33
Right-hand engine/transmission mounting:		
Mounting bracket to support bracket	60	44
Rubber mounting to body	60	44
Support bracket to engine	45	33
Roadwheels	90	66
Sump retaining bolts	8	6
Sump baffle plate bolts	20	15
Sump drain plug	30	22
Timing belt tensioner pulley bolt	21	15
Timing belt idler pulley bolt:		
Stage 1	15	11
Stage 2	37	27

Do not re-use

1 General information

How to use this Chapter

This Part of Chapter 2 describes those repair procedures that can reasonably be carried out on the engine, while it remains in the car. If the engine has been removed from the car and is being dismantled as described in Part F, any preliminary dismantling procedures can be ignored.

Note that, while it may be possible physically to overhaul items such as the piston/connecting rod assemblies while the engine is in the car, such tasks are not usually carried out as separate operations. Usually, several additional procedures (not to mention the cleaning of components and oilways) have to be carried out. For this reason, all such tasks are classed as major overhaul procedures, and are described in Part D of this Chapter.

Part F describes the removal of the engine/transmission unit from the vehicle, and the full overhaul procedures that can then be carried out.

EW series engine

The engine is of in-line four-cylinder, double-overhead camshaft, 16-valve type, mounted transversely at the front of the car. The clutch and transmission are attached to its left-hand end.

The engine is of conventional 'dry-liner' type, and the cylinder block is cast in aluminium.

The crankshaft runs in five main bearings. Thrustwashers are fitted to No 2 main bearing cap, to control crankshaft endfloat.

The connecting rods rotate on horizontally-split bearing shells at their big-ends. The pistons are attached to the connecting rods by gudgeon pins. The gudgeon pins are an interference fit in the connecting rod small-end eyes. The aluminium alloy pistons are fitted with three piston rings – two compression rings and an oil control ring.

The camshafts are driven by a toothed timing belt, and operate sixteen valves by followers located beneath each cam lobe. The valve clearances are self-adjusting by means of hydraulic tappets fitted to the cam followers. The camshaft runs in bearing cap housings which are bolted to the top of the cylinder head. The inlet and exhaust valves are each closed by coil springs, and operate in guides pressed into the cylinder head. Both the valve seats and guides can be renewed separately if worn.

The coolant pump is driven by the timing belt and located in the right-hand end of the cylinder block.

Lubrication is by means of an oil pump driven off the crankshaft right-hand end. It draws oil through a strainer located in the sump, and then forces it through an externally-mounted filter into galleries in the cylinder block/crankcase. From there, the oil is distributed to the crankshaft (main bearings) and camshaft. The big-end bearings are supplied with oil via internal drillings in the crankshaft; the camshaft bearings also receive a pressurised supply. The camshaft lobes and valves are lubricated by splash, as are all other engine components.

Throughout the manual, it is often necessary to identify the engines not only by their cubic capacity, but also by their engine code. The engine code consists of three digits (eg, RFN). The code is stamped on a plate attached to the front, left-hand end of the cylinder block, or stamped directly onto the front face of the cylinder block, on the machined surface located just to the left of the oil filter (next to the crankcase vent hose union).

Operations with engine in the car

The following work can be carried out with the engine in the car:

a) Compression pressure – testing.
b) Cylinder head covers – removal and refitting.
c) Crankshaft pulley – removal and refitting.
d) Timing belt covers – removal and refitting.
e) Timing belt – removal, refitting and adjustment.
f) Timing belt tensioner and sprockets – removal and refitting.
g) Camshaft oil seals – renewal.
h) Camshafts and followers – removal, inspection and refitting.
i) Cylinder head – removal and refitting.
j) Cylinder head and pistons – decarbonising.
k) Sump – removal and refitting.
l) Oil pump – removal, overhaul and refitting.
m) Crankshaft oil seals – renewal.
n) Engine/transmission mountings – inspection and renewal.
o) Flywheel/driveplate – removal, inspection and refitting.

2 Compression test – description and interpretation

Refer to Chapter 2A, Section 2.

3 Engine assembly/valve timing holes – general information and usage

Vehicles before RPO 9653

Note: *Do not attempt to rotate the engine whilst the crankshaft/camshaft are locked in position. If the engine is to be left in this state for a long period of time, it is a good idea to place suitable warning notices inside the vehicle, and in the engine compartment. This will reduce the possibility of the engine being accidentally cranked on the starter motor,* which is likely to cause damage with the locking pins in place.

1 Timing holes are drilled in the crankshaft sprocket end plate and in the two camshaft sprockets. The holes are used to ensure that the crankshaft and camshafts are correctly positioned when assembling the engine (to prevent the possibility of the valves contacting the pistons when refitting the cylinder head), or refitting the timing belt. When the timing holes are aligned with corresponding holes in the cylinder head and oil pump housing, suitable diameter pins or bolts can be inserted to lock both the camshafts and crankshaft in position, preventing them from rotating. To set the engine in the timing position, proceed as follows.

2 Remove the crankshaft pulley as described in Section 5.

3 Remove the timing belt upper (outer) and lower covers as described in Section 6.

4 Using a socket and extension bar fitted to the crankshaft sprocket centre bolt, turn the crankshaft in the normal direction of rotation (clockwise) until the timing holes in both camshaft sprockets are aligned with their corresponding holes in the cylinder head. The holes are aligned when the inlet camshaft sprocket hole is in approximately the 5 o'clock position and the exhaust camshaft sprocket hole is in approximately the 7 o'clock position, when viewed from the right-hand end of the engine. Use a small mirror to accurately observe the position of the holes.

5 With the camshaft sprocket holes correctly positioned, insert an 8.0 mm diameter drill bit or bolt through the timing hole in the crankshaft sprocket end plate, and locate it in the corresponding hole in the oil pump housing (see illustration). **Note:** *It may be found that an 8.0 mm drill is too large, in which case a 5/16 in drill may be required.*

6 The camshaft sprockets can now be locked in position using the Peugeot camshaft setting rods, or suitable home-made alternatives (see Tool Tip). With the crankshaft locked in position, insert the Peugeot special tools, or alternatives, through the timing hole in each camshaft sprocket and locate it in the

3.5 Insert an 8.0 mm drill bit or bolt through the hole in the crankshaft sprocket end plate, and into the corresponding hole in the oil pump housing

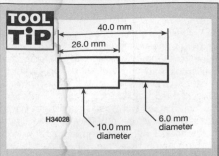

Camshaft sprocket locking tools can be made from 10.0 mm diameter steel bar, fabricated to the dimensions shown.

corresponding hole in the cylinder head (see illustration).

7 The crankshaft and camshafts are now locked in position, preventing rotation. In this position the crankshaft is at 90° BTDC and all the pistons are positioned half-way down their cylinder bores.

Vehicles from RPO 9653

Note: *Do not attempt to rotate the engine whilst the crankshaft/camshafts are locked in position. If the engine is to be left in this state for a long period of time, it is a good idea to place suitable warning notices inside the vehicle, and in the engine compartment. This will reduce the possibility of the engine being accidentally cranked on the starter motor, which is likely to cause damage with the locking rods/tool in place.*

8 Timing holes are drilled in the flywheel/

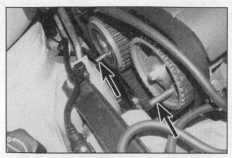

3.6 Camshaft sprocket locking tools (arrowed) inserted through the timing hole in each sprocket

cylinder block and in the two camshaft sprockets. The holes are used to ensure that the crankshaft and camshafts are correctly positioned when assembling the engine (to prevent the possibility of the valves contacting the pistons when refitting the cylinder head), or refitting the timing belt. When the timing holes are aligned with corresponding holes in the cylinder head and flywheel, suitable diameter pins or bolts can be inserted to lock both the camshafts and crankshaft in position, preventing them from rotating. To set the engine in the timing position, proceed as follows.

9 Undo the bolts and remove the timing belt upper cover (see Section 6).

10 Using a socket and extension bar fitted to the crankshaft sprocket centre bolt, turn the crankshaft in the normal direction of rotation until the timing holes in both camshaft sprockets are aligned with their corresponding

holes in the cylinder head. The holes are aligned when the intake camshaft sprocket hole is in approximately the 5 o'clock position and the exhaust camshaft sprocket hole is in approximately the 7 o'clock position, when viewed from the right-hand end of the engine. Use a small mirror to accurately observe the position of the holes.

11 With the camshaft sprocket holes correctly positioned, insert Peugeot tool (-).0189.R, or home-made equivalent, through the timing cylinder block transmission flange, and locate it in the corresponding hole in the flywheel.

12 The camshaft sprockets can now be locked in position using the Peugeot camshaft setting rods, or suitable home-made alternatives (see Tool Tip in this Section). With the crankshaft locked in position, insert the Peugeot special tools, or alternatives, through the timing hole in each camshaft sprocket and locate it in the corresponding hole in the cylinder head.

13 The crankshaft and camshafts are now locked in position, preventing rotation. In this position the crankshaft is at 90° BTDC and all the pistons are positioned half way down their cylinder bores.

---

4 Cylinder head covers – removal and refitting

Removal

1 Undo the six screws and remove the plastic cover from the top of the engine. Remove the crankcase ventilation hose and camshaft position sensor from the rear cylinder head cover (see illustrations).

2 Progressively unscrew the bolts securing the cylinder head covers to the cylinder head. The bolts must be unscrewed in a spiral sequence starting from the outside.

3 Remove the cylinder head covers and gaskets (see illustrations). Unless they are obviously damaged, do not attempt to remove the rubber gaskets from the covers.

Refitting

4 Thoroughly clean the surfaces of the covers and cylinder head.

5 If necessary, fit new seals and locate the

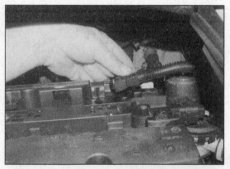

4.1a Disconnect the crankcase breather hose from the rear cylinder head cover

4.1b Disconnect the camshaft position sensor wiring connector . . .

4.1c . . . then undo the bolt and remove the sensor from the rear cylinder head cover

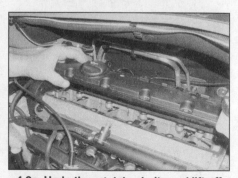

4.3a Undo the retaining bolts and lift off the front . . .

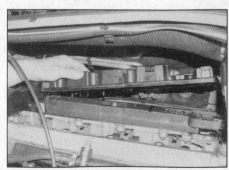

4.3b . . . and rear cylinder head covers

4.5 Locate the cylinder head cover seal in the groove, ensuring it is fully seated along its entire length

4.6 Cylinder head cover bolt tightening sequence

covers on the head **(see illustration)**. Insert the retaining bolts and finger-tighten them.

6 Progressively tighten the bolts in sequence **(see illustration)**.

7 Check the condition of the O-ring seal on the camshaft position sensor and renew the seal if it is in any way suspect.

8 Refit the camshaft position sensor and secure with the retaining bolt. Reconnect the sensor wiring connector.

9 Reconnect the breather hose to the rear cover.

10 The remainder of refitting is a reversal of removal.

5 Crankshaft pulley – removal and refitting

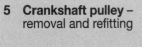

Removal

1 Remove the auxiliary drivebelt (Chapter 1A).

2 To prevent the crankshaft turning whilst the pulley retaining bolt is being slackened on manual transmission models, select 5th gear and have an assistant apply the brakes firmly. On automatic transmission models it will be necessary to remove the starter motor (Chapter 5A) and lock the driveplate with a suitable tool. If the engine has been removed from the vehicle, lock the flywheel ring gear as described in Section 8. *Do not* attempt to lock the pulley by inserting a bolt/drill through the timing hole. If the locking pin is in position, temporarily remove it prior to slackening the pulley bolt, then refit it once the bolt has been slackened.

Vehicles before RPO 9653

3 Undo the four crankshaft pulley retaining bolts and remove the pulley from the crankshaft sprocket end plate **(see illustrations)**.

Vehicles from RPO 9653

4 On these engines, the pulley can only be removed once the crankshaft sprocket bolt has been unscrewed. Removal of this

5.3a Undo the four crankshaft pulley retaining bolts . . .

bolt is only possible once the camshafts and crankshaft are locked in the reference position, as described in Section 3. Removal of the pulley is therefore described in the timing belt removal procedure (see Section 7).

Refitting

Vehicles before RPO 9653

5 Locate the pulley on the crankshaft sprocket end plate, refit the four retaining bolts and tighten them to the specified torque

6 Refit and tension the auxiliary drivebelt as described in Chapter 1A.

6 Timing belt covers – removal and refitting

Removal

Upper (outer) cover

1 Undo the screws and remove the engine undershield (where fitted).

2 Position a trolley jack under the engine, placing a block of wood between the jack head and the sump. Take the weight of the engine, undo the bolts/nuts and remove the right-hand engine mounting and bracket (see Section 16).

3 Undo the bolt securing the power steering

5.3b . . . and remove the pulley from the crankshaft end plate

pipe bracket adjacent to the coolant pump. Move the pipes to one side to improve access.

4 Remove the plastic cover from over the coolant and washer reservoirs. The cover is secured by plastic expanding rivets. Push in the centre pins a little, then prise out the complete rivets and release the side clip. Release the side retaining clip.

5 Undo the upper and lower retaining bolts securing the outer cover to the inner cover **(see illustration)**. Slide the cover retaining clip upwards to release it from its fasteners.

6 Ease the outer cover upwards and away

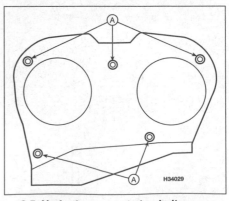

6.5 Undo the upper timing belt cover retaining bolts (A) . . .

6.6 . . . and withdraw the cover from the cylinder head

from the engine, freeing it from its lower locations **(see illustration)**.

Lower cover

7 Remove the crankshaft pulley as described in Section 5 or 7.

8 Remove the upper (outer) cover as described above.

9 Slacken and remove the retaining bolts, then remove the lower timing belt cover from the engine **(see illustration)**. Note that on some models it may be necessary to unbolt the auxiliary drivebelt tensioner assembly and remove it from the engine in order to allow the cover to be removed.

Upper (inner) cover

10 Remove the timing belt as described in Section 7.

11 Remove both camshaft sprockets as described in Section 8.

12 Remove the bolts securing the cover to the side of the cylinder head, and remove the cover from the engine **(see illustration)**.

Refitting

13 Refitting is a reversal of the relevant removal procedure, ensuring that each cover section is correctly located, and that the cover retaining nuts and/or bolts are securely tightened. When refitting the upper (inner) cover, apply thread locking compound to the retaining bolts.

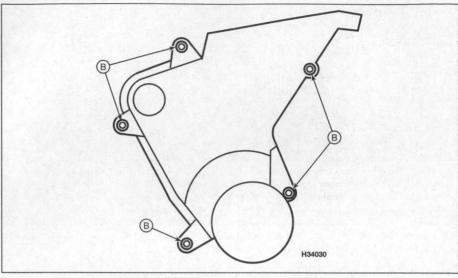

6.9 Undo the lower timing belt cover retaining bolts (B)

7 Timing belt – general information, removal and refitting

General information

1 The timing belt drives the camshafts and coolant pump from a toothed sprocket on the end of the crankshaft. If the belt breaks or slips in service, the pistons are likely to hit the valve heads, resulting in extensive (and expensive) damage.

2 The timing belt should be renewed at the specified intervals (see Chapter 1A), or earlier if it is contaminated with oil, or if it is at all noisy in operation (a 'scraping' noise due to uneven wear).

3 If the timing belt is being removed, it is a wise precaution to check the condition of the coolant pump at the same time (check for signs of coolant leakage). This may avoid the need to remove the timing belt again at a later stage, should the coolant pump fail.

4 On vehicles before RPO 9653, the crankshaft sprocket is a two-piece assembly consisting of the toothed sprocket itself and an outer end plate. The end plate is locked to the crankshaft by means of a conventional Woodruff key. When the sprocket retaining bolt is slackened, the sprocket is free to turn on the crankshaft within the limits afforded by an additional keyway within the end plate. When the sprocket retaining bolt is tightened the complete assembly is locked to the crankshaft. This arrangement allows accurate tensioning of the timing belt when refitting, provided that the procedures contained in this Section are strictly adhered to.

5 On vehicles from RPO 9653 the crankshaft sprocket is a one-piece assembly with integral flange. Once the pulley retaining bolt is slackened, the sprocket is free to revolve on the crankshaft. Again, this arrangement allows accurate tensioning of the timing belt when refitting, provided that the procedures contained in this Section are strictly adhered to.

Removal

6 On vehicles before RPO 9653 undo the 4 bolts and detach the auxiliary drive belt pulley from the crankshaft sprocket as described in Section 5.

7 Align the engine assembly/valve timing holes as described in Section 3, and lock the crankshaft sprocket and camshaft sprockets in position. *Do not* attempt to rotate the engine whilst the locking tools are in position.

8 On vehicles from RPO 9653, slacken and remove the crankshaft pulley bolt.

9 Undo the bolts and remove the timing belt lower cover.

Vehicles before RPO 9653

10 Loosen the timing belt tensioner pulley retaining bolt. Using an Allen key in the hole provided on the front of the pulley, rotate the pulley in a clockwise direction, to relieve the

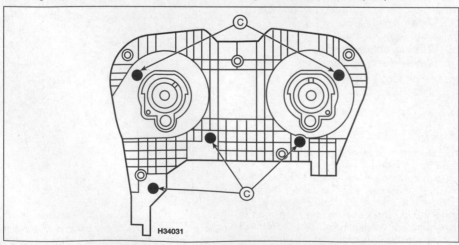

6.12 Upper (inner) timing belt cover retaining bolts (C)

7.10 Using an Allen key in the hole (arrowed) on the tensioner pulley, rotate it clockwise to relieve tension from the belt

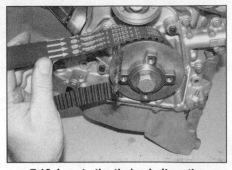

7.16 Locate the timing belt on the crankshaft sprocket, with the arrows on the belt pointing in the direction of rotation

7.17a Retain the belt on the crankshaft sprocket and feed it over the idler pulley . . .

7.17b . . . inlet camshaft sprocket . . .

7.17c . . . exhaust camshaft sprocket . . .

7.17d . . . coolant pump sprocket and tensioner pulley

tension from the timing belt **(see illustration)**. Retighten the tensioner pulley retaining bolt to secure it in the slackened position.

Vehicles from RPO 9653

11 Slacken the timing belt tensioner pulley retaining bolt. Rotate the tensioner roller clockwise.

All vehicles

12 If the timing belt is to be re-used, use white paint or chalk to mark the direction of rotation on the belt (if markings do not already exist), then slip the belt off the sprockets and pulleys. Note that the crankshaft must not be rotated whilst the belt is removed.

13 Check the timing belt carefully for any signs of uneven wear, splitting, or oil contamination. Pay particular attention to the roots of the teeth. Renew it if there is the slightest doubt about its condition. If the engine is undergoing an overhaul, it is advisable to renew the belt as a matter of course, regardless of its apparent condition. The cost of a new belt is nothing compared with the cost of repairs, should the belt break in service. If signs of oil contamination are found, trace the source of the oil leak and rectify it. Wash down the engine timing belt area and all related components, to remove all traces of oil.

Refitting

14 Before refitting, thoroughly clean the timing belt sprockets. Check that the tensioner and idler pulleys rotate freely, without any sign of roughness. If necessary, renew the relevant pulley as described in Section 8.

15 Ensure that the crankshaft and camshaft sprocket locking tools are still in position.

16 Locate the timing belt on the crankshaft sprocket, ensuring that any arrows on the belt are pointing in the direction of rotation (clockwise when viewed from the right-hand end of the engine) **(see illustration)**.

17 Retain the timing belt on the crankshaft sprocket then, keeping it taut, feed the belt over the remaining sprockets and pulleys in the following order, ensuring the belt is as flush as possible with the outer faces of the sprockets/rollers **(see illustrations)**:

a) Idler pulley.
b) Inlet camshaft.
c) Exhaust camshaft.
d) Coolant pump.
e) Tensioner pulley.

Note that there is a special Peugeot tool available (-).0189.K which clips over the belt, retaining it on the crankshaft sprocket. The use of this tool is not essential.

18 Remove the locking tool from the exhaust

7.19a Using an Allen key, turn the tensioner pulley anti-clockwise . . .

camshaft sprocket, and (where applicable) the clip securing the timing belt to the crankshaft sprocket.

Vehicles before RPO 9653

19 Slacken the tensioner retaining bolt, and using an 8 mm Allen key, rotate the pulley hub anti-clockwise until the tensioner index is positioned 10° below the notch in the backplate **(see illustrations)**. Note that if the index will not attain a position of at least 10° past the notch, then the tensioner pulley, or both the tensioner pulley and belt must be renewed.

20 Now rotate the hub clockwise until the index aligns with the centre of the notch in the backplate **(see illustration 7.19b)**. If the index is allowed to go past the notch, repeat the tensioning procedure.

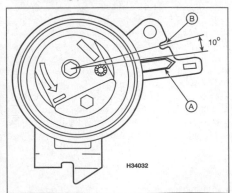

H34032

7.19b . . . until the upper edge of the index pointer (A) is positioned approximately 10° past the slot (B) in the backing plate

7.27a Hold the crankshaft sprocket end plate with the holding tool and tighten the retaining bolt to the specified torque . . .

7.27b . . . then through the specified angle

21 Tighten the tensioning roller retaining bolt to the specified torque, without allowing the roller hub to rotate. With the belt tensioned and the retaining bolt tightened, the Allen key slot should be just below the cylinder head gasket level. If not, renew the tensioner, or both the tensioner and belt.

22 Remove the camshaft and crankshaft locking tools, and rotate the crankshaft 10 complete revolutions clockwise (viewed from the right-hand end of the engine). Realign the engine assembly/valve timing holes and refit the intake camshaft sprocket locking tool.

23 Check that the tensioner pulley index pointer is still aligned with the slot in the backing plate. If not repeat the tensioning operation from paragraph 19 onward.

24 With the intake camshaft sprocket locking tool in place, it should now also be possible to fit the crankshaft sprocket locking tool. If so, continue with the refitting procedure from paragraph 30 onward. If the crankshaft sprocket locking tool will not engage, then the crankshaft sprocket end plate must be repositioned as follows.

25 Slacken the crankshaft sprocket retaining bolt while holding the sprocket end plate stationary using Peugeot special tool 6310-T or a suitable home-made alternative (see Tool Tip). Do not attempt to use only the sprocket locking tools inserted in the engine assembly/ valve timing holes to prevent rotation whilst the bolt is slackened.

26 With the sprocket retaining bolt slackened, turn the end plate until the sprocket locking tool can be fully inserted through the end plate and into the hole in the oil pump housing.

27 Hold the end plate with the holding tool and tighten the sprocket retaining bolt to the specified torque, then through the specified angle (see illustrations).

28 Remove the camshaft and crankshaft locking tools and refit the lower and upper (outer) timing belt covers, tightening the retaining bolts to the specified torque.

29 Refit the crankshaft pulley as described in Section 5.

Vehicles from RPO 9653

30 Refit the lower timing belt cover, and tighten the retaining bolts to the specified torque.

31 Using an Allen key, rotate the belt tensioner

hub anti-clockwise until the tensioner index is positioned at least 10° below the notch in the backplate (see illustration 7.19b). Note that if the index will not attain a position of at least 10° past the notch, then the tensioner pulley, or both the tensioner pulley and belt must be renewed.

32 Now rotate the tensioner hub clockwise until the index is aligned with the notch in the backplate (see illustration 7.19b). If the index is allowed to go past the notch, repeat the tensioning procedure.

33 Tighten the tensioning roller retaining bolt to the specified torque, without allowing the roller hub to rotate. With the belt tensioned and the retaining bolt tightened, the Allen key slot should be approximately 15° below the cylinder head gasket level. If not, renew the tensioner, or both the tensioner and belt.

34 Refit the crankshaft pulley, and tighten the retaining bolt to the specified torque.

35 Remove the camshaft and crankshaft locking tools, and rotate the crankshaft 10

To make a sprocket holding tool, obtain two lengths of steel strip about 6 mm thick by about 30 mm wide or similar, one 600 mm long, the other 200 mm long (all dimensions are approximate). Bolt the two strips together to form a forked end, leaving the bolt slack so that the shorter strip can pivot freely. At the other end of each 'prong' of the fork, drill a suitable hole and fit a nut and bolt to engage with the spokes of holes in the sprocket. The same tool can be used to hold both the inlet camshaft sprocket and the crankshaft sprocket.

complete revolutions clockwise (viewed from the right-hand end of the engine). Realign the engine assembly/valve timing holes and refit the intake camshaft sprocket locking tool.

36 Check that the tensioner pulley index pointer is still aligned with the slot in the backing plate. If not repeat the tensioning operation from paragraph 31 onward.

37 Remove the intake camshaft sprocket locking tool, then refit the upper timing belt cover, and the auxiliary drivebelt (see Chapter 1A).

8 Timing belt tensioners, sprockets and pulleys – removal, inspection and refitting

Note: The following procedures entail the use of certain Peugeot special tools. If the Peugeot tools are not available, details for fabricating suitable alternative are given in the text.

Camshaft sprockets removal

1 Remove the timing belt as described in Section 7

2 The camshafts must now be prevented from rotating to allow the sprocket retaining bolts to be slackened. If working on the exhaust camshaft sprocket, it will be necessary to remove the rear cylinder head cover (see Section 4) to allow a spanner to be engaged with a square section of the camshaft, provided for this purpose. This is because the sprocket contains a rubber vibration damper incorporated into the sprocket hub. If the sprocket itself is held as the bolt is slackened, the rubber hub will be damaged. The intake camshaft sprocket is conventional and can be held using Peugeot tool 6016-T, or an acceptable substitute can be fabricated at home (see Tool Tip). Alternatively, remove the front cylinder head cover and hold the camshaft with a spanner as described for the exhaust camshaft. Do not attempt to use the engine assembly/valve timing hole locking tools to prevent the sprockets from rotating whilst the bolts are slackened.

3 Remove the engine assembly/valve timing hole locking tool from the relevant sprocket, then slacken the centre retaining bolt. If a spanner is being used to prevent camshaft rotation, the spanner should be engaged with the square section of the camshaft adjacent to No 8 cam lobe (see illustration).

8.3 The camshafts can be held with a spanner engaged with the square section adjacent to the No 8 cam lobe

8.4a Remove the retaining bolt and washer . . .

8.4b . . . and withdraw the sprocket from the end of the camshaft

8.6 Hold the crankshaft sprocket end plate with the home-made tool while the retaining bolt is slackened

4 Remove the previously slackened sprocket retaining bolt and washer, and withdraw the relevant sprocket from the end of the camshaft **(see illustrations)**.

Crankshaft sprocket removal

5 Remove the timing belt as described in Section 7.

Vehicles before RPO 9653

6 Remove the crankshaft sprocket locking tool and slacken the crankshaft sprocket retaining bolt. Prevent the crankshaft from turning while the bolt is slackened using Peugeot special tool 6310-T or a suitable home-made alternative, such as that described in the previous sub-Section, bolted to the sprocket end plate **(see illustration)**. *Do not* attempt to use only the sprocket locking tools inserted in the engine assembly/valve timing holes to prevent rotation whilst the bolt is slackened.

7 Unscrew the retaining bolt and slide the

sprocket end plate and the sprocket itself off the end of the crankshaft. If loose, remove the Woodruff key from the crankshaft, and store it with the sprocket components for safe-keeping **(see illustrations)**.

8 Examine the crankshaft oil seal for signs of oil leakage and, if necessary, renew it as described in Section 14.

Vehicles from RPO 9653

9 Slide the sprocket from the crankshaft.

10 Examine the crankshaft oil seal for signs of oil leakage and, if necessary, renew it as described in Section 14.

Tensioner and idler pulleys removal

11 Remove the timing belt as described in Section 7.

12 Undo the tensioner and idler pulley retaining bolts and remove the relevant pulley from the engine **(see illustrations)**.

Inspection

13 Clean the camshaft/crankshaft sprockets thoroughly, and renew any that show signs of wear, damage or cracks. Check the condition of the rubber vibration damper in the exhaust camshaft sprocket and renew the sprocket if there is any sign of deterioration of the rubber.

14 Clean the tensioner/idler pulleys, but do not use any strong solvent which may enter the pulley bearings. Check that the pulleys rotate freely, with no sign of stiffness or free play. Renew them if there is any doubt about their condition, or if there are any obvious signs of wear or damage.

Camshaft sprockets refitting

15 Locate the relevant sprocket on the end of the camshaft, engaging the lug in the sprocket hub with the slot in the end of the camshaft.

16 Refit the sprocket retaining bolt and washer, and tighten it to the specified torque. Prevent the sprocket from turning as the bolt is tightened using the method employed for removal.

17 Realign the hole in the camshaft sprocket with the corresponding hole in the cylinder head, and refit the locking tool. Check that the crankshaft pulley locking tool is still in position.

18 Where removed, refit the cylinder head cover(s) as described in Section 4.

19 Refit and tension the timing belt as described in Section 7.

8.7a Withdraw the crankshaft sprocket end plate . . .

8.7b . . . and the sprocket itself

8.7c Remove the Woodruff key from the end of the crankshaft

8.12a Remove the timing belt tensioner pulley . . .

8.12b . . . and the idler pulley

8.27 Ensure the slot (arrowed) on the tensioner pulley body engages with the web on the cylinder block when refitting

Crankshaft sprocket refitting

Vehicles before RPO 9653

20 Refit the Woodruff key (if removed) to its slot in the crankshaft end.

21 Slide on the crankshaft sprocket followed by the sprocket end plate, then refit the retaining bolt.

22 Hold the end plate with the holding tool and tighten the sprocket retaining bolt to the specified torque, then through the specified angle.

23 Realign the hole in the sprocket end plate with the corresponding hole in the oil pump housing, and refit the locking tool. Check that the camshaft sprocket locking tools are still in position.

24 Refit and tension the timing belt as described in Section 7.

Vehicles from RPO 9653

25 Slide the sprocket onto the crankshaft.

9.3 Use pliers and a self-tapping screw to extract the camshaft oil seal

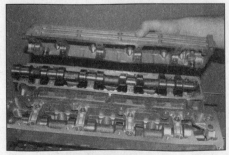

10.7 Progressively slacken and remove the retaining bolt, then lift off the camshaft bearing cap housing(s)

26 Refit the timing belt as described in Section 7.

Tensioner and idler pulleys refitting

27 Refit the tensioner and idler pulleys, ensuring that the slot on the tensioner pulley body correctly engages with the projecting web on the cylinder block (see illustration).

28 Secure the pulleys with the retaining bolts tightened to the specified torque.

29 Refit and tension the timing belt as described in Section 7.

9 Camshaft oil seals – renewal

1 Remove the camshaft sprockets as described in Section 8.

2 Note the fitted depth of the oil seals as a guide to fitting the new ones.

3 Punch or drill two small holes opposite each other in the oil seal. Screw a self-tapping screw into each, and pull on the screws with pliers to extract the seal (see illustration).

4 Clean the seal housing, and polish off any burrs or raised edges, which may have caused the seal to fail in the first place.

5 Lubricate the lips of the new seal with clean engine oil, and drive it into position until it seats on its locating shoulder (see illustration). Use a suitable tubular drift, such as a socket, which bears only on the hard outer edge of the seal. If available, use the Peugeot tool No 0189-D1/D2. Take care not to

9.5 Locate the new seal in position with the seal lips facing inwards

10.9 Carefully lift out the camshaft(s) up and out of their locations

damage the seal lips during fitting. Note that the seal lips should face inwards.

6 Refit the camshaft sprockets as described in Section 8.

10 Camshafts and followers – removal, inspection and refitting

Removal

1 Remove the timing belt as described in Section 7.

2 Progressively unscrew the bolts securing the cylinder head covers to the cylinder head. The bolts must be unscrewed in a spiral sequence starting from the outside (see Section 4).

3 Remove the cylinder head covers and gaskets.

4 Refer to Section 8 and remove both camshaft sprockets.

5 Unbolt and remove the inner timing cover from the cylinder head. At this stage, note the fitted depth of the oil seals as a guide to fitting new seals during reassembly.

6 Evenly and progressively slacken the camshaft bearing housing retaining bolts by one turn at a time, in a spiral sequence, starting from the outside. This will relieve the valve spring pressure on the bearing housing gradually and evenly. Once the pressure has been relieved, the bolts can be fully unscrewed, together with their washers.

7 Lift the camshaft bearing housings from the cylinder head, noting that the housings are located on dowels (see illustration).

8 Identify each camshaft for position – the exhaust camshaft is at the rear and the inlet camshaft is at the front of the cylinder head. Also note the TDC position of each camshaft for correct refitting.

9 Remove the camshafts by pressing on their transmission ends to release the opposite ends from the bearings. Withdraw the camshafts from the cylinder head and slide the oil seals from the ends (see illustration).

10 Obtain sixteen small, clean plastic containers, and number them inlet 1 to 8 and exhaust 1 to 8; alternatively, divide a larger container into sixteen compartments and number each compartment accordingly. Using a rubber sucker, withdraw each

10.10 Use a rubber sucker to withdraw the hydraulic tappets

10.14a Lubricate the hydraulic tappet bores and the tappets . . .

10.14b . . . then refit the tappets ensuring that each is refitted to its original bore

10.15 Liberally oil the camshaft bearings and lobes, then lay the camshaft in the cylinder head

hydraulic tappet in turn, and place it in its respective container **(see illustration)**. Do not interchange the tappets, or the rate of wear will be much-increased.

Inspection

11 Examine the camshaft bearing surfaces and cam lobes for signs of wear ridges and scoring. Renew the camshaft if any of these conditions are apparent. Examine the condition of the bearing surfaces, both on the camshaft journals and in the cylinder head and bearing housing. If the head bearing surfaces are worn excessively, the cylinder head will need to be renewed. If suitable measuring equipment is available, camshaft bearing journal wear can be checked by direct measurement, noting that No 1 journal is at the transmission end of the head.

12 Examine the hydraulic tappet bearing surfaces which contact the camshaft lobes for wear ridges and scoring. Renew any tappet where these conditions are apparent. If a tappet bearing surface is badly scored, also examine the corresponding lobe on the camshaft for wear, as it is likely that both will be worn. Renew worn components as necessary.

Refitting

13 Before commencing refitting, remove all traces of oil from the bearing housing retaining bolt holes in the cylinder head, using a clean rag. Also ensure that both the cylinder head and bearing housing mating faces are clean and free from oil.

14 Liberally oil the cylinder head hydraulic

tappet bores and the tappets. Carefully refit the tappets to the cylinder head, ensuring that each tappet is refitted to its original bore **(see illustrations)**. Some care will be required to enter the tappets squarely into their bores. Check that each tappet rotates freely in its bore.

15 Liberally oil the camshaft bearings in the cylinder head and the camshaft lobes, then refit the camshafts to the cylinder head in their previously-noted positions **(see illustration)**. Note that the exhaust camshaft has a sensor ring on its left-hand end and must be fitted at the rear of the cylinder head.

16 Ensure that the four locating dowels are in position, one at each corner of the cylinder head.

17 Apply a bead of silicone-based jointing compound (Peugeot E10 jointing paste) around the perimeter of the mating faces and around the retaining bolt hole locations **(see illustration)**.

18 Liberally oil the camshaft bearings and carefully locate the bearing housings over the camshafts. Refit the retaining bolts ensuring that each has a washer under its head **(see illustration)**. Note that the bearing housing with the sensor hole is located over the exhaust camshaft. Initially finger-tighten the bolts.

19 Progressively tighten the bearing housing retaining bolts to the specified torque, in the order given in Section 4. It is suggested that the bolts are initially tightened to 5 Nm (4 lbf ft), then tightened to their final torque.

20 Refit the inner timing cover to the cylinder head and tighten the retaining bolts securely.

21 Clean the jointing compound from the oil seal seatings in the cylinder head and camshaft housing.

22 Fit new oil seals with reference to Section 9.

23 Refit the sprockets to the camshafts with reference to Section 8.

24 Refit the cylinder head covers together with new gaskets, with reference to Section 4.

25 Refit the timing belt with reference to Section 7.

11 Cylinder head – removal and refitting

Removal

1 Disconnect the battery (see Chapter 5A).

2 Apply the handbrake, then jack up the front of the vehicle and support it on axle stands (see *Jacking and vehicle support*). Undo the screws and remove the engine undershield. For improved access, remove the bonnet as described in Chapter 11.

3 Drain the cooling system as described in Chapter 1A.

4 Unbolt the exhaust downpipe from the exhaust manifold on the rear of the engine with reference to Chapter 4A.

5 Undo the 6 screw fasteners and remove the plastic cover from the engine.

6 Release the fuel pressure from the fuel system by placing cloth rags around and over the Shrader valve on the fuel rail, and depressing the valve core.

7 Disconnect the fuel supply pipe from the fuel rail.

8 Remove the timing belt as described in Section 7.

9 Remove the timing belt tensioner roller as described in Section 8.

10 Remove the air cleaner and intake pipe with reference to Chapter 4A.

11 Remove the engine oil dipstick from its tube, then remove the tube itself from the block.

12 Disconnect the crankcase breather hose from the camshaft cover.

13 Note their fitted positions and routing, then disconnect all coolant hoses and wiring connectors/looms from the cylinder head.

14 Remove the camshaft position sensor

10.17 Apply a bead of sealing compound around the perimeter of the cylinder head mating faces

10.18 Carefully locate the bearing cap housings over the camshafts

11.20 Remove the cylinder head from the engine block

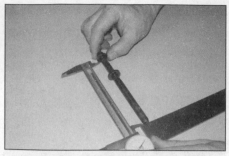

11.25 Measure the length of the cylinder head bolts from the underside of the head to the end of the bolt

from the left-hand end of the exhaust camshaft cover.

15 Remove the ignition coil module from the top of the cylinder head with reference to Chapter 5B.

16 Unscrew the bolts/nuts securing the inlet manifold to the front of the cylinder head, then support the manifold away from the cylinder head.

17 Remove both cylinder head covers and gaskets with reference to Section 4.

18 Refit the right-hand engine mounting support bracket to the cylinder head.

19 Using a Torx key socket and working in the *reverse* of the tightening sequence (see paragraph 33), progressively slacken the ten cylinder head bolts by half a turn at a time, until all bolts can be unscrewed by hand. Recover the washers where fitted.

20 With all the cylinder head bolts removed, the joint between the cylinder head and gasket, and the cylinder block/crankcase must now be broken. To break the joint, obtain two L-shaped metal bars which fit into the cylinder head bolt holes, and gently 'rock' the cylinder head free towards the front of the car. *Do not* try to swivel the head on the cylinder block/crankcase; it is located by dowels. When the joint is broken, lift the cylinder head away. Use a hoist or seek assistance if possible, as it is a heavy assembly **(see illustration)**. Remove the gasket from the top of the block, noting the two locating dowels. If the locating dowels are a loose fit, remove them and store them with the head for safe-keeping. Do not discard the gasket; it will be needed for identification purposes. During removal, check that the camshaft oil supply

non-return valve (located in the underside of the cylinder head at the timing belt end) does not drop out; it is easily lost if it does.

21 If the cylinder head is to be dismantled for overhaul, remove the camshafts as described in Section 10, then refer to Part F of this Chapter. Also remove the rigid pipe from the outlet housing.

Preparation for refitting

22 The mating faces of the cylinder head and cylinder block/crankcase must be perfectly clean before refitting the head. Use a hard plastic or wooden scraper to remove all traces of gasket and carbon and also clean the piston crowns. Make sure that the carbon is not allowed to enter the oil and water passages – this is particularly important for the lubrication system, as carbon could block the oil supply to the engine's components. Using adhesive tape and paper, seal the water, oil and bolt holes in the cylinder block/crankcase. To prevent carbon entering the gap between the pistons and bores, smear a little grease in the gap. After cleaning each piston, use a small brush to remove all traces of grease and carbon from the gap, then wipe away the remainder with a clean rag. Clean all the pistons in the same way.

23 Check the mating surfaces of the cylinder block/crankcase and the cylinder head for nicks, deep scratches and other damage. If slight, they may be removed carefully with a file, but if excessive, machining may be the only alternative to renewal. If warpage of the cylinder head gasket surface is suspected, use a straight-edge to check it for distortion. Refer to Part F of this Chapter if necessary.

24 Obtain a new cylinder head gasket before starting the refitting procedure. At the time of writing, there are two different thicknesses available – the standard gasket which is fitted at the factory, and a slightly thicker 'repair' gasket (+0.3 mm), for use once the head gasket face has been machined. If the cylinder head has been machined, it should be marked '–0.3' on the upper corner, on the inlet manifold side, at the timing belt end. Note that modifications to the cylinder head gasket material, type, and manufacturer are constantly taking place; seek the advice of a Peugeot dealer as to the latest recommendations.

25 Check the condition of the cylinder head bolts, and particularly their threads, whenever they are removed. Wash the bolts in a suitable solvent, and wipe them dry. Check each bolt for any sign of visible wear or damage, renewing them if necessary. Measure the length of each bolt from the underside of its head to the end of the bolt **(see illustration)**. The bolts may be re-used if their length does not exceed:

a) 147.0 mm for engine code RFN before RPO 09653.

b) 143.0 mm for engine code RFN from RPO 09653.

c) 130.0 mm for engine code RFJ.

If any one bolt is longer than the specified length, *all* of the bolts should be renewed as a complete set. Considering the stress which the cylinder head bolts are under, it is highly recommended that they are renewed, regardless of their apparent condition. Also check that the thickness of the head bolt washers is 4.00 ± 0.2 mm.

Refitting

26 Where removed, refit the camshafts, and the rigid pipe to the outlet housing on the cylinder head.

27 Wipe clean the mating surfaces of the cylinder head and cylinder block/crankcase. Check that the two locating dowels are in position at each end of the cylinder block/crankcase surface. Peugeot recommend that the camshaft oil supply non-return valve in the oil feed bore at the timing belt end of the cylinder head is renewed **(see illustrations)**.

28 Position a new gasket on the cylinder block/crankcase surface, ensuring that the TOP mark is uppermost and at the front of the block **(see illustration)**.

11.27a Check the cylinder head locating dowels (arrowed) are in place ...

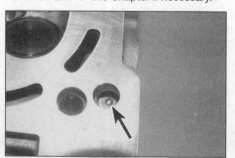

11.27b ... and the camshaft oil supply non-return valve (arrowed) is in place in the cylinder head

11.28 Position the cylinder head gasket with the work TOP uppermost and toward the oil filter side of the engine block

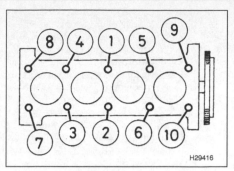

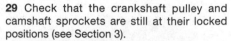

11.33 Cylinder head bolt tightening sequence

12.4 Undo the upper and lower retaining bolts and remove the dipstick guide tube

29 Check that the crankshaft pulley and camshaft sprockets are still at their locked positions (see Section 3).

30 With the aid of an assistant, carefully lower the cylinder head assembly onto the block, aligning it with the locating dowels.

31 Apply a smear of grease to the threads, and to the underside of the heads, of the cylinder head bolts. Peugeot recommend the use of Molykote G Rapid Plus (available from your Peugeot dealer); in the absence of the specified grease, any good-quality high melting-point grease may be used.

32 Carefully enter each bolt and washer into its relevant hole (*do not drop it in*) then screw them in finger-tight.

33 Working progressively and in sequence **(see illustration)**, tighten the cylinder head bolts to their Stage 1 torque setting.

34 Once all the bolts have been tightened to their Stage 1 torque setting, proceed to tighten them through the remaining stages as given in the Specifications. When carrying out Stage 3, slacken each bolt 1 turn working in the reverse of the tightening sequence. It is recommended that an angle-measuring gauge is used for the angle-tightening stages, however, if a gauge is not available, use white paint to make alignment marks between the bolt head and cylinder head prior to tightening; the marks can then by used to check that the bolt has rotated sufficiently. Where a maximum of 2 steps is given for angle-tightening, each step must be completed in one movement without stopping.

35 The remainder of the refitting procedure is a reversal of removal, referring to the relevant Chapters or Sections as required. On completion, refill the cooling system as described in Chapter 1A. Initialise the engine management ECU as follows. Start the engine and run to normal temperature. Carry out a road test during which the following procedure should be made. Engage third gear and stabilise the engine at 1000 rpm. Now accelerate fully to 3500 rpm.

12 Sump – removal and refitting

Removal

1 Apply the handbrake, then jack up the front of the vehicle and support it on axle stands (see *Jacking and vehicle support*). Undo the screws and remove the engine undershield (where fitted).

2 Drain the engine oil then clean and refit the engine oil drain plug, tightening it securely. If the engine is nearing its service interval when the oil and filter are due for renewal, it is recommended that the filter is also removed, and a new one fitted. After reassembly, the engine can then be refilled with fresh oil. Refer to Chapter 1A for further information.

3 Withdraw the engine oil dipstick from the guide tube.

4 Undo the bolt securing the upper end of the dipstick guide tube to the ancillary components mounting bracket. Undo the bolt securing the base of the guide tube to the sump and remove the guide tube **(see illustration)**. Collect the two O-rings from the base of the guide tube, noting that new O-rings will be required for refitting.

5 Where applicable, move the power steering pipe supports from the sump. Also disconnect the wiring from the oil temperature sender unit.

6 Progressively slacken and remove all the sump retaining bolts. Since there are nineteen 25.0 mm bolts and seven 110.0 mm bolts, remove each bolt in turn, and store it in its correct fitted order by pushing it through a clearly-marked cardboard template. This will avoid the possibility of installing the bolts in the wrong locations on refitting.

7 Break the joint by striking the sump with the palm of your hand. Lower the sump, and withdraw it from underneath the vehicle. While the sump is removed, take the opportunity to check the oil pump pick-up/strainer for signs of clogging or splitting. If necessary, remove the pump as described in Section 13, and clean or renew the strainer. Also unbolt the oil baffle plate from the bottom of the main bearing ladder, noting which way round it is fitted **(see illustrations)**. Note that the sump is located on a dowel.

Refitting

8 Where removed, refit the baffle plate to the main bearing ladder and tighten the bolts securely.

9 Where removed, refit the oil pump and pick-up/strainer with reference to Section 13.

10 Clean all traces of sealant/gasket from the mating surfaces of the main bearing ladder and sump, then use a clean rag to wipe out the sump and the engine's interior.

11 Ensure that the sump mating surfaces are clean and dry, then apply a thin coating of suitable sealant to the sump mating surface **(see illustration)**.

12 Check that the location dowel is in place, then refit the sump onto the main bearing ladder and insert the bolts and finger-tighten them at this stage, so that it is still possible to move the

12.7a Oil pump pick-up tube retaining nuts and retaining bolt locations (arrowed)

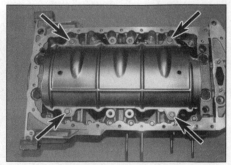

12.7b Crankcase baffle plate retaining bolts locations (arrowed)

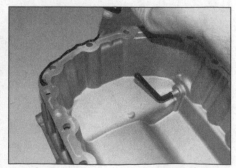

12.11 Apply a thin bead of RTV sealant to the sump mating surface

12.12a Four of the long sump retaining bolts are fitted at the transmission end . . .

12.12b . . . and three are fitted at the timing belt end on the oil filter side

12.13 Use a straight-edge to ensure the rear faces of the cylinder block and sump are flush

sump. Make sure the bolts are refitted in their correct locations **(see illustrations)**.

13 Using a straight-edge, align the flywheel end of the sump with the main bearing ladder and cylinder block, then progressively tighten the sump bolts to the specified torque **(see illustration)**.

14 Check that the oil drain plug is tightened securely, then refit the engine undershield (where applicable) and lower the vehicle to the ground.

15 Refill the engine with oil as described in Chapter 1A.

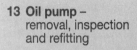

13 Oil pump –
removal, inspection and refitting

Removal

1 Remove the timing belt and crankshaft

sprocket as described in Sections 7 and 8.

2 Remove the sump and oil pump pick-up/strainer as described in Section 12.

3 Unscrew the nine bolts securing the oil pump to the main bearing ladder and cylinder block, then withdraw the oil pump over the nose of the crankshaft **(see illustration)**. Note it is located on dowels, and therefore it may be necessary to carefully prise it away to release it.

4 Slide the oil pump drive collar off the end of the crankshaft and collect the O-ring located behind the collar **(see illustrations)**.

5 With the oil pump removed, note the fitted depth of the crankshaft oil seal, then drive it from the oil pump housing. A new oil seal must be obtained for refitting.

Inspection

6 At the time of writing, checking specifications

for the oil pump were not available, however, if the oil pump is to be re-used, the internal gears should be cleaned. To do this, unbolt the cover, then mark the gears for location and remove them **(see illustrations)**. Clean the gears and inspect them for damage and excessive wear.

7 Lubricate the gears with oil, then refit them in their locations noted during removal. Refit the cover and tighten the bolts securely.

8 Thoroughly clean the oil pump strainer with a suitable solvent, and check it for signs of clogging or splitting. If the strainer is damaged, the strainer and cover assembly must be renewed.

Refitting

9 Clean the mating surfaces of the oil pump and main bearing ladder/cylinder block. Check that the locating dowels are in position on the

13.3 Oil pump housing retaining bolt locations (arrowed)

13.4a Slide the oil pump drive collar off the crankshaft . . .

13.4b . . . and collect the O-ring behind the collar

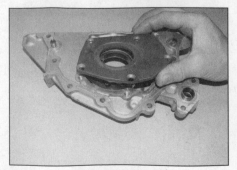

13.6a Undo the five screws and lift off the oil pump rear cover

13.6b Remove the inner rotor . . .

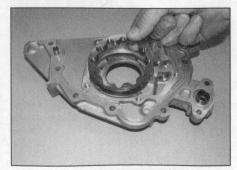

13.6c . . . and outer rotor from the pump housing

13.9 Locate a new O-ring over the oil pump outlet stub

13.10 Apply a thin bead of RTV sealant to the oil pump mating surface

13.13 Position a new oil pump drive collar O-ring on the end of the crankshaft

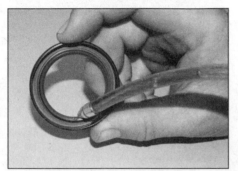

13.14a Lubricate the sealing lips of the new crankshaft right-hand oil seal . . .

13.14b . . . and carefully fit the seal over the oil pump drive collar

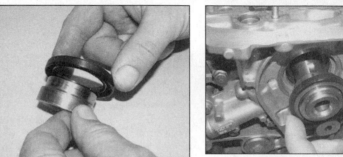

13.15 Slide the drive collar onto the crankshaft and engage it with the oil pump inner rotor

pump flange then locate a new O-ring over the oil pump outlet stub **(see illustration)**.

10 Apply a thin coating of suitable sealant to the mating face of the oil pump housing **(see illustration)**.

11 Prime the oil pump by injecting clean engine oil into the outlet stub, then place the pump in position on the cylinder block, engaging the locating dowels.

12 Apply thread locking compound to the threads of the nine oil pump retaining bolts, then refit the bolts and tighten them to the specified torque.

13 Position a new oil pump drive collar O-ring on the end of the crankshaft **(see illustration)**.

14 Lubricate the sealing lips of the new crankshaft right-hand oil seal and carefully fit the seal over the oil pump drive collar **(see illustrations)**. Note that the open part of the seal must be towards the shoulder of the drive collar.

15 Slide the drive collar over the end of the crankshaft and engage it with the oil pump inner rotor **(see illustration)**. As the collar engages with the pump inner rotor, push the oil seal initially into place in the oil pump housing. Tap the seal fully into position using a suitable drift.

16 Refit the pick-up/strainer and sump as described in Section 12, and the crankshaft sprocket and timing belt as described in Sections 7 and 8.

17 Before starting the engine, prime the oil pump as follows. Disconnect the fuel injector wiring connectors, then spin the engine

on the starter until the oil pressure light goes out. Reconnect the injector wiring on completion.

14 Crankshaft oil seals – renewal

Right-hand oil seal

1 Remove the crankshaft sprocket and (where fitted) spacer, referring to Section 8. Secure the timing belt clear of the working area, so that it cannot be contaminated with oil. Make a note of the correct fitted depth of the seal in its housing.

2 Punch or drill two small holes opposite each other in the seal. Screw a self-tapping screw into each, and pull on the screws with pliers to extract the seal. Alternatively, the seal can be levered out of position. Use a flat-bladed screwdriver, and take great care not to damage the crankshaft shoulder or seal housing.

3 Clean the seal housing, and polish off any burrs or raised edges, which may have caused the seal to fail in the first place.

4 Lubricate the lips of the new seal with clean engine oil, and carefully locate the seal on the end of the crankshaft. Note that its sealing lip must be facing inwards. Take care not to damage the seal lips during fitting.

5 Fit the new seal using a suitable tubular drift, such as a socket, which bears only on the hard outer edge of the seal. Tap the seal into position, to the same depth in the housing

as the original was prior to removal **(see illustration)**.

6 Wash off any traces of oil, then refit the crankshaft sprocket as described in Section 8.

Left-hand oil seal

7 Remove the flywheel/driveplate as described in Section 15. Make a note of the correct fitted depth of the seal in its housing.

8 Punch or drill two small holes opposite each other in the seal. Screw a self-tapping screw into each, and pull on the screws with pliers to extract the seal.

9 Clean the seal housing, and polish off any burrs or raised edges, which may have caused the seal to fail in the first place.

10 Lubricate the lips of the new seal with clean engine oil, and carefully locate the seal on the end of the crankshaft. The new seal will normally be supplied with a plastic fitting sleeve to protect the seal lips as the seal is

14.5 Tap the crankshaft right-hand oil seal into position using a suitable drift

14.10 Lubricate the crankshaft left-hand oil seal fitting sleeve and locate it over the end of the crankshaft

fitted. If so, lubricate the fitting sleeve and locate it over the end of the crankshaft **(see illustration)**.

11 Lubricate the lips of the new seal with clean engine oil, and carefully locate the seal over the fitting sleeve and onto the end of the crankshaft **(see illustration)**. Drive the seal into position, to the same depth in the housing as the original was prior to removal.

12 Wash off any traces of oil, then refit the flywheel/driveplate as described in Section 15.

15 Flywheel/driveplate – removal, inspection and refitting

Removal

Flywheel

1 Remove the transmission as described in Chapter 7A, then remove the clutch assembly as described in Chapter 6.

2 Prevent the crankshaft from turning by locking the flywheel with a wide-bladed screwdriver between the ring gear teeth and the transmission casing. Alternatively, bolt a strap between the flywheel and the cylinder block/crankcase. *Do not* attempt to lock the flywheel in position using the crankshaft pulley locking pin described in Section 3.

3 Slacken and remove the flywheel retaining bolts, and remove the flywheel from the end of the crankshaft. Be careful not to drop it; it is heavy. If the flywheel locating dowel is a loose fit in the crankshaft end, remove it and store it with the flywheel for safe-keeping. Discard the flywheel bolts; new ones must be used on refitting.

Driveplate

4 Remove the transmission as described in Chapter 7B. Lock the driveplate as described in paragraph 2. Mark the relationship between the torque converter plate and the driveplate, and slacken all the driveplate retaining bolts.

5 Remove the retaining bolts, along with the torque converter plate and (where fitted) the two shims (one fitted on each side of the torque converter plate). Note that the shims are of different thickness, the thicker one

14.11 Locate the oil seal over the fitting sleeve and over the end of the crankshaft

being on the outside of the torque converter plate. Discard the driveplate retaining bolts; new ones must be used on refitting.

6 Remove the driveplate from the end of the crankshaft. If the locating dowel is a loose fit in the crankshaft end, remove it and store it with the driveplate for safe-keeping.

Inspection

7 On models with manual transmission, examine the flywheel for scoring of the clutch face, and for wear or chipping of the ring gear teeth. If the clutch face is scored, the flywheel may be surface-ground, but renewal is preferable. Seek the advice of a Peugeot dealer or engine reconditioning specialist to see if machining is possible. If the ring gear is worn or damaged, the flywheel must be renewed, as it is not possible to renew the ring gear separately.

8 On models with automatic transmission, check the torque converter driveplate carefully for signs of distortion. Look for any hairline cracks around the bolt holes or radiating outwards from the centre, and inspect the ring gear teeth for signs of wear or chipping. If any sign of wear or damage is found, the driveplate must be renewed.

Refitting

Flywheel

9 Clean the mating surfaces of the flywheel and crankshaft. Remove any remaining locking compound from the threads of the crankshaft holes, using the correct-size tap, if available.

 HAYNES HiNT *If a suitable tap is not available, cut two slots into the threads of one of the old flywheel bolts and use the bolt to remove the locking compound from the threads.*

10 If the new flywheel retaining bolts are not supplied with their threads already precoated, apply a suitable thread-locking compound to the threads of each bolt.

11 Ensure the locating dowel is in position. Offer up the flywheel, locating it on the dowel, and fit the new retaining bolts.

12 Lock the flywheel using the method

employed on dismantling, and tighten the retaining bolts to the specified torque and angle.

13 Refit the clutch as described in Chapter 6. Remove the flywheel locking tool, and refit the transmission as described in Chapter 7A.

Driveplate

14 Carry out the operations described above in paragraphs 9 and 10, substituting 'driveplate' for all references to the flywheel.

15 Locate the driveplate on its locating dowel.

16 Offer up the torque converter plate, with the thinner shim positioned behind the plate and the thicker shim on the outside, and align the marks made prior to removal.

17 Fit the new retaining bolts, then lock the driveplate using the method employed on dismantling. Tighten the retaining bolts to the specified torque wrench setting and angle.

18 Remove the driveplate locking tool, and refit the transmission as described in Chapter 7B.

16 Engine/transmission mountings – inspection and renewal

Inspection

1 If improved access is required, raise the front of the car and support it securely on axle stands.

2 Check the mounting rubber to see if it is cracked, hardened or separated from the metal at any point; renew the mounting if any such damage or deterioration is evident.

3 Check that all the mounting's fasteners are securely tightened; use a torque wrench to check if possible.

4 Using a large screwdriver or a crowbar, check for wear in the mounting by carefully levering against it to check for free play. Where this is not possible, enlist the aid of an assistant to move the engine/transmission unit back-and-forth, or from side-to-side, while you watch the mounting. While some free play is to be expected even from new components, excessive wear should be obvious. If excessive free play is found, check first that the fasteners are correctly secured, then renew any worn components as described below.

Renewal

Right-hand mounting

5 Release all the relevant hoses and wiring from their retaining clips. Place the hoses/wiring clear of the mounting so that the removal procedure is not hindered.

6 Undo the screws and remove the engine undershield (where fitted), then place a jack beneath the engine, with a block of wood on the jack head. Raise the jack until it is supporting the weight of the engine.

7 Undo the bolts securing the engine mounting to the body and the support bracket.

8 If required, undo the bolts/nuts securing the support bracket to the cylinder head/cylinder block.

9 Check all components carefully for signs of wear or damage, and renew as necessary.

10 Where removed, refit the support bracket to the cylinder head, and tighten the bolts securely.

11 Refit the mount to the body and support bracket, then tighten the bolts to the specified torque.

12 Remove the jack from underneath the engine, and refit the engine undershield (where applicable).

Left-hand mounting

13 Remove the battery and battery tray (see Chapter 5A).

14 Undo the screws and remove the engine undershield (where fitted), then place a jack beneath the transmission, with a block of wood on the jack head. Raise the jack until it is supporting the weight of the transmission.

15 Slacken and remove the centre nut and washer from the left-hand mounting, then undo the nuts securing the mounting in position and remove it from the engine compartment. If necessary undo the nut/bolts and remove the mounting plate **(see illustrations)**.

16 If necessary, slide the spacer (where fitted) off the mounting stud, then unscrew the stud from the top of the transmission housing, and remove it along with its washer **(see illustration)**. If the mounting stud is tight, a universal stud extractor can be used to unscrew it.

17 Check all components carefully for signs of wear or damage, and renew as necessary.

18 Clean the threads of the mounting stud, and apply a coat of thread-locking compound to its threads. Refit the stud and washer to the top of the transmission, and tighten it securely.

19 Slide the spacer (where fitted) onto the mounting stud, then refit the rubber mounting. Tighten both the mounting-to-body bolts and the mounting centre nut to their specified torque settings, and remove the jack from underneath the transmission. Refit the engine undershield.

16.15a Slacken the centre nut (arrowed) then undo the mounting retaining nuts (arrowed)

16.15b Undo the nut/bolts (arrowed) and remove the mounting plate

16.16 Unscrew the mounting stud from the mounting

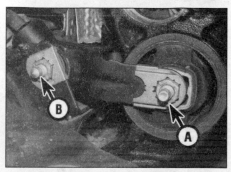

16.22 Undo the link-to-engine block bracket bolt (A) and the link-to-subframe bolt (B)

20 Refit the battery and tray as described in Chapter 5A.

Lower engine movement limiter

21 If not already done, chock the rear wheels, then jack up the front of the vehicle and support it securely on axle stands (see *Jacking and vehicle support*). Undo the screws and remove the engine undershield (where fitted).

22 Unscrew and remove the bolt securing the movement limiter link to the driveshaft intermediate bearing housing **(see illustration)**.

23 Remove the bolt securing the link to the subframe. Withdraw the link.

24 To remove the intermediate bearing housing assembly it will first be necessary to remove the right-hand driveshaft as described in Chapter 8.

25 With the driveshaft removed, undo the retaining bolts and remove the bearing housing from the rear of the cylinder block.

26 Check carefully for signs of wear or damage on all components, and renew them where necessary. The rubber bush fitted to the bearing housing is available as a separate item (at the time of writing), and can be pressed out of, and back into place.

27 On reassembly, fit the bearing housing assembly to the rear of the cylinder block, and tighten its retaining bolts securely. Refit the driveshaft as described in Chapter 8.

28 Refit the movement limiter link, and tighten both its bolts to their specified torque settings. Refit the engine undershield (where applicable).

29 Lower the vehicle to the ground.

Notes

Chapter 2 Part C:
1.4 and 2.0 litre SOHC diesel engine in-car repair procedures

Contents

Degrees of difficulty

| Easy, suitable for novice with little experience | | Fairly easy, suitable for beginner with some experience | | Fairly difficult, suitable for competent DIY mechanic | | Difficult, suitable for experienced DIY mechanic | 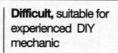 | Very difficult, suitable for expert DIY or professional | |

Specifications

General

Designation:
1.4 litre (1398cc engine)	DV4TD
2.0 litre (1997cc engine)	DW10TD
2.0 litre (1997cc engine)	DW10ATED

Engine codes*:
1.4 litre engine	8HZ
2.0 litre engine:	
DW10TD.	RHY
DW10ATED (without particle filter)	RHZ
DW10ATED (with particle filter).	RHS

Bore:
1.4 litre engine	73.70 mm
2.0 litre engine	85.00 mm

Stroke:
1.4 litre engine	82.00 mm
2.0 litre engine	88.00 mm

Direction of crankshaft rotation	Clockwise (viewed from the right-hand side of vehicle)
No 1 cylinder location.	At the transmission end of the block

Maximum power output:
1.4 litre engine	50 kW @ 4000 rpm
2.0 litre engine:	
Code RHY.	66 kW @ 4000 rpm
Code RHZ.	81 kW @ 4000 rpm
Code RHS.	80 kW @ 4000 rpm

Maximum torque output:
1.4 litre engine	160 Nm @ 2000 rpm
2.0 litre engine:	
Code RHY.	205 Nm @ 1900 rpm
Code RHZ and RHS	250 Nm @ 1750 rpm

Compression ratio:
1.4 litre engine	18.0 : 1
2.0 litre engine:	
Code RHZ.	17.6 : 1
Code RHS.	18.0 : 1

* The engine code is stamped on a plate attached to the front of the cylinder block, next to the oil filter

Compression pressures (engine hot, at cranking speed)
Normal . . . . 25 to 30 bars (363 to 435 psi)
Minimum. . . . . 18 bars (261 psi)
Maximum difference between any two cylinders . . . . 5 bars (73 psi)

Timing belt
Tension setting (see text – Section 7): **2.0 litre engine only**
  Initial setting . . . . 98 ± 2 SEEM units
  Final setting . . . . 54 ± 3 SEEM units

Camshaft
Drive . . . . Toothed belt

Lubrication system
Oil pump type:
  1.4 litre engine . . . . Gear type, driven directly by the right-hand end of the crankshaft, by two flats machined along the crankshaft journal
  2.0 litre engine . . . . Gear-type, chain-driven off the crankshaft right-hand end
Minimum oil pressure:
  1.4 litre engine . . . . 3.5 bars @ 4000 rpm, 2.3 bars @ 2000 rpm (110°C)
  2.0 litre engine . . . . 4.0 bars @ 4000 rpm, 2.0 bars @ 2000 rpm (80°C)
Oil pressure warning switch operating pressure . . . . 0.8 bars

Torque wrench settings

	Nm	lbf ft
1.4 litre engine		
Auxiliary drivebelt tensioner roller	20	15
Big-end bolts*:		
Stage 1	10	7
Stage 2	Slacken 180°	
Stage 3	10	7
Stage 4	Angle-tighten a further 100°	
Camshaft bearing housing	10	7
Camshaft position sensor bolt	5	4
Camshaft sprocket	45	33
Coolant outlet housing bolts	10	7
Crankshaft position/speed sensor bolt	5	4
Crankshaft pulley/sprocket bolt:		
Stage 1	30	22
Stage 2	Angle-tighten a further 180 °	
Cylinder head bolts:		
Stage 1	20	15
Stage 2	40	30
Stage 3	Angle-tighten a further 260°	
Cylinder head cover bolts	10	7
Engine-to-transmission fixing bolts	45	33
Flywheel bolts*:		
Stage 1	15	11
Stage 2	Angle-tighten a further 75°	
Fuel pump sprocket nut	50	37
Left-hand engine/transmission mounting:		
Mounting bracket-to-body bolts	20	15
Mounting stud-to-transmission bolts	20	15
Mounting to bracket	30	22
Rubber mounting centre nut	60	44
Main bearing ladder seam bolts:		
Stage 1	5	4
Stage 2	10	7
Main bearing ladder to cylinder block*:		
Stage 1	10	7
Stage 2	Slacken 180°	
Stage 3	30	22
Stage 4	Angle-tighten a further 140°	
Piston oil jet spray tube bolt	20	15
Oil pump to cylinder block	10	7
Rear engine/transmission mounting:		
Connecting link to mounting assembly	55	41
Connecting link-to-subframe nut/bolt	40	30
Mounting to engine	45	33

Torque wrench settings (continued)

	Nm	lbf ft
1.4 litre engine (continued)		
Right-hand engine mounting:		
Mounting to body	60	44
Mounting to support bracket	60	44
Support bracket to engine	55	41
Sump bolts/nuts	10	7
Sump plug	16	12
Timing belt idler pulley	35	26
Timing belt tensioner pulley	25	18
2.0 litre engine		
Big-end bearing cap nuts*		
Stage 1	20	15
Stage 2	Angle-tighten a further 70°	
Camshaft bearing housing bolts	10	7
Camshaft sprocket hub-to-camshaft bolt	43	32
Camshaft sprocket-to-hub bolts	20	15
Clutch bellhousing closure plate	18	13
Coolant outlet manifold:		
Stage 1 – studs	25	18
Stage 2 – stud nuts	20	15
Stage 3 – 3 bolts	20	15
Crankshaft pulley bolt:		
Early engines (see Section 7)		
Stage 1	50	37
Stage 2	Angle-tighten a further 62°	
Later engines (see Section 7)		
Stage 1	70	52
Stage 2	Angle-tighten a further 60°	
Crankshaft right-hand oil seal housing bolts	14	10
Cylinder head bolts:		
Stage 1	22	16
Stage 2	60	44
Stage 3	Angle-tighten a further 220° ± 5°	
Cylinder head cover bolts	10	7
Engine-to-transmission fixing bolts	45	33
Flywheel/driveplate bolts*	50	37
Fuel pump sprocket nut	50	37
Left-hand engine/transmission mounting:		
Mounting bracket-to-body bolts	20	15
Mounting stud-to-transmission bolts	20	15
Mounting to bracket	30	22
Rubber mounting centre nut	60	44
Main bearing cap bolts:		
Stage 1	25	18
Stage 2	Angle-tighten a further 60°	
Oil pump mounting bolts	18	13
Piston oil jet spray tube bolt	10	7
Rear engine/transmission mounting:		
Connecting link to mounting assembly	55	41
Connecting link-to-subframe nut/bolt	40	30
Mounting to engine	45	33
Right-hand engine mounting:		
Mounting to body	60	44
Mounting to support bracket	60	44
Support bracket to engine	55	41
Sump bolts	16	12
Sump plug	16	12
Timing belt idler roller bolt	25	18
Timing belt tensioner	23	17

* Do not re-use

1 General information

How to use this Chapter

This Part of Chapter 2 describes the repair procedures that can reasonably be carried out on the engine while it remains in the vehicle. If the engine has been removed from the vehicle and is being dismantled as described in Part F, any preliminary dismantling procedures can be ignored.

Note that, while it may be possible physically to overhaul items such as the piston/connecting rod assemblies while the engine is in the car, such tasks are not usually carried out as separate operations. Usually, several additional procedures are required (not to mention the cleaning of components and oilways); for this reason, all such tasks are classed as major overhaul procedures, and are described in Part F of this Chapter.

Part F describes the removal of the engine/transmission from the car, and the full overhaul procedures that can then be carried out.

DW and DV series engines

The DW series engine is based on the well-proven XUD series engine which has appeared in many Peugeot and Citroën vehicles. In particular, the cylinder block components are very similar to the XUD, however, the remainder of the engine has been completely redesigned. The 1.4 litre DV series engine is the result of development collaboration between Peugeot/Citroën and Ford.

Both engines are of single overhead camshaft 8-valve design. The turbocharged, four-cylinder engines are mounted transversely, with the transmission mounted on the left-hand side.

A toothed timing belt drives the camshaft, high-pressure fuel pump and coolant pump. The camshaft operates the inlet and exhaust valves via rocker arms which are supported at their pivot ends by hydraulic self-adjusting tappets. The camshaft is supported by bearings machined directly in the cylinder head and camshaft bearing housing.

The high-pressure fuel pump supplies fuel to the fuel rail, and subsequently to the electronically-controlled injectors which inject the fuel direct into the combustion chambers. This design differs from the previous type where an injection pump supplies the fuel at high-pressure to each injector. The earlier, conventional type injection pump required fine calibration and timing, and these functions are now completed by the high-pressure pump, electronic injectors and engine management ECU.

The crankshaft runs in five main bearings of the usual shell type. Endfloat is controlled by thrustwashers either side of No 2 main bearing.

The pistons are selected to be of matching weight, and incorporate fully-floating gudgeon pins retained by circlips.

On the 2.0 litre engine, the oil pump is chain-driven from the right-hand end of the crankshaft, whilst on the 1.4 litre engine, the gear type pump is fitted over the end of the crankshaft, and is driven by interlocking machined flats on the crankshaft and pump gear.

Throughout the manual, it is often necessary to identify the engines not only by their cubic capacity, but also by their engine code. The engine code, consists of three letters (eg, RHZ). The code is stamped on a plate attached to the front of the cylinder block.

Precautions

The engine is a complex unit with numerous accessories and ancillary components. The design of the engine compartment is such that every conceivable space has been utilised, and access to virtually all of the engine components is extremely limited. In many cases, ancillary components will have to be removed, or moved to one side, and wiring, pipes and hoses will have to be disconnected or removed from various cable clips and support brackets.

When working on this engine, read through the entire procedure first, look at the car and engine at the same time, and establish whether you have the necessary tools, equipment, skill and patience to proceed. Allow considerable time for any operation, and be prepared for the unexpected. Any major work on these engines is not for the faint-hearted!

Because of the limited access, many of the engine photographs appearing in this Chapter were, by necessity, taken with the engine removed from the vehicle.

 Warning: It is essential to observe strict precautions when working on the fuel system components of the engine, particularly the high-pressure side of the system. Before carrying out any engine operations that entail working on, or near, any part of the fuel system, refer to the special information given in Chapter 4B, Section 2.

Operations with engine in car

a) *Compression pressure – testing.*
b) *Cylinder head cover(s) – removal and refitting.*
c) *Crankshaft pulley – removal and refitting.*
d) *Timing belt covers – removal and refitting.*
e) *Timing belt – removal, refitting and adjustment.*
f) *Timing belt tensioner and sprockets – removal and refitting.*
g) *Camshaft oil seal – renewal.*
h) *Camshaft, rocker arms and hydraulic tappets – removal, inspection and refitting.*
i) *Sump – removal and refitting.*
j) *Oil pump – removal and refitting.*
k) *Crankshaft oil seals – renewal.*
l) *Engine/transmission mountings – inspection and renewal.*
m) *Flywheel/driveplate – removal, inspection and refitting.*

2 Compression and leakdown tests – description and interpretation

Compression test

Note: *A compression tester specifically designed for diesel engines must be used for this test.*

1 When engine performance is down, or if misfiring occurs which cannot be attributed to the fuel system, a compression test can provide diagnostic clues as to the engine's condition. If the test is performed regularly, it can give warning of trouble before any other symptoms become apparent.

2 A compression tester specifically intended for diesel engines must be used, because of the higher pressures involved. The tester is connected to an adapter which screws into the glow plug or injector hole. On these engines, an adapter suitable for use in the glow plug holes will be required, so as not to disturb the fuel system components. It is unlikely to be worthwhile buying such a tester for occasional use, but it may be possible to borrow or hire one – if not, have the test performed by a garage.

3 Unless specific instructions to the contrary are supplied with the tester, observe the following points:

a) *The battery must be in a good state of charge, the air filter must be clean, and the engine should be at normal operating temperature.*
b) *All the glow plugs should be removed as described in Chapter 5C before starting the test.*
c) *The wiring connector on the engine management system ECU (located in the plastic box behind the battery) must be disconnected.*

4 The compression pressures measured are not so important as the balance between cylinders. Values are given in the Specifications.

5 The cause of poor compression is less easy to establish on a diesel engine than on a petrol one. The effect of introducing oil into the cylinders ('wet' testing) is not conclusive, because there is a risk that the oil will sit in the swirl chamber or in the recess on the piston crown instead of passing to the rings. However, the following can be used as a rough guide to diagnosis.

6 All cylinders should produce very similar pressures; any difference greater than that specified indicates the existence of a fault. Note that the compression should build-up quickly in a healthy engine; low compression on the first stroke, followed by gradually-increasing pressure on successive strokes, indicates worn piston rings. A low compression reading on the first stroke, which does not build-up during successive strokes, indicates leaking valves or a blown head gasket (a cracked head could also be the cause). Deposits on the undersides of the valve heads can also cause low compression.

7 A low reading from two adjacent cylinders is almost certainly due to the head gasket having blown between them; the presence of coolant in the engine oil will confirm this.

8 If the compression reading is unusually high, the cylinder head surfaces, valves and pistons are probably coated with carbon deposits. If this is the case, the cylinder head should be removed and decarbonised (see Part F).

Leakdown test

9 A leakdown test measures the rate at which compressed air fed into the cylinder is lost. It is an alternative to a compression test, and in many ways it is better, since the escaping air provides easy identification of where pressure loss is occurring (piston rings, valves or head gasket).

10 The equipment needed for leakdown testing is unlikely to be available to the home mechanic. If poor compression is suspected, have the test performed by a suitably-equipped garage.

3 Engine assembly/ valve timing holes – general information and usage

Note: *Do not attempt to rotate the engine whilst the crankshaft and camshaft are locked in position. If the engine is to be left in this state for a long period of time, it is a good idea to place suitable warning notices inside the vehicle, and in the engine compartment. This will reduce the possibility of the engine being accidentally cranked on the starter motor, which is likely to cause damage with the locking pins in place.*

1 Timing holes or slots are located only in the flywheel/driveplate (2.0 litre) or crankshaft pulley flange (1.4 litre) and camshaft sprocket hub. The holes/slots are used to align the crankshaft and camshaft at the TDC position for Nos 1 and 4 on 2.0 litre models, or position the pistons halfway up the cylinder bores on the 1.4 litre models. This will ensure that the valve timing is maintained during operations that require removal and refitting of the timing belt. When the holes/slots are aligned with their corresponding holes in the cylinder block and cylinder head, suitable diameter bolts/pins can be inserted to lock the crankshaft and camshaft in position, preventing rotation. **Note:** *On 2.0 litre models, with the timing holes aligned, No 4 piston is at TDC on its compression stroke.*

3.7a Use a mirror to observe the camshaft sprocket hub timing slot (DW10 engine)

2 Note that the HDi type fuel system used on these engines does not have a conventional diesel injection pump, but instead uses a high-pressure fuel pump. On 2.0 litre engines, the alignment of the fuel pump sprocket (and hence the fuel pump itself) with respect to crankshaft and camshaft position, is irrelevant, however Peugeot include this procedure for late 1.4 litre engines fitted with a Bosch high-pressure fuel pump. Note: *On the Bosch pump, the drive sprocket is keyed to the shaft. In addition, note that on these 1.4 litre engines, the hole in the fuel pump sprocket only aligns correctly with the hole in the mounting bracket every 12 revolutions of the crankshaft (or every 6 revolutions of the camshaft sprocket).*

3 To align the engine assembly/valve timing holes, proceed as follows.

4 Apply the handbrake, then jack up the front of the vehicle and support it on axle stands (see *Jacking and vehicle support*). Remove the right-hand front roadwheel.

5 To gain access to the crankshaft pulley, to enable the engine to be turned, the wheel arch plastic liner must be removed. The liner is secured by several plastic expanding rivets. To remove the rivets, push in the centre pins a little, then prise the clips from place. Remove the liner from under the front wing. Where necessary, unclip the coolant hoses from under the wing to improve access further. The crankshaft can then be turned using a suitable socket and extension bar fitted to the pulley bolt.

6 Remove the upper and lower timing belt covers as described in Section 6.

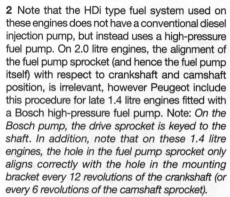

3.8 Tool required to lock the flywheel at TDC (2.0 litre engine)

3.7b Camshaft sprocket hub timing slot (A) aligned with the cylinder head timing hole (B) (DW10 engine)

7 Turn the crankshaft until the timing hole in the camshaft sprocket hub is aligned with the corresponding hole in the cylinder head. Note that the crankshaft must always be turned in a clockwise direction (viewed from the right-hand side of vehicle). Use a small mirror so that the position of the sprocket hub timing slot can be observed **(see illustrations)**. When the slot is aligned with the corresponding hole in the cylinder head, the camshaft is positioned correctly. **Note:** *On 2.0 litre engines, make sure that the centre part of the slot is aligned with the hole in the cylinder head, as it is possible to incorrectly align the area to each side of the slot.*

2.0 litre engines

8 Insert an 8 mm diameter bolt, rod or drill through the hole in the left-hand flange of the cylinder block by the starter motor; if necessary, carefully turn the crankshaft either way until the rod enters the timing hole in the flywheel/driveplate. Note that due to limited access, Peugeot technicians use a special tool as shown **(see illustration)** which can be home-made out of the correct diameter rod.

9 Insert an 8 mm bolt, rod or drill through the hole in the camshaft sprocket hub and into engagement with the cylinder head **(see illustration)**.

1.4 litre engines

10 Remove the crankshaft drivebelt pulley as described in Section 5.

11 Insert a 5 mm diameter bolt, rod or drill

3.9 Insert an 8 mm bolt (arrowed) through the sprocket timing slot and into the cylinder head to lock the camshaft (2.0 litre engine)

3.11 Insert a 5 mm drill through the hole in the crankshaft sprocket flange, and into the corresponding hole in the oil pump

3.12 Insert an 8 mm drill through the hole in the camshaft sprocket, and into the corresponding hole in the cylinder head

through the hole in crankshaft sprocket flange and into the corresponding hole in the oil pump **(see illustration)**, if necessary, carefully turn the crankshaft either way until the rod enters the timing hole in the block.

12 Insert an 8 mm bolt, rod or drill through the hole in the camshaft sprocket hub and into engagement with the cylinder head **(see illustration)**.

13 If using this procedure during refitting of the timing belt on late 1.4 litre engines fitted with a Bosch high-pressure fuel pump, insert a 5 mm diameter bolt, rod or drill through the hole in the fuel pump sprocket and into the corresponding hole in the cylinder head. Note the comment in paragraph 2 – if the fuel pump sprocket holes are not aligned during removal of the timing belt, it is of no consequence, however it is important to align the holes during the refitting procedure. If timing alignment alone is being *checked* there

is no need to check alignment of the pump sprocket.

4 Cylinder head cover – removal and refitting

Removal

1 Remove the plastic cover from the top of the engine. On 1.4 litre engines, the cover simply pulls up from place. On 2.0 litre models, the cover is retained by four fasteners, which simply unscrew **(see illustration)**

2 Carry out the following operations to remove the scuttle trim panel and cross-member **(see illustrations)**:

a) *Remove the wiper blades (see Chapter 12).*
b) *Push in the centre pins, and prise out the two plastic rivets at each end of the trim panel.*

c) *Pull the outer ends of the panel up, then pull the panel centre down and forwards to release it from the windscreen.*
d) *Undo the two screws securing the master cylinder upper fluid reservoir. Do not disconnect the fluid pipes.*
e) *Release the clips securing the sound insulation material, then undo the two bolts and remove the scuttle crossmember.*

3 Remove the timing belt upper cover, as described in Section 6.

2.0 litre engines

4 As applicable, slacken or release the clips securing the crankcase ventilation hoses to the cylinder cover and disconnect the hoses.

5 Undo the bolts and move the engine cover and cable guide support bracket clear of the right-hand end of the cylinder head cover.

6 Disconnect the camshaft position sensor wiring connector.

7 Release the wiring harness from the clip on the cylinder head cover and move the harness to one side.

8 Progressively unscrew the bolts securing the cylinder head cover to the camshaft carrier or inlet manifold (as applicable) and collect the washers. Carefully lift off the cover, taking care not to damage the camshaft position sensor as the cover is removed. Recover the seal from the cover.

1.4 litre engines

9 The cylinder head cover is integral with the inlet manifold and oil separator. Disconnect the mass airflow meter wiring plug **(see illustration)**.

4.1 Rotate the four fasteners (arrowed) 90° anti-clockwise and pull up the plastic cover

4.2a Push in the centre pin and prise out the complete rivet

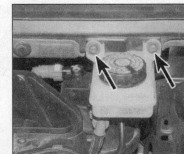

4.2b Undo the upper master cylinder fluid reservoir screws (arrowed)

4.2c Prise up the centre pin and lever out the complete plastic expanding rivet

4.2d Undo the bolt at each end and remove the scuttle crossmember

4.9 Disconnect the mass airflow meter wiring plug

4.10 Slacken the retaining clamps and disconnect the turbo outlet hose

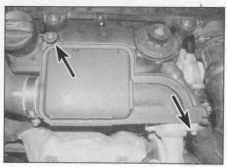

4.11a Undo the bolts (arrowed) and lift up the right-hand end . . .

4.11b . . . to disengage the resonator box from the turbocharger

4.13 Undo the two bolts (arrowed) and pull the air filter housing up from its place

4.17 Depress the locking buttons (arrowed) and disconnect the fuel feed and return hoses

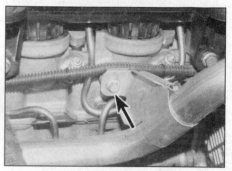

4.19 Undo the bolt securing the EGR pipe to the rear of the block (arrowed)

10 Slacken the retaining clip, and remove the turbocharger outlet elbow **(see illustration)**.
11 Undo the retaining bolts, lift up the right-hand end and remove the resonator **(see illustrations)**. Recover the O-ring seal.
12 Slacken the retaining clips and remove the air intake ducting and turbocharger intake hose. Slide up the plastic trim in the left-hand front corner of the engine compartment, push in the centre pin a little, prise out the rivet and remove the intake ducting from the bonnet slam panel.
13 Unscrew the air filter housing bolts, and the filter cover bolts, then remove the cover and filter element – refer to Chapter 4B **(see illustration)**. Release the diesel priming pump bulb from its retaining brackets at the right-hand end of the cylinder head, and remove the air filter housing. Disconnect any wiring plugs as

necessary as the housing is with-drawn, having first noted their fitted positions.
14 Remove the diesel fuel filter as described in Chapter 1B, then undo the 3 bolts securing the diesel filter support bracket.
15 Disconnect the wiring plugs from the top of each injector, then make sure all wiring harnesses are freed from any retaining brackets on the cylinder head cover/intake manifold. Disconnect any vacuum pipes as necessary, having first noted their fitted positions.
16 Prise out the retaining clips and disconnect the fuel return pipes from the injectors. Plug the openings to prevent dirt ingress.
17 Disconnect the fuel feed and return pipes at the right-hand end of the cylinder head cover. Undo the Torx screw securing the fuel pipes bracket **(see illustration)**.

18 Unclip the fuel temperature sensor from the retaining bracket and move the pipe/priming bulb assembly to the rear.
19 Undo the two screws securing the EGR pipe to the cylinder head cover, and the bolt securing the pipe to the rear of the cylinder head **(see illustration)**.
20 Undo the two bolts securing the EGR valve to the left-hand end of the cylinder head, disconnect the vacuum hose, then remove the valve along with the EGR pipe. Recover the O-ring seal from the pipe.
21 Undo the eight bolts securing the cylinder head cover and intake manifold at the front, and the two retaining bolts along the rear edge of the cover. Lift the assembly away **(see illustrations)**. Recover the manifold rubber seals.

4.21a Undo the 8 bolts (arrowed) at the front . . .

4.21b . . . and the two bolts (arrowed) at the rear

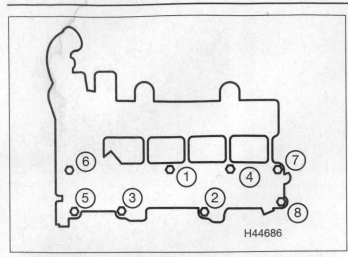

4.22 Cylinder head cover tightening sequence (1.4 litre engine)

5.1a Insert a drill or pin to lock the auxiliary drivebelt tensioner in position (2.0 litre engines) . . .

Refitting

22 Refitting is a reversal of removal, bearing in mind the following points:

a) *Examine the cover seal(s) for signs of damage and deterioration, and renew if necessary. On 1.4 litre engines, smear a little clean engine oil on the manifold seals.*

b) *Tighten the cylinder head cover bolts to the specified torque. On 1.4 litre engines, in the order shown* **(see illustration)**.

c) *On 2.0 litre engines, before refitting the timing belt upper cover, adjust the camshaft position sensor air gap as described in Chapter 4B, Section 13.*

5 Crankshaft pulley – removal and refitting

Removal

1 Remove the auxiliary drivebelt as described in Chapter 1B. Turn the tensioner anti-clockwise and insert a pin or drill to hold it away from the drivebelt **(see illustrations)**.

2.0 litre engines

2 To prevent crankshaft turning whilst the pulley retaining bolt is being slackened, the flywheel/driveplate ring gear can be locked using a suitable tool made from steel angle **(see illustration)**. Remove the cover plate from the base of the transmission bellhousing and bolt the tool to the bellhousing flange so it engages with the ring gear teeth. *Do not attempt to lock the pulley by inserting a bolt/drill through the timing hole. If the timing hole bolt/drill is in position from a previous operation, temporarily remove it prior to slackening the pulley bolt, then refit it once the bolt has been slackened.* **Note:** *On later 2.0 engines (see Section 7), it is essential that the crankshaft and camshaft timing pins are in place as described in Section 3. This is because, on these engines, the crankshaft sprocket has a wider keyway, to allow it to rotate a little independently of the crankshaft. Failure to lock the crankshaft and camshaft could result in the timing being lost.*

1.4 litre engines

3 To lock the crankshaft, working underneath the engine, insert Peugeot tool No 0194-C into the hole in the right-hand face of the engine block casting over the lower section of the flywheel. Rotate the crankshaft until the tool engages in the corresponding hole in the flywheel. In the absence of the Peugeot tool, insert a 12 mm rod or drill into the hole **(see illustration)**. **Note:** *The hole in the casting and the hole in the flywheel are provided purely to lock the crankshaft whilst the pulley bolt is undone, it does* **not** *position the crankshaft at TDC.*

All engines

4 Using a suitable socket and extension bar, unscrew the retaining bolt, remove the washer, then slide the pulley off the end of the crankshaft **(see illustration)**. If the pulley is tight fit, it can be drawn off the crankshaft using a suitable puller. If a puller is being used, refit the pulley retaining bolt without the washer, to avoid damaging the crankshaft as the puller is tightened.

Caution: On 1.4 litre engines, do not

5.1b . . . and 1.4 litre engine

5.2 Use a fabricated tool similar to this to lock the flywheel ring gear and prevent crankshaft rotation

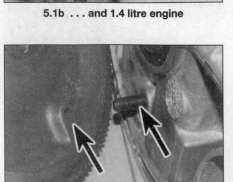

5.3 The locking pin/bolt (arrowed) must locate in the hole in the flywheel (arrowed) to prevent rotation

5.4 Undo the crankshaft pulley retaining bolt

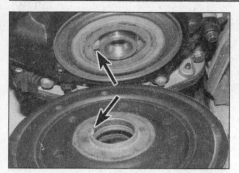

5.6 On 1.4 litre engines, the notch in the pulley (arrowed) must align with the key in the sprocket (arrowed)

touch the outer magnetic sensor ring of the sprocket with your fingers, or allow metallic particles to come into contact with it.

5 On 2.0 litre engines, if the pulley locating key is a loose fit, remove it and store it with the pulley for safe-keeping.

Refitting

6 Ensure that the key is correctly located in its crankshaft groove (2.0 litre engines only), then refit the pulley to the end of the crankshaft **(see illustration)**.

7 Thoroughly clean the threads of the pulley retaining bolt, then apply a coat of locking compound to the bolt threads. Peugeot recommend the use of Loctite (available from your Peugeot dealer); in the absence of this, any good-quality locking compound may be used.

8 Refit the crankshaft pulley retaining bolt and washer. Tighten the bolt to the specified torque, then through the specified angle, preventing the crankshaft from turning using the method employed on removal.

9 Refit and tension the auxiliary drivebelt as described in Chapter 1B.

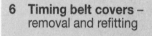

6 Timing belt covers –
removal and refitting

⚠️ **Warning: Refer to the pre-cautionary information contained in Section 1 before proceeding.**

6.7 Disconnect the fuel supply and return hose quick-release fittings

6.2 Release the wiring harness from the timing belt upper cover

Upper cover removal

1.4 litre engines

1 Remove the plastic covers from the top of the engine. The engine cover simply pulls up from its place, whilst the cover over the washer fluid reservoir is retained by two plastic rivets. Push the centre pins in a little then prise the complete rivet from place.

2 Release the wiring harness and fuel pipes from the upper cover **(see illustration)**.

3 Undo the five screws and remove the timing belt upper cover **(see illustration)**.

2.0 litre engines

4 Remove the plastic covers from the top of the engine, then undo the screws and remove the engine undershield. The cover over the engine is release by rotating the four fasteners anti-clockwise whilst gently pulling up the cover. Push in the centre pins and prise out the two plastic expanding rivets, release the side clip and remove the cover over the coolant/washer reservoirs.

5 Position a trolley jack under the engine and, using a piece of wood on the jack head, support the weight of the engine.

6 Undo the bolts and remove the right-hand engine mounting and support bracket – see Section 17.

7 At the connections above the fuel pump, disconnect the fuel supply and return hose quick-release fittings using a small screwdriver to press down and release the locking clip **(see illustration)**. Cover the open unions to prevent dirt entry, using small plastic bags, or fingers cut from clean rubber gloves.

6.8 Release the two fuel hoses from the retaining clips on the upper timing belt cover

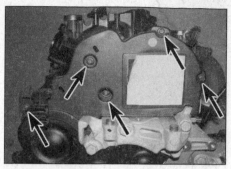

6.3 Undo the 5 screws (arrowed) and remove the upper timing belt cover

8 Release the two hoses from the retaining clips on the upper timing belt cover and move them to one side **(see illustration)**.

9 Release the EGR solenoid valve vacuum hose from the clip on the upper cover.

10 Undo the bolt securing the upper cover to the cylinder head cover **(see illustration)**.

11 Undo the upper bolt on the edge of the cover nearest to the engine compartment bulkhead.

12 Undo the lower bolt/nut on the bulkhead side of the cover at the join between the upper and lower covers. Note that this bolt/stud also retains the coolant pump. Where a bolt is fitted, to avoid coolant leakage after the upper cover is removed, refit the bolt fitted with a 17.0 mm spacer, and tighten it securely.

13 Undo the remaining bolt in the centre of the cover. Loosen the lower cover bolts to allow the upper cover to be released – the upper and intermediate covers share the lower cover mounting bolts, and have slotted holes to enable them to be withdrawn upwards.

14 Disengage the upper cover from the intermediate cover and manipulate the upper cover from its location.

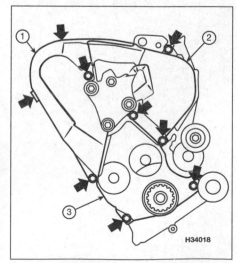

6.10 Timing belt cover retaining bolt locations (arrowed)

1 Upper cover
2 Intermediate cover
3 Lower cover

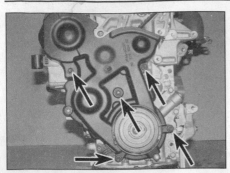

6.20 Lower cover retaining bolts (arrowed)

Intermediate cover removal

2.0 litre engines

15 Remove the upper cover as described previously.

16 Undo the upper bolt on the top edge of the intermediate cover.

17 Undo the two remaining bolts at the join between the intermediate cover and lower cover, then manipulate the intermediate cover from its location.

Lower cover removal

1.4 litre engines

18 Remove the upper cover as described previously.

19 Remove the crankshaft pulley as described in Section 5.

20 Undo the five bolts and remove the lower cover **(see illustration)**.

7.8 Undo the bolt securing the crankshaft position sensor (arrowed)

7.13 Insert an Allen key into the hole (arrowed), slacken the pulley bolt and allow the tensioner to rotate

2.0 litre engines

21 Remove the upper and intermediate covers as described previously.

22 Remove the crankshaft pulley as described in Section 5.

23 Undo the two remaining bolts on the edge of the cover, one on either side of the crankshaft pulley location.

24 Lift the cover off the front of the engine.

Refitting

25 Refitting of all the covers is a reversal of the relevant removal procedure, ensuring that each cover section is correctly located, and that the cover retaining bolts are securely tightened. Ensure that all disturbed hoses are reconnected and retained by their relevant clips.

---

7 Timing belt –
removal, inspection, refitting and tensioning

Note: *On 2.0 litre engines, Peugeot specify the use of an electronic belt tension checking tool (SEEM CTG 105.M) to correctly set the timing belt tension. The following procedure assumes that this equipment (or suitable alternative equipment calibrated to display belt tension in SEEM units) is available. Accurate tensioning of the timing belt is essential, and if the electronic equipment is not available, it is recommended that the work is entrusted to a Peugeot dealer or suitably-equipped garage.*

Note: *Early models are identified by three bolts securing the camshaft sprocket to the hub.*

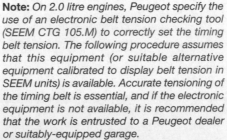

7.9 Timing belt protection bracket retaining bolt (arrowed)

7.15 Remove the turbocharger air inlet pipe

Later engines are identified by the camshaft sprocket being retained by one central bolt.

General

1 The timing belt drives the camshaft(s), high-pressure fuel pump, and coolant pump from a toothed sprocket on the end of the crankshaft. If the belt breaks or slips in service, the pistons are likely to hit the valve heads, resulting in expensive damage.

2 The timing belt should be renewed at the specified intervals, or earlier if it is contaminated with oil, or at all noisy in operation (a 'scraping' noise due to uneven wear).

3 If the timing belt is being removed, it is a wise precaution to check the condition of the coolant pump at the same time (check for signs of coolant leakage). This may avoid the need to remove the timing belt again at a later stage, should the coolant pump fail.

Removal

4 Apply the handbrake, then jack up the front of the vehicle and support it on axle stands (see *Jacking and vehicle support*). Remove the front right-hand roadwheel, wheel arch liner (to expose the crankshaft pulley) and the engine undershield. The wheel arch liner is secured by several plastic expanding rivets. Push the centre pins in a little then prise the rivet from place. The engine undershield is retained by several screw fasteners. Rotate the fasteners 90 degrees anti-clockwise and remove them.

5 Refer to Chapter 4B and remove the complete exhaust system.

Caution: If the exhaust system is not removed, the front pipe flexible section will be damaged when the right-hand engine mounting is detached.

6 Remove the auxiliary drivebelt as described in Chapter 1B.

1.4 litre engines

7 Remove the upper and lower timing belt covers, as described in Section 6.

8 Undo the screw and remove the crankshaft position sensor adjacent to the crankshaft sprocket flange, and move it to one side **(see illustration)**.

9 Undo the retaining screw and remove the timing belt protection bracket, again adjacent to the crankshaft sprocket flange **(see illustration)**.

10 Lock the crankshaft and camshaft in the correct position as described in Section 3. If necessary, temporarily refit the crankshaft pulley bolt to enable the crankshaft to be rotated.

11 Position a trolley jack under the engine, and using a block of wood on the jack head, take the weight of the engine.

12 Undo the bolts and remove the right hand engine mounting and support bracket – see Section 17.

13 Insert a hexagon key into belt tensioner pulley centre, slacken the pulley bolt, and allow the tensioner to rotate, relieving the belt

7.18a Unscrew the crankshaft pulley bolt . . .

7.18b . . . then remove the pulley

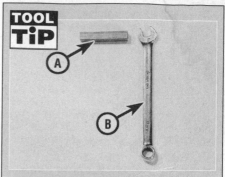

A square section tool to fit the timing belt tensioner pulley can be made from a length of standard 8 mm door handle rod (A), obtained from a DIY shop, and then cut to size. Once the rod has been fitted to the tensioner, the timing belt can be tensioned by turning the rod with an 8 mm spanner (B).

tension **(see illustration)**. With belt slack, temporarily tighten the pulley bolt.

14 Note its routing, then remove the timing belt from the sprockets.

2.0 litre engines

15 Remove the turbocharger air inlet pipe **(see illustration)**.

16 Unbolt the closure plate from the bottom of the clutch housing

17 Using a suitable tool, lock the flywheel/driveplate, then loosen the crankshaft pulley bolt. Peugeot technicians use a tool which engages the teeth of the starter ring gear and is bolted to the clutch bellhousing. A similar tool may be made out of a length of angle-iron, bent to engage the teeth, or alternatively an assistant may restrain the starter ring gear with a wide-bladed screwdriver.

18 Unscrew and remove the crankshaft pulley bolt, then remove the pulley from the crankshaft **(see illustrations)**. If it is tight, refit the bolt without its washer, leaving sufficient room to release the pulley. Using a puller, remove the pulley from the front of the crankshaft.

19 Unbolt the rear engine mounting link piece – see Section 17.

20 An 8.0 mm diameter flywheel/driveplate locking pin is now required, and may be obtained from a Peugeot dealer or car accessory shop.

21 Temporarily refit the crankshaft pulley bolt, then turn the engine until the TDC hole in the flywheel/driveplate is aligned with the hole in the front engine flange (next to the transmission bellhousing – see Section 3). Insert the locking pin to lock the engine.

22 Remove the upper, intermediate and lower timing belt covers as described in the previous Section.

23 As a precaution against damage to the radiator, place a card or piece of hardboard over it on the engine side.

24 Insert a suitable drill or metal dowel through the TDC hole in the camshaft sprocket flange, and into the cylinder head (see Section 3).

25 Loosen the bolt on the tensioner roller, and turn the tensioner clockwise to release the tension on the timing belt. If available, use an 8 mm square drive extension in the hole provided, to turn the tensioner bracket against

the spring tension **(see Tool Tip)**. Retighten the bolt sufficiently to hold the tensioner in its released position; do not fully tighten the bolt in this position.

26 Mark the timing belt with an arrow to indicate its running direction, if it is to be re-used. Remove the belt from the sprockets.

Inspection

27 Renew the belt as a matter of course, regardless of its apparent condition. The cost of a new belt is nothing compared with the cost of repairs, should the belt break in service. If signs of oil contamination are found, trace the source of the oil leak and rectify it. Wash down the engine timing belt area and all related components, to remove all traces of oil. Check that the tensioner and idler pulleys rotate freely without any sign of

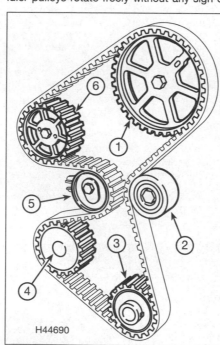

7.29 Timing belt routing (1.4 litre engine)

1	Camshaft sprocket	4	Coolant pump sprocket
2	Idler pulley	5	Tensioner pulley
3	Crankshaft sprocket	6	High-pressure fuel pump pulley

roughness, and also check that the coolant pump pulley rotates freely. If necessary, renew these items. **Note:** *Peugeot recommend that the tensioner and idler pulleys should not be re-used, regardless of apparent condition.*

Refitting and tensioning

28 Commence refitting by ensuring that the crankshaft and camshaft timing pins are still in position correctly.

1.4 litre engines

29 Locate the timing belt on the crankshaft sprocket then, keeping it taut, locate it around the idler pulley, camshaft sprocket, high-pressure pump sprocket, coolant pump sprocket, and the tensioner roller **(see illustration)**.

30 Refit the timing belt protection bracket and tighten the retaining bolt securely.

31 Slacken the tensioner pulley bolt and, using a hexagonal key, rotate the tensioner anti-clockwise, which moves the index arm clockwise, until the index arm is aligned **(see illustration)**.

32 Remove the camshaft and crankshaft timing pins and, using a socket on the crankshaft pulley bolt, rotate the engine clockwise 10 complete revolutions. Refit the crankshaft and camshaft locking pins.

7.31 Align the index arm (A) with the locating stud (B)

7.35 Slacken the three camshaft sprocket-to-sprocket hub retaining bolts

7.37a Retain the timing belt on the crankshaft sprocket and feed it around the idler roller . . .

7.37b . . . high pressure fuel pump sprocket . . .

7.37c . . . camshaft sprocket . . .

7.37d . . . coolant pump and tensioner pulley

33 Check that the tensioner index arm is still aligned between the edges of the area **(see illustration 7.31)**. If it is not, remove and belt and begin the refitting process again, starting at Paragraph 29.

34 The remainder of refitting is a reversal of removal. Tighten all fasteners to the specified torque where given.

Early 2.0 litre engines

35 Early models are identified by three bolts securing the camshaft sprocket to the hub. Loosen the three bolts securing the camshaft sprocket to the camshaft, so that the sprocket can be turned on its hub **(see illustration)**. To do this, either use a tool engaged with the holes in the sprocket, or alternatively, hold the sprocket with an old timing belt.

36 Finger-tighten the sprocket bolts, then slacken each bolt by one sixth of a turn. Turn the sprocket clockwise to the end of the slots.

37 Locate the timing belt on the crankshaft pulley splines then, keeping it taut, locate it around the idler pulley and onto the high-pressure pump pulley **(see illustrations)**. Peugeot technicians use a plastic clip to retain the belt on the crankshaft pulley; if necessary, use a plastic cable tie to hold it.

38 Locate the belt onto the camshaft pulley splines. If the teeth do not align correctly, turn the camshaft sprocket slightly anti-clockwise until the belt engages. **Note:** *Do not turn the pulley anti-clockwise more than one tooth space.*

39 Continue to locate the belt onto the tensioner pulley and coolant pump splines, then loosen the bolt and turn the tensioner *anti-clockwise* to tension the belt moderately. Pretighten the bolt to 1.0 Nm, then remove the holding clip or cable tie.

40 A timing belt tension setting tool is now required to apply the correct tension. A tool which checks SEEM units is necessary, and should be fitted to the belt run between the camshaft sprocket and high-pressure pump sprocket.

41 Loosen the bolt, then turn the tensioner *anti-clockwise* until 98.0 ± 2.0 SEEM units is read on the tool **(see illustrations)**. At this point, tighten the tensioner bolt to the specified torque.

42 Temporarily remove one of the three bolts securing the sprocket to the camshaft, and check that the bolts are not at the anti-clockwise limit of their slots. If they are, repeat the refitting procedure.

43 Tighten the camshaft sprocket bolts to the specified torque.

44 Remove the crankshaft and camshaft TDC setting pins. Also remove the tensioning tool.

45 Turn the engine clockwise 8 times. Do not turn the engine anti-clockwise during this operation.

46 Refit the crankshaft and camshaft TDC setting pins.

47 Loosen the camshaft sprocket bolts again, then finger-tighten them, and loosen each by one sixth of a turn.

48 Refit the tensioning tool midway between the camshaft and high-pressure pump sprocket.

49 Loosen the tensioner bolt, then turn the tensioner anti-clockwise until the tool reads 54.0 ± 2.0 SEEM units. With the tensioner held in this position, tighten the bolt to the specified torque. It is important to apply the correct tension to the timing belt, otherwise the belt may be noisy in operation, or worse still, may break.

50 Tighten the camshaft sprocket bolts to the specified torque.

51 Remove the tensioning tool to release its internal forces, then refit it and check the tension of the belt is between 51.0 and 57.0 SEEM units. If necessary, repeat the tensioning procedure.

52 Remove the tensioning tool and TDC setting pins.

53 Turn the engine clockwise 2 times. Do not turn the engine anti-clockwise during this operation.

54 Refit the crankshaft and camshaft TDC setting/locking pins.

7.41a Pivot the tensioner pulley anti-clockwise, then tighten the retaining bolt . . .

7.41b . . . when the specified tension value is shown on the measuring equipment

55 Visually check that the offset between the camshaft hub hole and the corresponding setting hole does not exceed 1.0 mm.

56 Remove the TDC setting/locking pins.

57 The remainder of refitting is a reversal of removal. Tighten all fasteners to the specified torque where given.

Later 2.0 litre engines

58 Later engines are identified by the camshaft sprocket being retained by one central bolt.

59 Set the crankshaft sprocket by inserting a 2 mm diameter rod on the left-hand side of the woodruff key **(see illustration)**. Check the flywheel and camshaft timing pins are still in place.

60 Locate the timing belt on the camshaft sprocket splines then, keeping it taut, locate it around the high-pressure pump pulley, idler pulley, crankshaft sprocket, coolant pump sprocket and tensioner pulley. Peugeot technicians use a plastic clip to retain the belt on the camshaft sprocket; if necessary, use a plastic cable tie to hold it.

61 Loosen the bolt and turn the tensioner *anti-clockwise* to tension the belt moderately. Pretighten the bolt to 1.0 Nm, then remove the holding clip or cable tie. Remove the 2 mm diameter rod from alongside the crankshaft sprocket key.

62 A timing belt tension setting tool is now required to apply the correct tension. A tool which checks SEEM units is necessary, and should be fitted to the belt run between the camshaft sprocket and high-pressure pump sprocket.

63 Loosen the bolt, then turn the tensioner *anti-clockwise* until 98.0 ± 2.0 SEEM units is read on the tool **(see illustrations 7.41a and 7.41b)**. At this point, tighten the tensioner bolt to the specified torque.

64 Immobilise the flywheel as described in Paragraph 17, then refit the crankshaft auxiliary belt pulley, and tighten its retaining bolt to 70 Nm.

65 Remove the crankshaft and camshaft timing pins, and the flywheel locking tool.

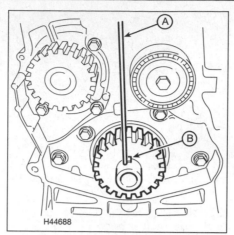

7.59 Insert a 2 mm rod (A) on the left-hand side of the Woodruff key (B)

66 Turn the engine clockwise 8 times. Do not turn the engine anti-clockwise during this operation.

67 Refit the crankshaft and camshaft TDC setting pins, then lock the flywheel as described in Paragraph 17.

68 Undo the bolt and remove the auxiliary drivebelt pulley.

69 Refit the tensioning tool midway between the camshaft and high-pressure pump sprocket.

70 Loosen the tensioner bolt, then turn the tensioner anti-clockwise until the tool reads 54.0 ± 2.0 SEEM units. With the tensioner held in this position, tighten the bolt to the specified torque. It is important to apply the correct tension to the timing belt, otherwise the belt may be noisy in operation, or worse still, may break.

71 Remove the tensioning tool to release its internal forces, then refit it and check the tension of the belt is between 51.0 and 57.0 SEEM units. If necessary, repeat the tensioning procedure.

72 Remove the crankshaft and camshaft timing pins, and the flywheel locking tool.

73 The remainder of refitting is a reversal of removal, noting the following points.

  a) Ensure the timing covers engage correctly with each other.

  b) When refitting the crankshaft auxiliary drivebelt pulley, apply a few drops of

thread locking compound to the pulley bolt.

  c) Tighten all fasteners to the specified torque where given.

8 Timing belt sprockets and tensioner – removal and refitting

Camshaft sprocket

Removal

1 Remove the timing belt as described in Section 7.

2 Remove the locking tool from the camshaft sprocket/hub. Slacken the sprocket hub retaining bolt, and the three sprocket-to-hub retaining bolts (where applicable). To prevent the camshaft rotating as the bolt(s) s are slackened, a sprocket holding tool will be required. In the absence of the special Peugeot tool, an acceptable substitute can be fabricated at home **(see Tool Tip 1)**. *Do not* attempt to use the engine assembly/valve timing locking tool to prevent the sprocket from rotating whilst the bolt is slackened.

3 Remove the sprocket hub retaining bolt and washer (where fitted), and slide the sprocket and hub off the end of the camshaft **(see illustration)**. If the Woodruff key is a loose fit in the camshaft on 2.0 litre engines, remove it for safe-keeping. Examine the camshaft oil seal for signs of oil leakage and, if necessary, renew it as described in Section 14.

4 If necessary on early 2.0 litre engines, the sprocket can be separated from the hub after removing the three retaining bolts.

5 Clean the camshaft sprocket thoroughly, and renew it if there are any signs of wear, damage or cracks.

Refitting

6 If removed on early 2.0 litre engines, refit the sprocket to the hub and secure with the three retaining bolts, tightened finger tight only at this stage.

7 Where applicable, refit the Woodruff key to the end of the camshaft, then refit the camshaft sprocket and hub **(see illustration)**.

8 Refit the sprocket hub retaining bolt and washer. Tighten the bolt to the specified

TOOL TiP 1

A sprocket holding tool can be made from two lengths of steel strip bolted together to form a forked end. Bend the end of the strip through 90° to form the fork 'prongs'.

8.3 Undo the retaining bolt and remove the camshaft sprocket (1.4 litre engine)

8.7 On 1.4 litre engines, align the sprocket lug with the notch in the end of the camshaft (arrowed)

8.13a Slide the crankshaft sprocket off the end of the crankshaft . . .

8.13b . . . and collect the Woodruff key (2.0 litre engine)

8.19 On 1.4 litre engines insert a suitable drill bit through the sprocket into the hole in the back plate

torque, preventing the camshaft from turning as during removal.

9 Align the engine assembly/valve timing slot in the camshaft sprocket hub with the hole in the cylinder head and refit the timing pin to lock the camshaft in position.

10 Fit the timing belt around the pump sprocket and camshaft sprocket, and tension the timing belt as described in Section 7.

Crankshaft sprocket

Removal

11 Remove the timing belt as described in Section 7.

12 Check that the engine assembly/valve timing holes are still aligned as described in Section 3, and the camshaft sprocket/hub and flywheel/driveplate are locked in position.

13 Slide the sprocket off the end of the crankshaft and collect the Woodruff key **(see illustrations)**.

14 Examine the crankshaft oil seal for signs of oil leakage and, if necessary, renew it as described in Section 14.

15 Clean the crankshaft sprocket thoroughly, and renew it if there are any signs of wear, damage or cracks. Recover the crankshaft locating key.

Refitting

16 Refit the key to the end of the crankshaft,

Make a sprocket releasing tool from a short strip of steel. Drill two holes in the strip to correspond with the two holes in the sprocket. Drill a third hole just large enough to accept the flats of the sprocket retaining nut.

then refit the crankshaft sprocket (with the flange nearest the cylinder block on the 2.0 litre engines, and facing the crankshaft pulley on the 1.4 litre engines).

17 Fit the timing belt around the crankshaft sprocket, and tension the timing belt as described in Section 7.

Fuel pump sprocket

Removal

18 Remove the timing belt as described in Section 7.

19 Using a suitable socket, undo the pump sprocket retaining nut. The sprocket can be held stationary by inserting a suitably-sized locking pin, drill or rod through the hole in the sprocket, and into the corresponding hole in the backplate **(see illustration)**, or by using a suitable forked tool engaged with the holes in the sprocket **(see Tool Tip 1** on previous page)**.

20 The pump sprocket is a taper fit on the pump shaft and it will be necessary to make up another tool to release it from the taper **(see Tool Tip 2)**.

21 Partially unscrew the sprocket retaining nut, fit the home-made tool, and secure it to the sprocket with two suitable bolts. Prevent the sprocket from rotating as before, and unscrew the sprocket retaining nut **(see illustration)**. The nut will bear against the tool as it is undone, forcing the sprocket off the shaft taper. Once the taper is released, remove the tool, unscrew the nut fully, and remove the sprocket from the pump shaft.

22 Clean the sprocket thoroughly, and renew

8.21 Using the home-made tools to remove the fuel pump sprocket (2.0 litre engine)

it if there are any signs of wear, damage or cracks.

Refitting

23 Refit the pump sprocket and retaining nut, and tighten the nut to the specified torque. Prevent the sprocket rotating as the nut is tightened using the sprocket holding tool.

24 Fit the timing belt around the pump sprocket, and tension the timing belt as described in Section 7.

Coolant pump sprocket

25 The coolant pump sprocket is integral with the pump, and cannot be removed. Coolant pump removal is described in Chapter 3.

Tensioner pulley

Removal

26 Remove the timing belt as described in Section 7.

27 Remove the tensioner pulley retaining bolt, and slide the pulley off its mounting stud.

28 Clean the tensioner pulley, but do not use any strong solvent which may enter the pulley bearings. Check that the pulley rotates freely, with no sign of stiffness or free play. Renew the pulley if there is any doubt about its condition, or if there are any obvious signs of wear or damage.

29 Examine the pulley mounting stud for signs of damage and if necessary, renew it.

Refitting

30 Refit the tensioner pulley to its mounting stud, and fit the retaining bolt.

31 Refit the timing belt as described in Section 7.

Idler pulley

Removal

32 Remove the timing belt as described in Section 7.

33 Undo the retaining bolt/nut and withdraw the idler pulley from the engine.

34 Clean the idler pulley, but do not use any strong solvent which may enter the bearings. Check that the pulley rotates freely, with no sign of stiffness or free play. Renew the idler pulley if there is any doubt about its condition, or if there are any obvious signs of wear or damage.

Refitting

35 Locate the idler pulley on the engine, and fit the retaining bolt/nut. Tighten the bolt/nut to the specified torque.

36 Refit the timing belt as described in Section 7.

9 Camshaft, rocker arms and hydraulic tappets – removal, inspection and refitting

Removal

1 Remove the cylinder head cover as described in Section 4.

2 Remove the camshaft sprocket as described in Section 8.

1.4 litre engines

3 Refit the right-hand engine mounting, but only tighten the bolts moderately; this will keep the engine supported during the camshaft removal.

4 Undo the bolts and remove the vacuum pump. Recover the pump O-ring seals **(see illustration)**.

5 Disconnect the wiring plug, unscrew the retaining bolt, and remove the camshaft position sensor from the cylinder head.

6 Working in a spiral pattern, progressively and evenly unscrew the camshaft upper bearing housing bolts **(see illustration)**. Carefully lift the housing away.

7 Note the orientation of the camshaft, then lift it upwards from the housing and slide off and discard the oil seal.

8 To remove the rocker arms and hydraulic tappets, undo the 13 bolts and remove the lower half of the camshaft bearing housing.

9 Obtain eight small, clean plastic containers, and number them 1 to 8; alternatively, divide a larger container into eight compartments.

10 Lift out each rocker arm. Place the rocker arms in their respective positions in the box or containers **(see illustration)**.

11 A compartmentalised container filled with engine oil is now required to retain the hydraulic tappets while they are removed from the cylinder head. Withdraw each hydraulic follower and place it in the container, keeping them each identified for correct refitting. The tappets must be totally submerged in the oil to prevent air entering them.

12 Recover the 5 O-ring seals between the housing and the cylinder head.

2.0 litre engines

13 Slacken the retaining clamps and disconnect the air intake hose from the left-hand end of the cylinder head. On the DW10ATED engine, remove the intercooler air duct from the left-hand end of the cylinder head.

14 Refit the right-hand engine mounting, but only tighten the bolts moderately; this will keep the engine supported during the camshaft removal.

9.4 Undo the vacuum pump bolts (arrowed)

9.10 Remove the rocker arms

15 Disconnect the vacuum pipe from the brake vacuum pump on the left-hand end of the cylinder head.

16 Remove the vacuum pump from the cylinder head with reference to Chapter 9.

17 Working in a spiral pattern from the outside-in, progressively loosen the camshaft bearing cap housing bolts until they can be removed.

18 Withdraw the bearing cap housing from the cylinder head. The housing is likely to be initially tight to release as it is located by two dowels on the forward-facing side of the cylinder head. If necessary, very carefully prise up the housing using a screwdriver inserted in the slotted lug adjacent to each dowel location. Once the bearing housing is free, lift it squarely from the cylinder head **(see illustration)**. The camshaft will rise up slightly under the pressure of the valve springs – be

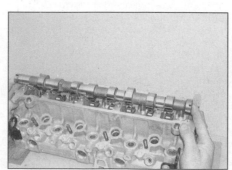

9.19 . . . then lift out the camshaft

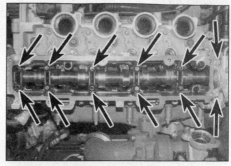

9.6 Upper camshaft bearing housing bolts (arrowed)

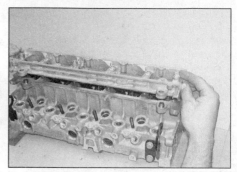

9.18 Remove the camshaft bearing housing from the cylinder head . . .

careful it doesn't tilt and jam in the cylinder head or bearing housing section.

19 Carefully lift the camshaft from its location and remove the oil seal **(see illustration)**. Discard the seal, a new one should be used on refitting.

20 Obtain eight small, clean plastic containers, and number them 1 to 8; alternatively, divide a larger container into eight compartments.

21 Lift out each rocker arm and release it from the spring clip on the tappet. Place the rocker arms in their respective positions in the box or containers **(see illustration)**.

22 A compartmentalised container filled with engine oil is now required to retain the hydraulic tappets while they are removed from the cylinder head. Using a rubber sucker, withdraw each hydraulic follower and place it in the container, keeping them each identified

9.21 Lift out the rocker arms . . .

9.22a ... followed by the hydraulic tappets ...

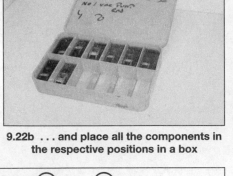

9.22b ... and place all the components in the respective positions in a box

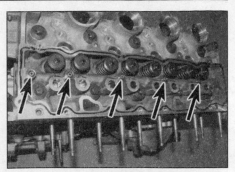

9.33 Apply a bead of sealant, and fit the new O-rings (arrowed)

9.34 Insert guide pins/rods into the guide holes (A), fit the housing and tighten the bolts in sequence

for correct refitting (see illustrations). The tappets must be totally submerged in the oil to prevent air entering them.

Inspection

23 Inspect the cam lobes and the camshaft bearing journals for scoring or other visible evidence of wear. Once the surface hardening of the cam lobes has been eroded, wear will occur at an accelerated rate. Note: If these symptoms are visible on the tips of the camshaft lobes, check the corresponding rocker arm, as it will probably be worn as well.
24 Examine the condition of the bearing surfaces in the cylinder head and camshaft bearing housing. If wear is evident, the cylinder head and bearing housing will both have to be

9.37 Lay the camshaft in position, and apply a bead of sealant to the housing mating face

renewed, as they are a matched assembly.
25 Inspect the rocker arms and tappets for scuffing, cracking or other damage and renew any components as necessary. Also check the condition of the tappet bores in the cylinder head. As with the camshafts, any wear in this area will necessitate cylinder head renewal.

Refitting

26 Thoroughly clean the sealant from the mating surfaces of the cylinder head and camshaft bearing housing. Use a suitable liquid gasket dissolving agent (available from Peugeot dealers) together with a soft putty knife; do not use a metal scraper or the faces will be damaged. As there is no conventional gasket used, the cleanliness of the mating faces is of the utmost importance.
27 Clean off any oil, dirt or grease from both components and dry with a clean lint-free cloth. Ensure that all the oilways are completely clean.
28 On 2.0 litre engines, to prevent any possibility of the valves contacting the pistons as the camshaft is refitted, remove the locking pin/drill from the flywheel/driveplate/crankshaft sprocket and turn the crankshaft a quarter turn in the opposite direction to normal rotation (ie, anti-clockwise), to position all the pistons at mid-stroke. On 1.4 litre engines, with the timing marks aligned as described in Section 3, the pistons are already positioned halfway down the cylinder bores.
29 Liberally lubricate the hydraulic tappet

bores in the cylinder head with clean engine oil.
30 Insert the hydraulic tappets into their original bores in the cylinder head unless they have been renewed.
31 Lubricate the rocker arms and place them over their respective tappets and valve stems. On 2.0 litre engines, ensure that the ends of the rocker arms engage with the spring clips on the tappets.
32 On 2.0 litre engines, lubricate the camshaft bearing journals in the cylinder head sparingly with oil, taking care not to allow the oil to spill over onto the camshaft bearing housing contact areas.

1.4 litre engines

33 Sparingly apply a bead of silicone sealant to the mating face of the cylinder head-to-camshaft lower bearing housing, and position the 5 new O-ring seals (see illustration).
34 Insert two 12 mm rods or drill bits into the locating holes in the cylinder head to guide the bearing housing into position. Suitable guide rods, No 194-N, are available from Peugeot dealers. Refit the lower bearing housing over the tools, insert the bolts and finger-tighten them in order (see illustration).
35 Remove the guide pins/rods and tighten the housing bolts in the sequence shown previously to the specified torque.
36 Lubricate the camshaft bearing journals with clean engine oil, and lay the camshaft in position.
37 Sparingly apply a bead of silicone sealant to the mating face of the camshaft lower bearing housing (see illustration).
38 Insert two 12 mm rods or drill bits into the locating holes in the lower camshaft bearing housing to guide the upper housing into position. Suitable guide rods, No 194-N, are available from Peugeot dealers.
39 Lower the upper housing over the guide pins/rods, and finger-tighten the bolts gradually and evenly, in sequence until the housing makes firm contact with the lower housing (see illustration).
40 Remove the guides pins/rods and tighten the housing to the specified torque in the same sequence.
41 Fit a new camshaft oil seal as described in Section 14.

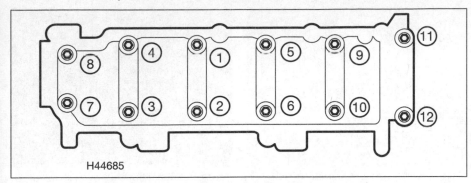

9.39 Upper camshaft housing bolts tightening sequence

9.43 When fitting a used sensor, the gap between the sensor end and the sensor ring web should be 1.2 mm

42 Ensure the key is fitted to the camshaft, then refit the camshaft sprocket to the camshaft and tighten the bolt to the specified torque.

43 Refit the camshaft position sensor to the camshaft housing, and position the sensor so that the gap between the sprocket and the sensor end is 1.2 mm for a used sensor. If fitting a new sensor, the small tip of the sensor must be just touching one of the three webs of the signal ring **(see illustration)**. Tighten the bolt to the specified torque.

44 Turn the camshaft sprocket the position where the timing tool can be inserted, then refit the timing belt as described in Section 7.

45 The remainder of refitting is a reversal of removal.

2.0 litre engines

46 Lay the camshaft in the cylinder head. On early engines position the camshaft so that the engine assembly/valve timing slot in the sprocket hub is approximately aligned with the timing hole in the cylinder head.

47 Ensure that the mating faces of the cylinder head and camshaft bearing housing are clean and free of any oil or grease.

48 Sparingly apply a bead of silicone sealant to the mating face of the camshaft bearing housing, taking care not to allow the product to contaminate the camshaft bearing journal areas **(see illustration)**.

49 Locate the bearing housing over the camshaft and into position on the cylinder head.

50 Insert all the bearing housing retaining bolts and *progressively* tighten them to the specified torque, in sequence **(see illustration)**.

51 Fit a new camshaft oil seal as described in Section 14.

52 Refit the camshaft hub and/or sprocket as described in Section 8.

53 Rotate the crankshaft clockwise until the timing rod can be re-inserted through the hole in the block and into the flywheel/driveplate (see Section 3).

54 Refit the timing belt as described in Section 7.

55 The remainder of refitting is a reversal of removal.

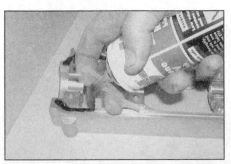

9.48 Apply a bead of silicone sealant to the mating face of the camshaft bearing housing

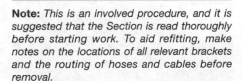

10 Cylinder head – removal and refitting

Note: *This is an involved procedure, and it is suggested that the Section is read thoroughly before starting work. To aid refitting, make notes on the locations of all relevant brackets and the routing of hoses and cables before removal.*

Removal

1 Apply the handbrake, then jack up the front of the vehicle and support it on axle stands (see *Jacking and vehicle support*). Remove the front right-hand roadwheel, the engine undershield, and the front wheel arch liner. The undershield is secured by several screws, and the wheel arch liner is secured by several plastic expanding rivets. Push the centre pins in a little, then prise the rivet from place.

2 Remove the battery (see Chapter 5A).

3 Drain the cooling system as described in Chapter 1B. For improved general access, remove the bonnet as described in Chapter 11.

1.4 litre engines

4 Remove the cylinder head cover as described in Section 4.

5 Remove the timing belt as described in Section 7.

6 Disconnect the exhaust front pipe from the manifold, as described in Chapter 4B. **Note:** *Do not allow any strain to be placed on the flexible section of the exhaust pipe, as damage will result.*

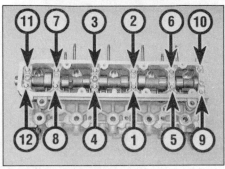

9.50 Camshaft bearing housing bolt tightening sequence

7 Remove the glow plugs as described in Chapter 5C.

8 Undo the three bolts and remove the auxiliary drivebelt tensioner from the front of the engine **(see illustration)**.

9 Remove the catalytic converter as described in Section 19 of Chapter 4B.

10 Remove the alternator (see Chapter 5A) and mounting bracket.

11 Undo the union bolts and remove the oil feed pipe from the engine block and the turbocharger. Recover the unions sealing washers.

12 Slacken the retaining clamp and disconnect the turbocharger oil return hose from the engine block.

13 Slacken and remove the high-pressure fuel pump rear support bracket bolts and front support bracket upper bolt **(see illustrations)**.

14 Remove the injectors as described in Chapter 4B.

10.8 Auxiliary drivebelt tensioner bolts (arrowed)

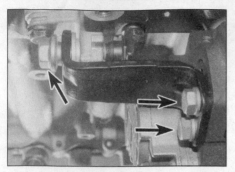

10.13a Fuel pump rear support bracket bolts (arrowed) . . .

10.13b . . . and front support bracket upper bolt

10.15 Coolant housing bolts (arrowed)

15 Undo the coolant outlet housing (left-hand end of the cylinder head) retaining bolts, slacken the two bolts securing the housing support bracket to the top of the transmission bellhousing, and move the outlet housing away from the cylinder head a little **(see illustration)**. There is no need to disconnect the hoses.

16 Disconnect the wiring plug, then undo the bolt and remove the camshaft position sensor from the cylinder head.

17 Undo the 13 bolts and remove the camshaft bearing housing from the cylinder head, complete with camshaft. Recover the 5 small O-ring seals between the housing and the cylinder head.

18 Obtain eight small, clean plastic containers, and number them 1 to 8; alternatively, divide a larger container into eight compartments.

19 Lift out each rocker arm. Place the rocker arms in their respective positions in the box or containers **(see illustration 9.10)**.

20 A compartmentalised container filled with engine oil is now required to retain the hydraulic tappets while they are removed from the cylinder head. Withdraw each hydraulic follower and place it in the container, keeping them each identified for correct refitting. The tappets must be totally submerged in the oil to prevent air entering them.

21 Working in the reverse of the tightening sequence **(see illustration 10.54)** undo the cylinder head bolts.

2.0 litre engines

22 Remove the air cleaner assembly, airflow meter and inlet air ducts, fuel injectors, common fuel rail and turbocharger as described in Chapter 4B.

23 Remove the EGR valve with reference to Chapter 4C.

24 Remove the timing belt as described in Section 7.

25 Temporarily refit the right-hand engine mounting to support the engine whilst the cylinder head is removed.

26 Note their fitted positions and routing, then disconnect all coolant and vacuum hoses from the cylinder head.

27 Unscrew the bolts securing the oil level dipstick tube to the cylinder head.

28 Unscrew the nuts on the two studs securing the coolant outlet manifold to the left-hand end of the cylinder head, then unscrew and remove the studs. Use a stud extractor or alternatively tighten two nuts together on the stud before unscrewing it. Note the location of brackets on the studs for correct refitting **(see illustrations)**.

29 Without disconnecting the hoses, unscrew the mounting bolts and move the coolant outlet manifold away from the left-hand end of the cylinder head **(see illustrations)**. If necessary, tie it to one side. Recover the seal. **Note:** *At the time of writing, the coolant outlet manifold seal was not available separately. If damaged, the complete outlet manifold must be renewed. Check with a Peugeot dealer.*

30 Disconnect the wiring from the camshaft position sensor then undo the screw and remove the sensor **(see illustration)**. Check that all relevant wiring is disconnected from the sensors on the cylinder head, then move the wiring harness to one side.

31 Remove the cylinder head cover as described in Section 4.

10.28a Unscrew the nuts . . .

10.28b . . . then remove the studs from the coolant outlet manifold

10.29a Unscrew the bolts . . .

10.29b . . . and move the coolant outlet manifold away from the cylinder head

10.30 Remove the camshaft position sensor

32 Progressively slacken the cylinder head bolts, in the reverse order to that for tightening **(see illustration 10.62)**. A Torx socket will be required for this.

33 When all the bolts are loose, unscrew them fully and remove them from the cylinder head.

All engines

34 Release the cylinder head from the cylinder block and location dowels by rocking it. The Peugeot tool for doing this consists simply of two metal rods with 90-degree angled ends **(see illustration)**. Do not prise between the mating faces of the cylinder head and block, as this may damage the gasket faces.

35 Lift the cylinder head from the block, and recover the gasket.

36 If necessary, remove the manifolds (if not already done so) with reference to Chapter 4B.

Preparation for refitting

37 The mating faces of the cylinder head and cylinder block must be perfectly clean before refitting the head. Peugeot recommend the use of a scouring agent for this purpose, but acceptable results can be achieved by using a hard plastic or wood scraper to remove all traces of gasket and carbon. The same method can be used to clean the piston crowns. Take particular care to avoid scoring or gouging the cylinder head/cylinder block mating surfaces during the cleaning operations, as aluminium alloy is easily damaged. Make sure that the carbon is not allowed to enter the oil and water passages – this is particularly important for the lubrication system, as carbon could block the oil supply to the engine's components. Using adhesive tape and paper, seal the water, oil and bolt holes in the cylinder block. To prevent carbon entering the gap between the pistons and bores, smear a little grease in the gap. After cleaning each piston, use a small brush to remove all traces of grease and carbon from the gap, then wipe away the remainder with a clean rag.

38 Check the mating surfaces of the cylinder block and the cylinder head for nicks, deep scratches and other damage. If slight, they may be removed carefully with a file, but if excessive, machining may be the only

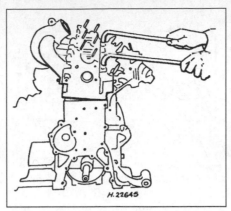

10.34 Free the cylinder head using angled rods

alternative to renewal. If warpage of the cylinder head gasket surface is suspected, use a straight-edge to check it for distortion. Refer to Part D of this Chapter if necessary.

39 Thoroughly clean the threads of the cylinder head bolt holes in the cylinder block. Ensure that the bolts run freely in their threads, and that all traces of oil and water are removed from each bolt hole.

Gasket selection

40 Remove the crankshaft timing pin, then turn the crankshaft until pistons 1 and 4 are at TDC (Top Dead Centre). Position a dial test indicator (dial gauge) on the cylinder block adjacent to the rear of No 1 piston, and zero it on the block face. Transfer the probe to the crown of No 1 piston (10.0 mm in from the rear edge), then slowly turn the crankshaft back-and-forth past TDC, noting the highest reading on the indicator. Record this reading as protrusion A.

41 Repeat the check described in para-graph 40, this time 10.0 mm in from the front edge of the No 1 piston crown. Record this reading as protrusion B.

42 Add protrusion A to protrusion B, then divide the result by 2 to obtain an average reading for piston No 1.

43 Repeat the procedure described in paragraphs 40 to 42 on piston 4, then turn the crankshaft through 180° and carry out the procedure on the piston Nos 2 and 3 **(see**

10.43 Measure the piston protrusion using a DTI gauge

illustration). Check that there is a maximum difference of 0.07 mm protrusion between any two pistons.

44 If a dial test indicator is not available, piston protrusion may be measured using a straight-edge and feeler blades or Vernier calipers. However, this is much less accurate, and cannot therefore be recommended.

45 Note the greatest piston protrusion measurement, and use this to determine the correct cylinder head gasket from the following table. The series of notches/holes on the side of the gasket are used for thickness identification **(see illustrations)**.

1.4 litre engines

Piston protrusion	Gasket identification
0.618 to 0.725 mm	*2 notches*
0.726 to 0.775 mm	*3 notches*
0.776 to 0.825 mm	*1 notch*
0.826 to 0.875 mm	*4 notches*
0.876 to 0.983 mm	*5 notches*

2.0 litre engines

Piston protrusion	Gasket identification
0.470 to 0.604 mm	*1 notch*
0.605 to 0.654 mm	*2 notches*
0.655 to 0.704 mm	*3 notches*
0.705 to 0.754 mm	*4 notches*
0.755 to 0.830 mm	*5 notches*

Head bolt examination

46 Carefully examine the cylinder head bolts for signs of damage to the threads or head, and for any sign of corrosion. If the bolts are in a satisfactory condition, measure the length of each bolt from the underside of the head, to the end of the shank. The bolts may be re-used

10.45a Cylinder head gasket thickness identification notches (arrowed) (1.4 litre engine) . . .

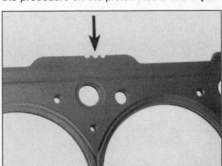

10.45b . . . and 2.0 litre engine (arrowed)

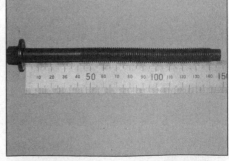

10.46 Measure the length of from under the bolt head to its end (1.4 litre engine)

10.49 Ensure the gasket fits correctly over the locating dowels

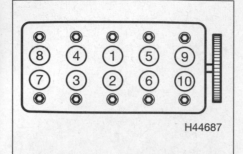

10.54 Cylinder head bolt tightening sequence (1.4 litre engine)

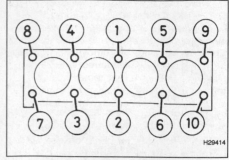

10.62 Cylinder head bolt tightening sequence (2.0 litre engine)

providing that the measured length does not exceed 149.0 mm on the 1.4 litre engine, and 133.3 mm on the 2.0 litre engine **(see illustration)**. *Note: Considering the stress to which the cylinder head bolts are subjected, it is highly recommended that they are all renewed, regardless of their apparent condition.*

Refitting

47 Turn the crankshaft and position Nos 1 and 4 pistons at TDC, then turn the crankshaft a quarter turn (90°) anti-clockwise.
48 Thoroughly clean the surfaces of the cylinder head and block.
49 Make sure that the locating dowels are in place, then fit the correct gasket the right way round on the cylinder block **(see illustration)**.

1.4 litre engines

50 If necessary refit the exhaust manifold to the cylinder head as described in Chapter 4B.
51 Carefully lower the cylinder head onto the gasket and block, making sure that it locates correctly onto the dowels.
52 Apply a smear of grease to the threads, and to the underside of the heads, of the cylinder head bolts. Peugeot recommend the use of Molykote G Rapid Plus (available from your Peugeot dealer); in the absence of the specified grease, any good-quality high melting-point grease may be used.
53 Carefully insert the cylinder head bolts into their holes (*do not drop them in*) and initially finger-tighten them.
54 Working progressively and in sequence, tighten the cylinder head bolts to their Stage 1 torque setting, using a torque wrench and suitable socket **(see illustration)**.
55 Once all the bolts have been tightened to their Stage 1 torque setting, working again in the specified sequence, tighten each bolt to the specified Stage 2 setting. Finally, angle-tighten the bolts through the specified Stage 3 angle. It is recommended that an angle-measuring gauge is used during this stage of tightening, to ensure accuracy. **Note:** *Retightening of the cylinder head bolts after running the engine is not required.*
56 Refit the hydraulic tappets, rocker arms, and camshaft housing (complete with camshaft) as described in Section 9.
57 Refit the timing belt as described in Section 7.

2.0 litre engines

58 If necessary, refit the inlet and exhaust manifolds with reference to Chapter 4B.
59 Check that the camshaft TDC timing pin is in position, then carefully lower the cylinder head onto the gasket and block, making sure that it locates correctly onto the dowels.
60 Apply a smear of grease to the threads, and to the underside of the heads, of the cylinder head bolts. Peugeot recommend the use of Molykote G Rapid Plus (available from your Peugeot dealer); in the absence of the specified grease, any good-quality high-melting-point grease may be used.
61 Carefully insert the cylinder head bolts into their holes (*do not drop them in*) and initially finger-tighten them.
62 Working progressively and in the sequence shown, tighten the cylinder head bolts to their Stage 1 torque setting, using a torque wrench and suitable socket **(see illustration)**.
63 Once all the bolts have been tightened to their Stage 1 torque setting, working again in the specified sequence, tighten each bolt to the specified Stage 2 setting. Finally, angle-tighten the bolts through the specified Stage 3 angle. It is recommended that an angle-measuring gauge is used during this stage of tightening, to ensure accuracy. **Note:** *Retightening of the cylinder head bolts after running the engine is not required.*
64 Refit the cylinder head cover with reference to Section 4.
65 Refit the timing belt as described in Section 7.

11.2 Undo the engine undershield screws

All models

66 The remainder of refitting is a reversal of removal, noting the following points.
 a) Use a new seal when refitting the coolant outlet housing.
 b) When refitting a cylinder head, it is good practice to renew the thermostat.
 c) Refit the camshaft position sensor and set the air gap with reference to Chapter 4B.
 d) Tighten all fasteners to the specified torque where given.
 e) Refill the cooling system as described in Chapter 1B.
 f) The engine may run erratically for the first few miles, until the engine management ECM relearns its stored values.

11 Sump – removal and refitting

Removal

1 Drain the engine oil, then clean and refit the engine oil drain plug, tightening it securely. If the engine is nearing its service interval when the oil and filter are due for renewal, it is recommended that the filter is also removed, and a new one fitted. After reassembly, the engine can then be refilled with fresh oil. Refer to Chapter 1B for further information.
2 Apply the handbrake, then jack up the front of the vehicle and support it on axle stands (see *Jacking and vehicle support*). Undo the screws and remove the engine undershield **(see illustration)**.
3 On 1.4 litre models, to improve access, remove the exhaust front pipe as described in Chapter 4B.
4 On 2.0 litre models with air conditioning, where the compressor is mounted onto the side of the sump, remove the drivebelt as described in Chapter 1B. Unbolt the compressor, and position it clear of the sump. Support the weight of the compressor by tying it to the vehicle, to prevent any excess strain being placed on the compressor lines. *Do not* disconnect the refrigerant lines from the compressor (refer to the warnings given in Chapter 3).
5 Where necessary, disconnect the wiring

connector from the oil temperature sender unit, which is screwed into the sump.

6 Progressively slacken and remove all the sump retaining bolts/nuts. Since the sump bolts vary in length, remove each bolt in turn, and store it in its correct fitted order by pushing it through a clearly-marked cardboard template. This will avoid the possibility of installing the bolts in the wrong locations on refitting.

7 Try to break the joint by striking the sump with the palm of your hand, then lower and withdraw the sump from under the car. If the sump is stuck (which is quite likely) use a putty knife, or similar, carefully inserted between the sump and block. Ease the knife along the joint until the sump is released. While the sump is removed, take the opportunity to check the oil pump pick-up/strainer for signs of clogging or splitting. If necessary, remove the pump as described in Section 12, and clean or renew the strainer. Note that on later 2.0 litre models, the oil dipstick tube extends to the bottom of the sump in order to allow the oil to sucked out of the tube using special equipment **(see illustration)**.

Refitting

8 Clean all traces of sealant/gasket from the mating surfaces of the cylinder block/crankcase and sump, then use a clean rag to wipe out the sump and the engine's interior.

9 On engines where the sump was fitted without a gasket, ensure that the sump mating surfaces are clean and dry, then apply a thin coating of suitable sealant to the sump or crankcase mating surface **(see illustration)**.

10 Offer up the sump to the cylinder block/crankcase. Refit its retaining bolts/nuts, ensuring that each bolt is screwed into its original location. Tighten the bolts evenly and progressively to the specified torque setting. On 2.0 litre engines, note the concealed bolts at one end of the sump **(see illustrations)**.

11 Where necessary, align the air conditioning compressor with its mountings on the sump, and insert the retaining bolts. Securely tighten the compressor retaining bolts, then refit the drivebelt as described in Chapter 1B.

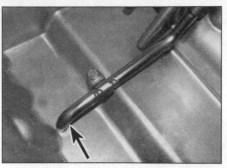

11.7 On later 2.0 litre models the dipstick tube extends to the bottom of the sump

11.10a Refit the sump and tighten the bolts (1.4 litre engine)

12 Reconnect the wiring connector to the oil temperature sensor (where fitted).

13 Lower the vehicle to the ground, then refill the engine with oil as described in Chapter 1B.

12 Oil pump – removal, inspection and refitting

Removal

1 Remove the sump as described in Section 11.

1.4 litre engines

2 Remove the crankshaft sprocket as described in Section 8. Recover the locating key from the crankshaft.

3 Disconnect the wiring plug, undo the bolts

11.9 Apply a bead of sealant to the sump of crankcase mating surface

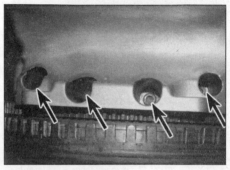

11.10b Concealed bolts (arrowed) at one end of the sump (2.0 litre engine)

and remove the crankshaft position sensor, located on the right-hand end of the cylinder block.

4 Undo the three Allen bolts and remove the oil pump pick-up tube from the pump/block, complete with the dipstick guide tube **(see illustration)**. Discard the oil seal, a new one must be fitted.

5 Undo the 8 bolts, and remove the oil pump **(see illustration)**.

2.0 litre engines

6 Unscrew and remove the bolts securing the oil pump to the base of the cylinder block/crankcase.

7 Disengage the pump sprocket from the chain, and remove the oil pump **(see illustration)**. Where necessary, also remove the spacer plate which is fitted behind the oil pump.

12.4 Undo the three Allen bolts (arrowed) and remove the oil pick-up tube

12.5 Undo the 8 bolts (arrowed) and remove the oil pump

12.7 Disengage the chain and remove the oil pump

12.8 Undo the Torx screws and remove the pump cover

12.9a Remove the circlip . . .

12.9b . . . cap . . .

12.9c . . . spring . . .

12.9d . . . and piston

Inspection

1.4 litre engine

8 Undo and remove the Torx screws securing the cover to the oil pump **(see illustration)**. Examine the pump rotors and body for signs of wear and damage. If worn, the complete pump must be renewed.

9 Remove the circlip, and extract the cap, valve piston and spring, noting which way around they are fitted **(see illustrations)**. The condition of the relief valve spring can only be measured by comparing it with a new one; if there is any doubt about its condition, it should also be renewed.

10 Refit the relief valve piston and spring, then secure them in place with the circlip.

11 Refit the cover to the oil pump, and tighten the Torx screws securely.

2.0 litre engines

12 Examine the oil pump sprocket for signs of damage and wear, such as chipped or missing teeth. If the sprocket is worn, the pump assembly must be renewed, since the sprocket is not available separately. It is also recommended that the chain and drive sprocket, fitted to the crankshaft, be renewed at the same time. To renew the chain and drive sprocket, first remove the crankshaft timing belt sprocket, then unbolt the oil seal carrier from the cylinder block. The sprocket, spacer (where fitted) and chain can then be slid off the end of the crankshaft.

13 Unscrew and remove the bolts (along with the baffle plate, where fitted) securing the strainer cover to the pump body. Lift off the strainer cover, and take off the relief valve

piston and spring, noting which way round they are fitted **(see illustrations)**.

14 Examine the pump rotors and body for signs of wear ridges or scoring. If worn, the complete pump assembly must be renewed.

15 Examine the relief valve piston for signs of wear or damage, and renew if necessary. The condition of the relief valve spring can only be measured by comparing it with a new one; if there is any doubt about its condition, it should also be renewed. Both the piston and spring are available individually.

16 Thoroughly clean the oil pump strainer with a suitable solvent, and check it for signs of clogging or splitting. If the strainer is damaged, the strainer and cover assembly must be renewed.

17 Locate the relief valve spring and piston in the strainer cover. Refit the cover to the pump body, aligning the relief valve piston with its bore in the pump. Refit the baffle plate (where fitted) and the cover retaining bolts, and tighten them securely.

18 Prime the pump by filling it with clean engine oil before refitting.

Refitting

1.4 litre engines

19 Remove all traces of sealant, and thoroughly clean the mating surfaces of the oil pump and cylinder block.

20 Apply a 4 mm wide bead of silicone sealant to the mating face of the cylinder block **(see illustration)**. Ensure that no sealant enters any of the holes in the block.

12.13a Remove the oil pump cover bolts . . .

12.13b . . . then lift off the cover and remove the spring . . .

12.13c . . . and relief valve piston, noting which way round it is fitted

21 With a new oil seal fitted, refit the oil pump over the end of the crankshaft, aligning the flats in the pump drive gear with the flats machined in the crankshaft **(see illustrations)**. Note that new oil pumps are supplied with the oil seal already fitted, and a seal protector sleeve. The sleeve fits over the end of the crankshaft to protect the seal as the pump is fitted.

22 Install the oil pump bolts and tighten them to the specified torque.

23 Refit the oil pick-up tube to the pump/cylinder block using a new O-ring seal. Ensure the oil dipstick guide tube is correctly refitted.

24 Refit the Woodruff key to the crankshaft, and slide the crankshaft sprocket into place.

25 The remainder of refitting is a reversal of removal.

2.0 litre engines

26 Offer up the spacer plate (where fitted), then engage the pump sprocket with its drive chain, and seat the pump on the base of the cylinder block/crankcase. Refit the pump retaining bolts, and tighten them to the specified torque setting.

27 Refit the sump as described in Section 11.

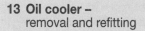

13 Oil cooler –
removal and refitting

Removal

1 Apply the handbrake, then jack up the front of the vehicle and support it on axle stands (see *Jacking and vehicle support*). Undo the screws and remove the engine undershield.

1.4 litre engine

2 The oil cooler is fitted to the front of the oil filter housing. Drain the coolant as described in Chapter 1B.

3 Drain the engine oil as described in Chapter 1B, or be prepared for fluid spillage.

4 Undo the bolts and remove the oil cooler. Recover the O-ring seals **(see illustrations)**.

2.0 litre engines

5 Drain the cooling system as described in Chapter 1B. Alternatively, clamp the oil cooler

12.20 Apply a bead of sealant to the cylinder block mating surface

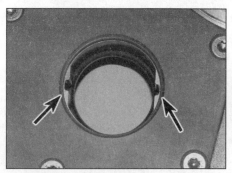

12.21b ... align the pump gear flats (arrowed) ...

coolant hoses directly above the cooler, and be prepared for some coolant loss as the hoses are disconnected.

6 Position a suitable container beneath the oil filter on the front of the engine. Unscrew the filter using an oil filter removal tool if necessary, and drain the oil into the container. If the oil filter is damaged or distorted during removal, it must be renewed. Given the low cost of a new oil filter relative to the cost of repairing the damage which could result if a re-used filter leaks, it is probably a good idea to renew the filter in any case.

7 Release the hose clips, and disconnect the coolant hoses from the oil cooler.

8 Unscrew the oil cooler/oil filter mounting bolt/stud from the cylinder block, and withdraw the cooler. Note the locating notch in the cooler flange, which fits over the lug on the cylinder block **(see illustration)**. Discard

12.21a Fit a new oil seal ...

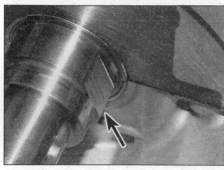

12.21c ... with those of the crankshaft (arrowed)

the oil cooler sealing ring; a new one must be used on refitting.

Refitting

1.4 litre engine

9 Fit new O-ring seals into the recesses in the oil filter housing, and refit the cooler. Tighten the bolts securely.

2.0 litre engines

10 Fit a new sealing ring to the recess in the rear of the cooler, then offer the cooler to the cylinder block.

11 Ensure that the locating notch in the cooler flange is correctly engaged with the lug on the cylinder block. Apply locking fluid to the threads of the mounting bolt/stud, then insert it through the oil cooler and tighten securely.

12 Fit the oil filter, then lower the vehicle to the ground.

13.4a Undo the bolts (arrowed), remove the oil cooler ...

13.4b ... and recover the O-ring seals

13.8 Oil cooler/oil filter mounting bolt (A) and locating notch (B)

14.3 Drill a hole then use a self-tapping screw and pliers to extract the oil seal

All engines

13 Refill or top-up the cooling system and engine oil level as described in Chapter 1B or *Weekly Checks* (as applicable). Start the engine, and check the oil cooler for signs of leakage.

14 Oil seals –
renewal

Crankshaft right-hand oil seal

1 Remove the crankshaft sprocket as described in Section 8.
2 Measure and note the fitted depth of the oil seal.
3 Pull the oil seal from the housing using a hooked instrument. Alternatively, drill a small hole in the oil seal, and use a self-tapping screw and a pair of pliers to remove it (see **illustration**).
4 Clean the oil seal housing and the crankshaft sealing surface.
5 On 2.0 litre engines, dip the new oil seal in clean engine oil, and press it into the housing (open end first) to the previously-noted depth, using a suitable tube or socket.

 HAYNES HiNT *A piece of thin plastic or tape wound around the front of the crankshaft is useful to prevent damage to the oil seal as it is fitted.*

14.21 Use a tube or socket to press the new seal into place

6 On 1.4 litre engines, the seal has a Teflon lip and must not be oiled or marked. The new seal should be supplied with a protector sleeve. which fits over the end of the crankshaft to prevent any damage to the seal lip. With the sleeve in place, press the seal (open end first) into the pump to the previously noted depth, using a suitable tube or socket.
7 Where applicable, remove the plastic or tape from the end of the crankshaft.
8 Refit the timing belt crankshaft sprocket as described in Section 8.

Crankshaft left-hand oil seal

9 Remove the flywheel/driveplate, as described in Section 16.
10 Measure and note the fitted depth of the oil seal.
11 Pull the oil seal from the housing using a hooked instrument. Alternatively, drill a small hole in the oil seal, and use a self-tapping screw and a pair of pliers to remove it (see **illustration 14.3**).
12 Clean the oil seal housing and the crankshaft sealing surface.
13 On 2.0 litre engines, dip the new oil seal in clean engine oil, and press it into the housing (open end first) to the previously-noted depth, using a suitable tube or socket. A piece of thin plastic or tape wound around the end of the crankshaft is useful to prevent damage to the oil seal as it is fitted.
14 On 1.4 litre engines, the seal has a Teflon lip and must not be oiled or marked. The new seal should be supplied with a protector sleeve, which fits over the end of the crankshaft to prevent any damage to the seal

14.14 The new oil seal comes with a protective sleeve (arrowed) which fits over the end of the crankshaft

14.22 The new oil seal comes with a protective sleeve (arrowed) which fits over the end of the camshaft

14.20 Locate the new seal in the cylinder head

lip (see illustration). With the sleeve in place, press the seal (open end first) into the housing to the previously noted depth, using a suitable tube or socket.
15 Where applicable, remove the plastic or tape from the end of the crankshaft.
16 Refit the flywheel/driveplate, as described in Section 16.

Camshaft right-hand oil seal

17 Remove the camshaft sprocket (and hub where applicable) as described in Section 8. In principle there is no need to remove the timing belt completely, but remember that if the belt has been contaminated with oil, it must be renewed.
18 Pull the oil seal from the housing using a hooked instrument. Alternatively, drill a small hole in the oil seal and use a self-tapping screw and a pair of pliers to remove it (see illustration 14.3).
19 Clean the oil seal housing and the camshaft sealing surface.

2.0 litre engines

20 Smear the new oil seal with clean engine oil, then fit it over the end of the camshaft, open end first (see illustration). A piece of thin plastic or tape wound around the front of the camshaft is useful to prevent damage to the oil seal as it is fitted.
21 Press the seal into the housing until it is flush with the end face of the cylinder head. Use an M10 bolt (screwed into the end of the camshaft), washers and a suitable tube or socket that bears only on the outer edge of the seal to press it into position (see illustration).

1.4 litre engines

22 The seal has a Teflon lip and must not be oiled or marked. The new seal should be supplied with a protector sleeve. which fits over the end of the camshaft to prevent any damage to the seal lip (see illustration). With the sleeve in place, press the seal (open end first) into the housing to the previously noted depth, using a suitable tube or socket which bears only of the outer edge of the seal.

All engines

23 Refit the camshaft sprocket (and hub where applicable) as described in Section 8.
24 Where necessary, fit a new timing belt with reference to Section 7.

Camshaft left-hand oil seal

2.0 litre engines

25 No oil seal is fitted to the left-hand end of the camshaft. The sealing is provided by an O-ring fitted to the endplate flange. The O-ring can be renewed after unbolting the plate from the cylinder head.

15 Oil pressure switch and level sensor – removal and refitting

Removal

Oil pressure switch

1 The oil pressure switch is located at the front of the cylinder block, adjacent to the oil dipstick guide tube (1.4 litre engines) or above the oil filter mounting (2.0 litre engines). Note that on some models, access to the switch may be improved if the vehicle is jacked up and supported on axle stands, then undo the screws and remove the engine undershield so that the switch can be reached from underneath (see *Jacking and vehicle support*).
2 Remove the protective sleeve from the wiring plug (where applicable), then disconnect the wiring from the switch.
3 Unscrew the switch from the cylinder block, and recover the sealing washer **(see illustrations)**. Be prepared for oil spillage, and if the switch is to be left removed from the engine for any length of time, plug the hole in the cylinder block.

Oil level sensor

4 The oil level sensor is located at the rear of the cylinder block. Jack up the front of the vehicle and support it securely on axle stands (see *Jacking and vehicle support*). Undo the screws and remove the engine undershield.
5 Reach up between the driveshaft and the cylinder block and disconnect the sensor wiring plug **(see illustration)**.
6 Using an open-ended spanner, unscrew the sensor and withdraw it from position. On 2.0 litre engines, discard the sealing washer, a new one must be fitted.

Refitting

Oil pressure switch

7 Examine the sealing washer for any signs of damage or deterioration, and if necessary renew.
8 Refit the switch, complete with washer, and tighten it securely.
9 Refit the engine undershield, and lower the vehicle to the ground.

Oil level sensor

10 Smear a little silicone sealant on the threads and refit the sensor to the cylinder block, tightening it securely. On 2.0 litre models renew the sealing washer prior to refitting the sensor.
11 Reconnect the sensor wiring plug.

15.3a On 1.4 litre engines, the oil pressure switch is on the front face of the cylinder block

12 Refit the engine undershield, and lower the vehicle to the ground.

16 Flywheel/driveplate – removal, inspection and refitting

Flywheel removal

1 Remove the transmission as described in Chapter 7A, then remove the clutch assembly as described in Chapter 6.
2 Prevent the flywheel from turning by locking the ring gear teeth **(see illustration 5.2)**. Alternatively, bolt a strap between the flywheel and the cylinder block/crankcase. *Do not* attempt to lock the flywheel in position using the crankshaft pulley locking tool described in Section 3. On 1.4 litre engines, insert a 12 mm diameter rod or drill bit through the hole in the flywheel cover casting, and into a slot in the flywheel **(see illustration 5.3)**
3 Make alignment marks between the flywheel and crankshaft to aid refitment. Slacken and remove the flywheel retaining bolts, and remove the flywheel from the end of the crankshaft. Be careful not to drop it; it is heavy. If the flywheel locating dowel (where fitted) is a loose fit in the crankshaft end, remove it and store it with the flywheel for safe-keeping. Discard the flywheel bolts; new ones must be used on refitting.

Driveplate removal

4 Remove the transmission as described in

15.5 Oil level sensor (arrowed)

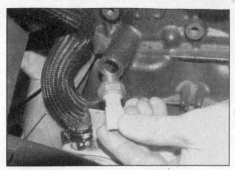

15.3b Oil pressure switch (2.0 litre engine)

Chapter 7B. Lock the driveplate as described in paragraph 2 of this Section. Mark the relationship between the torque converter plate and the driveplate, and slacken all the driveplate retaining bolts.
5 Remove the retaining bolts, along with the torque converter plate and the two shims (one fitted on each side of the torque converter plate). Note that the shims are of different thickness, the thicker one being on the outside of the torque converter plate. Discard the driveplate retaining bolts; new ones must be used on refitting.
6 Remove the driveplate from the end of the crankshaft. If the locating dowel is a loose fit in the crankshaft end, remove it and store it with the driveplate for safe-keeping.

Inspection

7 On models with manual transmission, examine the flywheel for scoring of the clutch face, and for wear or chipping of the ring gear teeth. If the clutch face is scored, the flywheel may be surface-ground, but renewal is preferable. Seek the advice of a Peugeot dealer or engine reconditioning specialist to see if machining is possible. If the ring gear is worn or damaged, the flywheel must be renewed, as it is not possible to renew the ring gear separately.
8 On models with automatic transmission, check the torque converter driveplate carefully for signs of distortion. Look for any hairline cracks around the bolt holes or radiating outwards from the centre, and inspect the ring gear teeth for signs of wear or chipping. If any sign of wear or damage is found, the driveplate must be renewed.

Flywheel refitting

9 Clean the mating surfaces of the flywheel and crankshaft. Remove any remaining locking compound from the threads of the crankshaft holes, using the correct size of tap, if available.

HAYNES HINT *If a suitable tap is not available, cut two slots along the threads of one of the old flywheel bolts, and use the bolt to remove the locking compound from the threads.*

16.10 If the new bolts are not supplied with their threads precoated, apply thread-locking compound to them . . .

10 If the new flywheel retaining bolts are not supplied with their threads already precoated, apply a suitable thread-locking compound to the threads of each bolt (see illustration).

DW10ATED with dual mass flywheel

11 The dual mass flywheel is designed to reduce harshness and vibration in the action of the engine, clutch and transmission. With this type of flywheel, two flywheel centralising tools are needed (0216-L – available from Peugeot dealers). These are screwed into two opposite flywheel bolt holes in the crankshaft. As the tools are screwed down, their conical shape centralises the flywheel with regard to the crankshaft.

12 With the flywheel centralised, fit the new bolts into the remaining flywheel holes, then lock the flywheel using the same method employed on dismantling, and tighten the bolts to the specified torque.

13 Remove the two centralising tools, fit the new bolts and tighten them to the specified torque.

All other engines

14 Ensure that the locating dowel is in position. Offer up the flywheel, locating it on the dowel (where fitted) and fit the new retaining bolts. Where no locating dowel is fitted, align the previously-made marks to ensure the flywheel is refitted in its original position.

15 Lock the flywheel using the method employed on dismantling, and tighten the retaining bolts to the specified torque (see illustration).

17.7 Undo the bolts (arrowed) and remove the engine mounting

16.15 . . . then refit the flywheel and tighten the bolts to the specified torque

All engines

16 Refit the clutch as described in Chapter 6. Remove the flywheel locking tool, and refit the transmission as described in Chapter 7A.

Driveplate refitting

17 Carry out the operations described above in paragraphs 9 and 10, substituting 'driveplate' for all references to the flywheel.

18 Locate the driveplate on its locating dowel.

19 Offer up the torque converter plate, with the thinner shim positioned behind the plate and the thicker shim on the outside, and align the marks made prior to removal.

20 Fit the new retaining bolts, then lock the driveplate using the method employed on dismantling. Tighten the retaining bolts to the specified torque wrench setting.

21 Remove the driveplate locking tool, and refit the transmission (see Chapter 7B).

---

17 Engine/transmission mountings –
inspection and renewal

Inspection

1 If improved access is required, firmly apply the handbrake, then jack up the front of the car and support it on axle stands (see *Jacking and vehicle support*). Undo the screws and remove the engine undershield.

2 Check the mounting rubbers to see if they

17.15a Undo the centre nut followed by the two mounting nuts (arrowed)

are cracked, hardened or separated from the metal at any point; renew the mounting if any such damage or deterioration is evident.

3 Check that all the mountings' fasteners are securely tightened; use a torque wrench to check if possible.

4 Using a large screwdriver or a crowbar, check for wear in each mounting by carefully levering against it to check for free play. Where this is not possible, enlist the aid of an assistant to move the engine/transmission back-and-forth, or from side-to-side, while you watch the mounting. While some free play is to be expected even from new components, excessive wear should be obvious. If excessive free play is found, check first that the fasteners are correctly secured, then renew any worn components as described below.

Renewal

Right-hand mounting

5 Release all the relevant hoses and wiring from their retaining clips. Place the hoses/wiring clear of the mounting so that the removal procedure is not hindered. Undo the screws and remove the engine undershield.

6 Place a jack beneath the engine, with a block of wood on the jack head. Raise the jack until it is supporting the weight of the engine.

7 Undo the bolts securing the engine mounting to the body and the support bracket (see illustration).

8 If required, undo the bolts/nuts securing the support bracket to the cylinder head/cylinder block.

9 Check all components carefully for signs of wear or damage, and renew as necessary.

10 Where removed, refit the support bracket to the cylinder head, and tighten the bolts securely.

11 Refit the mount to the body and support bracket, then tighten the bolts to the specified torque.

12 Remove the jack from underneath the engine.

Left-hand mounting

13 Remove the battery and battery tray (see Chapter 5A). Undo the screws and remove the engine undershield.

14 Place a jack beneath the transmission, with a block of wood on the jack head. Raise the jack until it is supporting the weight of the transmission.

15 Slacken and remove the centre nut and washer from the left-hand mounting, then undo the nuts securing the mounting in position and remove it from the engine compartment. If required, undo the bolts/nut and remove the support bracket (see illustrations).

16 If necessary, slide the spacer (where fitted) off the mounting stud, then unscrew the stud from the top of the transmission housing, and remove it along with its washer (see illustration). If the mounting stud is tight,

17.15b Undo the nut/bolts (arrowed) and remove the mounting support bracket

17.16 Unscrew the mounting stud and recover the washer

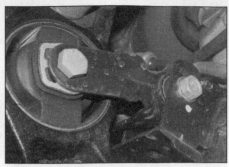

17.22 Lower engine movement limiter

a universal stud extractor can be used to unscrew it.

17 Check all components carefully for signs of wear or damage, and renew as necessary.

18 Clean the threads of the mounting stud, and apply a coat of thread-locking compound to its threads. Refit the stud and washer to the top of the transmission, and tighten it securely.

19 Slide the spacer (where fitted) onto the mounting stud, then refit the rubber mounting. Tighten both the mounting-to-body bolts and the mounting centre nut to their specified torque settings, and remove the jack from underneath the transmission.

20 Refit the battery and tray as described in Chapter 5A.

Lower engine movement limiter

21 If not already done, chock the rear wheels, then jack up the front of the vehicle and support it securely on axle stands (see *Jacking and vehicle support*). Undo the screws and remove the engine undershield.

22 Unscrew and remove the bolt securing the movement limiter link to the driveshaft intermediate bearing housing **(see illustration)**.

23 Remove the bolt securing the link to the subframe. Withdraw the link.

24 To remove the intermediate bearing housing assembly it will first be necessary to remove the right-hand driveshaft as described in Chapter 8.

25 With the driveshaft removed, undo the retaining bolts and remove the bearing housing from the rear of the cylinder block.

26 Check carefully for signs of wear or damage on all components, and renew them where necessary. The rubber bush fitted to the bearing housing is available as a separate item (at the time of writing), and can be pressed out of, and back into, place.

27 On reassembly, fit the bearing housing assembly to the rear of the cylinder block, and tighten its retaining bolts securely. Refit the driveshaft as described in Chapter 8.

28 Refit the movement limiter link, and tighten both its bolts to their specified torque settings. Refit the engine undershield.

29 Lower the vehicle to the ground.

Notes

Notes

Chapter 2 Part D:
1.6 litre DOHC diesel engine in-car repair procedures

Contents

Degrees of difficulty

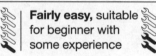

| **Easy,** suitable for novice with little experience | **Fairly easy,** suitable for beginner with some experience | **Fairly difficult,** suitable for competent DIY mechanic | **Difficult,** suitable for experienced DIY mechanic | **Very difficult,** suitable for expert DIY or professional |

Specifications

General

Designation:
Without intercooler DV6TED4
With intercooler DV6ATED4
Engine codes*:
DV6ATED4 . . . . 9HX
DV6TED4:
Without particulate filter 9HY
With particulate filter. 9HZ
Capacity . . . . 1560 cc
Bore . . . . 75.0 mm
Stroke . . . . 88.3 mm
Direction of crankshaft rotation . . . . Clockwise (viewed from the right-hand side of vehicle)
No 1 cylinder location. . . . . At the transmission end of block
Maximum power output. . . . . 80 kW @ 4000 rpm
Maximum torque output. . . . . 245 Nm @ 2000 rpm
Compression ratio . . . . 18.0 :1
* The engine code is stamped on a plate attached to the front of the cylinder block, next to the oil filter.

Compression pressures (engine hot, at cranking speed)

Normal . . . . 20 ± 5 bar
Minimum . . . . 15 bar
Maximum difference between any two cylinders. . . . . 5 bar

Camshaft

Drive:
Inlet camshaft	Toothed belt from crankshaft
Exhaust camshaft	Chain-drive from inlet camshaft
Number of teeth	19

Length:
Inlet camshaft	401.0 ± 0.15 mm
Exhaust camshaft	389.0 ± 0.5 mm
Endfloat	0.195 to 0.300 mm

Lubrication system

Oil pump type	Gear-type, driven directly by the right-hand end of the crankshaft, by two flats machined along the crankshaft journal

Minimum oil pressure at 80°C:
1000 rpm	1.3 bar
4000 rpm	3.5 bar

Torque wrench settings

	Nm	lbf ft
Ancillary drivebelt tensioner roller	20	15
Big-end bolts*:		
Stage 1	10	7
Stage 2	Slacken 180°	
Stage 3	30	22
Stage 4	Angle-tighten a further 140°	
Camshaft bearing caps	10	7
Camshaft cover/bearing ladder:		
Studs	10	7
Bolts	10	7
Camshaft position sensor bolt	5	4
Camshaft sprocket:		
Stage 1	20	15
Stage 2	Angle-tighten a further 50°	
Coolant outlet housing bolts	7	5
Crankshaft position/speed sensor bolt	5	4
Crankshaft pulley/sprocket bolt*:		
Stage 1	35	26
Stage 2	Angle-tighten a further 190 °	
Cylinder head bolts:		
Stage 1	20	15
Stage 2	40	30
Stage 3	Angle-tighten a further 230°	
Cylinder head cover/manifold	10	7
EGR valve	10	7
Engine-to-transmission fixing bolts	60	44
Flywheel bolt*:		
Dual mass flywheel:		
Stage 1	25	18
Stage 2	Fully slacken	
Stage 3	8	6
Stage 4	30	22
Stage 5	Angle-tighten a further 90°	
Normal flywheel:		
Stage 1	25	18
Stage 2	Fully slacken	
Stage 3	8	6
Stage 4	17	13
Stage 5	Angle-tighten a further 75°	
Fuel pump sprocket	50	37
Left-hand engine/transmission mounting:		
Mounting bracket to transmission	55	41
Mounting to bracket	60	44
Main bearing ladder outer seam bolts:		
Stage 1	5	4
Stage 2	10	7
Main bearing ladder to cylinder block:		
Stage 1	10	7
Stage 2	Slacken 180°	
Stage 3	30	22
Stage 4	Angle-tighten a further 140°	

Torque wrench settings (continued)

	Nm	lbf ft
Piston oil jet spray tube bolt	20	15
Oil filter cover	25	18
Oil pick-up pipe	10	7
Oil pressure switch	32	24
Oil pump to cylinder block	10	7
Rear engine/transmission mounting:		
Connecting link to mounting assembly	60	44
Connecting link-to-subframe nut/bolt	60	44
Mounting to engine	60	44
Right-hand engine mounting:		
Mounting to body	60	44
Mounting to support bracket	60	44
Support bracket to engine	55	41
Sump drain plug	25	18
Sump bolts/nuts	12	9
Timing belt idler pulley	35	26
Timing belt tensioner pulley	25	18
Timing chain tensioner	10	7
Vacuum pump:		
Stage 1	18	13
Stage 2	Angle-tighten a further 5°	

* Do not re-use

1 General information

How to use this Chapter

This Part of Chapter 2 describes the repair procedures that can reasonably be carried out on the engine whilst it remains in the vehicle. If the engine has been removed from the vehicle and is being dismantled as described in Part F, any preliminary dismantling procedures can be ignored.

Note that, while it may be possible physically to overhaul items such as the piston/connecting rod assemblies while the engine is in the car, such tasks are not usually carried out as separate operations. Usually, several additional procedures are required (not to mention the cleaning of components and oilways); for this reason, all such tasks are classed as major overhaul procedures, and are described in Part F of this Chapter.

Part F describes the removal of the engine/transmission from the car, and the full overhaul procedures that can then be carried out.

DV series engines

The 1.6 litre DV series engine is the result of development collaboration between Peugeot/Citroën and Ford. The engine is of double overhead camshaft (DOHC) 16-valve design. The direct injection, turbocharged, four-cylinder engine is mounted transversely, with the transmission mounted on the left-hand side.

A toothed timing belt drives the inlet camshaft, high-pressure fuel pump and coolant pump. The inlet camshaft drives the exhaust camshaft via a chain. The camshafts operate the inlet and exhaust valves via rocker arms which are supported at their pivot ends by hydraulic self-adjusting tappets. The camshafts are supported by bearings machined directly in the cylinder head and camshaft bearing housing.

The high-pressure fuel pump supplies fuel to the fuel rail, and subsequently to the electronically-controlled injectors which inject the fuel direct into the combustion chambers. This design differs from the previous type where an injection pump supplies the fuel at high-pressure to each injector. The earlier, conventional type injection pump required fine calibration and timing, and these functions are now completed by the high-pressure pump, electronic injectors and engine management ECM.

The crankshaft runs in five main bearings of the usual shell type. Endfloat is controlled by thrustwashers either side of No 2 main bearing.

The pistons are selected to be of matching weight, and incorporate fully-floating gudgeon pins retained by circlips.

Repair operations precaution

The engine is a complex unit with numerous accessories and ancillary components. The design of the engine compartment is such that every conceivable space has been utilised, and access to virtually all of the engine components is extremely limited. In many cases, ancillary components will have to be removed, or moved to one side, and wiring, pipes and hoses will have to be disconnected or removed from various cable clips and support brackets.

When working on this engine, read through the entire procedure first, look at the car and engine at the same time, and establish whether you have the necessary tools, equipment, skill and patience to proceed. Allow considerable time for any operation, and be prepared for the unexpected.

Because of the limited access, many of the engine photographs appearing in this Chapter were, by necessity, taken with the engine removed from the vehicle.

Warning: It is essential to observe strict precautions when working on the fuel system components of the engine, particularly the high-pressure side of the system. Before carrying out any engine operations that entail working on, or near, any part of the fuel system, refer to the special information given in Chapter 4B.

Operations with engine in vehicle

a) Compression pressure – testing.
b) Cylinder head cover – removal and refitting.
c) Crankshaft pulley – removal and refitting.
d) Timing belt covers – removal and refitting.
e) Timing belt – removal, refitting and adjustment.
f) Timing belt tensioner and sprockets – removal and refitting.
g) Camshaft oil seal – renewal.
h) Camshaft, rocker arms and hydraulic tappets – removal, inspection and refitting.
i) Sump – removal and refitting.
j) Oil pump – removal and refitting.
k) Crankshaft oil seals – renewal.
l) Engine/transmission mountings – inspection and renewal.
m) Flywheel – removal, inspection and refitting.

2 Compression and leakdown tests – description and interpretation

Compression test

Note: *A compression tester specifically designed for diesel engines must be used for this test.*

1 When engine performance is down, or if misfiring occurs which cannot be attributed to the fuel system, a compression test can provide diagnostic clues as to the engine's condition. If the test is performed regularly, it can give warning of trouble before any other symptoms become apparent.

2 A compression tester specifically intended for diesel engines must be used, because of the higher pressures involved. The tester is connected to an adapter which screws into the glow plug or injector hole. On this engine, an adapter suitable for use in the glow plug holes will be required, so as not to disturb the fuel system components. It is unlikely to be worthwhile buying such a tester for occasional use, but it may be possible to borrow or hire one – if not, have the test performed by a garage.

3 Unless specific instructions to the contrary are supplied with the tester, observe the following points:

a) *The battery must be in a good state of charge, the air filter must be clean, and the engine should be at normal operating temperature.*

b) *All the glow plugs should be removed as described in Chapter 5A before starting the test.*

c) *The wiring connectors on the engine management system ECM (located in the plastic box behind the battery) must be disconnected.*

4 The compression pressures measured are not so important as the balance between cylinders. Values are given in the Specifications.

5 The cause of poor compression is less easy to establish on a diesel engine than on a petrol one. The effect of introducing oil into the cylinders ('wet' testing) is not conclusive, because there is a risk that the oil will sit in the swirl chamber or in the recess on the piston crown instead of passing to the rings. However, the following can be used as a rough guide to diagnosis.

6 All cylinders should produce very similar pressures; any difference greater than that specified indicates the existence of a fault. Note that the compression should build-up quickly in a healthy engine; low compression on the first stroke, followed by gradually-increasing pressure on successive strokes, indicates worn piston rings. A low compression reading on the first stroke, which does not build-up during successive strokes, indicates leaking valves or a blown head gasket (a cracked head could also be the cause). Deposits on the undersides of the valve heads can also cause low compression.

7 A low reading from two adjacent cylinders is almost certainly due to the head gasket having blown between them; the presence of coolant in the engine oil will confirm this.

8 If the compression reading is unusually high, the cylinder head surfaces, valves and pistons are probably coated with carbon deposits. If this is the case, the cylinder head should be removed and decarbonised (see Part F).

Leakdown test

9 A leakdown test measures the rate at which compressed air fed into the cylinder is lost. It is an alternative to a compression test, and in many ways it is better, since the escaping air provides easy identification of where pressure loss is occurring (piston rings, valves or head gasket).

10 The equipment needed for leakdown testing is unlikely to be available to the home mechanic. If poor compression is suspected, have the test performed by a suitably-equipped garage.

3 Engine assembly/valve timing holes – general information and usage

Note: *Do not attempt to rotate the engine whilst the crankshaft and camshaft are locked in position. If the engine is to be left in this state for a long period of time, it is a good idea to place suitable warning notices inside the vehicle, and in the engine compartment. This will reduce the possibility of the engine being accidentally cranked on the starter motor, which is likely to cause damage with the locking pins in place.*

1 Timing holes or slots are located only in the crankshaft pulley flange and camshaft sprocket hub. The holes/slots are used to position the pistons halfway up the cylinder bores. This will ensure that the valve timing is maintained during operations that require removal and refitting of the timing belt. When the holes/slots are aligned with their corresponding holes in the cylinder block and cylinder head, suitable diameter bolts/pins can be inserted to lock the crankshaft and camshaft in position, preventing rotation.

2 Note that the HDi type fuel system used on these engines does not have a conventional diesel injection pump, but instead uses a high-pressure fuel pump. Although it may be argued that timing of the fuel pump is irrelevant because it merely pressurises the fuel in the fuel rail, Peugeot include this procedure for engines fitted with a Bosch high-pressure fuel pump, using the same timing rod/pin used for crankshaft sprocket timing. **Note:** *On the Bosch pump, the drive sprocket is keyed to the shaft.* In addition, note that the hole in the fuel pump sprocket only aligns correctly with the hole in the mounting bracket every 12 revolutions of the crankshaft (or every 6 revolutions of the camshaft sprocket).

3 To align the engine assembly/valve timing holes, proceed as follows.

4 Chock the rear wheels then jack up the front of the vehicle and support it on axle stands (see *Jacking and vehicle support*). Remove the right-hand front roadwheel.

5 To gain access to the crankshaft pulley, to enable the engine to be turned, the wheel arch plastic liner must be removed. The liner is secured by several plastic expanding rivets/nut/screws. To remove the rivets, push in the centre pins a little, then prise the clips from place. Remove the liner from under the front wing. The crankshaft can then be turned using a suitable socket and extension bar fitted to the pulley bolt.

6 Remove the upper and lower timing belt covers as described in Section 6.

7 Temporarily refit the crankshaft pulley bolt, remove the crankshaft locking tool, then turn the crankshaft until the timing hole in the camshaft sprocket hub is aligned with the corresponding hole in the cylinder head. Note that the crankshaft must always be turned in a clockwise direction (viewed from the right-hand side of vehicle). Use a small mirror so that the position of the sprocket hub timing slot can be observed. When the slot is aligned with the corresponding hole in the cylinder head, the camshaft is positioned correctly.

8 Remove the crankshaft drivebelt pulley as described in Section 5.

9 Insert a 5 mm diameter bolt, rod or drill through the hole in crankshaft sprocket flange and into the corresponding hole in the oil pump **(see illustration)**, if necessary, carefully turn the crankshaft either way until the rod enters the timing hole in the block.

10 Insert an 8 mm bolt, rod or drill through the hole in the camshaft sprocket hub and into engagement with the cylinder head. Note that a modified 3-segment camshaft sprocket is fitted to later models **(see illustrations)**.

11 If using this procedure during refitting of the timing belt, insert a 5 mm diameter bolt, rod or drill through the hole in the fuel pump sprocket and into the corresponding hole in

3.9 Insert a 5.0 mm drill bit/bolt through the round hole in the sprocket flange, into the hole in the oil pump housing (lower timing belt cover removed for clarity)

3.10a Insert an 8.0 mm drill bit/bolt through the hole in the camshaft sprocket into the corresponding hole in the cylinder head

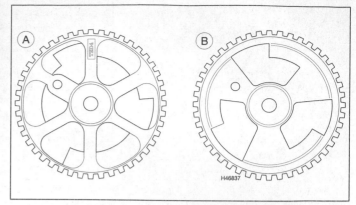

3.10b Early (A) and late (B) camshaft sprocket

3.11 Insert a 5.0 mm drill bit/bolt through the round hole in the fuel pump sprocket into the cylinder head

4.2 Release the clip (arrowed) and disconnect the mass airflow meter wiring plug

the cylinder head **(see illustration)**. Note: *On some engines, a hole is provided at the 5 o'clock position for locking purposes only, however, the timing hole is at the 12 o'clock position.* Note the comment in paragraph 2 – if the fuel pump sprocket holes are not aligned during removal of the timing belt, it is of no consequence, however it is important to align the holes during the refitting procedure. If timing alignment alone is being *checked* there is no need to check alignment of the pump sprocket.

12 The crankshaft and camshaft are now locked in position, preventing unnecessary rotation.

4 Cylinder head cover/manifold – removal and refitting

Removal

1 Pull the plastic cover upwards from the top of the engine. Carry out the following operations to remove the scuttle trim panel and crossmember:

a) *Remove the wiper arms (see Chapter 12).*
b) *Push in the centre pins, and prise out the two plastic rivets at each end of the trim panel.*

c) *Pull the outer ends of the panel up, then pull the panel centre down and forwards to release it from the windscreen.*
d) *Undo the two screws securing the master cylinder upper fluid reservoir. Do not disconnect the fluid pipes.*
e) *Release the clips securing the sound insulation material, then undo the two bolts and remove the scuttle crossmember.*

2 Disconnect the mass airflow meter wiring plug **(see illustration)**.

3 Remove the inlet and outlet air ducting from the air filter housing **(see illustrations)**.

4 Unscrew the air filter housing cover bolts,

4.3a Undo the screw (arrowed) and remove the inlet ducting

4.3b Disconnect the hose to the turbocharger . . .

4.3c . . . release the clips (arrowed) and disconnect the breather hose . . .

4.4a . . . then undo the cover screws (arrowed) . . .

4.4b . . . and remove the ducting/cover assembly

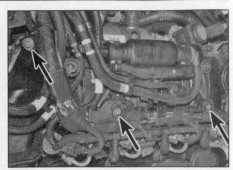

4.5 Undo the bolts (arrowed) and position the wiring harness/guide to one side

then remove the cover and filter element – refer to Chapter 4B **(see illustrations)**. Pull the air filter housing from its mountings.

5 Disconnect the wiring plugs from the top of

each injector, undo the guide bolts, then make sure all wiring harnesses are freed from any retaining brackets on the cylinder head cover/ inlet manifold **(see illustration)**. Disconnect

any vacuum pipes as necessary, having first noted their fitted positions.

6 Remove the EGR cooler as described in Chapter 4C.

7 Depress the release buttons and disconnect the fuel feed and return hoses at the right-hand end of the cylinder head, then disconnect the fuel temperature sensor wiring plug, and move the pipe/priming bulb assembly to the rear **(see illustrations)**.

8 Release the clamps, undo the bolts and remove the inlet ducting between the turbocharger and the inlet manifold. Make a note of their fitted positions, then disconnect the various wiring plugs as the assembly is withdrawn **(see illustrations)**.

9 Undo the retaining bolts and remove the oil separator from the top of the cylinder head **(see illustration)**. Recover the rubber seal.

10 Prise out the retaining clips and

4.7a Depress the release buttons (arrowed) and disconnect the fuel feed and return hoses

4.7b Disconnect the fuel temperature sensor wiring plug (arrowed) . . .

4.7c . . . then unclip the fuel priming bulb/ pipes (arrowed)

4.8a Slacken the left-hand turbocharger outlet hose bolt, undo the right-hand bolt (arrowed) . . .

4.8b . . . then slacken the hose clamps (arrowed), disconnect the wiring plugs . . .

4.8c . . . undo the bolt on the end (arrowed) . . .

4.8d . . . and the 2 at the front (arrowed), then remove the assembly

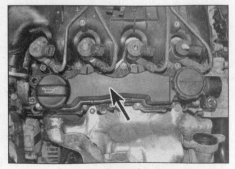

4.9 Undo the bolts and remove the oil separator (arrowed)

4.10a Prise out the clip and pull the return hose from the top of each injector

4.10b Use a second spanner to hold the injector port whilst slackening the fuel pipe unions

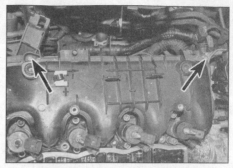

4.11 Undo the 2 remaining bolts (arrowed) and pull the cover/manifold upwards

disconnect the fuel return pipes from the injectors, then undo the unions and remove the high-pressure fuel pipes from the injectors and the common fuel rail at the rear of the cylinder head – counterhold the unions with a second spanner **(see illustrations)**. Plug the openings to prevent dirt ingress.

11 Undo the 2 bolts securing the cylinder head cover/inlet manifold. Lift the assembly away **(see illustration)**. Recover the manifold rubber seals.

Refitting

12 Refitting is a reversal of removal, bearing in mind the following points:
 a) *Examine the seals for signs of damage and deterioration, and renew if necessary. Smear a little clean engine oil on the manifold seals.*
 b) *Renew the fuel injector high-pressure pipes – see Chapter 4B.*

5 Crankshaft pulley – removal and refitting

Removal

1 Remove the auxiliary drivebelt as described in Chapter 1B.

2 To lock the crankshaft, working underneath the engine, insert Peugeot tool No 0194-C into the hole in the right-hand face of the engine block casting over the lower section of the flywheel. Rotate the crankshaft until the tool engages in the corresponding hole in the flywheel. In the absence of the Peugeot tool, insert a 12 mm rod or drill into the hole **(see illustration)**. Note: *The hole in the casting and the hole in the flywheel are provided purely to lock the crankshaft whilst the pulley bolt is undone, it does not position the crankshaft at TDC.*

3 Using a suitable socket and extension bar, unscrew the retaining bolt, remove the washer, then slide the pulley off the end of the crankshaft **(see illustration)**. If the pulley is tight fit, it can be drawn off the crankshaft using a suitable puller. If a puller is being used, refit the pulley retaining bolt without the washer to avoid damaging the crankshaft as the puller is tightened.
Caution: Do not touch the outer magnetic sensor ring of the sprocket with your fingers, or allow metallic particles to come into contact with it.

Refitting

4 Refit the pulley to the end of the crankshaft.
5 Thoroughly clean the threads of the pulley retaining bolt, then apply a coat of locking compound to the bolt threads. Peugeot recommend the use of Loctite (available from your Peugeot dealer); in the absence of this, any good-quality locking compound may be used.

6 Refit the crankshaft pulley retaining bolt and washer. Tighten the bolt to the specified torque, then through the specified angle, preventing the crankshaft from turning using the method employed on removal.
7 Refit and tension the auxiliary drivebelt as described in Chapter 1B.

6 Timing belt covers – removal and refitting

⚠️ *Warning: Refer to the precautionary information contained in Section 1 before proceeding.*

Removal

Upper cover

1 Remove the plastic cover from the top of the engine. Carry out the following operations to remove the scuttle trim panel and crossmember:
 a) *Remove the wiper blades (see Chapter 12).*
 b) *Push in the centre pins, and prise out the*

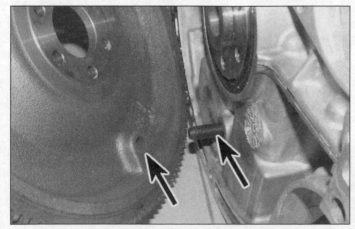

5.2 The locking pin/bolt (arrowed) must locate in the hole in the flywheel (arrowed) to prevent rotation

5.3 Undo the crankshaft pulley retaining bolt (arrowed)

6.2a Unclip the fuel pipes (arrowed) . . .

6.2b . . . and the wiring harness (arrowed) from the timing belt upper cover

6.3 Upper timing belt cover screws (arrowed)

two plastic rivets at each end of the trim panel.
c) Pull the outer ends of the panel up, then pull the panel centre down and forwards to release it from the windscreen.
d) Undo the two screws securing the master cylinder upper fluid reservoir. Do not disconnect the fluid pipes.
e) Release the clips securing the sound insulation material, then undo the two bolts and remove the scuttle crossmember.

2 Release the wiring harness and fuel pipes from the upper cover **(see illustrations)**.
3 Undo the five screws and remove the timing belt upper cover **(see illustration)**.

Lower cover

4 Remove the upper cover as described previously.
5 Remove the crankshaft pulley as described in Section 5.
6 Remove the auxiliary drivebelt tensioner locking tool (where applicable), then undo the five bolts and remove the lower cover **(see illustration)**.

Refitting

7 Refitting of all the covers is a reversal of the relevant removal procedure, ensuring that each cover section is correctly located, and that the cover retaining bolts are securely tightened. Ensure that all disturbed hoses are reconnected and retained by their relevant clips.

7 Timing belt – removal, inspection, refitting and tensioning

General

1 The timing belt drives the inlet camshaft, high-pressure fuel pump, and coolant pump from a toothed sprocket on the end of the crankshaft. If the belt breaks or slips in service, the pistons are likely to hit the valve heads, resulting in expensive damage.
2 The timing belt should be renewed at the specified intervals, or earlier if it is contaminated with oil, or at all noisy in operation (a 'scraping' noise due to uneven wear).
3 If the timing belt is being removed, it is a wise precaution to check the condition of the coolant pump at the same time (check for signs of coolant leakage). This may avoid the need to remove the timing belt again at a later stage should the coolant pump fail.

Removal

4 Chock the rear wheels then jack up the front of the vehicle and support it on axle stands (see *Jacking and vehicle support*). Remove the front right-hand roadwheel, wheel arch liner (to expose the crankshaft pulley), and the engine undershield. The wheel arch liner is secured by several plastic expanding rivets/nuts/plastic

clips. Push the centre pins in a little then prise the rivets from place. The engine undershield is retained by several screws.
5 Remove the auxiliary drivebelt as described in Chapter 1B.
6 Remove the upper and lower timing belt covers, as described in Section 6.
7 Refer to Chapter 4B and disconnect the front exhaust pipe at the flexible section.
8 Position a trolley jack under the engine, and using a block of wood on the jack head, take the weight of the engine.
9 Undo the bolts/nut and remove the right-hand engine mounting and support bracket – see Section 17.
10 Undo the screw and remove the crankshaft position sensor adjacent to the crankshaft sprocket flange, and move it to one side **(see illustration)**.
11 Undo the retaining screw and remove the timing belt protection bracket, again adjacent to the crankshaft sprocket flange **(see illustration)**.
12 Lock the crankshaft and camshaft in the correct position as described in Section 3. If necessary, temporarily refit the crankshaft pulley bolt to enable the crankshaft to be rotated. At this stage, it is of no consequence that the fuel pump sprocket aligns correctly with the hole in the pump mounting bracket.
13 Insert a hexagon key into the belt tensioner pulley centre, slacken the pulley bolt, and allow the tensioner to rotate, relieving the belt

6.6 Lower timing belt cover bolts (arrowed)

7.10 Undo the bolt (arrowed) and remove the crankshaft position sensor

7.11 Remove the timing belt protection bracket

7.13 Slacken the bolt and allow the tensioner to rotate, relieving the tension on the belt

7.17 Timing belt routing

7.19 The index arm must align with the lug (arrowed)

tension **(see illustration)**. With the belt slack, temporarily tighten the pulley bolt.

14 Note its routing, then remove the timing belt from the sprockets.

Inspection

15 Renew the belt as a matter of course, regardless of its apparent condition. The cost of a new belt is nothing compared with the cost of repairs should the belt break in service. If signs of oil contamination are found, trace the source of the oil leak and rectify it. Wash down the engine timing belt area and all related components, to remove all traces of oil. Check that the tensioner and idler pulleys rotate freely without any sign of roughness, and also check that the coolant pump pulley rotates freely. If necessary, renew these items.

Refitting and tensioning

16 Commence refitting by ensuring that the crankshaft and camshaft timing pins are still in position correctly. Also, where a Bosch high-pressure fuel pump is fitted, locate and lock the fuel pump sprocket in its correct position as described in Section 3.

17 Locate the timing belt on the crankshaft sprocket, then keeping it taut, locate it around the idler pulley, camshaft sprocket, high-pressure pump sprocket, coolant pump sprocket, and the tensioner pulley **(see illustration)**. If the timing belt has directional arrows on it, make sure that they point in the direction of normal engine rotation.

18 Refit the timing belt protection bracket and tighten the retaining bolt securely.

19 Slacken the tensioner pulley bolt, and using a hexagonal key, rotate the tensioner anti-clockwise, which moves the index arm clockwise, until the index arm is aligned as shown **(see illustration)**.

20 Remove the camshaft and crankshaft and fuel pump timing pins and, using a socket on the crankshaft pulley bolt, crankshaft clockwise 10 complete revolutions. Align the camshaft and crankshaft timing holes and check that the timing pins can be inserted, then remove them. There is no requirement to check the fuel pump sprocket alignment,

as it will only be aligned after 12 complete revolutions.

21 Check that the tensioner index arm is still aligned between the edges of the area shown **(see illustration 7.19)**. If it is not, remove and belt and begin the refitting process again, starting at Paragraph 19.

22 The remainder of refitting is a reversal of removal. Tighten all fasteners to the specified torque where given.

---

8 Timing belt sprockets and tensioner – removal and refitting

Camshaft sprocket

Removal

1 Remove the timing belt as described in Section 7.

2 Remove the locking tool from the camshaft sprocket/hub. Slacken the sprocket hub retaining bolt. To prevent the camshaft rotating as the bolt is slackened, a sprocket holding tool will be required. In the absence of the special Peugeot tool, an acceptable substitute can be fabricated at home **(see Tool Tip 1)**. *Do not* attempt to use the engine

A sprocket holding tool can be made from two lengths of steel strip bolted together to form a forked end. Drill holes and insert bolts in the ends of the fork to engage with the sprocket spokes.

assembly/valve timing locking tool to prevent the sprocket from rotating whilst the bolt is slackened.

3 Remove the sprocket hub retaining bolt, and slide the sprocket and hub off the end of the camshaft.

4 Clean the camshaft sprocket thoroughly, and renew it if there are any signs of wear, damage or cracks.

Refitting

5 Refit the camshaft sprocket to the camshaft **(see illustration)**.

6 Refit the sprocket hub retaining bolt. Tighten the bolt to the specified torque, preventing the camshaft from turning as during removal.

7 Align the engine assembly/valve timing slot in the camshaft sprocket hub with the hole in the cylinder head and refit the timing pin to lock the camshaft in position.

8 Fit the timing belt around the pump sprocket and camshaft sprocket, and tension the timing belt as described in Section 7.

Crankshaft sprocket

Removal

9 Remove the timing belt as described in Section 7.

10 Check that the engine assembly/valve timing holes are still aligned as described in Section 3, and the camshaft sprocket and flywheel are locked in position.

11 Slide the sprocket off the end of the

8.5 Ensure the lug on the sprocket hub engages with the slot on the end of the camshaft (arrowed)

8.11a Slide the sprocket from the crankshaft . . .

8.11b . . . and recover the Woodruff key

8.17 Insert a suitable drill bit through the sprocket into the hole in the backplate

crankshaft and collect the Woodruff key (see illustrations).

12 Examine the crankshaft oil seal for signs of oil leakage and, if necessary, renew it as described in Section 14.

13 Clean the crankshaft sprocket thoroughly, and renew it if there are any signs of wear, damage or cracks. Recover the crankshaft locating key.

Refitting

14 Refit the key to the end of the crankshaft, then refit the crankshaft sprocket (with the flange facing the crankshaft pulley).

15 Fit the timing belt around the crankshaft sprocket, and tension the timing belt as described in Section 7.

Fuel pump sprocket

Removal

16 Remove the timing belt as described in Section 7.

17 Using a suitable socket, undo the pump sprocket retaining nut. The sprocket can be held stationary by inserting a suitably-sized locking pin, drill or rod through the hole in the sprocket, and into the corresponding hole in the backplate (see illustration), or by using a suitable forked tool engaged with the holes in the sprocket (see Tool Tip 1). Note: *On some*

TOOL TiP 2

Make a sprocket releasing tool from a short strip of steel. Drill two holes in the strip to correspond with the two holes in the sprocket. Drill a third hole just large enough to accept the flats of the sprocket retaining nut.

engines, a hole is provided at the 5 o'clock position for locking purposes only, however, the timing position hole is at the 12 o'clock position.

18 The pump sprocket is a taper fit on the pump shaft and it will be necessary to make up another tool to release it from the taper (see Tool Tip 2).

19 On late models where the sprocket is keyed to the shaft, unscrew the retaining nut and remove the sprocket, then recover the Woodruff key. On early models where the sprocket is **not** keyed to the shaft, partially unscrew the sprocket retaining nut, then fit the home-made tool, and secure it to the sprocket with two suitable bolts. Prevent the sprocket from rotating as before, and unscrew the sprocket retaining nut. The nut will bear against the tool as it is undone, forcing the sprocket off the shaft taper. Once the taper is released, remove the tool, unscrew the nut fully, and remove the sprocket from the pump shaft.

20 Clean the sprocket thoroughly, and renew it if there are any signs of wear, damage or cracks.

Refitting

21 Refit the Woodruff key (late models only) then refit the pump sprocket and retaining nut, and tighten the nut to the specified torque. Prevent the sprocket rotating as the nut is tightened using the sprocket holding tool.

22 Fit the timing belt around the pump sprocket, and tension the timing belt as described in Section 7.

8.31 Timing belt idler pulley retaining nut (arrowed)

Coolant pump sprocket

23 The coolant pump sprocket is integral with the pump, and cannot be removed. Coolant pump removal is described in Chapter 3.

Tensioner pulley

Removal

24 Remove the timing belt as described in Section 7.

25 Remove the tensioner pulley retaining bolt, and slide the pulley off its mounting stud.

26 Clean the tensioner pulley, but do not use any strong solvent which may enter the pulley bearings. Check that the pulley rotates freely, with no sign of stiffness or free play. Renew the pulley if there is any doubt about its condition, or if there are any obvious signs of wear or damage.

27 Examine the pulley mounting stud for signs of damage and if necessary, renew it.

Refitting

28 Refit the tensioner pulley to its mounting stud, and fit the retaining bolt.

29 Refit the timing belt as described in Section 7.

Idler pulley

Removal

30 Remove the timing belt as described in Section 7.

31 Undo the retaining bolt/nut and withdraw the idler pulley from the engine (see illustration).

32 Clean the idler pulley, but do not use any strong solvent which may enter the bearings. Check that the pulley rotates freely, with no sign of stiffness or free play. Renew the idler pulley if there is any doubt about its condition, or if there are any obvious signs of wear or damage.

Refitting

33 Locate the idler pulley on the engine, and fit the retaining bolt/nut. Tighten the bolt/nut to the specified torque.

34 Refit the timing belt (see Section 7).

9.5 Vacuum pump bolts (arrowed)

9.7 Timing belt inner, upper cover bolts (arrowed)

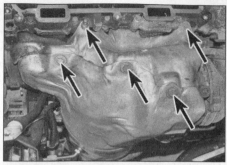

9.9a Undo the bolts (arrowed) and remove the rear section of the heat shield

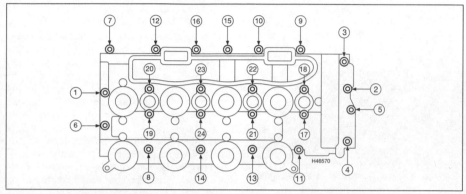

9.9b Camshaft cover/bearing ladder bolt slackening sequence

9.10 The camshaft bearing caps are numbered 1 to 4 from the flywheel end – A for Inlet, and E for exhaust (arrowed)

9 Camshafts, rocker arms and hydraulic tappets – removal, inspection and refitting

Removal

1 Remove the cylinder head cover/manifold as described in Section 4.

2 Remove the injectors as described in Chapter 4B.

3 Remove the camshaft sprocket as described in Section 8.

4 Refit the right-hand engine mounting, but only tighten the bolts moderately; this will keep the engine supported during the camshaft removal.

5 Undo the bolts and remove the vacuum pump. Recover the pump O-ring seals (see illustration).

6 Remove the fuel filter (see Chapter 1B), then undo the bolts and remove the fuel filter mounting bracket.

7 Release the wiring harness clips, then undo the 3 bolts and remove the timing belt inner, upper cover (see illustration).

8 Disconnect the wiring plug, unscrew the retaining bolt, and remove the camshaft position sensor from the camshaft cover/ bearing ladder.

9 Undo the 5 bolts and remove the upper rear section of the turbocharger heat shield, then working gradually and evenly, slacken and remove the bolts securing the camshaft cover/bearing ladder to the cylinder head in

sequence (see illustrations). Lift the cover/ ladder from position complete with the camshafts.

10 Undo the retaining bolts and remove the bearing caps. Note their fitted positions, as they must be refitted into their original positions (see illustration). Note that the bearing caps are marked A for inlet, and E for exhaust, and 1 to 4 from the flywheel end of the cylinder head.

11 Undo the bolts securing the chain tensioner assembly to the camshaft cover/ bearing ladder, then lift the camshafts, chain and tensioner from place (see illustrations). Discard the camshaft oil seal.

12 Obtain 16 small, clean plastic containers, and number them 1 to 8 inlet and 1 to 8 exhaust; alternatively, divide a larger container into 16 compartments.

13 Lift out each rocker arm. Place the rocker

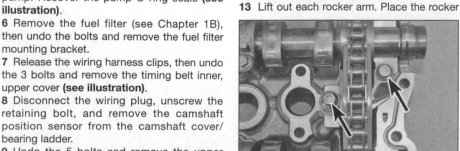

9.11a Undo the tensioner bolts (arrowed) . . .

arms in their respective positions in the box or containers.

14 A compartmentalised container filled with engine oil is now required to retain the hydraulic tappets while they are removed from the cylinder head. Withdraw each hydraulic follower and place it in the container, keeping them each identified for correct refitting. The tappets must be totally submerged in the oil to prevent air entering them.

Inspection

15 Inspect the cam lobes and the camshaft bearing journals for scoring or other visible evidence of wear. Once the surface hardening of the cam lobes has been eroded, wear will occur at an accelerated rate. Note: If these symptoms are visible on the tips of the camshaft lobes, check the corresponding rocker arm, as it will probably be worn as well.

9.11b . . . then lift the camshafts, chain and tensioner from place

9.21 Refit the hydraulic tappets . . .

9.22 . . . and rocker arms to their original locations

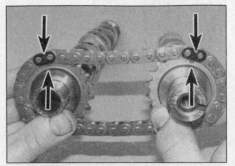

9.23 Align the marks on the sprockets with the centre of the black-coloured chain links (arrowed). There must be 12 link pins between the sprocket marks

9.24a Assemble the chain tensioner between the upper and lower runs of the chain . . .

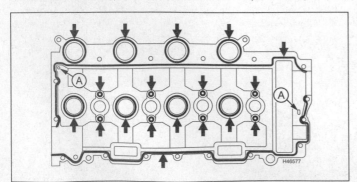

9.24b . . . and lower the camshafts, chain and tensioner into position

16 Examine the condition of the bearing surfaces in the cylinder head and camshaft bearing housing. If wear is evident, the cylinder head and bearing housing will both have to be renewed, as they are a matched assembly.

17 Inspect the rocker arms and tappets for scuffing, cracking or other damage and renew any components as necessary. Also check the condition of the tappet bores in the cylinder head. As with the camshafts, any wear in this area will necessitate cylinder head renewal.

Refitting

18 Thoroughly clean the sealant from the mating surfaces of the cylinder head and camshaft bearing housing. Use a suitable liquid gasket dissolving agent (available from Peugeot dealers) together with a soft putty knife; do not use a metal scraper or the faces will be

damaged. As there is no conventional gasket used, the cleanliness of the mating faces is of the utmost importance. Prise out the oil injector oil seals from the camshaft bearing housing.

19 Clean off any oil, dirt or grease from both components and dry with a clean lint-free cloth. Ensure that all the oilways are completely clean.

20 Liberally lubricate the hydraulic tappet bores in the cylinder head with clean engine oil.

21 Insert the hydraulic tappets into their original bores in the cylinder head unless they have been renewed **(see illustration)**.

22 Lubricate the rocker arms and place them over their respective tappets and valve stems **(see illustration)**.

23 Engage the timing chain around the camshaft sprockets, aligning the black-coloured links with the marked teeth on the camshaft sprockets **(see illustration)**. If the black

colouring has been lost, there must be 12 chain link pins between the marks on the sprockets.

24 Fit the chain tensioner between the upper and lower runs of the chain, then lubricate the bearing surfaces with clean engine oil, and fit the camshafts into position on the underside of the camshaft cover/bearing ladder. Refit the bearing caps to their original positions and tighten the retaining bolts to the specified torque **(see illustrations)**. Tighten the tensioner retaining bolts to the specified torque.

25 Apply a thin bead of sealant to the mating surface of the camshaft cover/bearing ladder as shown. Peugeot recommend the use of Autojoint Noir **(see illustration)**. Do not allow the sealant to obstruct the oil channels for the hydraulic chain tensioner.

26 Check that the black-coloured links on the chain are still aligned with the marks on the camshaft sprockets, then refit the camshaft cover/bearing ladder, and gradually and evenly tighten the retaining bolts until the cover/ladder is in contact with the cylinder head, then tighten the bolts to the specified torque in sequence **(see illustration)**. **Note:** *Ensure the cover/ladder is correctly located by checking the bores of the vacuum pump and camshaft oil seal at each end of the cover/ladder.*

27 Fit a new camshaft oil seal as described in Section 14.

28 Refit the camshaft sprocket, and tighten the retaining bolt finger-tight.

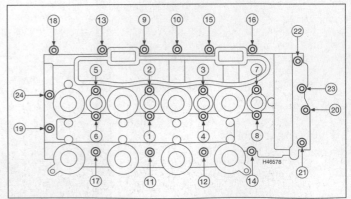

9.25 Apply sealant to the camshaft cover/bearing ladder as indicated by the heavy black lines. Ensure sealant does not enter the tensioner oil holes – marked A

9.26 Camshaft cover/bearing ladder bolt tightening sequence

29 Using a spanner on the camshaft sprocket bolt, rotate the camshafts approximately 40 complete revolutions clockwise. Check the black-coloured links on the chain still align with the marks on the camshaft sprockets.

30 If the marks still align, refit the camshaft sprocket as described in Section 8.

31 Refit and adjust the camshaft position sensor as described in Chapter 4B.

32 Press the new oil seals into the bearing housing, using a tube/socket of approximately 20 mm outside diameter, ensuring the inner lip of the seal fits around the injector guide tube **(see illustrations)**. Refit the injectors as described in Chapter 4B.

33 Refit the cylinder head cover/manifold as described in Section 4.

10 Cylinder head – removal and refitting

Removal

1 Chock the rear wheels then jack up the front of the vehicle and support it on axle stands (see *Jacking and vehicle support*). Remove the front right-hand roadwheel, the engine undershield, and the front wheel arch liner. The undershield is secured by several screws, and the wheel arch liner is secured by several plastic expanding rivets/nuts/plastic clips. Push the centre pins in a little, then prise the rivet from place.

9.32a Fit the new seal around a 20 mm outside diameter socket . . .

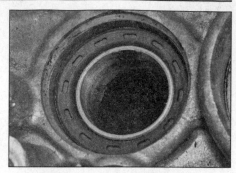

9.32b . . . and push it into place

2 Disconnect the battery negative lead as described in Chapter 5A.

3 Drain the cooling system as described in Chapter 1B.

4 Remove the camshafts, rocker arms and hydraulic tappets as described in Section 9.

5 Remove the turbocharger as described in Chapter 4B.

6 Remove the glow plugs as described in Chapter 5C.

7 Where applicable, undo the 3 mounting bolts and move the power steering pump to one side (there's no need to disconnect the hoses).

8 Undo the upper mounting bolts, and pivot the alternator away from the engine, undo the oil dipstick guide tube bolt, then undo the bolts securing the alternator/power steering pump mounting bracket to the cylinder head/block **(see illustration)**.

9 Undo the coolant outlet housing (left-hand end of the cylinder head) retaining bolts, slacken the two bolts securing the housing support bracket to the top of the transmission bellhousing, and move the outlet housing away from the cylinder head a little **(see illustration)**. There is no need to disconnect the hoses.

10 Disconnect the high-pressure fuel pipe from the common rail to the pump, and disconnect the fuel supply and return hoses. Remove the bracket at the rear of the pump, then undo the bolt/nut and remove the pump and mounting bracket as an assembly **(see illustrations)**. Note that a new high-pressure pipe must be fitted – see Chapter 4B.

11 Working in the **reverse** of the sequence shown **(see illustration 10.32)** undo the cylinder head bolts.

12 Release the cylinder head from the cylinder block and location dowels by rocking it. The Peugeot tool for doing this consists simply of two metal rods with 90-degree angled ends **(see illustration)**. Do not prise between the

10.8 The engine oil level dipstick is secured to the alternator bracket by a Torx bolt (arrowed)

10.9 Undo the bolts (arrowed) and pull the coolant outlet housing from the left-hand end of the cylinder head

10.10a Remove the high-pressure pipe (arrowed) . . .

10.10b . . . and the bracket (arrowed)

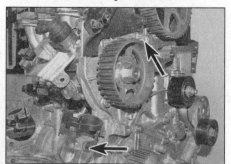

10.10c Pump mounting bracket upper nut and lower mounting bolt (arrowed)

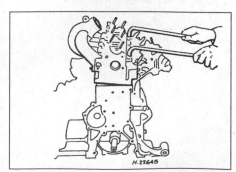

10.12 Free the cylinder head using angled rods

10.17a Pull the non-return valve from the cylinder head . . .

10.17b . . . and push a new one into place

10.21 Measure the piston protrusion using a DTI gauge

mating faces of the cylinder head and block, as this may damage the gasket faces.

13 Lift the cylinder head from the block, and recover the gasket.

14 If necessary, remove the exhaust manifold with reference to Chapter 4B.

Preparation for refitting

15 The mating faces of the cylinder head and cylinder block must be perfectly clean before refitting the head. Peugeot recommend the use of a scouring agent for this purpose, but acceptable results can be achieved by using a hard plastic or wood scraper to remove all traces of gasket and carbon. The same method can be used to clean the piston crowns. Take particular care to avoid scoring or gouging the cylinder head/cylinder block mating surfaces during the cleaning operations, as aluminium alloy is easily damaged. Make sure that the carbon is not allowed to enter the oil and water passages – this is particularly important for the lubrication system, as carbon could block the oil supply to the engine's components. Using adhesive tape and paper, seal the water, oil and bolt holes in the cylinder block. To prevent carbon entering the gap between the pistons and bores, smear a little grease in the gap. After cleaning each piston, use a small brush to remove all traces of grease and carbon from the gap, then wipe away the remainder with a clean rag.

16 Check the mating surfaces of the cylinder block and the cylinder head for nicks, deep scratches and other damage. If slight, they may be removed carefully with a file, but

if excessive, machining may be the only alternative to renewal. If warpage of the cylinder head gasket surface is suspected, use a straight-edge to check it for distortion. Refer to Part F of this Chapter if necessary.

17 Thoroughly clean the threads of the cylinder head bolt holes in the cylinder block. Ensure that the bolts run freely in their threads, and that all traces of oil and water are removed from each bolt hole. If required, pull the oil feed non-return valve from the cylinder head, and check the ball moves freely. Push a new valve into place if necessary **(see illustrations)**.

Gasket selection

18 Remove the crankshaft timing pin, then turn the crankshaft until pistons 1 and 4 are at TDC (Top Dead Centre). Position a dial test indicator (dial gauge) on the cylinder block adjacent to the rear of No 1 piston, and zero it on the block face. Transfer the probe to the crown of No 1 piston (10.0 mm in from the rear edge), then slowly turn the crankshaft back-and-forth past TDC, noting the highest reading on the indicator. Record this reading as protrusion A.

19 Repeat the check described in paragraph 18, this time 10.0 mm in from the front edge of the No 1 piston crown. Record this reading as protrusion B.

20 Add protrusion A to protrusion B, then divide the result by 2 to obtain an average reading for piston No 1.

21 Repeat the procedure described in paragraphs 18 to 20 on piston 4, then turn the

crankshaft through 180° and carry out the procedure on the piston Nos 2 and 3 **(see illustration)**. Check that there is a maximum difference of 0.07 mm protrusion between any two pistons.

22 If a dial test indicator is not available, piston protrusion may be measured using a straight-edge and feeler blades or Vernier calipers. However, this is much less accurate, and cannot therefore be recommended.

23 Note the greatest piston protrusion measurement, and use this to determine the correct cylinder head gasket from the following table. The series of notches/holes on the side of the gasket are used for thickness identification **(see illustration)**.

Piston protrusion	Gasket identification
0.6115 to 0.720 mm	2 notches
0.721 to 0.770 mm	3 notches
0.771 to 0.820 mm	1 notches
0.821 to 0.870 mm	4 notches
0.871 to 0.977 mm	5 notches

Head bolt examination

24 Carefully examine the cylinder head bolts for signs of damage to the threads or head, and for any sign of corrosion. If the bolts are in a satisfactory condition, measure the length of each bolt from the underside of the head to the end of the shank. The bolts may be re-used providing that the measured length does not exceed 149.0 mm **(see illustration)**. **Note:** *Considering the stress to which the cylinder head bolts are subjected, it is highly recommended that they are all renewed, regardless of their apparent condition.*

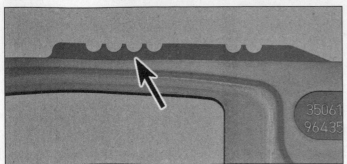

10.23 Cylinder head gasket thickness identification notches (arrowed)

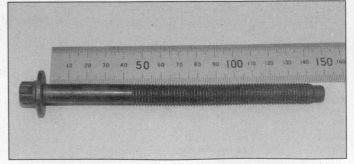

10.24 Measure the length from under the bolt head to its end

10.27 Ensure the gasket locates over the dowels (arrowed)

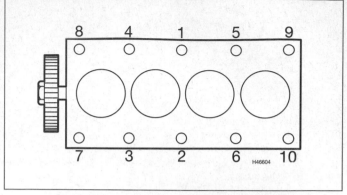

10.32 Cylinder head bolt tightening sequence

Refitting

25 Turn the crankshaft and position Nos 1 and 4 pistons at TDC, then turn the crankshaft a quarter turn (90°) anti-clockwise.

26 Thoroughly clean the surfaces of the cylinder head and block.

27 Make sure that the locating dowels are in place, then fit the correct gasket the right way round on the cylinder block **(see illustration)**.

28 If necessary, refit the exhaust manifold to the cylinder head as described in Chapter 4B.

29 Carefully lower the cylinder head onto the gasket and block, making sure that it locates correctly onto the dowels.

30 Apply a smear of grease to the threads, and to the underside of the heads, of the cylinder head bolts. Peugeot recommend the use of Molykote G Rapid Plus (available from your Peugeot dealer); in the absence of the specified grease, any good-quality high melting-point grease may be used.

31 Carefully insert the cylinder head bolts into their holes (*do not drop them in*) and initially finger-tighten them.

32 Working progressively and in sequence, tighten the cylinder head bolts to their Stage 1 torque setting, using a torque wrench and suitable socket **(see illustration)**.

33 Once all the bolts have been tightened to their Stage 1 torque setting, working again in the specified sequence, tighten each bolt to the specified Stage 2 setting. Finally,

angle-tighten the bolts through the specified Stage 3 angle. It is recommended that an angle-measuring gauge is used during this stage of tightening, to ensure accuracy. **Note:** *Retightening of the cylinder head bolts after running the engine is not required.*

34 Refit the hydraulic tappets, rocker arms, and camshaft housing (complete with camshafts) as described in Section 9.

35 Refit the timing belt as described in Section 7.

36 The remainder of refitting is a reversal of removal, noting the following points.

a) *Use a new seal when refitting the coolant outlet housing.*

b) *When refitting a cylinder head, it is good practice to renew the thermostat.*

c) *Refit the camshaft position sensor and set the air gap with reference to Chapter 4B.*

d) *Tighten all fasteners to the specified torque where given.*

e) *Refill the cooling system as described in Chapter 1B.*

f) *The engine may run erratically for the first few miles, until the engine management ECM relearns its stored values.*

11 Sump – removal and refitting

Removal

1 Drain the engine oil, then clean and refit the engine oil drain plug, tightening it securely. If the engine is nearing the service interval

11.8 Apply a bead of sealant to the sump or crankcase mating surface. Ensure the sealant is applied on the inside of the retaining bolt holes

11.9 Refit the sump and tighten the bolts

when the oil and filter are due for renewal, it is recommended that the filter is also removed, and a new one fitted. After reassembly, the engine can then be refilled with fresh oil. Refer to Chapter 1B for further information.

2 Chock the rear wheels then jack up the front of the vehicle and support it on axle stands (see *Jacking and vehicle support*). Undo the screws and remove the engine undershield.

3 Remove the exhaust front pipe as described in Chapter 4B.

4 Where necessary, disconnect the wiring connector from the oil temperature sender unit, which is screwed into the sump.

5 Progressively slacken and remove all the sump retaining bolts/nuts. Since the sump bolts vary in length, remove each bolt in turn, and store it in its correct fitted order by pushing it through a clearly-marked cardboard template. This will avoid the possibility of installing the bolts in the wrong locations on refitting.

6 Try to break the joint by striking the sump with the palm of your hand, then lower and withdraw the sump from under the car. If the sump is stuck (which is quite likely) use a putty knife or similar, carefully inserted between the sump and block. Ease the knife along the joint until the sump is released. While the sump is removed, take the opportunity to check the oil pump pick-up/strainer for signs of clogging or splitting. If necessary, remove the pump as described in Section 12, and clean or renew the strainer.

Refitting

7 Clean all traces of sealant from the mating surfaces of the cylinder block/crankcase and sump, then use a clean rag to wipe out the sump and the engine's interior.

8 On engines where the sump was fitted without a gasket, ensure that the sump mating surfaces are clean and dry, then apply a thin coating of suitable sealant to the sump or crankcase mating surface **(see illustration)**.

9 Offer up the sump to the cylinder block/crankcase. Refit its retaining bolts/nuts, ensuring that each bolt is screwed into its original location. Tighten the bolts evenly and progressively to the specified torque setting **(see illustration)**.

12.4 Oil pick-up tube Allen screws (arrowed)

12.5 Oil pump retaining bolts (arrowed)

10 Where necessary, align the air conditioning compressor with its mountings on the sump, and insert the retaining bolts. Securely tighten the compressor retaining bolts, then refit the drivebelt as described in Chapter 1B.
11 Reconnect the wiring connector to the oil temperature sensor (where fitted).
12 Lower the vehicle to the ground, then refill the engine with oil as described in Chapter 1B.

12 Oil pump – removal, inspection and refitting

Removal

1 Remove the sump as described in Section 11.
2 Remove the crankshaft sprocket as described in Section 8. Recover the locating key from the crankshaft.
3 Disconnect the wiring plug, undo the bolts and remove the crankshaft position sensor, located on the right-hand end of the cylinder block.
4 Undo the three Allen screws and remove the oil pump pick-up tube from the pump/block **(see illustration)**. Discard the oil seal, a new one must be fitted.

5 Undo the 8 bolts, and remove the oil pump **(see illustration)**.

Inspection

6 Undo and remove the Torx bolts securing the cover to the oil pump **(see illustration)**. Examine the pump rotors and body for signs of wear and damage. If worn, the complete pump must be renewed.
7 Remove the circlip, and extract the cap, valve piston and spring, noting which way around they are fitted **(see illustrations)**. The condition of the relief valve spring can only be measured by comparing it with a new one;

if there is any doubt about its condition, it should also be renewed.
8 Refit the relief valve piston and spring, then secure them in place with the circlip.
9 Refit the cover to the oil pump, and tighten the Torx bolts securely.

Refitting

10 Remove all traces of sealant, and thoroughly clean the mating surfaces of the oil pump and cylinder block.
11 Apply a 4 mm wide bead of silicone sealant to the mating face of the cylinder

12.6 Undo the Torx bolts and remove the pump cover

12.7a Remove the circlip . . .

12.7b . . . cap . . .

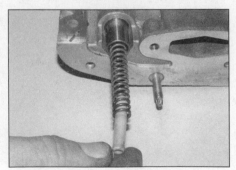

12.7c . . . spring . . .

12.7d . . . and piston

12.11 Apply a bead of sealant to the cylinder block mating surface

12.12a Fit a new seal . . .

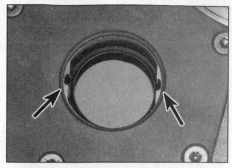

12.12b . . . align the pump gear flats (arrowed) . . .

block **(see illustration)**. Ensure that no sealant enters any of the holes in the block.

12 With a new oil seal fitted, refit the oil pump over the end of the crankshaft, aligning the flats in the pump drivegear with the flats machined in the crankshaft **(see illustrations)**. Note that new oil pumps are supplied with the oil seal already fitted, and a seal protector sleeve. The sleeve fits over the end of the crankshaft to protect the seal as the pump is fitted.

13 Install the oil pump bolts and tighten them to the specified torque.

14 Refit the oil pick-up tube to the pump/ cylinder block using a new O-ring seal. Ensure the oil dipstick guide tube is correctly refitted.

15 Refit the Woodruff key to the crankshaft, and slide the crankshaft sprocket into place.

16 The remainder of refitting is a reversal of removal.

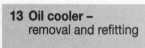

13 Oil cooler – removal and refitting

Removal

1 Chock the rear wheels then jack up the front of the vehicle and support it on axle stands (see *Jacking and vehicle support*). Undo the screws and remove the engine undershield.

2 The oil cooler is fitted to the front of the oil

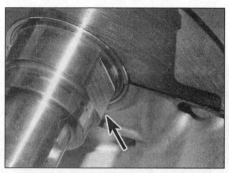

12.12c . . . with those of the crankshaft (arrowed)

filter housing. Drain the coolant as described in Chapter 1B.

3 Drain the engine oil as described in Chapter 1B, or be prepared for fluid spillage.

4 Undo the 5 bolts/stud and remove the oil cooler. Recover the O-ring seals **(see illustrations)**.

Refitting

5 Fit new O-ring seals into the recesses in the oil filter housing, and refit the cooler. Tighten the bolts securely.

6 Refill or top-up the cooling system and engine oil level as described in Chapter 1B or *Weekly Checks* (as applicable). Start the engine, and check the oil cooler for signs of leakage.

13.4a Undo the oil cooler bolts/stud (arrowed)

14 Oil seals – renewal

Crankshaft

Right-hand oil seal

1 Remove the crankshaft sprocket and Woodruff key as described in Section 8.

2 Measure and note the fitted depth of the oil seal.

3 Pull the oil seal from the housing using a screwdriver. Alternatively, drill a small hole in the oil seal, and use a self-tapping screw and a pair of pliers to remove it **(see illustration)**.

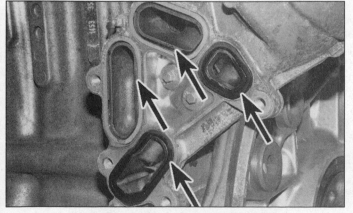

13.4b Renew the O-ring seals (arrowed)

14.3 Take great care not to mark the crankshaft whilst levering out the oil seal

14.5a Slide the seal and protective sleeve over the end of the crankshaft . . .

14.5b . . . and press the seal into place

14.12 Slide the seal and protective sleeve over the left-hand end of the crankshaft

4 Clean the oil seal housing and the crankshaft sealing surface.

5 The seal has a Teflon lip and must not be oiled or marked. The new seal should be supplied with a protector sleeve, which fits over the end of the crankshaft to prevent any damage to the seal lip. With the sleeve in place, press the seal (open end first) into the pump to the previously-noted depth, using a suitable tube or socket (see illustrations).

6 Where applicable, remove the plastic sleeve from the end of the crankshaft.

7 Refit the timing belt crankshaft sprocket as described in Section 8.

Left-hand oil seal

8 Remove the flywheel, as described in Section 16.

9 Measure and note the fitted depth of the oil seal.

10 Pull the oil seal from the housing using a screwdriver. Alternatively, drill a small hole in the oil seal, and use a self-tapping screw and a pair of pliers to remove it (see illustration 14.3).

11 Clean the oil seal housing and the crankshaft sealing surface.

12 The seal has a Teflon lip and must not be oiled or marked. The new seal should be supplied with a protector sleeve, which fits over the end of the crankshaft to prevent any damage to the seal lip (see illustration). With the sleeve in place, press the seal (open end first) into the housing to the previously-noted depth, using a suitable tube or socket.

13 Where applicable, remove the plastic sleeve from the end of the crankshaft.

14 Refit the flywheel, as described in Section 16.

Camshaft

15 Remove the camshaft sprocket as described in Section 8. In principle there is no need to remove the timing belt completely, but remember that if the belt has been contaminated with oil, it must be renewed.

16 Pull the oil seal from the housing using a hooked instrument. Alternatively, drill a small hole in the oil seal and use a self-tapping screw and a pair of pliers to remove it (see illustration).

17 Clean the oil seal housing and the camshaft sealing surface.

18 The seal has a Teflon lip and must not be oiled or marked. The new seal should be supplied with a protector sleeve. which fits over the end of the camshaft to prevent any damage to the seal lip (see illustration). With the sleeve in place, press the seal (open end first) into the housing, using a suitable tube or socket which bears only of the outer edge of the seal.

19 Refit the camshaft sprocket as described in Section 8.

20 Where necessary, fit a new timing belt with reference to Section 7.

15 Oil pressure switch and level sensor – removal and refitting

Removal

Oil pressure switch

1 The oil pressure switch is located at the front of the cylinder block, adjacent to the oil dipstick guide tube. Note that on some models, access to the switch may be improved if the vehicle is jacked up and supported on axle stands, then undo the screws and remove the engine undershield so that the switch can be reached from underneath (see *Jacking and vehicle support*).

2 Remove the protective sleeve from the wiring plug (where applicable), then disconnect the wiring from the switch.

3 Unscrew the switch from the cylinder block, and recover the sealing washer (see illustration). Be prepared for oil spillage, and if the switch is to be left removed from the engine for any length of time, plug the hole in the cylinder block.

Oil level sensor

4 The oil level sensor is located at the rear of the cylinder block. Jack up the front of the vehicle and support it securely on axle stands (see *Jacking and vehicle support*). Undo the screws and remove the engine undershield.

14.16 Drill a hole, insert a self-tapping screw, and pull the seal from place using pliers

14.18 Fit the protective sleeve and seal over the end of the camshaft

15.3 The oil pressure switch is located on the front face of the cylinder block (arrowed)

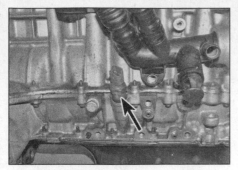

15.5 The oil level sensor is located on the rear face of the cylinder block (arrowed)

5 Reach up between the driveshaft and the cylinder block and disconnect the sensor wiring plug **(see illustration)**.

6 Using an open-ended spanner, unscrew the sensor and withdraw it from position.

Refitting

Oil pressure switch

7 Examine the sealing washer for any signs of damage or deterioration, and if necessary renew.

8 Refit the switch, complete with washer, and tighten it to the specified torque.

9 Refit the engine undershield, and lower the vehicle to the ground.

Oil level sensor

10 Smear a little silicone sealant on the threads and refit the sensor to the cylinder block, tightening it securely.

11 Reconnect the sensor wiring plug.

12 Refit the engine undershield, and lower the vehicle to the ground.

16 Flywheel – removal, inspection and refitting

Removal

1 Remove the transmission as described in Chapter 7A, then remove the clutch assembly as described in Chapter 6.

2 Prevent the flywheel from turning by locking the ring gear teeth **(see illustration 5.2)**. Alternatively, bolt a strap between the flywheel and the cylinder block/crankcase. *Do not* attempt to lock the flywheel in position using the crankshaft pulley locking tool described in Section 3. Insert a 12 mm diameter rod or drill bit through the hole in the flywheel cover casting, and into a slot in the flywheel.

3 Make alignment marks between the flywheel and crankshaft to aid refitting. Slacken and remove the flywheel retaining bolts, and remove the flywheel from the end of the crankshaft. Be careful not to drop it; it is heavy. If the flywheel locating dowel (where fitted) is a loose fit in the crankshaft end,

16.8 Flywheel retaining Torx bolts

remove it and store it with the flywheel for safe-keeping. Discard the flywheel bolts; new ones must be used on refitting.

Inspection

4 Examine the flywheel for scoring of the clutch face, and for wear or chipping of the ring gear teeth. If the clutch face is scored, the flywheel may be surface-ground, but renewal is preferable. Seek the advice of a Peugeot dealer or engine reconditioning specialist to see if machining is possible. If the ring gear is worn or damaged, the flywheel must be renewed, as it is not possible to renew the ring gear separately.

Refitting

5 Clean the mating surfaces of the flywheel and crankshaft. Remove any remaining locking compound from the threads of the crankshaft holes, using the correct size of tap, if available.

6 If the new flywheel retaining bolts are not supplied with their threads already pre-coated, apply a suitable thread-locking compound to the threads of each bolt.

HAYNES HINT *If a suitable tap is not available, cut two slots along the threads of one of the old flywheel bolts, and use the bolt to remove the locking compound from the threads.*

All models except engines with dual mass flywheel

7 Ensure that the locating dowel is in position. Offer up the flywheel, locating it on the dowel (where fitted), and fit the new retaining bolts. Where no locating dowel is fitted, align the previously-made marks to ensure the flywheel is refitted in its original position.

8 Lock the flywheel using the method employed on dismantling, and tighten the retaining bolts to the specified torque **(see illustration)**.

Engines with dual mass flywheel

9 The dual mass flywheel is designed to

reduce harshness and vibration in the action of the engine, clutch and transmission. With this type of flywheel, two flywheel centralising tools are needed (available from Peugeot dealers). These are screwed into two opposite flywheel bolt holes in the crankshaft. As the tools are screwed down, their conical shape centralises the flywheel with regard to the crankshaft.

10 With the flywheel centralised, fit the new bolts into the remaining flywheel holes, then lock the flywheel using the same method employed on dismantling, and tighten the bolts to the specified torque.

11 Remove the two centralising tools, fit the new bolts and tighten them to the specified torque.

All models

12 Refit the clutch as described in Chapter 6. Remove the flywheel locking tool, and refit the transmission as described in Chapter 7A.

17 Engine/transmission mountings – inspection and renewal

Inspection

1 If improved access is required, chock the rear wheels then jack up the front of the car and support it on axle stands (see *Jacking and vehicle support*). Undo the screws and remove the engine undershield.

2 Check the mounting rubbers to see if they are cracked, hardened or separated from the metal at any point; renew the mounting if any such damage or deterioration is evident.

3 Check that all the mountings' fasteners are securely tightened; use a torque wrench to check if possible.

4 Using a large screwdriver or a crowbar, check for wear in each mounting by carefully levering against it to check for free play. Where this is not possible, enlist the aid of an assistant to move the engine/transmission back-and-forth, or from side-to-side, while you watch the mounting. While some free play is to be expected even from new components, excessive wear should be obvious. If excessive free play is found, check first that the fasteners are correctly secured, then renew any worn components as described below.

Renewal

Right-hand mounting

5 Release all the relevant hoses and wiring from their retaining clips. Place the hoses/wiring clear of the mounting so that the removal procedure is not hindered. Undo the screws and remove the engine undershield.

6 Place a jack beneath the engine, with a block of wood on the jack head. Raise the jack until it is supporting the weight of the engine.

7 Undo the bolts/nut securing the engine

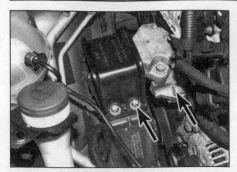

17.7 Undo the right-hand engine mounting bolts/nut (arrowed)

17.15 Left-hand engine/transmission mounting bolts (arrowed)

17.20 Lower engine torque rod bracket

mounting to the body and the support bracket **(see illustration)**.

8 If required, undo the bolts/nuts securing the support bracket to the cylinder head/cylinder block.

9 Check all components carefully for signs of wear or damage, and renew as necessary.

10 Where removed, refit the support bracket to the cylinder head, and tighten the bolts securely.

11 Refit the mount to the body and support bracket, then tighten the bolts to the specified torque.

12 Remove the jack from underneath the engine.

Left-hand mounting

13 Remove the engine management ECM and module box as described in Chapter 4B.

14 Undo the screws and remove the engine undershield, then place a jack beneath the transmission, with a block of wood on the jack

head. Raise the jack until it is supporting the weight of the transmission.

15 Slacken and remove the bolts securing the mounting to the support bracket and vehicle body. If required, undo the bolts/nut and remove the support bracket **(see illustration)**.

16 Check all components carefully for signs of wear or damage, and renew as necessary.

17 Refit the mounting, tighten the bolts to the specified torque settings, and remove the jack from underneath the transmission.

18 Refit the module box and ECM as described in Chapter 4B.

Lower engine torque rod

19 If not already done, chock the rear wheels, then jack up the front of the vehicle and support it securely on axle stands (see *Jacking and vehicle support*). Undo the screws and remove the engine undershield.

20 Unscrew and remove the bolt securing the movement limiter link to the driveshaft intermediate bearing housing **(see illustration)**.

21 Remove the bolt securing the link to the subframe. Withdraw the link.

22 To remove the intermediate bearing housing assembly it will first be necessary to remove the right-hand driveshaft as described in Chapter 8.

23 With the driveshaft removed, undo the retaining bolts and remove the bearing housing from the rear of the cylinder block.

24 Check carefully for signs of wear or damage on all components, and renew them where necessary. The rubber bush fitted to the bearing housing is available as a separate item (at the time of writing), and can be pressed out of, and back into place.

25 On reassembly, fit the bearing housing assembly to the rear of the cylinder block, and tighten its retaining bolts securely. Refit the driveshaft as described in Chapter 8.

26 Refit the movement limiter link, and tighten both its bolts to their specified torque settings. Refit the engine undershield.

27 Lower the vehicle to the ground.

Chapter 2 Part E:
2.0 litre DOHC diesel engine in-car repair procedures

Contents

Degrees of difficulty

Easy, suitable for novice with little experience	**Fairly easy,** suitable for beginner with some experience	**Fairly difficult,** suitable for competent DIY mechanic	**Difficult,** suitable for experienced DIY mechanic	**Very difficult,** suitable for expert DIY or professional

Specifications

General

Designation	DW10BTED4
Engine code*	RHR
Bore	85.00 mm
Stroke	88.00 mm
Direction of crankshaft rotation	Clockwise (viewed from the right-hand side of vehicle)
No 1 cylinder location	At the transmission end of block
Maximum power output	100 kW @ 4000 rpm
Maximum torque output	320 Nm @ 2000 rpm
Compression ratio	18.0 : 1

* The engine code is stamped on a plate attached to the front of the cylinder block, next to the oil filter

Compression pressures (engine hot, at cranking speed)

Normal	20 ± 5 bar
Maximum difference between any two cylinders	5 bar

Camshaft

Drive	Toothed belt

Lubrication system

Oil pump type	Gear-type, chain-driven off the crankshaft right-hand end
Minimum oil pressure @ 80°C:	
1000 rpm	1.9 bar
4000 rpm	4.0 bar
Oil pressure warning switch operating pressure	0.8 bar

Torque wrench settings

	Nm	lbf ft
Big-end bearing cap nuts*:		
Stage 1	20	15
Stage 2	Angle-tighten a further 70°	
Camshaft bearing housing bolts	10	7
Camshaft position sensor bolt	6	4
Camshaft sprocket bolt:		
Stage 1	20	15
Stage 2	Angle-tighten a further 60°	
Clutch bellhousing closure plate	18	13
Coolant outlet housing	18	13
Crankshaft pulley bolt:		
Stage 1	70	52
Stage 2	Angle-tighten a further 60°	
Crankshaft right-hand oil seal housing bolts	14	10
Crankshaft sensor bolt	7	5
Cylinder head bolts:		
Stage 1	15	11
Stage 2	60	44
Stage 3	Angle-tighten a further 220° ± 5°	
Cylinder head cover bolts	10	7
Driveplate bolts*:		
Stage 1	20	15
Stage 2	66	49
Engine-to-transmission fixing bolts	60	44
Exhaust manifold nuts	25	18
Flywheel bolts*	50	37
High-pressure fuel pump bolts	20	15
Left-hand engine/transmission mounting:		
Bracket-to-transmission bolts	45	33
Bracket-to-transmission nut	55	41
Mounting to body/bracket	27	20
Main bearing cap bolts:		
Stage 1	25	18
Stage 2	Angle-tighten a further 60°	
Oil filter cap	25	18
Oil pressure switch	20	15
Oil pump mounting bolts	16	12
Piston oil jet spray tube bolt	10	7
Rear engine mounting/torque rod:		
Torque rod to mounting assembly	50	37
Torque rod-to-subframe nut/bolt	50	37
Mounting to engine	60	44
Right-hand engine mounting:		
Connecting link to body	50	37
Connecting link to bracket	50	37
Bracket-to-mounting nut	45	33
Bracket-to-engine bracket Torx	60	44
Engine bracket to engine	56	41
Sump bolts	16	12
Sump drain plug	30	22
Timing belt idler roller bolt	56	41
Timing belt tensioner	21	15
Timing chain tensioner bolts	6	4

* Do not re-use

1 General information

How to use this Chapter

This Part of Chapter 2 describes the repair procedures that can reasonably be carried out on the engine while it remains in the vehicle. If the engine has been removed from the vehicle and is being dismantled as described in Part F, any preliminary dismantling procedures can be ignored.

Note that, while it may be possible physically to overhaul items such as the piston/connecting rod assemblies while the engine is in the car, such tasks are not usually carried out as separate operations. Usually, several additional procedures are required (not to mention the cleaning of components and oilways); for this reason, all such tasks are classed as major overhaul procedures, and are described in Part F of this Chapter.

Part F describes the removal of the engine/transmission from the car, and the full overhaul procedures that can then be carried out.

DW10BTED4 engines

This engine is based on the DW10 SOHC direct injection engine described in Chapter 2C and which has appeared in many Peugeot and Citroën vehicles. In particular, the cylinder block components are very similar, however, the remainder of the engine has been completely redesigned. The engine is of double overhead camshaft (DOHC) 16-valve design. The turbocharged, four-cylinder engine is mounted transversely, with the transmission mounted on the left-hand side.

A toothed timing belt drives the exhaust camshaft and coolant pump. The exhaust camshaft drives the intake camshaft via a chain at the timing belt end. The camshafts operate the intake and exhaust valves via rocker arms which are supported at their pivot ends by hydraulic self-adjusting tappets. The camshafts are supported by bearings machined directly in the cylinder head and camshaft bearing housing.

The high-pressure fuel pump is driven from the left-hand end of the exhaust camshaft. The high-pressure fuel pump supplies fuel to the fuel rail, and subsequently to the electronically-controlled injectors which inject the fuel direct into the combustion chambers. This design differs from the previous type where an injection pump supplies the fuel at high pressure to each injector. The earlier, conventional type injection pump required fine calibration and timing, and these functions are now completed by the high-pressure pump, electronic injectors and engine management ECM.

The crankshaft runs in five main bearings of the usual shell type. Endfloat is controlled by thrustwashers either side of No 2 main bearing.

The pistons are selected to be of matching weight, and incorporate fully-floating gudgeon pins retained by circlips.

The oil pump is chain-driven from the right-hand end of the crankshaft.

Throughout the manual, it is often necessary to identify the engines not only by their cubic capacity, but also by their engine code. The engine code consists of three letters (eg, RHR). The code is stamped on a plate attached to the front of the cylinder block.

Repair operations precaution

The engine is a complex unit with numerous accessories and ancillary components. The design of the engine compartment is such that every conceivable space has been utilised, and access to virtually all of the engine components is extremely limited. In many cases, ancillary components will have to be removed, or moved to one side, and wiring, pipes and hoses will have to be disconnected or removed from various cable clips and support brackets.

When working on this engine, read through the entire procedure first, look at the car and engine at the same time, and establish whether you have the necessary tools, equipment, skill and patience to proceed. Allow considerable time for any operation, and be prepared for the unexpected. Any major work on these engines is not for the faint-hearted!

Because of the limited access, many of the engine photographs appearing in this Chapter were, by necessity, taken with the engine removed from the vehicle.

 Warning: It is essential to observe strict precautions when working on the fuel system components of the engine, particularly the high-pressure side of the system. Before carrying out any engine operations that entail working on, or near, any part of the fuel system, refer to the special information given in Chapter 4B, Section 2.

Operations with engine in vehicle

a) Compression pressure – testing.
b) Cylinder head cover(s) – removal and refitting.
c) Crankshaft pulley – removal and refitting.
d) Timing belt covers – removal and refitting.
e) Timing belt/chain – removal, refitting and adjustment.
f) Timing belt tensioner and sprockets – removal and refitting.
g) Camshaft oil seal – renewal.
h) Camshafts, rocker arms and hydraulic tappets – removal, inspection and refitting.
i) Sump – removal and refitting.
j) Oil pump – removal and refitting.
k) Crankshaft oil seals – renewal.
l) Engine/transmission mountings – inspection and renewal.
m) Flywheel/driveplate – removal, inspection and refitting.

2 Compression and leakdown tests – description and interpretation

Compression test

Note: A compression tester specifically designed for diesel engines must be used for this test.

1 When engine performance is down, or if misfiring occurs which cannot be attributed to the fuel system, a compression test can provide diagnostic clues as to the engine's condition. If the test is performed regularly, it can give warning of trouble before any other symptoms become apparent.

2 A compression tester specifically intended for diesel engines must be used, because of the higher pressures involved. The tester is connected to an adapter which screws into the glow plug or injector hole. On these engines, an adapter suitable for use in the glow plug holes will be required, so as not to disturb the fuel system components. It is unlikely to be worthwhile buying such a tester for occasional use, but it may be possible to borrow or hire one – if not, have the test performed by a garage.

3 Unless specific instructions to the contrary are supplied with the tester, observe the following points:

a) The battery must be in a good state of charge, the air filter must be clean, and the engine should be at normal operating temperature.
b) All the glow plugs should be removed as described in Chapter 5C before starting the test.
c) The wiring connector on the engine management system ECU (see Chapter 4B) must be disconnected.

4 The compression pressures measured are not so important as the balance between cylinders. Values are given in the Specifications.

5 The cause of poor compression is less easy to establish on a diesel engine than on a petrol one. The effect of introducing oil into the cylinders ('wet' testing) is not conclusive, because there is a risk that the oil will sit in the swirl chamber or in the recess on the piston crown instead of passing to the rings. However, the following can be used as a rough guide to diagnosis.

6 All cylinders should produce very similar pressures; any difference greater than that specified indicates the existence of a fault. Note that the compression should build-up quickly in a healthy engine; low compression on the first stroke, followed by gradually-increasing pressure on successive strokes, indicates worn piston rings. A low compression reading on the first stroke, which does not build-up during successive strokes, indicates leaking valves or a blown head gasket (a cracked head could also be the cause). Deposits on the undersides of the valve heads can also cause low compression.

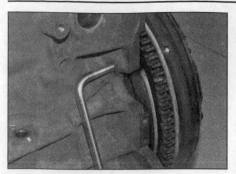

3.7a The tool fits through the hole in the cylinder block flange . . .

3.7b . . . and into a hole in the rear of the flywheel

3.8 Fit the tool through the hole in the exhaust camshaft sprocket, into the timing hole in the cylinder head

7 A low reading from two adjacent cylinders is almost certainly due to the head gasket having blown between them; the presence of coolant in the engine oil will confirm this.

8 If the compression reading is unusually high, the cylinder head surfaces, valves and pistons are probably coated with carbon deposits. If this is the case, the cylinder head should be removed and decarbonised (see Part F).

Leakdown test

9 A leakdown test measures the rate at which compressed air fed into the cylinder is lost. It is an alternative to a compression test, and in many ways it is better, since the escaping air provides easy identification of where pressure loss is occurring (piston rings, valves or head gasket).

10 The equipment needed for leakdown testing is unlikely to be available to the home mechanic. If poor compression is suspected, have the test performed by a suitably-equipped garage.

3 Engine assembly/valve timing holes – general information and usage

Note: *Do not attempt to rotate the engine whilst the crankshaft and camshaft are locked in position. If the engine is to be left in this state for a long period of time, it is a good idea to place suitable warning notices inside the vehicle, and in the engine compartment. This will reduce the possibility of the engine being accidentally cranked on the starter motor, which is likely to cause damage with the locking pins in place.*

1 Timing holes or slots are located only in the flywheel/driveplate and camshaft sprocket hub. The holes/slots are used to align the crankshaft and camshaft at the TDC position for Nos 1 and 4. This will ensure that the valve timing is maintained during operations that require removal and refitting of the timing belt. When the holes/slots are aligned with their corresponding holes in the cylinder block and cylinder head, suitable diameter bolts/pins can be inserted to lock the crankshaft and

camshaft in position, preventing rotation. Note that with the timing holes aligned, No 4 piston is at TDC on its compression stroke.

2 To align the engine assembly/valve timing holes, proceed as follows.

3 Apply the handbrake, then jack up the front of the vehicle and support it on axle stands (see *Jacking and vehicle support*). Remove the right-hand front roadwheel.

4 To gain access to the crankshaft pulley, to enable the engine to be turned, the wheelarch plastic liner must be removed. The liner is secured by several plastic expanding rivets. To remove the rivets, push in the centre pins a little, then prise the clips from place. Remove the liner from under the front wing. Where necessary, unclip the coolant hoses from under the wing to improve access further. The crankshaft can then be turned using a suitable socket and extension bar fitted to the pulley bolt.

5 Remove the upper timing belt cover as described in Section 6.

6 Turn the crankshaft until the timing hole in the camshaft sprocket is aligned with the corresponding hole in the cylinder head. Note that the crankshaft must always be turned in a clockwise direction (viewed from the right-hand side of vehicle). Use a small mirror so that the position of the sprocket timing slot can be observed. When the slot is aligned with the corresponding hole in the cylinder head, the camshaft is positioned correctly.

7 Insert Peugeot tool No. (-).0188.X or an 8 mm diameter bolt, rod or drill through the hole in the left-hand flange of the cylinder block by the starter motor; if necessary, carefully turn the crankshaft either way until the rod enters the timing hole in the flywheel/driveplate **(see illustrations)**. Note that if an 8.0 mm bolt/rod/drill bit is used, it must be flat (not tapered at all) at the end. If improved access is required, remove the starter motor as described in Chapter 5A.

8 Insert an 8 mm bolt, rod or drill through the hole in the camshaft sprocket hub and into engagement with the cylinder head **(see illustration)**.

9 The crankshaft and camshaft are now locked in position, preventing unnecessary rotation.

4 Cylinder head cover – removal and refitting

Removal

1 Remove the plastic cover from the top of the engine. The cover simply pulls up from its rubber mountings. Carry out the following operations to remove the scuttle trim panel and crossmember:

  a) *Remove the wiper arms (see Chapter 12).*
  b) *Push in the centre pins, and prise out the two plastic rivets at each end of the trim panel.*
  c) *Pull the outer ends of the panel up, then pull the panel centre down and forwards to release it from the windscreen.*
  d) *Undo the two screws securing the master cylinder upper fluid reservoir. Do not disconnect the fluid pipes.*
  e) *Release the clips securing the sound insulation material, then undo the two bolts and remove the scuttle crossmember.*

2 The cylinder head cover is integral with the intake manifold. Begin by releasing the wiring harness from the timing belt upper cover.

3 Disconnect the wiring plug, then unscrew the camshaft position sensor from the cover **(see illustration)**.

4 Undo the bolts securing the upper timing belt cover to the cylinder head cover/intake manifold.

4.3 Undo the bolt and remove the camshaft position sensor (arrowed)

4.5 Release the clips (arrowed) and detach the injector wiring harness duct

4.6a Release the clamps and disconnect the breather hose (arrowed) from the cylinder head cover . . .

4.6b . . . the EGR pipe from the intake manifold . . .

5 Disconnect the injectors' wiring plugs, then detach the harness duct from the intake manifold/cover and position it to one side **(see illustration)**.

6 Disconnect the crankcase ventilation hoses from the intake manifold/cover, then release the clamp and disconnect the EGR pipe from the intake manifold **(see illustrations)**.

7 Release the glow plugs' wiring harness from the 2 clips on the cover.

8 Slacken the clamps and disconnect the intake hoses from the manifold.

9 Unclip the fuel temperature sensor from the underside of the manifold.

10 Undo the manifold/cover retaining bolts in the **reverse** of the sequence shown in illustration 4.12. Discard the gaskets, new ones must be fitted.

Refitting

11 Clean the sealing surfaces of the manifold/cover and the cylinder head.

12 Fit the new seals to the intake manifold/cover, then fit it to the cylinder head. Use a little petroleum jelly on the manifold O-rings to ease

reassembly. Tighten the bolts to the specified torque in sequence **(see illustration)**.

13 The remainder of refitting is a reversal of removal, noting the following points:

a) *Tighten all fasteners to their specified torque.*

b) *Before refitting the timing belt upper cover, adjust the camshaft position sensor air gap as described in Chapter 4B, Section 13.*

5 Crankshaft pulley – removal and refitting

Removal

1 Remove the auxiliary drivebelt as described in Chapter 1B.

2 Position the camshaft and crankshaft at TDC for No. 1 cylinder, as described in Section 3. **Note:** *It is essential that the crankshaft and camshaft timing pins are in place as described in Section 3. This is because on these engines, the crankshaft sprocket has a wider keyway,*

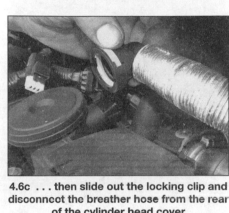

4.6c . . . then slide out the locking clip and disconnect the breather hose from the rear of the cylinder head cover

to allow it to rotate a little independently of the crankshaft during the belt tensioning procedure. Failure to lock the crankshaft and camshaft could result in the timing being lost.

3 To prevent crankshaft turning whilst the pulley retaining bolt is being slackened the flywheel/driveplate ring gear can be locked using (Peugeot tool No. (-).0188.F) or a suitable tool made from steel angle. Remove the starter motor as described in Chapter 5A, and bolt the tool to the bellhousing flange so it engages with the ring gear teeth **(see illustration)**. *Do not* attempt to lock the pulley by only inserting a bolt/drill through the timing hole.

4 Using a suitable socket and extension bar, unscrew the retaining bolt, remove the washer, then slide the pulley off the end of

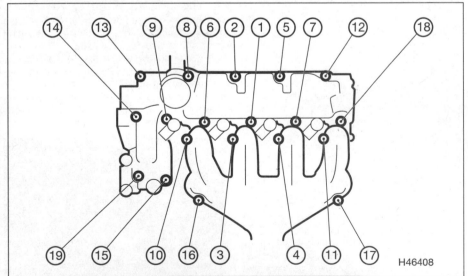

4.12 Intake manifold/cylinder head cover bolt tightening sequence
Note that the 55 mm bolt is fitted in position 14, and the 70 mm bolts are fitted in positions 16 and 17

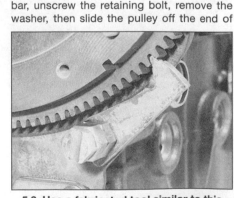

5.3 Use a fabricated tool similar to this to lock the flywheel ring gear and prevent crankshaft rotation

5.4 Undo the bolt and remove the crankshaft pulley

6.4 Depress the clips and disconnect the fuel pipes (arrowed)

6.6 Upper timing belt fasteners (arrowed)

the crankshaft **(see illustration)**. If the pulley is tight fit, it can be drawn off the crankshaft using a suitable puller. If a puller is being used, refit the pulley retaining bolt without the washer, to avoid damaging the crankshaft as the puller is tightened.

Refitting

5 Ensure the camshaft and crankshaft are positioned at TDC as described previously, and the flywheel/driveplate ring gear is locked in position, as described in paragraph 3.
6 Thoroughly clean the threads of the pulley retaining bolt, then apply a coat of locking compound to the bolt threads. Peugeot recommend the use of Loctite (available from your Peugeot dealer); in the absence of this, any good-quality locking compound may be used.
7 Refit the crankshaft pulley retaining bolt and washer. Tighten the bolt to the specified torque, then through the specified angle.
8 Remove the crankshaft, camshaft and flywheel/driveplate locking tools.
9 Refit and tension the auxiliary drivebelt as described in Chapter 1B.

6 Timing belt covers – removal and refitting

 Warning: Refer to the precautionary information contained in Section 1 before proceeding.

Removal

Upper cover

1 Pull up the plastic cover from the top of the engine, then undo the screws and remove the engine undershield. Carry out the following operations to remove the scuttle trim panel and crossmember:
a) Remove the wiper arms (see Chapter 12).
b) Push in the centre pins, and prise out the two plastic rivets at each end of the trim panel.
c) Pull the outer ends of the panel up, then pull the panel centre down and forwards to release it from the windscreen.
d) Undo the two screws securing the master

cylinder upper fluid reservoir. Do not disconnect the fluid pipes.
e) Release the clips securing the sound insulation material, then undo the two bolts and remove the scuttle crossmember.

2 Position a trolley jack under the engine, and using a piece of wood on the jack head, support the weight of the engine.
3 Undo the bolts and remove the right-hand engine mounting and support bracket – see Section 17.
4 At the connections at the right-hand end of the cylinder head, disconnect the fuel supply and return hose quick-release fittings using a small screwdriver to press down and release the locking clip **(see illustration)**. Cover the open unions to prevent dirt entry, using small plastic bags, or fingers cut from clean rubber gloves.
5 Release the two fuel hoses from the retaining clips at the right-hand end of the cylinder head.
6 Move the electrical harness to one side, then undo the screws/nut and remove the upper timing belt cover **(see illustration)**.

Lower cover

7 Remove the upper cover as described previously.
8 Remove the crankshaft pulley as described in Section 5.
9 Undo the bolt and position the crankshaft sensor to one side **(see illustration)**.
10 Carefully pull the crankshaft sensor signal disc from the crankshaft **(see illustration)**. If the disc is reluctant to move, screw in two

6.9 Crankshaft position sensor bolt (arrowed)

6.0 mm bolts into the threaded holes in the disc and force it from place.
11 Undo the bolts and remove the lower timing belt cover.

Refitting

12 Refitting of all the covers is a reversal of the relevant removal procedure, ensuring that each cover section is correctly located, and that the cover retaining bolts are securely tightened. Ensure that all disturbed hoses are reconnected and retained by their relevant clips.

7 Timing belt – removal, inspection, refitting and tensioning

General

1 The timing belt drives the camshaft and coolant pump from a toothed sprocket on the end of the crankshaft. If the belt breaks or slips in service, the pistons are likely to hit the valve heads, resulting in expensive damage.
2 The timing belt should be renewed at the specified intervals, or earlier if it is contaminated with oil, or at all noisy in operation (a 'scraping' noise due to uneven wear).
3 If the timing belt is being removed, it is a wise precaution to check the condition of the coolant pump at the same time (check for signs of coolant leakage). This may avoid the need to remove the timing belt again at a later stage, should the coolant pump fail.

6.10 Sensor signal disc

Removal

4 Apply the handbrake, then jack up the front of the vehicle and support it on axle stands (see *Jacking and vehicle support*). Remove the front right-hand roadwheel, wheelarch liner (to expose the crankshaft pulley), and the engine undershield. The wheelarch liner is secured by several plastic expanding rivets, or push-in clips. Push the centre pins in a little then prise the rivet from place. The engine undershield is retained by several screw fasteners. Rotate the fasteners 90 degrees anti-clockwise and remove them.

5 Remove the crankshaft pulley as described in Section 5, then use 6.0 mm bolts to draw the sensor wheel from the end of the crankshaft **(see illustration 6.10)**.

6 Remove the upper and lower timing belt covers as described in the previous Section.

7 Ensure the engine is positioned at TDC as described in Section 3, with the camshaft and crankshaft locking tools described in place.

8 Loosen the bolt on the tensioner roller, and turn the tensioner clockwise to release the tension on the timing belt. Use an Allen key in the hole provided to turn the tensioner bracket against the spring tension. Retighten the bolt sufficiently to hold the tensioner in its released position; do not fully tighten the bolt in this position.

9 Mark the timing belt with an arrow to indicate its running direction, if it is to be re-used. Remove the belt from the sprockets.

Inspection

10 Renew the belt as a matter of course, regardless of its apparent condition. The cost of a new belt is nothing compared with the cost of repairs, should the belt break in service. If signs of oil contamination are found, trace the source of the oil leak and rectify it. Wash down the engine timing belt area and all related components, to remove all traces of oil. Check that the tensioner and idler pulleys rotate freely without any sign of roughness, and also check that the coolant pump pulley rotates freely. If necessary, renew these items.

Refitting and tensioning

11 Commence refitting by ensuring that the TDC timing pins are still in position correctly.

12 Centre the crankshaft sprocket by inserting Peugeot tool (-).0188.AH either side

7.12 Position the crankshaft sprocket so that equal gaps exists each side of the key (arrowed)

of the crankshaft key, and into the keyway in the sprocket. In the absence of the tool, position the sprocket centrally, ensuring a gap exists each side of the key **(see illustration)**.

13 Fit the timing belt to the camshaft sprocket. Peugeot technicians use a clip to retain the belt on the sprocket; if necessary, use a plastic cable tie to hold it.

14 Continue to fit the belt in the following order, keeping the belt taut between as it's fitted around the idler roller and the crankshaft sprocket **(see illustration)**:

a) Idler roller.
b) Crankshaft sprocket.
c) Coolant pump sprocket.
d) Tensioner roller.

15 Remove the tool/cable tie securing the belt to the camshaft sprocket, and the crankshaft sprocket centring tool.

16 Slacken the tensioner roller retaining bolt, then using an Allen key, rotate the tensioner anti-clockwise until the index pointer is aligned with the lower, outside edge of the reference plate **(see illustrations)**. Tighten the tensioner roller retaining bolt to the specified torque.

17 Ensure the crankshaft/flywheel ring gear locking tool is still in place, then refit the lower timing belt cover, sensor wheel and crankshaft pulley, and tighten the retaining bolt to 70 Nm (52 lbf ft).

18 Remove the camshaft sprocket and crankshaft locking/timing tools.

19 Rotate the crankshaft 10 times in the normal direction of rotation, and refit the

7.14 Timing belt routing

camshaft sprocket and crankshaft locking/timing tools.

20 With the flywheel ring gear locked, slacken the crankshaft pulley bolt.

21 Slacken the timing belt tensioner retaining bolt, then use an Allen key to rotate the tensioner clockwise until the index pointer aligns with the notch in the reference plate **(see illustration)**. Tighten the tensioner roller bolt to the specified torque.

22 Tighten the crankshaft pulley bolt to 70 Nm (52 lbf ft).

23 Remove the camshaft sprocket, and crankshaft/flywheel ring gear locking/aligning tools, and rotate the crankshaft 2 complete revolutions in the normal direction of rotation (clockwise).

24 Check that the camshaft sprocket and crankshaft/flywheel aligning tools can still be inserted, and that the tensioner index pointer is still aligned with the notch in the reference plate. If necessary, repeat the tensioning procedure until the pointer and notch align.

25 Lock the flywheel ring gear using the previously described tool, undo the crankshaft pulley bolt.

26 Refit the crankshaft sensor. Tighten the retaining bolt securely.

27 Apply a little thread-locking compound to the threads, then tighten the crankshaft pulley retaining bolt to the specified torque and angle.

28 Remove the camshaft sprocket, and crankshaft/flywheel ring gear locking/aligning tools.

29 The remainder of refitting is a reversal of removal.

7.16a Use an Allen key in the tensioner (arrowed)

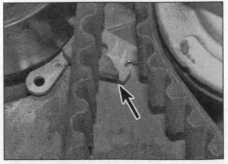

7.16b Rotate the tensioner anti-clockwise until the index pointer is aligned with the lower edge of the reference plate (arrowed)

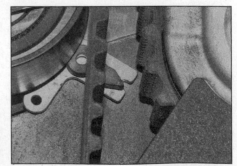

7.21 Align the index pointer with the notch in the reference plate

TOOL TiP

To make a sprocket holding tool, obtain two lengths of steel strip about 6.0 mm thick by about 30 mm wide or similar, one 600 mm long, the other 200 mm long (all dimensions approximate). Bolt the two strips together to form a forked end, leaving the bolt slack so that the shorter strip can pivot freely. At the other end of each 'prong' of the fork, drill a suitable hole and fit a nut and bolt to engage with the spokes or holes in the sprocket. It may be necessary to cut-off or grind the side slightly to allow them to fit in the sprocket holes.

8.10a Slide off the crankshaft pulley . . .

8.10b . . . and recover the Woodruff key

8 Timing belt sprockets and tensioner – removal and refitting

Camshaft sprocket

Removal

1 Remove the timing belt as described in Section 7.
2 Remove the locking tool from the camshaft sprocket, then slacken the sprocket retaining bolt. To prevent the camshaft rotating as the bolt is slackened, Peugeot technicians use tool No. 6016-T. In the absence of this tool, fabricate a substitute as described **(see Tool Tip)**. *Do not* attempt to use the camshaft sprocket locking tool to prevent the sprocket from rotating whilst the bolt is slackened. **Note:** *Take care not to damage the sensor signal disc integral with the sprocket.*
3 Remove the bolt, and slide the sprocket from the camshaft. If the Woodruff key is a loose fit in the camshaft, remove it for safe-keeping. Examine the camshaft oil seal for signs of oil leakage and, if necessary, renew it as described in Section 14.
4 Clean the camshaft sprocket thoroughly, and renew it if there are any signs of wear, damage or cracks.

Refitting

5 Where applicable, refit the Woodruff key to the end of the camshaft, then refit the camshaft sprocket and hub.
6 Refit the sprocket retaining bolt and washer. Tighten the bolt to the specified torque,

preventing the camshaft from turning as during removal.
7 Align the timing slot in the camshaft sprocket with the hole in the cylinder head and refit the tool lock the camshaft in position.
8 Refit the timing belt as described in Section 7.

Crankshaft sprocket

Removal

9 Remove the timing belt as described in Section 7.
10 Slide the sprocket off the end of the crankshaft and collect the Woodruff key **(see illustrations)**.
11 Examine the crankshaft oil seal for signs of oil leakage and, if necessary, renew it as described in Section 14.
12 Clean the crankshaft sprocket thoroughly, and renew it if there are any signs of wear, damage or cracks.

Refitting

13 Refit the Woodruff key to the end of the crankshaft, then refit the crankshaft sprocket (with the flange nearest the cylinder block).
14 Refit the timing belt as described in Section 7.

Coolant pump sprocket

15 The coolant pump sprocket is integral with the pump, and cannot be removed.

Tensioner pulley

Removal

16 Remove the timing belt as described in Section 7.
17 Remove the tensioner pulley retaining bolt, and slide the pulley off its mounting stud.
18 Clean the tensioner pulley, but do not use any strong solvent which may enter the pulley bearings. Check that the pulley rotates freely, with no sign of stiffness or free play. Renew the pulley if there is any doubt about its condition, or if there are any obvious signs of wear or damage.

Refitting

19 Refit the tensioner pulley, and insert the retaining bolt.
20 Refit the timing belt as described in Section 7.

Idler roller

Removal

21 Remove the timing belt as described in Section 7.
22 Undo the retaining bolt and withdraw the idler roller from the engine.
23 Clean the idler roller, but do not use any strong solvent which may enter the bearings. Check that the roller rotates freely, with no sign of stiffness or free play. Renew the idler roller if there is any doubt about its condition, or if there are any obvious signs of wear or damage.

Refitting

24 Locate the idler roller on the engine, and fit the retaining bolt. Tighten the bolt to the specified torque.
25 Fit the timing belt around the idler roller, and tension the timing belt as described in Section 7.

9 Camshafts, rocker arms and hydraulic tappets – removal, inspection and refitting

Removal

1 Remove the cylinder head cover as described in Section 4.
2 Remove the camshaft sprocket as described in Section 8.
3 Slacken the retaining clamps and disconnect the air intake hose from the left-hand end of the cylinder head. Remove the intercooler air duct from the left-hand end of the cylinder head.
4 Remove the air cleaner assembly, high-pressure fuel pump, and fuel injectors as described in Chapter 4B.
5 Refit the right-hand engine mounting, but only tighten the bolts moderately; this will keep the engine supported during the camshaft removal.
6 Disconnect the vacuum pipe from the brake vacuum pump on the left-hand end of the cylinder head.
7 Remove the vacuum pump from the cylinder head with reference to Chapter 9.
8 Compress the timing chain tensioner and

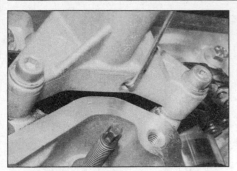

9.8 Lift up the upper chain guide rail and insert a 2.0 mm diameter rod/drill bit into the hole in the tensioner body

9.9 Undo the tensioner retaining bolts (arrowed)

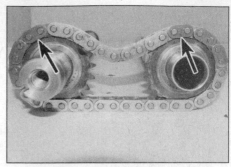

9.12a The coloured links on the chain (arrowed) align with the marks on the camshaft sprockets . . .

insert a 2.0 mm drill bit into the tensioner body to the lock the piston in the compressed state **(see illustration)**.

9 Undo the bolts and remove the timing chain tensioner **(see illustration)**.

10 Working in a spiral pattern from the outside-in, progressively loosen the camshaft bearing cap housing bolts until they can be removed.

11 Withdraw the bearing cap housing from the cylinder head. The housing is likely to be initially tight to release as it is located by two dowels on the forward facing side of the cylinder head. If necessary, very carefully prise up the housing using a screwdriver inserted in the slotted lug adjacent to each dowel location. Once the bearing housing is free, lift it squarely from the cylinder head. The camshaft will rise up slightly under the pressure of the valve springs – be careful it doesn't tilt and jam in the cylinder head or bearing housing section.

12 Check that the camshafts and chain are marked in relation to each other – the chain should have two black or copper links which align with marks on the teeth. If necessary, mark the chain and teeth with dabs of paint. The marks on the teeth are the most important as they determine the valve timing, however the chain links can be marked as they are 7 links (inclusive) apart **(see illustrations)**.

13 Simultaneously lift the camshafts and chain from the cylinder head. Release the camshafts from the chain.

14 Obtain sixteen small, clean plastic

containers, and number them 1 to 16; alternatively, divide a larger container into sixteen compartments.

15 Lift out each rocker arm and release it from the spring clip on the tappet **(see illustration)**. Place the rocker arms in their respective positions in the box or containers.

16 A compartmentalised container filled with engine oil is now required to retain the hydraulic tappets while they are removed from the cylinder head. Using a rubber sucker, withdraw each hydraulic follower and place it in the container, keeping them each identified for correct refitting. The tappets must be totally submerged in the oil to prevent air entering them.

Inspection

17 Inspect the cam lobes and the camshaft bearing journals for scoring or other visible evidence of wear. Once the surface hardening of the cam lobes has been eroded, wear will occur at an accelerated rate. **Note:** *If these symptoms are visible on the tips of the camshaft lobes, check the corresponding rocker arm, as it will probably be worn as well.*

18 Examine the condition of the bearing surfaces in the cylinder head and camshaft bearing housing. If wear is evident, the cylinder head and bearing housing will both have to be renewed, as they are a matched assembly.

19 Inspect the rocker arms and tappets for scuffing, cracking or other damage and renew any components as necessary. Also check the condition of the tappet bores in the cylinder head. As with the camshafts, any wear in this area will necessitate cylinder head renewal.

Refitting

20 Thoroughly clean the sealant from the mating surfaces of the cylinder head and camshaft bearing housing. Use a suitable liquid gasket dissolving agent (available from Peugeot dealers) together with a soft putty knife; do not use a metal scraper or the faces will be damaged. As there is no conventional gasket used, the cleanliness of the mating faces is of the utmost importance.

21 Clean off any oil, dirt or grease from both components and dry with a clean lint-free cloth. Ensure that all the oilways are completely clean.

22 To prevent any possibility of the valves contacting the pistons as the camshaft is refitted, remove the locking pin/drill from the flywheel/driveplate and turn the crankshaft a quarter turn in the *opposite* direction to normal rotation (ie, anti-clockwise), to position all the pistons at mid-stroke.

23 Liberally lubricate the hydraulic tappet bores in the cylinder head with clean engine oil.

24 Insert the hydraulic tappets into their original bores in the cylinder head unless they have been renewed **(see illustration)**.

25 Lubricate the rocker arms and place them over their respective tappets and valve stems. Ensure that the ends of the rocker arms engage with the spring clips on the tappets.

26 Lubricate the camshaft bearing journals in the cylinder head sparingly with oil, taking care not to allow the oil to spill over onto the camshaft bearing housing contact areas.

9.12b . . . the mark on the sprockets is a dot and a line

9.15 Lift out the rocker arms with the hydraulic tappets

9.24 Insert the tappets and rocker arms into their original locations

9.27 Position the camshafts so the mark on the intake camshaft (arrowed) is in the 12 o'clock position

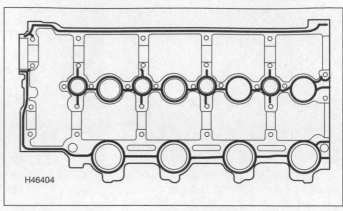

9.32a Apply a thin bead of sealant as indicated by the heavy black line

9.32b We inserted a tapered rod (arrowed) into the tensioner oil supply hole to prevent any sealant from entering

27 Engage the camshafts with the chain, making sure that the coloured links are aligned with the marked teeth, fit the tensioner between the chain runs, then lower them into position. The longer exhaust camshaft must go at the rear of the cylinder head. Rotate the camshaft so the mark on the intake camshaft is in the 12 o'clock position **(see illustration)**.

28 Fit a new camshaft oil seal as described in Section 14.

29 Refit the camshaft sprocket, lightly tighten the retaining bolt, then fit the camshaft sprocket locking tool.

30 Check the marks on the camshaft sprockets still align with the coloured links on the chain.

31 Ensure that the mating faces of the cylinder head and camshaft bearing housing are clean and free of any oil or grease.

32 Sparingly apply a bead of suitable sealant (Loctite 518) to the mating face of the camshaft bearing housing, taking care not to allow the product to contaminate the camshaft bearing journal areas **(see illustrations)**.

33 Lower the housing into place, then insert and tighten the camshaft bearing housing bolts to the specified torque, in the sequence shown **(see illustration)**.

34 Refit the chain tensioner, tighten the retaining bolts to the specified torque, then pull out the locking pin and allow the tensioner to act upon the chain.

35 The remainder of refitting is a reversal of removal.

10 Cylinder head – removal and refitting

Note: *This is an involved procedure, and it is suggested that the Section is read thoroughly before starting work. To aid refitting, make notes on the locations of all relevant brackets and the routing of hoses and cables before removal.*

Removal

1 Apply the handbrake, then jack up the front of the vehicle and support it on axle stands (see *Jacking and vehicle support*). Remove the front right-hand roadwheel, the engine undershield, and the front wheelarch liner. The undershield is secured by several screws, and the wheelarch liner is secured by several plastic expanding rivets. Push the centre pins in a little, then prise the rivet from place.

2 Remove the battery (see Chapter 5A).

3 Drain the cooling system as described in Chapter 1B.

4 Remove the camshafts, rocker arms and hydraulic tappets as described in Section 9.

5 Remove the timing chain pad at the right-hand side of the cylinder head **(see illustration)**.

6 Remove the fuel filter and bracket.

7 Remove the common (fuel) rail as described in Chapter 4B.

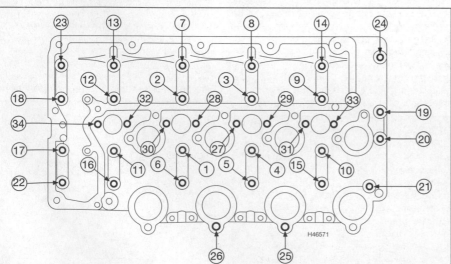

9.33 Camshaft bearing cap housing bolts tightening sequence

10.5 Remove the timing chain pad from the cylinder head

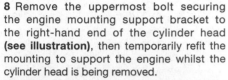

10.8 Undo the bracket upper bolt (arrowed)

10.10 Undo the nuts (arrowed) and remove the coolant outlet housing

10.19 Zero the DTI on the gasket face

8 Remove the uppermost bolt securing the engine mounting support bracket to the right-hand end of the cylinder head **(see illustration)**, then temporarily refit the mounting to support the engine whilst the cylinder head is being removed.

9 Note their fitted positions and routing, then disconnect all coolant and vacuum hoses from the cylinder head.

10 Undo the bolts/studs securing the coolant outlet housing to the left-hand end of the cylinder head. Pull the housing away from the cylinder head **(see illustration)**.

11 Remove the turbocharger and exhaust manifold as described in Chapter 4B.

12 Progressively slacken the cylinder head bolts, in the **reverse** order to that shown for tightening **(see illustration 10.33)**. A Torx socket will be required for this.

13 When all the bolts are loose, unscrew them fully and remove them from the cylinder head.

14 Release the cylinder head from the cylinder block and location dowels by rocking it. The Peugeot tool for doing this consists simply of two metal rods with 90-degree angled ends. Do not prise between the mating faces of the cylinder head and block, as this may damage the gasket faces.

15 Lift the cylinder head from the block, and recover the gasket.

Preparation for refitting

16 The mating faces of the cylinder head and cylinder block must be perfectly clean before refitting the head. Peugeot recommend the use of a scouring agent for this purpose, but acceptable results can be achieved by using a hard plastic or wood scraper to remove all traces of gasket and carbon. The same method can be used to clean the piston crowns. Take particular care to avoid scoring or gouging the cylinder head/cylinder block mating surfaces during the cleaning operations, as aluminium alloy is easily damaged. Make sure that the carbon is not allowed to enter the oil and water passages – this is particularly important for the lubrication system, as carbon could block the oil supply to the engine's components. Using adhesive tape and paper, seal the water, oil and bolt holes in the cylinder block. To prevent carbon entering the gap between the pistons

and bores, smear a little grease in the gap. After cleaning each piston, use a small brush to remove all traces of grease and carbon from the gap, then wipe away the remainder with a clean rag.

17 Check the mating surfaces of the cylinder block and the cylinder head for nicks, deep scratches and other damage. If slight, they may be removed carefully with a file, but if excessive, machining may be the only alternative to renewal. If warpage of the cylinder head gasket surface is suspected, use a straight-edge to check it for distortion. Refer to Part F of this Chapter if necessary.

18 Thoroughly clean the threads of the cylinder head bolt holes in the cylinder block. Ensure that the bolts run freely in their threads, and that all traces of oil and water are removed from each bolt hole. If possible, use a M12 x 150 tap to clean out the threads.

Gasket selection

19 Turn the crankshaft until pistons 1 and 4 are at TDC (Top Dead Centre). Position a dial test indicator (dial gauge) on the cylinder block adjacent to the rear of No 1 piston, and zero it on the block face **(see illustration)**. Transfer the probe to the crown of No 1 piston (10.0 mm in from the rear edge), then slowly turn the crankshaft back-and-forth past TDC, noting the highest reading on the indicator. Record this reading as protrusion A.

20 Repeat the check described in paragraph 19, this time 10.0 mm in from the front edge of the No 1 piston crown. Record this reading as protrusion B.

21 Add protrusion A to protrusion B, then divide the result by 2 to obtain an average reading for piston No 1.

22 Repeat the procedure described in paragraphs 19 to 21 on piston 4, then turn the crankshaft through 180° and carry out the procedure on the piston Nos 2 and 3. Check that there is a maximum difference of 0.07 mm protrusion between any two pistons.

23 If a dial test indicator is not available, piston protrusion may be measured using a straight-edge and feeler blades or Vernier calipers. However, this is much less accurate, and cannot therefore be recommended.

24 Note the greatest piston protrusion measurement, and use this to determine

the correct cylinder head gasket from the following table. The series of holes on the front side of the gasket are used for thickness identification.

Piston protrusion	Gasket identification
0.55 to 0.60 mm	1 hole
0.61 to 0.65 mm	2 holes
0.66 to 0.70 mm	3 holes
0.71 to 0.75 mm	4 holes

Head bolt examination

25 Carefully examine the cylinder head bolts for signs of damage to the threads or head, and for any sign of corrosion. If the bolts are in a satisfactory condition, measure the length of each bolt from the underside of the head to the end of the shank. Two different types of bolts may be fitted. The older type do not have integral, captive washers; on these bolts, they may be re-used providing that the measured length from beneath the head to the very end of the bolt, does not exceed 129.0 mm ± 0.5 mm **(see illustration)**. On the later type of bolt, there is a washer which is captive under the head of the bolt; on these bolts, they may be re-used providing the measured length from beneath head (not the washer) to the end of the bolt does not exceed 134.5 mm ± 0.05 mm. **Note:** *Considering the stress to which the cylinder head bolts are subjected, it is highly recommended that they are all renewed, regardless of their apparent condition.*

Refitting

26 Turn the crankshaft and position Nos 1

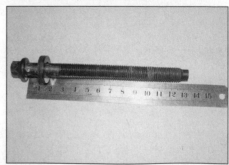

10.25 Measure the length of the cylinder head bolts from under the bolt head, not the washer

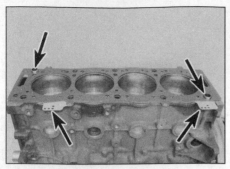

10.28 Fit the new gasket over the dowels, with the thickness identification holes at the front (arrowed)

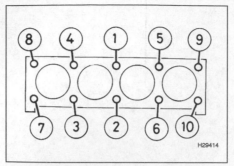

10.33 Cylinder head bolt tightening sequence

b) Refit the camshaft position sensor and set the air gap with reference to Chapter 4B.
c) Tighten all fasteners to the specified torque where given.
d) Refill the cooling system as described in Chapter 1B.
e) The engine may run erratically for the first few miles, until the engine management ECM relearns its stored values.

11 Sump – removal and refitting

Removal

1 Drain the engine oil, then clean and refit the engine oil drain plug, tightening it securely. If the engine is nearing the interval when the oil and filter are due for renewal, it is recommended that the filter is also removed, and a new one fitted. After reassembly, the engine can then be refilled with fresh oil. Refer to Chapter 1B for further information.
2 Apply the handbrake, then jack up the front of the vehicle and support it on axle stands (see *Jacking and vehicle support*). Undo the screws and remove the engine undershield.
3 On models with air conditioning, where the compressor is mounted onto the side of the sump, remove the drivebelt as described in Chapter 1B. Unbolt the compressor, and position it clear of the sump. Support the weight of the compressor by tying it to the vehicle, to prevent any excess strain being placed on the compressor lines. Do not disconnect the refrigerant lines from the compressor (refer to the warnings given in Chapter 3).
4 Undo the 4 Torx screws, release the retaining clips and remove the sump shield (where fitted) **(see illustrations)**.
5 Slacken the clamps, undo the bolts and remove the charge air pipe from under the sump **(see illustration)**.
6 Where necessary, disconnect the wiring connector from the oil temperature sender unit, which is screwed into the sump.
7 Progressively slacken and remove all the sump retaining bolts **(see illustrations)**. Since the sump bolts vary in length, remove each bolt in turn, and store it in its correct fitted

and 4 pistons at TDC, then turn the crankshaft a quarter turn (90°) anti-clockwise.
27 Thoroughly clean the surfaces of the cylinder head and block.
28 Make sure that the locating dowels are in place, then fit the correct gasket the right way round on the cylinder block **(see illustration)**.
29 If necessary, refit the exhaust manifold with reference to Chapter 4B.
30 Carefully lower the cylinder head onto the gasket and block, making sure that it locates correctly onto the dowels.
31 Apply a light smear of grease to the threads, and to the underside of the heads, of the cylinder head bolts. Peugeot recommend the use of Molykote G Rapid Plus (available from your Peugeot dealer); in the absence of the specified grease, any good-quality high melting-point grease may be used.
32 Carefully insert the cylinder head bolts into

their holes (*do not drop them in*) and initially finger-tighten them.
33 Working progressively and in the sequence shown, tighten the cylinder head bolts to their Stage 1 torque setting, using a torque wrench and suitable socket **(see illustration)**.
34 Once all the bolts have been tightened to their Stage 1 torque setting, working again in the specified sequence, tighten each bolt to the specified Stage 2 setting. Finally, angle-tighten the bolts through the specified Stage 3 angle. It is recommended that an angle-measuring gauge is used during this stage of tightening, to ensure accuracy. **Note:** *Retightening of the cylinder head bolts after running the engine is not required.*
35 The remainder of refitting is a reversal of removal, noting the following points.
a) Use a new seal when refitting the coolant outlet housing.

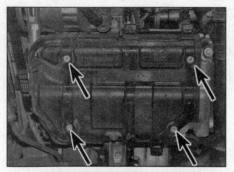

11.4a Undo the 4 Torx screws (arrowed) . . .

11.4b . . . release the clips around the edge, and remove the sump shield

11.5 Remove the charge air pipe (arrowed)

11.7a Undo the 2 bolts securing the sump to the transmission (arrowed) . . .

11.7b . . . access to the sump end bolts is through the holes (arrowed)

order by pushing it through a clearly-marked cardboard template. This will avoid the possibility of installing the bolts in the wrong locations on refitting.

8 Try to break the joint by striking the sump with the palm of your hand, then lower and withdraw the sump from under the car. If the sump is stuck (which is quite likely) use a putty knife or similar carefully inserted between the sump and block. Ease the knife along the joint until the sump is released. While the sump is removed, take the opportunity to check the oil pump pick-up/strainer for signs of clogging or splitting. If necessary, remove the pump as described in Section 12, and clean or renew the strainer.

Refitting

9 Clean all traces of sealant/gasket from the mating surfaces of the cylinder block/crankcase and sump, then use a clean rag to wipe out the sump and the engine's interior.

10 Ensure that the sump mating surfaces are clean and dry, then apply a thin coating of suitable sealant (E10 – available from Peugeot dealers) to the sump or crankcase mating surface (**see illustration**).

11 Offer up the sump to the cylinder block/crankcase. Refit its retaining bolts, ensuring that each bolt is screwed into its original location. Tighten the bolts evenly and progressively to the specified torque setting.

12 The remainder of refitting is a reversal of removal, remembering to refill the engine with oil as described in Chapter 1B.

12 Oil pump – removal, inspection and refitting

Removal

1 Remove the timing belt as described in Section 7, then slide off the crankshaft sprocket. Recover the Woodruff key from the end of the crankshaft.

2 Remove the sump as described in Section 11.

3 Undo the retaining bolts and remove the front cover and crankshaft seal. Note the original locations of the cover screws – they are different lengths.

4 Undo the bolt securing the oil level pipe (**see illustration**).

5 Pull out the key from the end of the crankshaft sprocket, then undo the pump mounting bolts, slide the pump, chain and crankshaft sprocket from the end of the engine (**see illustrations**). Recover the O-ring between the sprocket and crankshaft.

Inspection

6 Examine the oil pump sprocket for signs of damage and wear, such as chipped or missing teeth. If the sprocket is worn, the pump assembly must be renewed, since the sprocket is not available separately. It is also recommended that the chain and drive sprocket, fitted to the crankshaft, be renewed at the same time.

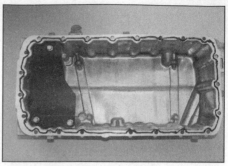

11.10 Apply a bead of sealant around the inside of the bolt holes

7 Undo the retaining screws and remove the cover from the oil pump (**see illustration**). Note the location of any identification marks on the inner and outer rotors for refitting.

8 Unscrew the plug and remove the pressure relief valve, spring and plunger, clean out and check the condition of the components (**see illustration**).

9 Examine the pump rotors and body for signs of wear ridges or scoring. If worn, the complete pump assembly must be renewed.

10 Examine the relief valve piston for signs of wear or damage, and renew if necessary. The condition of the relief valve spring can only be measured by comparing it with a new one; if there is any doubt about its condition, it should also be renewed. Both the piston and spring are available individually.

11 Thoroughly clean the oil pump strainer with a suitable solvent, and check it for

12.4 Oil level pipe bracket bolt (arrowed)

12.5a Remove the sprocket key . . .

12.5b . . . undo the pump mounting bolts (arrowed), slide the assembly from the crankshaft . . .

12.5c . . . and recover the O-ring between the sprocket and the crankshaft (arrowed)

12.7 Oil pump cover screws

12.8 Oil pressure relief valve plug

12.15 Fit the O-ring to the end of the crankshaft

13.2 Oil cooler retaining bolts (arrowed)

13 Oil cooler – removal and refitting

Note: *New sealing rings will be required on refitting – check for availability prior to commencing work.*

Removal

1 The cooler is fitted to the oil filter housing on the front of the cylinder block. Access is from under the vehicle. Undo the fasteners and remove the engine undershield. To further improve access, undo the mounting bolts and move the air conditioning compressor to one side. Suspend the compressor using wire or straps. There is no need to disconnect the refrigerant pipes.

2 Undo the 4 retaining bolts and detach the cooler from the housing **(see illustration)**. Recover the sealing rings and be prepared for coolant/oil spillage.

Refitting

3 Refitting is a reversal of removal, bearing in mind the following points:
a) Use new sealing rings.
b) Tighten the cooler mounting bolts securely.
c) On completion lower the car to the ground. Check and if necessary top-up the oil and coolant levels, then start the engine and check for signs of oil or coolant leakage.

---

signs of clogging or splitting. If the strainer is damaged, the strainer and cover assembly must be renewed.

12 Locate the relief valve spring and piston in the strainer cover. Refit the cover to the pump body, aligning the relief valve plunger with its bore in the pump. Refit the baffle plate (where fitted) and the cover retaining bolts, and tighten them securely.

13 Prime the pump by filling it with clean engine oil before refitting.

Refitting

14 Before refitting the oil pump, ensure the mating faces of the pump and engine block are completely clean.

15 Fit the O-ring to the end of the crankshaft **(see illustration)**.

16 Engage the drive chain with the oil pump and crankshaft sprockets, then slide the crankshaft sprocket into place (aligning the slot in the sprocket with the keyway in the crankshaft) as the pump is refitted. Refit the crankshaft key.

17 Refit the mounting bolts and tighten them to the specified torque. Note that the front, left-hand bolt is slightly longer than the others.

18 Apply a 3 mm bead of sealant to the oil seal carrier flange. Refit the carrier and tighten the bolts to the specified torque.

19 Fit a new oil seal to the carrier as described in Section 14.

20 Refit the bolt securing the oil level pipe.

21 The remainder of refitting is a reversal of removal.

---

14 Oil seals – renewal

Crankshaft

Right-hand oil seal

1 Remove the crankshaft sprocket as described in Section 8.

2 Measure and note the fitted depth of the oil seal.

3 Pull the oil seal from the housing using a hooked instrument. Alternatively, drill a small hole in the oil seal, and use a self-tapping screw and a pair of pliers to remove it **(see illustrations)**.

4 Clean the oil seal housing and the crankshaft sealing surface.

5 Press the new seal into the housing (open end first) to the previously-noted depth, using a suitable tube or socket. A piece of thin plastic or tape wound around the front of the crankshaft is useful to prevent damage to the oil seal as it is fitted. Note that special tools to guide the seal onto the crankshaft and drive it into place may be available from Peugeot **(see illustrations)**.

6 Where applicable, remove the plastic or tape from the end of the crankshaft.

14.3a Drill a small hole in the seal . . .

14.3b . . . insert a self-tapping screw and pull out the seal

14.5a Locate the new seal and guide over the end of the crankshaft . . .

14.5b . . . then drive the seal home until it's flush with carrier

14.10a Drill a hole in the seal . . .

14.10b . . . then insert a self-tapping screw and pull out the seal

14.19a Use a socket or similar to drive the seal into place . . .

7 Refit the crankshaft sprocket as described in Section 8.

Left-hand oil seal

8 Remove the flywheel/driveplate, as described in Section 16.

9 Measure and note the fitted depth of the oil seal.

10 Pull the oil seal from the housing using a hooked instrument. Alternatively, drill a small hole in the oil seal, and use a self-tapping screw and a pair of pliers to remove it **(see illustrations)**.

11 Clean the oil seal housing and the crankshaft sealing surface.

12 Press the new seal into the housing (open end first) to the previously-noted depth, using a suitable tube or socket. A piece of thin plastic or tape wound around the end of the crankshaft is useful to prevent damage to the oil seal as it is fitted.

13 Where applicable, remove the plastic or tape from the end of the crankshaft.

14 Refit the flywheel/driveplate, as described in Section 16.

Camshaft

Right-hand oil seal

15 Remove the camshaft sprocket as described in Section 8. In principle there is no need to remove the timing belt completely, but remember that if the belt has been contaminated with oil, it must be renewed.

16 Pull the oil seal from the housing using a

hooked instrument. Alternatively, drill a small hole in the oil seal and use a self-tapping screw and a pair of pliers to remove it **(see illustration 14.3b)**.

17 Clean the oil seal housing and the camshaft sealing surface.

18 Fit it over the end of the camshaft, open end first. Note that the seal must not be oiled prior to fitting. A piece of thin plastic or tape wound around the front of the camshaft is useful to prevent damage to the oil seal as it is fitted.

19 Press the seal into the housing until it is flush with the end face of the cylinder head. Use an M10 bolt (screwed into the end of the camshaft), washers and a suitable tube or socket that bears only on the outer edge of the seal to press it into position **(see illustrations)**.

20 Refit the camshaft sprocket as described in Section 8.

21 Where necessary, fit a new timing belt with reference to Section 7.

---

15 Oil pressure switch – removal and refitting

Removal

1 The switch is screwed into the oil filter housing **(see illustration)**. Access is from under the vehicle. Undo the fasteners and remove the engine undershield. To further improve access, undo the mounting bolts

and move the air conditioning compressor to one side. Suspend the compressor from the radiator crossmember using wire or straps. There is no need to disconnect the refrigerant pipes.

2 Remove the protective sleeve from the wiring plug (where applicable), then disconnect the wiring from the switch.

3 Unscrew the switch from the cylinder block, and recover the sealing washer. Be prepared for oil spillage, and if the switch is to be left removed from the engine for any length of time, plug the hole in the cylinder block.

Refitting

4 Examine the sealing washer for any signs of damage or deterioration, and if necessary renew.

5 Refit the switch, complete with washer, and tighten it to the specified torque where given.

6 Refit all components removed for access to the switch.

7 Check the engine oil level, and top-up as required (see *Weekly checks*).

8 Check for correct operation of the warning light, and for signs of oil leaks once the engine has been started and warmed-up to normal operating temperature.

---

16 Flywheel/driveplate – removal, inspection and refitting

Removal

Flywheel

1 Remove the transmission as described in Chapter 7A, then remove the clutch assembly as described in Chapter 6.

2 Prevent the flywheel from turning by locking the ring gear teeth **(see illustration 5.3)**. Alternatively, bolt a strap between the flywheel and the cylinder block/crankcase. *Do not attempt to lock the flywheel in position using the crankshaft pulley locking tool described in Section 3.*

3 Slacken and remove the flywheel retaining bolts, and remove the flywheel from the end

14.19b . . . until it's flush with the casing surface

15.1 Oil pressure warning light switch (arrowed)

16.3 Flywheel retaining bolts

16.11 Note the locating dowel and the corresponding hole (arrowed)

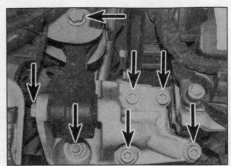

17.7 Right-hand engine mounting bolts/ nuts (arrowed)

of the crankshaft (see illustration). Be careful not to drop it; it is heavy. If the flywheel locating dowel is a loose fit in the crankshaft end, remove it and store it with the flywheel for safe-keeping. Discard the flywheel bolts; new ones must be used on refitting.

Driveplate

4 Remove the transmission as described in Chapter 7B. Lock the driveplate as described in paragraph 2 of this Section. Mark the relationship between the torque converter plate and the driveplate, and slacken all the driveplate retaining bolts.

5 Remove the retaining bolts, along with the torque converter plate and the two shims (one fitted on each side of the torque converter plate). Note that the shims are of different thickness, the thicker one being on the outside of the torque converter plate. Discard the driveplate retaining bolts; new ones must be used on refitting.

6 Remove the driveplate from the end of the crankshaft. If the locating dowel is a loose fit in the crankshaft end, remove it and store it with the driveplate for safe-keeping.

Inspection

7 On models with manual transmission, examine the flywheel for scoring of the clutch face, and for wear or chipping of the ring gear teeth. If the clutch face is scored, the flywheel may be surface-ground, but renewal is preferable. Seek the advice of a Peugeot dealer or engine reconditioning specialist to see if machining is possible. If the ring gear is worn or damaged, the flywheel must be renewed, as it is not possible to renew the ring gear separately.

8 On models with automatic transmission, check the torque converter driveplate carefully for signs of distortion. Look for any hairline cracks around the bolt holes or radiating outwards from the centre, and inspect the ring gear teeth for signs of wear or chipping. If any sign of wear or damage is found, the driveplate must be renewed.

Refitting

Flywheel

9 Clean the mating surfaces of the flywheel and crankshaft. Remove any remaining

locking compound from the threads of the crankshaft holes, using the correct size of tap, if available.

> **HAYNES HiNT** *If a suitable tap is not available, cut two slots along the threads of one of the old flywheel bolts, and use the bolt to remove the locking compound from the threads.*

10 If the new flywheel retaining bolts are not supplied with their threads already pre-coated, apply a suitable thread-locking compound to the threads of each bolt.

11 Ensure that the locating dowel is in position. Offer up the flywheel, locating it on the dowel, and fit the new retaining bolts (see illustration).

12 Lock the flywheel using the method employed on dismantling, and tighten the retaining bolts to the specified torque.

13 Refit the clutch as described in Chapter 6. Remove the flywheel locking tool, and refit the transmission as described in Chapter 7A.

Driveplate

14 Carry out the operations described above in paragraphs 9 and 10, substituting 'driveplate' for all references to the flywheel.

15 Locate the driveplate on its locating dowel.

16 Offer up the torque converter plate, with the thinner shim positioned behind the plate and the thicker shim on the outside, and align the marks made prior to removal.

17 Fit the new retaining bolts, then lock the driveplate using the method employed on dismantling. Tighten the retaining bolts to the specified torque wrench setting.

18 Remove the driveplate locking tool, and refit the transmission (see Chapter 7B).

17 Engine/transmission mountings – inspection and renewal

Inspection

1 If improved access is required, firmly apply the handbrake, then jack up the front of the

car and support it on axle stands (see *Jacking and vehicle support*). Undo the screws and remove the engine undershield.

2 Check the mounting rubbers to see if they are cracked, hardened or separated from the metal at any point; renew the mounting if any such damage or deterioration is evident.

3 Check that all the mountings' fasteners are securely tightened; use a torque wrench to check if possible.

4 Using a large screwdriver or a crowbar, check for wear in each mounting by carefully levering against it to check for free play. Where this is not possible, enlist the aid of an assistant to move the engine/transmission back-and-forth, or from side-to-side, while you watch the mounting. While some free play is to be expected even from new components, excessive wear should be obvious. If excessive free play is found, check first that the fasteners are correctly secured, then renew any worn components as described below.

Renewal

Right-hand mounting

5 Release all the relevant hoses and wiring from their retaining clips. Place the hoses/ wiring clear of the mounting so that the removal procedure is not hindered. Undo the screws and remove the engine undershield.

6 Place a jack beneath the engine, with a block of wood on the jack head. Raise the jack until it is supporting the weight of the engine.

7 Undo the bolts/nuts securing the engine mounting to the body and the support bracket (see illustration).

8 If required, undo the bolts/nuts securing the support bracket to the cylinder head/cylinder block.

9 Check all components carefully for signs of wear or damage, and renew as necessary.

10 Where removed, refit the support bracket to the cylinder head, and tighten the bolts securely.

11 Refit the mount to the body and support bracket, then tighten the bolts to the specified torque.

12 Remove the jack from underneath the engine.

Left-hand mounting

13 Remove the battery (see Chapter 5A).

Undo the screws and remove the engine undershield.

14 Remove the diesel engine management ECM and module box as described in Chapter 4B.

15 Place a jack beneath the transmission, with a block of wood on the jack head. Raise the jack until it is supporting the weight of the transmission.

16 Undo the nuts securing the mounting in position and remove it from the engine compartment. If required, undo the bolts/nut and remove the support bracket **(see illustration)**.

17 Check all components carefully for signs of wear or damage, and renew as necessary.

18 Clean the threads of the mounting stud (where applicable), and apply a coat of thread-locking compound to its threads.

19 Refit the support bracket and mounting, tightening the bolts/nuts to the specified torque.

20 The remainder of refitting is a reversal of removal.

Rear engine torque rod

21 If not already done, chock the rear wheels, then jack up the front of the vehicle and support it securely on axle stands (see *Jacking*

17.16 Left-hand engine/transmission mounting assembly

and vehicle support). Undo the screws and remove the engine undershield.

22 Unscrew and remove the bolt securing the torque rod to the driveshaft intermediate bearing housing **(see illustration)**.

23 Remove the bolt securing the torque rod to the subframe. Withdraw the torque rod.

24 To remove the intermediate bearing housing assembly it will first be necessary to remove the right-hand driveshaft as described in Chapter 8.

25 With the driveshaft removed, undo the retaining bolts and remove the bearing housing from the rear of the cylinder block.

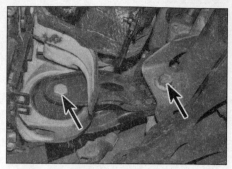

17.22 Rear engine torque rod mounting bolts (arrowed)

26 Check carefully for signs of wear or damage on all components, and renew them where necessary. The rubber bush fitted to the bearing housing is available as a separate item (at the time of writing), and can be pressed out of, and back into place.

27 On reassembly, fit the bearing housing assembly to the rear of the cylinder block, and tighten its retaining bolts securely. Refit the driveshaft as described in Chapter 8.

28 Refit the torque rod, and tighten both its bolts to their specified torque settings. Refit the engine undershield.

29 Lower the vehicle to the ground.

Chapter 2 Part F:
Engine removal and overhaul procedures

Contents

Degrees of difficulty

Easy, suitable for novice with little experience 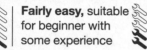	**Fairly easy,** suitable for beginner with some experience	**Fairly difficult,** suitable for competent DIY mechanic	**Difficult,** suitable for experienced DIY mechanic	**Very difficult,** suitable for expert DIY or professional

Specifications

Engine identification

Petrol engines		Designation	Engine code
1.4 litre		TU3JP	KFW
1.4 litre		ET3JP4	KFU
1.6 litre		TU5JP4	NFU
2.0 litre		EW10J4 IFL5	RFN
2.0 litre		EW10A	RFJ

Diesel engines			
1.4 litre		DV4TD	8HZ
1.6 litre		DV6ATED4	9HX
1.6 litre		DV6TED4	9HY and 9HZ
2.0 litre		DW10TD	RHY
2.0 litre		DW10ATED	RHZ and RHS
2.0 litre		DW10BTED4	RHR

Cylinder block

Cylinder bore diameter:	
Petrol engines:	
1.4 litre	75.00 mm (nominal)
1.6 litre	78.50 mm (nominal)
2.0 litre	85.00 mm (nominal)
Diesel engines:	
1.4 litre	73.70 mm (nominal)
1.6 litre (reboring not possible)	75.00 mm (nominal)
2.0 litre	85.00 mm (nominal)
Liner protrusion – 1.4 litre petrol engine:	
Standard	0.03 to 0.10 mm
Maximum difference between any two liners	0.05 mm

Cylinder head

Maximum gasket face distortion	0.05 mm

New cylinder head height:

Petrol engines:

1.4 litre	111.20 mm
1.6 litre	N/A

2.0 litre:

EW10J4 before RPO 09653	138.0 mm
EW10J4 from RPO 09653.	137.0 mm
EW10A	137.0 mm

Diesel engines:

1.4 litre	88.0 mm
1.6 litre	124.0 ± 0.05 mm
2.0 litre	133.0 mm

Minimum cylinder head height after machining:

Petrol engines:

1.4 litre	111.0 mm
1.6 litre	N/A

2.0 litre:

EW10J4 before RPO 09653	137.7 mm
EW10J4 from RPO 09653.	136.7 mm
EW10A	136.7 mm

Diesel engines:

1.4 litre	87.60 mm
1.6 litre	N/A

2.0 litre:

Except DW10BTED4.	132.80 mm
DW10BTED4.	132.60 mm

Valve head-to-cylinder head measurement – diesel engines:

1.4 litre	1.25 mm maximum
1.6 litre	N/A
2.0 litre	0.20 mm maximum

Valves

	Inlet	Exhaust
Valve head diameter:		
Petrol engines:		
1.4 litre	36.7 mm	29.4 mm
1.6 litre	N/A	N/A
2.0 litre	33.3 mm	29.0 mm
Diesel engines:		
1.4 litre	32.8 mm	30.3 mm
1.6 litre	N/A	N/A
2.0 litre	35.6 mm	33.8 mm
Valve stem diameter:		
Petrol engines:		
1.4 litre	6.965 to 6.980 mm	6.945 to 6.960 mm
1.6 litre	N/A	N/A
2.0 litre	5.985 to 5.970 mm	5.975 to 5.960 mm
Diesel engines:		
1.4 litre	N/A	N/A
1.6 litre	5.485 +0.0, -0.015 mm	5.475 +0.0, -0.015 mm
2.0 litre	5.978 ± 0.05 mm	5.973 ± 0.05 mm

Pistons

Piston diameter:

Petrol engines:

1.4 litre	74.950 mm (nominal)
1.6 litre	78.455 mm (nominal)
2.0 litre	84.948 mm (nominal)

Diesel engines:

1.4 litre	73.520 mm (nominal)
2.0 litre	84.210 mm (nominal)

Check with your Peugeot dealer or engine specialist regarding piston oversizes

Piston rings
End gaps:
  Petrol engines:
    Top compression ring . . . .   0.20 to 0.45 mm
    Second compression ring . . . .   0.30 to 0.50 mm
    Oil control ring . . . .   0.30 to 0.50 mm
  Diesel engines:
    1.4 litre:
      Top compression ring . . . .   0.20 to 0.35 mm
      Second compression ring . . . .   0.20 to 0.40 mm
      Oil control ring . . . .   0.80 to 1.00mm
    1.6 litre: . . . .
      Top compression ring . . . .   0.15 to 0.25 mm
      Second compression ring . . . .   0.30 to 0.50 mm
      Oil control ring . . . .   0.35 to 0.55 mm
    2.0 litre:
      Top compression ring . . . .   0.20 to 0.35 mm
      Second compression ring . . . .   0.80 to 1.00 mm
      Oil control ring . . . .   0.25 to 0.50 mm

Crankshaft
Endfloat:
  Petrol engines:
    1.4 litre . . . .   0.07 to 0.27 mm
    1.6 litre . . . .   0.07 to 0.27 mm
    2.0 litre . . . .   0.07 to 0.32 mm
  Diesel engines:
    1.4 litre . . . .   0.10 to 0.30 mm
    1.6 litre . . . .   0.10 to 0.30 mm (thrustwasher thickness 2.40 ± 0.05 mm)
    2.0 litre . . . .   0.07 to 0.32 mm
Main bearing journal diameter:
  Petrol engines:
    1.4 litre . . . .   49.965 to 49.981 mm
    1.6 litre . . . .   49.965 to 49.981 mm
    2.0 litre . . . .   60.00 mm (nominal)
  Diesel engines:
    1.4 and 1.6 litre . . . .   49.962 to 49.981 mm
    2.0 litre . . . .   59.977 to 60.000 mm
Big-end bearing journal diameter:
  Petrol engines:
    1.4 litre . . . .   44.975 to 44.991 mm
    1.6 litre . . . .   44.975 to 44.991 mm
    2.0 litre . . . .   60.00 mm (nominal)
  Diesel engines:
    1.4 litre . . . .   44.975 to 44.991 mm
    1.6 litre . . . .   46.975 to 46.991 mm
    2.0 litre . . . .   49.980 to 50.000 mm
Maximum bearing journal out-of-round (all models) . . . .   0.007 mm

Torque wrench settings

1.4 and 1.6 litre petrol engines
Refer to Chapter 2A Specifications

2.0 litre petrol engines
Refer to Chapter 2B Specifications

2.0 litre SOHC diesel engines
Refer to Chapter 2C Specifications

1.6 litre DOHC diesel engines
Refer to Chapter 2D Specifications

2.0 litre DOHC diesel engines
Refer to Chapter 2E Specifications

1 General information

Included in this Part of Chapter 2 are details of removing the engine/transmission from the car and general overhaul procedures for the cylinder head, cylinder block/crankcase and all other engine internal components.

The information given ranges from advice concerning preparation for an overhaul and the purchase of parts, to detailed step-by-step procedures covering removal, inspection, renovation and refitting of engine internal components.

After Section 5, all instructions are based on the assumption that the engine has been removed from the car. For information concerning in-car engine repair, as well as the removal and refitting of those external components necessary for full overhaul, refer to Part A, B, C, D or E of this Chapter, as applicable and to Section 5. Ignore any preliminary dismantling operations that are no longer relevant once the engine has been removed from the car.

Apart from torque wrench settings, which are given at the beginning of Parts A, B, C, D and E, all specifications relating to engine overhaul are at the beginning of this Part of Chapter 2.

2 Engine overhaul – general information

1 It is not always easy to determine when, or if, an engine should be completely overhauled, as a number of factors must be considered.

2 High mileage is not necessarily an indication that an overhaul is needed, while low mileage does not preclude the need for an overhaul. Frequency of servicing is probably the most important consideration. An engine which has had regular and frequent oil and filter changes, as well as other required maintenance, should give many thousands of miles of reliable service. Conversely, a neglected engine may require an overhaul very early in its life.

3 Excessive oil consumption is an indication that piston rings, valve seals and/or valve guides are in need of attention. Make sure that oil leaks are not responsible before deciding that the rings and/or guides are worn. Perform a compression test, as described in Part A, B, C, D or E of this Chapter (as applicable), to determine the likely cause of the problem.

4 Check the oil pressure with a gauge fitted in place of the oil pressure switch, and compare it with that specified. If it is extremely low, the main and big-end bearings, and/or the oil pump, are probably worn out.

5 Loss of power, rough running, knocking or metallic engine noises, excessive valve gear noise, and high fuel consumption may also point to the need for an overhaul, especially if they are all present at the same time. If a complete service does not remedy the situation, major mechanical work is the only solution.

6 A full engine overhaul involves restoring all internal parts to the specification of a new engine. During a complete overhaul, the pistons and the piston rings are renewed. New main and big-end bearings are generally fitted; if necessary, the crankshaft may be reground, to compensate for wear in the journals. The valves are also serviced as well, since they are usually in less-than-perfect condition at this point. While the engine is being overhauled, other components, such as the starter and alternator, can be overhauled as well. Always pay careful attention to the condition of the oil pump when overhauling the engine, and renew it if there is any doubt as to its serviceability. The end result should be an as-new engine that will give many trouble-free miles.

7 Critical cooling system components such as the hoses, thermostat and water pump should be renewed when an engine is overhauled. The radiator should be checked carefully, to ensure that it is not clogged or leaking. Also, it is a good idea to renew the oil pump whenever the engine is overhauled.

8 Before beginning the engine overhaul, read through the entire procedure, to familiarise yourself with the scope and requirements of the job. Overhauling an engine is not difficult if you follow carefully all of the instructions, have the necessary tools and equipment, and pay close attention to all specifications. It can, however, be time-consuming. Plan on the car being off the road for a minimum of two weeks, especially if parts must be taken to an engineering works for repair or reconditioning. Check on the availability of parts and make sure that any necessary special tools and equipment are obtained in advance. Most work can be done with typical hand tools, although a number of precision measuring tools are required for inspecting parts to determine if they must be renewed. Often the engineering works will handle the inspection of parts and offer advice concerning reconditioning and renewal.

9 Always wait until the engine has been completely dismantled, and until all components (especially the cylinder block/crankcase and the crankshaft) have been inspected, before deciding what service and repair operations must be performed by an engineering works. The condition of these components will be the major factor to consider when determining whether to overhaul the original engine, or to buy a reconditioned unit. Do not, therefore, purchase parts or have overhaul work done on other components until they have been thoroughly inspected. As a general rule, time is the primary cost of an overhaul, so it does not pay to fit worn or sub-standard parts.

10 As a final note, to ensure maximum life and minimum trouble from a reconditioned engine, everything must be assembled with care, in a spotlessly-clean environment.

3 Engine removal – methods and precautions

1 If you have decided that the engine must be removed for overhaul or major repair work, several preliminary steps should be taken.

2 Locating a suitable place to work is extremely important. Adequate work space, along with storage space for the car, will be needed. Engine/transmission removal is extremely complicated and involved on these vehicles. It must be stated, that unless the vehicle can be positioned on a ramp, or raised and supported on axle stands over an inspection pit, it will be very difficult to carry out the work involved.

3 Cleaning the engine compartment and engine/transmission before beginning the removal procedure will help keep tools clean and organised.

4 An engine hoist or A-frame will also be necessary. Make sure the equipment is rated in excess of the weight of the engine. Safety is of primary importance, considering the potential hazards involved in lifting the engine/transmission out of the car.

5 The help of an assistant is essential. Apart from the safety aspects involved, there are many instances when one person cannot simultaneously perform all of the operations required during engine/transmission removal.

6 Plan the operation ahead of time. Before starting work, arrange for the hire of or obtain all of the tools and equipment you will need. Some of the equipment necessary to perform engine/transmission removal and installation safely and with relative ease (in addition to an engine hoist) is as follows: a heavy duty trolley jack, complete sets of spanners and sockets (see *Tools and working facilities*), wooden blocks, and plenty of rags and cleaning solvent for mopping-up spilled oil, coolant and fuel. If the hoist must be hired, make sure that you arrange for it in advance, and perform all of the operations possible without it beforehand. This will save you money and time.

7 Plan for the car to be out of use for quite a while. An engineering machine shop or engine reconditioning specialist will be required to perform some of the work which cannot be accomplished without special equipment. These places often have a busy schedule, so it would be a good idea to consult them before removing the engine, in order to accurately estimate the amount of time required to rebuild or repair components that may need work.

8 During the engine/transmission removal procedure, it is advisable to make notes of the locations of all brackets, cable ties, earthing points, etc, as well as how the wiring harnesses, hoses and electrical connections are attached and routed around the engine and engine compartment. An effective way of doing this is to take a series of photographs of the various components before they are disconnected or removed; the resulting photographs will prove invaluable when the engine/transmission is refitted.

9 On all models, the engine must be removed complete with the transmission as an assembly. There is insufficient clearance in the engine compartment to remove the engine leaving the transmission in the vehicle. The assembly is removed by raising the front of the vehicle, and lowering the assembly from the engine compartment.

10 Always be extremely careful when removing and refitting the engine/transmission. Serious injury can result from careless actions. Plan ahead and take your time, and a job of this nature, although major, can be accomplished successfully.

Note: *Such is the complexity of the power unit arrangement on these vehicles, and the variations that may be encountered according to model and optional equipment fitted, that the following should be regarded as a guide to the work involved, rather than a step-by-step procedure. Where differences are encountered, or additional component disconnection or removal is necessary, make notes of the work involved as an aid to refitting.*

4 Engine – removal and refitting

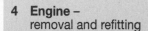

Note: *Such is the complexity of the power unit arrangement on these vehicles, and the variations that may be encountered according to model and optional equipment fitted, the following should be regarded as a guide to the work involved, rather than a step-by-step procedure. Where differences are encountered, or additional component disconnection or removal is necessary, make notes of the work involved as an aid to refitting.*

Removal

1 Remove the battery and battery support tray (see Chapter 5A).

2 Apply the handbrake, then jack up the front of the vehicle and support it on axle stands (see *Jacking and vehicle support*). Remove both front roadwheels. Undo the screws and remove the engine undershield.

3 Where fitted, remove the plastic covers from the top of the engine. On 1.4 and 1.6 litre diesel engines, the engine cover simply pulls up from place. Other covers are retained by either plastic nut type fasteners or plastic expanding rivets. Rotate the nuts 90° anti-clockwise, or push in the centre pins a little and prise up the complete rivets

4 Unbolt the brake fluid reservoir, and move it to one side **(see illustration).**

5 To improve access, remove the bonnet as described in Chapter 11.

6 Remove the wiper arms (Chapter 12), and remove the plastic scuttle trim and crossmember. The trim is retained by an

4.4 Undo the bolts (arrowed) and move the master cylinder upper reservoir to one side

expanding plastic rivet at each end, then pull up each end of the trim and slide the trim down and off the lower edge of the windscreen. The crossmember is secured by one screw at each end, and expanding plastic rivets securing it to the sound insulation material **(see illustrations).**

7 Drain the cooling system with reference to Chapter 1A or 1B.

8 Drain the transmission oil/fluid as described in Chapter 7A or 7B. Refit the drain and filler plugs, and tighten them to their specified torque settings.

9 If the engine is to be dismantled, drain the engine oil and remove the oil filter as described in Chapter 1A or 1B. Clean and refit the drain plug, tightening it securely.

10 Push the centre pins in a little, then prise out the complete plastic expanding rivets and remove the front wheelarch liners from both sides.

4.6a The scuttle trim is secured at each end by a plastic expanding rivet

4.6c . . . and to the sound insulation material by plastic expanding rivets

11 Refer to Chapter 8 and remove both front driveshafts.

12 Remove the front bumper and bumper bar as described in Chapter 11. Also, remove the headlamps (see Chapter 12).

13 Refer to Chapter 1A or 1B and remove the auxiliary drivebelt.

14 Remove the cooling fan and front panel assembly as described in Chapter 3. On air conditioned models, tie the condenser to one side. **Do not** disconnect the refrigerant pipes.

15 Undo the four nuts (two each side) and remove the front panel lower crossmember **(see illustration).**

16 On 1.6 litre diesel engines, remove the auxiliary drivebelt (see Chapter 1B) then remove the air hoses leading from the intercooler to the turbocharger located on the right-hand side of the radiator, and to the inlet manifold.

17 On 2.0 litre diesel engines with an intercooler, remove the air duct leading from the turbocharger to the intercooler.

18 Remove the air cleaner housing and ducting, then remove the exhaust system with reference to Chapter 4A or 4B.

19 Note their fitted positions and harness routing, then disconnect all wiring plugs from the transmission. If necessary label the connectors as they are unplugged. On diesel models, undo the nut and remove the heater control box (still connected) from the front of the plastic electrical box in the front left-hand corner of the engine compartment.

20 Disconnect the engine wiring harness plugs at the fusebox or ECM depending on

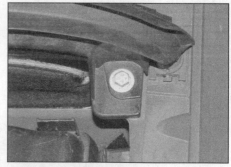

4.6b The scuttle crossmember is bolted at each end . . .

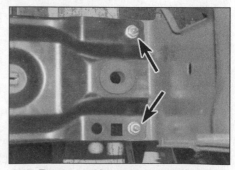

4.15 Front panel lower crossmember nuts (arrowed)

model **(see illustration)**. Release the wiring harness from the retaining clips on the timing cover at the right-hand end of the engine (where applicable).

21 Disconnect the hose from the vacuum pump on the left-hand end of the cylinder head (diesel models) or the brake servo unit vacuum pipe (petrol models) – see Chapter 9.

22 Disconnect the accelerator cable (where fitted) with reference to Chapter 4A or 4B.

23 Disconnect the fuel feed and return hoses. Plug the end of the hoses to prevent dirt ingress.

24 Disconnect the selector cable(s) from the transmission as described in Chapter 7A or 7B.

25 On manual transmission models, unbolt the clutch slave cylinder, then tie it to one side, without disconnecting the fluid pipe (see Chapter 6). Use an elastic band around the cylinder to prevent the piston from coming out.

26 From underneath the vehicle, slacken and remove the nuts and bolts securing the rear engine mounting connecting link to the mounting assembly and subframe, and remove the connecting link. Refer to Chapter 2A, 2B, 2C, 2D or 2E.

27 On 2.0 litre diesel models, remove the torque reaction link from under the centre of the engine/transmission assembly.

28 On models with air conditioning, refer to Chapter 3 and unbolt the compressor from the engine. **Do not** disconnect the refrigerant lines. Support or tie the compressor to one side.

29 Using a hoist attached to the lifting eyes on the cylinder head, take the weight of the engine and transmission.

30 Remove the right-hand and left-hand engine mountings and support brackets as described in Chapter 2A, 2B, 2C, 2D or 2E.

31 Completely pull out the wire retaining clips and disconnect the heater hoses at the engine compartment bulkhead.

32 Make a final check to ensure all wiring, hoses and brackets that would prevent the removal of the assembly have been disconnected.

33 Move the engine/transmission forwards and out from the front of the vehicle. Enlist the help of an assistant during this procedure, as it may be necessary to tilt and twist the assembly slightly to clear the body panels and adjacent components. Move the unit clear of the car and lower it to the ground

Separation

34 With the engine/transmission assembly removed, support the assembly on suitable blocks of wood on a workbench (or failing that, on a clean area of the workshop floor).

35 Undo the retaining bolts, and remove the flywheel lower cover plate (where fitted) from the transmission.

36 Slacken and remove the retaining bolts, and remove the starter motor from the transmission.

37 Disconnect any remaining wiring connectors at the transmission, then move the main engine wiring harness to one side.

38 On automatic transmission models, locate the access hole at the lower rear of the cylinder block, then turn the crankshaft by means of a socket on the crankshaft pulley bolt, until one of the three torque converter retaining nuts is accessible through the access hole. Undo the accessible torque converter bolt, then turn the crankshaft as necessary and undo the remaining two bolts.

39 Ensure that both engine and transmission are adequately supported, then slacken and remove the remaining bolts securing the transmission housing to the engine. Note the correct fitted positions of each bolt (and the relevant brackets) as they are removed, to use as a reference on refitting. On 1.4 and 1.6 litre diesel models, the left-hand catalytic converter mounting stud must be removed to access the front transmission-to-engine bolt **(see illustration)**.

40 Carefully withdraw the transmission from the engine, ensuring that the weight of the transmission is not allowed to hang on the input shaft while it is engaged with the clutch friction disc (manual transmission models) or that the torque converter does not slip from the input shaft (automatic transmission models).

41 If they are loose, remove the locating dowels from the engine or transmission, and keep them in a safe place.

Refitting

42 If the engine and transmission have not been separated, perform the operations described below from paragraph 49 onwards.

43 Apply a smear of high melting-point grease (Peugeot recommend the use of Molykote BR2 plus – available from your Peugeot dealer) to the splines of the transmission input shaft. Do not apply too much, otherwise there is a possibility of the grease contaminating the clutch friction disc. **Note:** *On late models, Peugeot recommend **no** grease is applied.*

44 On automatic transmission models, prior to reconnection it is necessary to make a simple tool to align the torque converter with the driveplate as the transmission is refitted. To make the tool, carry out the following:

a) *Obtain a bolt of the same size as the torque converter retaining bolts, but long enough to extend through the access hole in the cylinder block when the transmission is refitted.*

b) *Cut the head off the bolt and cut a slot (to enable it to be unscrewed) in the plain end. Check that the tool will slide easily through the torque converter retaining bolt hole in the driveplate.*

c) *Turn the engine crankshaft so that one of the torque converter retaining bolt holes in the driveplate, is aligned with the access hole in the cylinder block. Screw the alignment tool (finger-tight only) into one of the retaining bolt holes in the torque converter. Turn the torque converter so that the alignment tool is*

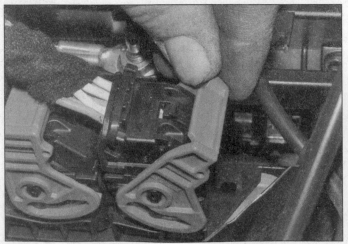

4.20 Disconnect the ECM wiring plugs

4.39 On 1.4 and 1.6 litre diesel models, the stud must be removed to access the front transmission-to-engine bolt

in approximately the correct position, relative to the cylinder block access hole. As the transmission is refitted, the alignment tool will pass through the retaining bolt hole in the driveplate and through the access hole. It can then be unscrewed with a screwdriver and the first torque converter retaining bolt fitted in its place.

d) Check that the torque converter support bush fitted to the centre of the crankshaft is in good condition, and in place.

45 Ensure that the locating dowels are correctly positioned in the engine or transmission, then carefully offer the transmission to the engine until the locating dowels are engaged. On manual transmission models, ensure that the weight of the transmission is not allowed to hang on the input shaft as it is engaged with the clutch friction disc. On automatic transmission models, ensure the torque converter studs engage correctly with the corresponding holes in the driveplate.

46 Refit the transmission housing-to-engine bolts, ensuring that all the necessary brackets are correctly positioned, and tighten them securely.

47 Refit the starter motor, and securely tighten its retaining bolts.

48 Refit the lower flywheel cover plate (where fitted) to the transmission, and securely tighten the bolts.

49 Reconnect the hoist and lifting tackle to the engine lifting brackets. With the aid of an assistant, lift the assembly into the engine compartment, taking care not to damage surrounding components.

50 Refit the right-hand engine mounting and support bracket, but leave the bolts finger-tight at this stage.

51 Working on the left-hand mounting, refit the rubber mounting to the body over the stud, and tighten the bolts, then refit the centre nut and washer and finger-tighten.

52 Remove the hoist.

53 From underneath the vehicle, refit the rear mounting connecting link and finger-tighten the bolts.

54 Rock the engine to settle it on its mountings, then go around and tighten all the mounting nuts and bolts to their specified torque settings.

55 The remainder of the refitting procedure is a direct reversal of the removal sequence, with reference to the relevant chapters and noting the following points:

a) Ensure that the wiring loom is correctly routed and retained by all the relevant retaining clips; all connectors should be correctly and securely reconnected.

b) Prior to refitting the driveshafts to the transmission, renew the driveshaft oil seals as described in Chapter 7A or 7B.

c) Ensure that all coolant hoses are correctly reconnected, and securely retained by their retaining clips.

d) Refill the engine and transmission with the correct quantity and type of lubricant, as described in Chapters 1A or 1B, and 7A or 7B.

e) Refill the cooling system as described in Chapter 1A or 1B.

f) Initialise the engine management ECU as follows. Start the engine and run to normal temperature. Carry out a road test during which the following procedure should be made. Engage third gear and stabilise the engine at 1000 rpm. Now accelerate fully to 3500 rpm.

5 Engine overhaul – dismantling sequence

1 It is much easier to dismantle and work on the engine if it is mounted on a portable engine stand. These stands can often be hired from a tool hire shop. Before the engine is mounted on a stand, the flywheel/driveplate should be removed, so that the stand bolts can be tightened into the end of the cylinder block/crankcase.

2 If a stand is not available, it is possible to dismantle the engine with it blocked up on a sturdy workbench, or on the floor. Be extra careful not to tip or drop the engine when working without a stand.

3 If you are going to obtain a reconditioned engine, all the external components must be removed first, to be transferred to the new engine (just as they will if you are doing a complete engine overhaul yourself). These components include the following:

a) Ancillary unit mounting brackets (oil filter, starter, alternator, power steering pump (where fitted), etc)

b) Thermostat and housing (Chapter 3).

c) Dipstick tube/sensor.

d) All electrical switches and sensors.

e) Inlet and exhaust manifolds – where applicable (Chapter 4A or 4B).

f) Ignition coils and spark plugs – as applicable (Chapter 5B and 1A).

g) Flywheel/driveplate (Part A, B, C, D or E of this Chapter).

Note: *When removing the external components from the engine, pay close attention to details that may be helpful or important during refitting. Note the fitted position of gaskets, seals, spacers, pins, washers, bolts, and other small items.*

4 If you are obtaining a 'short' engine (which consists of the engine cylinder block/crankcase, crankshaft, pistons and connecting rods all assembled), then the cylinder head, sump, oil pump, and timing belt will have to be removed also.

5 If you are planning a complete overhaul, the engine can be dismantled, and the internal components removed, in the order given below, referring to Part A, B, C, D or E of this Chapter unless otherwise stated.

a) Inlet and exhaust manifolds – where applicable (Chapter 4A or 4B).

b) Timing belts, sprockets and tensioner(s).

c) Cylinder head.

d) Flywheel/driveplate.

e) Sump.

f) Oil pump.

g) Piston/connecting rod assemblies (Section 9). **Note:** *On 1.4 and 1.6 litre diesel engines, remove the crankshaft before the pistons.*

h) Crankshaft (Section 10).

6 Before beginning the dismantling and overhaul procedures, make sure that you have all of the correct tools necessary. Refer to *Tools and working facilities* for further information.

6 Cylinder head – dismantling

Note: *New and reconditioned cylinder heads are available from the manufacturer, and from engine overhaul specialists. Be aware that some specialist tools are required for the dismantling and inspection procedures, and new components may not be readily available. It may therefore be more practical and economical for the home mechanic to purchase a reconditioned head, rather than dismantle, inspect and recondition the original head.*

1 Remove the cylinder head as described in Part A, B, C, D or E of this Chapter (as applicable).

2 If not already done, remove the inlet and exhaust manifolds with reference to Chapter 4A or 4B. Remove any remaining brackets or housings as required.

3 Remove the camshaft(s), hydraulic tappets and rockers (as applicable) as described in Part A, B, C, D or E of this Chapter. On the 2.0 litre DOHC diesel engines, remove the camshaft drive chain guide from the cylinder head.

4 If not already done on petrol models, remove the spark plugs as described in Chapter 1A.

5 If not already done on diesel models, remove the glow plugs as described in Chapter 5C.

6 On all models, using a valve spring compressor, compress each valve spring in turn until the split collets can be removed. Release the compressor, and lift off the spring retainer, spring and, where fitted, the spring seat. Using a pair of pliers, carefully extract the valve stem oil seal from the top of the guide. On 16-valve engines, the valve stem oil seal also forms the spring seat and is deeply recessed in the cylinder head. It is also a tight fit on the valve guide making it difficult to remove with pliers or a conventional valve stem oil seal removal tool. It can be easily removed, however, using a self-locking nut of suitable diameter screwed onto the end of a bolt and locked with a second nut. Push the nut down onto the top of the seal; the locking portion of the nut will grip the seal allowing it to be withdrawn from the top of the valve guide.

6.6a Compress the valve spring using a spring compressor . . .

6.6b . . . then extract the collets and release the spring compressor

6.6c Remove the spring retainer . . .

6.6d . . . followed by the valve spring . . .

6.6e . . . and the spring seat (not all models)

6.6f Use a pair of pliers to remove the valve stem oil seal. On 1.4 and 1.6 litre diesel and 2.0 litre petrol models the spring seat is integral with the seal

Access to the valves is limited, and it may be necessary to make up an adapter out of metal tube – cut out a 'window' so that the valve collets can be removed **(see illustrations)**.

7 If, when the valve spring compressor is screwed down, the spring retainer refuses to free and expose the split collets, gently tap the top of the tool, directly over the retainer, with a light hammer. This will free the retainer.

8 Withdraw the valve from the combustion chamber. Remove the valve stem oil seal from the top of the guide, then lift out the spring seat where fitted.

9 It is essential that each valve is stored together with its collets, retainer, spring, and spring seat. The valves should also be kept in their correct sequence, unless they are so badly worn that they are to be renewed. If they are going to be kept and used again, place each valve assembly in a labelled polythene bag or similar small container **(see**

6.9 Place each valve and its associated components in a labelled bag

illustration). Note that No 1 valve is nearest to the transmission (flywheel/driveplate) end of the engine.

---

7 Cylinder head and valves – cleaning and inspection

1 Thorough cleaning of the cylinder head and valve components, followed by a detailed inspection, will enable you to decide how much valve service work must be carried out during the engine overhaul. **Note:** *If the engine has been severely overheated, it is best to assume that the cylinder head is warped – check carefully for signs of this.*

Cleaning

2 Scrape away all traces of old gasket material from the cylinder head.

7.5 Check the cylinder head gasket surface for distortion

3 Scrape away the carbon from the combustion chambers and ports, then wash the cylinder head thoroughly with paraffin or a suitable solvent.

4 Scrape off any heavy carbon deposits that may have formed on the valves, then use a power-operated wire brush to remove deposits from the valve heads and stems.

Inspection

Note: *Be sure to perform all the following inspection procedures before concluding that the services of a machine shop or engine overhaul specialist are required. Make a list of all items that require attention.*

Cylinder head

5 Inspect the head very carefully for cracks, evidence of coolant leakage, and other damage. If cracks are found, a new cylinder head should be obtained. Use a straight-edge and feeler blade to check that the cylinder head gasket surface is not distorted **(see illustration)**. If it is, it may be possible to have it machined, provided that the cylinder head height is not significantly reduced.

6 Examine the valve seats in each of the combustion chambers. If they are severely pitted, cracked, or burned, they will need to be renewed or recut by an engine overhaul specialist. If they are only slightly pitted, this can be removed by grinding-in the valve heads and seats with fine valve-grinding compound, as described below. If in any doubt, have the cylinder head inspected by an engine overhaul specialist.

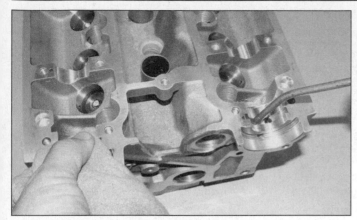

7.9a Apply compressed air to the oil feed bore of the inlet camshaft, seal the bore in the exhaust camshaft bore with a rag . . .

7.9b . . . and the camshaft oil supply non-return valve will be ejected from the underside of the cylinder head

7 Check the valve guides for wear by inserting the relevant valve, and checking for side-to-side motion of the valve. A very small amount of movement is acceptable. If the movement seems excessive, remove the valve. Measure the valve stem diameter (see below), and renew the valve if it is worn. If the valve stem is not worn, the wear must be in the valve guide, and the guide must be renewed. The renewal of valve guides is best carried out by a Peugeot dealer or engine overhaul specialist, who will have the necessary tools available. Where no valve stem diameter is specified, seek the advice of a Peugeot dealer on the best course of action.

8 If renewing the valve guides, the valve seats should be recut or reground only *after* the guides have been fitted.

9 Where applicable, examine the camshaft oil supply non-return valve in the oil feed bore at the timing belt end of the cylinder head. Check that the valve is not loose in the cylinder head and that the ball is free to move within the valve body. If the valve is a loose fit in its bore, or if there is any doubt about its condition, it should be renewed. The non-return valve can be removed (assuming it is not loose), using compressed air, such as that generated by a tyre foot pump. Place the pump nozzle over the oil feed bore of the camshaft bearing journal and seal the corresponding oil feed bore with a rag. Apply the compressed air and the valve will be forced out of its location

in the underside of the cylinder head **(see illustrations)**. Fit the new non-return valve to its bore on the underside of the head ensuring it is fitted the correct way. Oil should be able to pass upwards through the valve to the camshafts, but the ball in the valve should prevent the oil from returning back to the cylinder block. Use a thin socket or similar to push the valve fully into position.

Valves

10 Examine the head of each valve for pitting, burning, cracks, and general wear. Check the valve stem for scoring and wear ridges. Rotate the valve, and check for any obvious indication that it is bent. Look for pits or excessive wear on the tip of each valve stem. Renew any valve that shows any such signs of wear or damage.

11 If the valve appears satisfactory at this stage, measure the valve stem diameter at several points using a micrometer **(see illustration)**. Any significant difference in the readings obtained indicates wear of the valve stem. Should any of these conditions be apparent, the valve must be renewed.

12 If the valves are in satisfactory condition, they should be ground (lapped) into their respective seats, to ensure a smooth, gas-tight seal. If the seat is only lightly pitted, or if it has been recut, fine grinding compound *only* should be used to produce the required finish. Coarse valve-grinding compound should *not*

be used, unless a seat is badly burned or deeply pitted. If this is the case, the cylinder head and valves should be inspected by an expert, to decide whether seat recutting, or even the renewal of the valve or seat insert (where possible) is required.

13 Valve grinding is carried out as follows. Place the cylinder head upside-down on a bench.

14 Smear a trace of (the appropriate grade of) valve-grinding compound on the seat face, and press a suction grinding tool onto the valve head **(see illustration)**. With a semi-rotary action, grind the valve head to its seat, lifting the valve occasionally to redistribute the grinding compound. A light spring placed under the valve head will greatly ease this operation.

15 If coarse grinding compound is being used, work only until a dull, matt even surface is produced on both the valve seat and the valve, then wipe off the used compound, and repeat the process with fine compound. When a smooth unbroken ring of light grey matt finish is produced on both the valve and seat, the grinding operation is complete. *Do not* grind-in the valves any further than absolutely necessary, or the seat will be prematurely sunk into the cylinder head.

16 When all the valves have been ground-in, carefully wash off *all* traces of grinding compound using paraffin or a suitable solvent, before reassembling the cylinder head.

Valve components

17 Examine the valve springs for signs of damage and discoloration. No minimum free length is specified by Peugeot, so the only way of judging valve spring wear is by comparison with a new component.

18 Stand each spring on a flat surface, and check it for squareness. If any of the springs are damaged, distorted or have lost their tension, obtain a complete new set of springs. It is normal to renew the valve springs as a matter of course if a major overhaul is being carried out.

19 Renew the valve stem oil seals regardless of their apparent condition.

7.11 Measure the valve stem diameter with a micrometer

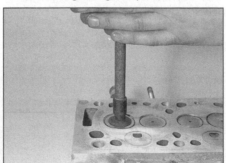

7.14 Grinding-in a valve

8.1a Locate the valve stem oil seal on the valve guide . . .

8.1b . . . and press the seal firmly onto the guide using a suitable socket

8.1c On 1.4 and 1.6 litre diesel and 2.0 litre petrol models, the valve stem oil seal is integral with the spring seat

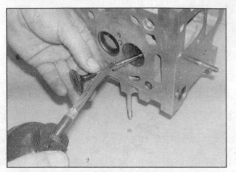

8.2 Lubricate the stem of the valve and insert it into the guide

8 Cylinder head – reassembly

1 Working on the first valve assembly, refit the spring seat then dip the new valve stem oil seal in fresh engine oil. Locate the seal on the valve guide and press the seal firmly onto the guide using a suitable socket **(see illustrations)**. Note that on 2.0 litre diesel engines no spring lower seat is fitted, whilst on 1.4 and 1.6 litre diesel and 2.0 litre petrol engines, the seal is integral with the lower spring seat.

2 Lubricate the stem of the first valve, and insert it in the guide **(see illustration)**.

3 Locate the valve spring on top of its seat, then refit the spring retainer. Note that on the 2.0 litre petrol engines, the larger diameter of the spring must face the cylinder head.

4 Compress the valve spring, and locate the split collets in the recess in the valve stem. Release the compressor, then repeat the procedure on the remaining valves. Ensure that each valve is inserted into its original location. If new valves are being fitted, insert them into the locations to which they have been ground.

5 With all the valves installed, support the cylinder head and, using a hammer and interposed block of wood, tap the end of each valve stem to settle the components.

6 Refit the camshafts, hydraulic tappets and rocker arms (as applicable) as described in Part A, B, C, D or E of this Chapter.

7 Refit any remaining components using the reverse of the removal sequence and with new seals or gaskets as necessary.

8 The cylinder head can then be refitted as described in Part A, B, C, D or E of this Chapter.

9 Piston/connecting rod assembly – removal

1 Remove the cylinder head, sump and oil pump as described in Part A, B, C, D or E of this Chapter.

2 If there is a pronounced wear ridge at the top of any bore, it may be necessary to remove it with a scraper or ridge reamer, to avoid piston damage during removal. Such a ridge indicates excessive wear of the cylinder bore.

3 Using quick-drying paint, mark each connecting rod and big-end bearing cap with its respective cylinder number on the flat machined surface provided; if the engine has been dismantled before, note carefully any identifying marks made previously **(see illustration)**. Note that No 1 cylinder is at the transmission (flywheel) end of the engine.

4 Turn the crankshaft to bring pistons 1 and 4 to BDC (bottom dead centre). On 1.4 and 1.6 litre diesel engines, remove the main bearing ladder as described in Section 10 of this Chapter.

5 Unscrew the nuts or bolts, as applicable, from No 1 piston big-end bearing cap. Take off the cap, and recover the bottom half bearing shell **(see illustration)**. If the bearing shells are to be re-used, tape the cap and the shell together.

6 Where applicable, to prevent the possibility of damage to the crankshaft bearing journals, tape over the connecting rod stud threads **(see illustration)**.

7 Using a hammer handle, push the piston up through the bore, and remove it from the top of the cylinder block. Recover the bearing shell, and tape it to the connecting rod for safe-keeping.

8 Loosely refit the big-end cap to the connecting rod, and secure with the nuts/bolts – this will help to keep the components in their correct order.

9 Remove No 4 piston assembly in the same way.

10 Turn the crankshaft through 180° to bring pistons 2 and 3 to BDC (bottom dead centre), and remove them in the same way.

9.3 Connecting rod and big-end bearing cap identification marks (No 3 shown)

9.5 Remove the big-end bearing shell and cap

9.6 To protect the crankshaft journals, tape over the connecting rod stud threads

10 Crankshaft – removal

1 Remove the crankshaft sprocket and the oil pump as described in Part A, B, C, D or E of this Chapter (as applicable).

2 Remove the pistons and connecting rods, as described in Section 9. If no work is to be done on the pistons and connecting rods, there is no need to remove the cylinder head, or to push the pistons out of the cylinder bores. The pistons should just be pushed far enough up the bores so that they are positioned clear of the crankshaft journals. **Note:** *On 1.4 and 1.6 litre diesel engines, the main bearing ladder must be removed before the piston/connecting rods.*

3 Check the crankshaft endfloat as described in Section 13, then proceed as follows.

1.4 litre petrol engine

4 Work around the outside of the cylinder block, and unscrew all the small (M6) bolts securing the main bearing ladder to the base of the cylinder block. Note the correct fitted depth of both the left- and right-hand crankshaft oil seals in the cylinder block/main bearing ladder.

5 Working in a diagonal sequence, evenly and progressively slacken the ten large (M11) main bearing ladder retaining bolts by a turn at a time. Once all the bolts are loose, remove them from the ladder.

6 With all the retaining bolts removed, carefully lift the main bearing ladder casting away from the base of the cylinder block. Recover the lower main bearing shells, and tape them to their respective locations in the casting. If the two locating dowels are a loose fit, remove them and store them with the casting for safe-keeping.

7 Lift out the crankshaft, and discard both the oil seals. Remove the oil pump drive chain from the end of the crankshaft. Where necessary, slide off the drive sprocket, and recover the Woodruff key.

8 Recover the upper main bearing shells, and store them along with the relevant lower bearing shell. Also recover the two thrustwashers (one fitted either side of No 2 main bearing) from the cylinder block.

1.6 litre petrol engine

9 Unbolt and remove the crankshaft left- and right-hand oil seal housings from each end of the cylinder block, noting the correct fitted locations of the locating dowels. If the locating dowels are a loose fit, remove them and store them with the housings for safe-keeping.

10 Remove the oil pump drive chain, and slide the drive sprocket off the end of the crankshaft. Remove the Woodruff key, and store it with the sprocket for safe-keeping.

11 The main bearing caps should be numbered 1 to 5 from the transmission (flywheel/driveplate) end of the engine. If not, mark them accordingly using a centre-punch or paint.

12 Unscrew and remove the main bearing cap retaining bolts, and withdraw the caps. Recover the lower main bearing shells, and tape them to their respective caps for safe-keeping.

13 Carefully lift out the crankshaft, taking care not to displace the upper main bearing shell.

14 Recover the upper bearing shells from the cylinder block, and tape them to their respective caps for safe-keeping. Remove the thrustwasher halves from the side of No 2 main bearing, and store them with the bearing cap.

2.0 litre petrol engine

15 Work around the outside of the cylinder block, and unscrew all the small bolts securing the main bearing ladder to the base of the cylinder block. Note the correct fitted depth of the left-hand crankshaft oil seal in the cylinder block/main bearing ladder.

16 Working in a diagonal sequence, evenly and progressively slacken the large main bearing ladder retaining bolts by a turn at a time. Once all the bolts are loose, remove them from the ladder.

17 With all the retaining bolts removed, carefully lift the main bearing ladder casting away from the base of the cylinder block. Recover the lower main bearing shells, and tape them to their respective locations in the casting. If the two locating dowels are a loose fit, remove them and store them with the casting for safe-keeping.

18 Lift out the crankshaft, and discard both the oil seals.

19 Recover the upper main bearing shells, and store them along with the relevant lower bearing shell. Also recover the two thrustwashers (one fitted either side of No 2 main bearing) from the cylinder block.

1.4 and 1.6 litre diesel engine

20 Work around the outside of the cylinder block, and unscrew all the small bolts securing the main bearing ladder to the base of the cylinder block. Note the correct fitted depth of

10.21 On 1.4 and 1.6 litre diesel engines, prise up the two caps to expose the main bearing bolts at the flywheel end

the left-hand crankshaft oil seal in the cylinder block/main bearing ladder.

21 Working in a diagonal sequence, evenly and progressively slacken the large main bearing ladder retaining bolts by a turn at a time. Once all the bolts are loose, remove them from the ladder. **Note:** *Prise up the two caps at the flywheel end of the ladder to expose the two end main bearing bolts (see illustration).*

22 With all the retaining bolts removed, carefully lift the main bearing ladder casting away from the base of the cylinder block. Recover the lower main bearing shells, and tape them to their respective locations in the casting. If the two locating dowels are a loose fit, remove them and store them with the casting for safe-keeping. Undo the big-end bolts and remove the pistons/connecting rods as described in Section 9.

23 Lift out the crankshaft, and discard both the oil seals.

24 Recover the upper main bearing shells, and store them along with the relevant lower bearing shell. Also recover the two thrustwashers (one fitted either side of No 2 main bearing) from the cylinder block.

2.0 litre diesel engine

25 Slacken and remove the retaining bolts, and remove the oil seal housing from the right-hand (timing belt) end of the cylinder block **(see illustration)**.

26 Remove the oil pump drive chain, and slide the drive sprocket and spacer (where fitted) off from the crankshaft. Remove the Woodruff key, and store it with the sprocket for safe-keeping then remove the sealing ring (where fitted) from the crankshaft.

27 The main bearing caps should be numbered 1 to 5, starting from the transmission (flywheel) end of the engine. If not, mark them accordingly using a centre-punch. Also note the correct fitted depth of the crankshaft oil seal in the bearing cap.

28 Slacken and remove the main bearing cap retaining bolts, and lift off each bearing cap. Recover the lower bearing shells, and tape them to their respective caps for safe-keeping. Also recover the lower thrustwasher halves from the side of No 2 main bearing cap (see

10.25 Remove the oil seal housing from the right-hand end of the block

10.28 Note the thrustwashers (arrowed) fitted to the No 2 bearing cap

illustration). Remove the sealing strips from the sides of No 1 main bearing cap, and discard them.

29 Lift out the crankshaft, and discard the left-hand (flywheel end) oil seal.

30 Recover the upper bearing shells from the cylinder block, and tape them to their respective caps for safe-keeping. Remove the upper thrustwasher halves from the side of No 2 main bearing, and store them with the lower halves.

11 Cylinder block/crankcase – cleaning and inspection

Cleaning

1 Remove all external components and electrical switches/sensors from the block. For complete cleaning, the core plugs should ideally be removed **(see illustration)**. Drill a small hole in the plugs, then insert a self-tapping screw into the hole. Pull out the plugs by pulling on the screw with a pair of grips, or by using a slide hammer.

2 On aluminium block petrol engines with wet liners (1.4 litre), remove the liners – see paragraph 18.

3 Where applicable, undo the retaining bolts and remove the piston oil jet spray tubes (there is one for each piston) from inside the cylinder block **(see illustration)**.

4 Scrape all traces of gasket from the cylinder block/crankcase, and from the main bearing

ladder/caps (as applicable), taking care not to damage the gasket/sealing surfaces.

5 Remove all oil gallery plugs (where fitted). The plugs are usually very tight – they may have to be drilled out, and the holes retapped. Use new plugs when the engine is reassembled.

6 If any of the castings are extremely dirty, all should be steam-cleaned.

7 After the castings are returned, clean all oil holes and oil galleries one more time. Flush all internal passages with warm water until the water runs clear. Dry thoroughly, and apply a light film of oil to all mating surfaces, to prevent rusting. On cast-iron block engines, also oil the cylinder bores. If you have access to compressed air, use it to speed up the drying process, and to blow out all the oil holes and galleries.

⚠ **Warning: Wear eye protection when using compressed air.**

8 If the castings are not very dirty, you can do an adequate cleaning job with hot (as hot as you can stand), soapy water and a stiff brush. Take plenty of time, and do a thorough job. Regardless of the cleaning method used, be sure to clean all oil holes and galleries very thoroughly, and to dry all components well. On cast-iron block engines, protect the cylinder bores as described above, to prevent rusting.

9 All threaded holes must be clean, to ensure accurate torque readings during reassembly. To clean the threads, run the correct-size tap into each of the holes to remove rust, corrosion, thread sealant or sludge, and to restore damaged threads **(see illustration)**. If possible, use compressed air to clear the holes of debris produced by this operation.

10 Apply suitable sealant to the new oil gallery plugs, and insert them into the holes in the block. Tighten them securely. Also apply suitable sealant to new core plugs, and drive them into the block using a tube or socket.

11 Where applicable, clean the threads of the piston oil jet retaining bolts, and apply a drop of thread-locking compound (Peugeot recommend Loctite Frenetanch) to each bolt threads. Refit the piston oil jet spray tubes to the cylinder block, and tighten the retaining bolts to the specified torque setting.

12 If the engine is not going to be reassembled right away, cover it with a large

plastic bag to keep it clean; protect all mating surfaces and the cylinder bores as described above, to prevent rusting.

Inspection

Cast-iron cylinder block

13 Visually check the castings for cracks and corrosion. Look for stripped threads in the threaded holes. If there has been any history of internal water leakage, it may be worthwhile having an engine overhaul specialist check the cylinder block/crankcase with special equipment. If defects are found, have them repaired if possible, or renew the assembly.

14 Check each cylinder bore for scuffing and scoring. Check for signs of a wear ridge at the top of the cylinder, indicating that the bore is excessively worn.

15 If the necessary measuring equipment is available, measure the bore diameter of each cylinder at the top (just under the wear ridge), centre, and bottom of the cylinder bore, parallel to the crankshaft axis.

16 Next, measure the bore diameter at the same three locations, at right-angles to the crankshaft axis. Compare the results with the figures given in the Specifications. If there is any doubt about the condition of the cylinder bores, seek the advice of a Peugeot dealer or suitable engine reconditioning specialist.

17 At the time of writing, it was not clear whether oversize pistons were available for all models. Consult your Peugeot dealer or engine specialist for the latest information on piston availability. If oversize pistons are available, then it may be possible to have the cylinder bores rebored and fit the oversize pistons. If oversize pistons are not available, and the bores are worn, renewal of the block seems to be the only option.

Aluminium cylinder block

18 Remove the liner clamps (where used), then use a hardwood drift to tap out each liner from the inside of the cylinder block. When all the liners are released, tip the cylinder block/crankcase on its side and remove each liner from the top of the block. As each liner is removed, stick masking tape on its left-hand (transmission side) face, and write the cylinder number on the tape. No 1 cylinder is at the transmission (flywheel/driveplate) end of the

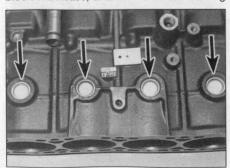

11.1 Cylinder block core plugs (arrowed)

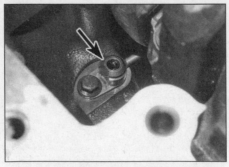

11.3 Piston oil jet spray tube (arrowed) in the cylinder block

11.9 Use a suitable tap to clean the cylinder block threaded holes

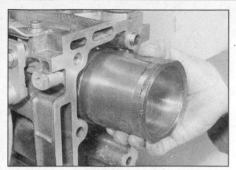

11.18a On aluminium block engines, remove each liner . . .

11.18b . . . and recover the bottom O-ring seal (arrowed)

12.2 Remove the piston rings with the aid of a feeler gauge

engine. Remove the sealing ring from the base of each liner, and discard (see illustrations).

19 Check each cylinder liner for scuffing and scoring. Check for signs of a wear ridge at the top of the liner, indicating that the bore is excessively worn.

20 Take the liners to a Peugeot dealer or engine reconditioning specialist and have their bores measured to determine if renewal is necessary. If it is, the dealer or specialist will be able to advise you regarding piston/liner availability.

21 Prior to installing the liners, check the liner protrusion as follows. Thoroughly clean the mating surfaces of the liner and cylinder block. Insert the liners into the block, without a sealing ring, ensuring each one is correctly seated; if the original liners are being refitted, ensure the liners are fitted in their original locations. With all four liners correctly installed, use a dial gauge (or a straight-edge and feeler blade) to check that the protrusion of each liner above the upper surface of the cylinder block is within the limits given in the Specifications. The maximum difference between any two liners must not be exceeded. Note: If new liners are being fitted, it is permissible to interchange them to bring the difference in protrusion within limits. Remember to keep each piston with its respective liner. If liner protrusion is not within the specified limits, seek the advice of a Peugeot dealer or engine reconditioning specialist before proceeding with the engine rebuild.

22 Once the protrusions have been checked, remove the liners from the block and fit a new sealing ring carefully to the base of each liner. Lubricate the base of each liner with a smear of oil to aid installation.

23 Insert each liner into the cylinder block, taking care not to damage the O-ring, and press it home as far as possible by hand. Using a hammer and a block of wood, tap each liner lightly but fully onto its locating shoulder. If the original liners are being refitted, use the marks made on removal to ensure that each is refitted the correct way round, and is inserted into its original bore.

24 Wipe clean, then lightly oil all exposed liner surfaces, to prevent rusting. Where necessary, clamp the liners back in position.

12 Piston/connecting rod assembly – inspection

1 Before the inspection process can begin, the piston/connecting rod assemblies must be cleaned, and the original piston rings removed from the pistons.

2 Carefully expand the old rings over the top of the pistons. The use of two or three old feeler blades will be helpful in preventing the rings dropping into empty grooves (see illustration). Be careful not to scratch the piston with the ends of the ring. The rings are brittle, and will snap if they are spread too far. They are also very sharp – protect your hands and fingers. Note that the third ring incorporates an expander. Always remove the rings from the top of the piston. Keep each set of rings with its piston if the old rings are to be re-used.

3 Scrape away all traces of carbon from the top of the piston. A hand-held wire brush (or a piece of fine emery cloth) can be used, once the majority of the deposits have been scraped away.

4 Remove the carbon from the ring grooves in the piston, using an old ring. Break the ring in half to do this (be careful not to cut your fingers – piston rings are sharp). Be careful to remove only the carbon deposits – do not remove any metal, and do not nick or scratch the sides of the ring grooves.

5 Once the deposits have been removed, clean the piston/connecting rod assembly with paraffin or a suitable solvent, and dry thoroughly. Make sure that the oil return holes in the ring grooves are clear.

6 If the pistons and cylinder bores are not damaged or worn excessively, and if the cylinder block does not need to be rebored (where possible), the original pistons can be refitted. Normal piston wear shows up as even vertical wear on the piston thrust surfaces, and slight looseness of the top ring in its groove. New piston rings should always be used when the engine is reassembled.

7 Carefully inspect each piston for cracks around the skirt, around the gudgeon pin holes, and at the piston ring 'lands' (between the ring grooves).

8 Look for scoring and scuffing on the piston skirt, holes in the piston crown, and burned areas at the edge of the crown. If the skirt is scored or scuffed, the engine may have been suffering from overheating, and/or abnormal combustion which caused excessively high operating temperatures. The cooling and lubrication systems should be checked thoroughly. Scorch marks on the sides of the pistons show that blow-by has occurred. A hole in the piston crown, or burned areas at the edge of the piston crown, indicates that abnormal combustion (pre-ignition, knocking, or detonation) has been occurring. If any of the above problems exist, the causes must be investigated and corrected, or the damage will occur again. The causes may include incorrect ignition/injection pump timing, or a faulty injector (as applicable).

9 Corrosion of the piston, in the form of pitting, indicates that coolant has been leaking into the combustion chamber and/or the crankcase. Again, the cause must be corrected, or the problem may persist in the rebuilt engine.

10 On aluminium block engines with wet liners, it is not possible to renew the pistons separately; pistons are only supplied with piston rings and a liner, as a part of a matched assembly (see Section 11). On iron-block engines, pistons can be purchased from a Peugeot dealer or engine reconditioning specialist.

11 Examine each connecting rod carefully for signs of damage, such as cracks around the big-end and small-end bearings. Check that the rod is not bent or distorted. Damage is highly unlikely, unless the engine has been seized or badly overheated. Detailed checking of the connecting rod assembly can only be carried out by a Peugeot dealer or engine specialist with the necessary equipment.

12 The connecting rod big-end cap bolts/nuts must be renewed whenever they are disturbed. Although Peugeot do not specify that the bolts must also be renewed, it is recommended that the nuts and bolts are renewed as a complete set.

Petrol engines

13 On petrol engines, the gudgeon pins are an interference fit in the connecting rod

12.15a Prise out the circlip . . .

12.15b . . . and withdraw the gudgeon pin

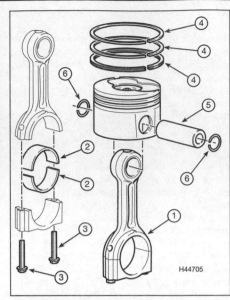

12.19 Piston and connecting rod assembly – 1.4 and 1.6 litre diesel engine

1 Connecting rod
2 Big-end shells
3 Big-end bolt
4 Piston rings
5 Gudgeon pin
6 Circlips

small-end bearing. Therefore, piston and/or connecting rod renewal should be entrusted to a Peugeot dealer or engine repair specialist, who will have the necessary tooling to remove and install the gudgeon pins.

Diesel engines

14 On diesel engines, the gudgeon pins are of the floating type, secured in position by two circlips. On these engines, the pistons and connecting rods can be separated as described in the following paragraphs.

15 Using a small flat-bladed screwdriver, prise out the circlips, and push out the gudgeon pin **(see illustrations)**. Hand pressure should be sufficient to remove the pin. Identify the piston and rod to ensure correct reassembly. Discard the circlips – new ones *must* be used on refitting.

16 Examine the gudgeon pin and connecting rod small-end bearing for signs of wear or damage. Wear can be cured by renewing both the pin and bush (where possible) or connecting rod. Bush renewal, however, is a specialist job – press facilities are required, and the new bush must be reamed accurately.

17 The connecting rods themselves should not be in need of renewal, unless seizure or some other major mechanical failure has occurred. Check the alignment of the connecting rods visually, and if the rods are not straight, take them to an engine overhaul specialist for a more detailed check.

18 Examine all components, and obtain any new parts from your Peugeot dealer. If new pistons are purchased, they will be supplied complete with gudgeon pins and circlips.

Circlips can also be purchased individually.

19 On 1.4 and 1.6 litre diesel engines, position the piston as shown **(see illustration)**.

20 On 2.0 litre diesel engines, position the piston so that the valve recesses on the piston crown are on the opposite side to the connecting rod big-end bearing shell cut-outs.

21 Ensure the piston and connecting rod are correctly positioned then apply a smear of clean engine oil to the gudgeon pin. Slide it into the piston and through the connecting rod small-end. Check that the piston pivots freely on the rod, then secure the gudgeon pin in position with two new circlips. Ensure that each circlip is correctly located in its groove in the piston.

13 Crankshaft – inspection

Checking endfloat

1 If the crankshaft endfloat is to be checked, this must be done when the crankshaft is still installed in the cylinder block/crankcase, but is free to move (see Section 10).

2 Check the endfloat using a dial gauge in contact with the end of the crankshaft. Push the crankshaft fully one way, and then zero the gauge. Push the crankshaft fully the other way, and check the endfloat. The result can be compared with the specified amount, and will give an indication as to whether new thrustwashers are required **(see illustration)**.

3 If a dial gauge is not available, feeler blades

can be used. First push the crankshaft fully towards the flywheel end of the engine, then use feeler blades to measure the gap between the web of No 2 crankpin and the thrustwasher **(see illustration)**.

Inspection

4 Clean the crankshaft using paraffin or a suitable solvent, and dry it, preferably with compressed air if available. Be sure to clean the oil holes with a pipe cleaner or similar probe, to ensure that they are not obstructed.

⚠️ *Warning: Wear eye protection when using compressed air.*

5 Check the main and big-end bearing journals for uneven wear, scoring, pitting and cracking.

6 Big-end bearing wear is accompanied by distinct metallic knocking when the engine is running (particularly noticeable when the engine is pulling from low speed) and some loss of oil pressure.

7 Main bearing wear is accompanied by severe engine vibration and rumble – getting progressively worse as engine speed increases – and again by loss of oil pressure.

8 Check the bearing journal for roughness by running a finger lightly over the bearing surface. Any roughness (which will be accompanied by obvious bearing wear) indicates that the crankshaft requires regrinding (where possible) or renewal.

9 Check the oil seal contact surfaces at each end of the crankshaft for wear and damage. If the seal has worn a deep groove in the surface of the crankshaft, consult an engine overhaul specialist; repair may be possible, but otherwise a new crankshaft will be required.

13.2 The crankshaft endfloat can be checked with a dial gauge . . .

13.3 . . . or with feeler gauges

10 Take the crankshaft to a Peugeot dealer or engine reconditioning specialist to have it measured for journal wear. If excessive wear is evident, they will be able to advise you with regard to regrinding the crankshaft and supplying new bearing shells.

11 If the crankshaft has been reground, check for burrs around the crankshaft oil holes (the holes are usually chamfered, so burrs should not be a problem unless regrinding has been carried out carelessly). Remove any burrs with a fine file or scraper, and thoroughly clean the oil holes as described previously.

12 At the time of writing, it was not clear whether Peugeot produce undersize bearing shells for all of these engines. On some engines, if the crankshaft journals have not already been reground, it may be possible to have the crankshaft reconditioned, and to fit undersize shells. If no undersize shells are available and the crankshaft has worn beyond the specified limits, it will have to be renewed. Consult your Peugeot dealer or engine specialist for further information on parts availability.

14 Main and big-end bearings – inspection

1 Even though the main and big-end bearings should be renewed during the engine overhaul, the old bearings should be retained for close examination, as they may reveal valuable information about the condition of the engine. The bearing shells are graded by thickness, the grade of each shell being indicated by the colour code marked on it.

2 Bearing failure can occur due to lack of lubrication, the presence of dirt or other foreign particles, overloading the engine, or corrosion **(see illustration)**. Regardless of the cause of

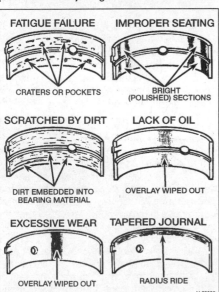

14.2 Typical bearing failures

bearing failure, the cause must be corrected (where applicable) before the engine is reassembled, to prevent it from happening again.

3 When examining the bearing shells, remove them from the cylinder block/crankcase, the main bearing ladder/caps (as appropriate), the connecting rods and the connecting rod big-end bearing caps. Lay them out on a clean surface in the same general position as their location in the engine. This will enable you to match any bearing problems with the corresponding crankshaft journal. *Do not* touch any shell's bearing surface with your fingers while checking it, or the delicate surface may be scratched.

4 Dirt and other foreign matter gets into the engine in a variety of ways. It may be left in the engine during assembly, or it may pass through filters or the crankcase ventilation system. It may get into the oil, and from there into the bearings. Metal chips from machining operations and normal engine wear are often present. Abrasives are sometimes left in engine components after reconditioning, especially when parts are not thoroughly cleaned using the proper cleaning methods. Whatever the source, these foreign objects often end up embedded in the soft bearing material, and are easily recognised. Large particles will not embed in the bearing, and will score or gouge the bearing and journal. The best prevention for this cause of bearing failure is to clean all parts thoroughly, and keep everything spotlessly-clean during engine assembly. Frequent and regular engine oil and filter changes are also recommended.

5 Lack of lubrication (or lubrication breakdown) has a number of interrelated causes. Excessive heat (which thins the oil), overloading (which squeezes the oil from the bearing face) and oil leakage (from excessive bearing clearances, worn oil pump or high engine speeds) all contribute to lubrication breakdown. Blocked oil passages, which usually are the result of misaligned oil holes in a bearing shell, will also oil-starve a bearing, and destroy it. When lack of lubrication is the cause of bearing failure, the bearing material is wiped or extruded from the steel backing of the bearing. Temperatures may increase to the point where the steel backing turns blue from overheating.

6 Driving habits can have a definite effect on bearing life. Full-throttle, low-speed operation (labouring the engine) puts very high loads on bearings, tending to squeeze out the oil film. These loads cause the bearings to flex, which produces fine cracks in the bearing face (fatigue failure). Eventually, the bearing material will loosen in pieces, and tear away from the steel backing.

7 Short-distance driving leads to corrosion of bearings, because insufficient engine heat is produced to drive off the condensed water and corrosive gases. These products collect in the engine oil, forming acid and sludge. As the oil is carried to the engine bearings, the acid attacks and corrodes the bearing material.

8 Incorrect bearing installation during engine assembly will lead to bearing failure as

well. Tight-fitting bearings leave insufficient bearing running clearance, and will result in oil starvation. Dirt or foreign particles trapped behind a bearing shell result in high spots on the bearing, which lead to failure.

9 *Do not* touch any shell's bearing surface with your fingers during reassembly; there is a risk of scratching the delicate surface, or of depositing particles of dirt on it.

10 As mentioned at the beginning of this Section, the bearing shells should be renewed as a matter of course during engine overhaul; to do otherwise is false economy.

15 Engine overhaul – reassembly sequence

1 Before reassembly begins, ensure that all new parts have been obtained, and that all necessary tools are available. Read through the entire procedure to familiarise yourself with the work involved, and to ensure that all items necessary for reassembly of the engine are at hand. In addition to all normal tools and materials, thread-locking compound will be needed. A tube of suitable liquid sealant will also be required for the joint faces that are fitted without gaskets. It is recommended that Peugeot's own product(s) are used, which are specially formulated for this purpose; the relevant product names are quoted in the text of each Section where they are required.

2 In order to save time and avoid problems, engine reassembly can be carried out in the following order, referring to Part A, B, C, D or E of this Chapter unless otherwise stated:

   a) *Crankshaft (See Section 17).* **Note:** *On 1.4 litre diesel engines, the piston/ connecting rods must be fitted before the crankshaft.*
   b) *Piston/connecting rod assemblies (See Section 18).*
   c) *Oil pump.*
   d) *Sump.*
   e) *Flywheel/driveplate.*
   f) *Cylinder head.*
   g) *Injection pump and mounting bracket – diesel engine (Chapter 4B).*
   h) *Timing belt tensioner pulley(s) and sprockets, and timing belt.*
   i) *Engine external components.*

3 At this stage, all engine components should be absolutely clean and dry, with all faults repaired. The components should be laid out (or in individual containers) on a completely clean work surface.

16 Piston rings – refitting

1 Before fitting new piston rings, the ring end gaps must be checked as follows.

2 Lay out the piston/connecting rod assemblies and the new piston ring sets, so that the ring

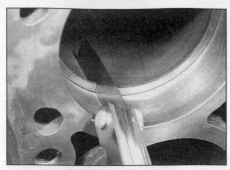

16.5 Measure the piston rings end gaps with a feeler gauge

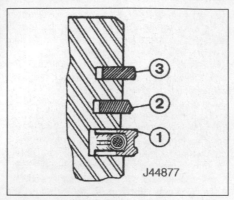

16.9a Piston ring fitting diagram (typical)

1 Oil control ring
2 Second compression ring
3 Top compression ring

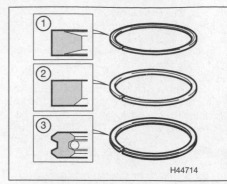

16.9b Piston rings (1.4 and 1.6 litre diesel engine)

1 Top compression ring
2 Second compression ring
3 Oil control ring

sets will be matched with the same piston and cylinder during the end gap measurement and subsequent engine reassembly.

3 Insert the top ring into the first cylinder, and push it down the bore using the top of the piston. This will ensure that the ring remains square with the cylinder walls. Position the ring near the bottom of the cylinder bore, at the lower limit of ring travel. Note that the top and second compression rings are different. The second ring can be identified by its taper; on petrol engines it also has a step on its lower surface. On 1.4 and 1.6 litre diesel engines, the top ring has a chamfer on its upper/outer edge.

4 Measure the end gap using feeler blades.

5 Repeat the procedure with the ring at the top of the cylinder bore, at the upper limit of its travel (see illustration), and compare the measurements with the figures given in the Specifications. If the end gaps are incorrect, check that you have the correct rings for your engine and for the cylinder bore size.

6 Repeat the checking procedure for each ring in the first cylinder, and then for the rings in the remaining cylinders. Remember to keep rings, pistons and cylinders matched up.

7 Once the ring end gaps have been checked and if necessary corrected, the rings can be fitted to the pistons.

8 Fit the oil control ring expander (where fitted) then install the ring. The ring gap should be positioned 180° from the expander gap.

9 The second and top rings are different and can be identified from their cross-sections; the top ring is symmetrical whilst the second ring is tapered. Fit the second ring, ensuring its

identification (TOP) marking is facing upwards, then install the top ring (see illustrations). Arrange the second and top ring end gaps so they are equally spaced 120° apart. Note: *Always follow any instructions supplied with the new piston ring sets – different manufacturers may specify different procedures. Do not mix up the top and second compression rings, as they have different cross-sections.*

17 Crankshaft – refitting

Selection of bearing shells

1 Have the crankshaft inspected and measured by a Peugeot dealer or engine reconditioning specialist. They will be able to carry out any regrinding/repairs, and supply suitable main and big-end bearing shells.

Crankshaft refitting

Note: *New main bearing cap/lower crankcase bolts must be used when refitting the crankshaft.*

2 Where applicable, ensure that the oil spray jets are fitted to the bearing locations in the cylinder block.

1.4 litre petrol engine

3 Using a little grease, stick the upper thrustwashers to each side of the No 2 main

bearing upper location; ensure that the oilway grooves on each thrustwasher face outwards (away from the block).

4 Clean the backs of the bearing shells, and the bearing locations in both the cylinder block/crankcase and the main bearing ladder/bearing caps.

5 Press the bearing shells into their locations, ensuring that the tab on each shell engages in the notch in the cylinder block/crankcase or main bearing ladder/bearing cap. Take care not to touch any shell's bearing surface with your fingers. Note that the grooved bearing shells, both upper and lower, are fitted to Nos 2 and 4 main bearings (see illustration).

6 Liberally lubricate each bearing shell in the cylinder block/crankcase with clean engine oil.

7 Refit the Woodruff key, then slide on the oil pump drive sprocket, and locate the drive chain on the sprocket (see illustration). Lower the crankshaft into position so that Nos 2 and 3 cylinder crankpins are at TDC; Nos 1 and 4 cylinder crankpins will be at BDC, ready for fitting No 1 piston. Check the crankshaft endfloat as described in Section 13.

8 Thoroughly degrease the mating surfaces of the cylinder block/crankcase and the main bearing ladder. Apply a thin bead of suitable sealant to the cylinder block mating surface of the main bearing ladder casting, then spread to an even film (see illustration).

17.5 Fit the grooved bearing shells to No 2 and 4 main bearings (1.4 and 1.6 litre petrol engine)

17.7 Fit the oil pump drive chain and sprocket

17.8 Apply a thin film of sealant to the cylinder block mating surface

17.10 Tighten the ten main bearing bolts to the specified torque

17.17 Fit the thrustwashers to either side of the No 2 main bearing, with the oilway grooves facing outwards

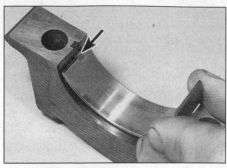

17.18 Ensure the tab (arrowed) is located in the cut-out when fitting the bearing shells

9 Ensure the locating dowels are in position then lubricate the lower bearing shells with clean engine oil. Refit the main bearing ladder to the cylinder block, ensuring that the lower bearings remain correctly fitted.

10 Install the main bearing ladder retaining bolts, and tighten them all by hand only. Working in a spiral pattern from the centre bolts outwards, evenly and progressively tighten the bolts to the specified Stage 1 torque wrench setting. Once all the bolts have been tightened to the Stage 1 setting, working in the same sequence, angle-tighten the bolts through the specified Stage 2 angle using a socket and extension bar. It is recommended that an angle-measuring gauge is used during this stage of the tightening, to ensure accuracy **(see illustration)**. If a gauge is not available, use a dab of white paint to make alignment marks between the bolt head and casting prior to tightening; the marks can then be used to check that the bolt has been rotated sufficiently during tightening.

11 Refit all the smaller bolts securing the main bearing ladder to the base of the cylinder block, and tighten them to the specified torque. Check that the crankshaft rotates freely.

12 Refit the piston/connecting rod assemblies to the crankshaft as described in Section 18.

13 Ensuring that the drive chain is correctly located on the sprocket, refit the oil pump and sump as described in Part A of this Chapter.

14 Fit two new crankshaft oil seals as described in Part A.

15 Refit the flywheel/driveplate as described in Part A of this Chapter.

16 Refit the cylinder head (where removed) as described in Part A. Also refit the crankshaft sprocket and timing belt (see Part A).

1.6 litre petrol engine

17 Using a little grease, stick the upper thrustwashers to each side of the No 2 main bearing upper location. Ensure that the oilway grooves on each thrustwasher face outwards (away from the cylinder block) **(see illustration)**.

18 Place the bearing shells in their locations as described in paragraphs 4 and 5 **(see illustration)**. If new shells are being fitted, ensure that all traces of protective grease are cleaned off using paraffin. Wipe dry the shells and connecting rods with a lint-free cloth. Liberally lubricate each bearing shell in the cylinder block/crankcase and cap with clean engine oil.

19 Lower the crankshaft into position so that Nos 2 and 3 cylinder crankpins are at TDC; Nos 1 and 4 cylinder crankpins will be at BDC, ready for fitting No 1 piston. Check the crankshaft endfloat as described in Section 13.

20 Lubricate the lower bearing shells in the main bearing caps with clean engine oil. Make sure that the locating lugs on the shells engage with the corresponding recesses in the caps.

21 Fit the main bearing caps to their correct locations, ensuring that they are fitted the correct way round (the bearing shell lug recesses in the block and caps must be on the same side).

22 Lightly lubricate the threads and the underside of the heads of the main bearing cap bolts with engine oil then refit the bolts. Working in a spiral sequence from the centre bolts outwards, tighten the main bearing cap bolts evenly and progressively to the specified Stage 1 torque wrench setting. Once all the bolts have been tightened to the Stage 1 setting, working in the same sequence, angle-tighten the bolts through the specified Stage 2 angle, using a socket and extension bar. It is recommended that an angle-measuring gauge is used during this stage of the tightening, to ensure accuracy. If a gauge is not available, use a dab of white paint to make alignment marks between the bolt head and casting prior to tightening; the marks can then be used to check that the bolt has been rotated sufficiently during tightening.

23 Check that the crankshaft rotates freely.

24 Refit the piston/connecting rod assemblies to the crankshaft as described in Section 18.

25 Refit the Woodruff key to the crankshaft groove, and slide on the oil pump drive sprocket. Locate the drive chain on the sprocket.

26 Ensure that the mating surfaces of right-hand (timing belt end) oil seal housing and cylinder block are clean and dry. Note the correct fitted depth of the oil seal then, using a large flat-bladed screwdriver, lever the seal out of the housing.

27 Apply a smear of suitable sealant to the oil seal housing mating surface, and make sure that the locating dowels are in position. Slide the housing over the end of the crankshaft, and into position on the cylinder block. Tighten the housing retaining bolts securely.

28 Repeat the operations in paragraphs 26 and 27, and fit the left-hand (flywheel/driveplate end) oil seal housing.

29 Fit new crankshaft oil seals as described in Part A of this Chapter.

30 Ensuring that the chain is correctly located on the drive sprocket, refit the oil pump and sump as described in Part A of this Chapter.

31 Refit the flywheel/driveplate as described in Part A of this Chapter.

32 Refit the cylinder head (where removed) and install the crankshaft sprocket and timing belt as described in the relevant Sections of Part A.

2.0 litre petrol engine

33 Clean the backs of the bearing shells in both the cylinder block/crankcase and the main bearing ladder. If new shells are being fitted, ensure that all traces of protective grease are cleaned off using paraffin. Wipe dry the shells with a lint-free cloth.

34 Press the bearing shells into their locations, ensuring that the tab on each shell engages in the notch in the cylinder block/crankcase and bearing ladder. Take care not to touch any shell's bearing surface with your fingers. Note that the upper bearing shells all have a grooved surface, whereas the lower shells have a plain bearing surface.

35 Liberally lubricate each bearing shell in the cylinder block with clean engine oil then lower the crankshaft into its position.

36 Insert the thrustwashers to either side of No 2 main bearing upper location and push them around the bearing journal until their edges are horizontal **(see illustration)**. Ensure

17.36 Insert the thrustwashers to either side of the No 2 main bearing upper location

17.37 Apply a thin bead of RTV sealant to the bearing cap housing mating surface

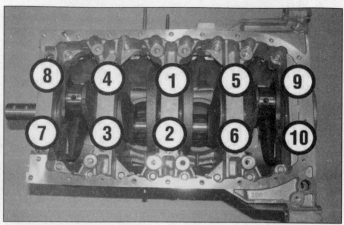

17.40 Main bearing ladder retaining bolt tightening sequence (2.0 litre petrol engine)

that the oilway grooves on each thrustwasher face outwards (away from the cylinder block).

37 Thoroughly degrease the mating surfaces of the cylinder block and the crankshaft bearing cap housing/main bearing ladder. Apply a thin bead of RTV sealant to the bearing cap housing mating surface **(see illustration)**. Peugeot recommend the use of Loctite Autojoint Noir for this purpose.

38 Lubricate the lower bearing shells with clean engine oil, then refit the bearing cap housing, ensuring that the shells are not displaced, and that the locating dowels engage correctly.

39 Install the large and small crankshaft bearing cap housing/ladder retaining bolts, and screw them in until they are just making contact with the housing.

40 Working in sequence, tighten all the M11 bolts to the Stage 1 torque setting given in the Specifications **(see illustration)**. Now

tighten all the M6 bolts to the Stage 2 torque setting (finger-tight).

41 Fully slacken all the M11 bolts (Stage 3), then tighten them to the Stage 4 setting, working in the correct sequence.

42 Finally tighten all the M11 bolts, in the correct sequence, through the specified Stage 5 angle, using an angle tightening gauge.

43 The M6 bolts can now be tightened to the Stage 6 torque setting.

44 With the bearing cap housing in place, check that the crankshaft rotates freely.

45 Refit the piston/connecting rod assemblies to the crankshaft as described in Section 18.

46 Refit the oil pump and sump as described in Part B.

47 Fit a new crankshaft left-hand oil seal, then refit the flywheel as described in Part B.

48 Where removed, refit the cylinder head, crankshaft sprocket and timing belt also as described in Part B.

1.4 litre diesel engine

49 Clean the backs of the bearing shells in both the cylinder block/crankcase and the main bearing ladder. If new shells are being fitted, ensure that all traces of protective grease are cleaned off using paraffin. Wipe dry the shells with a lint-free cloth.

50 Press the bearing shells into their locations, ensuring that the tab on each shell engages in the notch in the cylinder block/crankcase and bearing ladder. Take care not to touch any shell's bearing surface with your fingers. Note that the upper bearing shells all have a grooved surface, whereas the lower shells have a plain bearing surface. It is essential that the lower bearing shell halves are centrally located in the ladder. To ensure this use Peugeot tool No 0194-Q positioned over the ladder, and insert the bearing shells through the slots in the tool **(see illustration)**.

51 Liberally lubricate each bearing shell in the cylinder block with clean engine oil then lower the crankshaft into position.

52 Insert the thrustwashers to either side of No 2 main bearing upper location and push them around the bearing journal until their edges are horizontal. Ensure that the oilway grooves on each thrustwasher face outwards (away from the cylinder block). Now refit the piston and connecting rod assemblies as described in Section 18.

53 Thoroughly degrease the mating surfaces of the cylinder block and the crankshaft bearing cap housing/main bearing ladder. Apply a thin bead of RTV sealant to the bearing cap housing mating surface. Peugeot recommend the use of Loctite Autojoint Noir for this purpose. Use two aligning pins (available from Peugeot) inserted into the main bearing ladder, to ensure the correct positioning of the assembly.

54 Lubricate the lower bearing shells with clean engine oil, then refit the bearing cap housing, ensuring that the shells are not displaced, and that the locating dowels engage correctly. Remove the aligning pins from the bearing ladder.

1 Bearing shell
2 Main bearing ladder
3 Peugeot tool
4 Aligning pins

H44713

17.50 Main bearing shell refitment (1.4 and 1.6 litre diesel engine)

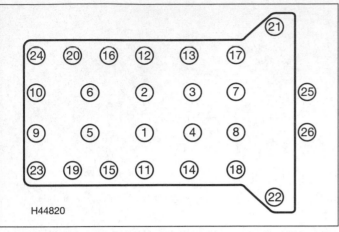

17.56 Main bearing ladder bolts tightening sequence (1.4 and 1.6 litre diesel engine)

17.65 Place the thrustwashers each side of the No 2 bearing upper location

55 Install the large and small crankshaft bearing cap housing/ladder retaining bolts, and screw them in until they are just making contact with the housing. Note that new large (M11) bolts must be used.

56 Tighten all the main bearing ladder bolts to their Stage 1 setting in the sequence shown **(see illustration)**.

57 Slacken (Stage 2) the large diameter bearing ladder bolts half a turn (180°), then tighten them in sequence to the Stage 3 torque setting, followed by the Stage 4 angle-tightening setting. Apply sealant to the two new bearing ladder bolt caps, and tap them into place over the two flywheel end bolts.

58 Finally, tighten the small diameter bearing ladder bolts to their Stage 2 setting.

59 With the bearing cap housing in place, check that the crankshaft rotates freely.

60 Refit the oil pump and sump as described in Part C.

61 Fit a new crankshaft left-hand oil seal, then refit the flywheel as described in Part C.

62 Where removed, refit the cylinder head, crankshaft sprocket and timing belt also as described in Part C.

1.6 litre diesel engine

63 Place the bearing shells in their locations. If new shells are being fitted, ensure that all traces of protective grease are cleaned off using paraffin. Wipe dry the shells with a lint-free cloth. On 1.6 litre diesel engines, the upper bearing shells all have a grooved surface, whereas the lower shells have a plain surface. On these engines, it's essential that the lower bearing shells are centrally located in the bearing cap housing/ladder. To ensure this use Peugeot tool No 0194-QZ positioned over the housing/ladder, and insert the bearing shells through the slots in the tool **(see illustration 17.50)**.

64 Liberally lubricate each bearing shell in the cylinder block with clean engine oil then lower the crankshaft into position.

65 Insert the thrustwashers to either side of No 2 main bearing upper location and push them around the bearing journal until their edges are horizontal **(see illustration)**. Ensure that the oilway grooves on each thrustwasher face outwards (away from the bearing journal).

66 Thoroughly degrease the mating surfaces of the cylinder block and the crankshaft bearing cap housing. Apply a thin bead of RTV sealant to the bearing cap housing mating surface **(see illustration 17.37)**. Peugeot recommend the use of Loctite Autojoint Noir for this purpose.

67 Lubricate the lower bearing shells with clean engine oil, then refit the bearing cap housing, ensuring that the shells are not displaced, and that the locating dowels engage correctly.

68 Install the ten large diameter and sixteen smaller diameter crankshaft bearing cap housing retaining bolts, and screw them in until they are just making contact with the housing.

69 Working in sequence, tighten the bolts to the torque settings given in the Specifications **(see illustration 17.56)**.

70 With the bearing cap housing in place, check that the crankshaft rotates freely.

71 Refit the piston/connecting rod assemblies to the crankshaft as described in Section 18.

72 Refit the oil pump and sump.

73 Fit a new crankshaft left-hand oil seal, then refit the flywheel.

74 Where removed, refit the cylinder head, crankshaft sprocket and timing belt.

2.0 litre diesel engine

75 Using a little grease, stick the thrustwashers to each side of No 2 main bearing upper location and bearing cap **(see illustration 17.65)**. Ensure that the oilway grooves on each thrustwasher face outwards (away from the cylinder block).

76 Place the bearing shells in their locations **(see illustrations)**. If new shells are being fitted, ensure that all traces of protective grease are cleaned off using paraffin. Wipe dry the shells and connecting rods with a lint-free cloth. Liberally lubricate each bearing shell in the cylinder block/crankcase and cap with clean engine oil.

77 Lower the crankshaft into position so that Nos 2 and 3 cylinder crankpins are at TDC; Nos 1 and 4 cylinder crankpins will be at BDC, ready for fitting No 1 piston. Check the crankshaft endfloat, referring to Section 13.

78 Lubricate the lower bearing shells in the main bearing caps with clean engine oil. Make sure that the locating lugs on the shells engage with the corresponding recesses in the caps.

79 Fit main bearing caps Nos 2 to 5 to their correct locations, ensuring that they are fitted the correct way round (the bearing shell tab recesses in the block and caps must be on

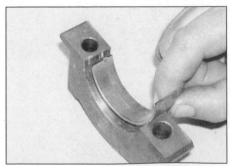

17.76a Ensure the grooved main bearing shells are fitted to the cylinder block . . .

17.76b . . . and plain bearing shells to the bearing caps (2.0 litre diesel engine)

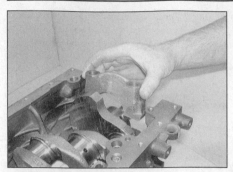

17.79 Fit the No 2 to 5 bearing caps and install the bearing cap bolts (2.0 litre diesel engine)

17.80 Apply sealant to the No 1 main bearing cap mating face on the cylinder block, around the sealing strip holes and in the corners

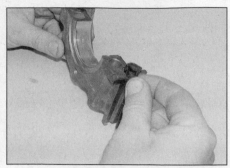

17.81a Fit the sealing strips to each side of No 1 main bearing cap, ensuring they are correctly engaged with the pins

the same side) **(see illustration)**. Ensure the thrustwashers remain correctly fitted to No 2 bearing cap then refit the bearing cap bolts, tightening them only lightly at this stage.

80 Apply a small amount of sealant to the No 1 main bearing cap mating face on the cylinder block, around the sealing strip holes **(see illustration)**.

81 Locate the tab of each sealing strip over the pins on the base of No 1 bearing cap, and press the strips into the bearing cap grooves. It is now necessary to obtain two thin metal strips, of 0.25 mm thickness or less, in order to prevent the strips moving when the cap is being fitted. Peugeot garages use the tool shown, which acts as a clamp. Metal strips (such as old feeler blades) can be used, provided all burrs which may damage the sealing strips are first removed **(see illustrations)**.

82 Where applicable, oil both sides of the metal strips, and hold them on the sealing strips. Fit the No 1 main bearing cap, insert the bolts loosely, then carefully pull out the metal strips in a horizontal direction, using a pair of pliers **(see illustration)**.

83 Working in sequence **(see illustration)**, tighten the main bearing cap bolts evenly and progressively to the specified Stage 1 torque wrench setting. Once all the bolts have been tightened to the Stage 1 setting, working in the specified sequence, angle-tighten

the bolts through the specified Stage 2 angle, using a socket and extension bar. It is recommended that an angle-measuring gauge is used during this stage of the tightening, to ensure accuracy. If a gauge is not available, use a dab of white paint to make alignment marks between the bolt head and casting prior to tightening; the marks can then be used to check that the bolt has been rotated sufficiently during tightening.

84 Check that the sealing strips protrude slightly from above the cylinder block/ crankcase mating surface by approximately 1 mm. If not, remove the bearing cap again and refit; the seals are supplied the correct length and should not be cut. Also check that the crankshaft rotates freely.

85 Fit a new crankshaft left-hand (flywheel end) oil seal as described in Part C or E.

86 Refit the piston/connecting rod assemblies to the crankshaft as described in Section 18.

87 Fit a new sealing ring (where fitted) the crankshaft then refit the Woodruff key and slide on the oil pump drive sprocket and spacer. Locate the drive chain on the sprocket.

88 Ensure that the mating surfaces of the right-hand (timing belt end) oil seal housing and cylinder block are clean and dry. Note the correct fitted depth of the oil seal then, using a large flat-bladed screwdriver, lever the old seal out of the housing.

89 Apply a smear of suitable sealant to the oil seal housing mating surface. Ensure that the locating dowels are in position, then slide the

housing over the end of the crankshaft and into position on the cylinder block. Tighten the housing retaining bolts to the specified torque.

90 Fit a new crankshaft right-hand (timing belt end) oil seal as described in Part C or E.

91 Ensuring that the drive chain is correctly located on the sprocket, refit the oil pump and sump as described in Part C or E.

92 Refit the flywheel as described in Part C or E of this Chapter.

93 Refit the cylinder head (where removed) as described in Part C or E. Also refit the crankshaft sprocket and timing belt (see Part C or E).

18 Piston/connecting rod assembly – refitting

Note: *New big-end cap nuts/bolts must be used on refitting.*

1 Note that the following procedure assumes that the cylinder liners (aluminium block petrol engines) are in position in the cylinder block/ crankcase as described in Section 11, and that the crankshaft and main bearing ladder/ caps are in place – except on the 1.4 litre diesel engine where the crankshaft is fitted after the pistons (see Section 17).

2 Clean the backs of the bearing shells, and the bearing locations in both the connecting rod and bearing cap.

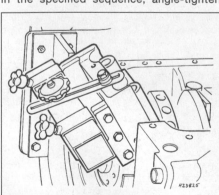

17.81b Using the Peugeot special tool to fit the No 1 main bearing cap

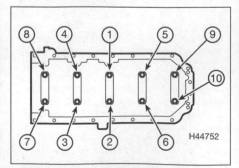

17.82 Fit the No 1 main bearing cap using metal strips to retain the sealing strips

17.83 Main bearing cap bolt tightening sequence (2.0 litre diesel engines)

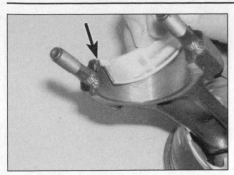

18.3 Ensure the bearing shell tab (arrowed) locates correctly in the cut-out

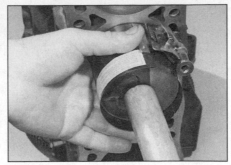

18.7 Tap the piston into the bore using a hammer handle

18.8 Fit the big-end bearing cap, ensuring it is fitted the right way around, and screw on the new nuts

All engines except 1.4 and 1.6 litre diesel

3 Press the bearing shells into their locations, ensuring that the tab on each shell engages in the notch in the connecting rod and cap. Take care not to touch any shell's bearing surface with your fingers (see illustration).

All engines

4 Lubricate the cylinder bores, the pistons, and piston rings, then lay out each piston/connecting rod assembly in its respective position.
5 Start with assembly No 1. Make sure that the piston rings are still spaced as described in Section 16, then clamp them in position with a piston ring compressor.
6 Insert the piston/connecting rod assembly into the top of cylinder/liner No 1, ensuring the piston is correctly positioned as follows:
a) On petrol engines, ensure that the arrow on the piston crown is pointing towards the timing belt end of the engine.
b) On 1.4 and 1.6 litre diesel engines, ensure that the DIST mark or arrow on the piston crown is towards the timing belt end of the engine.

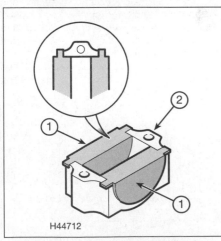

18.12 Big-end bearing shell positioning (1.4 and 1.6 litre diesel engine)

1 Peugeot tool No 0194-P
2 Bearing shell

c) On 2.0 litre diesel engines, ensure that the valve recesses on the piston crown are towards the rear of the cylinder block.
7 Once the piston is correctly positioned, using a block of wood or hammer handle against the piston crown, tap the assembly into the cylinder/liner until the piston crown is flush with the top of the cylinder/liner (see illustration).

All engines except 1.4 and 1.6 litre diesel

8 Ensure that the bearing shell is still correctly installed. Liberally lubricate the crankpin and both bearing shells. Taking care not to mark the cylinder/liner bores, pull the piston/connecting rod assembly down the bore and onto the crankpin. Refit the big-end bearing cap and fit the new nuts, tightening them finger-tight at first (see illustration). Note that the faces with the identification marks must match (which means that the bearing shell locating tabs abut each other).
9 On petrol engines, tighten the bearing cap retaining nuts evenly and progressively to the specified torque setting.
10 On 2.0 litre diesel engines, tighten the bearing cap retaining nuts evenly and progressively to the Stage 1 torque setting. Once both nuts have been tightened to the Stage 1 setting, angle-tighten them through the specified Stage 2 angle, using a socket and extension bar. It is recommended that an angle-measuring gauge is used during this stage of the tightening, to ensure accuracy. If a gauge is not available, use a dab of white paint to make alignment marks between the nut and bearing cap prior to tightening; the marks can then be used to check that the nut has been rotated sufficiently during tightening.

1.4 and 1.6 litre diesel engine

11 On these engines, the connecting rod is made in one piece, and the big-end bearing cap is 'cracked' off. This ensures that the cap fits onto the connecting rod only in one position, and with maximum rigidity. Consequently, there are no locating notches for the bearing shells to fit into.
12 To ensure that the big-end bearing shells are centrally located in the connecting rod

and cap, two special tools are available from Peugeot. These half-moon shaped tools are pressed in from either side of the rod/cap and locate the shell exactly in the centre (see illustration). Fit the shells into the connecting rods and big-end caps and lubricate them with plenty of clean engine oil.
13 Pull the connecting rods and pistons down the bores and onto the crankshaft journals. Fit the big-end caps – they will only fit properly one way round (see paragraph 11), and insert the new bolts.
14 Tighten the bolts to the Stage 1 torque setting, then slacken them 180° (Stage 2). Tighten the bolts to the Stage 3 setting, followed by the Stage 4 angle-tightening setting.
15 Continue refitting the main bearing shells and ladder as described in Section 17.

All engines

16 Once the bearing cap retaining nuts have been correctly tightened, rotate the crankshaft. Check that it turns freely; some stiffness is to be expected if new components have been fitted, but there should be no signs of binding or tight spots.
17 Refit the cylinder head and oil pump as described in Part A, B, C, D or E of this Chapter (as applicable).

19 Engine – initial start-up after overhaul

1 With the engine refitted in the vehicle, double-check the engine oil and coolant levels. Make a final check that everything has been reconnected, and that there are no tools or rags left in the engine compartment.

Petrol engine models

2 Remove the spark plugs and disable the fuel system by disconnecting the wiring connectors from the fuel injectors, referring to Chapter 4A for further information.
3 Turn the engine on the starter until the oil pressure warning light goes out. Refit the spark plugs, and reconnect the wiring.

Diesel engine models

4 On the models covered in this Manual, the oil pressure warning light is linked to the STOP warning light, and is not illuminated when the ignition is initially switched on. Therefore it is not possible to check the oil pressure warning light when turning the engine on the starter motor.

5 Prime the fuel system (refer to Chapter 4B).

6 Fully depress the accelerator pedal, turn the ignition key to position M, and wait for the preheating warning light to go out.

All models

7 Start the engine, noting that this may take a little longer than usual, due to the fuel system components having been disturbed.

8 While the engine is idling, check for fuel, water and oil leaks. Don't be alarmed if there are some odd smells and smoke from parts getting hot and burning off oil deposits.

9 Assuming all is well, keep the engine idling until hot water is felt circulating through the top hose, then switch off the engine.

10 After a few minutes, recheck the oil and coolant levels as described in *Weekly checks*, and top-up as necessary.

11 Note that there is no need to retighten the cylinder head bolts once the engine has first run after reassembly.

12 If new pistons, rings or crankshaft bearings have been fitted, the engine must be treated as new, and run-in for the first 500 miles. Do not operate the engine at full-throttle, or allow it to labour at low engine speeds in any gear. It is recommended that the oil and filter be changed at the end of this period.

Chapter 3
Cooling, heating and ventilation systems

Contents

Degrees of difficulty

| **Easy,** suitable for novice with little experience | | **Fairly easy,** suitable for beginner with some experience | | **Fairly difficult,** suitable for competent DIY mechanic | | **Difficult,** suitable for experienced DIY mechanic | | **Very difficult,** suitable for expert DIY or professional | |

Specifications

General

Maximum system pressure	1.4 bars

Engine coolant temperature sensor resistance (approx):

All petrol engines:

20°C	6100 Ω
80°C	620 Ω

1.4 and 1.6 litre diesel engines:

60°C	1266 Ω
80°C	642 Ω

2.0 litre SOHC diesel engine:

20°C	6200 Ω
30°C	1920 Ω

2.0 litre DOHC diesel engine:

20°C	6200 Ω

Thermostat

Start of opening temperature:

Petrol engine models	89°C
1.4 litre diesel engine models.	88°C
1.6 and 2.0 litre diesel engine models	83°C

Air conditioning compressor oil

Quantity:

All except 2.0 litre diesel engine.	135 cc
2.0 litre diesel engine	265 cc

Type:

All except 2.0 litre diesel engine.	SP10
2.0 litre diesel engine	Planet Elf 488

Refrigerant

Quantity	585 ± 25 g
Type	R134a

Torque wrench settings

	Nm	lbf ft
Air conditioning compressor mounting bolts:		
2.0 litre petrol engine	45	33
1.4 and 1.6 litre diesel engine.	25	18
2.0 litre diesel engine	40	30
Coolant outlet housing	10	7
Coolant pump:		
Petrol engines.	14	10
1.4 and 1.6 litre diesel engine.	10	7
2.0 litre diesel engine	16	12

1 General information and precautions

General information

1 The cooling system is of pressurised type, comprising a coolant pump driven by the timing belt, an aluminium radiator, an expansion tank, an electric cooling fan, a thermostat, a heater matrix, and all associated hoses and switches.

2 The system functions as follows. Cold coolant in the bottom of the radiator passes through the bottom hose to the coolant pump, where it is pumped around the cylinder block and head passages. After cooling the cylinder bores, combustion surfaces and valve seats, the coolant reaches the underside of the thermostat, which is initially closed. The coolant passes through the heater, and is returned via the cylinder block to the coolant pump.

3 When the engine is cold, the coolant circulates only through the cylinder block, cylinder head, and heater. When the coolant reaches a predetermined temperature, the thermostat opens, and the coolant passes through the top hose to the radiator. As the coolant passes down through the radiator, it is cooled by the inrush of air when the car is in forward motion. The airflow is supplemented by the action of the electric cooling fan when necessary. Upon reaching the bottom of the radiator, the coolant has now cooled, and the cycle is repeated.

4 On models with automatic transmission, a proportion of the coolant is recirculated through the transmission fluid cooler mounted on the transmission. On models fitted with an engine oil cooler, the coolant is also passed through the oil cooler.

5 The operation of the electric cooling fan(s) is controlled by the engine management control unit.

6 On 2.0 litre diesel models up to RPO 10261 fitted with the DW10BTED4 engine, additional cooling is provided when required by a degas solenoid valve located on the right-hand side of the radiator which allows circulation from the thermostat housing to the expansion tank. Also on these models, a coolant flow solenoid is fitted to the thermostat housing to open the engine by-pass circuit when required. Both of these solenoids are additional to a conventional wax pellet thermostat located in the housing. However, from RPO 10262 the degas solenoid valve was no longer fitted.

Precautions

⚠️ *Warning: Do not attempt to remove the expansion tank filler cap, or to disturb any part of the cooling system, while the engine is hot, as there is a high risk of scalding. If the expansion tank filler cap must be removed before the engine and radiator have fully cooled (even though this is not recommended), the pressure in the cooling system must first be relieved. Cover the cap with a thick layer of cloth to avoid scalding, and slowly unscrew the filler cap until a hissing sound is heard. When the hissing has stopped, indicating that the pressure has reduced, slowly unscrew the filler cap until it can be removed; if more hissing sounds are heard, wait until they have stopped before unscrewing the cap. At all times keep well away from the filler cap opening, and protect your hands.*

⚠️ *Warning: Do not allow antifreeze to come into contact with your skin, or with the painted surfaces of the vehicle. Rinse off spills immediately, with plenty of water. Never leave antifreeze lying around in an open container, or in a puddle in the driveway or on the garage floor. Children and pets are attracted by its sweet smell, but antifreeze can be fatal if ingested.*

⚠️ *Warning: If the engine is hot, the electric cooling fan(s) may start rotating even if the engine is not running. Be careful to keep your hands, hair, and any loose clothing well clear when working in the engine compartment.*

⚠️ *Warning: Refer to Section 11 for precautions to be observed when working on models equipped with air conditioning.*

2 Cooling system hoses – disconnection and renewal

Note: *Refer to the warnings given in Section 1 of this Chapter before proceeding. Hoses should only be disconnected once the engine has cooled sufficiently to avoid scalding.*

1 If the checks described in the *Hose and fluid leak check* Section in Chapter 1A or 1B reveal a faulty hose, it must be renewed as follows.

2 First drain the cooling system (see Chapter 1A or 1B). If the coolant is not due for renewal, it may be re-used, providing it is collected in a clean container.

3 To disconnect a hose, proceed as follows, according to the type of hose connection.

Conventional connections

4 On conventional connections, the clips used to secure the hoses in position may be either standard worm-drive clips, spring clips or disposable crimped types. The crimped type of clip is not designed to be re-used and should be renewed with a worm drive type on reassembly.

5 To disconnect a hose, release the retaining clips and move them along the hose, clear of the relevant inlet/outlet. Carefully work the hose free. The hoses can be removed with relative ease when new – on an older car, they may have stuck **(see illustration)**.

6 If a hose proves to be difficult to remove, try to release it by rotating its ends before attempting to free it. Gently prise the end of the hose with a blunt instrument (such as a flat-bladed screwdriver), but do not apply too much force, and take care not to damage the pipe stubs or hoses. Note in particular that the radiator inlet stub is fragile; do not use excessive force when attempting to remove the hose. If all else fails, cut the hose with a sharp knife, then slit it so that it can be peeled off in two pieces. Although this may prove expensive if the hose is otherwise undamaged, it is preferable to buying a new radiator. Check first, however, that a new hose is readily available.

7 When fitting a hose, first slide the clips onto the hose, then work the hose into position. If crimped-type clips were originally fitted, use

2.5 Release the retaining clip and move it along the hose

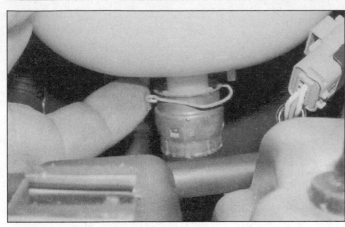

2.12 Where click-fit connectors are used, prise out the circlip then disconnect the hose

2.13 Ensure the sealing ring and circlip (arrowed) are correctly fitted to the hose union before reconnecting a connector

standard worm-drive clips when refitting the hose.

8 Work the hose into position, checking that it is correctly routed, then slide each clip back along the hose until it passes over the flared end of the relevant inlet/outlet, before tightening the clip securely.

> **HAYNES HiNT** *If the hose is stiff, use a little soapy water as a lubricant or soften the hose by soaking it in hot water. Do not use oil or grease as these may attack the rubber.*

9 Refill the cooling system (see Chapter 1A or 1B).
10 Check thoroughly for leaks as soon as possible after disturbing any part of the cooling system.

Click-fit connections

Note: *New sealing ring should be used when reconnecting the hose.*
11 On certain models, some cooling system hoses are secured in position with click-fit connectors where the hose is retained by a large circlip.
12 To disconnect this type of hose fitting, carefully prise the wire clip out of position then disconnect the hose connection **(see**

illustration). Once the hose has been disconnected, refit the wire clip to the hose union. Inspect the hose unit sealing ring for signs of damage or deterioration and renew if necessary.
13 On refitting, ensure that the sealing ring is in position and wire clip is correctly located in the groove in the union **(see illustration)**. Lubricate the sealing ring with a smear of soapy water, to ease installation, then push the hose into its union until it is heard to click into position.
14 Ensure the hose is securely retained by the wire clip then refill the cooling system as described in Chapter 1A or 1B.
15 Check thoroughly for leaks as soon as possible after disturbing any part of the cooling system.

3 Coolant expansion tank – removal and refitting

Removal

1 Referring to Chapter 1A or 1B, drain the cooling system sufficiently to empty the contents of the expansion tank. Do not drain any more coolant than is necessary.
2 Remove the plastic cover from over the coolant and washer reservoirs. The cover is

secured by two plastic expanding rivets. Push the centre pins in a little, then prise out the complete rivets.
3 Slide out the retaining clips, or squeeze together the collar, then pull the plastic hoses from the expansion tank. On some models, the hoses may be secured by expanding clamps **(see illustrations)**.
4 Disconnect the level sensor wiring plug – where fitted **(see illustration)**.
5 Unscrew the mounting bolt and free the tank from its mount. Take care not to lose the mounting rubber.
6 Slacken the clip and disconnect the remaining hose as the expansion tank is removed.

Refitting

7 Refitting is the reverse of removal, ensuring the hoses are securely reconnected. On completion, top-up the coolant level as described in *Weekly checks*.

4 Radiator – removal, inspection and refitting

Note: *If leakage is the reason for removing the radiator, bear in mind that minor leaks can often be cured using a radiator sealant with the radiator in situ.*

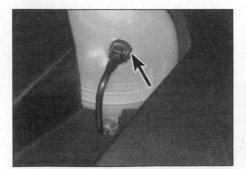

3.3a Slide up the retaining clip (arrowed) and pull out the hose

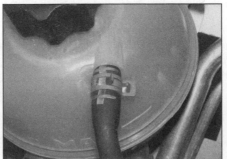

3.3b Some hoses are secured by expanding clamps

3.4 Disconnect the level sensor wiring plug

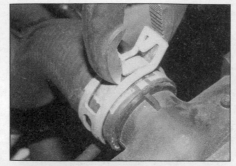

4.2a Slide the expansion tank hose clip up and pull out the hose

4.2b Release the upper and lower hose retaining clips

4.4a Undo the retaining screws (arrowed) . . .

4.4b . . . and remove the radiator upper brackets

4.5 Recover the radiator lower mounting rubbers

Removal

1 Drain the cooling system (see Chapter 1A or 1B).

2 Release the retaining clips and disconnect the expansion tank hose and the upper and lower coolant hoses from the radiator. The expansion tank hose clip slides up from place. Once disconnected, refit the clip to the hose end fitting **(see illustrations)**.

3 Remove the front bumper as described in Chapter 11.

4 Slacken and remove the retaining screws securing the radiator upper mounting brackets to the front panel. Unclip both brackets from the panel and remove them from the radiator **(see illustrations)**.

5 Carefully lift the radiator out of position, taking care not to damage the radiator fins. Recover the radiator lower mounting rubbers **(see illustration)**.

Inspection

6 If the radiator has been removed due to suspected blockage, reverse-flush it as described in Chapter 1A or 1B. Clean dirt and debris from the radiator fins, using an air line (in which case, wear eye protection) or a soft brush. Be careful, as the fins are sharp, and easily damaged.

7 If necessary, a radiator specialist can perform a 'flow test' on the radiator, to establish whether an internal blockage exists.

8 A leaking radiator must be referred to a specialist for permanent repair. Do not attempt to weld or solder a leaking radiator,

as damage to the plastic components may result.

9 Inspect the condition of the radiator mounting rubbers, and renew them if necessary.

Refitting

10 Refitting is a reversal of removal, bearing in mind the following points:
 a) *Ensure that the lower lugs on the radiator are correctly engaged with the mounting rubbers in the body panel.*
 b) *Reconnect the hoses with reference to Section 2, using new sealing rings where applicable.*
 c) *On completion, refill the cooling system as described in Chapter 1A or 1B.*

5 Thermostat –
removal, testing and refitting

Removal

1 Drain the cooling system (see Chapter 1A or 1B).

2 The thermostat is located on the coolant outlet housing on the left-hand end of the cylinder head. On some engines removal of the thermostat only requires the removal of the coolant outlet pipe, however on others the thermostat is integral with the housing requiring removal of the housing. The various arrangements are as follows:

Petrol engines
1.4 litre TU3JP up to RPO 10249
  Coolant outlet pipe.
1.4 litre TU3JP from RPO 10250
  Coolant outlet housing.
1.4 litre ET3JP4 up to RPO 10436
  Coolant outlet pipe.
1.4 litre ET3JP4 from RPO 10437
  Coolant outlet housing.
1.6 litre TU5JP4 up to RPO 10436
  Coolant outlet pipe.
1.6 litre TU5JP4 from RPO 10437
  Coolant outlet housing.
2.0 litre
  Coolant outlet pipe.
Diesel engines
1.4 litre and 1.6 litre
  Coolant outlet housing.
2.0 litre DW10TD and DW10ATED
  Separate (renewable) thermostat located beneath coolant outlet housing.
2.0 litre DW10BTED4 up to RPO 10261
  Coolant outlet pipe, plus electrically-operated coolant flow solenoid and degas solenoid in coolant outlet housing.
2.0 litre DW10BTED4 from RPO 10262
  Coolant outlet housing, plus electrically-operated coolant flow solenoid.

3 Remove the engine top cover. Remove the battery and battery tray as described in Chapter 5A, then remove the air cleaner and air ducting as described in Chapter 4A or 4B. In the following paragraphs, note that some of the hoses are disconnected after pressing down on the white-coloured release button **(see illustration)**.

4 On engines where the thermostat is integral

5.3 Press down the release button and disconnect the hose

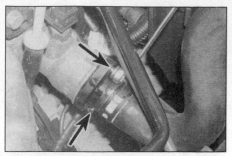

5.4 Unscrew the retaining bolts (arrowed) and free the outlet union from the coolant housing

5.5a Lift the thermostat from its housing . . .

5.5b . . . and remove the sealing ring

with the coolant outlet, disconnect the coolant hose, then unscrew the two bolts and remove the outlet **(see illustration)**. Recover the sealing ring.

5 On engines where the thermostat is beneath the coolant outlet, disconnect the coolant hose, unscrew the bolts, remove the coolant outlet, and lift the thermostat from the housing noting which way round it is fitted. Recover the sealing ring **(see illustrations)**.

6 On engines where the thermostat is integral with the coolant housing, disconnect the wiring from the temperature sensor and solenoid (where fitted), then disconnect all hoses having noted their fitted locations. Unscrew the retaining bolts and remove the housing **(see illustration)**. Recover the gasket.

Testing

7 A rough test of the thermostat may be made by suspending it with a piece of string in a container full of water. Heat the water to

bring it to the boil – the thermostat must open by the time the water boils. If not, renew it.

8 If a thermometer is available, the precise opening temperature of the thermostat may be determined; compare with the figures given in the Specifications. The opening temperature is also marked on the thermostat.

9 A thermostat which fails to close as the water cools must also be renewed.

Refitting

10 Refitting is a reversal of removal, bearing in mind the following points.

   a) Renew the coolant housing gasket where removed.
   b) Examine the sealing ring for damage or deterioration, and if necessary, renew.
   c) Where a separate thermostat is fitted, ensure that it is fitted the correct way round.
   d) On completion, refill the cooling system as described in Chapter 1A or 1B.

5.6 Undo the coolant outlet housing retaining bolts (arrowed)

6 Electric cooling fan – removal and refitting

Removal

1 The cooling fan can be removed on its own or complete with the front panel assembly. Proceed as described under the relevant sub-heading.

Cooling fan

2 Remove the front bumper as described in Chapter 11.

3 Slacken and remove the four bolts and washers securing the cooling fan to the front panel. Recover the collar from the rear of each mounting rubber **(see illustration)**.

4 Release the retaining clips and remove the louvered panel to the right of the fan, then lift the retaining clip then disconnect the wiring connector. Manoeuvre the fan assembly out of position **(see illustrations)**.

Cooling fan and front panel

5 Remove the radiator as described in Section 4. On models with air conditioning, move the condenser and dehydrator slightly to the rear – there is no need to disconnect the refrigerant pipes.

6 Undo the two bolts securing the bonnet lock to the front panel, then remove the retaining clips and free the bonnet release cable from the front panel **(see illustration)**.

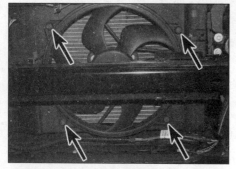

6.3 Undo the four cooling fan screws (arrowed)

6.4a Release the retaining clips and remove the louvered panel . . .

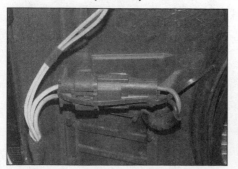

6.4b . . . then disconnect the fan wiring plug

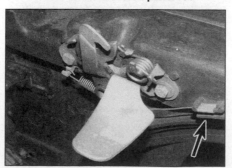

6.6 Undo the bonnet locks bolts, and free the cable from its retaining clips (arrowed)

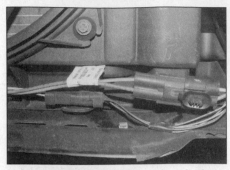

6.7 Disconnect the wiring plugs in the left-hand corner of the cooling fan panel

6.8a Undo the screw on the right . . .

6.8b . . . and the left-hand side

6.12 Cooling fan relays

6.15 Cooling fan resistor

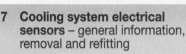

7 Cooling system electrical sensors – general information, removal and refitting

7 Disconnect the wiring plugs at the left-hand lower edge of the panel **(see illustration)**.
8 Slacken and remove the two retaining screws securing the front trim panel in position. Carefully remove the panel from the vehicle **(see illustrations)**.

7.1a Coolant temperature sensors (arrowed) (1.6 litre petrol engine, 1.4 litre similar) . . .

Refitting
9 Refitting is a reversal of removal.

Cooling fan relays
10 The relays are fitted to the front panel and are located behind the cover on the right-hand side of the cooling fan.
11 To gain access to the relays, remove the front bumper as described in Chapter 11.
12 Release the clips and remove the cover from the front panel. The relays can then be removed **(see illustration)**.

Cooling fan resistor
Models with air conditioning
13 The cooling fan resistor is fitted to the front panel and is also located on the right-hand side of the cooling fan.
14 To gain access to the resistor, remove the front bumper as described in Chapter 11.
15 Disconnect the wiring connector then undo the retaining screw and remove the resistor from the front panel **(see illustration)**.

General information
1 There is only one coolant temperature sensor on most models, which is fitted to the coolant outlet housing on the left-hand end of the cylinder head **(see illustrations)**. The coolant temperature gauge and the cooling fan are all operated by the engine management ECU using the signal supplied by this sensor. However, on some 1.4 and 1.6 litre petrol models, two sensors are fitted. The one fitted to the outlet housing is for the temperature gauge, and the one screwed into the left-hand end of the cylinder head is for the engine management ECU.

Removal
Note: *Ensure the engine is cold before removing a temperature sensor.*
2 Partially drain the cooling system to just below the level of the sensor (as described in Chapter 1A or 1B). Alternatively, have ready a suitable bung to plug the sensor aperture whilst the sensor is removed. If this method is used, take great care not to damage the switch aperture or use anything which will allow foreign matter to enter the cooling system. On diesel models, to improve access, remove the battery as described in Chapter 5A.
3 Disconnect the wiring connector from the sensor.
4 On some engines, the sensor is clipped in place. Prise out the sensor retaining circlip

7.1b . . . 2.0 litre petrol engine . . .

7.1c . . . 2.0 litre diesel engine . . .

7.1d . . . and 1.4 litre diesel engine

7.4 Prise out the clip (arrowed) and pull out the sensor

then remove the sensor and sealing ring from the housing **(see illustration)**. If the system has not been drained, plug the sensor aperture to prevent further coolant loss.

5 On all other engines, unscrew the sensor and recover the sealing washer (where applicable). If the system has not been drained, plug the sensor aperture to prevent further coolant loss.

Refitting

6 Where the sensor was clipped in place, fit a new sealing ring to the sensor. Push the sensor firmly into the housing and secure it in position with the circlip, ensuring it is correctly located in the housing groove.

7 On all other engines, if the sensor was originally fitted using sealing compound, clean the sensor threads thoroughly, and coat them with fresh sealing compound. If the sensor was originally fitted using a sealing washer, use a new sealing washer. Fit the sensor and tighten securely.

8 Reconnect the wiring connector then refit any components removed for access. If removed, refit the battery.

9 Top-up the cooling system as described in *Weekly checks*.

8 Coolant pump – removal and refitting

Removal

1 Drain the cooling system (see Chapter 1A or 1B).

2 Remove the timing belt as described in Chapter 2A, 2B, 2C, 2D or 2E as applicable.

All except 2.0 litre SOHC petrol engine

3 Slacken and remove the retaining bolts and withdraw the pump assembly from the engine. Recover the pump sealing ring/gasket (as applicable) and discard it; a new one must be used on refitting **(see illustrations)**. Note that on some engines, the sealing ring is not

available separately from the pump – check with your Peugeot dealer.

2.0 litre SOHC petrol engine

4 Remove the heat shield from the pump, then undo the bolts securing the pump to the cylinder block **(see illustration)**. Do not undo the bolts securing the two halves of the pump together. Withdraw the pump.

Refitting

5 Ensure that the pump and cylinder block/housing mating surfaces are clean and dry.

6 Fit the new sealing ring/gasket (as applicable) to the pump then refit the pump assembly, tightening its retaining bolts securely.

7 Refit the timing belt as described in Chapter 2A, 2B, 2C, 2D or 2E (as applicable).

8 Refill the cooling system as described in Chapter 1A or 1B (as applicable).

9 Heating and ventilation system – general information

Note: *Refer to Section 11 for information on the air conditioning side of the system.*

Manually-controlled system

1 The heating/ventilation system consists of a four-speed blower motor (housed behind

8.3a Remove the coolant pump ...

8.3b ... and recover the sealing ring (1.4 litre petrol engine)

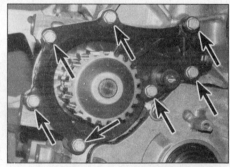

8.3c Undo the coolant pump bolts (arrowed) (1.4 litre diesel engine)

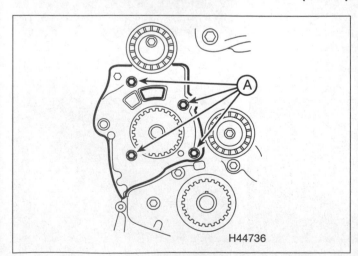

8.3d Coolant pump bolts (A) (2.0 litre diesel engine)

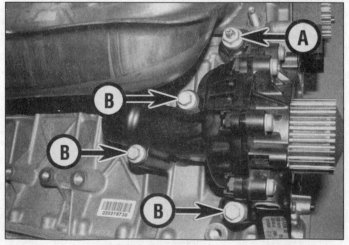

8.4 Coolant pump retaining nut (A) and bolts (B)

the facia), face level vents in the centre and at each end of the facia, and air ducts to the front footwells.

2 The control unit is located in the facia, and the controls operate flap valves to deflect and mix the air flowing through the various parts of the heating/ventilation system. The flap valves are contained in the air distribution housing, which acts as a central distribution unit, passing air to the various ducts and vents.

3 Cold air enters the system through the grille in the scuttle. If required, the airflow is boosted by the blower, and then flows through the various ducts, according to the settings of the controls. Stale air is expelled through ducts at the rear of the vehicle. If warm air is required, the cold air is passed over the heater matrix, which is heated by the engine coolant.

4 A recirculation lever enables the outside air supply to be closed off, while the air inside the vehicle is recirculated. This can be useful to prevent unpleasant odours entering from outside the vehicle, but should only be used briefly, as the recirculated air inside the vehicle will soon become stale.

5 On some diesel engine models an electric heater is fitted into the heater housing. When the coolant temperature is cold, the heater warms the air before it enters the heater matrix. This quickly increases the temperature of the heater matrix on cold starts, resulting in warm air being available to heat the vehicle interior soon after start-up.

Automatic climate control

6 A fully automatic electronic climate control system was offered as an option on some models. The main components of the system are exactly the same as those described for the manual system, the only major difference being that the temperature and distribution flaps in the heating/ventilation housing are operated by electric motors rather than cables.

7 The operation of the system is controlled by the electronic control module (which is incorporated in the blower motor assembly) along with the following sensors.
  a) *The passenger compartment sensor – informs the control module of the temperature of the air inside the passenger compartment.*
  b) *Evaporator temperature sensor – informs the control module of the evaporator temperature.*
  c) *Heater matrix temperature sensor – informs the control module of the heater matrix temperature.*

8 Using the information from the above sensors, the control module determines the appropriate settings for the heating/ventilation system housing flaps to maintain the passenger compartment at the desired setting on the control panel.

9 If the system develops a fault, the vehicle should be taken to a Peugeot dealer. A complete test of the system can then be carried out, using a special electronic diagnostic test unit which is simply plugged into the system's diagnostic connector (located next to the fusebox).

10 Heater/ventilation components – removal and refitting

Control panel

Removal

1 Remove the audio unit (see Chapter 12).

2 Press down the retaining clip, and remove the ashtray from the centre console.

3 Undo the two screws below the control panel, and remove the storage compartment rubber trim **(see illustration)**.

4 On models equipped with manual transmission, unclip the gear lever gaiter from the centre console. On models with automatic transmission, carefully unclip the selector lever display surround trim from place **(see illustrations)**.

5 Starting at the top, carefully unclip the trim panel from around the heater controls, and pass the gear lever gaiter/selector lever through the panel **(see illustration)**.

6 Undo the four retaining screws, release the two retaining clips and tilt the control panel forward, then manoeuvre it from the console **(see illustrations)**.

7 On models with a manual control panel, disconnect the wiring connectors from the rear of the control panel. Note the correct fitted location of each control cables (the end fittings are colour-coded) then unhook the cable retaining clips. Detach the cables and remove the control panel from the vehicle.

10.3 Undo the two screws (arrowed) below the control panel

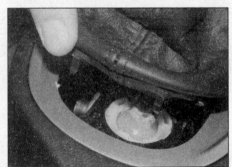

10.4a Unclip the gear lever gaiter . . .

10.4b . . . or unclip the selector lever display surround trim

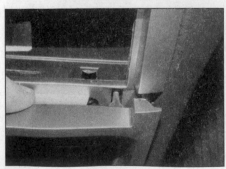

10.5 Starting at the top, unclip the trim panel

10.6a Undo the four heater control panel retaining screws (arrowed) . . .

10.6b . . . and release the retaining clips (arrowed)

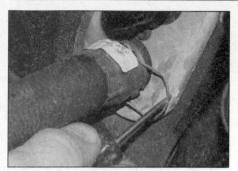

10.15 Prise out the wire retaining clip and disconnect the heater hose

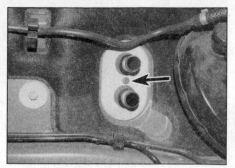

10.16 Undo the heater pipes retaining plate screw (arrowed)

10.18a Undo the screws securing the pipes to the housing (arrowed) . . .

8 On models with an automatic climate control system, disconnect the wiring connectors and remove the control panel from the vehicle.

Refitting

9 Refitting is the reverse of removal. On models with a manual control panel, ensure the control cables are correctly reconnected and securely held by the retaining clips; check the operation of the control knobs before securing the control panel to the facia.

Control cables

Removal

10 Remove the facia (see Chapter 11).
11 Release the retaining clip and detach the relevant cable from the rear of the control panel and the heating/ventilation housing. Remove the cable, noting its correct routing.

Refitting

12 Refitting is the reverse of removal, ensuring the cable is securely retained by its clips. Check the operation of the control panel and cables before refitting the facia (see Chapter 11).

Heater matrix

Removal

13 To improve access to the matrix unions on the bulkhead, remove the battery and battery tray as described in Chapter 5A. Where

necessary also remove the air cleaner housing intake duct (see Chapter 4A or 4B).
14 Drain the cooling system (see Chapter 1A or 1B). Alternatively, clamp the heater matrix coolant hoses to minimise coolant loss.
15 Release the retaining clips and disconnect the coolant hoses from the heater matrix pipe unions on the engine compartment bulkhead **(see illustration)**.
16 Slacken and remove the screw securing the heater matrix pipes to the bulkhead and remove the retaining plate and seal **(see illustration)**.
17 Position a container beneath the heater matrix pipe union on the left-hand side of the heating/ventilation housing to catch any spilt coolant.
18 Slacken and remove the screws securing the matrix pipes to the housing and release the clips securing the pipes to the matrix **(see illustrations)**.
19 Free the pipes from the matrix, catching the coolant in the container, then free them from the bulkhead and remove them from the vehicle. Recover the sealing rings fitted to the pipe unions and discard them; new ones should be used on refitting. Take care not to lose the bulkhead seal or retaining plate from the pipes.
20 Release the retaining clips then slide the matrix out from the housing. Keep the matrix unions uppermost as the matrix is removed to prevent coolant spillage **(see illustration)**.

Refitting

21 Ease the matrix into the housing and clip it into position.
22 Ensure the bulkhead seal and retaining plate are correctly fitted to the matrix pipes and fit a new sealing ring to each of the pipe unions. Manoeuvre the pipe assembly into position and secure it to the matrix.
23 Working in the engine compartment, refit the seal and retaining plate to the heater matrix pipes and securely tighten the retaining screw. Remove the clamps (where fitted) then reconnect the coolant hoses, securing them in position with the retaining clips.
24 Refit the battery (see Chapter 5A).
25 Refill the cooling system (see Chapter 1A or 1B).

Heater blower motor

Removal

26 The blower motor is fitted to the top of the heating/ventilation housing, on the left-hand side.
27 On right-hand drive models, remove the glovebox (see Section 27 of Chapter 11). Access to the motor can then be gained through the glovebox aperture.
28 On left-hand drive models, remove the steering column as described in Chapter 10 to gain access to the motor.
29 Where necessary, slacken and remove the retaining screw securing the motor to the housing (this screw may not be fitted).

10.18b . . . and the matrix (arrowed) . . .

10.18c . . . then release the retaining clips

10.20 Slide the matrix from the housing

10.31a Rotate the motor cover clockwise . . .

10.31b . . . and withdraw the blower motor

10.34 Reach through the blower motor aperture, and rotate the resistor (arrowed) to remove it

30 Disconnect the wiring connector(s) from the blower motor.

31 Rotate the motor clockwise to free it from the housing then manoeuvre it out of position **(see illustrations)**.

Refitting

32 Refitting is the reverse of removal. If the motor is not a secure fit in the housing, fix it in position by fitting a self-tapping screw to the hole provided.

Heater blower motor resistor

Removal

33 Remove the heater blower motor as previously described.

34 Reach through the blower motor aperture and rotate the resistor to free it, and pull it down into the duct. Disconnect the wiring connector and remove the resistor from the housing **(see illustration)**.

Refitting

35 Manoeuvre the resistor into position and connect it to the wiring connector. Once the connector is securely fitted, locate the resistor in the duct and clip it in position. Refit any components removed for access.

Housing assembly

Models without air conditioning – removal

36 To improve access to the matrix unions on the bulkhead, remove the battery and battery tray as described in Chapter 5A. Where necessary also remove the air cleaner housing intake duct (see Chapter 4A or 4B).

37 Drain the cooling system (see Chapter 1A or 1B). Alternatively, working in the engine compartment, clamp the heater matrix coolant hoses to minimise coolant loss.

38 Release the retaining clips and disconnect the coolant hoses from the heater matrix pipe unions on the engine compartment bulkhead **(see illustration 10.15)**.

39 Slacken and remove the screw securing the heater matrix pipes to the bulkhead and remove the retaining plate and seal **(see illustrations 10.16)**.

40 Slacken and remove the bolt securing the heating/ventilation housing to the bulkhead **(see illustration)**.

41 Remove the facia assembly as described in Chapter 11.

42 Disconnect the wiring connectors from the heating/ventilation housing components then remove the housing and control panel assembly from the vehicle. Keep the heater matrix pipe unions uppermost as the assembly is removed to prevent coolant spillage.

43 Recover the seal and retaining plate from the heater matrix pipes, and the seal from the housing mounting. Renew the seals if they show signs of damage or deterioration.

Models without air conditioning – refitting

44 Refitting is the reverse of removal ensuring the seals are in position on the pipes and housing mounting. On completion, refill the cooling system (see Chapter 1A or 1B).

Models with air conditioning – removal

⚠ **Warning: Refer to Section 11 for precautions to be observed when working on models equipped with air conditioning. Do not attempt the following procedure unless the system has been professionally discharged.**

45 Have the air conditioning system discharged by an air conditioning specialist and obtain some plugs to seal the air conditioning pipe unions whilst the system is disconnected.

46 Carry out the operations described in paragraphs 36 to 39.

47 Unscrew the two nuts securing the air conditioning pipe union to the bulkhead **(see illustration)**. Separate the pipes from the

10.40 Heater/ventilation housing retaining bolt (arrowed)

evaporator and quickly seal the pipe and evaporator unions to prevent the entry of moisture into the refrigerant circuit. Discard the sealing rings, new ones must be used on refitting.

⚠ **Warning: Failure to seal the refrigerant pipe unions will result in the dehydrator reservoir become saturated, necessitating its renewal.**

48 Remove the heating/ventilation housing assembly as described in paragraphs 40 to 43 and recover the seal from the evaporator.

Models with air conditioning – refitting

49 Ensure the bulkhead seals are correctly fitted to the evaporator, matrix pipes and housing mounting. Manoeuvre the housing assembly into position, locating the housing drain hose correctly in its hole in the floor.

50 Loosely refit the housing mounting bolt then refit the retaining plate to the heater matrix pipe and loosely install the retaining screw.

51 Lubricate the new evaporator union sealing rings with compressor oil. Remove the plugs and install the sealing rings then quickly fit the refrigerant pipe union to the evaporator. Ensure the refrigerant pipes and evaporator are correctly joined then refit the retaining nuts, tighten them securely.

52 Tighten the matrix pipe retaining screw securely and securely tighten the housing mounting bolt.

53 The remainder of refitting is the reverse of removal. On completion, refill the cooling system (see Chapter 1A or 1B).

10.47 Undo the two nuts securing the air conditioning pipes to the engine compartment bulkhead

10.55 Unclip the passenger compartment air temperature sensor from the audio unit aperture (arrowed)

Interior air temperature sensor

54 Remove the audio unit as described in Chapter 12.

55 Unclip the sensor from the exposed aperture, and disconnect the wiring plug (see illustration).

56 Refitting is a reversal of removal.

Additional heater – diesel models

Removal

57 On right-hand drive models, remove the glovebox and passenger side central kick panel as described in Chapter 11.

58 On left-hand drive models, remove the trim panel above the pedals, undo the two fasteners and remove the trim panel at the front of the centre console, adjacent to the pedals.

59 Undo the bolt securing the heater earth connection.

60 Disconnect the heater wiring plug, then undo the screw, release the retaining clip at the base of the unit, and slide the heater from the housing (see illustration).

Refitting

61 Refitting is the reverse of removal.

Air recirculation motor

62 On right-hand drive models, remove the lower facia trim panel, then undo the two fasteners and remove the centre console side panel at the front (adjacent to the pedals).

63 Disconnect the motor wiring plug, undo the bolts, and remove the motor (see illustration).

64 Refitting is a reversal of removal.

Ambient temperature sensor

65 The ambient temperature sensor is located on the underside of the passenger's side exterior mirror. To remove the sensor, remove the mirror cover as described in Chapter 11.

66 Unclip the sensor from the mirror housing. To disconnect the wiring plug, it is necessary to remove the door trim panel as described in Chapter 11.

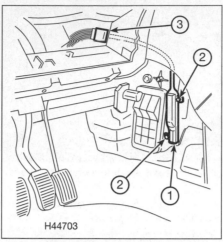

H44703

10.60 Additional heater on diesel models (LHD)

1 Wiring plug   3 Heater
2 Screw and clip

---

11 Air conditioning system – general information and precautions

General information

1 An air conditioning system is available on certain models. It enables the temperature of incoming air to be lowered, and also dehumidifies the air, which makes for rapid demisting and increased comfort.

2 The cooling side of the system works in the same way as a domestic refrigerator. Refrigerant gas is drawn into a belt-driven compressor, and passes into a condenser mounted on the front of the radiator, where it loses heat and becomes liquid. The liquid passes through an expansion valve to an evaporator, where it changes from liquid under high pressure to gas under low pressure. This change is accompanied by a drop in temperature, which cools the evaporator. The refrigerant returns to the compressor, and the cycle begins again.

3 Air blown through the evaporator passes to the heating/ventilation housing, where it is mixed with hot air blown through the heater matrix to achieve the desired temperature in the passenger compartment.

4 The heating side of the system works in the same way as on models without air conditioning (see Section 9).

5 The operation of the system is controlled electronically by the ECU integral with the control panel. Any problems with the system should be referred to a Peugeot dealer, or suitably-equipped specialist.

Precautions

6 When an air conditioning system is fitted, it is necessary to observe special precautions whenever dealing with any part of the system,

10.63 Air recirculation motor

or its associated components. The refrigerant is potentially dangerous, and should only be handled by qualified persons. Uncontrolled discharging of the refrigerant is dangerous and damaging to the environment for the following reasons.

a) *If it is splashed onto the skin, it can cause frostbite.*

b) *The refrigerant is heavier then air and so displaces oxygen. In a confined space which is not adequately ventilated this could lead to a risk of suffocation. The gas is odourless and colourless so there is no warning of its presence in the atmosphere.*

c) *Although not poisonous, in the presence of a naked flame (including a cigarette) it forms a noxious gas which causes headaches, nausea, etc.*

⚠ *Warning: Never attempt to open any air conditioning system refrigerant pipe/hose union without first having the system fully discharged by an air conditioning specialist. On completion of work, have the system recharged with the correct type and amount of fresh refrigerant.*

⚠ *Warning: Always seal disconnected refrigerant pipe/hose unions as soon as they are disconnected. Failure to form an air-tight seal on any union will result in the dehydrator reservoir become saturated, necessitating its renewal. Also renew all sealing rings disturbed.*

Caution: Do not operated the air conditioning system if it is known to be short of refrigerant as this could damage the compressor.

---

12 Air conditioning system components – removal and refitting

⚠ *Warning: Refer to the precautions given in Section 11 and have the system discharged by an air conditioning specialist before carrying out any work on the air conditioning system*

12.4 Unscrew the refrigerant pipes retaining plates nuts

12.5 Remove the compressor mounting bolts (arrowed)

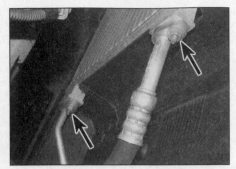

12.14 Undo the nuts (arrowed) securing the refrigerant pipes to the condenser

Compressor

Removal

1 Have the air conditioning system fully discharged and evacuated by an air conditioning specialist.

2 Remove the auxiliary drivebelt as described in Chapter 1A or 1B (as applicable).

3 Disconnect the compressor wiring connector from the engine harness.

4 Unscrew the nuts securing the refrigerant pipes retaining plates to the compressor **(see illustration)**. Separate the pipes from the compressor and quickly seal the pipe and compressor unions to prevent the entry of moisture into the refrigerant circuit. Discard the sealing rings, new ones must be used on refitting.

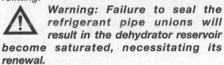

⚠ *Warning: Failure to seal the refrigerant pipe unions will result in the dehydrator reservoir become saturated, necessitating its renewal.*

5 Unscrew the compressor mounting bolts and nuts then free the compressor from its mounting bracket and remove it from the engine **(see illustration)**. Take care not to lose the spacers from the compressor rear mountings (where fitted).

6 If the compressor is to be renewed, drain the refrigerant oil from the old compressor. The specialist who recharges the refrigerant system will need to add this amount of oil to the system.

Refitting

7 If a new compressor is being fitted, drain the refrigerant oil.

8 Ensure the spacers are correctly fitted to the rear mountings then manoeuvre the com-pressor into position and fit the mounting bolts and nuts. Tighten the compressor front (drivebelt pulley) end mounting bolts to the specified torque first then tighten the rear bolts.

9 Lubricate the new refrigerant pipe sealing rings with compressor oil. Remove the plugs and install the sealing rings then quickly fit the refrigerant pipes to the compressor. Ensure the refrigerant pipes are correctly joined then refit the retaining bolt, tighten it securely.

10 Reconnect the wiring connector then refit the auxiliary drivebelt (see Chapter 1A or 1B).

11 Have the air conditioning system recharged with the correct type and amount of refrigerant by a specialist before using the system. Remember to inform the specialist which components have been renewed, so they can add the correct amount of oil.

Condenser

Removal

12 Have the air conditioning system fully discharged by an air conditioning specialist.

13 Remove the radiator as described in Section 4.

14 Undo the retaining nuts and disconnect the refrigerant pipes from the right-hand side of the condenser. Recover the O-ring seals **(see illustration)**.

⚠ *Warning: Failure to seal the refrigerant pipe unions will result in the dehydrator reservoir become saturated, necessitating its renewal.*

15 Move the top of the condenser to the rear and remove it.

Refitting

16 Refitting is a reversal of removal. Noting the following points:

a) *Ensure the upper and lower mounting rubbers are correctly fitted then seat the condenser in position in the front panel* **(see illustrations)**.

b) *Lubricate the sealing rings with compressor oil. Remove the plugs and install the sealing rings then quickly fit the refrigerant pipes to the condenser. Securely tighten the dehydrator pipe union nut and ensure the compressor pipe is correctly joined.*

c) *Have the air conditioning system recharged with the correct type and amount of refrigerant by a specialist before using the system.*

12.16a Ensure the condenser upper (arrowed) . . .

12.16b . . . and lower (arrowed) mountings are correctly fitted

12.19a Undo the screw and remove the clip (arrowed) . . .

12.19b . . . then unscrew the receiver/drier cartridge

12.19c Renew the cartridge seal

Receiver/drier

Removal

17 The receiver/drier is located on the left-hand side of the condenser. Have the air conditioning system fully discharged and evacuated by an air conditioning specialist.

18 Remove the radiator as described in Section 4.

19 Undo the screw and remove the clip at the top then pull the top of the condenser rearwards slightly, and unscrew the receiver/drier cartridge using a Torx T70 bit. Take great care not to pull the condenser too far and damage the refrigerant pipes **(see illustrations)**.

⚠️ *Warning: Prior to slackening the clamp, clean the dehydrator and wipe it dry, to avoid moisture/ debris entering the air conditioning circuit*

Refitting

20 Refitting is a reversal of removal noting the following points:

a) *Lubricate the cartridge seals with compressor oil.*

b) *Have the air conditioning system recharged with the correct type and amount of refrigerant by a specialist prior to using the system.*

Evaporator

Removal

21 Have the air conditioning system fully discharged and evacuated by an air conditioning specialist.

22 Remove the heating/ventilation housing as described in Section 10.

24 Note their fitted positions, then disconnect the wiring plugs and harness from the housing.

25 Release the retaining clips, undo the screws and separate the two halves of the heater housing **(see illustrations)**.

12.25a Undo the various screws and clips around the housing (arrowed) . . .

12.25c . . . remove the base cover . . .

26 With the two halves of the housing separated, undo the 2 screws, remove the pipe cover, then slide the evaporator from the housing **(see illustrations)**.

12.25b . . . including the ones hidden at the sides (arrowed) . . .

12.25d . . . and separate the 2 halves of the housing

12.26a Undo the screws (arrowed), remove the pipe cover . . .

12.26b . . . then slide the evaporator from the housing

12.26c Ensure the nut plate is in place when refitting the evaporator

12.31a Undo the 2 studs (arrowed) using a Torx socket

12.31b Renew the expansion valve seals on the pipes

Refitting

27 Refitting is a reversal of removal but have the air conditioning system recharged with the correct type and amount of refrigerant by a specialist prior to using the system.

Expansion valve

Removal

28 Have the air conditioning system fully discharged and evacuated by an air conditioning specialist.

29 Remove the sound insulation material/ heatshield from the engine compartment bulkhead (where fitted).

30 Undo the nuts securing the refrigerant pipes to the connection at the engine compartment bulkhead. Plug/cover the openings to prevent contamination/saturation. Recover and discard the O-ring seals – new ones must be fitted.

⚠️ **Warning: Failure to seal the refrigerant pipe unions will result in the receiver/drier becoming saturated, necessitating its renewal**

31 Pull the seal from around the pipes connection at the bulkhead, then undo the 2 studs using a Torx socket, and remove the expansion valve **(see illustrations)**. Recover and discard the O-ring seals – new ones must be fitted.

Refitting

32 Refitting is a reversal of removal but have the air conditioning system recharged with the correct type and amount of refrigerant by a specialist prior to using the system.

Chapter 4 Part A:
Fuel and exhaust systems – petrol models

Contents

Degrees of difficulty

Easy, suitable for novice with little experience | **Fairly easy,** suitable for beginner with some experience | **Fairly difficult,** suitable for competent DIY mechanic 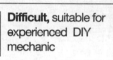 | **Difficult,** suitable for experienced DIY mechanic | **Very difficult,** suitable for expert DIY or professional

Specifications

Engine identification

		Designation	Engine code
1.4 litre		TU3JP	KFW
1.4 litre		ET3JP4	KFU
1.6 litre		TU5JP4	NFU
2.0 litre		EW10J4 IFL5	RFN
2.0 litre		EW10A	RFJ

System type

1.4 litre models:	
TU3	Sagem S2000
ET3	Marelli 6LP
1.6 litre models	Bosch Motronic ME7.4.4
2.0 litre models	Magneti Marelli 4.8P, 4.8P2, 4MP2, 6LP1 or 6LPB

Fuel system data

Fuel pump type	Electric, immersed in tank
Fuel pump regulated constant pressure	3.5 ± 0.2 bars
Specified idle speed	850 ± 100 rpm (not adjustable – controlled by ECU)
Idle mixture CO content	Less than 1.0% (not adjustable – controlled by ECU)

Recommended fuel

Minimum octane rating	95 RON unleaded (UK unleaded premium). Leaded/lead replacement fuel (LRP) must **not** be used

Torque wrench settings

	Nm	lbf ft
Exhaust manifold to catalytic converter	15	11
Exhaust manifold-to-cylinder head nuts	20	15
Inlet manifold nuts:		
M6	10	7
M8	20	15
Roadwheel bolts	90	66

2.1 Slacken the retaining clips and remove the air intake duct

1 General information and precautions

1 The fuel supply system consists of a fuel tank (which is mounted under the rear of the car, with an electric fuel pump immersed in it), a fuel filter, fuel feed and return lines. The fuel pump supplies fuel to the fuel rail, which acts as a reservoir for the four fuel injectors which inject fuel into the inlet tracts. The fuel filter incorporated in the feed line from the pump to the fuel rail ensures that the fuel supplied to the injectors is clean.

2 Refer to Section 6 for further information on the operation of the engine management system, and to Section 16 for information on the exhaust system.

⚠️ *Warning: Many of the procedures in this Chapter require the removal of fuel lines and connections, which may result in some fuel spillage. Before carrying out any operation on the fuel system, refer to the precautions given in 'Safety first!' at the beginning of this manual, and follow them implicitly. Petrol is a highly dangerous and volatile liquid, and the precautions necessary when handling it cannot be overstressed.*

Note: *Residual pressure will remain in the fuel lines long after the vehicle was last used. When disconnecting any fuel line, first depressurise the fuel system as described in Section 7.*

3.1 Remove the spring clip (arrowed) from the outer cable

2.2 Depress the retaining clip (arrowed) and lift the air cleaner housing from its bracket

2 Air cleaner assembly and intake ducts – removal and refitting

Removal

1 Slacken the retaining clips then free the duct from the manifold and air cleaner housing, and remove it from the engine compartment **(see illustration)**.

2 Depress the retaining clip at the side, then lift the air cleaner housing assembly off of its mounting bracket and remove it from the engine compartment. Recover the mounting rubber fitted to the housing lower locating peg and the sealing ring from the housing intake duct **(see illustration)**.

3 To remove the intake duct, firmly apply the handbrake then jack up the front of the car and support it on axle stands (see *Jacking and vehicle support*). Push in the centre pins a little, then prise out the complete expanding plastic rivets, and remove the left-hand wheel arch liner. Remove the retaining bolts and remove the duct assembly from the vehicle (on 1.6 and 2.0 litre engines a resonator chamber is incorporated into the duct to reduce intake noise).

Refitting

4 Refitting is a reversal of the removal procedure, ensuring that all hoses and ducts are properly reconnected and correctly seated and, where necessary, securely held by their retaining clips.

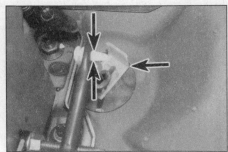

3.4 Squeeze the tabs (arrowed), detach the inner cable from the accelerator pedal, then pull out the grommet clip (arrowed)

3 Accelerator cable – removal, refitting and adjustment

Removal

1 Working in the engine compartment, free the accelerator inner cable from the throttle housing cam, then pull the outer cable out from its mounting bracket rubber grommet. Recover the spring clip from the outer cable **(see illustration)**.

2 Working back along the length of the cable, free it from any retaining clips or ties, noting its correct routing.

3 Working inside the vehicle, prise up the centre pins a little, then lever out the complete plastic rivets, and remove the trim above the driver's pedals.

4 Reach up behind the facia, squeeze together the sides of the retaining clip, then detach the inner cable from the top of the accelerator pedal and pull out the clip securing the bulkhead grommet **(see illustration)**.

5 Tie a length of string to the end of the cable.

6 Return to the engine compartment, release the cable grommet from the bulkhead and withdraw the cable. When the end of the cable appears, untie the string and leave it in position – it can then be used to draw the cable back into position on refitting.

Refitting

7 Tie the string to the end of the cable, then use the string to draw the cable into position through the bulkhead. Once the cable end is visible, untie the string, then secure the inner cable into the pedal end.

8 Refit the bulkhead grommet clip.

9 From within the engine compartment, ensure the outer cable is correctly seated in the bulkhead grommet, then work along the cable, securing it in position with the retaining clips and ties, and ensuring that the cable is correctly routed.

10 Pass the outer cable through its mounting bracket grommet, and reconnect the inner cable to the throttle cam. Adjust the cable as described below.

Adjustment

11 Remove the spring clip from the accelerator outer cable **(see illustration 3.1)**. Ensuring that the throttle cam is fully against its stop, gently pull the cable out of its grommet until all free play is removed from the inner cable.

12 With the cable held in this position, refit the spring clip to the last exposed outer cable groove in front of the rubber grommet. When the clip is refitted and the outer cable is released, there should be only a small amount of free play in the inner cable.

13 Have an assistant depress the accelerator pedal, and check that the throttle cam opens fully and returns smoothly to its stop.

4 Accelerator pedal – removal and refitting

Removal

Models with accelerator cable

1 Detach the accelerator cable from the pedal as described in the previous Section.
2 On right-hand drive models, remove the retaining clip then slide out the bush and remove the accelerator pedal from the pedal pivot shaft **(see illustration)**.
3 On left-hand drive models, remove the retaining clip then slide the pedal off its pivot shaft. The pivot shaft is a screw fit in the body.

Models without accelerator cable

4 Release the fasteners and remove trim panel above the pedals (see Chapter 11).
5 Disconnect the accelerator pedal position sensor wiring plug from the top of the pedal.
6 Undo the three nuts and remove the pedal assembly **(see illustration)**.

Refitting

7 Refitting is a reversal of the removal procedure. On models fitted with a cable, apply a little multi-purpose grease to the pedal pivot point, and adjust the accelerator cable as described in Section 3.

5 Unleaded petrol – general information and usage

Note: *The information given in this Chapter is correct at the time of writing. If updated information is thought to be required, check with a Peugeot dealer. If travelling abroad, consult one of the motoring organisations (or a similar authority) for advice on the fuel available.*

1 The fuel recommended by Peugeot is given in the Specifications Section of this Chapter, followed by the equivalent petrol currently on sale in the UK.
2 All models are designed to run on fuel with a minimum octane rating of 95 (RON). All models have a catalytic converter, and so must be run on unleaded fuel only. Under no circumstances should leaded/lead replacement fuel (UK 4-star/LRP) be used, as this may damage the converter.
3 Super unleaded petrol (98 octane) can also be used in all models if wished, though there is no advantage in doing so.

6 Engine management system – general information

Note: *The fuel injection ECU is of the 'self-learning' type, meaning that as it operates, it also monitors and stores the settings which give optimum engine performance under all operating conditions. When the battery is*

4.2 Remove the clip (arrowed) and slide out the bush

disconnected, these settings are lost and the ECU reverts to the base settings programmed into its memory at the factory. On restarting, this may lead to the engine running/idling roughly for a short while, until the ECU has relearned the optimum settings. This process is best accomplished by taking the vehicle on a road test (for approximately 15 minutes), covering all engine speeds and loads, concentrating mainly in the 2500 to 3500 rpm region.

On all engines, the fuel injection and ignition functions are combined into a single engine management system. The systems fitted are manufactured by Bosch, Magneti Marelli and Sagem, and are very similar to each other in most respects, the only significant differences being in the software contained in the system ECU, and specific component location according to engine type. Each system incorporates a closed-loop catalytic converter and an evaporative emission control system, and complies with the latest emission control standards. Refer to Chapter 5B for information on the ignition side of each system; the fuel side of the system operates as follows.

The fuel pump supplies fuel from the tank to the fuel rail, via a renewable cartridge filter mounted on the side of the fuel tank. The pump itself is mounted inside the tank, with the pump motor permanently immersed in fuel, to keep it cool. The fuel rail is mounted directly above the fuel injectors and acts as a fuel reservoir.

Fuel rail supply pressure is controlled by the pressure regulator, also located in the fuel tank. The regulator contains a spring-loaded valve, which lifts to allow excess fuel to recirculate within the tank when the optimum operating

4.6 Accelerator pedal mounting nuts (arrowed)

pressure of the fuel system is exceeded (eg, during low speed, light load cruising).

The fuel injectors are electromagnetic pintle valves, which spray atomised fuel into the intake manifold tracts under the control of the engine management system ECU. There are four injectors, one per cylinder, mounted in the inlet manifold close to the cylinder head. Each injector is mounted at an angle that allows it to spray fuel directly onto the back of the inlet valve(s). The ECU controls the volume of fuel injected by varying the length of time for which each injector is held open. The fuel injection systems are typically of the sequential type, whereby each injector operates individually in cylinder sequence.

The electrical control system consists of the ECU, along with the following sensors:

a) *Throttle potentiometer – informs the ECU of the throttle valve position, and the rate of throttle opening/closing (not all models)*.
b) *Coolant temperature sensor – informs the ECU of engine temperature.*
c) *Inlet air temperature sensor – informs the ECU of the temperature of the air passing through the throttle housing.*
d) *Oxygen sensors – inform the ECU of the oxygen content of the exhaust gases (explained in greater detail in Part C of this Chapter).*
e) *Manifold pressure sensor – informs the ECU of the load on the engine (expressed in terms of inlet manifold vacuum).*
f) *Crankshaft position sensor – informs the ECU of engine speed and crankshaft angular position.*
g) *Vehicle speed sensor – informs the ECU of the vehicle speed (not all models).*
h) *Knock sensor – informs the ECU of pre-ignition (detonation) within the cylinders (not all models).*
i) *Camshaft sensor – informs the ECU of which cylinder is on the firing stroke on systems with sequential injection (not all models).*
j) *Accelerator pedal position sensor – informs the ECU of the pedal position and rate of change (not all models)*.
k) *Throttle valve positioner motor – allows the ECU to control the throttle valve position (not all models)*.
l) *Engine oil temperature sensor – informs the ECU of the engine oil temperature (not all models).*
m) *Clutch and brake pedal position sensor – informs the ECU of the pedal positions (not all models).*

* *2.0 litre petrol engines may be fitted with a manual throttle body with an accelerator cable, or a motorised throttle body with no cable.*

Signals from each of the sensors are compared by the ECU and, based on this information, the ECU selects the response appropriate to those values, and controls the fuel injectors (varying the pulse width – the length of time the injectors are held open – to provide a richer or weaker air/fuel mixture, as

7.2 Fuel pressure relief valve (arrowed)

appropriate). The air/fuel mixture is constantly varied by the ECU, to provide the best settings for cranking, starting (with either a hot or cold engine) and engine warm-up, idle, cruising and acceleration.

The ECU also has full control over the engine idle speed, via a stepper motor fitted to the throttle housing. The stepper motor either controls the amount of air passing through a bypass drilling at the side of the throttle or controls the position of the throttle valve itself, depending on model. On some models, a sensor informs the ECU of the position, and rate of change, of the accelerator pedal. The ECU then controls the throttle valve by means of a throttle positioning motor integral with the throttle body – no accelerator cable is fitted. On 1.6 litre models, the accelerator cable is connected to a sensor in the left-hand front corner of the engine compartment, which informs the ECU of the accelerator pedal position. The ECU also carries out 'fine tuning' of the idle speed by varying the ignition timing to increase or reduce the torque of the engine as it is idling. This helps to stabilise the idle speed when electrical or mechanical loads (such as headlights, air conditioning, etc) are switched on and off.

The throttle housing is also fitted with an electric heating element. The heater is supplied with current by the ECU, warming the throttle housing on cold starts to help prevent icing of the throttle valve.

The exhaust and evaporative loss emission control systems are described in more detail in Chapter 4C.

If there is any abnormality in any of the readings obtained from the coolant tem-perature sensor, the inlet air temperature sensor or the lambda sensor, the ECU enters its 'back-up' mode. If this happens, the erroneous sensor signal is overridden, and the ECU assumes a preprogrammed 'back-up' value, which will allow the engine to continue running, albeit at reduced efficiency. If the ECU enters this mode, the warning lamp on the instrument panel will be illuminated, and the relevant fault code will be stored in the ECU memory.

If the warning light illuminates, the vehicle should be taken to a Peugeot dealer or specialist at the earliest opportunity. Once there, a complete test of the engine management system can be carried out, using a special electronic diagnostic test unit, which is plugged into the system's diagnostic connector, located behind the trim panel to the right of the steering column.

7 Fuel system – depressurisation and pressurising

Note: *Refer to the warning note in Section 1 before proceeding.*

Depressurisation

⚠️ **Warning: The following procedure will merely relieve the pressure in the fuel system – remember that fuel will still be present in the system components and take precautions accordingly before disconnecting any of them.**

1 The fuel system referred to in this Section is defined as the tank-mounted fuel pump, the fuel filter, the fuel injectors, the fuel rail and the pipes of the fuel lines between these components. All these contain fuel which will be under pressure while the engine is running, and/or while the ignition is switched on. The pressure will remain for some time after the ignition has been switched off, and must be relieved in a controlled fashion when any of these components are disturbed for servicing work.

2 Some models are equipped with a pressure relief valve on the fuel rail **(see illustration)**.

On these models, unscrew the cap from the valve and position a container beneath the valve. Hold a wad of rag over the valve and relieve the pressure in the system by depressing the valve core with a suitable screwdriver. Be prepared for the squirt of fuel as the valve core is depressed and catch it with the rag. Hold the valve core down until no more fuel is expelled from the valve. Once the pressure is relieved, securely refit the valve cap.

3 Where no valve is fitted to the fuel rail, it will be necessary to release the pressure as the fuel pipe is disconnected. Place a container beneath the union and position a large rag around the union to catch any fuel spray which may be expelled. Slowly release and disconnect the fuel pipe and catch any spilt fuel in the container. Plug the pipe/union to minimise fuel loss and prevent the entry of dirt into the fuel system.

Pressurising

4 After any work is carried out on the fuel system, the system should be pressurised as follows.

5 Depress the accelerator pedal fully then switch on the ignition. Hold the pedal depressed for approximately 1 second then release it. The ECU should then operate the fuel pump for between 20 and 30 seconds to refill the fuel system. Once the fuel pump stops the ignition can be switched off.

8 Fuel pump – removal and refitting

Removal

1 For access to the fuel pump, tilt or remove the right-hand rear seat cushion (see Chapter 11).

2 Using a screwdriver, carefully release the three plastic access cover retaining clips at the points indicated by the small arrows, and remove the cover from the floor to expose the fuel pump/sender unit **(see illustration)**.

3 Disconnect the wiring connector from the fuel pump, and tape the connector to the vehicle body, to prevent it from disappearing behind the tank **(see illustration)**.

4 Depress the retaining clip and detach the fuel pipe(s) from the top of the pump, bearing in mind the information given in Section 7 on depressurising the fuel system. Plug the pipe end(s) to minimise fuel loss and prevent the entry of dirt. On diesel models, note the pipes are identified with arrows indicating the fuel feed and return **(see illustrations)**.

5 Noting the alignment marks on the tank, pump cover and the locking ring, unscrew the ring and remove it from the tank. This is best accomplished by using a screwdriver on the raised ribs of the locking ring. Carefully tap the screwdriver to turn the ring anti-clockwise until it can be unscrewed by hand **(see**

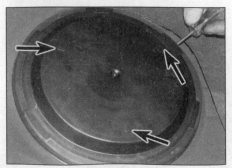

8.2 Fuel pump access cover retaining clips release points (arrowed)

8.3 Disconnect the pump wiring plug

8.4a Depress the release button and disconnect the fuel pipe

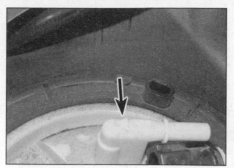

8.4b Note the fuel flow arrows on diesel models (arrowed)

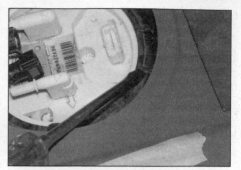

8.5 Tap the screwdriver to rotate the locking ring anti-clockwise

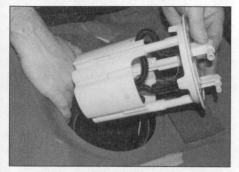

8.6 Lift the fuel pump assembly, taking care not to damage the float arm

8.8 Fit a new sealing ring to the top of the tank

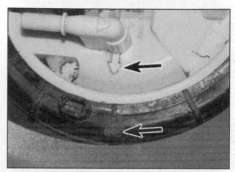

8.11 Rotate the locking ring until the mark aligns with the pump cover mark (arrowed)

illustration). Alternatively, a Peugeot special tool is available which fits over the collar and allows it to be released using a ratchet and extension.

6 Carefully lift the fuel pump assembly out of the fuel tank, taking great care not to damage the fuel gauge sender unit float arm, or to spill fuel onto the interior of the vehicle **(see illustration)**. Recover the rubber sealing ring and discard it – a new one must be used on refitting.

7 Note that the fuel pump is only available as a complete assembly – no components are available separately.

Refitting

8 Fit the new sealing ring to the top of the fuel tank **(see illustration)**.

9 Carefully manoeuvre the pump assembly into the fuel tank, taking care not to damage the float arm.

10 Align the arrow on the fuel pump cover with previously noted mark on the fuel tank and clip the pump assembly into position.

11 Refit the locking ring and tighten it securely until its alignment mark aligns with the pump cover arrow **(see illustration)**.

12 Securely reconnect the fuel pipe(s) to the pump cover then reconnect the pump wiring connector.

13 Pressurise the fuel system (see Section 7). Start the engine and check the fuel pump feed and return hoses unions for signs of leakage.

14 If all is well, refit the plastic access cover ensuring its locating tab is at the front.

15 Refit the rear seat cushion (see Chapter 11).

9 Fuel gauge sender unit – removal and refitting

The fuel gauge sender unit is an integral part of the fuel pump assembly and is not available separately. Refer to Section 8 for removal and refitting details.

10 Fuel tank – removal and refitting

Note: *Refer to the warning note in Section 1 before proceeding.*

Removal

1 Before removing the fuel tank, all fuel must be drained from the tank. Since a fuel

10.6a Push in the centre pins a little, then prise out the complete plastic expanding rivets . . .

tank drain plug is not provided, it is therefore preferable to carry out the removal operation when the tank is nearly empty. Before proceeding, disconnect the battery (see Chapter 5A) and syphon or hand-pump the remaining fuel from the tank.

2 Remove the rear seat cushion and, using a screwdriver, carefully release the three access cover retaining clips at the points indicated by the small arrows, and remove the cover from the floor to expose the fuel pump **(see illustration 8.2)**.

3 Disconnect the wiring connector from the fuel pump, and tape the connector to the vehicle body, to prevent it from disappearing behind the tank **(see illustration 8.3)**.

4 Depress the retaining clip and detach the fuel pipe(s) from the top of the pump, bearing in mind the information given in Section 7 on depressurising the fuel system **(see illustration 8.4)**. Plug the pipe end(s) to minimise fuel loss and prevent the entry of dirt.

5 Chock the front wheels then jack up the rear of the vehicle and support it on axle stands (*see Jacking and vehicle support*). Remove the right-hand rear roadwheel.

6 Remove the retaining nuts and fasteners (push in the centre pin a little then remove the complete fasteners) and remove the right-hand rear wheel arch liner **(see illustrations)**.

7 Remove the exhaust system as described in Section 16.

8 Unscrew the centre pins a little, then lever out the complete expanding plastic rivets, and remove the heat shield from the tank underside. On petrol models, undo the nuts,

10.6b ... undo the nuts (arrowed) ...

10.6c ... and remove the wheel arch liner

securing the fuel tank to the body and the bolts securing the filler neck **(see illustrations)**. Release the filler neck seal from the body at the filler cap aperture.

12 Slowly lower the fuel tank, ensuring the filler neck assembly is guided out of position without placing any stress on it.

13 If the tank is contaminated with sediment or water, remove the fuel pump (Section 8), and swill the tank out with clean fuel. The tank is injection-moulded from a synthetic material – if seriously damaged, it should be renewed. However, in certain cases, it may be possible to have small leaks or minor damage repaired. Seek the advice of a specialist before attempting to repair the fuel tank.

14 It is not possible to separate the filler neck from the tank. If damaged, the complete assembly must be renewed.

Refitting

15 Refitting is the reverse of the removal procedure, noting the following points:
  a) Ensure the wiring connector and fuel pipes are securely reconnected and retained by all the relevant clips. When lifting the tank back into position, take care to ensure that the pipes/wiring do not become trapped between the tank and vehicle body.
  b) Refit the rear suspension springs as described in Chapter 10.
  c) Refit the exhaust as described in Section 16.
  d) On completion, refill the tank with a small amount of fuel and pressurise the fuel system as described in Section 7. Check for signs of leakage prior to taking the vehicle out on the road.

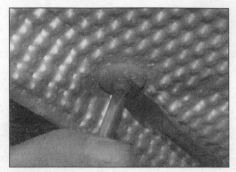

10.8a Unscrew the centre pin a little, then prise out the fastener

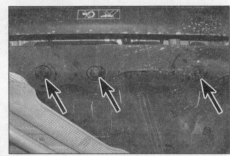

10.8b Undo the nuts, prise out the plastic rivets (arrowed) and remove the plastic undershield

release the plastic rivets and remove the plastic undershield(s) from the fuel tank **(see illustrations)**.

9 Remove the rear suspension coil springs as described in Chapter 10.

10 Place a trolley jack with an interposed block of wood beneath the tank, then raise the jack until it is supporting the weight of the tank.

11 Slacken and remove the four bolts

---

11 Engine management system – testing and adjustment

Testing

1 If a fault appears in the engine management system, first ensure that all the system wiring connectors are securely connected and free of corrosion. Ensure that the fault is not due to poor maintenance; ie, check that the air

10.11a Fuel tank strap bolts (arrowed) ...

10.11b ... right-hand ...

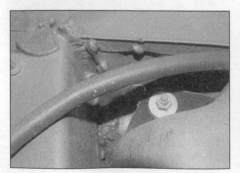

10.11c ... and left-hand corner bolts

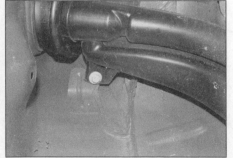

10.11d Fuel filler neck upper ...

10.11e ... and lower fixing bolts

cleaner filter element is clean, the spark plugs are in good condition and correctly gapped, the cylinder compression pressures are correct and that the engine breather hoses are clear and undamaged, referring to Chapters 1A, 2A, 2B and 5B for further information.

2 If these checks fail to reveal the cause of the problem, the vehicle should be taken to a suitably-equipped Peugeot dealer or specialist for testing using a diagnostic tester, which is connected into the diagnostic socket located behind the trim panel to the right of the steering column **(see illustration)**. The tester will locate the fault quickly and simply, alleviating the need to test all the system components individually, which is a time-consuming operation that carries a risk of damaging the ECU.

Adjustment

3 Whilst it is possible to check the exhaust CO level and the idle speed, if these are found to be in need of adjustment, the car *must* be taken to a suitably-equipped Peugeot dealer or specialist for further testing. Neither the mixture adjustment (exhaust gas CO level) nor the idle speed are adjustable, and should either be incorrect, a fault must be present in the engine management system.

12 Throttle housing –
removal and refitting

Removal

1 On 2.0 litre models, rotate the 6 fasteners 90° anti-clockwise, and remove the plastic cover from the top of the engine. On all models, remove the scuttle trim panel and crossmember as described in Section 13, Paragraph 1.

2 Slacken the retaining clips then free the air duct from the throttle housing and air cleaner housing and remove it from the engine compartment.

3 Free the accelerator inner cable from the throttle cam (where fitted).

4 Note their fitted positions, then depress the retaining clip and disconnect the wiring connectors from the throttle body **(see illustration)**.

5 Slacken and remove the three retaining screws and remove the throttle housing from the inlet manifold **(see illustrations)**. Recover the sealing ring from manifold and discard it; a new one must be used on refitting.

Refitting

6 Refitting is a reversal of the removal procedure, noting the following points:
  a) Fit a new sealing ring to the manifold, then refit the throttle housing and securely tighten its retaining screws.
  b) Ensure all wiring is correctly routed, and that the connectors are securely reconnected.

11.2 Diagnostic socket

c) On completion, adjust the accelerator cable (where fitted) as described in Section 3.

13 Engine management system components –
removal and refitting

Fuel rail and injectors

Note: *Refer to the warning note in Section 1 before proceeding.*

Note: *If a faulty injector is suspected, before condemning the injector, it is worth trying the effect of one of the proprietary injector-cleaning treatments which are available from car accessory shops.*

1 Slacken the retaining clips then free the duct from the throttle housing and air cleaner housing and remove it from the engine

12.5a Undo the three retaining screws (arrowed) . . .

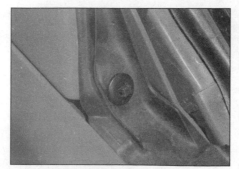

13.1a Push in the centre pins a little and prise out the rivets

12.4 Disconnect the wiring connectors from the throttle housing components

compartment. **Note:** *In order to improve access, remove the wiper blades and plastic scuttle trim. The trim is secured by plastic expanding rivets at each end – push in the centre pins a little, then prise out the complete rivet. Undo the two screws and move the master cylinder upper reservoir to one side. Release the sound insulation trim from the scuttle crossmember, undo the bolt at each end, and remove the crossmember from the vehicle (see illustrations).*

1.4 litre models

2 Remove the ignition HT coil as described in Chapter 5B.

3 Free the accelerator inner cable (where fitted) from the throttle housing cam, then pull the outer cable out from its mounting bracket rubber grommet, complete with its spring clip **(see illustration 3.1)**.

4 Unscrew the bolts and remove the

12.5b . . . then remove the throttle housing from the manifold and recover the sealing ring (1.4 litre engine)

13.1b Undo the screws (arrowed) and move the master cylinder reservoir to one side

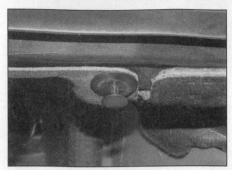

13.1c Prise up the centre pin and prise out the rivet securing the insulation material

13.1d The plastic crossmember is secured by a bolt at each end

13.5 Depress the retaining clip (arrowed) and disconnect the fuel hose from the fuel rail

accelerator cable bracket (where fitted) from the manifold/cylinder head.

5 Depress the retaining clip and disconnect the fuel pipe from the right-hand end of the fuel rail, bearing in mind the information given in Section 7 on depressurising the fuel system (see illustration).

6 Slacken and remove the two bolts securing the fuel rail to the cylinder head, and the nut securing the rail to the manifold. Loosen the bolt securing the fuel rail centre bracket to the inlet manifold, then lift off the bracket (the bracket is slotted to ease removal) (see illustrations).

7 Disconnect the injector wiring harness connector, then unclip the connector from the rear of the inlet manifold. Also disconnect the wiring connectors from the throttle housing and position the wiring harness clear of the manifold so that it does not hinder fuel rail removal.

8 Carefully ease the fuel rail and injector assembly out from the cylinder head and manoeuvre it out of position. Remove the seals from the end of each injector and discard them; they must be renewed whenever they are disturbed (see illustration).

9 Refitting is a reversal of the removal procedure, noting the following points.
  a) Fit new seals to all disturbed injector unions.
  b) Apply a smear of engine oil to the seals to aid installation, then ease the injectors and fuel rail into position ensuring that none of the seals are displaced.
  c) On completion, pressurise the fuel system as described in Section 7. Start the engine and check for fuel leaks.

1.6 litre models

10 Remove the inlet manifold as described in Section 14.

11 Undo the two bolts and remove the fuel rail with injectors from the manifold (see illustration).

12 Disconnect the wiring connector(s) then slide out the retaining clip(s) and remove the relevant injector(s) from the fuel rail. Remove the seals from each disturbed injector and discard; all disturbed seals must be renewed (see illustration).

13 Refitting is a reversal of the removal procedure, noting the following points.
  a) Fit new seals to all disturbed injector unions (see illustration).
  b) Apply a smear of engine oil to the seals to aid installation, then ease the injectors and fuel rail into position ensuring that none of the seals are displaced.
  c) On completion, pressurise the fuel system as described in Section 7. Start the engine and check for fuel leaks.

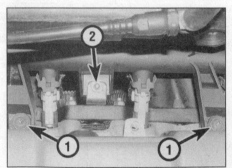

13.6a Unscrew the fuel rail mounting bolts (1) and the nut (2) . . .

13.6b . . . then slacken the bolt (arrowed) and lift off the centre bracket

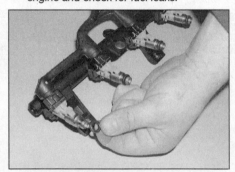

13.8 Remove the seal from the end of each injector

13.11 Undo the two bolts (arrowed) and remove the injectors and fuel rail from the manifold

13.12 Slide off the retaining clip and remove the injector from the fuel rail

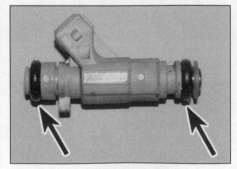

13.13 Renew all injector seals (arrowed) disturbed on removal

13.14 Undo the screws (arrowed) and remove the engine top cover

2.0 litre models

14 Unbolt and remove the engine top cover **(see illustration)**, then disconnect the air duct from between the air cleaner and throttle body.

15 Disconnect the wiring from the inlet air temperature sensor.

16 Unbolt the wiring tray from the top of the inlet manifold, and position to one side.

17 Depress the release button and disconnect the fuel supply hose from the fuel rail **(see illustration)**

18 Depress the retaining clip(s), and disconnect the wiring connector(s) from the injector(s) **(see illustration)**.

19 Unscrew the mounting bolts and carefully ease the fuel rail, complete with injectors, from the inlet manifold **(see illustration)**. Remove the O-rings from the end of each injector, and discard them; these must be renewed whenever they are disturbed.

20 Slide out the retaining clip(s) and remove the relevant injector(s) from the fuel rail. Remove the upper O-ring from each disturbed injector and discard; all disturbed O-rings must be renewed.

21 Refitting is a reversal of the removal procedure, noting the following points.

 a) *Fit new O-rings to all disturbed injector unions.*

 b) *Apply a smear of engine oil to the O-rings to aid installation then ease the injectors and fuel rail into position ensuring that none of the O-rings are displaced.*

 c) *On completion start the engine and check for fuel leaks.*

13.24 . . . then undo the retaining screws (arrowed) and remove it from the throttle housing (1.4 litre engine)

13.17 Depress the button (arrowed) and disconnect the fuel supply hose from the fuel rail

Fuel pressure regulator

22 The fuel pressure regulator is an integral part of the fuel pump assembly and is not available separately. Refer to Section 8 for removal and refitting details.

Throttle potentiometer

23 Depress the retaining clip and disconnect the wiring connector from the throttle potentiometer **(see illustration)**.

24 Slacken and remove the two retaining screws, then disengage the potentiometer from the throttle valve spindle and remove it from the vehicle **(see illustration)**.

25 Refit in the reverse order of removal.

26 Ensure that the potentiometer is correctly engaged with the throttle valve spindle.

Electronic Control Unit (ECU)

Note: *If a new ECU is being fitted, the vehicle*

13.19 Undo the fuel rail mounting bolts (arrowed)

13.28 Release the lever catches and disconnect the ECU wiring plugs

13.18 Release the clips and disconnect the injector wiring plugs (centre plugs arrowed)

will not start until the immobiliser ECU has been matched to the engine management ECU. This can only be performed using dedicated test equipment. Consequently, entrust the procedure to a Peugeot dealer or suitably-equipped specialist.

27 The ECU is located on the left-hand side of the engine compartment.

28 Remove the electrical box lid, and disconnect the wiring plugs **(see illustration)**.

29 The ECU lifts up from the electrical box **(see illustration)**.

30 Refitting is a reverse of the removal procedure ensuring the wiring connectors are securely reconnected.

Idle speed stepper motor

31 The idle speed stepper motor is fitted to the rear of the throttle housing.

32 Disconnect the wiring connector from the motor **(see illustration)**.

13.23 Disconnect the throttle potentiometer wiring plug . . .

13.29 Lift the ECU up from the electrical box

13.32 Disconnect the idle speed stepper motor wiring plug (arrowed) (1.4 litre engine)

33 Slacken and remove the retaining screws then remove the motor from the throttle housing **(see illustration)**. If necessary, remove the throttle potentiometer to improve access to the motor lower screw.

34 Refitting is a reversal of the removal procedure ensuring the seal is in good condition.

Manifold pressure sensor

35 The MAP sensor is mounted on the inlet manifold.

36 Disconnect the wiring connector then undo the screw and remove the sensor from the manifold **(see illustrations)**.

37 Refitting is a reversal of the removal procedure ensuring the sensor seal is in good condition.

Coolant temperature sensor

38 The coolant temperature sensor is screwed into the coolant outlet housing on the left-hand

end of the cylinder head. Refer to Chapter 3, Section 7, for removal and refitting information.

Intake air temperature sensor

39 The intake air temperature sensor is integral with the throttle housing and is not available separately.

Crankshaft position sensor

40 The crankshaft sensor is situated on the front face of the transmission clutch housing.

41 Disconnect the sensor wiring connector and unclip the wiring. Undo the retaining bolt and remove the sensor and bracket assembly from the transmission unit **(see illustrations)**.

42 Refitting is reverse of the removal procedure.

Throttle housing heating element

Note: *The heating element is only fitted to aluminium throttle housings. Plastic housings do not need a heater.*

43 The heating element is fitted to the top of the throttle housing.

44 Disconnect the wiring connector then unscrew the retaining screw and remove the heating element from the throttle housing **(see illustration)**.

45 Refitting is the reverse of removal.

Vehicle speed sensor

46 The vehicle speed sensor is an integral part of the speedometer drive on 1.4 litre TU engine models. Refer to Chapter 7A for removal and refitting details. On other models,

13.33 Undo the retaining screw(s) and remove the motor from the housing

the ECU receives vehicle speed data from the wheel speed sensors, via the ABS ECU.

Knock sensor

47 Refer to Chapter 5B.

Air conditioning pressure switch

48 The air conditioning pressure switch is fitted to the refrigerant pipe located on the right-hand side of the engine compartment. Switch renewal requires the air conditioning system to be discharged and drained (see Chapter 3).

Camshaft position sensor

49 The camshaft position sensor is located on the left-hand end of the exhaust camshaft cylinder head cover on 2.0 litre models only.

50 Rotate the 6 fasteners 90° anti-clockwise and remove the plastic cover from the top of the engine.

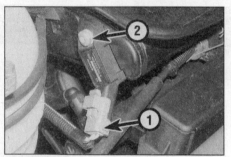

13.36a Disconnect the wiring connector (1) then undo the retaining screw (2) and remove the MAP sensor (1.4 litre engine) . . .

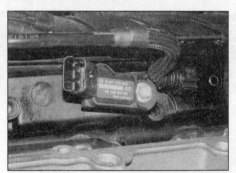

13.36b . . . 1.6 litre engine . . .

13.36c . . . and 2.0 litre engine

13.41a Disconnect the wiring plug then undo the retaining screw (arrowed) . . .

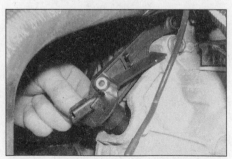

13.41b . . . then remove the crankshaft position sensor from the front of the transmission housing

13.44 Remove the throttle housing heating element (1.4 litre engine)

51 Disconnect the wiring plug, then undo the bolt and remove the sensor from the cylinder head cover **(see illustration)**.

52 Refitting is the reverse of removal ensuring the sensor seal is in good condition.

Throttle valve positioner motor

53 The throttle valve positioner motor (where fitted) is integral with the throttle body, and is not available separately.

Accelerator pedal position sensor

54 The sensor is integral with the accelerator pedal assembly – see Section 4.

14 Inlet manifold – removal and refitting

Removal

Note: *Refer to the warning note in Section 1 before proceeding.*

1.4 litre models

1 Remove the fuel rail and injectors as described in Section 13.

2 If not already done, disconnect the wiring connectors from the throttle housing components then unclip the harness and position it clear of the manifold

1.6 and 2.0 litre models

3 Remove the throttle housing as described in Section 12.

14.4c . . . and 2.0 litre engine (arrowed)

14.8c Withdraw the manifold (2.0 litre engine)

13.51 Camshaft position sensor (2.0 litre engine)

All models

4 Release the retaining clips and disconnect the vacuum servo unit pipe and purge valve pipe from the inlet manifold **(see illustration)**.

5 Disconnect all wiring connectors from the

14.4a Disconnect the vacuum servo pipe . . .

14.8a Inlet manifold nuts (arrowed) (1.4 litre engine)

14.9a Ensure new manifold seals are fitted (1.4 litre engine) . . .

manifold, having first noted their fitted positions. Release the wiring from any retaining clips.

6 Depress the release button and disconnect the fuel pipe and position it clear of the manifold.

7 Where necessary, undo the retaining bolts and remove the support bracket from the underside of the manifold.

8 Undo the manifold retaining nuts and withdraw the manifold from the engine compartment. Recover the four manifold seals and discard them; new ones must be used on refitting **(see illustrations)**.

Refitting

9 Refitting is a reverse of the relevant removal procedure, noting the following points:
   a) Ensure that the manifold and cylinder head mating surfaces are clean and dry, then locate the new seals in their recesses in the manifold **(see illustrations)**. Refit

14.4b . . . and purge valve pipe from the manifold (1.6 litre engine) . . .

14.8b Note the centre bracket (arrowed) fitted to the 1.6 litre engine

14.9b . . . 1.6 litre engine . . .

the manifold and tighten its retaining nuts to the specified torque.

b) Ensure that all relevant hoses are reconnected to their original positions and are securely held (where necessary) by the retaining clips.

c) Ensure the wiring is correctly routed and all connectors are securely reconnected.

d) Adjust the accelerator cable (where fitted) as described in Section 3.

15 Exhaust manifold – removal and refitting

Removal

1.4 and 1.6 litre models

1 Disconnect the battery, as described in Chapter 5A.

2 Slacken and remove the retaining screws and remove the shroud from the top of the exhaust manifold. It may be necessary to remove the engine lifting eye bracket from the left-hand end of the cylinder head, and undo the bolt and remove the oil dipstick tube **(see illustrations)**.

3 Firmly apply the handbrake, then jack up the front of the vehicle and support it on axle stands (see *Jacking and vehicle support*). Release the screws and remove the engine undershield (where fitted).

4 On some models, a second heat shield is fitted on the underside of the manifold, above the oil filter. Undo the bolts and remove the heat shield.

5 Trace the oxygen sensors wiring back to the connectors and disconnect them.

6 Undo the nuts securing the exhaust front pipe to the manifold, then remove the bolt securing the front pipe to its mounting bracket. Disconnect the front pipe from the manifold, and recover the gasket.

Caution: Do not place any strain on the flexible section of the exhaust front pipe (where fitted), it is easily damaged.

7 Undo the retaining nuts securing the manifold to the head. Manoeuvre the manifold out of the engine compartment, and discard the manifold gasket(s).

14.9c . . . and 2.0 litre engine

2.0 litre models

8 Rotate the 6 fasteners 90° anti-clockwise and remove the plastic cover from the top of the engine.

9 Remove the right-hand driveshaft as described in Chapter 8.

10 Undo the bolts and remove the heat shield from the exhaust manifold and right-hand driveshaft.

11 Undo the bolt and remove the exhaust pipe-to-manifold clamp.

12 Trace the oxygen sensors wiring back to the connectors and unplug them.

13 Release the exhaust system from its mounting points and lower the front pipe. Support the front pipe with a block of wood – do not let it hang unsupported.

14 Working underneath the vehicle, undo the bolts and remove the engine movement limiter link (see Chapter 2B).

15 Place a sheet of thick cardboard over the rear face of the radiator, and tilt the engine forward a little. Wedge it in this position using a block of wood.

16 Undo the manifold-to-cylinder head nuts, and manoeuvre the manifold from the vehicle. Discard the gasket.

Refitting

17 Refitting is the reverse of the removal procedure, noting the following points:

a) Examine all the exhaust manifold studs for signs of damage and corrosion; remove all traces of corrosion, and repair or renew any damaged studs.

b) Ensure that the manifold and cylinder

head sealing faces are clean and flat, and fit the new manifold gasket(s). Tighten the manifold retaining nuts to the specified torque.

c) Reconnect the front pipe to the manifold using the information given in Section 16.

d) Where necessary, renew the oil dipstick tube O-ring.

16 Exhaust system – general information, removal and refitting

General information

1 The exhaust system consists three sections; the front pipe with integral catalytic converter, the intermediate pipe, and rear silencer with tailpipe. On 1.4 and 1.6 litre models, the front pipe and intermediate pipe sections are joined by flanged joints. All other joints are secured by clamping rings.

2 The system is suspended throughout its entire length by rubber mountings.

3 Each exhaust section can be removed individually or, alternatively, the complete system can be removed as a unit. Even if only one part of the system needs attention, it is often easier to remove the whole system and separate the sections on the bench.

4 To remove the system or part of the system, first jack up the front or rear of the car and support it on axle stands (see *Jacking and vehicle support*). Alternatively, position the car over an inspection pit or on car ramps. Undo the screws and remove the engine undershield.

Front pipe removal

Note: *The catalytic converter is integral with the front pipe.*

5 Trace the wiring back from the oxygen sensors to their wiring connectors. Disconnect the connectors and free the wiring from all its clips and ties so the sensors are free to be removed with the front pipe. On 1.4 and 1.6 litre models, it is only necessary to disconnect the post-catalyst sensor.

1.4 and 1.6 litre models

6 Undo the bolts securing the transmission support bracket to the underside of the transmission casing.

7 Undo the nuts securing the front pipe flange joint to the manifold, and the single bolt securing the front pipe to its mounting bracket. Separate the flange joint and collect the gasket.

8 Slacken and remove the two nuts securing the front pipe flange joint to the intermediate pipe, and recover the spring cups and springs. Remove the bolts and collars, then withdraw the front pipe from underneath the vehicle. Recover the wire mesh gasket.

2.0 litre models

9 Undo the bolt and remove the front pipe-to-manifold clamp.

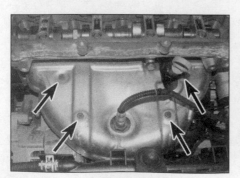

15.2a Undo the heat shield bolts (arrowed) . . .

15.2b . . . and the dipstick guide tube bolt

10 Undo the bolt and remove the front-to-intermediate pipe clamp. Manoeuvre the pipe/catalytic converter from the vehicle.

Intermediate pipe removal

1.4 and 1.6 litre models

11 Undo the two nuts securing the front pipe flange joint to the intermediate pipe. Recover the springs and spring cups, and withdraw the bolts and collars.

12 Slacken and remove the nut, washer and bolt from the intermediate pipe-to-rear silencer clamping ring and disengage the clamp from the joint.

13 Free the intermediate pipe and withdraw it from underneath the vehicle. Recover the wire mesh gasket from the front pipe joint.

2.0 litre models

14 Undo the clamp bolts at each end of the intermediate pipe.

15 Release the pipe from the rubber mounting, and manoeuvre the pipe from under the vehicle.

Tailpipe/rear silencer removal

16 Slacken the tailpipe/silencer-to-intermediate pipe clamp bolt.

17 Unhook the tailpipe/silencer from its mounting rubbers and remove it from the vehicle.

Complete system removal (minus front pipe)

18 On 1.4 and 1.6 litre models, undo the two nuts securing the front pipe flange joint to the intermediate pipe. Recover the springs and spring cups, and withdraw the bolts and collars.

19 On 2.0 litre models, slacken the front pipe-to-intermediate pipe clamp bolt.

20 Free the system from all its mounting rubbers and lower it from under the vehicle. On 1.4 and 1.6 litre models, recover the wire mesh gasket from the front pipe joint.

Heat shield(s) removal

21 The heat shields are secured to the underside of the body by various nuts and fasteners. If a shield is being removed to gain access to a component located behind it, remove the retaining nuts and/or fastener (unscrew the centre screw then pull out the complete fastener), and manoeuvre the shield out of position **(see illustration 10.8b)**. On some models it may be necessary to free the exhaust system from its mountings to gain the clearance necessary to remove the larger heat shield.

Refitting

22 Each section is refitted by reversing the removal sequence, noting the following points:

   a) *Ensure that all traces of corrosion have been removed from the flanges and renew all necessary gaskets.*

   b) *Inspect the rubber mountings for signs of damage or deterioration, and renew as necessary.*

   c) *Where joints are secured together by a clamping ring, apply a smear of exhaust system jointing paste to the flange joint to ensure a gas-tight seal. Insert the bolt through the clamping ring and fit the washer. Ensure the bolt and washer cut-outs are correctly engaged with the clamping ring then securely tighten the nut.*

   d) *Prior to tightening the exhaust system fasteners, ensure that all rubber mountings are correctly located, and that there is adequate clearance between the exhaust system and vehicle underbody.*

Notes

Chapter 4 Part B:
Fuel and exhaust systems – diesel models

Contents

Degrees of difficulty

Easy, suitable for novice with little experience	**Fairly easy,** suitable for beginner with some experience	**Fairly difficult,** suitable for competent DIY mechanic	**Difficult,** suitable for experienced DIY mechanic	**Very difficult,** suitable for expert DIY or professional

Specifications

Engine identification

Engine identification

Engine identification	Designation	Engine code
1.4 litre	DVTD	8HZ
1.6 litre	DV6ATED4	9HX
1.6 litre	DV6TED4	9HY and 9HZ
2.0 litre SOHC	DW10TD	RHY
2.0 litre SOHC	DW10ATED	RHZ and RHS
2.0 litre DOHC	DW10BTED4	RHR

General

System type . . . . HDi (High-pressure Diesel injection) with full electronic control, direct injection and turbocharger

Designation:
   1.4 litre . . . . Bosch EDC 16
   2.0 litre:
      SOHC . . . . Bosch EDC 15 C2
      DOHC . . . . Siemens SID 803
Firing order . . . . 1-3-4-2 (No 1 at flywheel end)
Fuel system operating pressure . . . . 200 to 1800 bars (according to engine speed)
Idle speed:
   1.4 litre . . . . 800 ± 20 rpm (controlled by ECU)
   2.0 litre . . . . 800 ± 20 rpm (controlled by ECU)
Engine cut-off speed:
   1.4 litre . . . . 5000 rpm (controlled by ECU)
   2.0 litre . . . . 5000 rpm (controlled by ECU)

High-pressure fuel pump

Type:
   1.4 litre CP3.2
   2.0 litre . . . . Bosch CP 1
Direction of rotation . . . . Clockwise, viewed from sprocket end

Injectors

Type . . . . Electromagnetic or Piezo

Turbocharger

Type:

1.4 litre	KKK
1.6 litre engine	Garrett GT1544V
2.0 litre engines:	
SOHC	Garrett GT15 or KKK K03
DOHC	Garrett GT1749V

Boost pressure (approximate):

1.4 and 1.6 litre engine	0.9 bar @ 3500 rpm
2.0 litre engines:	
SOHC	1.2 bar @ 3000 rpm
DOHC	1.0 bar @ 4000 rpm

Torque wrench settings

	Nm	lbf ft
Accumulator rail mounting bolts	23	17
Accumulator rail-to-fuel injector fuel pipe unions*:		
1.4 litre engine:		
Stage 1	17	13
Stage 2	22	16
1.6 and 2.0 litre engines:		
Injector end union:		
Stage 1	25	18
Stage 2	27	20
Rail end union:		
Stage 1	24	18
Stage 2	26	19
Camshaft position sensor bolt	5	4
Clamping ring nuts	20	15
Crankshaft speed/position sensor	5	4
Exhaust manifold nuts	20	15
Exhaust system fasteners:		
Catalytic converter-to-manifold nuts	40	30
Clamping ring nuts	20	15
Fuel injector clamp bolt:		
1.4 litre engine	20	15
1.6 litre engine:		
Stage 1	4	3
Stage 2	Angle-tighten a further 65°	
2.0 litre engines:		
SOHC	30	22
DOHC:		
Stage 1	4	3
Stage 2	Angle-tighten a further 65°	
Fuel injector clamp stud	7	5
Fuel pressure sensor to accumulator rail	45	33
Fuel pump-to-accumulator rail fuel pipe unions*:		
1.4 litre engine:		
Stage 1	17	13
Stage 2	22	16
1.6 litre engine	25	18
2.0 litre engines:		
SOHC	20	15
DOHC	25	18
High-pressure fuel pump mounting bolts		
1.4 litre engine	25	18
1.6 litre engine	23	17
2.0 litre engines	20	15
High-pressure fuel pump rear mounting bolts/nut (8 mm)	17	13
High-pressure fuel pump sprocket nut	50	37
Inlet manifold bolts	10	7
Turbocharger mounting bolts/nuts	25	18
Turbocharger oil feed pipe banjo bolts:		
1.4 litre and 2.0 litre SOHC engines	25	18
1.6 litre engine	30	20
2.0 litre DOHC engine:		
Engine pipe to cylinder block	40	30
All other connections	25	18

* These torque settings are using Peugeot crow-foot adapters – see Section 2

1 General information and system operation

The fuel system consists of a rear-mounted fuel tank and fuel lift pump, a fuel filter with integral water separator, on some models a fuel cooler mounted under the car, and an electronically-controlled High-pressure Diesel injection (HDi) system, together with a turbocharger.

The exhaust system is conventional, but to meet the latest emission levels an unregulated catalytic converter and an exhaust gas recirculation system are fitted to all models. On some 1.6 and 2.0 litre models, an exhaust emission particulate filter is fitted – refer to Chapter 4C for further details.

The HDi system (generally known as a 'common rail' system) derives its name from the fact that a common rail (referred to as an accumulator rail), or fuel reservoir, is used to supply fuel to all the fuel injectors. Instead of an in-line or distributor type injection pump, which distributes the fuel directly to each injector, a high-pressure pump is used, which generates a very high fuel pressure (1350 bars at high engine speed) in the accumulator rail. The accumulator rail stores fuel, and maintains a constant fuel pressure, with the aid of a pressure control valve. Each injector is supplied with high-pressure fuel from the accumulator rail, and the injectors are individually controlled via signals from the system electronic control unit (ECU). The injectors are electronically-operated.

In addition to the various sensors used on models with a conventional fuel injection pump, common rail systems also have a fuel pressure sensor. The fuel pressure sensor allows the ECU to maintain the required fuel pressure, via the pressure control valve.

System operation

For the purposes of describing the operation of a common rail injection system, the components can be divided into three sub-systems; the low-pressure fuel system, the high-pressure fuel system and the electronic control system.

Low-pressure fuel system

The low-pressure fuel system consists of the following components:
a) Fuel tank.
b) Fuel lift pump.
c) Fuel cooler (not all models).
d) Fuel heater (not all models).
e) Fuel filter/water trap.
f) Low-pressure fuel lines.

The low-pressure system (fuel supply system) is responsible for supplying clean fuel to the high-pressure fuel system.

High-pressure fuel system

The high-pressure fuel system consists of the following components:
a) High-pressure fuel pump with pressure control valve.
b) High-pressure fuel accumulator rail.
c) Fuel injectors.
d) High-pressure fuel lines.

After passing through the fuel filter, the fuel reaches the high-pressure pump, which forces it into the accumulator rail. As diesel fuel has a certain elasticity, the pressure in the accumulator rail remains constant, even though fuel leaves the rail each time one of the injectors operates. Additionally, a pressure control valve mounted on the high-pressure pump ensures that the fuel pressure is maintained within preset limits.

The pressure control valve is operated by the ECU. When the valve is opened, fuel is returned from the high-pressure pump to the tank, via the fuel return lines, and the pressure in the accumulator rail falls. To enable the ECU to trigger the pressure control valve correctly, the pressure in the accumulator rail is measured by a fuel pressure sensor.

The electronically-controlled fuel injectors are operated individually, via signals from the ECU, and each injector injects fuel directly into the relevant combustion chamber. The fact that high fuel pressure is always available allows very precise and highly flexible injection in comparison to a conventional injection pump: for example combustion during the main injection process can be improved considerably by the pre-injection of a very small quantity of fuel.

Electronic control system

The electronic control system consists of the following components:
a) Electronic control unit (ECU).
b) Crankshaft speed/position sensor.
c) Camshaft position sensor.
d) Accelerator pedal position sensor.
e) Coolant temperature sensor.
f) Fuel temperature sensor.
g) Air mass meter.
h) Fuel pressure sensor.
i) Fuel injectors.
j) Fuel pressure control valve.
k) Preheating control unit.
l) EGR solenoid valve.
m) Air temperature sensor
n) Atmospheric pressure sensor – integral with the ECU (DV6TED4, DW10ATED and DW10BTED4 engines only).
o) Inlet manifold pressure sensor (DV6TED4 and DW10BTED4 engines only).

The information from the various sensors is passed to the ECU, which evaluates the signals. The ECU contains electronic 'maps' which enable it to calculate the optimum quantity of fuel to inject, the appropriate start of injection, and even pre- and post-injection fuel quantities, for each individual engine cylinder under any given condition of engine operation.

Additionally, the ECU carries out monitoring and self-diagnostic functions. Any faults in the system are stored in the ECU memory, which enables quick and accurate fault diagnosis using appropriate diagnostic equipment (such as a suitable fault code reader).

System components

Fuel lift pump

The fuel lift pump (2.0 litre models with particulate filter only) and integral fuel gauge sender unit is electrically-operated, and is mounted in the fuel tank.

High-pressure pump

The high-pressure pump is mounted on the engine in the position normally occupied by the conventional distributor fuel injection pump. The pump is driven at half engine speed by the timing belt, and is lubricated by the fuel which it pumps.

The fuel lift pump forces the fuel into the high-pressure pump chamber, via a safety valve.

The high-pressure pump consists of three radially-mounted pistons and cylinders. The pistons are operated by an eccentric cam mounted on the pump drive spindle. As a piston moves down, fuel enters the cylinder through an inlet valve. When the piston reaches bottom dead centre (BDC), the inlet valve closes, and as the piston moves back up the cylinder, the fuel is compressed. When the pressure in the cylinder reaches the pressure in the accumulator rail, an outlet valve opens, and fuel is forced into the accumulator rail. When the piston reaches top dead centre (TDC), the outlet valve closes, due to the pressure drop, and the pumping cycle is repeated. The use of multiple cylinders provides a steady flow of fuel, minimising pulses and pressure fluctuations.

As the pump needs to be able to supply sufficient fuel under full-load conditions, it will supply excess fuel during idle and part-load conditions. This excess fuel is returned from the high-pressure circuit to the low-pressure circuit (to the tank) via the pressure control valve.

The pump incorporates a facility to effectively switch off one of the cylinders to improve efficiency and reduce fuel consumption when maximum pumping capacity is not required. When this facility is operated, a solenoid-operated needle holds the inlet valve in the relevant cylinder open during the delivery stroke, preventing the fuel from being compressed.

Accumulator rail

As its name suggests, the accumulator rail (also known as common rail) acts as an accumulator, storing fuel and preventing pressure fluctuations. Fuel enters the rail from the high-pressure pump, and each injector has its own connection to the rail. The fuel pressure sensor is mounted in the rail, and the rail also has a connection to the fuel pressure control valve on the pump.

Pressure control valve

The pressure control valve is operated by the ECU, and controls the system pressure.

The valve is integral with the high-pressure pump and cannot be separated.

If the fuel pressure is excessive, the valve opens, and fuel flows back to the tank. If the pressure is too low, the valve closes, enabling the high-pressure pump to increase the pressure.

The valve is an electronically-operated ball valve. The ball is forced against its seat, against the fuel pressure, by a powerful spring, and also by the force provided by the electromagnet. The force generated by the electromagnet is directly proportional to the current applied to it by the ECU. The desired pressure can therefore be set by varying the current applied to the electromagnet. Any pressure fluctuations are damped by the spring.

Fuel pressure sensor

The fuel pressure sensor is mounted in the accumulator rail, and provides very precise information on the fuel pressure to the ECU.

Fuel injector

The injectors are mounted on the engine in a similar manner to conventional diesel fuel injectors. The injectors are electronically-operated via signals from the ECU, and fuel is injected at the pressure existing in the accumulator rail. The injectors are high-precision instruments and are manufactured to very high tolerances.

Fuel flows into the injector from the accumulator rail, via an inlet valve and an inlet throttle, and an electromagnet causes the injector nozzle to lift from its seat, allowing injection. Excess fuel is returned from the injectors to the tank via a return line. The injector operates on a hydraulic servo principle: the forces resulting inside the injector due to the fuel pressure effectively amplify the effects of the electromagnet, which does not provide sufficient force to open the injector nozzle directly. The injector functions as follows. Five separate forces are essential to the operation of the injector.

a) *A nozzle spring forces the nozzle needle against the nozzle seat at the bottom of the injector, preventing fuel from entering the combustion chamber.*

b) *In the valve at the top of the injector, the valve spring forces the valve ball against the opening to the valve control chamber. The fuel in the chamber is unable to escape through the fuel return.*

c) *When triggered, the electromagnet exerts a force which overcomes the valve spring force, and moves the valve ball away from its seat. This is the triggering force for the start of injection. When the valve ball moves off its seat, fuel enters the valve control chamber.*

d) *The pressure of the fuel in the valve control chamber exerts a force on the valve control plunger, which is added to the nozzle spring force.*

e) *A slight chamfer towards the lower end of the nozzle needle causes the fuel in the*

control chamber to exert a force on the nozzle needle.

When these forces are in equilibrium, the injector is in its rest (idle) state, but when a voltage is applied to the electromagnet, the forces work to lift the nozzle needle, injecting fuel into the combustion chamber. There are four phases of injector operation as follows:

a) *Rest (idle) state – all forces are in equilibrium. The nozzle needle closes off the nozzle opening, and the valve spring forces the valve ball against its seat.*

b) *Opening – the electromagnet is triggered which opens the nozzle and triggers the injection process. The force from the electromagnet allows the valve ball to leave its seat. The fuel from the valve control chamber flows back to the tank via the fuel return line. When the valve opens, the pressure in the valve control chamber drops, and the force on the valve plunger is reduced. However, due to the effect of the input throttle, the pressure on the nozzle needle remains unchanged. The resulting force in the valve control chamber is sufficient to lift the nozzle from its seat, and the injection process begins.*

c) *Injection – within a few milliseconds, the triggering current in the electromagnet is reduced to a lower holding current. The nozzle is now fully open, and fuel is injected into the combustion chamber at the pressure present in the accumulator rail.*

d) *Closing – the electromagnet is switched off, at which point the valve spring forces the valve ball firmly against its seat, and in the valve control chamber, the pressure is the same as that at the nozzle needle. The force at the valve plunger increases, and the nozzle needle closes the nozzle opening. The forces are now in equilibrium once more, and the injector is once more in the idle state, awaiting the next injection sequence.*

ECU and sensors

The ECU and sensors are described earlier in this Section – see *Electronic control system*.

Air inlet sensor and turbocharger

An airflow sensor is fitted downstream of the air filter to monitor the quantity of air supplied to the turbocharger. On 1.6 and 2.0 litre models, air from the high-pressure side of the turbocharger is either channelled through the intercooler, or into the manifold without being intercooled, depending on the air temperature (see illustration 4.27). The flow and routing of intake air is controlled by the engine management ECU. On these models, an engine coolant-heated matrix is fitted to the base of the air cleaner housing, to warm the incoming air, which decreases harmful exhaust emissions.

The turbochargers are of the fixed-geometry type on 2.0 litre SOHC models, and variable nozzle geometry type on other models.

2 High-pressure diesel injection system – special information

Warnings and precautions

1 It is essential to observe strict precautions when working on the fuel system components, particularly the high-pressure side of the system. Before carrying out any operations on the fuel system, refer to the precautions given in *Safety first!* at the beginning of this manual, and to the following additional information.

• Do not carry out any repair work on the high-pressure fuel system unless you are competent to do so, have all the necessary tools and equipment required, and are aware of the safety implications involved.

• Before starting any repair work on the fuel system, wait at least 30 seconds after switching off the engine to allow the fuel circuit pressure to reduce.

• Never work on the high-pressure fuel system with the engine running.

• Keep well clear of any possible source of fuel leakage, particularly when starting the engine after carrying out repair work. A leak in the system could cause an extremely high-pressure jet of fuel to escape, which could result in severe personal injury.

• Never place your hands or any part of your body near to a leak in the high-pressure fuel system.

• Do not use steam cleaning equipment or compressed air to clean the engine or any of the fuel system components.

Procedures and information

2 Strict cleanliness must be observed at all times when working on any part of the fuel system. This applies to the working area in general, the person doing the work, and the components being worked on.

3 Before working on the fuel system components, they must be thoroughly cleaned with a suitable degreasing fluid. Specific cleaning products may be obtained from Peugeot dealers. Alternatively, a suitable brake cleaning fluid may be used. Cleanliness is particularly important when working on the fuel system connections at the following components:

a) *Fuel filter.*
b) *High-pressure fuel pump.*
c) *Accumulator rail.*
d) *Fuel injectors.*
e) *High-pressure fuel pipes.*

4 After disconnecting any fuel pipes or components, the open union or orifice must be immediately sealed to prevent the entry of dirt or foreign material. Plastic plugs and caps in various sizes are available in packs from motor factors and accessory outlets, and are particularly suitable for this application

2.4 Typical plastic plug and cap set for sealing disconnected fuel pipes and components

2.7 Two crow-foot adapters will be necessary for tightening the fuel pipe unions

3.1 Operate the hand priming pump until fuel clear of bubbles appears in the fuel pipe (arrowed) (1.4 litre engine)

3.2 Attach a hose to the filter outlet and bleed the fuel into a container

(see illustration). Fingers cut from disposable rubber gloves should be used to protect components such as fuel pipes, fuel injectors and wiring connectors, and can be secured in place using elastic bands. Suitable gloves of this type are available at no cost from most petrol station forecourts.

5 Whenever any of the high-pressure fuel pipes are disconnected or removed, new pipes must be obtained for refitting.

6 On the completion of any repair on the high-pressure fuel system, Peugeot recommend the use of a leak-detecting compound. This is a powder which is applied to the fuel pipe unions and connections and turns white when dry. Any leak in the system will cause the product to darken indicating the source of the leak.

7 The torque wrench settings given in the Specifications must be strictly observed when tightening component mountings and connections. This is particularly important when tightening the high-pressure fuel pipe unions. To enable a torque wrench to be used on the fuel pipe unions, two Peugeot crow-foot adapters are required. Suitable alternatives are available from motor factors and accessory outlets (see illustration).

3 Fuel system – priming and bleeding

1 Should the fuel supply system be disconnected between the fuel tank and high-pressure pump, it is necessary to prime

the fuel system. This is achieved by operating the hand priming pump (where fitted) until resistance is felt (1.6 and 2.0 litre models) or fuel appears in the transparent fuel supply pipe in the engine compartment (1.4 litre models) (see illustration). Remove the plastic cover from the top of the engine to access the priming pump.

2 Note that where a hand priming pump is not fitted, priming is achieved by connecting a suitable hose (if necessary, a special Peugeot hose No 444-T may be available) from the fuel filter outlet pipe to the fuel return pipe and forcing fuel through the filter, into the return system. If the suitable hose is not available, it will suffice to connect a length of hose to the filter outlet, with the other end of the hose in a suitable container (see illustration). The method of forcing the fuel through differs according to engine type:

DV6TED4 and DV6ATED4 – Operate the hand priming pump for approximately 2 minutes.

DW10TD – Operate the hand priming pump for approximately 2 minutes.

DW10ATED – Turn the ignition key to the ON position, allow the tank-mounted fuel pump to operate (it will only operate momentarily), then turn it off. Repeat a total of 10 times, then remove the by-pass hose, reconnect the normal fuel hoses, and turn the ignition key to the ON position. Allow the pump to operate, and turn the key OFF. Repeat the key ON-OFF procedure once more.

DW10BTED4 – Operate the hand priming pump for approximately 1 minute.

3 With the system primed, reconnect the hoses, then operate the starter until the engine starts.

4 Air cleaner assembly and inlet ducts – removal and refitting

Air cleaner and inlet ducts removal

1.4 litre models

1 Pull the plastic engine cover up and remove it.

2 Slacken the turbocharger inlet hose clip, and release the diesel priming bulb from its brackets at the right-hand end of the housing.

3 Slacken the clip securing the turbo outlet hose, undo the bolt securing the resonator box, and the bolt securing the resonator box to the turbocharger, swivel the box up and remove it (see illustrations). Note: *In order*

4.3a Slacken the clip and disconnect the turbo outlet hose (arrowed) . . .

4.3b . . . then undo the retaining bolts (arrowed) . . .

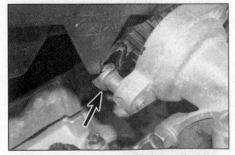

4.3c . . . pivot the right-hand end of the box up and disengage it from the turbo outlet stud (arrowed)

4.4a Undo the two air cleaner housing screws (arrowed)

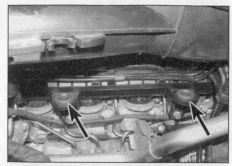

4.4b The rear of the air cleaner housing locates in two rubber mountings (arrowed)

4.5 Push in the centre pin, then prise the complete plastic rivet (arrowed) from place, and remove the air inlet ducting

to improve access, remove the wiper blades and plastic scuttle trim. The trim is secured by plastic expanding rivets at each end – push in the centre pins a little, then prise out the complete rivets. Release the sound insulation trim from the scuttle crossmember, undo the bolt at each end, and remove the crossmember from the vehicle (see illustrations 14.3a, 14.3b and 14.3c).

4 Undo the two screws and remove the air cleaner housing, disconnecting any wiring plugs as necessary as the housing is withdrawn (see illustrations).

5 To remove the air inlet ducting, slacken the retaining clips and remove the relevant section of ducting. The air ducting in the left-hand front corner of the engine compartment is retained by a plastic expansion rivet. Push down the centre pin then pull the entire rivet from place (see illustration). The air deflector in the left-hand front corner of the engine

compartment simply lifts from place and, upon refitting, locates over a clip on the front of the electrical box. The ducting at the rear of the engine is only accessible once the battery tray has been removed (see Chapter 5A).

1.6 litre models

6 Remove the windscreen wiper arms (Chapter 12), then unclip the plastic scuttle panel. The trim is secured by plastic expanding rivets at each end – push in the centre pins a little, then prise out the complete rivets. Pull up the ends of the panel to release it from the windscreen clips, the pull the centre of the panel down to release it from the centre windscreen clip. Undo the two bolts securing the brake/clutch master cylinder upper reservoir and move it to one side. Release the sound insulation trim from the scuttle crossmember, undo the bolt at each end, and remove the crossmember from the vehicle.

7 Undo the screw and remove the air inlet ducting from the front of the engine compartment to the air filter housing (see illustration).

8 Undo the two screws securing the air filter cover to the housing, disconnect the mass airflow sensor wiring plug, slacken the clamp securing the air inlet ducting to the turbocharger, release the clips securing the breather tube to the cylinder head cover, then manoeuvre the inlet ducting/filter cover assembly from position (see illustrations).

9 Pull the air filter housing upwards from the rubber mounting grommets.

2.0 litre models

10 Undo the four fasteners and lift off the engine cover (see illustration).

11 Disconnect the air mass meter wiring plug.

12 Slacken the retaining clips and disconnect

4.7 Undo the screw (arrowed) and remove the inlet duct

4.8a Undo the air filter cover screws (arrowed) . . .

4.8b . . . disconnect the turbocharger inlet duct . . .

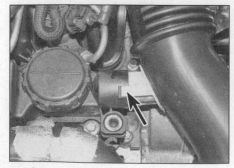

4.8c . . . release the clip (arrowed) and disconnect the breather . . .

4.8d . . . then remove the cover/duct assembly

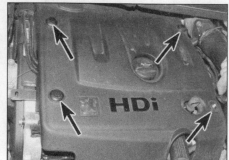

4.10 Undo the fasteners (arrowed) and remove the plastic engine cover

4.12 Slacken the clip (arrowed) and disconnect the flexible ducting from the air mass meter

4.15 Undo the five screws (arrowed) securing the heater matrix into the air cleaner housing

4.16 Depress the clip (arrowed) and slide the housing up from the bracket

the flexible air inlet duct from the air mass meter **(see illustration)**.

13 Where fitted, disconnect the wiring plug from the accelerator pedal position sensor, adjacent to the air cleaner housing.

14 Rotate the accelerator pedal position sensor quadrant, and release the inner cable from the quadrant.

15 On intercooled models (DW10ATED), disconnect the water valve wiring plug, then undo the five screws securing the valve and heater matrix to the air cleaner housing **(see illustration)**.

16 Release the retaining clip, then lift up the housing. Where fitted, slide the heater matrix out from the housing, and disconnect the water drain hose **(see illustration)**.

17 To remove the air cleaner air inlet duct, depress the retaining lug and slide the duct from the bracket **(see illustration)**.

18 Remove the front bumper as described in Chapter 11.

19 Push in the centre pins a little, then prise out the complete plastic rivets securing the inlet ducting to the bumper bar.

20 Manoeuvre the ducting from the engine compartment.

Intake air resonator removal

1.4 litre models

21 To remove the resonator, pull up and remove the plastic cover from the top of the engine, then make a note of its fitted position, and slacken the outlet ducting clamp. It must be refitted into its original position.

4.17 Depress the lug (arrowed) and slide the duct from the bracket

22 Undo the bolt securing the resonator box, and the bolt securing the turbocharger outlet pipe to the box **(see illustrations 4.3a, 4.3b and 4.3c)**.

23 Lift up the right-hand end of the ducting, and remove the box and ducting from position.

Turbocharger ducting removal

Note: For 1.4 and 1.6 litre models, see Air cleaner and inlet ducts removal.

2.0 litre models

24 On 2.0 litre engines, the rigid ducts at the rear of the engine, connecting the turbocharger to the air inlet duct and to the inlet manifold are inaccessible with the engine in the car. To gain access it will be necessary to remove the front suspension subframe as described in Chapter 10.

25 Once access has been gained, undo the bolt securing the duct to the inlet manifold elbow.

26 At the lower end, undo the bolt securing the duct to the turbocharger. Lift off the duct and recover the seal from the lower end.

27 On DW10TD (non-intercooled) engines, to remove the turbocharger-to-inlet manifold rigid plastic duct, slacken the clamps, and release the connecting hose from the inlet manifold elbow. Slacken the clip securing the connecting hose at the lower end of the duct to the turbocharger. Release the attachment strap from the lug on the turbocharger and withdraw the duct from the engine **(see illustration)**.

28 On DW10ATED engines, the intake air exits the turbocharger and enters an intermediate manifold, where the air flows though the non-intercooled or intercooled route **(see**

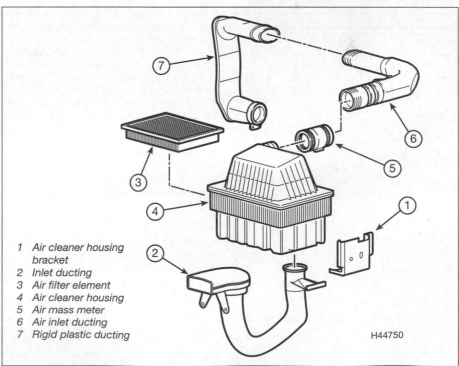

1 Air cleaner housing bracket
2 Inlet ducting
3 Air filter element
4 Air cleaner housing
5 Air mass meter
6 Air inlet ducting
7 Rigid plastic ducting

H44750

4.27 Air inlet ducting (non-intercooled, 2.0 litre DW10TD engine)

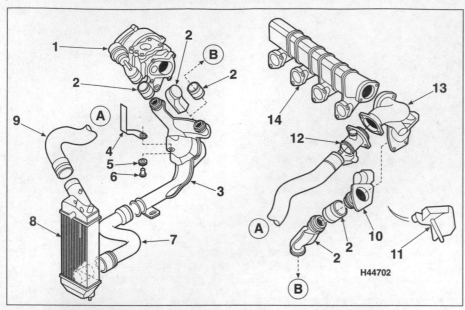

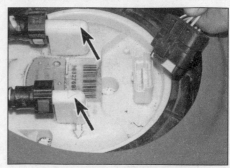

7.1 The arrows on the pump cover indicate supply and return (arrowed)

4.28 Turbocharger-to-manifold air ducting (2.0 litre DW10ATED engine)

1	Turbocharger	5	Grommet
2	Connecting piece	6	Sleeve
3	Intermediate manifold	7	Ducting
		8	Intercooler
4	Support bracket	9	Ducting
10	Valve housing		
11	Heat shield		
12	Valve housing		
13	Intake elbow		
14	Intake manifold		

illustration). To remove this intermediate manifold, jack up the front of the vehicle and support it on axle stands (see *Jacking and vehicle support*). Undo the screws and remove the engine undershield.

29 Slacken the clamps securing the intake ducting to the intermediate manifold, undo the bolt and manoeuvre the assembly from position.

30 The remaining ducting is secured by hose clamps. Prior to removing any ducting, note the fitted positions of any vacuum hoses or electrical wiring/connections to aid refitting.

Refitting

31 Refitting is a reverse of the removal procedure. Examine the condition of the seals and retaining clips and renew if necessary.

32 Where applicable, refit the front suspension subframe as described in Chapter 10.

33 Where necessary, reconnect and adjust the accelerator cable as described in Section 5.

5 Accelerator cable – removal, refitting and adjustment

Note: *The accelerator cable is only fitted to some 2.0 litre models*

Removal

1 Undo the four fasteners and lift off the engine cover.

2 Rotate the accelerator pedal position sensor quadrant, and release the inner cable from the quadrant.

3 Withdraw the outer cable from the grommet in the pedal position sensor body, recover the flat washer from the end of the cable and remove the spring clip.

4 Release the cable from the remaining clips and brackets in the engine compartment, noting its routing.

5 Working in the passenger compartment, reach up under the facia, depress the ends of the cable end fitting, and detach the inner cable from the top of the accelerator pedal.

6 Release the outer cable grommet from the pedal mounting bracket, then tie a length of string to the end of the cable.

7 Return to the engine compartment, release the cable grommet from the bulkhead and withdraw the cable. When the end of the cable appears, untie the string and leave it in position – it can then be used to draw the cable back into position on refitting.

Refitting

8 Refitting is a reversal of removal, but ensure that the cable is routed as noted before removal and, on completion, adjust the cable as follows.

Adjustment

9 Remove the spring clip from the accelerator outer cable. Ensuring that the pedal position sensor quadrant is against its stop, gently pull the cable out of its grommet until all free play is removed from the inner cable.

10 With the cable held in this position, refit the spring clip to the last exposed outer cable groove in front of the rubber grommet and washer. When the clip is refitted and the outer cable is released, there should be only a small amount of free play in the inner cable.

11 Have an assistant depress the accelerator pedal, and check that the pedal position sensor quadrant opens fully and returns smoothly to its stop.

12 Refit the engine cover on completion.

6 Accelerator pedal – removal and refitting

Refer to Chapter 4A.

7 Fuel lift pump – removal and refitting

The diesel fuel lift pump is located in the same position as the conventional fuel pump on petrol models, and the removal and refitting procedures are virtually identical (**see illustration**). Refer to Chapter 4A. **Note:** *No lift pump is fitted to the 1.4 litre engine, but the fuel gauge sender unit is located in the fuel tank – the same position as other models.*

8 Fuel gauge sender unit – removal and refitting

The fuel gauge sender unit is integral with the fuel lift pump. Refer to Section 7.

9 Fuel tank and cooler – removal and refitting

Fuel tank

Refer to Chapter 4A.

Fuel cooler

Removal

1 The fuel cooler is located under the right-hand side of the vehicle. Jack up the rear of the vehicle, and support it on axle stands (see *Jacking and vehicle support*).

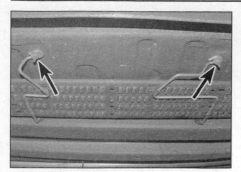

9.2 Undo the two nuts (arrowed) securing the fuel cooler

2 Working underneath the vehicle, undo the two retaining nuts, and release the cooler from the locating holes **(see illustration)**.

3 Depress the release buttons and disconnect the fuel feed and return hoses from the cooler. Be prepared for fuel spillage, and plug the hose and cooler openings to prevent dirt ingress **(see illustration)**.

Refitting

4 Refitting is a reversal of removal,

10 High-pressure fuel pump – removal and refitting

> ⚠️ **Warning: Refer to the information contained in Section 2 before proceeding.**

10.3 Depress the release buttons (arrowed) and disconnect the fuel supply and return hoses from the pump

10.6 Counterhold the pump union with a second spanner whilst slackening the accumulator-to-pump pipe union

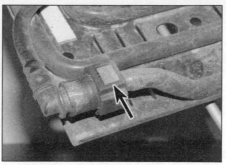

9.3 Depress the release button (arrowed) and disconnect the hose

Note: *A new fuel pump-to-accumulator rail high-pressure fuel pipe will be required for refitting.*

Removal

1.4 litre SOHC engine

1 Disconnect the battery (see Chapter 5A) and remove the timing belt as described in Chapter 2C. After removal of the timing belt, temporarily refit the right-hand engine mounting but do not fully tighten the bolts.

2 Remove the cylinder head cover/air filter housing as described in Chapter 2C.

3 Depress the clip buttons and disconnect the fuel supply and return hoses from the pump **(see illustration)**. Plug the end of the hoses to prevent dirt ingress.

4 Hold the pump sprocket stationary, and

10.4 Stop the fuel pump sprocket from rotating by inserting an 8 mm drill bit or pin through the sprocket into the backplate

10.8a Undo the pump rear support bracket bolts/nut (arrowed) . . .

loosen the centre nut securing it to the pump shaft. The manufacturers recommend using an 8 mm pin inserted through the pulley and into the pump support **(see illustration)**.

5 The fuel pump sprocket is a taper fit on the pump shaft and it will be necessary to make up a tool to release it from the taper **(see Tool Tip 1)**. Partially unscrew the sprocket retaining nut, fit the home-made tool, and secure it to the sprocket with two 7.0 mm bolts and nuts. Prevent the sprocket from rotating as before, and screw down the nuts, forcing the sprocket off the shaft taper. Once the taper is released, remove the tool, unscrew the nut fully, and remove the sprocket from the pump shaft.

6 Undo the unions and remove the pump-to-accumulator rail metal pipe. Counterhold the pump union with a second spanner – the union screwed into the pump must not be allowed to unscrew **(see illustration)**. Discard the pipe, a new one must be fitted.

7 Disconnect the wiring plugs from the pump, noting their fitted positions.

8 Undo the nuts/bolts and remove the pump support bracket from the rear of the pump, and the bracket on the cylinder head **(see illustrations)**.

9 Remove the EGR valve with reference to Chapter 4C.

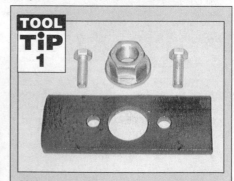

TOOL TiP 1

Make a sprocket releasing tool from a short strip of steel. Drill two holes in the strip to correspond with the two holes in the sprocket. Drill a third hole just large enough to accept the flats of the sprocket retaining nut.

10.8b . . . and the bolts securing the bracket to the cylinder head

10.10 Unscrew the three bolts (arrowed) and remove the pump

10.14a Remove the air filter support bracket (arrowed) . . .

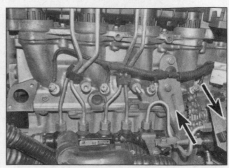

10.14b . . . and the brackets around the fuel pump (arrowed)

TOOL TiP 2

A sprocket holding tool can be made from two lengths of steel strip bolted together to form a forked end. Bend the ends of the strip through 90° to form the fork 'prongs'.

10 Undo the three bolts, and remove the pump **(see illustration)**.

Caution: The high-pressure fuel pump is manufactured to extremely close tolerances and must not be dismantled in any way. Do not unscrew the fuel pipe male union on the rear of the pump, or attempt to remove the sensor, piston de-activator switch, or the seal on the pump shaft. No parts for the pump are available separately and if the unit is in any way suspect, it must be renewed.

1.6 litre DOHC engine

11 Disconnect the battery (see Chapter 5A) and remove the timing belt as described in Chapter 2D. After removal of the timing belt, temporarily refit the right-hand engine mounting but do not fully tighten the bolts.

12 Remove the air filter assembly as described in Section 4.

13 Remove the EGR cooler as described in Chapter 4C.

14 Undo the bolts/nuts and remove the 3 support brackets above the fuel accumulator rail and the high-pressure pump **(see illustrations)**.

15 Undo the union nuts and remove the high-pressure fuel pipe between the fuel accumulator rail and the high-pressure pump. Plug the openings to prevent contamination.

16 Disconnect the wiring plug from the high-pressure fuel pump.

17 Depress the release buttons and disconnect the fuel supply and return hoses from the pump. Note that the hoses may have a release button on each side of the fitting. Plug the openings to prevent contamination.

18 Hold the pump sprocket stationary, and loosen the centre nut securing it to the pump shaft **(see Tool Tip 1)**.

19 The fuel pump sprocket is a taper fit on the pump shaft and it will be necessary to make up a tool to release it from the taper **(see Tool Tip 2)**. Partially unscrew the sprocket retaining nut, fit the home-made tool, and secure it to the sprocket with two 7.0 mm bolts and nuts. Prevent the sprocket from rotating as before, and screw down the nuts, forcing the sprocket off the shaft taper. Once the taper is released, remove the tool, unscrew the nut fully, and remove the sprocket from the pump shaft.

20 Undo the three bolts, and remove the pump from the mounting bracket.

Caution: The high-pressure fuel pump is manufactured to extremely close tolerances and must not be dismantled in any way. Do not unscrew the fuel pipe male union on the rear of the pump, or attempt to remove the sensor, piston de-activator switch, or the seal on the pump shaft. No parts for the pump are available separately and if the unit is in any way suspect, it must be renewed.

2.0 litre SOHC engine

21 Disconnect the battery (see Chapter 5A) and remove the timing belt as described in Chapter 2C. After removal of the timing belt, temporarily refit the right-hand engine mounting but do not fully tighten the bolts.

22 Undo the bolts securing the plastic wiring harness guide to the front of the engine **(see illustration)**. It will be necessary to lift up the wiring harness as far as possible for access to the rear of the fuel pump. If necessary, disconnect the relevant wiring connectors to enable the harness and guide assembly to be moved further for additional access.

23 Remove the fuel filter as described in Chapter 1B, then undo the bolts and remove the fuel filter bracket.

24 Thoroughly clean the high-pressure fuel pipe unions on the fuel pump and accumulator rail. Using an open-ended spanner, unscrew the union nuts securing the high-pressure fuel pipe to the fuel pump and accumulator rail. Counterhold the unions on the pump and accumulator rail with a second spanner, while unscrewing the union nuts. Withdraw the high-pressure fuel pipe and plug or cover the open unions to prevent dirt entry **(see illustration)**. Note that a

10.22 Undo the bolt (arrowed) to release the plastic wiring harness guide

10.24a Press in the buttons (arrowed) and disconnect the fuel supply and return hose quick-release fitting at the connections

10.24b Unscrew the unions and remove the high-pressure fuel pipe

new high-pressure fuel pipe will be required for refitting. **Note:** *The fuel lines must be renewed every time they are removed, as it is possible for minute metal particles to enter them as a result of tightening the union nuts. If these particles enter the fuel injectors, fuel at high-pressure can enter the combustion chambers unrestricted.*

25 Disconnect the low pressure hoses from the fuel pump, then tape over the openings. Move the hoses to one side.

26 Unscrew the nut and bolt securing the fuel pump rear mounting to the mounting bracket **(see illustration)**.

27 Disconnect the wiring connector at the pressure control valve on the rear of the fuel pump, and at the piston de-activator switch on the top of the pump.

28 Hold the pump pulley/sprocket stationary, and loosen the centre nut securing it to the pump shaft. The manufacturers recommend using a pin inserted through the pulley and into the cylinder head, however, a home-made forked tool engaged with the pulley holes can be used instead **(see illustration)**.

29 The fuel pump sprocket is a taper fit on the pump shaft and it will be necessary to make up a tool to release it from the taper **(see Tool Tip 1**. Partially unscrew the sprocket retaining nut, fit the home-made tool, and secure it to the sprocket with two 7.0 mm bolts. Prevent the sprocket from rotating as before, and unscrew the sprocket retaining nut. The nut will bear against the tool as it is undone, forcing the sprocket off the shaft taper. Once the taper is released, remove the tool, unscrew the nut fully, and remove the sprocket from the pump shaft.

30 Unscrew the nut and two bolts securing the front of the fuel pump to the mounting bracket **(see illustrations)**. Withdraw the pump and lift it off the engine.

Caution: The high-pressure fuel pump is manufactured to extremely close tolerances and must not be dismantled in any way. Do not unscrew the fuel pipe male union on the rear of the pump, or attempt to remove the pressure control valve, piston de-activator switch, or the seal on the pump shaft. No parts for the pump are available separately and if the unit is in any way suspect, it must be renewed.

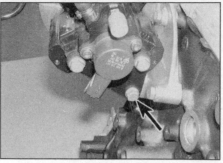
10.26 Undo the nut and bolt (arrowed) securing the fuel pump rear mounting to the mounting bracket

10.30a Fuel pump front mounting bolts (arrowed) . . .

2.0 litre DOHC engine

31 Disconnect the battery negative lead as described in Chapter 5A.
32 Remove the plastic cover from the top of the engine.
33 Remove the air filter assembly as described in Section 4.
34 Slacken the clamps and detach the breather pipe from the left-hand end of the cylinder head cover.
35 Thoroughly clean the high-pressure fuel pipe unions on the fuel pump and accumulator rail. Using an open-ended spanner, unscrew the union nuts securing the high-pressure fuel pipe to the fuel pump and accumulator rail. Counterhold the unions on the pump and accumulator rail with a second spanner, while unscrewing the union nuts. Withdraw the high-pressure fuel pipe and plug or cover the open unions to prevent dirt entry **(see**

10.28 Use the home-made tools to remove the fuel pump sprocket

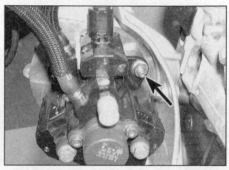
10.30b . . . and mounting nut (arrowed)

illustration). Note that a new high-pressure fuel pipe will be required for refitting. **Note:** *The fuel lines must be renewed every time they are removed, as it is possible for minute metal particles to enter them as a result of tightening the union nuts. If these particles enter the fuel injectors, fuel at high-pressure can enter the combustion chambers unrestricted.*

36 Disconnect the fuel supply and return hoses from the high-pressure pump. Plug the openings to prevent contamination.
37 Note their fitted positions, and disconnect the wiring plugs from the pump. Move the wiring harness to one side.
38 Undo the retaining bolt and move the turbocharger inlet duct to one side **(see illustration)**.
39 Undo the bolts/nuts and remove the support bracket from the pump.
40 Undo the 3 bolts and remove the pump **(see illustration)**.

10.35 Remove the pipe (arrowed) between the pump and accumulator rail

10.38 Move the inlet duct (arrowed) to one side

10.40 Undo the 3 bolts (arrowed) and remove the pump

Caution: *The high-pressure fuel pump is manufactured to extremely close tolerances and must not be dismantled in any way. Do not unscrew the fuel pipe male union on the rear of the pump, or attempt to remove the pressure control valve, piston de-activator switch, or the seal on the pump shaft. No parts for the pump are available separately and if the unit is in any way suspect, it must be renewed.*

Refitting

41 Refitting is a reversal of removal, noting the following points:

a) *Always renew the pump-to-accumulator rail high-pressure pipe.*

b) *On engines with a camshaft driven pump (ie, DW10BTED4), renew the drive seal.*

c) *With everything reassembled and reconnected, and observing the precautions listed in Section 2, start the engine and allow it to idle. Check for leaks at the high-pressure fuel pipe unions with the engine idling. If satisfactory, increase the engine speed to 3000 rpm and check again for leaks.*

d) *Take the car for a short road test and check for leaks once again on return. If any leaks are detected, obtain and fit another new high-pressure fuel pipe.* **Do not** *attempt to cure even the slightest leak by further tightening of the pipe unions. During the road test, initialise the engine management ECU as follows –*

engage third gear and stabilise the engine at 1000 rpm, then accelerate fully up to 3500 rpm.

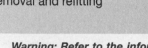

11 Accumulator rail – removal and refitting

> **Warning: Refer to the information contained in Section 2 before proceeding.**

Note: *A complete new set of high-pressure fuel pipes will be required for refitting.*

Removal

1 Disconnect the battery (refer to Chapter 5A).

2 Remove the plastic cover from the top of the engine.

1.4 litre models

3 Remove the cylinder head cover/air filter housing as described in Chapter 2C.

4 Clean the area around the high-pressure fuel pipes to and from the accumulator rail, then unscrew the pump-to-accumulator rail pipe unions. Use a second spanner to counterhold the union screwed in to the pump body **(see illustration 10.6)**. The screwed-in union must not be allowed to move. Remove the pipe.

5 Repeat the procedure on the accumulator rail-to-injector fuel pipes. Use a second

spanner to counterhold the unions screwed in to the injectors **(see illustration)**. These unions must not be allowed to move. Note their fitted locations and remove the pipes.

6 Plug the openings in the accumulator rail and fuel pump to prevent dirt ingress.

7 Disconnect the pressure sensor wiring plug from the accumulator rail **(see illustration)**.

8 Disconnect the fuel return pipe from the rail **(see illustration)**.

9 Unscrew the two rail mounting bolts and manoeuvre it from place **(see illustration)**.

Note: *Peugeot insist that the fuel pressure sensor on the accumulator rail must not be removed.*

1.6 litre engine

10 Remove the cylinder head cover/inlet manifold as described in Chapter 2D.

11 Drain the cooling system as described in Chapter 1B.

12 Remove the EGR cooler as described in Chapter 4C.

13 Undo the 2 mounting bolts, slacken the clamps, and move the coolant pump outlet assembly aside **(see illustration)**.

14 Clean around the pipe, then undo the unions and remove the high-pressure pipe from the accumulator rail to the high-pressure pump. Plug the openings to prevent contamination.

15 Disconnect the pressure sensor wiring plug from the accumulator rail **(see illustration)**.

11.5 Use a second spanner to counterhold the fuel injector unions whilst slackening the pipe unions

11.7 Disconnect the accumulator rail pressure sensor wiring plug

11.8 Depress the release button (arrowed) and disconnect the fuel return pipe

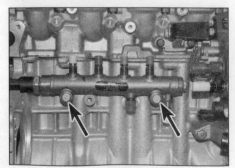

11.9 Remove the accumulator rail mounting bolts (arrowed)

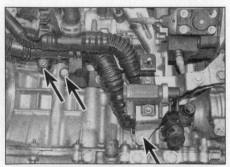

11.13 Undo the bolts (arrowed) and move the coolant pump outlet assembly aside

11.15 The pressure sensor is located at the end of the accumulator rail (arrowed)

11.16 Accumulator rail mounting bolt/stud (arrowed)

11.17a Disconnect the wiring connectors at the fuel injectors . . .

11.17b . . . and at the piston de-activator switch on top of the fuel pump

16 Unscrew the two rail mounting bolts and manoeuvre it from place **(see illustration)**. Note: *Peugeot insist that the fuel pressure sensor on the accumulator rail must not be removed.*
Caution: Do not attempt to remove the four high-pressure fuel pipe male unions from the accumulator rail. These parts are not available separately and if disturbed are likely to result in fuel leakage on reassembly.

2.0 litre SOHC engine

17 Disconnect the wiring connectors at the fuel injectors and at the piston de-activator switch on the top of the fuel pump or at the sensor in the middle of the accumulator rail **(see illustrations)**.
18 Undo the two nuts securing the plastic wiring harness guide to the cylinder head. Lift the guide off the two mounting studs and move it to one side **(see illustration)**. Disconnect any additional wiring connectors as necessary to enable the harness and guide assembly to be moved further for increased access.
19 Release the retaining clip and disconnect the crankcase ventilation hose from the cylinder head cover. Position it to one side.
20 At the connections above the fuel pump, disconnect the fuel supply and return hose quick-release fittings using a small screwdriver to release the locking clip. Suitably plug or cover the open unions to prevent dirt entry.
21 Similarly disconnect the supply and return hose quick-release fittings at the fuel filter and plug or cover the open unions. Release the fuel hoses from the relevant retaining clips, then undo the fasteners and move the fuel filter support bracket to one side.
22 Disconnect the fuel temperature sensor wiring plug from the left-hand end of the accumulator rail.
23 Thoroughly clean all the high-pressure fuel pipe unions on the accumulator rail, fuel pump and injectors. Using an open-ended spanner, unscrew the union nuts securing the high-pressure fuel pipe to the fuel pump and accumulator rail. Counterhold the unions on the pump and accumulator rail with a second spanner, while unscrewing the union nuts. Withdraw the high-pressure fuel pipe and plug or cover the open unions to prevent dirt entry.
24 Again using two spanners, hold the unions

and unscrew the union nuts securing the high-pressure fuel pipes to the fuel injectors and accumulator rail **(see illustrations)**. Withdraw the high-pressure fuel pipes and plug or cover the open unions to prevent dirt entry.
25 Undo the three bolts securing the accumulator rail to the cylinder head and withdraw the rail from its location **(see illustration)**.
Caution: Do not attempt to remove the four high-pressure fuel pipe male unions from the accumulator rail. These parts are not available separately and if disturbed are likely to result in fuel leakage on reassembly.

2.0 litre DOHC engine

26 Disconnect the engine breather hose from the cylinder head cover.
27 Remove the air filter as described in Section 4.

11.18 Undo the nuts and lift off the plastic wiring harness guide

11.24b . . . and at each injector

28 Remove the inlet manifold as described in Section 14.
29 Move the oil filler neck to one side.
30 Thoroughly clean all the high-pressure fuel pipe unions on the accumulator rail, fuel pump and injectors. Using an open-ended spanner, unscrew the union nuts securing the high-pressure fuel pipe to the fuel pump and accumulator rail. Counterhold the unions on the pump and accumulator rail with a second spanner, while unscrewing the union nuts. Withdraw the high-pressure fuel pipe and plug or cover the open unions to prevent dirt entry.
31 Again using two spanners, hold the unions and unscrew the union nuts securing the high-pressure fuel pipes to the fuel injectors and accumulator rail **(see illustrations 11.24a and 11.24b)**. Withdraw the high-pressure fuel pipes and plug or cover the open unions to prevent dirt entry.

11.24a Using two spanners, unscrew the fuel pipe unions at the accumulator rail . . .

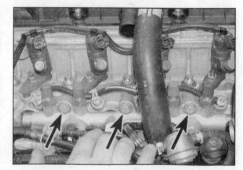

11.25 Accumulator rail mounting bolts (arrowed)

32 Undo the 2 mounting nuts and manoeuvre the accumulator rail from position. Recover the mounting spacers. Disconnect the sensor wiring plug(s) as the accumulator rail is withdrawn.

Refitting

33 Locate the accumulator rail in position, refit and finger-tighten the mounting bolts/nuts.

34 Reconnect the accumulator rail wiring plug(s).

35 Fit the new pump-to-rail high-pressure pipe, and only finger-tighten the unions at first, then tighten the unions to the specified torque setting. Use a second spanner to counterhold the union screwed into the pump body.

36 Fit the new set of rail-to-injector high-pressure pipes, and finger tighten the unions. If it's not possible to fit the new pipes to the injector unions, remove and refit the injectors as described in Section 12. and try again.

37 Tighten the accumulator rail mounting bolts/nuts to the specified torque.

38 Tighten the rail-to-injector pipe unions to the specified torque setting. Use a second spanner to counterhold the injector unions.

39 The remainder of refitting is a reversal of removal, noting the following points:
- a) Ensure all wiring connectors and harnesses are correctly refitting and secured.
- b) Reconnect the battery as described in Chapter 5A.
- c) Observing the precautions listed in

Section 2, start the engine and allow it to idle. Check for leaks at the high-pressure fuel pipe unions with the engine idling. If satisfactory, increase the engine speed to 3000 rpm and check again for leaks. Take the car for a short road test and check for leaks once again on return. If any leaks are detected, obtain and fit additional new high-pressure fuel pipes as required. Do not attempt to cure even the slightest leak by further tightening of the pipe unions.

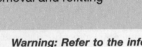

12 Fuel injectors – removal and refitting

 Warning: Refer to the information contained in Section 2 before proceeding.

Removal

1 Remove the plastic cover from the top of the engine.

1.4 litre models

Note: The following procedure describes the removal and refitting of the injectors as a complete set, however each injector may be removed individually if required. New copper washers, upper seals, injector clamp retaining nuts and a high-pressure fuel pipe will be required for each disturbed injector when refitting.

2 Remove the cylinder head cover/air filter housing as described in Chapter 2C.

3 Clean the area around the high-pressure fuel pipes between the injectors and the accumulator rail, then unscrew the pipe unions. Use a second spanner to counterhold the union screwed in to the injector body **(see illustration 11.5)**. The injectors screwed-in unions must not be allowed to move. Remove the pipes. Plug the openings in the accumulator rail and injectors to prevent dirt ingress.

4 Extract the retaining circlip and disconnect the leak-off pipe from each fuel injector **(see illustration)**.

5 Unscrew the injector retaining bolt, and remove the clamp. If loose, recover the clamp locating dowel from the cylinder head **(see illustrations)**.

6 Carefully pull or lever the injector from place. Do not lever against or pull on the solenoid housing at the top of the injector.

7 Remove the copper washer and the upper seal from each injector, or from the cylinder head if they remained in place during injector removal **(see illustration)**. New copper washers and upper seals will be required for refitting. Cover the injector hole in the cylinder head to prevent dirt ingress.

8 Examine each injector visually for any signs of obvious damage or deterioration. If any defects are apparent, renew the injector(s).

9 If the injectors are in a satisfactory condition, plug the fuel pipe union (if not already done) and suitably cover the electrical element and the injector nozzle.

Caution: The injectors are manufactured to extremely close tolerances and must not be dismantled in any way. Do not unscrew the fuel pipe union on the side of the injector, or separate any parts of the injector body. Do not attempt to clean carbon deposits from the injector nozzle or carry out any form of ultrasonic or pressure testing.

1.6 litre engine

Note: The following procedure describes the removal and refitting of the injectors as a complete set, however each injector may be removed individually if required. New copper washers, upper seals, and a high-pressure fuel pipe will be required for each disturbed injector when refitting.

10 Remove the EGR cooler as described in Chapter 4C.

12.4 Prise out the circlip and disconnect the fuel leak-off pipe

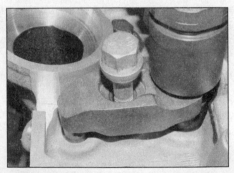

12.5a Undo the injector clamp bolt . . .

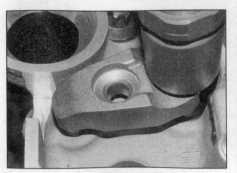

12.5b . . . and remove the clamp

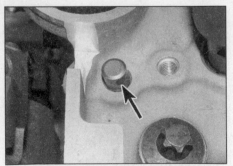

12.5c If it's loose, remove the locating dowel (arrowed)

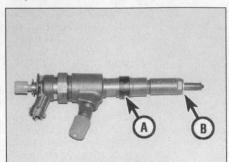

12.7 Fuel injector upper seal (A) and copper washer (B)

12.11a Inlet ducting clamps (arrowed) . . .

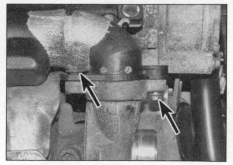

12.11b . . . and bolts (arrowed)

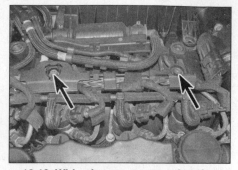

12.13 Wiring harness support bracket bolts (arrowed)

11 Undo the bolts, slacken the clamps and remove the air inlet ducting assembly from between the turbocharger and the inlet manifold. Note their fitted positions, and disconnect the various wiring plugs as the assembly is withdrawn **(see illustrations)**.

12 Disconnect the injector wiring plugs.

13 Undo the bolts and move aside the wiring harness support bracket **(see illustration)**.

14 Release the manual fuel priming pump and its support.

15 Extract the retaining circlip and disconnect the leak-off pipe from each fuel injector **(see illustration)**.

16 Clean the area around the high-pressure fuel pipes between the injectors and the accumulator rail, then unscrew the pipe unions. Use a second spanner to counterhold the union screwed into the injector body **(see illustration)**. The injectors screwed-in unions must not be allowed to move. Remove the bracket above the accumulator rail unions, then remove the pipes. Plug the openings in the accumulator rail and injectors to prevent dirt ingress.

17 Unscrew the injector retaining nuts, and carefully pull or lever the injector from place. If necessary, use an open-ended spanner and twist the injector to free it from position **(see illustrations)**. Do not lever against or pull on the solenoid housing at the top of the injector. Note down the injectors position – if the injectors are to be refitted, they must be refitted to their original locations. If improved access is required, undo the bolts and remove

the oil separator housing from the front of the cylinder head cover.

18 Remove the copper washer and the upper seal from each injector, or from the cylinder head if they remained in place during injector removal. New copper washers and upper seals will be required for refitting. Cover the injector hole in the cylinder head to prevent dirt ingress.

19 Examine each injector visually for any signs of obvious damage or deterioration. If any defects are apparent, renew the injector(s). Note down the 8-digit injector classification number – this may be needed during the refitting procedure if the ECU has been renewed **(see illustration)**.

20 If the injectors are in a satisfactory condition, plug the fuel pipe union (if not already done) and suitably cover the electrical element and the injector nozzle.

Caution: The injectors are manufactured to extremely close tolerances and must not be dismantled in any way. Do not unscrew the fuel pipe union on the side of the injector, or separate any parts of the injector body. Do not attempt to clean carbon deposits from the injector nozzle or carry out any form of ultrasonic or pressure testing.

2.0 litre SOHC engine

Note: *The following procedure describes the removal and refitting of the injectors as a complete set, however each injector may be removed individually if required. New copper washers, upper seals, clamp bolt/nut, and a high-pressure fuel pipe will be required for each disturbed injector when refitting.*

21 Disconnect the wiring connectors at

12.15 Prise out the clip and pull the return pipe from each injector

12.16 Use a second spanner to counterhold the high-pressure pipe union nuts

12.17a Injector retaining nuts (arrowed)

12.17b Use a spanner to twist the injector and free it from position

12.19 Note the injector classification number

12.21 Disconnect the injector wiring plugs

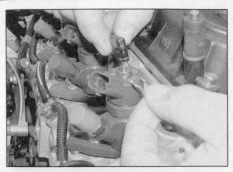

12.23 Extract the clip and disconnect the leak-off pipes

12.25a Undo the injector retaining nut . . .

12.25b . . . and remove the washer

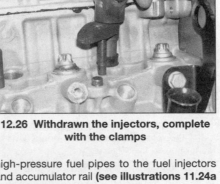

12.26 Withdrawn the injectors, complete with the clamps

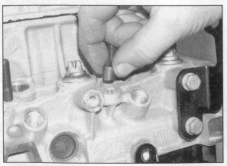

12.27 Recover the clamp locating dowel from the cylinder head

12.33 Use a second spanner to counterhold the injector port when slackening the union nut

the fuel injectors **(see illustration)**. Where necessary, release the retaining clip and disconnect the crankcase ventilation hose from the cylinder head cover. Position it to one side.

22 Undo the two nuts securing the plastic wiring harness guide to the cylinder head. Lift the guide off the two mounting studs and move it clear. Disconnect any additional wiring connectors as necessary to enable the harness and guide assembly to be moved to one side.

23 Extract the retaining circlip and disconnect the leak-off pipe from each fuel injector **(see illustration)**.

24 Thoroughly clean all the high-pressure fuel pipe unions on the fuel injectors and accumulator rail. Using two open-ended spanners, unscrew the union nuts securing the

high-pressure fuel pipes to the fuel injectors and accumulator rail **(see illustrations 11.24a and 11.24b)**. Withdraw the high-pressure fuel pipes and plug or cover the open unions on the injectors and accumulator rail to prevent dirt entry. Note that a new high-pressure fuel pipe will be required for each removed injector when refitting.

25 Unscrew the bolt/nut securing each injector clamp to its cylinder head **(see illustrations)**. Note that new clamp bolt/nut will be required for refitting.

26 Withdraw the injectors, together with their clamps, from the cylinder head. Slide the clamp off the injector once it is clear of the mounting stud. If the injectors are a tight fit in the cylinder head and cannot be released, two screwdrivers may be used to carefully lever them out **(see illustration)**. Alternatively,

unscrew one mounting stud (where fitted) using a stud extractor and slide off the injector clamp. Using an open-ended spanner engaged with the clamp locating slot on the injector body, free the injector by twisting it and at the same time lifting it upwards.

27 Recover the injector clamp locating dowel from the cylinder head **(see illustration)**.

28 Remove the copper washer and the upper seal from each injector, or from the cylinder head if they remained in place during injector removal. New copper washers and upper seals will be required for refitting.

29 Examine each injector visually for any signs of obvious damage or deterioration. If any defects are apparent, renew the injector(s).

Caution: The injectors are manufactured to extremely close tolerances and must not be dismantled in any way. Do not unscrew the fuel pipe union on the side of the injector, or separate any parts of the injector body. Do not attempt to clean carbon deposits from the injector nozzle or carry out any form of ultrasonic or pressure testing.

30 If the injectors are in a satisfactory condition, plug the fuel pipe union (if not already done) and suitably cover the electrical element and the injector nozzle.

2.0 litre DOHC engine

Note: *New copper washers, upper seals, and a high-pressure fuel pipe will be required for each disturbed injector when refitting.*

31 Remove the inlet manifold as described in Section 14.

32 Disconnect the wiring plugs from the injectors.

33 Thoroughly clean all the high-pressure fuel pipe unions on the fuel injectors and accumulator rail. Using two open-ended spanners, unscrew the union nuts securing the high-pressure fuel pipes to the fuel injectors and accumulator rail **(see illustration)**. Withdraw the high-pressure fuel pipes and plug or cover the open unions on the injectors and accumulator rail to prevent dirt entry. Note that a new high-pressure fuel pipe will be required for each removed injector when refitting.

34 Release the retaining clip and disconnect

12.34a Prise down the lower edge of the retaining clip (shown with the leak-off hose disconnected for clarity) . . .

12.34b . . . then pull the hose from the injector

12.35 Injector clamp nuts (arrowed)

the leak-off pipe from each fuel injector **(see illustrations)**.

35 Progressively and evenly slacken and remove the injector retaining nuts **(see illustration)**.

36 Carefully pull the injectors upwards from the cylinder head. Note down the injectors' positions – if the injectors are to be refitted, they must be refitting to their original locations.

37 Remove the lower copper washer and upper seal from each injector.

38 Examine each injector visually for any signs of obvious damage or deterioration. If any defects are apparent, renew the injector(s). Note down the 8-digit injector classification number – this may be needed during the refitting procedure if the ECU has been renewed **(see illustration 12.19)**.

Caution: The injectors are manufactured to extremely close tolerances and must not be dismantled in any way. Do not unscrew the fuel pipe union on the side of the injector, or separate any parts of the injector body. Do not attempt to clean carbon deposits from the injector nozzle or carry out any form of ultrasonic or pressure testing.

39 If the injectors are in a satisfactory condition, plug the fuel pipe union (if not already done) and suitably cover the electrical element and the injector nozzle.

Refitting

40 Locate a new upper seal on the body of each injector, and place a new copper washer on the injector nozzle **(see illustrations)**.

41 Refit the injector clamp locating dowels (where fitted) to the cylinder head.

1.4 and 2.0 litre SOHC engine

42 Place the injector clamp in the slot on each injector body and refit the injectors to the cylinder head. Guide the clamp over the mounting stud and onto the locating dowel as each injector is inserted. Ensure the upper injector seals are correctly located in the cylinder head.

43 Fit the washer and a new injector clamp retaining nut to each mounting stud. Tighten the nuts finger-tight only at this stage.

12.40a Ensure the circlip (arrowed) is in place on the 1.6 litre engine injectors . . .

1.6 litre and 2.0 litre DOHC engines

44 Ensure the injector clamps are in place over their respective circlips on the injector bodies, then fit the injectors into place in the cylinder head. If the original injectors are being refitted, ensure they are fitted into their original positions **(see illustration)**.

45 Fit the injector retaining bolts/nuts, but only finger-tighten them at this stage. When tightening the nuts/bolts, ensure the clamps stay horizontal.

All engines

46 Working on one fuel injector at a time, remove the blanking plugs from the fuel pipe unions on the accumulator rail and the relevant injector. Locate a new high-pressure fuel pipe over the unions and screw on the union nuts. Take care not to cross-thread the nuts or strain the fuel pipes as they are fitted. Once

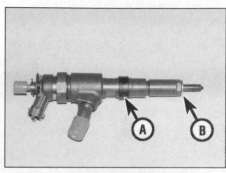

12.40b . . . then fit the upper seal (A) and copper washer (B)

the union nut threads have started, finger-tighten the nuts to the ends of the threads.

47 When all the fuel pipes are in place, tighten the injector clamp retaining nuts/bolts to the specified torque (and angle where applicable).

48 Using an open-ended spanner, hold each fuel pipe union in turn and tighten the union nut to the specified torque using a torque wrench and crow-foot adapter **(see illustration)**. Tighten all the disturbed union nuts in the same way.

49 On 1.6 litre and 2.0 litre DOHC engines, if new injectors have been fitted, their classification numbers must be programmed into the engine management ECU using dedicated diagnostic equipment/scanner. If this equipment is not available, entrust this task to a Peugeot dealer or suitably-equipped repairer. Note that it should be possible to drive the vehicle, albeit with reduced performance/

12.44 Fit the injectors into their original locations

12.48 Tighten the high-pressure pipe union nuts using a crow-foot adapter

13.6a Depress the retaining tab (arrowed) . . .

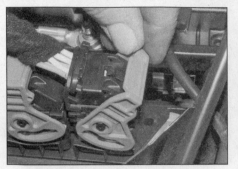

13.6b . . . and move the lever from the vertical to horizontal position

13.7 Lift the ECU from the electrical box

increased emissions, to a repairer for the numbers to be programmed.

50 The remainder of refitting is a reversal of removal, following the points listed in Paragraph 39 of the previous Section.

13 Electronic control system components – testing, removal and refitting

Testing

1 If a fault is suspected in the electronic control side of the system, first ensure that all the wiring connectors are securely connected and free of corrosion. Ensure that the suspected problem is not of a mechanical nature, or due to poor maintenance; ie, check that the air cleaner filter element is clean, the engine breather hoses are clear and undamaged, and that the cylinder compression pressures are correct, referring to Chapters 1B and 2C, D or E for further information.

2 If these checks fail to reveal the cause of the problem, the vehicle should be taken to a Peugeot dealer or suitably-equipped garage for testing. A diagnostic socket is located behind the trim panel to the right of the steering column, to which a fault code reader or other suitable test equipment can be connected. By using the code reader or test equipment, the engine management ECU (and the various other vehicle system ECUs) can be interrogated, and any stored fault codes can be retrieved.

3 This will allow the fault to be quickly and simply traced, alleviating the need to test all the system components individually, which is a time-consuming operation that carries a risk of damaging the ECU.

Electronic control unit (ECU)

Note: *If a new ECU is to be fitted, this work must be entrusted to a Peugeot dealer or suitably-equipped specialist. It is necessary to initialise the new ECU after installation, which requires the use of dedicated Peugeot diagnostic equipment.*

Note: *Before carrying out the following procedure, disconnect the battery (see Chapter 5A). Reconnect the battery on completion of refitting.*

4 The ECU is located in a plastic box which is mounted on the left-hand front wheel arch.

5 Lift off the ECU module box lid.

6 Release the wiring connector(s) by depressing the tab and moving the locking lever on top of the connector from the vertical to the fully horizontal position. Carefully withdraw the connector from the ECU pins **(see illustrations)**.

7 Lift the ECU upwards and remove it from its location **(see illustration)**.

8 To remove the ECU module box, undo the internal and external retaining bolts and remove the module box.

9 Refitting is a reversal of removal.

Crankshaft speed/position sensor

Note: *Before carrying out the following*

procedure, disconnect the battery (refer to Chapter 5A). Reconnect the battery on completion of refitting.

1.4 litre engine

10 The crankshaft position sensor is located adjacent to the crankshaft pulley on the right-hand end of the engine. Slacken the right-hand front roadwheel bolts, then jack the front of the vehicle up and support it on axle stands (see *Jacking and vehicle support*). Remove the right-hand front roadwheel.

11 Push in the centre pins a little, then prise out the rivets and remove the wheel arch liner.

12 Disconnect the sensor wiring plug **(see illustration)**.

13 Undo the bolt and remove the sensor.

14 Refitting is a reversal of removal, tightening the sensor retaining bolt securely.

2.0 litre SOHC engine

15 The crankshaft speed/position sensor is located at the top of the transmission bellhousing, directly above the engine flywheel. To gain access, remove the air cleaner assembly as described in Section 4, then remove the battery and battery tray (see Chapter 5A).

16 Undo the retaining nuts and bolts and release the plastic wiring harness guide from its mountings **(see illustration)**.

17 Working below the thermostat housing, disconnect the wiring connector from the crankshaft speed/position sensor.

18 Slacken the bolt securing the sensor to the bellhousing **(see illustration)**. It is not

13.12 Disconnect the crankshaft position sensor wiring plug

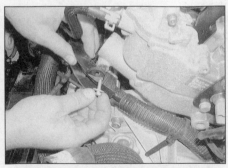

13.16 Release the plastic wiring harness guide for access to the crankshaft position sensor

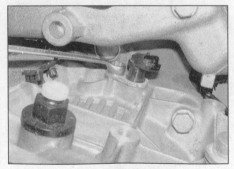

13.18 Slacken the bolt securing the sensor to the bellhousing

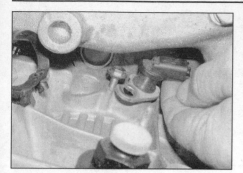

13.19 Turn the sensor body to clear the bolt and withdraw it from the bellhousing

13.23 Crankshaft position sensor (arrowed) (1.6 litre and 2.0 litre DOHC engines)

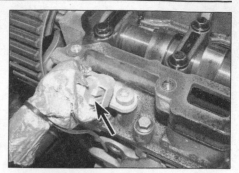

13.28 Disconnect the camshaft position sensor wiring plug (arrowed)

13.30 The gap between the end of the sensor and the webs of the signal wheel must be 1.2 mm (used sensor only)

13.34 Undo the camshaft sensor retaining bolt (arrowed) (1.6 litre engine)

necessary to remove the bolt completely as the sensor mounting flange is slotted.

19 Turn the sensor body to clear the mounting bolt, then withdraw the sensor from the bellhousing **(see illustration)**.

20 Refitting is reverse of the removal procedure, ensuring the sensor retaining bolt is securely tightened.

1.6 litre and 2.0 litre DOHC engines

21 The crankshaft position sensor is located adjacent to the crankshaft pulley on the right-hand end of the engine. Slacken the right-hand front roadwheel bolts, then jack the front of the vehicle up and support it on axle stands (see *Jacking and vehicle support*). Remove the right-hand front roadwheel.

22 Push in the centre pins a little, then prise out the rivets and remove the wheel arch liner.

23 Disconnect the sensor wiring plug **(see illustration)**.

24 Undo the bolt and remove the sensor.

25 Refitting is a reversal of removal, tightening the sensor retaining bolt securely.

Camshaft position sensor

Note: *Before carrying out the following procedure, disconnect the battery (refer to Chapter 5A). Reconnect the battery on completion of refitting.*

26 The camshaft position sensor is mounted on the right-hand end of the cylinder head cover, directly behind the camshaft sprocket.

1.4 litre engine

27 Remove the upper timing belt cover, as described in Chapter 2C.

28 Unplug the sensor wiring connector **(see illustration)**.

29 Undo the bolt and pull the sensor from position.

30 Upon refitting, position the sensor so that the air gap between the sensor end and the webs of the signal wheel is 1.2 mm, measured with feeler gauges, for a used sensor. If fitting a new sensor, the small tip of the sensor must be just touching one of the three webs of the signal wheel. Tighten the sensor retaining bolt to the specified torque **(see illustration)**.

31 The remainder of refitting is a reversal of removal.

1.6 litre engine

32 Remove the upper timing belt cover, as described in Chapter 2D.

33 Unplug the sensor wiring connector.

34 Undo the bolt and pull the sensor from position **(see illustration)**.

35 Upon refitting, position the sensor so that the air gap between the sensor end and the webs of the signal wheel is 1.2 mm, measured with feeler gauges **(see illustrations)**. If a new sensor is being fitted, position it so the nipple of the sensor is just in contact with the camshaft signal wheel. Tighten the sensor retaining bolt to the specified torque.

36 The remainder of refitting is a reversal of removal.

2.0 litre SOHC engine

37 Remove the timing belt upper covers as described in Chapter 2C.

38 Disconnect the sensor wiring connector **(see illustration)**.

13.35a The gap between the used sensor and the signal wheel (arrowed) . . .

13.35b . . . must be 1.2 mm measured with a feeler gauge

13.38 Disconnect the wiring . . .

13.39 . . . and remove the sensor

13.41 Insert feeler gauges bent 90° through the sprocket to measure the camshaft position sensor air gap

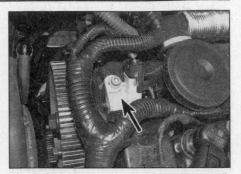

13.45 Camshaft position sensor (arrowed)

39 Undo the retaining bolt and lift the sensor off the cylinder head cover **(see illustration)**.

40 To refit and adjust the sensor position, locate the sensor on the cylinder head cover and loosely refit the retaining bolt.

41 The air gap between the tip of the sensor and the signal wheel at the rear of the camshaft sprocket hub must be set to 1.2 mm, using feeler blades. Clearance for the feeler blades is limited with the timing belt and camshaft sprocket in place, but it is just possible if the feeler blades are bent through 90° so they can be inserted through the holes in the sprocket to rest against the inner face of the signal wheel. Note that if a new sensor is being fitted, position it so the nipple on the end of the sensor is just in contact with the signal wheel **(see illustration)**.

42 Hold the sensor in this position and tighten the retaining bolt.

43 With the gap correctly adjusted, reconnect the sensor wiring connector, then refit the

timing belt upper and intermediate covers as described in Chapter 2C.

2.0 litre DOHC engine

44 Remove the plastic cover from the top of the engine.

45 Disconnect the sensor wiring plug **(see illustration)**.

46 Undo the retaining bolt and remove the sensor.

47 To refit and adjust the sensor position, locate the sensor on the cylinder head cover and loosely refit the retaining bolt.

48 When refitting a used sensor, position it against the camshaft sprocket spoke, then pull it back 1.2 mm **(see illustrations)**. Tighten the retaining bolt securely.

49 When fitting a new sensor, position the sensor so the nipple on the tip is just in contact with the signal wheel. Tighten the retaining bolt securely.

Accelerator pedal position sensor

Note: *Before carrying out the following procedure, disconnect the battery (refer to Chapter 5A). Reconnect the battery on completion of refitting.*

Models without accelerator cable

50 On these models, the pedal sensor is integral with the accelerator pedal assembly. Refer to the relevant Section of Chapter 4A for the pedal removal procedure.

Models with accelerator cable

51 The accelerator pedal position sensor is located in the left-hand front corner of the engine compartment.

52 Remove the air cleaner assembly as described in Section 4.

53 Undo the two nuts and bolts and remove the sensor assembly from the mounting bracket on the side of the air cleaner housing.

54 Refitting is reverse of the removal procedure.

Coolant temperature sensor

55 Refer to Chapter 3, Section 7.

Fuel temperature sensor

⚠ **Warning: Refer to the information contained in Section 2 before proceeding.**

Note: *Before carrying out the following procedure, disconnect the battery (refer to Chapter 5A). Reconnect the battery on completion of refitting.*

1.4 and 1.6 litre engines

56 The sensor is clipped in to the plastic fuel manifold at the right-hand rear end of the cylinder head. To remove the sensor, disconnect the wiring plug, then unclip the sensor from the manifold. Be prepared for fuel spillage **(see illustration)**.

57 Refitting is a reversal of removal. Observing the precautions listed in Section 2, start the engine and allow it to idle. Check for leaks at the fuel temperature sensor with the engine idling. If satisfactory, increase the engine speed to 4000 rpm and check again for leaks. Take the car for a short road test and check for leaks once again on return. If any leaks are detected, obtain and fit a new sensor.

2.0 litre engine

58 The fuel temperature sensor is located to the left-hand side of the oil filler cap **(see illustration)**.

13.48a Position the sensor against the camshaft sprocket spoke . . .

13.48b . . . then pull it back 1.2 mm

13.56 Fuel temperature sensor (arrowed) (1.4 litre engine)

13.58 Fuel temperature sensor (arrowed) (2.0 litre engine)

59 Undo the four plastic fasteners and lift off the engine cover.

60 Disconnect the fuel temperature sensor wiring connector.

61 Thoroughly clean the area around the sensor and its location.

62 Suitably protect the components below the sensor and have plenty of clean rags handy. Be prepared for considerable fuel spillage.

63 Release the retaining clips and detach the sensor from the fuel pipes.

64 Refit the sensor to the fuel pipes, ensuring the clips fully engage.

65 Reconnect the sensor wiring plug.

66 Refit the engine plastic cover.

All models

67 Observing the precautions listed in Section 2, start the engine and allow it to idle. Check for leaks at the fuel temperature sensor with the engine idling. If satisfactory, increase the engine speed to 4000 rpm and check again for leaks. Take the car for a short road test and check for leaks once again on return. If any leaks are detected, obtain and fit a new sensor.

Air mass meter

Note: *Before carrying out the following procedure, disconnect the battery (refer to Chapter 5A). Reconnect the battery on completion of refitting.*

68 Air mass meter is located in the intake ducting from the air cleaner housing. On 1.4 litre engines, pull the plastic cover from its mountings on top of the engine.

69 Disconnect the meter wiring plug **(see illustrations)**.

70 Slacken the retaining clips and disconnect the air inlet ducting from either side of the air mass meter. Suitably plug or cover the turbocharger inlet duct, using clean rag to prevent any dirt or foreign material from entering. On 1.4 litre engines, the air cleaner outlet is bolted to the air mass meter.

71 Refitting is reverse of the removal procedure.

Fuel pressure sensor

72 The fuel pressure sensor is integral with the accumulator rail, and is not available separately. Peugeot insist that the sensor is not removed from the rail.

Fuel pressure control valve

73 The fuel pressure control valve is integral with the high-pressure fuel pump and cannot be separated.

Preheating system control unit

74 Refer to Chapter 5C.

EGR solenoid valve

75 Refer to Chapter 4C, Section 2.

Vehicle speed sensor

76 The engine management ECU receives the vehicle speed signal from the wheels speed

13.69a Air mass meter wiring plug (arrowed) (1.4 litre engine)

sensors via the ABS ECU. Refer to Chapter 9 for wheel speed sensor removal.

14 Inlet manifold – removal and refitting

All except 2.0 litre SOHC engine

1 The inlet manifold is integral with the cylinder head cover.

2.0 litre SOHC engine

Note: *Renew the manifold gasket when refitting.*

Removal

2 The inlet manifold is located on the rear of the cylinder head, together with the exhaust

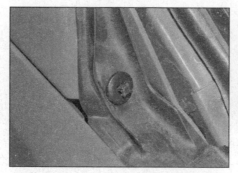

14.3a Push in the centre pins a little, then prise out the complete plastic rivet

14.3c . . . then undo the bolts (one at each end), and remove the plastic scuttle crossmember

13.69b Air mass meter wiring plug (2.0 litre engine)

manifold. First, remove the exhaust manifold as described in Section 15.

3 Remove the windscreen wiper arms (Chapter 12), then unclip the plastic scuttle panel. The trim is secured by plastic expanding rivets at each end – push in the centre pins a little, then prise out the complete rivets. Pull up the ends of the panel to release it from the windscreen clips, the pull the centre of the panel down to release it from the centre windscreen clip. Undo the two bolts securing the brake/clutch master cylinder upper reservoir and move it to one side. Release the sound insulation trim from the scuttle crossmember, undo the bolt at each end, and remove the crossmember from the vehicle **(see illustrations)**.

4 Undo the four bolts and four nuts securing the inlet manifold flanges to the cylinder head **(see illustration)** and recover the washers.

14.3b Lever up the centre pins, prise out the plastic rivet, and detach the insulation material from the crossmember . . .

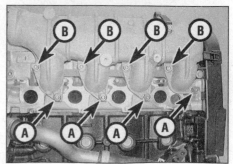

14.4 Inlet manifold retaining nuts (A) and bolts (B)

If preferred, the lower mounting nuts may be loosened and not removed, as the lower inlet manifold holes are slotted to allow the manifold to be lifted upwards once the upper bolts have been removed.

5 Lift the manifold off the cylinder head studs and recover the gasket.

Refitting

6 Refitting is reverse of the removal procedure, bearing in mind the following points.
  a) *Ensure that the manifold and cylinder head mating faces are clean, with all traces of old gasket removed.*
  b) *Use a new gasket when refitting the manifold.*
  c) *Ensure that all fixings and attachments are securely tightened.*
  d) *Refit the exhaust manifold as described in Section 15.*

15 Exhaust manifold – removal and refitting

Removal

All except 2.0 litre SOHC engine

1 Remove the turbocharger as described in Section 17.

2 Undo the retaining nuts, recover the spacers, and remove the manifold. Recover the gasket **(see illustrations)**.

15.2a Undo the exhaust manifold nuts, recover the spacers, and remove the manifold

15.2b Recover the manifold gasket

2.0 litre SOHC engine

3 The exhaust manifold is located on the rear of the cylinder head and access is very limited. First, apply the handbrake, then jack up the front of the vehicle and support it on axle stands (see *Jacking and vehicle support*).

4 Disconnect the battery (see Chapter 5A).

5 Remove the exhaust front pipe with reference to Section 19.

6 Remove the turbocharger inlet and outlet ducts as described in Section 4.

7 Unscrew the union nut securing the turbocharger oil feed pipe to the cylinder block, then withdraw the pipe from its location **(see illustration)**.

8 Remove the filter from the end of the oil feed pipe, and examine it for contamination

(see illustration). Clean or renew if necessary.

9 Undo the two bolts securing the oil return pipe flange to the turbocharger. Separate the flange and recover the gasket **(see illustrations)**.

10 Remove the exhaust gas recirculation (EGR) valve and connecting pipe from the exhaust manifold as described in Chapter 4C.

11 Undo the exhaust manifold retaining nuts and recover the spacers from the studs **(see illustrations)**.

12 Undo the nut and bolt securing the base of the turbocharger to the support bracket on the cylinder block.

13 Withdraw the turbocharger and exhaust manifold off the mounting studs and remove the assembly from the

15.7 Unscrew the turbocharger oil feed pipe union nut

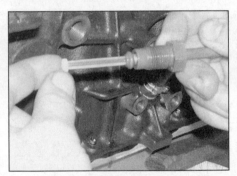

15.8 Withdraw the oil feed pipe and remove the filter

15.9a Undo the oil return pipe flange securing bolts (arrowed) . . .

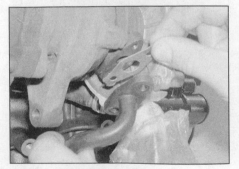

15.9b . . . separate the flange and recover the gasket

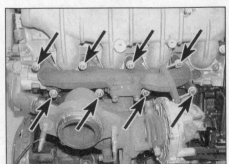

15.11a Undo the exhaust manifold retaining nuts (arrowed) . . .

15.11b . . . and recover the spacers

engine. Recover the manifold gasket **(see illustrations).**

Refitting

14 Refitting is a reverse of the removal procedure, bearing in mind the following points:
a) *Ensure that the manifold and cylinder head mating faces are clean, with all traces of old gasket removed.*
b) *Use new gaskets when refitting the manifold to the cylinder head and, on 2.0 litre SOHC engines, the oil return pipe flange to the turbocharger.*
c) *Tighten the exhaust manifold retaining nuts to the specified torque.*
d) *On 2.0 litre SOHC engines, refit the EGR valve and connecting pipe as described in Chapter 4C, Section 2.*
e) *Refit the turbocharger rear inlet and outlet ducts as described in Section 4.*
f) *Refit the exhaust front pipe as described in Section 19.*

16 Turbocharger – description and precautions

Description

1 A turbocharger is fitted to increase engine efficiency by raising the pressure in the inlet manifold above atmospheric pressure. Instead of the air simply being sucked into the cylinders, it is forced in.
2 Energy for the operation of the turbocharger comes from the exhaust gas. The gas flows through a specially-shaped housing (the turbine housing) and, in so doing, spins the turbine wheel. The turbine wheel is attached to a shaft, at the end of which is another vaned wheel known as the compressor wheel. The compressor wheel spins in its own housing, and compresses the inlet air on the way to the inlet manifold.
3 Boost pressure (the pressure in the inlet manifold) is limited by a wastegate, which diverts the exhaust gas away from the turbine wheel in response to a pressure-sensitive

15.13a Withdraw the turbocharger and manifold . . .

actuator. On later models, the turbocharger incorporates a variable intake nozzle to improve boost pressure at low engine speeds.
4 The turbo shaft is pressure-lubricated by an oil feed pipe from the main oil gallery. The shaft 'floats' on a cushion of oil. A drain pipe returns the oil to the sump.

Precautions

5 The turbocharger operates at extremely high speeds and temperatures. Certain precautions must be observed, to avoid premature failure of the turbo, or injury to the operator.
● Do not operate the turbo with any of its parts exposed, or with any of its hoses removed. Foreign objects falling onto the rotating vanes could cause excessive damage, and (if ejected) personal injury.
● Do not race the engine immediately after start-up, especially if it is cold. Give the oil a few seconds to circulate.
● Always allow the engine to return to idle speed before switching it off – do not blip the throttle and switch off, as this will leave the turbo spinning without lubrication.
● Allow the engine to idle for several minutes before switching off after a high-speed run.
● Observe the recommended intervals for oil and filter changing, and use a reputable oil of the specified quality. Neglect of oil changing, or use of inferior oil, can cause carbon formation on the turbo shaft, leading to subsequent failure.

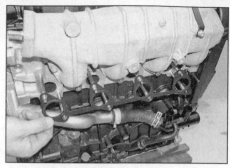

15.13b . . . and recover the gasket

17 Turbocharger – removal, inspection and refitting

Removal

1 Apply the handbrake, then jack up the front of the vehicle and support it on axle stands (see *Jacking and vehicle support*). Undo the screws and remove the engine undershield. Disconnect the battery negative lead as described in Chapter 5A, Section 4.

1.4 litre engine

2 Undo the two bolts and four clips, then lift the bonnet slam panel slightly, and move it forward, tilting the radiator **(see illustrations)**. Place a sheet of thick cardboard over the rear of the radiator to protect it from accidental damage.
3 Undo the heat shield mounting bolts **(see illustration)**, and remove the heat shield from above.
4 Release the clips and remove the turbocharger air intake pipe and resonator box.
5 Undo the bolts and remove the upper heat shield from the manifold.
6 Slacken the clip securing the front pipe/catalytic converter to the turbocharger.
7 Undo the oil supply pipe banjo bolts

17.2a Undo the two bolts (one each side – arrowed) . . .

17.2b . . . prise out the four plastic rivets, and move the bonnet slam panel forward slightly

17.3 Undo the heat shield retaining bolts (arrowed)

17.7a Undo the turbocharger oil supply pipe banjo bolts from the cylinder block . . .

17.7b . . . and the turbocharger

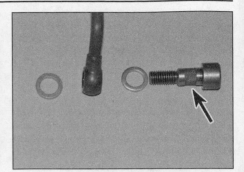

17.7c Note the filter incorporated into the banjo bolt (arrowed)

and recover the sealing washers **(see illustrations)**.

8 Slacken the retaining clip and disconnect the oil return pipe from the turbocharger **(see illustration)**.

17.8 Slacken the oil return hose clip (arrowed)

9 Unscrew the four nuts, and remove the turbocharger from the exhaust manifold **(see illustrations)**.

1.6 litre engine

10 Place a sheet of thick cardboard over the rear of the radiator to protect it from accidental damage.

11 Slacken the clamps, undo the bolts, and remove the air ducts to and from the turbocharger and inlet manifold. Note their fitted positions and disconnect the various wiring plugs as the assembly is withdrawn.

12 Disconnect the vacuum hose from the turbocharger wastegate control assembly **(see illustration)**.

13 Undo the mounting bolts **(see illustration)**, and remove the heat shield from above turbocharger.

14 Remove the catalytic converter/particle

filter (where applicable) as described in Section 19.

15 Undo the oil supply pipe banjo bolts and recover the sealing washers **(see illustration)**.

16 Slacken the retaining clip and disconnect the oil return pipe from the turbocharger and cylinder block.

17 Unscrew the four nuts, and the nut securing the support bracket, then remove the turbocharger from the exhaust manifold **(see illustration)**.

2.0 litre SOHC engine

18 Remove the exhaust system as described in Section 19. **Note:** *This is necessary to prevent damage to the exhaust flexible joint.*

19 Remove the front floor tunnel heat shield, and steering rack heat shield.

20 Remove the turbocharger inlet and outlet ducting as described in Section 4. Also, on DW10ATED (intercooled) engines, remove the

17.9a Undo the lower nuts (arrowed) . . .

17.9b . . . and upper nuts securing the turbocharger

17.12 Disconnect the vacuum pipe from the wastegate control assembly (arrowed)

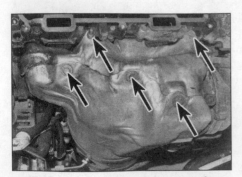

17.13 Undo the bolts and remove the turbocharger heat shield (arrowed)

17.15 Turbocharger oil supply and return pipes (arrowed)

17.17 Undo the 3 nuts (arrowed – one hidden) and remove the support bracket (arrowed)

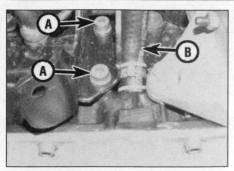

17.21 Turbocharger lower mounting bracket bolts (A) and oil return pipe (B)

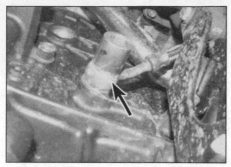

17.22 Turbocharger oil supply pipe banjo (arrowed) on the rear of the cylinder block

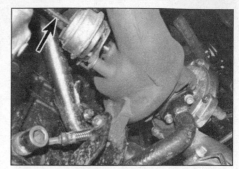

17.23 Turbocharger vacuum control pipe (arrowed)

turbocharger air inlet ducting intermediate manifold, as described in Section 4.
21 Unbolt the turbocharger upper and lower mounting brackets **(see illustration)**.
22 Unscrew the union nuts and disconnect the oil supply and return pipes from the turbocharger and engine cylinder block **(see illustration)**. Tape over the openings.
23 Disconnect the vacuum control pipe **(see illustration)**.
24 On models without an intercooler, unscrew the three retaining nuts and withdraw the turbocharger from the exhaust manifold studs.
25 Undo the three nuts securing the turbocharger to the exhaust manifold, then remove the turbocharger down through the exhaust tunnel **(see illustration)**. Recover the gasket from the manifold.

2.0 litre DOHC engine

26 Remove the air filter assembly as described in Section 4.
27 Remove the front subframe as described in Chapter 10.
28 Remove the right-hand driveshaft as described in Chapter 8.
29 Remove the particulate emission filter and the steering rack heat shield.
30 Move the EGR valve and cooler assembly to one side without disconnecting the coolant hoses (refer to Chapter 4C).
31 Undo the bolts and remove the heat shield over the turbocharger.
32 Detach the right-hand driveshaft intermediate bearing housing from the cylinder block.

33 Remove the heat shields over the pre-catalyst, then undo the fasteners, remove the pre-catalyst support bracket at the right-hand end, undo the mounting bolt at the left-hand end, slacken the clamp securing the pre-catalyst to the turbocharger, and remove the pre-catalyst.
34 Disconnect the turbocharger air inlet and outlet ducts.
35 Remove the support bracket beneath the turbocharger.
36 Disconnect the vacuum pipe and wiring plug from the turbocharger control.
37 Disconnect the oil supply and return pipes from the engine cylinder block. Tape over the openings.
38 Undo the nuts/bolt securing the turbocharger to the exhaust manifold, lift the assembly slightly, then lower the turbocharger downwards from position.

Inspection

39 With the turbocharger removed, inspect the housing for cracks or other visible damage.
40 Spin the turbine or the compressor wheel, to verify that the shaft is intact and to feel for excessive shake or roughness. Some play is normal, since in use, the shaft is 'floating' on a film of oil. Check that the wheel vanes are undamaged.
41 If oil contamination of the exhaust or induction passages is apparent, it is likely that turbo shaft oil seals have failed.
42 No DIY repair of the turbo is possible

and none of the internal or external parts are available separately. If the turbocharger is suspect in any way a complete new unit must be obtained. Do not attempt to dismantle the turbocharger control assemblies.

Refitting

43 Refitting is a reverse of the removal procedure, bearing in mind the following points:
  a) *Renew the turbocharger retaining nuts and gaskets.*
  b) *If a new turbocharger is being fitted, change the engine oil and filter. Also renew the filter in the oil feed pipe.*
  c) *Prime the turbocharger by injecting clean engine oil through the oil feed pipe union before reconnecting the union.*

---

18 Intercooler and air inlet heater – removal and refitting

Note: *The following applies to DV6ATED4, DW10ATED and DW10BTED4 engines only.*

Intercooler

Removal

1 The intercooler is located at the front of the engine compartment, on the left-hand side of the radiator on 2.0 litre models, or on the right-hand side of the radiator on 1.6 litre models. First apply the handbrake, then jack up the front of the vehicle and support it on axle stands (see *Jacking and vehicle support*). Undo the screws and remove the engine undershield.
2 Remove the engine top cover.
3 On 2.0 litre models, remove the air filter assembly as described in Section 4.
4 Remove the front bumper as described in Chapter 11.
5 On 1.6 litre models, loosen the clips and disconnect the inlet and outlet ducts from the top of the intercooler **(see illustration)**.
6 On 2.0 litre models, loosen the clip and disconnect the outlet air duct from the intercooler, then working under the car, loosen

17.25 Turbocharger-to-exhaust manifold retaining nuts (arrowed)

18.5 On 1.6 litre models, loosen the inlet and outlet duct clips

18.6 On 2.0 litre models, loosen the inlet duct clip (arrowed)

18.7 Intercooler top mounting bolts on 1.6 litre models

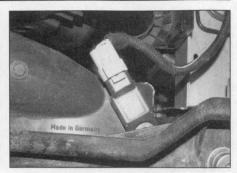

18.8 Disconnect the sensor wiring plug

18.12 Release the clip (arrowed) and disconnect the hoses from the matrix and valve

the clip and disconnect the inlet air duct from the intercooler (see illustration).

7 Undo the bolt(s) securing the intercooler to the engine compartment front crossmember (see illustration).

8 Disconnect the wiring plug from the sensor on the top of the intercooler (see illustration).

9 Lift the intercooler from its lower mountings and remove from the vehicle.

Refitting

10 Refitting is a reversal of removal.

Air inlet heater

Removal

11 Drain the coolant as described in Chapter 1B.

12 Disconnect the hoses from the matrix and valve (see illustration).

13 Remove the air cleaner housing as described in Section 4, sliding the matrix from the housing.

Refitting

14 Refitting is a reversal of removal. Refill the coolant as described in Chapter 1B.

---

19 Exhaust system – general information and component renewal

General information

1 According to model, the exhaust system consists of either two, three or four sections. Three-section systems consist of a catalytic converter, an intermediate pipe, and a tailpipe. The three- or four-section system consists of a pre-catalyst after the turbocharger, followed by a catalytic converter, particulate filter (not all models), intermediate pipe, and tailpipe. On two-section systems, the catalytic converter and intermediate pipe are combined to form a single section.

2 The exhaust joints are of either the spring-loaded ball type (to allow for movement in the exhaust system) or clamp-ring type.

3 The system is suspended throughout its entire length by rubber mountings.

4 Each exhaust section can be removed individually, or alternatively, the complete system can be removed as a unit. Even if only one part of the system needs attention, it is often easier to remove the whole system and separate the sections on the bench.

5 To remove the system or part of the system, first jack up the front or rear of the car, and support it on axle stands (see *Jacking and vehicle support*). Alternatively, position the car over an inspection pit, or on car ramps.

Catalytic converter removal

1.4 litre SOHC engine

6 Undo the screws and remove the engine undershield.

7 Undo the bolts and remove the heat shield from the catalytic converter (see illustration 17.3).

8 Slacken the retaining clamps joining the catalytic converter to the turbocharger and exhaust pipe. Take care not to damage the flexible section of the front exhaust pipe (see illustration).

9 Undo the bolts securing the catalytic converter to the cylinder block and manoeuvre it down and out of the engine compartment (see illustration).

2.0 litre SOHC DW10TD engine

10 The catalytic converter is integral with the front section of the exhaust pipe. Undo the screws and remove the engine undershield.

11 Slacken the retaining clamps securing the

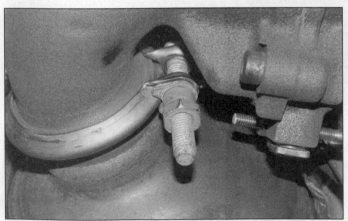

19.8 Catalytic converter-to-turbocharger clamp bolt

19.9 Catalytic converter mounting bolts (arrowed)

19.14a Unscrew the pressure take-off union from the side of the catalyst/filter . . .

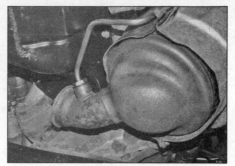

19.14b . . . and the one at the base

19.17 Exhaust pipe-to-catalyst/filter clamp (arrowed)

front pipe to the manifold and intermediate pipe.

12 Release the pipe from the rubber mountings and manoeuvre is from under the vehicle.

Catalytic converter/ particulate filter removal

1.6 litre engine

13 Undo the screws and remove the engine undershield.

14 Unscrew the pressure take off unions from the side and base of the assembly **(see illustrations)**.

15 Disconnect the sensor wiring plug on the side of the catalytic converter.

16 Undo the bolts and remove the heat shield from the catalytic converter/particulate filter.

17 Slacken the retaining clamps joining the catalytic converter to the turbocharger, and exhaust pipe. Take care not to damage the flexible section of the front exhaust pipe **(see illustration)**.

18 Slacken the clamp securing the catalytic converter to the turbocharger.

19 Undo the 2 nuts securing the catalytic converter to the cylinder block and manoeuvre it down and out of the engine compartment **(see illustration)**.

20 If required, note its fitted position, then slacken the clamp and detach the particulate filter from the base of the catalytic converter **(see illustration)**.

2.0 litre SOHC DW10ATED and DOHC engines

21 Disconnect the wiring connector from the particulate filter.

19.19 Catalytic converter/particulate filter retaining nuts (arrowed)

22 Mark or label the additive/pressure pipes to aid refitting, then disconnect them at the connectors **(see illustration)**. Be prepared for fluid spillage.

23 Unscrew the temperature sensor from the assembly **(see illustration)**. Take care not to damage the sensor probe during removal.

24 Unscrew the assembly front and rear clamp bolts, and carefully lower it from the vehicle.

25 From production number RPO 09436, it is possible to separate the particle filter from the catalytic converter. With the assembly on a bench undo the four bolts/nuts and separate the two halves. Recover the gasket.

Pre-catalytic converter removal

2.0 litre DOHC engine

26 The pre-catalyst removal procedure is

19.20 Undo the clamp (arrowed) and slide the particulate filter from the catalytic converter

described within the turbocharger removal procedure – see Section 17.

Intermediate pipe removal

27 Slacken the clamping ring bolts, and disengage both clamps from the flange joints.

28 Release the pipe from its mounting rubber and remove it from underneath the vehicle. Alternatively, undo the nuts/bolts securing the mountings to the vehicle body **(see illustration)**.

Tailpipe removal

29 Slacken the tailpipe clamping ring bolts, and disengage the clamp from the flange joint.

30 Unhook the tailpipe from its mounting rubbers, and remove it from the vehicle **(see**

19.22 Particulate filter additive/pressure pipes

19.23 Unscrew the temperature sensor

19.28 Undo the nuts (arrowed) and remove the pipe along with the mountings

19.30 Unhook the tail pipe from the mountings, or undo the mounting nuts (arrowed)

illustration). Alternatively, undo the nuts/bolts securing the mountings to the vehicle body.

Complete system removal

31 Unscrew the front clamp ring bolt and release the catalytic converter or front pipe from the turbocharger **(see illustration 19.8)**. On models with a particulate filter, note their fitted positions, and disconnect the various pipes/sensors from the system. Free the system from its mounting rubbers and remove it from underneath the vehicle. Alternatively, undo the nuts/bolts securing the mountings to the vehicle body.

Heat shield(s) removal

32 The heat shields are secured to the underside of the body by various nuts and bolts. Each shield can be removed once the relevant exhaust section has been removed. If a shield is being removed to gain access to a component located behind it, it may prove sufficient in some cases to remove the retaining nuts and/or bolts, and simply lower the shield, without disturbing the exhaust system.

Refitting

33 Each section is refitted by reversing the removal sequence, noting the following points:

a) *Ensure that all traces of corrosion have been removed from the flanges, and renew all necessary gaskets.*

b) *Inspect the rubber mountings for signs of damage or deterioration, and renew as necessary.*

c) *On joints secured together by a clamping ring, apply a smear of exhaust system jointing paste to the flange joint, to ensure a gas-tight seal. Tighten the clamping ring nuts evenly and progressively, so that the clearance between the clamp halves remains equal on either side.*

d) *Prior to tightening the exhaust system fasteners, ensure that all rubber mountings are correctly located, and that there is adequate clearance between the exhaust system and vehicle underbody.*

e) *On models fitted with a particulate filter, fill the additive reservoir as described in Chapter 1B.*

Chapter 4 Part C:
Emission control systems

Contents

Degrees of difficulty

Easy, suitable for novice with little experience	**Fairly easy,** suitable for beginner with some experience	**Fairly difficult,** suitable for competent DIY mechanic	**Difficult,** suitable for experienced DIY mechanic	**Very difficult,** suitable for expert DIY or professional

1 General information

All petrol engines use unleaded petrol and also have various other features built into the fuel system to help minimise harmful emissions. In addition, all engines are equipped with the crankcase emission control system described below. All engines are also equipped with a catalytic converter and an evaporative emission control system. Some 2.0 litre petrol engines equipped to emission standard L4 also utilise a secondary air injection system to quickly bring the catalytic converter up to normal working temperature.

All diesel engines are also designed to meet the strict emission requirements and are equipped with a crankcase emission control system and a catalytic converter. To further reduce exhaust emissions, all diesel engines are also fitted with an exhaust gas recirculation (EGR) system. Additionally, 2.0 litre DW10ATED diesel models may be equipped with a particulate emission filter which uses porous silicon carbide substrate to trap particulates of carbon as the exhaust gases pass through.

The emission control systems function as follows.

Petrol engines

Crankcase emission control

To reduce the emission of unburned hydrocarbons from the crankcase into the atmosphere, the engine is sealed and the blow-by gases and oil vapour are drawn from inside the crankcase, through a wire mesh oil separator, into the inlet tract to be burned by the engine during normal combustion.

Under all conditions the gases are forced out of the crankcase by the (relatively) higher crankcase pressure; if the engine is worn, the raised crankcase pressure (due to increased blow-by) will cause some of the flow to return under all manifold conditions.

Exhaust emission control

To minimise the amount of pollutants which escape into the atmosphere, a catalytic converter is fitted in the exhaust system. On all models where a catalytic converter is fitted, the system is of the closed-loop type, in which lambda (oxygen) sensors in the exhaust system provides the fuel-injection/ignition system ECU with constant feedback, enabling the ECU to adjust the mixture to provide the best possible conditions for the converter to operate.

The lambda sensors have a heating element built-in that is controlled by the ECU through the lambda sensor relay to quickly bring the sensor's tip to an efficient operating temperature. The sensor's tip is sensitive to oxygen and sends the ECU a varying voltage depending on the amount of oxygen in the exhaust gases; if the inlet air/fuel mixture is too rich, the exhaust gases are low in oxygen so the sensor sends a low-voltage signal, the voltage rising as the mixture weakens and the amount of oxygen rises in the exhaust gases. Peak conversion efficiency of all major pollutants occurs if the inlet air/fuel mixture is maintained at the chemically-correct ratio for the complete combustion of petrol of 14.7 parts (by weight) of air to 1 part of fuel (the 'stoichiometric' ratio). The sensor output voltage alters in a large step at this point, the ECU using the signal change as a reference point and correcting the inlet air/fuel mixture accordingly by altering the fuel injector pulse width.

Evaporative emission control

To minimise the escape into the atmosphere of unburned hydrocarbons, an evaporative emission control system is fitted to models equipped with a catalytic converter. The fuel tank filler cap is sealed and a charcoal canister is mounted behind the wheel arch liner under the right-hand side front wing to collect the petrol vapours generated in the tank when the car is parked. It stores them until they can be cleared from the canister (under the control of the fuel-injection/ignition system ECU) via the purge valve into the inlet tract to be burned by the engine during normal combustion.

To ensure that the engine runs correctly when it is cold and/or idling and to protect the catalytic converter from the effects of an over-rich mixture, the purge control valve is not opened by the ECU until the engine has warmed-up, and the engine is under load; the valve solenoid is then modulated on and off to allow the stored vapour to pass into the inlet tract.

Secondary air injection

2.0 litre petrol engines equipped to emission standard L4 are also equipped with a secondary air injection system. This system is designed to reduce exhaust emissions in the period between first starting the engine and until the catalytic converter reaches operating (functioning) temperature. Introduction of air into the exhaust system during the initial start-up period, creates an 'afterburner' effect which quickly increases the temperature in the exhaust system front pipe, thus bringing the catalytic converter up to normal operating temperatures very quickly.

The system consists of an air pump, mounted at the front left-hand side of the car, an air injection valve, mounted on a bracket at the front of the cylinder head, a connecting pipe linking the valve to the exhaust manifold, and interconnecting air hoses.

The system operates for between 10 and 45 seconds after engine start-up, dependant on coolant temperature.

Diesel models

Crankcase emission control

Refer to the description for petrol engines.

Exhaust emission control

To minimise the level of exhaust pollutants released into the atmosphere, a catalytic converter is fitted in the exhaust system of all models.

The catalytic converter consists of a canister containing a fine mesh impregnated with a catalyst material, over which the hot exhaust gases pass. The catalyst speeds up

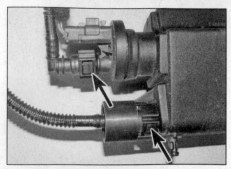

2.5 Depress the quick-release buttons, and disconnect the hoses (arrowed)

the oxidation of harmful carbon monoxide, unburnt hydrocarbons and soot, effectively reducing the quantity of harmful products released into the atmosphere via the exhaust gases.

Exhaust gas recirculation system

This system is designed to recirculate small quantities of exhaust gas into the inlet tract, and therefore into the combustion process. This process reduces the level of oxides of nitrogen present in the final exhaust gas which is released into the atmosphere.

The volume of exhaust gas recirculated is controlled by the system electronic control unit.

A vacuum-operated valve is fitted to the exhaust manifold, to regulate the quantity of exhaust gas recirculated. The valve is operated by the vacuum supplied by the solenoid valve.

Particulate filter system

The particulate filter is combined with the catalytic converter in the exhaust system, and its purpose it to trap particulates of carbon (soot) as the exhaust gases pass through, in order to comply with latest emission regulations.

The filter can be automatically regenerated (cleaned) by the system's ECU on-board the vehicle. The engine's high pressure injection system is utilized to inject fuel into the exhaust gases during the post-injection period; this causes the filter temperature to increase sufficient to oxidize the particulates, leaving an ash residue. The regeneration period is

2.12 Lambda sensor (1.6 litre model)

automatically controlled by the on-board ECU. Subsequently, at the correct service interval the filter must be removed from the exhaust system, and renewed.

To assist the combustion of the trapped carbon (soot) during the regeneration process, a fuel additive (cerium-based Eolys) is automatically mixed with the diesel fuel in the fuel tank. The additive is stored in a 5 litre container attached to the bottom of the fuel tank, and the ECU regulates the amount of additive to send to the fuel tank by means of an additive injector located on the top of the fuel tank.

---

2 Emission control systems – testing and component renewal

Petrol models

Crankcase emission control

1 The components of this system require no attention other than to check that the hose(s) are clear and undamaged at regular intervals.

Evaporative emission control

2 If the system is thought to be faulty, disconnect the hoses from the charcoal canister and purge control valve and check that they are clear by blowing through them. If the purge control valve or charcoal canister are thought to be faulty, they must be renewed.

Charcoal canister renewal

3 The charcoal canister is located under the wheel arch on the right-hand side. To gain access, slacken the right-hand front roadwheel bolts, jack up the front of the car and support it on axle stands. Remove the roadwheel, push in the centre pins then prise out the plastic expanding rivets, and remove the wheel arch liner.
4 Gently prise the canister from its three retaining clips and lower it from the top of the wheel arch.
5 Identify the location of the two hoses then depress the quick-release button and disconnect hoses from the purge valve and the canister. Disconnect the purge valve wiring plug **(see illustration)**.
6 Refitting is a reverse of the removal

2.16 Secondary air injection pump

procedure ensuring that the hoses are correctly reconnected.

Purge valve renewal

7 The purge valve is integral with the canister, and cannot be renewed separately.

Exhaust emission control

8 The performance of the catalytic converter can be checked only by measuring the exhaust gases using a good-quality, carefully-calibrated exhaust gas analyser.
9 If the CO level at the tailpipe is too high, the vehicle should be taken to a Peugeot dealer or specialist so that the complete fuel injection and ignition systems, including the lambda sensor, can be thoroughly checked using the special diagnostic equipment. Once these have been checked and are known to be free from faults, the fault must be in the catalytic converter, which must be renewed as described in Part A of this Chapter.

Catalytic converter renewal

10 Refer to Part A of this Chapter.

Lambda sensor renewal

Note: *The lambda sensor is delicate and will not work if it is dropped or knocked, if its power supply is disrupted, or if any cleaning materials are used on it.*
11 Trace the wiring back from the lambda sensor(s), which are located before and after the catalytic converters. On 1.4 and 1.6 litre petrol engines to emission level L4, one sensor is located in the exhaust manifold, and one after the catalytic converter. On 2.0 litre petrol engines one sensor is screwed into the top of the exhaust front pipe, and one after the catalytic converter. Disconnect both wiring connectors and free the wiring from any relevant retaining clips or ties.
12 Unscrew the sensor from the exhaust system front pipe/manifold and remove it along with its sealing washer **(see illustration)**.
13 Refitting is a reverse of the removal procedure using a new sealing washer. Prior to installing the sensor apply a smear of high temperature grease to the sensor threads. Ensure that the sensor is securely tightened and that the wiring is correctly routed and in no danger of contacting either the exhaust system or engine.

Testing secondary air injection

14 The components of this system require no attention other than to check that the hose(s) are clear and undamaged at regular intervals.
15 Accurate testing of the system operation entails the use of diagnostic test equipment and should be entrusted to a Peugeot dealer or specialist.

Air pump renewal

16 The air pump is located at the front right-hand corner of the engine **(see illustration)**.
17 Slacken and remove the three nuts and withdraw the pump from the mounting bracket.
18 Disconnect the air hoses and wiring connector and remove the pump.

2.23 Secondary air injection valve

2.37a The EGR pipe is secured to the manifold by two screws (arrowed) . . .

2.37b . . . and to the cylinder block by one bolt (arrowed)

19 Refitting is a reverse of the removal procedure, ensuring that the hoses are correctly reconnected.

Air injection valve renewal

20 Disconnect the battery (see Chapter 5A).
21 Slacken and remove the retaining screws, and remove the shroud from the top of the exhaust manifold.
22 Undo the two bolts securing the connecting pipe flange to the exhaust manifold.
23 Undo the two bolts securing the valve mounting bracket to the cylinder head **(see illustration)**.
24 Withdraw the valve and connecting pipe, disconnect the air hose and remove the air injection valve and connecting pipe as an assembly.
25 If necessary, the air pipe can be removed from the valve and the valve removed from the mounting bracket after undoing the two retaining nuts. Collect the flange gasket after removal.
26 Refitting is a reverse of the removal procedure, but use a new gasket between the valve and mounting bracket.

Diesel models

Crankcase emission control

27 The components of this system require no attention other than to check that the hose(s) are clear and undamaged at regular intervals.

Exhaust emission control

28 The performance of the catalytic converter can be checked only by measuring the exhaust gases using a good-quality, carefully-calibrated exhaust gas analyser.
29 If the catalytic converter is thought to be faulty, before assuming the catalytic converter is faulty, it is worth checking the problem is not due to a faulty injector(s). Refer to your Peugeot dealer for further information.

Catalytic converter renewal

30 Refer to Part B of this Chapter.

Exhaust gas recirculation system

31 Testing of the system should ideally be entrusted to a Peugeot dealer since a vacuum pump and vacuum gauge are required.

2.37c A new EGR pipe-to-manifold O-ring seal must be fitted

EGR valve renewal – 1.4 litre engine

32 Remove the windscreen scuttle trim panel and crossmember as described in paragraph 47 of this Section. Disconnect the battery negative lead as described in Chapter 5A.
33 Carefully pull the plastic cover upwards from the top of the engine.
34 Remove the air cleaner housing as described in Chapter 4B.
35 Note its fitted location, then disconnect the vacuum pipe from the EGR valve.
36 Release the two retaining clamps fitted to the EGR pipe.
37 There are three bolts securing the EGR pipe, and two bolts securing the EGR valve. Undo the bolts and remove the pipe complete with valve. Discard the metal gasket from the valve, and the O-ring seal from the pipe – new ones must be fitted **(see illustrations)**.
38 To remove the EGR solenoid valve,

2.38 EGR solenoid valve retaining bolts (arrowed)

disconnect the two vacuum hoses and the wiring connector. Undo the mounting bracket bolts and remove the valve from the engine compartment **(see illustration)**.
39 Refitting is a reversal of removal.

EGR valve renewal – 1.6 litre engine

40 The EGR valve is located on the left-hand rear of the cylinder head. First, remove the windscreen scuttle trim panel and crossmember as described in paragraph 53 of this Section.
41 Remove the battery as described in Chapter 5A.
42 Remove the air cleaner housing as described in Chapter 4B.
43 Release the clamps securing the EGR pipe to the EGR cooler, and the EGR cooler to the EGR valve **(see illustrations)**.
44 Disconnect the EGR valve wiring plug.

2.43a EGR cooler-to-valve clamp (arrowed) . . .

2.43b . . . EGR cooler-to-pipe clamp (arrowed)

2.45 EGR valve mounting bolts (arrowed – one hidden)

2.47a Push in the centre pins a little, then prise out the complete plastic expanding rivets . . .

2.47b Lever up the centre pins, remove the rivets, and detach the sound insulation material from the crossmember . . .

45 Undo the 2 EGR valve mounting bolts, move the EGR cooler to one side, and manoeuvre the valve from position **(see illustration)**.

46 Recover the gasket/seal. If required, then 'CLIC' type clamps can be replaced by normal worm drive clips.

EGR valve renewal – 2.0 litre engine

47 Undo the four fasteners and remove the plastic cover from the top of the engine. Remove the wiper blades (Chapter 12), then release the clips and remove the plastic scuttle trim panel. The trim is secured by a plastic expanding rivet at each end. Push the centre pins in a little, then prise out the complete rivets. Pull up the ends of the trim to release it from the windscreen clips, then pull the trim down and forward to release it from the centre of the windscreen. Undo the two screws securing the brake/clutch master cylinder reservoir, and move it to one side. Release the sound insulation material from the plastic scuttle crossmember, then undo the two screws and remove the crossmember **(see illustrations)**.

48 Place a sheet of thick cardboard over the rear face of the radiator to prevent any accidental damage.

49 Jack up the front of the vehicle and support it securely on axle stands (see *Jacking and vehicle support*). Undo the screws and remove the engine undershield.

50 Undo the nuts/bolts and remove the rear engine mounting link rod.

51 Disconnect the exhaust pipe in front of the catalytic converter/particle filter. This

is to allow the engine to tip forward without damaging the exhaust system.

52 Use an engine lighting hoist attached to the right-hand engine of the cylinder head, then remove the bolts/nuts and detach the right-hand engine mounting and bracket (see Chapter 2C). Allow the engine to tip forward slightly.

53 Undo the two retaining bolts and remove the turbo air inlet ducting to allow access to the EGR valve.

54 Note its fitted location, then disconnect the vacuum pipe from the EGR valve.

55 Release the EGR valve pipe collar, undo the two nuts and remove the valve. Discard the EGR valve seal – a new one must be fitted.

56 To remove the EGR solenoid valve, disconnect the two vacuum hoses and the wiring connector. Undo the mounting bracket bolts and remove the valve from the engine compartment.

57 Refitting is a reversal of removal.

EGR heat exchanger renewal

58 Drain the cooling system (see Chapter 1B). Alternatively, fit hose clamps to the hoses connected to the EGR heat exchanger.

59 Proceed as described in paragraphs 41 to 47.

60 Loosen the clips and disconnect the coolant hoses from the EGR heat exchanger **(see illustration)**.

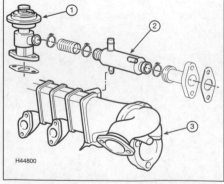

2.60 EGR valve and heat exchanger (2.0 litre models)

1 EGR valve   -   3 Inlet manifold
2 Heat exchanger

61 Unscrew the bolt(s) securing the heat exchanger.

62 Loosen the clips and separate the heat ex-changer from the EGR valve and the EGR pipe.

63 Refitting is a reversal of removal.

Particle filter fuel additive system

64 It is possible to check the fuel additive pump delivery pressure, however, this should be made by a Peugeot dealer or specialist.

Fuel additive reservoir renewal

Note: *Ideally, the additive reservoir should be empty before removing it, otherwise take precautions against spillage.*

> **Warning: Wear protective gloves and eye protection when handling the reservoir.**

65 To remove the fuel additive reservoir, chock the front wheels then jack up the rear of the vehicle and support on axle stands (see *Jacking and vehicle support*). The reservoir is attached to the left-hand side of the fuel tank.

66 Remove the undershield beneath the fuel tank (where fitted).

67 Undo the three nuts and remove the shield from beneath the additive reservoir **(see illustration)**.

68 Note the location of the additive pipes on the reservoir, then depress the release buttons and disconnect them **(see illustration)**. Tape over or plug the openings to prevent dirt ingress.

69 Disconnect the wiring from the level sensor on the rear of the reservoir.

2.47c . . . then undo the screws and remove the crossmember

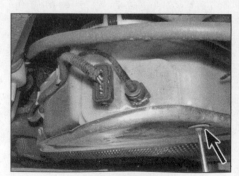

2.67 Additive reservoir heat shield retaining bolt (arrowed)

2.68 Depress the buttons and disconnect the pipes from the reservoir (arrowed)

2.75a The pressure differential sensor is located at the top, right-hand corner of the radiator – 1.6 litre models

2.75b On 2.0 litre models, the pressure differential sensor is located at the engine compartment bulkhead

70 Undo the two nuts and remove the tank retaining strap. Remove the heat shield under the tank.

71 Have a suitable container available to catch spilled additive, undo the two retaining screws and detach the reservoir.

72 Refitting is a reversal of removal.

73 Have the reservoir refilled by a Peugeot dealer or specialist.

Particulate filter

74 Renewal of the particulate filter is described in part B of this Chapter.

Pressure differential sensor

75 This sensor measures the pressure at the entrance and exit of the particulate filter, and is located in the engine compartment **(see illustrations)**.

76 Note their fitted positions, then disconnect the rubber hoses and wiring plug from the sensor.

77 Undo the mounting bolts and remove the sensor.

3 Catalytic converter – general information and precautions

1 The catalytic converter is a reliable and simple device which needs no maintenance in itself, but there are some facts of which an owner should be aware if the converter is to function properly for its full service life.

Petrol models

a) *DO NOT use leaded petrol or LRP – the lead will coat the precious metals, and will eventually destroy the converter.*

b) *Always keep the ignition and fuel systems well-maintained to the service schedule.*

c) *If the engine develops a misfire, do not drive the car at all (or at least as little as possible) until the fault is cured.*

d) *DO NOT push- or tow-start the car – this will soak the catalytic converter in unburned fuel, causing it to overheat when the engine does start.*

e) *DO NOT switch off the ignition at high engine speeds.*

f) *DO NOT use fuel or engine oil additives – these may contain substances harmful to the catalytic converter.*

g) *DO NOT continue to use the car if the engine burns oil to the extent of leaving a visible trail of blue smoke.*

h) *Remember that the catalytic converter operates at very high temperatures. DO NOT, therefore, park the car in dry undergrowth, over long grass or piles of dead leaves after a long run.*

i) *Remember that the catalytic converter is FRAGILE – do not strike it with tools.*

j) *In some cases a sulphurous smell (like that of rotten eggs) may be noticed from the exhaust. This is common to many catalytic converter-equipped cars and once the car has covered a few thousand miles the problem should disappear.*

k) *If the converter is no longer effective it must be renewed.*

Diesel models

2 Refer to parts f, g, h and i of the *petrol models* information given above.

Chapter 5 Part A:
Starting and charging systems

Contents

Degrees of difficulty

Easy, suitable for novice with little experience	Fairly easy, suitable for beginner with some experience	Fairly difficult, suitable for competent DIY mechanic	Difficult, suitable for experienced DIY mechanic	Very difficult, suitable for expert DIY or professional

Specifications

System type .... 12 volt, negative earth

Battery
Type .... Low maintenance or 'maintenance-free' sealed for life

Charge condition:
  Poor .... 12.5 volts
  Normal .... 12.6 volts
  Good .... 12.7 volts

Alternator
Type .... Denso, Bosch, Magneti Marelli, Valeo or Mitsubishi (depending on model)

Rating:
  1.4 and 1.6 litre petrol models .... 70, 80, 90 or 120 amp
  2.0 litre petrol models .... 80, 90, 120 or 150 amp
  Diesel models .... 150 amp

Starter motor
Type .... Mitsubishi, Valeo, Ducellier, Iskra, or Bosch (depending on model)

Torque wrench settings	Nm	lbf ft
Alternator mounting bolts	40	30
Oil pressure switch	30	22
Starter motor:		
1.4 and 1.6 litre diesel models	20	15
All other models	35	26

1 General information and precautions

General information

The engine electrical system consists mainly of the charging and starting systems. Because of their engine-related functions, these components are covered separately from the body electrical devices such as the lights, instruments, etc (which are covered in Chapter 12). On petrol engine models refer to Part B for information on the ignition system, and on diesel models refer to Part C for information on the preheating system.

The electrical system is of the 12 volt negative earth type.

The battery is of the low maintenance or 'maintenance-free' (sealed for life) type and is charged by the alternator, which is belt-driven from the crankshaft pulley.

The starter motor is of the pre-engaged type incorporating an integral solenoid. On starting, the solenoid moves the drive pinion into engagement with the flywheel ring gear before the starter motor is energised. Once the engine has started, a one-way clutch prevents the motor armature being driven by the engine until the pinion disengages from the flywheel.

Precautions

Further details of the various systems are given in the relevant Sections of this Chapter. While some repair procedures are given, the usual course of action is to renew the component concerned. The owner whose interest extends beyond mere component renewal should obtain a copy of the *Automotive Electrical & Electronic Systems Manual*, available from the publishers of this manual.

It is necessary to take extra care when working on the electrical system to avoid damage to semi-conductor devices (diodes and transistors), and to avoid the risk of personal injury. In addition to the precautions given in *Safety first!* at the beginning of this manual, observe the following when working on the system:

• *Always remove rings, watches, etc, before working on the electrical system. Even with the battery disconnected, capacitive discharge could occur if a component's live terminal is earthed through a metal object. This could cause a shock or nasty burn.*
• *Do not reverse the battery connections. Components such as the alternator, electronic control units, or any other components having semi-conductor circuitry could be irreparably damaged.*
• *If the engine is being started using jump leads and a slave battery, connect the batteries positive-to-positive and negative-to-negative (see 'Jump starting'). This also applies when connecting a battery charger.*
• *Never disconnect the battery terminals, the alternator, any electrical wiring or any test instruments when the engine is running.*
• *Do not allow the engine to turn the alternator when the alternator is not connected.*
• *Never 'test' for alternator output by 'flashing' the output lead to earth.*
• *Never use an ohmmeter of the type incorporating a hand-cranked generator for circuit or continuity testing.*
• *Always ensure that the battery negative lead is disconnected when working on the electrical system.*
• *Before using electric-arc welding equipment on the car, disconnect the battery, alternator and components such as the fuel injection/ignition electronic control unit to protect them from the risk of damage.*

2 Electrical fault finding – general information

Refer to Chapter 12.

3 Battery – testing and charging

Testing

Standard and low maintenance battery

1 If the vehicle covers a small annual mileage, it is worthwhile checking the specific gravity of the electrolyte every three months to determine the state of charge of the battery. Use a hydrometer to make the check and compare the results with the following table. Note that the specific gravity readings assume an electrolyte temperature of 15°C; for every 10°C below 15°C subtract 0.007. For every 10°C above 15°C add 0.007.

	Above 25°C	Below 25°C
Fully-charged	1.210 to 1.230	1.270 to 1.290
70% charged	1.170 to 1.190	1.230 to 1.250
Discharged	1.050 to 1.070	1.110 to 1.130

2 If the battery condition is suspect, first check the specific gravity of electrolyte in each cell. A variation of 0.040 or more between any cells indicates loss of electrolyte or deterioration of the internal plates.
3 If the specific gravity variation is 0.040 or more, the battery should be renewed. If the cell variation is satisfactory but the battery is discharged, it should be charged as described later in this Section.

Maintenance-free battery

4 In cases where a 'sealed for life' maintenance-free battery is fitted, topping-up and testing of the electrolyte in each cell is not possible. The condition of the battery can therefore only be tested using a battery condition indicator or a voltmeter.
5 Certain models may be fitted with a 'Delco' type maintenance-free battery, with a built-in charge condition indicator. The indicator is located in the top of the battery casing, and indicates the condition of the battery from its colour. If the indicator shows green, then the battery is in a good state of charge. If the indicator shows black, then the battery requires charging, as described later in this Section. If the indicator shows blue, then the electrolyte level in the battery is too low to allow further use, and the battery should be renewed.
Caution: Do not attempt to charge, load or jump start a battery when the indicator shows clear/yellow.

All battery types

6 If testing the battery using a voltmeter, connect the voltmeter across the battery and compare the result with those given in the Specifications under 'charge condition'. The test is only accurate if the battery has not been subjected to any kind of charge for the previous six hours. If this is not the case, switch on the headlights for 30 seconds, then wait four to five minutes before testing the battery after switching off the headlights. All other electrical circuits must be switched off, so check that the doors and tailgate are fully shut when making the test.
7 If the voltage reading is less than 12.2 volts, then the battery is discharged, whilst a reading of 12.2 to 12.4 volts indicates a partially-discharged condition.
8 If the battery is to be charged, remove it from the vehicle (Section 4) and charge it as described later in this Section.

Charging

Note: *The following is intended as a guide only. Always refer to the manufacturer's recommendations (often printed on a label attached to the battery) before charging a battery.*

Standard and low maintenance battery

9 Charge the battery at a rate of 3.5 to 4 amps and continue to charge the battery at this rate until no further rise in specific gravity is noted over a four hour period.
10 Alternatively, a trickle charger charging at the rate of 1.5 amps can safely be used overnight.
11 Specially rapid 'boost' charges which are claimed to restore the power of the battery in 1 to 2 hours are not recommended, as they can cause serious damage to the battery plates through overheating.
12 While charging the battery, note that the temperature of the electrolyte should never exceed 38°C.

Maintenance-free battery

13 This battery type takes considerably longer to fully recharge than the standard type, the time taken being dependent on the extent of discharge, but it can take anything up to three days.
14 A constant voltage type charger is required to be set, when connected, to 13.9 to 14.9 volts with a charger current below 25 amps. Using this method, the battery should be usable within three hours, giving a voltage reading of 12.5 volts, but this is for a partially-discharged battery and, as mentioned, full charging can take considerably longer.
15 If the battery is to be charged from a fully discharged state (condition reading less than 12.2 volts), have it recharged by your Peugeot dealer or local automotive electrician, as the charge rate is higher and constant supervision during charging is necessary.

4 Battery – removal and refitting

Note: *The radio/cassette/CD player/auto-changer unit fitted as standard equipment by Peugeot is equipped with an anti-theft system, to deter thieves. If the power source is disconnected, the radio/cassette will automatically recode itself as long as it is still fitted to the correct vehicle. If the unit is removed it will not operate in another vehicle.*
Note: *Prior to disconnecting the battery, wait 15 minutes after switching off the ignition to allow the vehicle's ECUs to store all learnt values in their memories.*

Removal

1 Prior to disconnecting the battery, close all windows and the sunroof, and ensure that the vehicle alarm system is deactivated (see Owner's Handbook or Chapter 12, Section 20).
2 The battery is located on the left-hand side of the engine compartment.

3 Lift off the battery positive terminal cover then lift up the quick-release lever (coloured black) and remove the lead. On 2.0 litre diesel models, remove the air filter top cover as described in Chapter 1B. On petrol models, remove the air filter housing as described in Chapter 4A. Remove the cover and insulation from the battery **(see illustrations)**.
4 Disconnect the negative terminal connector (coloured green) in the same way **(see illustration)**.
5 Unscrew the bolt and remove the battery retaining clamp **(see illustration)**.
6 Lift the battery out of the engine compartment.
7 Slacken the left-hand front roadwheel bolts, then jack up the front of the vehicle and support it securely on axle stands (see *Jacking and vehicle support*).
8 Push down the centre pins a little, then prise out the complete rivets and remove the wheel arch liner.
9 Undo the internal bolts securing the battery box/tray to the mounting bracket, including the one from the outer side of the inner wheel arch **(see illustrations)**.
10 On automatic transmission models, slide out the locking catch and disconnect the transmission ECU wiring plug, or undo the nuts and remove the ECU from the battery box/tray **(see illustrations)**.
11 Carefully move aside all cables and hoses, then lift the battery box out of the engine compartment.

Refitting

12 Refitting is a reversal of removal, but

4.3a Lift up the quick-release lever and disconnect the positive lead . . .

smear petroleum jelly on the terminals after reconnecting the leads, and reconnect the negative lead first, and positive the lead last.
13 With the battery reconnected, switch on the ignition and wait at least 1 minute before starting the engine. This will allow the vehicle electronic systems and control units to stabilise. Also refer to Chapter 12, Section 20, on models with the anti-theft alarm system.
14 On models with a sunroof, after reconnecting the battery, re-initialise the sunroof mechanism as follows:
a) *Turn the switch to the maximum-partial opening position (3rd position to the right).*
b) *Keep the control switch pressed in. The sunroof will reach the maximum-partially open position, then close slightly.*
c) *Release the switch within 6 seconds.*
d) *Press the switch within 6 seconds. The sunroof starts to close after 4 seconds from the switch being pressed, then opens completely, then closes completely.*

4.3b . . . then lift off the cover from the battery

5 Charging system – testing

Note: *Refer to the warnings given in 'Safety first!' and in Section 1 of this Chapter before starting work.*
1 If the ignition warning light fails to illuminate when the ignition is switched on, first check the alternator wiring connections for security. If satisfactory, check that the warning light bulb has not blown, and that the bulbholder is secure in its location in the instrument panel. If the light still fails to illuminate, check the continuity of the warning light feed wire from the alternator to the bulbholder. If all is satisfactory, the alternator is at fault and should be renewed or taken to an auto-electrician for testing and repair.
2 If the ignition warning light illuminates when the engine is running, stop the engine and

4.4 Lift the lever and disconnect the negative lead

4.5 Undo the battery clamp bolt (arrowed)

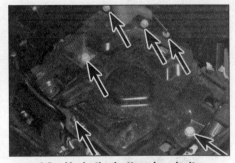

4.9a Undo the battery box bolts (arrowed) . . .

4.9b . . . including the one from the wheel arch

4.10a Slide out the locking catch (arrowed) and disconnect the automatic transmission ECU connector . . .

4.10b . . . or undo the nuts (arrowed) and remove the ECU

check that the drivebelt is correctly fitted and tensioned (see Chapter 1A or 1B) and that the alternator connections are secure. If all is so far satisfactory, have the alternator checked by an auto-electrician for testing and repair.

3 If the alternator output is suspect even though the warning light functions correctly, the regulated voltage may be checked as follows.

4 Connect a voltmeter across the battery terminals and start the engine.

5 Increase the engine speed until the voltmeter reading remains steady; the reading should be approximately 12 to 13 volts, and no more than 14 volts.

6 Switch on as many electrical accessories (eg, the headlights, heated rear window and heater blower) as possible, and check that the alternator maintains the regulated voltage of around 13 to 14 volts.

7 If the regulated voltage is not as stated, the fault may be due to worn brushes, weak brush springs, a faulty voltage regulator, a faulty diode, a severed phase winding or worn or damaged slip-rings. The alternator should be renewed or taken to an auto-electrician for testing and repair.

6 Alternator drivebelt –
removal, refitting and tensioning

Refer to the procedure given for the auxiliary drivebelt in Chapter 1A or 1B.

7 Alternator –
removal and refitting

Removal

1 Disconnect the battery (see Section 4).

2 Remove the auxiliary drivebelt as described in Chapter 1A or 1B. On 1.6 litre petrol models, undo the bolts and remove the auxiliary drivebelt idler pulley bracket bolts, which obscures the lower alternator mounting bolt.

3 Push in the centre pins a little, then prise out the complete plastic rivets, release the side clip, and remove the plastic cover from the top of the washer and coolant reservoirs.

1.4 and 1.6 litre diesel models

4 Remove the rubber cover from the alternator terminal, then unscrew the retaining nut and disconnect the wiring from the rear of the alternator **(see illustration)**. Prise out the retaining clip to release the wiring harness routed around the left-hand end of the alternator.

5 Undo the three bolts and remove the auxiliary drivebelt tensioner assembly **(see illustration)**.

6 Unscrew the alternator mounting bolts **(see illustrations)**. To access the left-hand lower mounting bolt, unbolt the air conditioning compressor (where fitted) and move it to one side. **Do not** disconnect the refrigerant pipes. Manoeuvre the alternator away from its

7.4 Prise out the rubber cover, then disconnect the alternator wiring and plug

7.6a Alternator right-hand mounting bolts (arrowed) . . .

mounting brackets and out from the engine compartment.

All other models

7 Remove the rubber covers (where fitted) from the alternator terminals, then unscrew the retaining nuts and disconnect the wiring from the rear of the alternator **(see illustration)**. Prise out the retaining clip to release the wiring harness routed around the left-hand end of the alternator.

8 Unscrew the lower nut(s) and/or mounting bolt(s), or undo the nut securing the adjuster bolt bracket to the alternator (as applicable). Note that, where a long through-bolt is used to secure the alternator in position, the bolt does not need to be fully removed; the alternator can be disengaged from the bolt once it has been slackened sufficiently. On some models, it may be necessary to remove the drivebelt idler/tensioner pulley to gain access to the

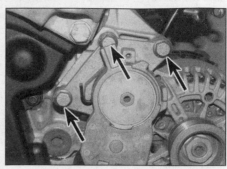

7.5 Undo the auxiliary drivebelt tensioner bolts (arrowed)

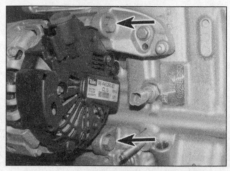

7.6b . . . and left-hand mounting bolts (arrowed)

alternator mounting nuts and bolts (depending on specification). On 2.0 litre diesel models, the lower front mounting bolt also carries the auxiliary drivebelt idler pulley which can be left in position on the bolt as it is removed **(see illustration)**. On 2.0 litre petrol models equipped with secondary air injection, undo the bolts and move the air pump and auxiliary drivebelt idler pulley bracket to one side.

9 Manoeuvre the alternator away from its mounting brackets and out from the engine compartment **(see illustration)**.

Refitting

10 Refitting is a reversal of removal, tensioning the auxiliary drivebelt as described in Chapter 1A or 1B, and ensuring that the alternator mountings are securely tightened. Note that on diesel models, the upper bolt acts as a centraliser and should be tightened first **(see illustration)**.

7.7 Alternator wiring connections

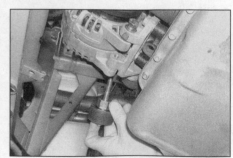

7.8 On 2.0 litre diesel models, the lower mounting bolt also carries the auxiliary drivebelt pulley

7.9 Remove the alternator from its bracket

7.10 On diesel engines, the upper bolts acts as a centraliser

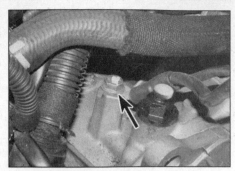

9.3 Engine/transmission earth strap connection (arrowed)

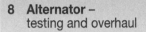

8 Alternator – testing and overhaul

If the alternator is thought to be suspect, it should be removed from the vehicle and taken to an auto-electrician for testing. Most auto-electricians will be able to supply and fit brushes at a reasonable cost. However, check on the cost of repairs before proceeding as it may prove more economical to obtain a new or exchange alternator.

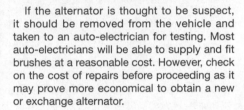

9 Starting system – testing

Note: *Refer to the precautions given in 'Safety first!' and in Section 1 of this Chapter before starting work.*

1 If the starter motor fails to operate when the ignition key is turned to the appropriate position, the following possible causes may be to blame.

  a) *The engine immobiliser is faulty.*

  b) *The battery is faulty.*

  c) *The electrical connections between the switch, solenoid, battery and starter motor are somewhere failing to pass the necessary current from the battery through the starter to earth.*

  d) *The solenoid is faulty.*

  e) *The starter motor is mechanically or electrically defective.*

2 To check the battery, switch on the headlights. If they dim after a few seconds, this indicates that the battery is discharged – recharge (see Section 3) or renew the battery. If the headlights glow brightly, operate the ignition switch and observe the lights. If they dim, then this indicates that current is reaching the starter motor, therefore the fault must lie in the starter motor. If the lights continue to glow brightly (and no clicking sound can be heard from the starter motor solenoid), this indicates that there is a fault in the circuit or solenoid – see following paragraphs. If the starter motor turns slowly when operated, but the battery is in good condition, then this indicates that

either the starter motor is faulty, or there is considerable resistance somewhere in the circuit.

3 If a fault in the circuit is suspected, disconnect the battery leads (including the earth connection to the body), the starter/solenoid wiring and the engine/ transmission earth strap – located on the to of transmission housing **(see illustration)**. Thoroughly clean the connections and reconnect the leads and wiring, then use a voltmeter or test lamp to check that full battery voltage is available at the battery positive lead connection to the solenoid, and that the earth is sound. Smear petroleum jelly around the battery terminals to prevent corrosion – corroded connections are amongst the most frequent causes of electrical system faults.

4 If the battery and all connections are in good condition, check the circuit by disconnecting the wire from the solenoid blade terminal. Connect a voltmeter or test lamp between the wire end and a good earth (such as the battery negative terminal), and check that the wire is live when the ignition switch is turned to the 'start' position. If it is, then the circuit is sound – if not the circuit wiring can be checked as described in Chapter 12.

5 The solenoid contacts can be checked by connecting a voltmeter or test lamp between the battery positive feed connection on the starter side of the solenoid, and earth. When the ignition switch is turned to the 'start' position, there should be a reading or lighted bulb, as applicable. If there is no reading or

lighted bulb, the solenoid is faulty and should be renewed.

6 If the circuit and solenoid are proved sound, the fault must lie in the starter motor. In this event, it may be possible to have the starter motor overhauled by a specialist, but check on the cost of spares before proceeding, as it may prove more economical to obtain a new or exchange motor.

10 Starter motor – removal and refitting

Removal

1 Disconnect the battery (see Section 4).

2 So that access to the motor can be gained both from above and below, apply the handbrake then jack up the front of the vehicle and support it on axle stands (see *Jacking and vehicle support*). Release the screws and remove the engine undershield (where fitted).

3 On 1.4 and 1.6 litre engines, remove the battery and the battery tray.

4 Slacken and remove the two retaining nuts and disconnect the wiring from the starter motor solenoid. Recover the washers under the nuts. On 1.4 and 1.6 litre diesel engines, release the wiring loom from the retaining clips, then undo the bolt securing the wiring loom support plate above the starter motor **(see illustrations)**.

5 Undo the three mounting bolts (two at the rear of the motor, and one which comes through from the top of the transmission

10.4a Undo the two nuts (arrowed) and disconnect the starter motor wiring

10.4b Undo the bolt (arrowed) securing the wiring loom support plate

10.5 Starter motor mounting bolts (arrowed)

housing), supporting the motor as the bolts are withdrawn. Recover the washers from under the bolt heads and note the locations of any wiring or hose brackets secured by the bolts **(see illustration)**.

6 Manoeuvre the starter motor out from underneath the engine and recover the locating dowel(s) from the motor/transmission (as applicable).

Refitting

7 Refitting is a reversal of removal, ensuring that the locating dowel(s) are correctly positioned. Also make sure that any wiring or hose brackets are in place under the bolt heads as noted prior to removal.

13.3a The oil pressure switch is located at the front of the cylinder block . . .

13.3b . . . at the base of the oil filter housing (2.0 litre model) . . .

11 Starter motor – testing and overhaul

If the starter motor is thought to be suspect, it should be removed from the vehicle and taken to an auto-electrician for testing. Most auto-electricians will be able to supply and fit brushes at a reasonable cost. However, check on the cost of repairs before proceeding as it may prove more economical to obtain a new or exchange motor.

12 Ignition switch – removal and refitting

The ignition switch is integral with the steering column lock, and can be removed as described in Chapter 10.

13 Oil pressure warning light switch – removal and refitting

Removal

1 The switch is fitted at the front of the cylinder block, in the following locations:
Petrol engines:
  Screwed into the base of the oil filter housing.
1.4 and 1.6 litre diesel engines:
  Adjacent to the oil dipstick guide tube
2.0 litre DW10TD/ATED diesel engines
  Above the oil filter mounting.
2.0 litre DW10BTED diesel engines
  Screwed into the oil filter housing.
Note that on some models access to the switch may be improved if the vehicle is jacked up and supported on axle stands, and the engine undershield removed (where fitted), so that the switch can be reached from underneath (see *Jacking and vehicle support*).

13.3c . . . or above the oil filter housing

2 Remove the protective sleeve from the wiring plug (where applicable), then disconnect the wiring from the switch.
3 Unscrew the switch from the cylinder block, and recover the sealing washer **(see illustrations)**. Be prepared for oil spillage, and if the switch is to be left removed from the engine for any length of time, plug the hole in the cylinder block.

Refitting

4 Examine the sealing washer for signs of damage or deterioration and if necessary renew.
5 Refit the switch, complete with washer, and tighten it securely. Reconnect the wiring connector.
6 Lower the vehicle to the ground then check and, if necessary, top-up the engine oil as described in *Weekly Checks*.

14 Oil level sensor – removal and refitting

1 The sensor is fitted in the following locations:
1.4 and 1.6 litre petrol engines:
  Front side of the cylinder block adjacent to the oil filter housing.
2.0 litre petrol engines:
  Rear side of the cylinder block at the sump-to-block joint.
1.4 and 1.6 litre diesel engines:
  Rear side of the cylinder block, between cylinders 2 and 3.
2.0 litre SOHC diesel engines:
  Rear side of the cylinder block, adjacent to the transmission housing.
2.0 litre DOHC diesel engines
  Front side of the cylinder block, adjacent to the transmission housing.
2 The removal and refitting procedure is as described for the oil pressure switch in Section 13. Access is most easily obtained from underneath the vehicle **(see illustration)**.

14.2 Oil level sensor (arrowed)

Chapter 5 Part B:
Ignition system – petrol models

Contents

Degrees of difficulty

Easy, suitable for novice with little experience	**Fairly easy,** suitable for beginner with some experience	**Fairly difficult,** suitable for competent DIY mechanic	**Difficult,** suitable for experienced DIY mechanic	**Very difficult,** suitable for expert DIY or professional 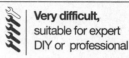

Specifications

General

System type	Static (distributorless) ignition system controlled by engine management ECU
Firing order...	1-3-4-2 (No 1 cylinder at transmission end)
Spark plugs	See Chapter 1A Specifications
Ignition timing......................................	Controlled by engine management ECU

Torque wrench setting	**Nm**	**lbf ft**
Knock sensor securing bolt	20	15

---

1 Ignition system – general information

The ignition system is integrated with the fuel injection system to form a combined engine management system under the control of one ECU (see Chapter 4A for further information). The ignition side of the system is of the static (distributorless) type, consisting of the ignition coils and spark plugs. The ignition coils are housed in a single unit mounted directly above the spark plugs. The coils are integral with the spark plug caps and are pushed directly onto the spark plugs, one for each plug. This removes the need for any HT leads connecting the coils to the plugs.

Under the control of the ECU, the ignition coils operate on the 'wasted spark' principle, ie, each plug sparks twice for every cycle of the engine, once during the compression stroke and once during the exhaust stroke. The spark voltage is greatest in the cylinder which is under compression; in the cylinder on its exhaust stroke the compression is low and this produces a very weak spark which has no effect on the exhaust gases.

The ECU uses its inputs from the various sensors to calculate the required ignition advance setting and coil charging time, depending on engine temperature, load and speed. At idle speeds, the ECU varies the ignition timing to alter the torque characteristic of the engine, enabling the idle speed to be controlled. This system operates in conjunction with the idle speed control motor – see Chapter 4A for additional details.

A knock sensor is also incorporated into the ignition system. Mounted onto the cylinder block, the sensor detects the high-frequency vibrations caused when the engine starts to pre-ignite, or 'pink'. Under these conditions, the knock sensor sends an electrical signal to the ECU which in turn retards the ignition advance setting in small steps until the 'pinking' ceases.

2 Ignition system – testing

Warning: Voltages produced by an electronic ignition system are considerably higher than those produced by conventional ignition systems. Extreme care must be taken when working on the system with the ignition switched on. Persons with surgically-implanted cardiac pacemaker devices should keep well clear of the ignition circuits, components and test equipment.

If a fault appears in the engine management (fuel injection/ignition) system, first ensure that the fault is not due to a poor electrical connection or poor maintenance; ie, check that the air cleaner filter element is clean, the spark plugs are in good condition and correctly gapped, that the engine breather hoses are clear and undamaged, referring to Chapter 1A for further information. Also check that the accelerator cable is correctly adjusted as described in Chapter 4A. If the engine is running very roughly, check the compression pressures and the valve clearances as described in Chapter 2A or 2B, where applicable.

If these checks fail to reveal the cause of the problem the vehicle should be taken to a suitably-equipped Peugeot dealer or specialist for testing. A wiring block diagnostic connector is incorporated in the engine management circuit into which a special electronic diagnostic tester can be plugged. The tester will locate the fault quickly and simply alleviating the need to test all the system components individually which is a time-consuming operation that carries a high risk of damaging the ECU.

The only ignition system checks which can be carried out by the home mechanic are those described in Chapter 1A relating to the spark plugs.

3.1 Disconnect the breather hose from the cylinder head cover

3.2 Disconnect the wiring plug from the ignition HT coil

3.3 Undo the coil retaining bolts (arrowed) . . .

3 Ignition coil unit – removal, testing and refitting

Removal

1.4 litre engines

1 Disconnect the engine breather hose at the quick-release connections on the air cleaner air inlet duct, cylinder head cover and inlet manifold **(see illustration)**. Move the hose to one side.
2 Unplug the wiring connector from the top of the ignition coil unit **(see illustration)**.
3 Undo the nut securing each end of the ignition coil unit to the mounting studs **(see illustration)**. Note that it is quite likely that the stud will be released with the nut.

4 Lift the ignition coil unit upwards off the mounting studs and at the same time carefully ease the HT extension pillars away from the tops of the spark plugs. Lift the unit off the plugs and withdraw it from the engine **(see illustration)**.

1.6 litre engines

5 Undo the six screws and remove the plastic coil pack cover from the top of the engine between the two camshaft covers.
6 Disconnect the wiring plug from the left-hand end of the ignition coil unit **(see illustration)**.
7 Depress the clips and remove the two breather pipes from between the camshaft covers **(see illustration)**.
8 Undo the four mounting screws securing the coil pack **(see illustration)**.

9 Lift the ignition coil unit upwards and at the same time carefully ease the HT extension pillars away from the tops of the spark plugs. Lift the unit off the plugs and withdraw it from the engine.

2.0 litre engines

10 Undo the six screws and lift off the plastic cover from the top of the engine.
11 Disconnect the wiring connector at the left-hand end of the ignition coil unit. Undo the three retaining bolts and lift the coil unit upwards, off the spark plugs and from its location between the cylinder head covers **(see illustration)**.

Testing

12 The circuitry arrangement of the ignition coil unit on these engines is such that testing of an individual coil in isolation from the remainder of the engine management system is unlikely to prove effective in diagnosing a particular fault. Should there be any reason to suspect a faulty individual coil, the engine management system should be tested by a Peugeot dealer or specialist using diagnostic test equipment (see Section 2).

Refitting

13 Refitting is a reversal of the relevant removal procedure ensuring the wiring connectors are securely reconnected.

3.4 . . . then ease the ignition HT coil assembly off the spark plugs and remove it from the engine

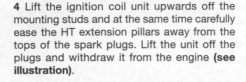

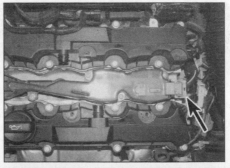

3.6 Disconnect the wiring plug from the HT coils (arrowed)

3.7 Depress the clips (arrowed) and disconnect the breather pipes

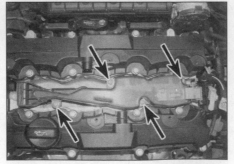

3.8 Undo the four coil pack retaining screws (arrowed)

3.11 Disconnect the HT coil wiring plug (arrowed)

4 Ignition timing – checking and adjustment

1 There are no timing marks on the flywheel or crankshaft pulley. The timing is constantly being monitored and adjusted by the engine management ECU, and nominal values cannot be given. Therefore, it is not possible for the home mechanic to check the ignition timing.

2 The only way in which the ignition timing can be checked is using special electronic test equipment, connected to the engine management system diagnostic connector (refer to Chapter 4A for further information).

5 Knock sensor – removal and refitting

Removal

1 On 1.4 and 1.6 litre engines, the knock sensor is screwed into the rear face of the cylinder block, and, on 2.0 litre engines, into the front face.

2 Firmly apply the handbrake, then jack up the front of the vehicle and support it securely on axle stands (see *Jacking and vehicle support*). Undo the screws and remove the engine undershield (where fitted).

3 Trace the wiring back from the sensor to its wiring connector, and disconnect it from the main loom.

4 Undo the sensor securing bolt and remove the sensor from the cylinder block.

Refitting

5 Refitting is a reversal of the removal procedure, ensuring that the sensor securing bolt is tightened to the specified torque.

Chapter 5 Part C:
Pre/post-heating system – diesel models

Contents

Degrees of difficulty

Easy, suitable for novice with little experience	**Fairly easy,** suitable for beginner with some experience	**Fairly difficult,** suitable for competent DIY mechanic	**Difficult,** suitable for experienced DIY mechanic	**Very difficult,** suitable for expert DIY or professional 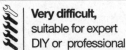

Specifications

Preheating system

Note: *At the time of writing no information concerning the 1.4 litre DV4TD engine was available.*

Preheating period at coolant temperatures of (approximate values):

1.6 litre engine:
- -30°C .... 15 seconds
- -10°C .... 5 seconds
- 0°C .... 0.5 seconds
- 20°C .... 0 seconds

2.0 litre SOHC engine:
- -30°C .... 20 seconds
- -10°C .... 5 seconds
- 0°C .... 0.5 seconds
- 18°C .... 0 seconds

2.0 litre DOHC engine:
- -30°C .... 30 seconds
- -10°C .... 15 seconds
- 0°C .... 10 seconds
- 20°C .... 10 seconds
- 80°C .... 5 seconds

Post-heating system

Note: *At the time of writing no information concerning the 1.4 litre DV4TD engine was available.*

Post-heating period at coolant temperatures of (approximate values):

1.6 litre engine:
- -30°C .... 3 minutes
- -10°C .... 3 minutes
- 0°C .... 3 minutes
- 20° .... 0.5 seconds
- 80° .... 0 seconds

2.0 litre SOHC engine:
- -30°C .... 3 minutes
- -10°C .... 3 minutes
- 0°C .... 1 minute
- 18° .... 30 seconds
- 40° .... 0 seconds

2.0 litre DOHC engine:
- -30°C .... 3 minutes
- -10°C .... 3 minutes
- 0°C .... 3 minutes
- 20° .... 3 minutes
- 40° .... 70 seconds
- 80° .... 0 seconds

Torque wrench settings

Glow plugs:	Nm	lbf ft
1.4 litre engine	8	6
1.6 litre engine	10	7
2.0 litre engines	22	16

1 Pre/post-heating system – description and testing

Description

1 To assist cold starting, diesel engines are fitted with a preheating system, which consists of four of glow plugs (one per cylinder), a glow plug relay unit, a facia-mounted warning lamp, the engine management ECU, and the associated electrical wiring.

2 The glow plugs are miniature electric heating elements, encapsulated in a metal case with a probe at one end and electrical connection at the other. Each combustion chamber has one glow plug threaded into it, with the tip of the glow plug probe positioned directly in line with incoming spray of fuel from the injectors. When the glow plug is energised, it heats up rapidly, causing the fuel passing over the glow plug probe to be heated to its optimum temperature, ready for combustion. In addition, some of the fuel passing over the glow plugs is ignited and this helps to trigger the combustion process.

3 The preheating system begins to operate as soon as the ignition key is switched to the second position, but only if the engine coolant temperature is below 20°C and the engine is turned at more than 70 rpm for 0.2 seconds. A facia-mounted warning lamp informs the driver that preheating is taking place. The lamp extinguishes when sufficient preheating has taken place to allow the engine to be started, but power will still be supplied to the glow plugs for a further period until the engine is started. If no attempt is made to start the engine, the power supply to the glow plugs is switched off after 10 seconds, to prevent battery drain and glow plug burn-out.

4 With the electronically-controlled diesel injection systems fitted to models in this manual, the glow plug relay unit is controlled by the engine management system ECU, which determines the necessary preheating time based on inputs from the various system sensors. The system monitors the temperature of the intake air, then alters the preheating time (the length for which the glow plugs are supplied with current) to suit the conditions.

5 Post-heating takes place after the ignition key has been released from the 'start' position, but only if the engine coolant temperature is below 20°C, the injected fuel flow is less than a certain rate, and the engine speed is less than 2000 rpm. The glow plugs continue to operate for a maximum of 60 seconds, helping to improve fuel combustion whilst the engine is warming-up, resulting in quieter, smoother running and reduced exhaust emissions.

Testing

6 If the system malfunctions, testing is ultimately by substitution of known good units, but some preliminary checks may be made as follows.

7 Connect a voltmeter or 12 volt test lamp between the glow plug supply cable and earth (engine or vehicle metal). Make sure that the live connection is kept clear of the engine and bodywork.

8 Have an assistant switch on the ignition, and check that voltage is applied to the glow plugs. Note the time for which the warning light is lit, and the total time for which voltage is applied before the system cuts out. Switch off the ignition.

9 Compare the results with the information given in the Specifications. Warning light time will increase with lower temperatures and decrease with higher temperatures.

10 If there is no supply at all, the control unit or associated wiring is at fault.

11 To gain access to the glow plugs for further testing, remove the following components, according to model:

1.4 and 1.6 litre engine:
  Remove the cylinder head cover/manifold assembly as described in Chapter 2C.

2.0 litre SOHC engines:
  Undo the four plastic fasteners and remove the engine cover from the top of the engine. Disconnect the injector wiring plugs and move the wiring harness tray to one side after undoing the two retaining nuts. For access to No 4 glow plug, undo the three bolts and move the fuel pipe support bracket to one side (see illustrations).

2.0 litre DOHC engines:
  Working as described in Chapter 4C, undo the bolts and move the EGR heat exchanger and valve assembly to one side. There's no need to disconnect the coolant hoses, so no need to drain the cooling system.

12 Disconnect the main supply cable and the interconnecting wire or strap from the top of the glow plugs. Be careful not to drop the nuts and washers.

13 Use a continuity tester, or a 12 volt test lamp connected to the battery positive terminal, to check for continuity between each glow plug terminal and earth. The resistance of a glow plug in good condition is very low (less than 1 ohm), so if the test lamp does not light or the continuity tester shows a high resistance, the glow plug is certainly defective.

1.11a Rotate the four fasteners (arrowed) 90° anti-clockwise and pull the plastic cover from place

1.11b Undo the two nuts (arrowed) and move the wiring harness tray to one side

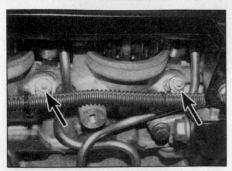

2.2 Undo the nuts securing the glow plug connections (arrowed)

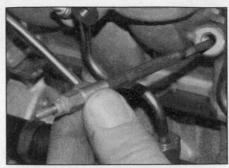

2.4 Unscrew the glow plugs from the cylinder head

3.3 Undo the glow plug control unit mounting nut (arrowed)

14 If an ammeter is available, the current draw of each glow plug can be checked. After an initial surge of 15 to 20 amps, each plug should draw 12 amps. Any plug which draws much more or less than this is probably defective.

15 As a final check, the glow plugs can be removed and inspected as described in the following Section. On completion, refit any components removed for access.

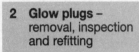

2 Glow plugs – removal, inspection and refitting

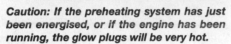

Caution: If the preheating system has just been energised, or if the engine has been running, the glow plugs will be very hot.

Removal

1 Ensure the ignition is turned off. To gain access to the glow plugs, remove the components described in Section 1, according to engine.

2 Unscrew the nuts from the glow plug terminals, and recover the washers. Note that on some 2.0 litre models, an interconnecting wire/shunt is fitted between the four plugs **(see illustration)**.

3 Where applicable, carefully move any obstructing pipes or wires to one side to enable access to the relevant glow plug(s).

4 Unscrew the glow plug(s) and remove from the cylinder head **(see illustration)**.

Inspection

5 Inspect each glow plug for physical damage. Burnt or eroded glow plug tips can be caused by a bad injector spray pattern. Have the injectors checked if this sort of damage is found.

6 If the glow plugs are in good physical condition, check them electrically using a 12 volt test lamp or continuity tester as described in the previous Section.

7 The glow plugs can be energised by applying 12 volts to them to verify that they heat up evenly and in the required time. Observe the following precautions.

a) Support the glow plug by clamping it carefully in a vice or self-locking pliers. Remember it will become red-hot.

b) Make sure that the power supply or test lead incorporates a fuse or overload trip to protect against damage from a short-circuit.

c) After testing, allow the glow plug to cool for several minutes before attempting to handle it.

8 A glow plug in good condition will start to glow red at the tip after drawing current for 5 seconds or so. Any plug which takes much longer to start glowing, or which starts glowing in the middle instead of at the tip, is defective.

Refitting

9 Refit by reversing the removal operations. Apply a smear of copper-based anti-seize compound to the plug threads and tighten the glow plugs to the specified torque. Do not overtighten, as this can damage the glow plug element.

10 Refit any components removed for access.

3 Pre/post-heating system relay unit – removal and refitting

Removal

1 The unit is located on the left-hand front side of the engine compartment where it is mounted on a bracket just in front of the fuse/relay box.

2 Disconnect the battery (see Chapter 5A).

3 Unscrew the retaining nut securing the unit to the mounting bracket **(see illustration)**.

4 Unscrew the two retaining nuts and free the main feed and supply wires from the base of the unit, then disconnect the wiring connector. Remove the unit from the engine compartment.

Refitting

5 Refitting is a reversal of removal, ensuring that the wiring connectors are correctly connected.

Chapter 6
Clutch

Contents

Degrees of difficulty

Easy, suitable for novice with little experience	Fairly easy, suitable for beginner with some experience	Fairly difficult, suitable for competent DIY mechanic	Difficult, suitable for experienced DIY mechanic	Very difficult, suitable for expert DIY or professional

Specifications

Type

All models . . . . Single dry disc with diaphragm spring, hydraulic operation

Clutch operation

All models . . . . Hydraulic

Friction disc diameter

Petrol engine models:

1.4 litre	180 mm
1.6 litre	200 mm
2.0 litre	230 mm
Diesel engine models	230 mm

Torque wrench setting	**Nm**	**lbf ft**
Pressure plate retaining bolts	20	15

1 General information

The clutch consists of a friction disc, a pressure plate assembly, a release bearing and release fork; all of these components are contained in the large cast-aluminium alloy bellhousing, sandwiched between the engine and the transmission. The release mechanism is hydraulic on all models.

The friction disc is fitted between the engine flywheel and the clutch pressure plate, and is allowed to slide on the transmission input shaft splines.

The pressure plate assembly is bolted to the engine flywheel. When the engine is running, drive is transmitted from the crank-shaft, via the flywheel, to the friction disc (these components being clamped securely together by the pressure plate assembly) and from the friction disc to the transmission input shaft.

To interrupt the drive, the spring pressure must be relaxed. This is done by means of the clutch release bearing, fitted concentrically around the transmission input shaft. The bearing is pushed onto the pressure plate assembly by means of the release fork actuated by clutch slave cylinder pushrod.

The clutch pedal is connected to the clutch master cylinder by a short pushrod. The master cylinder is mounted on the engine side of the bulkhead in front of the driver and receives its hydraulic fluid supply from the brake master cylinder reservoir. Depressing the clutch pedal moves the piston in the master cylinder forwards, so forcing hydraulic fluid through the clutch hydraulic pipe to the slave cylinder. The piston in the slave cylinder moves forward on the entry of the fluid and actuates the clutch release fork by means of a short pushrod. The release fork pivots on its mounting stud, and the other end of the fork then presses the release bearing against the pressure plate spring fingers. This causes the springs to deform and releases the clamping force on the pressure plate.

On all models the clutch operating mechanism is self-adjusting, and no manual adjustment is required.

2.4 Remove the dust cap from the bleed screw

2 Clutch hydraulic system – bleeding

⚠️ *Warning: Hydraulic fluid is poisonous; wash off immediately and thoroughly in the case of skin contact, and seek immediate medical advice if any fluid is swallowed or gets into the eyes. Certain types of hydraulic fluid are inflammable, and may ignite when allowed into contact with hot components; when servicing any hydraulic system, it is safest to assume that the fluid IS inflammable, and to take precautions against the risk of fire as though it is petrol that is being handled. Hydraulic fluid is also an effective paint stripper, and will attack plastics; if any is spilt, it should be washed off immediately, using copious quantities of clean water. When topping-up or renewing the fluid, always use the recommended type, and ensure that it comes from a freshly-opened sealed container.*

1 Obtain a clean jar, a suitable length of rubber or clear plastic tubing, which is a tight fit over the bleed screw on the clutch slave cylinder, and a tin of the specified hydraulic fluid. The help of an assistant will also be required. (If a one-man do-it-yourself bleeding kit for bleeding the brake hydraulic system is available, this can be used quite satisfactorily for the clutch also. Full information on the use of these kits may be found in Chapter 9.)

2 On all models, except the 1.4 litre diesel, remove the air cleaner housing as described in Chapter 4A or 4B.
3 Remove the filler cap from the brake master cylinder reservoir, and if necessary top-up the fluid. Keep the reservoir topped-up during subsequent operations.
4 Remove the dust cap from the slave cylinder bleed screw, located on the lower front facing side of the transmission **(see illustration)**.
5 Connect one end of the bleed tube to the bleed screw, and insert the other end of the tube in the jar containing sufficient clean hydraulic fluid to keep the end of the tube submerged.
6 Open the bleed screw half a turn and have your assistant depress the clutch pedal and then slowly release it. Continue this procedure until clean hydraulic fluid, free from air bubbles, emerges from the tube. Now tighten the bleed screw at the end of a downstroke. Make sure that the brake master cylinder reservoir is checked frequently to ensure that the level does not drop too far, allowing air into the system.
7 Check the operation of the clutch pedal. After a few strokes it should feel normal. Any sponginess would indicate air still present in the system.
8 On completion remove the bleed tube and refit the dust cover. Top-up the master cylinder reservoir if necessary and refit the cap. Fluid expelled from the hydraulic system should now be discarded as it will be contaminated with moisture, air and dirt, making it unsuitable for further use.

3 Clutch master cylinder – removal and refitting

Note: *Before starting work, refer to the note at the beginning of Section 2 concerning the dangers of hydraulic fluid.*

Removal

1 Prise up the centre pins, lever out the complete expanding plastic rivets, and remove the trim panel above the driver.s pedals.

2 Depress the clutch pedal, then prise the master cylinder pushrod end from the pedal pin **(see illustration 5.2)**.
3 To minimise hydraulic fluid loss, remove the brake master cylinder reservoir filler cap then tighten it down onto a piece of polythene to obtain an airtight seal.
4 Place absorbent rags under the clutch master cylinder pipe connections in the engine compartment and be prepared for hydraulic fluid loss.
5 Release the master cylinder hydraulic pressure pipe from its retaining clips on the engine compartment bulkhead, then prise out the retaining wire clip and disconnect the pipe from the master cylinder **(see illustration)**. Suitably plug or cap the pipe end to prevent further fluid loss and dirt entry.
6 Depress the quick-release connector tabs and disconnect the hydraulic fluid supply hose **(see illustration)**. Suitably plug or cap the hose end.
7 Rotate the master cylinder 90 degrees clockwise, and remove it from the bulkhead **(see illustration)**.

Refitting

8 Refitting the master cylinder is the reverse sequence to removal, bearing in mind the following points.
  a) *Ensure all retaining clips are correctly refitted.*
  b) *Bleed the clutch hydraulic system as described in Section 2 on completion.*

4 Clutch slave cylinder – removal and refitting

Note: *Before starting work, refer to the note at the beginning of Section 2 concerning the dangers of hydraulic fluid.*

Removal

1 To minimise hydraulic fluid loss, remove the brake master cylinder reservoir filler cap then tighten it down onto a piece of polythene to obtain an airtight seal.
2 On all models except 1.4 and 1.6 litre diesel, remove the air cleaner housing as described in Chapter 4A or 4B.

3.5 Prise out the clip, and disconnect the pipe from the master cylinder

3.6 Squeeze together the sides of the quick-release coupling and disconnect the supply hose

3.7 Turn the master cylinder 90° clock-wise, and remove it from the bulkhead

3 Place absorbent rags under the clutch slave cylinder located on the lower front facing side of the transmission. Be prepared for hydraulic fluid loss.

4 Where necessary for access, release the wiring harness from the retaining clips and move the harness clear of the slave cylinder.

5 Lever out the retaining clip a little, then disconnect the hydraulic pipe from the side of the slave cylinder **(see illustration)**. Suitably plug or cap the pipe end to prevent further fluid loss and dirt entry.

6 On MA5 and BE4/5 transmissions, undo the two retaining bolts and remove the cylinder from the transmission housing **(see illustration)**. On the ML6CL transmission, release the slave cylinder from the transmission by pushing it in by hand and at the same time turning it 90° anti-clockwise.

Refitting

7 Refitting the slave cylinder is the reverse sequence to removal, bearing in mind the following points.
  a) *Apply a little Molykote BR2 Plus grease to the end of the slave cylinder pushrod.*
  b) *Bleed the clutch hydraulic system as described in Section 2 on completion.*

5 Clutch pedal – removal and refitting

Removal

1 Working inside the car, prise up the centre pins, then prise out the complete expanding plastic rivets, and remove the facia lower trim panel above the pedals on the driver's side.

2 Depress the clutch pedal until the end of the master cylinder pushrod is visible though the hole in the side of the pedal bracket. Using a screwdriver, prise the end of the pushrod from the pedal pin **(see illustration)**.

3 Using a screwdriver, compress the helper spring a little, and remove it from the pedal and pedal bracket.

4 Undo the nut from the clutch pedal pivot bolt and withdraw the bolt **(see illustration)**. Note that the bolt also provides a pivot for the brake pedal.

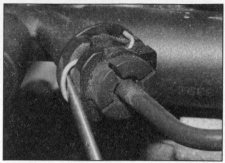
4.5 Lever out the hydraulic pipe retaining clip

5 Remove the clutch pedal from the pedal bracket and recover the bush from the pedal pivot.

6 Check the condition of the pedal, pivot bush and helper spring assembly and renew any components as necessary.

Refitting

7 Lubricate the pedal pivot bolt with multi-purpose grease, then locate the pedal in the bracket and insert the pivot bolt. Refit the pivot bolt nut and tighten it securely.

8 Reconnect the helper spring to the pedal and pedal bracket.

9 Depress the pedal two or three times and check the operation of the clutch release mechanism.

10 Refit the facia lower trim panel and secure with the plastic clips.

6 Clutch assembly – removal, inspection and refitting

⚠️ *Warning: Dust created by clutch wear and deposited on the clutch components may contain asbestos, which is a health hazard. DON'T blow it out with compressed air, nor inhale any of it. DO NOT use petrol or petroleum-based solvents to clean off the dust. Brake system cleaner or methylated spirit should be used to flush the dust into a suitable receptacle. After the clutch components are wiped clean with*

4.6 Undo the two bolts (arrowed) and remove the clutch slave cylinder

rags, dispose of the contaminated rags and cleaner in a sealed, marked container.
Note: *Although most friction materials no longer contain asbestos, it is safest to assume that some still do, and to take precautions accordingly.*

Removal

1 Unless the complete engine/transmission unit is to be removed from the car and separated for major overhaul (see Chapter 2F), the clutch can be reached by removing the transmission as described in Chapter 7A.

2 Before disturbing the clutch, use chalk or a marker pen to mark the relationship of the pressure plate assembly to the flywheel.

3 Working in a diagonal sequence, slacken the pressure plate bolts by half a turn at a time, until spring pressure is released and the bolts can be unscrewed by hand **(see illustration)**.

4 Prise the pressure plate assembly off its locating dowels, and collect the friction disc, noting which way round the disc is fitted.

Inspection

Note: *Due to the amount of work necessary to remove and refit clutch components, it is considered good practice to renew the clutch friction disc, pressure plate assembly and release bearing as a matched set, even if only one of these is worn enough to require renewal. It is worth considering the renewal of the clutch components on a preventative basis if the engine and/or transmission have been removed for some other reason.*

5 When cleaning clutch components, read

5.2 Prise the end of the pushrod from the pedal pin

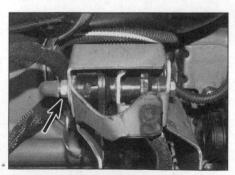
5.4 The clutch pedal bolt (arrowed) is also the pivot for the brake pedal

6.3 Undo the pressure plate bolts (arrowed)

6.13 Fit the disc so the spring hub assembly faces away from the flywheel

6.16 Using a clutch aligning tool to centralise the friction disc

first the warning at the beginning of this Section; remove dust using a clean, dry cloth, and working in a well-ventilated atmosphere.

6 Check the friction disc facings for signs of wear, damage or oil contamination. If the friction material is cracked, burnt, scored or damaged, or if it is contaminated with oil or grease (shown by shiny black patches), the friction disc must be renewed.

7 If the friction material is still serviceable, check that the centre boss splines are unworn, that the torsion springs are in good condition and securely fastened, and that all the rivets are tight. If any wear or damage is found, the friction disc must be renewed.

8 If the friction material is fouled with oil, this must be due to an oil leak from the crankshaft left-hand oil seal, from the sump-to-cylinder block joint, or from the transmission input shaft. Renew the seal or repair the joint, as appropriate, as described in the relevant Part of Chapter 2 or 7, before installing the new friction disc.

9 Check the pressure plate assembly for obvious signs of wear or damage; shake it to check for loose rivets or worn or damaged fulcrum rings, and check that the drive straps securing the pressure plate to the cover do not show signs (such as a deep yellow or blue discoloration) of overheating. If the diaphragm spring is worn or damaged, or if its pressure is in any way suspect, the pressure plate assembly should be renewed.

10 Examine the machined bearing surfaces of the pressure plate and of the flywheel; they should be clean, completely flat, and free from scratches or scoring. If either is discoloured

from excessive heat, or shows signs of cracks, it should be renewed – although minor damage of this nature can sometimes be polished away using emery paper.

11 Check that the release bearing contact surface rotates smoothly and easily, with no sign of noise or roughness. Also check that the surface itself is smooth and unworn, with no signs of cracks, pitting or scoring. If there is any doubt about its condition, the bearing must be renewed.

Refitting

12 On reassembly, ensure that the bearing surfaces of the flywheel and pressure plate are completely clean, smooth, and free from oil or grease. Use solvent to remove any protective grease from new components.

13 Fit the friction disc so that its spring hub assembly faces away from the flywheel; there may be a marking showing which way round the disc is to be refitted (see illustration).

14 Refit the pressure plate assembly, aligning the marks made on dismantling (if the original pressure plate is re-used), and locating the pressure plate on its three locating dowels. Fit the pressure plate bolts, but tighten them only finger-tight, so that the friction disc can still be moved.

15 The friction disc must now be centralised, so that when the transmission is refitted, its input shaft will pass through the splines at the centre of the friction disc.

16 Centralisation can be achieved by passing a screwdriver or other long bar through the friction disc and into the hole in the crankshaft;

the friction disc can then be moved around until it is centred on the crankshaft hole. Alternatively, a clutch-aligning tool can be used to eliminate the guesswork; these can be obtained from most accessory shops (see illustration).

> **HAYNES HINT** *A home-made aligning tool can be fabricated from a length of metal rod or wooden dowel which fits closely inside the crankshaft hole, and has insulating tape wound around it to match the diameter of the friction disc splined hole.*

17 When the friction disc is centralised, tighten the pressure plate bolts evenly and in a diagonal sequence to the specified torque setting.

18 Apply a **thin** smear of molybdenum disulphide grease (Peugeot recommend the use of Molykote BR2 Plus – available from your dealer) to the splines of the friction disc and the transmission input shaft, and also to the release bearing bore and release fork shaft.

19 Refit the transmission as described in Chapter 7A.

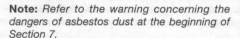

7 Clutch release mechanism – removal, inspection and refitting

Note: *Refer to the warning concerning the dangers of asbestos dust at the beginning of Section 7.*

Removal

1 Unless the complete engine/transmission unit is to be removed from the car and separated for major overhaul (see Chapter 2F), the clutch release mechanism can be reached by removing the transmission only, as described in Chapter 7A.

2 With the transmission removed, squeeze together the tabs of the retaining clip and pull the release fork off the pivot ball-stud. Recover the shim where fitted. The mounting stud unscrews from the transmission housing (see illustrations).

7.2a Squeeze the tabs of the retaining clip together and remove the release fork ...

7.2b ... recover the shim (arrowed) ...

7.2c ... then unscrew the pivot ball-stud

3 Slide the release bearing off the guide tube and disengage the arms of the release fork **(see illustration)**.

Inspection

4 Check that the release bearing contact surface rotates smoothly and easily, with no sign of noise or roughness, and that the surface itself is smooth and unworn, with no signs of cracks, pitting or scoring. If there is any doubt about its condition, the bearing must be renewed.

5 Check the bearing surfaces and points of contact on the release fork and pivot ball-stud, renewing any component which is worn or damaged.

Refitting

6 Apply a smear of molybdenum disulphide grease to the pivot ball-stud.

7 Insert the outer end of the release fork

7.3 Disengage the release bearing from the release fork

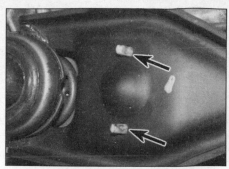

7.9 Ensure the retaining tabs (arrowed) engage correctly with the release fork

through the rubber boot in the side of the transmission bellhousing.

8 Engage the arms of the release fork with the release bearing collar, then slide the release bearing onto the guide tube.

9 Position the shim over the tabs of the pivot ball-stud clip, then push the fork over the stud, ensuring the tabs of the retaining clip engage correctly with the fork **(see illustration)**.

10 Refit the transmission as described in Chapter 7A.

Chapter 7 Part A:
Manual transmission

Contents

Degrees of difficulty

Easy, suitable for novice with little experience	Fairly easy, suitable for beginner with some experience 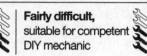	Fairly difficult, suitable for competent DIY mechanic	Difficult, suitable for experienced DIY mechanic	Very difficult, suitable for expert DIY or professional

Specifications

General

Type . . . . Manual, five or six forward speeds and reverse. Synchromesh on all forward speeds

Designation:
Petrol engine models:
1.4 and 1.6 litre MA5
2.0 litre BE4/5
Diesel engine models:
Except DW10BTED4 . . . . BE4/5
DW10BTED4 . . . . ML6CL

Lubrication
Capacity:
MA5 . . . . 2.0 litres
BE4/5 . . . . 1.9 litres
ML6CL:
Without cooling fins on the gearbox casing . . . . . 2.6 litres
With cooling fins on the gearbox casing . . . . . 1.9 litres
Recommended oil type . . . . See *Lubricants and fluids*

Torque wrench settings

	Nm	lbf ft
MA5 transmission		
Clutch release bearing guide sleeve bolts	12	9
Engine-to-transmission fixing bolts	40	30
Gearchange lever mounting nuts	8	6
Left-hand engine/transmission mounting	Refer to Chapter 2A	
Oil drain plug	25	18
Oil filler/level plug	25	18
Rear mounting link	Refer to Chapter 2A	
Reversing light switch	25	18
Roadwheel bolts	90	66
Speedometer drive pinion bracket	10	7

Torque wrench settings (continued)

	Nm	lbf ft
BE4/5 transmission		
Clutch release bearing guide sleeve bolts	12	9
Engine-to-transmission fixing bolts	45	33
Gearchange lever mounting nuts	8	6
Left-hand engine/transmission mounting	Refer to Chapter 2B, 2C or 2D	
Oil drain plug	35	26
Oil filler/level plug	20	15
Rear mounting link	Refer to Chapter 2B, 2C or 2D	
Reversing light switch	25	18
Roadwheel bolts.	90	66
Speedometer drive housing bolts	15	11
ML6CL transmission		
Clutch release bearing guide sleeve bolts	10	7
Engine movement limiter to subframe	65	48
Engine-to-transmission fixing bolts	60	44
Gearchange lever housing bolts.	7	5
Left-hand engine/transmission mounting:		
Mounting bracket to transmission	45	33
Mounting to bracket.	45	33
Mounting to vehicle body.	27	20
Oil drain plug	30	22
Reversing light switch	25	18
Roadwheel bolts.	90	66

1 General information

1 The transmission is contained in a cast-aluminium alloy casing bolted to the engine's left-hand end, and consists of the gearbox and final drive differential – often called a transaxle.

2 Drive is transmitted from the crankshaft via the clutch to the input shaft, which has a splined extension to accept the clutch friction disc, and rotates in sealed ball-bearings. From the input shaft, drive is transmitted to the output shaft, which rotates in a roller bearing at its right-hand end, and a sealed ball-bearing at its left-hand end. From the output shaft, the drive is transmitted to the differential crownwheel, which rotates with the differential case and planetary gears, thus driving the sun gears and driveshafts. The rotation of the planetary gears on their shaft allows the inner roadwheel to rotate at a slower speed than the outer roadwheel when the car is cornering.

3 The input and output shafts are arranged side-by-side, parallel to the crankshaft and driveshafts, so that their gear pinion teeth are in constant mesh. In the neutral position, the output shaft gear pinions rotate freely, so that drive cannot be transmitted to the crownwheel.

4 Gear selection is via a floor-mounted lever and cable mechanism **(see illustration)**. The selector/gearchange cables causes the appropriate selector fork to move its respective synchro-sleeve along the shaft, to lock the gear pinion to the synchro-hub. Since the synchro-hubs are splined to the output shaft, this locks the pinion to the shaft, so that drive can be transmitted. To ensure that gearchanging can be made quickly and quietly, a synchromesh system is fitted to all forward gears, consisting of baulk rings and spring-loaded fingers, as well as the gear pinions and synchro-hubs. The synchromesh cones are formed on the mating faces of the baulk rings and gear pinions.

5 Three different manual transmissions are used on the models covered in this manual. 1.4 and 1.6 litre petrol engine models have the MA5 transmission. 2.0 litre petrol and 2.0 litre SOHC diesel engine models have the BE4/5 unit, and 2.0 litre DOHC diesel engine models have the ML6CL unit. The ML6CL transmission was specially developed to cope with the high torque output of the later 2.0 litre diesel engines. With 6 forward speeds and capable of handling 350 Nm of torque, the transmission is 'filled for life' with fluid – there's no recommended interval for changing the fluid, although it may be prudent to do so at some stage in the vehicle's life.

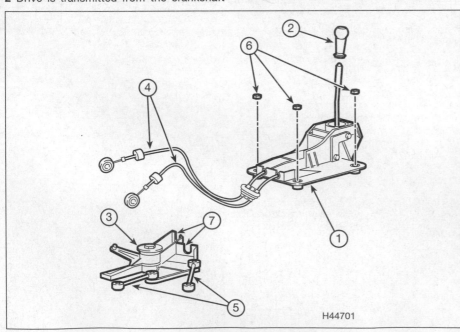

H44701

1.4 Gearchange lever and cables

1 *Gearchange lever and housing*	3 *Bracket*	6 *Nuts*
2 *Gearchange lever knob*	4 *Cables*	7 *Horseshoe clips*
	5 *Gearchange links*	

2 Manual transmission – draining and refilling

Note: *A suitable square section wrench may be required to undo the transmission filler/level and drain plugs on some models. These wrenches can be obtained from most motor factors or your Peugeot dealer.*

1 This operation is much quicker and more efficient if the car is first taken on a journey of sufficient length to warm the engine/transmission up to normal operating temperature.

2 Park the car on level ground, switch off the ignition and apply the handbrake firmly. For improved access, jack up the front of the car and support it securely on axle stands (see *Jacking and vehicle support*). Note that the car must be level to ensure accuracy when refilling and checking the oil level. Undo the screws and remove the engine undershield (where fitted).

3 To improve access to the filler/level plug, remove the plastic rivets (push in the centre pin a little then remove the complete plastic rivet) and remove the left-hand wheel arch liner.

4 Wipe clean the area around the filler/level plug. On the MA5 transmission, the filler/level plug is situated on the left-hand end of the transmission, next to the end cover. On the BE4/5 transmission, the filler/level plug is the largest bolt among those securing the end cover to the transmission. Remove the filler/level plug from the transmission and recover the sealing washer **(see illustrations)**. On the ML6CL transmission, fluid is added through the breather valve on the top face of the transmission.

5 Position a suitable container under the drain plug (situated on the final drive casing at the rear of the transmission) and unscrew the plug **(see illustrations)**

6 Allow the oil to drain completely into the container. If the oil is hot, take precautions against scalding. Clean both the filler/level and the drain plugs, being especially careful to wipe any metallic particles off the magnetic inserts. Discard the original sealing washers; they should be renewed whenever they are disturbed.

7 When the oil has finished draining, clean the drain plug threads and those of the transmission casing, fit a new sealing washer and refit the drain plug, tightening it to the specified torque wrench setting. Refit the undercover (where fitted) then lower the vehicle to the ground.

8 Refilling the transmission is an extremely awkward operation. Above all, allow plenty of time for the oil level to settle properly before checking it. Note that the car must be parked on flat level ground when checking the oil level.

MA5 and BE4/5 transmissions

9 Refill the transmission with the exact amount of the specified type of oil then check

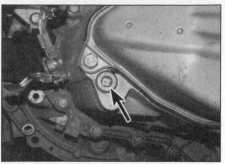

2.4a Oil filler/level plug (arrowed) (MA5 transmission)

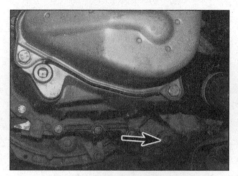

2.5a Oil drain plug (arrowed) (MA5 transmission)

the oil level as described in the relevant part of Chapter 1; if the correct amount was poured into the transmission and a large amount flows out on checking the level, refit the filler/level plug and take the car on a short journey so that the new oil is distributed fully around the transmission components, then check the level again on your return. Once the oil level is correct, securely refit the inner cover/wheel arch liner (as applicable).

ML6CL transmission

10 Remove the air cleaner assembly as described in Chapter 4B.

11 Carefully prise off the breather from the top of the transmission casing, and add the exact amount specified.

12 Refit the breather cap.

13 Refit the air cleaner assembly, and the engine/transmission undershield, and lower the vehicle to the ground.

3.5 Remove the air ducts from above the gear lever housing

2.4b Oil filler/level plug (BE4/5 transmission)

2.5b Oil drain plug (BE4/5 transmission)

3 Gearchange lever and cables – removal and refitting

Removal

1 Firmly apply the handbrake, then jack up the front of the vehicle and support it on axle stands (see *Jacking and vehicle support*).

2 Unclip the gearchange lever gaiter from the centre console.

3 Pull the gearchange lever knob sharply upwards, and remove it with the gaiter.

4 Remove the centre console as described in Chapter 11.

5 Carefully pull the rear passenger compartment air ducts from above the gear lever housing **(see illustration)**.

6 Undo the four nuts securing the gearchange lever housing to the floor **(see illustration)**.

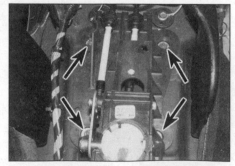

3.6 Undo the four nuts (arrowed) securing the gear lever housing to the floor

3.11a Depress the clip tabs and lever the cable outer upwards

3.11b The cable retaining clip tabs (arrowed) – shown with the cable removed

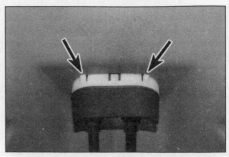

3.12 Depress the clips (arrowed) and release the cable sealing grommet from the floor

3.13a Lever the cable balljoint from the lever . . .

3.13b . . . then depress the clips and pull the cable up from the housing

Refitting

17 Refitting is a reversal of the removal procedure, noting the following points:
  a) *Tie the two cables together to make it easier to pass them through the floor to their correct locations..*
  b) *Apply grease to the balljoints before refitting.*
  c) *On the ML6CL transmission, renew the reverse gear unlocking device O-ring.*
  d) *No adjustment of the gearchange cables is possible.*

4 Oil seals – renewal

Driveshaft oil seals

7 On all models except the 1.4 and 1.6 litre diesel, remove the air cleaner housing as described in Chapter 4A or 4B. On 1.4 and 1.6 litre diesel models, remove the air cleaner intake ducting.

8 Remove the battery and battery box, as described in Chapter 5A.

9 Working in the engine compartment, note their fitted locations, then carefully prise the two gearchange cable balljoints from the selector levers on the transmission.

10 Working underneath the vehicle, remove the front exhaust pipe heat shield fasteners, and allow the heat shield to rest on the exhaust pipe.

MA5 and BE4/5 transmissions

11 Using a small screwdriver, press down the two horseshoe-shaped retaining clips upper tangs, then lever or pull the cables upwards and release them from the support bracket **(see illustrations)**.

12 Release the cable sealing grommet from the floor, and manoeuvre the lever, housing and cables assembly from the vehicle **(see illustration)**.

13 To release the cables from the lever housing, lever the cable balljoint from the lever, then depress the clips and pull the cable up from the housing **(see illustrations)**.

14 The gearchange lever is integral with the housing, and is not available separately.

ML6CL transmission

15 Undo the bolt and remove the reverse gear unlocking device from the left-hand rear upper edge of the transmission housing. Unclip the cable from the support bracket. Discard the O-ring seal, a new one must be fitted.

16 Note their fitted positions, then carefully prise the end of the gear engagement control cables from the lever. Prise out the retaining clip and pull the cables from the housing.

1 Remove the appropriate driveshaft as described in Chapter 8.

2 Carefully prise the oil seal out of the transmission, using a large flat-bladed screwdriver **(see illustration)**.

3 Remove all traces of dirt from the area around the oil seal aperture, then apply a smear of grease to the outer lip of the new oil seal. Fit the new seal into its aperture, and drive it squarely into position using a suitable tubular drift (such as a socket) which bears only on the hard outer edge of the seal, until it abuts its locating shoulder. If the seal was supplied with a plastic protector sleeve, leave this in position until the driveshaft has been refitted **(see illustrations)**.

4.2 Use a large flat-bladed screwdriver to prise out the driveshaft oil seals

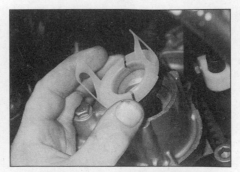

4.3a Fit the new seal to the transmission, noting the plastic seal protector . . .

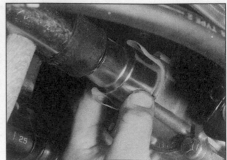

4.3b . . . and tap it into position using a tubular drift

4.7 Undo the three bolts (arrowed) securing the guide sleeve

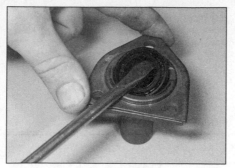

4.8 Remove the input shaft seal from the guide sleeve

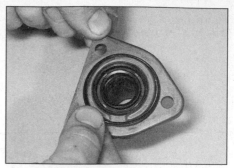

4.11 Fit a new O-ring/gasket (as applicable) to the guide sleeve

4 Apply a thin film of grease to the oil seal lip.
5 Refit the driveshaft as described in Chapter 8.

Input shaft oil seal

6 Remove the transmission as described in Section 7, and the clutch release mechanism as described in Chapter 6.
7 Undo the three bolts securing the clutch release bearing guide sleeve in position, and slide the guide off the input shaft, along with its sealing ring or gasket (as applicable) **(see illustration)**. Recover any shims or thrust-washers which have stuck to the rear of the guide sleeve, and refit them to the input shaft. Note that on the ML6CL transmission, the oil seal appears to be integral with the guide sleeve. Check with your Peugeot parts specialist.
8 Carefully lever the oil seal out of the guide using a suitable flat-bladed screwdriver **(see illustration)**.
9 Before fitting a new seal, check the input shaft's seal rubbing surface for signs of burrs, scratches or other damage, which may have caused the seal to fail in the first place. It may be possible to polish away minor faults of this sort using fine abrasive paper; however, more serious defects will require the renewal of the input shaft. Ensure that the input shaft is clean and greased, to protect the seal lips on refitting.
10 Dip the new seal in clean oil, and fit it to the guide sleeve.
11 Fit a new sealing ring or gasket (as applicable) to the rear of the guide sleeve, then carefully slide the sleeve into position over the input shaft. Refit the retaining bolts and tighten them to the specified torque setting **(see illustration)**.
12 Take the opportunity to inspect the clutch components if not already done (Chapter 6). Finally, refit the transmission as described in Section 7.

Selector shaft oil seal

MA5 transmissions

13 On these models, to renew the selector shaft seal, the transmission must be dismantled. This task should therefore be entrusted to a Peugeot dealer or transmission specialist.

BE4/5 transmissions

14 Park the car on level ground, apply the handbrake, slacken the left-hand front roadwheel bolts, then jack up the front of the vehicle and support it on axle stands (see *Jacking and vehicle support*). Remove the left-hand front roadwheel.
15 Using a large flat-bladed screwdriver, lever the link rod balljoint off the transmission selector shaft, and disconnect the link rod.
16 Using a large flat-bladed screwdriver, carefully prise the selector shaft seal out of the housing, and slide it off the end of the shaft.
17 Before fitting a new seal, check the selector shaft's seal rubbing surface for signs of burrs, scratches or other damage, which may have caused the seal to fail in the first place. It may be possible to polish away minor faults of this sort using fine abrasive paper; however, more serious defects will require the renewal of the selector shaft.
18 Apply a smear of grease to the new seal's outer edge and sealing lip, then carefully slide the seal along the selector rod. Press the seal fully into position in the transmission housing.
19 Refit the link rod to the selector shaft, ensuring that its balljoint is pressed firmly onto the shaft. Lower the car to the ground.

---

5 Reversing light switch – testing, removal and refitting

Testing

1 The reversing light circuit is controlled by a

5.4 Unscrew the reversing light switch from the transmission casing

plunger-type switch screwed into the top of the transmission casing. If a fault develops, first ensure that the circuit fuse has not blown.
2 To test the switch, disconnect the wiring connector, and use a multimeter (set to the resistance function) or a battery-and-bulb test circuit to check that there is continuity between the switch terminals only when reverse gear is selected. If this is not the case, and there are no obvious breaks or other damage to the wires, the switch is faulty, and must be renewed.

Removal

3 Where necessary, to improve access to the switch, remove the air cleaner housing intake duct assembly/battery and battery box (as applicable – see the relevant part of Chapters 4 and 5A).
4 Disconnect the wiring connector, then unscrew the switch from the transmission casing along with its sealing washer **(see illustration)**.

Refitting

5 Fit a new sealing washer to the switch, then screw it back into position in the top of the transmission housing and tighten it to the specified torque setting. Refit the wiring plug, and test the operation of the circuit. Refit any components removed for access.

---

6 Speedometer drive – removal and refitting

Note: *According to Peugeot, only the transmission fitted to the 1.4 petrol model is equipped with a speedometer drive pinion. On other models, the speedometer receives vehicle speed data from the engine management ECU, supplied by the wheel speed sensors and the ABS ECU.*

Removal

1 Chock the rear wheels, firmly apply the handbrake, then jack up the front of the car and support it on axle stands (see *Jacking and vehicle support*). The speedometer drive is on the rear of the transmission housing, next to the inner end of the right-hand driveshaft.

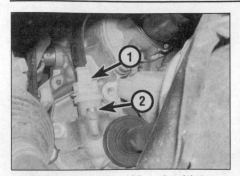

6.2 Disconnect the wiring plug (1) then undo the retaining bolt (2) and withdraw the speedometer drive assembly

7.15a Undo the centre nut (arrowed), followed by the mounting retaining nuts (arrowed) . . .

7.15b . . . then undo the nut/bolts (arrowed) securing the bracket to the body

Undo the screws and remove the engine/transmission undershield (where fitted).

2 Disconnect the wiring connector from the speedometer drive **(see illustration)**.

3 Slacken and remove the retaining bolt and remove the heat shield (where fitted). Withdraw the speedometer drive and driven pinion assembly from the transmission housing, along with its sealing ring.

4 If necessary, the pinion can be slid out of the housing, and the oil seal removed from the top of the housing. Examine the pinion for signs of damage, and renew if necessary. Renew the housing sealing ring as a matter of course.

5 If the driven pinion is worn or damaged, also examine the drive pinion in the transmission housing for similar signs.

6 To renew the drive pinion, the transmission must be dismantled and the differential gear removed. This task should therefore be entrusted to a Peugeot dealer or a transmission specialist.

Refitting

7 Apply a smear of grease to the lips of the seal and to the driven pinion shaft, and slide the pinion into position in the speedometer drive.

8 Fit a new sealing ring to the speedometer drive and refit it to the transmission, ensuring that the drive and driven pinions are correctly engaged. Refit the drive retaining bolt, complete with heat shield (where fitted), and tighten securely.

9 Reconnect the wiring connector to the speedometer drive then lower the vehicle to the ground.

7.17 Remove the mounting stud and washer from the transmission casing

---

7 Manual transmission – removal and refitting

Removal

1 Chock the rear wheels, then firmly apply the handbrake. Slacken both front roadwheel bolts. Jack up the front of the vehicle, and securely support it on axle stands (see *Jacking and vehicle support*). Remove both front roadwheels.

2 Drain the transmission oil as described in Section 2, then refit the drain and filler plugs, and tighten to their specified torque settings.

3 Remove both driveshafts as described in Chapter 8.

4 In order to prevent any damage, remove the exhaust system as described in Chapter 4A or 4B.

5 Remove the battery and battery box (see Chapter 5A).

6 On all models except the 1.4 and 1.6 litre diesel, remove the air cleaner housing and intake duct as described in the relevant part of Chapter 4. On 1.4 and 1.6 litre diesel models, remove the air intake ducting above the transmission.

7 Remove the starter motor (Chapter 5A).

8 Detach the clutch slave cylinder from the transmission as described in Chapter 6. Note there is no need to disconnect the fluid pipe from the cylinder.

7.19 Undo the nuts and bolts securing the rear engine mounting link

---

9 Disconnect the gearchange cables from the transmission and support bracket as described in Section 3.

10 Note their fitted positions, then disconnect all wiring plugs from the transmission. Note the harness routing and move the harness to one side.

11 Undo the retaining bolt(s), and remove the flywheel lower cover plate (where fitted) from the transmission.

12 On 2.0 litre diesel engines, remove the engine/transmission support bracket from under the vehicle.

13 Place a jack with a block of wood beneath the engine, to take the weight of the engine. Alternatively, attach a couple of lifting eyes to the engine, and fit a hoist or support bar to take the engine weight. If using a support bar, it may be necessary to remove the wiper arms, and remove the scuttle plastic trim panel.

14 Place a jack and block of wood beneath the transmission, and raise the jack to take the weight of the transmission.

15 Slacken and remove the centre nut and washer from the left-hand engine/transmission mounting then undo the mounting nuts and remove the mounting. Unscrew the nut/bolts securing the mounting bracket to the body and remove the bracket **(see illustrations)**.

16 On MA5 transmissions, undo the three retaining nuts and remove the mounting plate from the top of the transmission.

17 On BE4/5 transmissions, slide the spacer off the mounting stud (where fitted), then unscrew the stud from the top of the transmission housing and remove it, along with its washer **(see illustration)**.

18 On the ML6CL transmission, undo the 3 nuts/1 bolt and remove the gearbox impact absorber from the end of the transmission casing, then undo the bolt, prise apart the balljoint, and remove the counterweight from the transmission.

19 On all models, unscrew the nuts and bolts and remove the mounting link securing the rear engine/transmission mounting to the subframe **(see illustration)**.

20 With the jack positioned beneath the transmission taking the weight, slacken and

7.20 On 1.4 and 1.6 litre diesel engines, remove the mounting stud (arrowed) which obscures the transmission-to-engine bolt

remove the remaining bolts securing the transmission housing to the engine. Note the correct fitted positions of each bolt and the necessary brackets, as they are removed, to use as a reference on refitting. On 1.4 and 1.6 litre diesel engines, unscrew the left-hand catalytic converter mounting stud to allow access to the front transmission-to-engine bolt **(see illustration)**.

21 Make a final check that all components have been disconnected, and are positioned clear of the transmission so that they will not hinder the removal procedure.

22 With the bolts removed, move the trolley jack and transmission to the left, to free it from its locating dowels. Lower the engine slightly to enable the transmission to be freed.

Caution: Take great care not to damage the radiator if the engine is moved – place a sheet of thick cardboard over the rear face of the radiator. On models equipped with air conditioning, care must also be taken to ensure the auxiliary drivebelt pulleys do not damage the air conditioning pipes on the right-hand side of the engine compartment.

23 Once the transmission is free, lower the jack and manoeuvre the unit out from under the car. Remove the locating dowels from the transmission or engine if they are loose, and keep them in a safe place.

Refitting

24 The transmission is refitted by a reversal of the removal procedure, bearing in mind the following points:

a) *Prior to refitting, check the clutch assembly and release mechanism components (see Chapter 6). Lubricate the release bearing guide with a little high melting-point grease (Peugeot recommend the use of Molykote BR2 Plus). Do not apply too much grease, otherwise there is a possibility of the grease contaminating the clutch friction disc, and ensure no grease is applied to the input shaft/friction disc splines.*

b) *Ensure that the locating dowels are correctly positioned prior to installation.*

c) *On BE4/5 transmissions, apply thread-locking fluid to the left-hand engine/transmission mounting stud threads, prior to refitting it to the transmission. Tighten the stud to the specified torque.*

d) *Tighten all nuts and bolts to the specified torque (where given).*

e) *Renew the driveshaft oil seals, then refit the driveshafts (see Chapter 8).*

f) *Refit the slave cylinder (see Chapter 6).*

g) *On completion, refill the transmission with the specified type and quantity of lubricant, as described in Section 2.*

8 Manual transmission overhaul – general information

1 Overhauling a manual transmission is a difficult and involved job for the DIY home mechanic. In addition to dismantling and reassembling many small parts, clearances must be precisely measured and, if necessary, changed by selecting shims and spacers. Internal transmission components are also often difficult to obtain, and in many instances, extremely expensive. Because of this, if the transmission develops a fault or becomes noisy, the best course of action is to have the unit overhauled by a specialist repairer, or to obtain an exchange reconditioned unit.

2 Nevertheless, it is not impossible for the more experienced mechanic to overhaul the transmission, provided the special tools are available, and the job is done in a deliberate step-by-step manner, so that nothing is overlooked.

3 The tools necessary for an overhaul include internal and external circlip pliers, bearing pullers, a slide hammer, a set of pin punches, a dial test indicator, and possibly a hydraulic press. In addition, a large, sturdy workbench and a vice will be required.

4 During dismantling of the transmission, make careful notes of how each component is fitted, to make reassembly easier and more accurate.

5 Before dismantling the transmission, it will help if you have some idea what area is malfunctioning. Certain problems can be closely related to specific areas in the transmission, which can make component examination and replacement easier. Refer to the *Fault finding* Section for more information.

Notes

Chapter 7 Part B:
Automatic transmission

Contents

Degrees of difficulty

Easy, suitable for novice with little experience	**Fairly easy,** suitable for beginner with some experience	**Fairly difficult,** suitable for competent DIY mechanic	**Difficult,** suitable for experienced DIY mechanic	**Very difficult,** suitable for expert DIY or professional 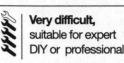

Specifications

General

Type	Auto-adaptive four-speed electronically-controlled automatic with three (normal, sport and snow) driving modes
Designation	AL4

Lubrication

Capacity:	
Refilling after draining	3.0 litres*
From dry	6.0 litres
Recommended fluid	See *Lubricants and fluids* on page 0•18

* If the torque converter is also removed and drained, add a further 2 litres

Torque wrench settings

	Nm	lbf ft
Engine-to-transmission fixing bolts	35	26
Fluid cooler centre bolt	50	37
Fluid drain plug	33	24
Fluid filler plug	24	18
Fluid level plug:		
To RPO 9855 (hexagonal)	24	18
From RPO 9856 (socket key)	9	7
Fluid pressure sensor bolts	9	7
Input shaft speed sensor bolt	10	7
Left-hand engine/transmission mounting	Refer to Chapter 2A, 2B or 2C	
Multi-function switch retaining bolts	10	7
Output shaft speed sensor bolt	10	7
Rear mounting link	Refer to Chapter 2A, 2B or 2C	
Roadwheel bolts	90	66
Torque converter-to-driveplate nuts:		
Stage 1	10	7
Stage 2	30	22

1 General information

1 Certain models were offered with the option of a four-speed electronically-controlled automatic transmission, consisting of a torque converter, an epicyclic geartrain, and hydraulically-operated clutches and brakes. The unit is controlled by the electronic control unit (ECU) via the electrically-operated solenoid valves in the hydraulic block within the transmission unit. The transmission has three driving modes: normal, sport and snow; the mode buttons are situated on the right-hand side of the selector lever and the mode indicator lights are incorporated in the instrument panel.

2 The normal mode is the standard mode for driving in which the transmission shifts up at relatively low engine speeds to combine reasonable performance with economy. If the transmission unit is switched into sport mode, the transmission will shift up only at high engine speeds, giving improved acceleration and overtaking performance. In snow mode, the transmission will select 2nd gear when the vehicle pulls away from a standing start; this helps maintain traction on slippery surfaces.

3 The torque converter provides a fluid coupling between the engine and transmission, which acts as an automatic clutch, and also provides a degree of torque multiplication when accelerating.

4 The epicyclic geartrain provides either of the four forward or one reverse gear ratios, according to which of its component parts are held stationary or allowed to turn. The components of the geartrain are held or released by brakes and clutches which are controlled by the ECU via the electrically-operated solenoid valves in the hydraulic unit. A fluid pump within the transmission provides the necessary hydraulic pressure to operate the brakes and clutches.

5 Driver control of the transmission is by a six-position selector lever. The transmission has a 'drive' position, and a 'hold' facility on the first three gear ratios. The 'drive' position D provides automatic changing throughout the range of all four gear ratios, and is the one to select for normal driving. An automatic kickdown facility shifts the transmission down a gear if the accelerator pedal is fully depressed. The 'hold' facility is very similar, but limits the number of gear ratios available – ie, when the selector lever is in the 3 position, only the first three ratios can be selected; in the 2 position, only the first two can be selected. When the lever is in the 2 position, the transmission can be locked in first gear using the button on the right-hand side of the selector lever. These lower ratio 'hold' settings are useful for providing engine braking when travelling down steep gradients, or for preventing unwanted selection of top gear on twisty roads. Note, however, that the transmission should *never* be shifted down at high engine speeds.

6 On some models, the selector lever is equipped with a shift-lock function. This prevents the selector lever being moved from the P position unless the brake pedal is depressed.

7 Due to the complexity of the automatic transmission, any repair or overhaul work must be left to a Peugeot dealer with the necessary special equipment for fault diagnosis and repair. The contents of the following Sections are therefore confined to supplying general information, and any service information and instructions that can be used by the owner.

Note: *The automatic transmission unit is of the 'auto-adaptive' type. This means that it takes into account your driving style and modifies the transmission shift points to provide optimum performance and economy to suit. When the battery is disconnected, the transmission will lose its memory and will resort to one of its many base shift programs. The transmission will then relearn the optimum shift points when the vehicle is driven a few miles. During these first few miles of driving, there maybe a noticeable difference in performance whilst the transmission adapts to your individual style.*

2 Automatic transmission fluid – draining and refilling

Note: *A suitable square section wrench may be required to undo the transmission filler plug. These wrenches can be obtained from most motor factors or your Peugeot dealer.*

Note: *The transmission unit is equipped with a fluid wear sensor to inform the driver when the fluid needs renewing (the ECU flashes the Sport and Snow mode indicator lights when fluid renewal is necessary). If the transmission unit is drained and refilled with new fluid, this sensor should be reset. This can only be done using the Peugeot diagnostic test box.*

Draining

1 This operation is much quicker and more efficient if the car is first taken on a journey of sufficient length to warm the engine/transmission up to normal operating temperature.

2 Park the car on level ground, switch off the ignition and apply the handbrake firmly. For improved access, jack up the front of the car and support it securely on axle stands (see *Jacking and vehicle support*). Undo the screws and remove the engine/transmission undershield (where fitted).

3 Position a suitable container under the drain plug, situated on the base of the transmission. Unscrew the drain plug (the smaller plug in the centre of the drain plug is the level plug – see Chapter 1A or 1B) and recover the sealing washer **(see illustration)**. Allow the fluid to drain completely into the container.

⚠ *Warning: If the fluid is hot, take precautions against scalding.*

4 Clean the drain plug, being especially careful to wipe off any metallic particles. Discard the sealing washer; it should be renewed whenever it is disturbed.

5 When the fluid has finished draining, clean the drain plug threads and those of the transmission casing, fit a new sealing washer and refit the drain plug, tightening it to the specified torque wrench setting. If the car was raised for the draining operation, now lower it to the ground.

Refilling

6 To improve access to the filler plug, remove air cleaner housing (Chapter 4A or 4B), and the battery and battery box as described in Chapter 5A. If necessary, also unclip the selector cable end fitting from its balljoint on the transmission lever.

7 Wipe clean the area around the filler plug which is situated directly behind the transmission selector lever **(see illustration)**. Unscrew the filler plug from the transmission and recover the sealing washer.

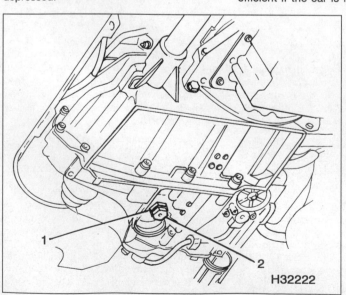

2.3 Transmission fluid drain plug (1) and oil level plug (2), inside the drain plug

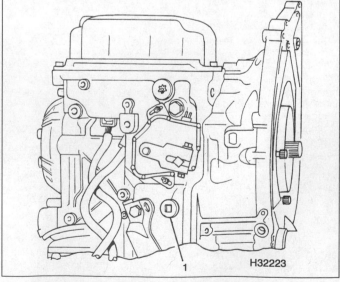

2.7 Transmission fluid filler plug (1) as viewed from above

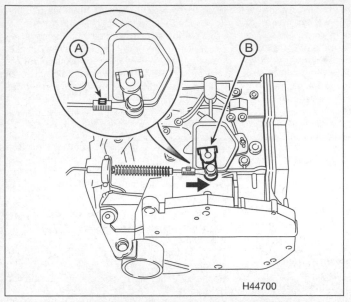

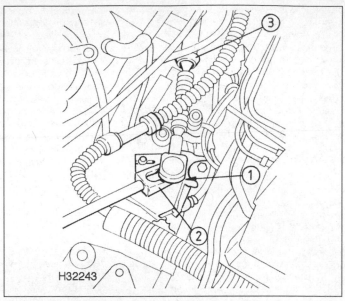

3.3 Press the yellow plastic part (A) to unlock the adjuster, then push the selector lever (B) fully to the front

4.3 Prise off the selector cable balljoint (1) using a forked tool (2), then remove the cable from the bracket (3)

Caution: Do not unscrew the selector shaft bolt (located in front of the selector lever).

8 Carefully refill the transmission with the correct amount of the specified type of fluid. Fit the new sealing washer to the filler plug then refit the plug, tightening it to the specified torque. Reconnect the selector cable to the lever (where disconnected – support the lever when pressing the cable onto its balljoint to prevent the lever being bent) then refit the battery (see Chapter 5A) and air cleaner housing (Chapter 4A or 4B).

9 Take the vehicle on a short journey to warm the transmission up to normal operating temperature.

10 On your return, check the transmission fluid level as described in Chapter 1A or 1B.

3 Selector cable – adjustment

1 To gain access to the transmission end of the selector cable, remove the battery and battery box as described in Chapter 5A.

2 Position the selector lever firmly against its detent in the P (park) position.

3 Press the yellow plastic part on the cable end fitting to unlock the adjustment system **(see illustration)**.

4 Ensure that the selector lever on top of the transmission is fully forward, then press the yellow part on the selector cable again, to lock it in position.

5 Check the operation of the selector lever before refitting the battery box and battery (see Chapter 5A) and air cleaner housing (Chapter 4A or 4B).

4 Selector lever and cable – removal and refitting

Removal

1 Firmly apply the handbrake, then jack up the front of the vehicle and support it on axle stands (see *Jacking and vehicle support*). Position the selector lever in the P position.

2 To gain access to the transmission end of

the selector cable, remove the battery and battery box/tray as described in Chapter 5A.

3 Unclip the selector cable end fitting from the balljoint on the transmission lever. Remove the retaining clip and free the cable from the transmission bracket **(see illustration)**.

4 Remove the centre console as described in Chapter 11.

5 Carefully pull the plastic rear air vents from place **(see illustration)**.

6 Note their fitted positions and disconnect all wiring plugs from the lever housing.

7 Undo the four nuts and manoeuvre the lever housing and cables from the vehicle **(see illustration)**. Prise the cable sealing grommet from the floor as the assembly is withdrawn.

8 Lever the selector cable off the selector lever balljoint then pull out the spring-loaded black pin and pull the outer cable from the front of the housing **(see illustrations)**. Note that at the time of writing, the lever and housing was only available as a complete assembly – check with your Peugeot dealer for parts availability.

4.5 Move the plastic air vents to one side

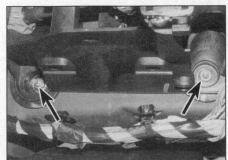

4.7 Undo the four nuts (arrowed – two each side) and remove the housing

4.8a Lever the selector cable end fitting from the balljoint

4.8b Pull out the pin (arrowed) a little, then slide up the outer cable fitting

Refitting

9 Refitting is the reverse of removal, noting the following points.
  a) *Support the transmission selector lever when pressing the cable onto its balljoint to prevent the lever being bent.*
  b) *Adjust the cable as described in Section 3 before refitting all components removed for access.*

5 Speedometer drive – removal and refitting

Refer to Chapter 7A, Section 6.

6 Oil seals – renewal

Driveshaft oil seals

1 Remove the appropriate driveshaft as described in Chapter 8.

Right-hand seal

2 Remove the O-ring from the differential sun gear shaft then carefully remove the oil seal from of the transmission, taking care not to damage the shaft or housing. To remove the seal, carefully punch or drill two small holes opposite each other into the seal. Screw a self-tapping screw into each hole and pull on the screws to extract the seal.

6.12 Unscrew the nut and clamp bolt (arrowed) and free the selector lever from the transmission shaft

3 Remove all traces of dirt from the area around the oil seal aperture, then apply a smear of grease to the outer edge and sealing lip of the new oil seal. Ease the new seal onto the shaft, taking care not to damage its lip, and into its aperture. Drive the seal squarely into position using a suitable tubular drift (such as a socket) which bears only on the hard outer edge of the seal.
4 Once the seal is correctly installed, fit a new O-ring to the sun gear shaft and slide along until it abuts the seal.
5 Refit the driveshaft as described in Chapter 8.

Left-hand seal

6 Carefully prise the oil seal out of the transmission, using a large flat-bladed screw-driver.
7 Remove all traces of dirt from the area around the oil seal aperture, then apply a smear of grease to the outer lip of the new oil seal. Fit the new seal into its aperture, and drive it squarely into position using a suitable tubular drift (such as a socket) which bears only on the hard outer edge of the seal, until it abuts its locating shoulder. If the seal was supplied with a plastic protector sleeve, leave this in position until the driveshaft has been refitted.
8 Apply a thin film of grease to the oil seal lip.
9 Refit the driveshaft as described in Chapter 8.

Selector shaft oil seal

10 To gain access to the transmission selector shaft, remove the battery and battery tray as described in Chapter 5A.
11 Position the selector lever firmly against its detent mechanism in the P position.
12 Slacken and remove the nut and clamp bolt securing the selector lever to the transmission shaft **(see illustration)**. Make alignment marks between the shaft and lever then free the lever from the shaft.
13 Remove the retaining clip and free the selector cable from transmission bracket **(see illustration 4.3)**. Position the cable clear of the selector shaft.
14 Make alignment marks between the multi-function switch and transmission unit then unscrew the retaining bolts and remove the switch.
15 Carefully remove the oil seal from of the transmission, taking care not to damage the shaft or housing. To remove the seal, carefully punch or drill two small holes opposite each other into the seal. Screw a self-tapping screw into each hole and pull on the screws to extract the seal.
16 Remove all traces of dirt from the area around the oil seal aperture, then apply a smear of grease to the outer edge and sealing lip of the new oil seal. Ease the new seal onto the shaft, taking care not to damage its lip, and press it squarely into its aperture.
17 Locate the multi-function switch back on the selector shaft. Align the marks made

prior to removal then refit the switch bolts, tightening them to the specified torque.
18 Seat the selector cable in the transmission bracket and engage the selector lever with the transmission shaft. Ensure the marks made on removal are correctly aligned then refit the lever clamp bolt and nut and tighten securely.
19 Secure the selector cable in position with the retaining clip then adjust the cable as described in Section 3.
20 Refit all components removed for access.

Torque converter seal

21 Remove the transmission unit as described in Section 9.
22 Carefully slide the torque converter off the transmission shaft whilst being prepared for fluid spillage.
23 Note the correct fitted position of the seal in the housing then carefully lever it out of position, taking care not to mark the housing or shaft.
24 Remove all traces of dirt from the area around the oil seal aperture. Ease the new seal into its aperture, ensuring its sealing lip is facing inwards, then press it squarely into position.
25 Engage the torque converter with the transmission shaft splines and slide it into position, taking care not to damage the oil seal.
26 Refit the transmission unit as described in Section 9.

7 Fluid cooler – removal and refitting

Caution: Be careful not to allow dirt into the transmission unit during this pro-cedure.

Removal

1 The fluid cooler is mounted on the rear of the transmission housing. To gain access to the cooler, remove the battery and battery box as described in Chapter 5A.
2 Remove all traces of dirt from around the fluid cooler before proceeding.
3 Using a hose clamp or similar, clamp both the fluid cooler coolant hoses to minimise coolant loss during subsequent operations.
4 Release the retaining clips, and disconnect both coolant hoses from the fluid cooler – be prepared for some coolant spillage **(see illustration)**. Wash off any spilt coolant immediately with cold water, and dry the surrounding area before proceeding further.
5 Slacken and remove the fluid cooler centre bolt, and remove the cooler from the transmission. Remove the seal from the centre bolt, and the two seals fitted to the rear of the cooler, and discard them; new ones must be used on refitting **(see illustration)**.

Refitting

6 Lubricate the new seals with clean automatic transmission fluid, then fit the two new seals to the rear of the fluid cooler, and a new seal to the centre bolt.

7 Locate the fluid cooler on the rear of transmission housing then refit the centre bolt. Ensure the cooler is correctly positioned then tighten the centre bolt to the specified torque setting.

8 Reconnect the coolant hoses to the fluid cooler, and secure them in position with their retaining clips. Remove the hose clamps.

9 Refit the battery and battery box (see Chapter 5A).

10 Top-up the cooling system as described in *Weekly checks* and check the trans-mission unit fluid level as described in Chapter 1A or 1B.

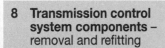

8 Transmission control system components – removal and refitting

Electronic control unit (ECU)

Note: *The automatic transmission electronic control system relies on accurate communication between the engine management ECU and the automatic transmission ECU. If the accelerator cable (where fitted) is removed and/or adjusted, or if either ECU is renewed, then both ECUs must be 'initialised'. The initialisation procedure requires access to specialised electronic test equipment and so it is recommended that this operation is entrusted to a suitably-equipped Peugeot dealer or specialist.*

Removal

1 Remove the battery and battery box (see Chapter 5A).

2 Slide out the locking catch and disconnect the wiring connector from the ECU **(see illustration)**.

3 Undo the two mounting nuts and remove the ECU from the mounting plate **(see illustration)**.

Refitting

4 Refitting is the reverse of removal, ensuring the wiring connector is securely reconnected.

Output shaft speed sensor

Caution: Be careful not to allow dirt into the transmission unit during this procedure.

Removal

5 The output shaft sensor is fitted to the rear of the transmission unit.

6 To gain access to the sensor, jack up the front of the vehicle and support it securely on axle stands (see *Jacking and vehicle support*). Undo the screws and remove the engine/transmission undershield (where fitted).

7 Trace the sensor wiring back to its connector, located next to the transmission main wiring harness connector. Unclip the connector from its bracket then disconnect it.

7.4 Release the retaining clips and disconnect the coolant hoses (arrowed) from the fluid cooler (viewed from above)

8 Wipe clean the area around the sensor then slacken and remove the sensor retaining bolt. Remove the sensor along with its sealing ring; discard the sealing ring, a new one must be used on refitting.

Refitting

9 Refitting is the reverse of removal, noting the following points.
   a) *Fit a new sealing ring to the sensor and tighten the sensor bolt to the specified torque.*
   b) *On completion, check the transmission fluid level as described in Chapter 1A or 1B.*

Input shaft speed sensor

Caution: Be careful not to allow dirt into the transmission unit during this procedure.

Removal

10 The input shaft speed sensor is located on the left-hand end of the transmission unit.

11 To gain access to the sensor, chock the rear wheels, firmly apply the handbrake, then jack up the front of the vehicle and securely support it on axle stands (see *Jacking and vehicle support*).

12 To gain access to the main wiring connector, remove the battery and battery box (see Chapter 5A).

13 Lift the retaining clip and disconnect the main wiring connector from the top of the transmission unit.

14 Unscrew the two bolts and free the main wiring connector from the transmission unit.

8.2 Slide out the locking catch (arrowed) and disconnect the ECU wiring plug

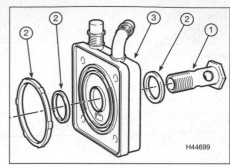

7.5 Fluid cooler

1 Bolt   3 Fluid cooler
2 Seals

Cut the cable tie securing the wiring to the connector cover then release the clips and slide the cover off the connector.

15 Trace the wiring back from the sensor being removed, freeing it from all the relevant retaining clips and ties, to the main wiring connector. Carefully release the retaining clips then slide the sensor connector out from the rear of the main connector, noting which way around it is fitted.

16 Wipe clean the area around the sensor. Slacken and remove the retaining bolt then remove the sensor, along with its sealing ring. Discard the sealing ring, a new one must be used on refitting.

Refitting

17 Refitting is the reverse of removal, noting the following points.
   a) *Fit a new sealing ring to the sensor and tighten the sensor bolt to the specified torque.*
   b) *Ensure the sensor wiring is correctly routed and retained by all the necessary clips and ties.*
   c) *Clip the sensor wiring back into the main wiring connector, ensuring it is fitted the right way around. Slide the cover back onto the main connector, ensuring it is clipped securely in position, and secure the wiring to the cover with a new cable tie. Secure the connector to the transmission unit with the retaining bolts.*
   d) *On completion, check the transmission fluid level as described in Chapter 1A or 1B.*

8.3 Undo the ECU mounting nuts (arrowed)

Fluid pressure sensor

Caution: Be careful not to allow dirt into the transmission unit during this procedure.

Removal

18 The fluid pressure sensor is located on the base of the transmission unit.

19 To gain access to the sensor, chock the rear wheels, firmly apply the handbrake then jack up the front of the vehicle and securely support it on axle stands (see *Jacking and vehicle support*).

20 Remove the battery and battery box as described in Chapter 5A.

21 Unscrew the two bolts and free the main wiring connector from the transmission unit. Cut the cable tie securing the wiring to the connector cover then release the clips and slide the cover off the connector.

22 Trace the wiring back from the sensor being removed, freeing it from all the relevant retaining clips and ties, to the main wiring connector. Carefully release the retaining clips then slide the green 3-way sensor connector out from the rear of the main connector, noting which way around it is fitted.

23 Wipe clean the area around the sensor. Slacken and remove the retaining bolts then remove the sensor, along with its sealing ring **(see illustration)**. Discard the sealing ring, a new one must be used on refitting. Be prepared for fluid spillage, and plug the opening to minimise fluid loss.

Refitting

24 Refitting is the reverse of removal, noting the following points.

  a) *Fit a new sealing ring to the sensor and tighten the sensor bolts to the specified torque.*

  b) *Ensure the sensor wiring is correctly routed and retained by all the necessary clips and ties.*

  c) *Clip the sensor wiring back into the main wiring connector, ensuring it is fitted the right way around. Slide the cover back onto the main connector, ensuring it is clipped securely in position, and secure the wiring to the cover with a new cable tie.*

  d) *On completion, check the transmission fluid level as described in Chapter 1A or 1B.*

Multi-function switch

Note: *The multi-function switch is slotted to allow for adjustment. Accurate adjustment requires the use an accurate multi-meter – see the text later in this Section.*

Removal

25 Remove the battery and battery box/tray (see Chapter 5A).

26 Position the selector lever firmly against its detent mechanism in the P position.

27 Slacken and remove the nut and clamp bolt securing the selector lever to the transmission shaft **(see illustration 6.12)**. Make alignment marks between the shaft and lever then free the lever from the shaft.

8.23 The fluid pressure sensor is secured to the base of the transmission by two bolts (arrowed)

28 Remove the retaining clip and free the selector cable from transmission bracket. Position the cable clear of the selector shaft.

29 Unscrew the two bolts and free the main wiring connector from the transmission unit. Cut the cable tie securing the wiring to the connector cover then release the clips and slide the cover off the connector.

30 Trace the wiring back from the switch to the main wiring connector, freeing it from all the relevant retaining clips and ties. Carefully release the retaining clips then slide the green 12-way connector out from the rear of the main connector, noting which way around it is fitted.

31 Make accurate alignment marks between the multi-function switch and transmission unit then unscrew the retaining bolts and remove the switch.

Refitting

32 Locate the multi-function switch back on the selector shaft. Align the marks made prior to removal then refit the switch bolts, tightening them to the specified torque.

33 Clip the wiring back into the main wiring connector, ensuring it is fitted the right way around. Slide the cover back onto the main connector, ensuring it is clipped securely in

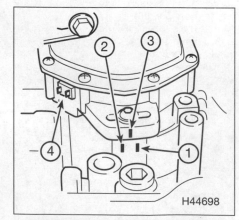

8.42 Multi-function switch adjustment

  1 *1st alignment mark*
  2 *2nd alignment mark*
  3 *Switch body alignment mark*
  4 *Switch external contacts*

position, and secure the wiring to the cover with a new cable tie. Locate the connector on the transmission unit and securely tighten its retaining bolts.

34 Reconnect the main wiring connector to the transmission unit.

35 Seat the selector cable in the transmission bracket and engage the selector lever with the transmission shaft. Ensure the marks made on removal are correctly aligned then refit the lever clamp bolt and nut, and tighten securely.

36 Secure the selector cable in position with the retaining clip then adjust the cable as described in Section 3, and the multi-function switch as described next.

Adjustment

37 Slacken the switch mounting bolts and rotate the switch fully anti-clockwise as far as it will go.

38 Set the multi-meter to measure ohms, and connect meter terminals to the external switch contacts.

39 Slowly rotate the switch clockwise until the switch contacts close (the meter should register zero ohms – no resistance).

40 In this position, make an alignment mark between the switch and the transmission casing.

41 Continue to rotate the switch clockwise until the contacts open (the meter should register infinite ohms or similar)

42 Make another alignment mark between the transmission casing and the mark made previously on the switch **(see illustration)**.

43 Rotate the switch until the alignment mark on the switch body is exactly half-way between the two marks made on the transmission casing. Tighten the switch mounting bolts to the specified torque.

44 Refit the battery and battery box/tray as described in Chapter 5A.

45 Check that the selector lever position corresponds to the display on the instrument panel.

---

9 Automatic transmission – removal and refitting

Removal

1 Chock the rear wheels, then firmly apply the handbrake. Slacken both front roadwheel bolts. Jack up the front of the vehicle, and securely support it on axle stands (see *Jacking and vehicle support*). Remove both front roadwheels.

2 Remove both driveshafts as described in Chapter 8.

3 Remove the air cleaner housing and intake duct as described in Chapter 4A or 4B.

4 Remove the automatic transmission ECU as described in Section 8.

5 Remove the starter motor (Chapter 5A).

6 Remove the exhaust system as described in Chapter 4A or 4B.

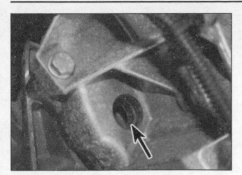

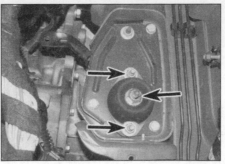

9.12 Access to the torque converter nuts is gained via the access hole (arrowed) above the driveshaft

9.16a Undo the centre nut (arrowed), followed by the mounting retaining nuts (arrowed) . . .

9.16b . . . then undo the nut/bolts (arrowed) securing the bracket to the body

7 Unclip the selector cable end fitting off the balljoint on the transmission lever. Remove the retaining clip then free the outer cable from its bracket and position it clear of the transmission unit **(see illustration 4.3)**.

8 Using a hose clamp or similar, clamp both the fluid cooler coolant hoses to minimise coolant loss. Release the retaining clips and disconnect both coolant hoses from the fluid cooler – be prepared for some coolant spillage. Wash off any spilt coolant immediately with cold water, and dry the surrounding area before proceeding further.

9 Lift the retaining clip and disconnect the main wiring connector from the transmission wiring block, located at the rear of the unit. Also disconnect the output shaft speed sensor wiring connector (located next to the main connector) then position the wiring harness clear of the transmission unit.

10 Undo the retaining nut/bolt(s), and disconnect the earth straps from the top of the transmission housing. Free the wiring from any relevant retaining clips, and position it clear of the transmission.

11 Undo the retaining bolts and remove the lower driveplate cover plate (where fitted) from the transmission.

12 Access to the torque converter retaining nuts is gained via an access hole above the right-hand driveshaft on the back of the cylinder block. Use a socket and extension bar to rotate the crankshaft pulley to align the first nut with the aperture **(see illustration)**. Unscrew the nut then rotate the crankshaft 120°. Remove the second nut then rotate the crankshaft another 120° Unscrew the third and final nut and discard all three nuts; new ones must be used on refitting.

13 To ensure that the torque converter does not fall out as the transmission is removed, secure it in position using a length of metal strip bolted to one of the starter motor bolt holes.

14 Place a jack with a block of wood beneath the engine, to take the weight of the engine. Alternatively, attach a couple of lifting eyes to the engine, and fit a hoist or support bar to take the engine weight.

15 Place a jack and block of wood beneath

the transmission, and raise the jack to take the weight of the transmission.

16 Slacken and remove the centre nut and washer from the left-hand engine/ trans-mission mounting then undo the mounting bolts and remove the mounting. Unscrew the bolts securing the mounting bracket to the body and remove the bracket **(see illustrations)**.

17 Slide the spacer off the mounting stud, then unscrew the stud from the top of the transmission housing and remove it along with its washer. If the mounting stud is tight, a universal stud extractor can be used to unscrew it.

18 Unscrew the nuts and bolts and remove the mounting link securing the rear engine/ transmission mounting to the subframe **(see illustration)**.

19 With the jack positioned beneath the transmission taking the weight, slacken and remove the remaining bolts securing the transmission housing to the engine. Note the correct fitted positions of each bolt and the necessary brackets as they are removed, to use as a reference on refitting. Make a final check that all components have been disconnected, and are positioned clear of the transmission so that they will not hinder the removal procedure.

20 With the bolts removed, move the trolley jack and transmission to the left, to free it from its locating dowels. If necessary, lower the engine slightly to enable the transmission to be freed.

21 Once the transmission is free, lower the jack and manoeuvre the unit out from under the car. Remove the locating dowels from the transmission or engine if they are loose, and keep them in a safe place.

Refitting

22 Ensure that the bush fitted to the centre of the crankshaft is in good condition, and apply a little Molykote BR2 grease to the torque converter centring pin.
Caution: Do not apply too much, otherwise there is a possibility of the grease contaminating the torque converter.

23 Ensure that the engine/transmission locating dowels are correctly positioned then

raise the transmission unit into position. Align the torque converter studs with the driveplate holes then engage the transmission unit with the engine.
Caution: Do not allow the weight of the transmission unit to hang on the torque converter as the unit is installed.

24 With the transmission and engine correctly joined, refit the transmission-to-engine unit bolts and tighten them to the specified torque.

25 Screw the new nuts onto the torque converter studs, tightening them lightly only, rotating the crankshaft as necessary. Tighten all three nuts to the specified Stage 1 torque setting. Once all have been tightened to the Stage 1 torque, go around and tighten them to the specified Stage 2 torque setting.

26 The remainder of refitting is the reverse of removal, noting the following.

a) Apply thread-locking fluid to the left-hand engine/transmission mounting stud threads, prior to refitting it to the transmission. Tighten the stud to the specified torque.

b) Tighten all nuts and bolts to the specified torque (where given).

c) Renew the driveshaft oil seals, then refit the driveshafts (see Chapter 8).

d) Reconnect the selector cable and adjust as described in Section 3.

e) On completion, check the transmission fluid level as described in Chapter 1A or 1B.

9.18 Undo the nuts and bolts securing the engine rear mounting link

10 Automatic transmission overhaul – general information

1 In the event of a fault occurring with the transmission, it is first necessary to determine whether it is of an electrical, mechanical or hydraulic nature and, to do this, special test equipment is required. It is therefore essential to have the work carried out by a Peugeot dealer or specialist if a transmission fault is suspected.

2 Do not remove the transmission from the car for possible repair before professional fault diagnosis has been carried out, since most tests require the transmission to be in the vehicle.

Chapter 8
Driveshafts

Contents

Degrees of difficulty

Easy, suitable for novice with little experience	**Fairly easy,** suitable for beginner with some experience	**Fairly difficult,** suitable for competent DIY mechanic	**Difficult,** suitable for experienced DIY mechanic	**Very difficult,** suitable for expert DIY or professional

Specifications

Lubrication (overhaul only – see text)

Lubricant type/specification. . . . .   Use only special grease supplied in sachets with gaiter kits – joints are otherwise pre-packed with grease and sealed

Torque wrench settings	Nm	lbf ft
Driveshaft retaining nut	325	240
Right-hand driveshaft intermediate bearing retaining bolt nuts.	10	7
Roadwheel bolts.	90	66
Suspension strut-to-hub carrier bolts	90	66

1 General information

Drive is transmitted from the differential to the front wheels by means of two solid-steel driveshafts of unequal length.

Both driveshafts are splined at their outer ends, to accept the wheel hubs, and are threaded so that each hub can be fastened by a large nut. The inner end of each driveshaft is splined, to accept the differential sun gear.

Constant velocity (CV) joints are fitted to each end of the driveshafts, to ensure that the smooth and efficient transmission of power at all suspension and steering angles. The outer constant velocity joints are of the ball-and-cage type, and the inner constant velocity joints are of the tripod type.

On the right-hand side, due to the length of the driveshaft, the inner constant velocity joint is situated approximately halfway along the shaft's length, and an intermediate support bearing is mounted in the engine/transmission rear mounting bracket. The inner end of the driveshaft passes through the bearing (which prevents any lateral movement of the driveshaft inner end) and the inner constant velocity joint outer member. On automatic transmission models, the inboard end of the right-hand driveshaft fits over a splined shaft from the transmission differential.

2 Driveshafts – removal and refitting

Note: *A new suspension lower balljoint nut will be required on refitting.*

Removal

1 Remove the wheel trim/hub cap (as applicable) then withdraw the R-clip and remove the locking cap from the driveshaft retaining nut. Slacken the driveshaft nut with the vehicle resting on its wheels. Also slacken the wheel bolts.

2 Chock the rear wheels of the car, firmly apply the handbrake, then jack up the front of the car and support it on axle stands (see *Jacking and vehicle support*). Remove the appropriate front roadwheel.

3 On manual transmission models drain the transmission oil as described in Chapter 7A. On automatic transmission models there is no need to drain the fluid.

4 Remove the wheel sensor as described in Chapter 9, Section 19.

5 Slacken and remove the driveshaft retaining nut. If the nut was not slackened with the wheels on the ground (see paragraph 1), withdraw the R-clip and remove the locking cap **(see illustration)**. Refit at least two roadwheel bolts to the front hub, tightening them securely, then have an assistant firmly depress the brake pedal to prevent the front hub from rotating, whilst you slacken and remove the driveshaft retaining nut. Alternatively, a tool can be fabricated from

2.5 Use a screwdriver to prise out the R-clip

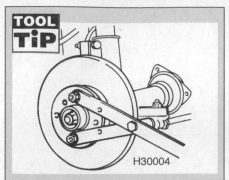

Using a fabricated tool to hold the front hub stationary whilst the driveshaft nut is slackened.

two lengths of steel strip (one long, one short) and a nut and bolt; the nut and bolt forming the pivot of a forked tool **(see Tool tip)**.

6 Undo the brake caliper guide pin bolts and slide the caliper from the disc. Suspend the caliper from the suspension coil spring using a cable tie to prevent straining the brake hose. Discard the guide pin bolts, new ones must be fitted.

Left-hand driveshaft

7 Slacken and remove the two bolts securing the steering hub carrier to the base of the suspension strut. Pull the hub carrier outwards to free it from the strut. **Note:** *After releasing the hub carrier, rotate the base of the strut 90° towards the rear of the vehicle to minimise the chances of damaging the rubber driveshaft gaiter* **(see illustrations)**.

8 Turn the steering to full left-hand lock, and carefully pull the swivel hub assembly outwards, and withdraw the driveshaft outer constant velocity joint from the hub assembly. If necessary, the shaft can be tapped out of the hub using a soft-faced mallet.

9 Support the driveshaft, then withdraw the inner constant velocity joint from the transmission, taking care not to damage the driveshaft oil seal. Remove the driveshaft from the vehicle. **Note:** *Do not allow the vehicle to rest on its wheels with one or both driveshafts removed, as damage to the wheel bearing(s) may result. If moving the vehicle is unavoidable, temporarily insert the outer end*

2.10a Slacken the two intermediate bearing retaining nuts (arrowed) . . .

2.7a Remove the two bolts securing the base of the suspension strut to the hub carrier

of the driveshaft(s) in the hub(s) and tighten the driveshaft nut(s). Support the inner end(s) of the driveshaft(s) to avoid damage.

Right-hand driveshaft

10 Loosen the two intermediate bearing retaining bolt nuts, then rotate the bolts through 90°, so that their offset heads are clear of the bearing outer race **(see illustrations)**.

11 Slacken and remove the two bolts securing the steering hub carrier to the base of the suspension strut. Pull the hub carrier outwards to free it from the strut. **Note:** *After releasing the hub carrier, rotate the base of the strut 90° towards the rear of the vehicle to minimise the chances of damaging the rubber driveshafts gaiter* **(see illustrations 2.7a and 2.7b)**.

12 Carefully pull the swivel hub assembly outwards, and withdraw the driveshaft outer constant velocity joint from the hub assembly. If necessary, the shaft can be tapped out of the hub using a soft-faced mallet.

13 Support the outer end of the driveshaft, then pull on the inner end of the shaft to free the intermediate bearing from its mounting bracket.

14 Once the driveshaft end is free from the transmission, slide the dust seal (where fitted) off the inner end of the shaft, noting which way around it is fitted, and remove the driveshaft from the vehicle. On automatic transmission models, the inboard end of the shaft fits over a splined shaft from the differential. Check the condition of the

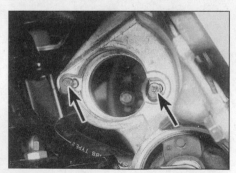

2.10b . . . rotate the bolts through 90° so the offset heads (arrowed) are clear of the outer race (driveshaft removed for clarity)

2.7b Rotate the base of the strut 90° towards the rear to minimise any chance of damaging the driveshaft gaiter

splined shaft O-ring. **Note:** *Do not allow the vehicle to rest on its wheels with one or both driveshafts removed, as damage to the wheel bearing(s) may result. If moving the vehicle is unavoidable, temporarily insert the outer end of the driveshaft(s) in the hub(s) and tighten the driveshaft nut(s). Support the inner end(s) of the driveshaft(s) to avoid damage.*

Refitting

15 Before installing the driveshaft, examine the driveshaft oil seal in the transmission for signs of damage or deterioration and, if necessary, renew it as described in Chapter 7A or 7B. It is highly recommended that the seal is renewed, regardless of its apparent condition.

16 Thoroughly clean the driveshaft splines, and the apertures in the transmission and hub assembly. Apply a thin film of grease to the oil seal lips, and to the driveshaft splines and shoulders. Check that all gaiter clips are securely fastened.

Left-hand driveshaft

17 Offer up the driveshaft, and locate the joint splines with those of the differential sun gear, taking great care not to damage the oil seal. Push the joint fully into position.

18 Locate the outer constant velocity joint splines with those of the swivel hub, and slide the joint back into position in the hub.

19 Rotate the base of the strut 90° and align the hub carrier with the brackets on the strut. Insert the bolts and tighten them to the specified torque.

20 Lubricate the inner face and threads of the driveshaft nut with clean engine oil, and refit it to the end of the driveshaft. Use the method employed on removal to prevent the hub from rotating (see paragraph 5), and tighten the driveshaft retaining nut to the specified torque. Check that the hub rotates freely then engage the locking cap with the driveshaft nut, so that one of its cut-outs is aligned with the driveshaft hole, and secure the cap in position with the R-clip **(see illustrations)**. Alternatively, lightly tighten the nut at this stage, and tighten it to the specified torque once the car is resting on its wheels again.

21 Refit the ABS wheel sensor and brake caliper as described in Chapter 9.

22 Refit the roadwheel, then lower the vehicle to the ground and tighten the roadwheel bolts to the specified torque. If not already done, tighten the driveshaft retaining nut to the specified torque then refit the locking cap, aligning its cut-outs with the driveshaft hole, and secure it in position with the R-clip.

23 Refill the transmission with the specified type and amount of oil, and check the level using the information given in the relevant Part of Chapter 1.

Right-hand driveshaft

24 Check that the intermediate bearing rotates smoothly, without any sign of roughness or undue free play between its inner and outer races. If necessary, renew the bearing as described in Section 5. Examine the dust seal for signs of damage or deterioration, and renew if necessary. Check the condition of the differential splined shaft O-ring seal and renew if necessary.

25 Apply a smear of grease to the outer race of the intermediate bearing, and to the inner lip of the dust seal (where fitted).

26 Pass the inner end of the shaft through the bearing mounting bracket then, where necessary, carefully slide the dust seal into position on the driveshaft, ensuring that its flat surface is facing the transmission **(see illustration)**.

27 On manual transmission models, carefully locate the inner driveshaft splines with those of the differential sun gear, taking care not to damage the oil seal.

28 On automatic transmission models, located the end of the driveshaft over the differential splined shaft.

29 On all models, align the intermediate bearing with its mounting bracket, and push the driveshaft fully into position. If necessary, use a soft-faced mallet to tap the outer race of the bearing into position in the mounting bracket.

30 Locate the outer constant velocity joint splines with those of the swivel hub, and slide the joint back into position in the hub.

31 Ensure that the intermediate bearing is correctly seated, then rotate its retaining bolts back through 90°, so that their offset heads are resting against the bearing outer race. Tighten the retaining nuts to the specified torque. Where necessary, ensure that the dust seal is tight against the driveshaft oil seal **(see illustration)**.

32 Carry out the operations described above in paragraphs 18 to 23.

---

3 Driveshaft rubber gaiters – renewal

Outer joint

1 Remove the driveshaft from the vehicle as described in Section 2.

2.20a Tighten the driveshaft nut to the specified torque, then refit the locking cap . . .

2.26 Locate the dust seal (where fitted) on the inner end of the right-hand driveshaft, ensuring it is fitted the right-way around

2 Secure the driveshaft in a vice equipped with soft jaws, and release the two outer gaiter retaining clips. If necessary, the gaiter retaining clips can be cut to release them.

3 Slide the rubber gaiter down the shaft, to expose the outer constant velocity joint. Scoop out the excess grease.

4 Using a hammer and suitable soft metal drift, sharply strike the inner member of the outer joint to drive it off the end of the shaft. The joint is retained on the driveshaft by a circlip, and striking the joint in this manner forces the circlip into its groove, so allowing the joint to slide off.

5 Once the joint assembly has been removed, remove the circlip from the groove in the driveshaft splines, and discard it. A new circlip must be fitted on reassembly.

6 Withdraw the rubber gaiter from the driveshaft. Where necessary, slide off the gaiter inner end plastic bush.

7 With the constant velocity joint removed from the driveshaft, thoroughly clean the joint using paraffin, or a suitable solvent, and dry it thoroughly. Carry out a visual inspection of the joint.

8 Move the inner splined driving member from side-to-side, to expose each ball in turn at the top of its track. Examine the balls for cracks, flat spots, or signs of surface pitting.

9 Inspect the ball tracks on the inner and outer members. If the tracks have widened, the balls will no longer be a tight fit. At the same time, check the ball cage windows for wear or cracking between the windows.

2.20b . . . and secure it in position with the R-clip

2.31 Secure the intermediate bearing in position then (if necessary) slide the dust seal up tight against the driveshaft oil seal

10 If, on inspection, any of the constant velocity joint components are found to be worn or damaged, it will be necessary to renew the complete joint assembly (where available), or even the complete driveshaft (where no joint components are available separately). Refer to your Peugeot dealer for further information on parts availability. If the joint is in satisfactory condition, obtain a repair kit consisting of a new gaiter, circlip, retaining clips, and the correct type and quantity of grease.

11 To install the new gaiter, perform the operations shown **(see illustrations)**. Be sure to stay in order, and follow the captions carefully. Note that the hard plastic rings and plastic bushes are not fitted to all gaiters, and the gaiter retaining clips supplied with the repair kit may be different to those shown in

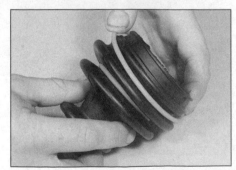

3.11a Fit the hard plastic rings to the outer CV joint gaiter . . .

3.11b . . . then slide on the new plastic bush (arrowed – where fitted), and seat it in its recess in the shaft. Slide the gaiter onto the shaft . . .

3.11c . . . and seat the gaiter inner end on top of the plastic bush (as applicable)

3.11d Fit the new circlip to its groove in the driveshaft splines . . .

3.11e . . . then locate the joint outer member on the splines, and slide it into position over the circlip. Ensure that the joint is securely retained by the circlip

3.11f Pack the joint with grease, working it into the ball tracks while twisting the joint, then locate the gaiter outer lip in its groove on the outer member

3.11g Fit the outer gaiter retaining clip and, using a hook fabricated out of welding rod and a pair of pliers, pull the clip tight to remove all the slack

3.11h Bend the clip end back over the buckle, then cut off the excess

3.11i Fold the clip end underneath the buckle . . .

3.11j . . . then fold the buckle firmly down onto the clip to secure the clip in position

3.11k Carefully lift the gaiter inner end to equalise the air pressure in the gaiter, then secure the inner gaiter retaining clip in position using the same method

3.16a Release the inner gaiter retaining clips, and remove the joint outer member

3.16b Slide the gaiter off the end of the driveshaft . . .

the sequence. To secure this other type of clip in position, lock the ends of the clip together, then remove any slack in the clip by carefully compressing the raised section of the clip using a pair of side-cutters.

12 Check that the constant velocity joint moves freely in all directions, then refit the driveshaft to the vehicle as described in Section 2.

Inner joint

13 Remove the driveshaft from the vehicle as described in Section 2.

14 Remove the outer constant velocity joint as described above in paragraphs 1 to 5.

15 Tape over the splines on the driveshaft, and carefully remove the outer constant velocity joint rubber gaiter, and (where fitted) the gaiter inner end plastic bush. It is recommended that the outer joint gaiter is also renewed, regardless of its apparent condition.

16 Release the retaining clips, then slide the inner gaiter off the shaft and (where fitted) remove its plastic bush. As the gaiter is released, the joint outer member will also be freed from the end of the shaft **(see illustrations)**.

17 Thoroughly clean the joint using paraffin, or a suitable solvent, and dry it thoroughly. Check the tripod joint bearings and joint outer member for signs of wear, pitting or scuffing on their bearing surfaces. Check that the bearing rollers rotate smoothly and easily around the tripod joint, with no traces of roughness.

18 If, on inspection, the tripod joint or outer member reveal signs of wear or damage, it will be necessary to renew the complete driveshaft assembly, since the joint is not available separately. If the joint is in satisfactory condition, obtain a repair kit consisting of a new gaiter, retaining clips, and the correct type and quantity of grease.

19 On reassembly, pack the inner joint with the grease supplied in the gaiter kit. Work the grease well into the bearing tracks and rollers, while twisting the joint.

20 Clean the shaft, using emery cloth to remove any rust or sharp edges which may damage the gaiter, then slide the plastic bush (where fitted) and inner joint gaiter along the driveshaft. Locate the plastic bush in its recess on the shaft, and seat the inner end of the gaiter on top of the bush; where no bush is fitted, seat the inner end of the driveshaft in the recess on the shaft.

21 Fit the outer member over the end

3.16c . . . and remove the plastic bush

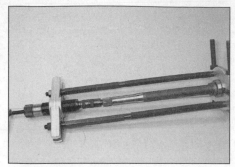

5.3 Using a long-reach bearing puller to remove the intermediate bearing from the right-hand driveshaft

of the shaft, and locate the gaiter in the groove on the joint outer member. Push the outer member onto the joint, so that its spring-loaded plunger is compressed, then lift the outer edge of the gaiter to equalise air pressure in the gaiter. Fit both the inner and outer retaining clips, securing them in position using the information given in paragraph 11. Ensure that the gaiter retaining clips are securely tightened, then check that the joint moves freely in all directions.

22 Refit the outer constant velocity joint components using the information given in paragraph 11.

4 Driveshaft overhaul – general information

1 If any of the checks described in Chapter 1A or 1B reveal wear in any driveshaft joint, first remove the roadwheel trim or centre cap (as appropriate).

2 If the R-clip is still in position, the driveshaft nut should be correctly tightened; if in doubt, remove the R-clip and locking cap, and use a torque wrench to check that the nut is securely fastened. Once tightened, refit the locking cap and R-clip, then refit the centre cap or trim. Repeat this check on the remaining driveshaft nut.

3 Road test the vehicle, and listen for a metallic clicking from the front as the vehicle is driven slowly in a circle on full-lock. If a clicking noise is heard, this indicates wear in the outer constant velocity joint. This means that the joint must be renewed; reconditioning is not possible.

4 If vibration, consistent with road speed, is felt through the car when accelerating, there is a possibility of wear in the inner joints.

5 To check the joints for wear, remove the driveshafts, then dismantle them as described in Section 3; if any wear or free play is found, the affected joint must be renewed. In the case of the inner joints (and on some models, the outer joints), this means that the complete driveshaft assembly must be renewed, as the joints are not available separately. Refer to your Peugeot dealer for latest information on the availability of driveshaft components.

5 Right-hand driveshaft intermediate bearing – renewal

Note: *A suitable bearing puller will be required, to draw the bearing and collar off the driveshaft end.*

1 Remove the right-hand driveshaft as described in Section 2 of this Chapter.

2 Check that the bearing outer race rotates smoothly and easily, without any signs of roughness or undue free play between the inner and outer races. If necessary, renew the bearing as follows.

3 Using a long-reach universal bearing puller, carefully draw the collar and intermediate bearing off the driveshaft inner end **(see illustration)**. Apply a smear of grease to the inner race of the new bearing, then fit the bearing over the end of the driveshaft. Using a hammer and suitable piece of tubing which bears only on the bearing inner race, tap the new bearing into position on the driveshaft, until it abuts the constant velocity joint outer member. Once the bearing is correctly positioned, tap the bearing collar onto the shaft until it contacts the bearing inner race.

4 Check that the bearing rotates freely, then refit the driveshaft as described in Section 2.

Chapter 9
Braking system

Contents

Degrees of difficulty

| **Easy,** suitable for novice with little experience | | **Fairly easy,** suitable for beginner with some experience | | **Fairly difficult,** suitable for competent DIY mechanic | | **Difficult,** suitable for experienced DIY mechanic | | **Very difficult,** suitable for expert DIY or professional | |

Specifications

Front brakes

Type	Disc, with single-piston sliding caliper
Disc diameter:	
1.4 litre models	266 mm
All other models	283 mm
Disc thickness:	
1.4 litre models:	
New.	22.0 mm
Minimum	20.0 mm
All other models:	
New.	26.0 mm
Minimum	24.0 mm
Maximum disc run-out	0.05 mm
Brake pad friction material thickness:	
New	13.0 mm
Minimum.	2.0 mm

Rear disc brakes

Disc diameter	247 mm
Disc thickness:	
New	9.0 mm
Minimum thickness.	7.0 mm
Maximum disc run-out	0.05 mm
Brake pad friction material thickness:	
New	11.0 mm
Minimum.	2.0 mm

Torque wrench settings

	Nm	lbf ft
ABS system components:		
Regulator unit nuts	20	15
Wheel sensor retaining bolts*	10	7
Crossover linkage housing nuts and bolts (right-hand drive models) . .	25	18
Disc retaining screws	10	7
Front brake caliper:		
Guide pin bolts*	30	22
Mounting bracket bolts*	105	77
Handbrake lever nuts	15	11
Hydraulic hose/pipe union nuts	15	11
Master cylinder retaining nuts	20	15
Rear brake caliper:		
Guide pin bolts*	30	22
Mounting bracket bolts*	50	37
Roadwheel bolts.	90	66
Vacuum servo unit mounting nuts	20	15

Do not re-use.

1 General information

The braking system is of the servo-assisted, dual-circuit hydraulic type. The arrangement of the hydraulic system is such that each circuit operates one front and one rear brake from a tandem master cylinder. Under normal circumstances, both circuits operate in unison. However, in the event of hydraulic failure in one circuit, full braking force will still be available at two wheels.

All models are equipped with disc brakes on all wheels. ABS is fitted as standard (refer to Section 18 for further information on ABS operation).

The disc brakes are actuated by single-piston sliding type calipers, which ensure that equal pressure is applied to each disc pad.

On all models, the handbrake provides an independent mechanical means of rear brake application. All models are fitted with rear brake calipers with an integral handbrake function. The handbrake cable operates a lever on the caliper which forces the piston to press the pad against the disc surface. A self-adjust mechanism is incorporated, to automatically compensate for brake pad wear.

On diesel engines, there is insufficient vacuum in the inlet manifold to operate the braking system servo effectively at all times. To overcome this problem, a vacuum pump is fitted to the engine, to provide sufficient vacuum to operate the servo unit. The vacuum pump is mounted on the end of the cylinder head, and is driven directly off the end of the camshaft.

Note: *When servicing any of the system, work carefully and methodically; also observe scrupulous cleanliness when overhauling any of the hydraulic system. Always renew components (in axle sets, where applicable) if in doubt about their condition, and use only genuine Peugeot replacement parts, or at least those of known good quality. Note the* warnings given in 'Safety first!' and at relevant points in this Chapter concerning the dangers of asbestos dust and hydraulic fluid.

2 Hydraulic system – bleeding

⚠ *Warning: Hydraulic fluid is poisonous; wash off immediately and thoroughly in the case of skin contact, and seek immediate medical advice if any fluid is swallowed or gets into the eyes. Certain types of hydraulic fluid are inflammable, and may ignite when allowed into contact with hot components; when servicing any hydraulic system, it is safest to assume that the fluid is inflammable, and to take precautions against the risk of fire as though it is petrol that is being handled. Hydraulic fluid is also an effective paint stripper, and will attack plastics; if any is spilt, it should be washed off immediately, using copious quantities of fresh water. Finally, it is hygroscopic (it absorbs moisture from the air) – old fluid may be contaminated and unfit for further use. When topping-up or renewing the fluid, always use the recommended type, and ensure that it comes from a freshly-opened sealed container.*

Caution: Ensure the ignition is switched off before starting the bleeding procedure, to avoid any possibility of voltage being applied to the hydraulic modulator before the bleeding procedure is complete. Ideally, the battery should be disconnected. If voltage is applied to the modulator before the bleeding procedure is complete, this will effectively drain the hydraulic fluid in the modulator, rendering the unit unserviceable. Do not, therefore, attempt to 'run' the modulator in order to bleed the brakes.
Note: *If difficulty is experienced in bleeding the braking circuit, this maybe due to air being* trapped in the ABS regulator unit. If this is the case then the vehicle should be taken to a Peugeot dealer or suitably-equipped specialist so that the system can be bled using special electronic test equipment.
Note: *A hydraulic clutch shares its fluid reservoir with the braking system, and may also need to be bled (see Chapter 6).*

General

1 The correct operation of any hydraulic system is only possible after removing all air from the components and circuit; this is achieved by bleeding the system.

2 During the bleeding procedure, add only clean, unused hydraulic fluid of the recommended type; never re-use fluid that has already been bled from the system. Ensure that sufficient fluid is available before starting work.

3 If there is any possibility of incorrect fluid being already in the system, the brake components and circuit must be flushed completely with uncontaminated, correct fluid, and new seals should be fitted to the various components.

4 If hydraulic fluid has been lost from the system, or air has entered because of a leak, ensure that the fault is cured before proceeding further.

5 Park the vehicle on level ground, switch off the engine and select first or reverse gear, then chock the wheels and release the handbrake.

6 Check that all pipes and hoses are secure, unions tight and bleed screws closed. Clean any dirt from around the bleed screws.

7 Unscrew the master cylinder reservoir cap, and top the master cylinder reservoir up to the MAX level line; refit the cap loosely, and remember to maintain the fluid level at least above the MIN/DANGER level line throughout the procedure, or there is a risk of further air entering the system.

8 There is a number of one-man, do-it-yourself brake bleeding kits currently available from motor accessory shops. It is recommended that one of these kits is used

whenever possible, as they greatly simplify the bleeding operation, and also reduce the risk of expelled air and fluid being drawn back into the system. If such a kit is not available, the basic (two-man) method must be used, which is described in detail below.

9 If a kit is to be used, prepare the vehicle as described previously, and follow the kit manufacturer's instructions, as the procedure may vary slightly according to the type being used; generally, they are as outlined below in the relevant sub-section.

10 Whichever method is used, the same sequence must be followed (paragraphs 11 and 12) to ensure that the removal of all air from the system.

Bleeding

Sequence

11 If the system has been only partially disconnected, and suitable precautions were taken to minimise fluid loss, it should be necessary only to bleed that of the system (ie, the primary or secondary circuit).

12 If the complete system is to be bled, then it should be done working in the following sequence:
   a) *Left-hand front brake.*
   b) *Right-hand front brake.*
   c) *Left-hand rear brake.*
   d) *Right-hand rear brake.*

Basic (two-man) method

13 Collect a clean glass jar, a suitable length of plastic or rubber tubing which is a tight fit over the bleed screw, and a ring spanner to fit the screw. The help of an assistant will also be required.

14 Remove the dust cap from the first screw in the sequence. Fit the spanner and tube to the screw, place the other end of the tube in the jar, and pour in sufficient fluid to cover the end of the tube.

15 Ensure that the master cylinder reservoir fluid level is maintained at least above the MIN/DANGER level line throughout the procedure.

16 Have the assistant fully depress the brake pedal several times to build up pressure, then maintain it on the final downstroke.

17 While pedal pressure is maintained, unscrew the bleed screw (approximately one turn) and allow the compressed fluid and air to flow into the jar. The assistant should maintain pedal pressure, following it down to the floor if necessary, and should not release it until instructed to do so. When the flow stops, tighten the bleed screw again, have the assistant release the pedal slowly, and recheck the reservoir fluid level.

18 Repeat the steps given in paragraphs 16 and 17 until the fluid emerging from the bleed screw is free from air bubbles. If the master cylinder has been drained and refilled, and air is being bled from the first screw in the sequence, allow approximately five seconds between cycles for the master cylinder passages to refill.

19 When no more air bubbles appear, tighten the bleed screw securely, remove the tube and spanner, and refit the dust cap. Do not overtighten the bleed screw.

20 Repeat the procedure on the remaining screws in the sequence, until all air is removed from the system and the brake pedal feels firm again.

Using a one-way valve kit

21 As their name implies, these kits consist of a length of tubing with a one-way valve fitted, to prevent expelled air and fluid being drawn back into the system; some kits include a translucent container, which can be positioned so that the air bubbles can be more easily seen flowing from the end of the tube.

22 The kit is connected to the bleed screw, which is then opened **(see illustration)**. The user returns to the driver's seat, depresses the brake pedal with a smooth, steady stroke, and slowly releases it; this is repeated until the expelled fluid is clear of air bubbles.

23 Note that these kits simplify work so much that it is easy to forget the master cylinder reservoir fluid level; ensure that this is maintained at least above the MIN/DANGER level line at all times.

Using a pressure-bleeding kit

24 These kits are usually operated by the reservoir of pressurised air contained in the spare tyre. However, note that it will probably be necessary to reduce the pressure to a lower level than normal; refer to the instructions supplied with the kit.

25 By connecting a pressurised, fluid-filled container to the master cylinder reservoir, bleeding can be carried out simply by opening each screw in turn (in the specified sequence), and allowing the fluid to flow out until no more air bubbles can be seen in the expelled fluid.

26 This method has the advantage that the large reservoir of fluid provides an additional safeguard against air being drawn into the system during bleeding.

27 Pressure-bleeding is particularly effective when bleeding 'difficult' systems, or when bleeding the complete system at the time of routine fluid renewal.

All methods

28 When bleeding is complete, and firm pedal feel is restored, wash off any spilt fluid, tighten the bleed screws securely, and refit their dust caps.

29 Check the hydraulic fluid level in the master cylinder reservoir, and top-up if necessary (see *Weekly checks*).

30 Discard any hydraulic fluid that has been bled from the system; it will not be fit for re-use.

31 Check the feel of the brake pedal. If it feels at all spongy, air must still be present in the system, and further bleeding is required. Failure to bleed satisfactorily after a reasonable repetition of the bleeding procedure may be due to worn master cylinder seals.

2.22 Connect the kit to the bleed screw

3 Hydraulic pipes and hoses – renewal

Caution: Ensure the ignition is switched off before disconnecting any braking system hydraulic union and do not switch it on until after the hydraulic system has been bled. Failure to do this could lead to air entering the regulator unit requiring the unit to be bled using special Peugeot test equipment (see Section 2).

Note: *Before starting work, refer to the note at the beginning of Section 2 concerning the dangers of hydraulic fluid.*

1 If any pipe or hose is to be renewed, minimise fluid loss by first removing the master cylinder reservoir cap, then tightening it down onto a piece of polythene to obtain an airtight seal. Alternatively, flexible hoses can be sealed, if required, using a proprietary brake hose clamp; metal brake pipe unions can be plugged (if care is taken not to allow dirt into the system) or capped immediately they are disconnected. Place a wad of rag under any union that is to be disconnected, to catch any spilt fluid.

2 If a flexible hose is to be disconnected, unscrew the brake pipe union nut before removing the spring clip which secures the hose to its mounting bracket.

3 To unscrew the union nuts, it is preferable to obtain a brake pipe spanner of the correct size; these are available from most large motor accessory shops. Failing this, a close-fitting open-ended spanner will be required, though if the nuts are tight or corroded, their flats may be rounded-off if the spanner slips. In such a case, a self-locking wrench is often the only way to unscrew a stubborn union, but it follows that the pipe and the damaged nuts must be renewed on reassembly. Always clean a union and surrounding area before disconnecting it. If disconnecting a component with more than one union, make a careful note of the connections before disturbing any of them.

4 If a brake pipe is to be renewed, it can be obtained, cut to length and with the union nuts and end flares in place, from Peugeot dealers. All that is then necessary is to bend

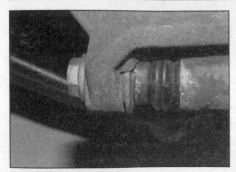

4.3 Remove the caliper lower guide pin bolt . . .

4.4 . . . then pivot the caliper upwards and away from the brake pads, and tie it to the suspension strut

4.5 Withdraw the brake pads from the caliper mounting bracket

it to shape, following the line of the original, before fitting it to the car. Alternatively, most motor accessory shops can make up brake pipes from kits, but this requires very careful measurement of the original, to ensure that the replacement is of the correct length. The safest answer is usually to take the original to the shop as a pattern.

5 On refitting, do not overtighten the union nuts. It is not necessary to exercise brute force to obtain a sound joint.

6 Ensure that the pipes and hoses are correctly routed, with no kinks, and that they are secured in the clips or brackets provided. After fitting, remove the polythene from the reservoir, and bleed the hydraulic system as described in Section 2. Wash off any spilt fluid, and check carefully for fluid leaks.

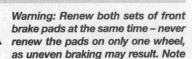

4 Front brake pads – renewal

⚠ *Warning: Renew both sets of front brake pads at the same time – never renew the pads on only one wheel, as uneven braking may result. Note that the dust created by wear of the pads may contain asbestos, which is a health hazard. Never blow it out with compressed air, and don't inhale any of it. An approved filtering mask should be worn when working on the brakes. DO NOT use petrol or petroleum-based solvents to clean brake parts; use brake cleaner or methylated spirit only.*

Note: *New guide pin bolts must be used on refitting.*

1 Apply the handbrake, slacken the front roadwheel bolts, then jack up the front of the vehicle and support it on axle stands. Remove the front roadwheels.

2 Push the piston into its bore by pulling the caliper outwards.

3 Slacken and remove the caliper lower guide pin bolt **(see illustration)**. Discard the guide pin bolt – a new one must be used on refitting.

4 With the lower guide pin bolt removed, pivot the caliper away from the brake pads and mounting bracket, and tie it to the suspension strut using a suitable piece of wire **(see illustration)**.

5 Withdraw the two brake pads from the caliper mounting bracket; the shims (where fitted) should be bonded to the pad, but may have come unstuck in use **(see illustration)**.

6 First measure the thickness of each brake pad's friction material **(see illustration)**. If either pad is worn at any point to the specified minimum thickness or less, all four pads must be renewed. Also, the pads should be renewed if any are fouled with oil or grease; there is no satisfactory way of degreasing friction material, once contaminated. If any of the brake pads are worn unevenly, or are fouled with oil or grease, trace and rectify the cause before reassembly.

7 If the brake pads are still serviceable, carefully clean them using a clean, fine wire brush or similar, paying particular attention to the sides and back of the metal backing.

Clean out the grooves in the friction material, and pick out any large embedded particles of dirt or debris. Carefully clean the pad locations in the caliper mounting bracket.

8 Prior to fitting the pads, check that the guide pins are free to slide easily in the caliper mounting bracket, and check that the rubber guide pin gaiters are undamaged **(see illustration)**. Brush the dust and dirt from the caliper and piston, but **do not** inhale it, as it is a health hazard. Inspect the dust seal around the piston for damage, and the piston for evidence of fluid leaks, corrosion or damage. If attention to any of these components is necessary, refer to Section 8.

9 If new brake pads are to be fitted, the caliper piston must be pushed back into the cylinder to make room for them. Either use a G-clamp or similar tool, or use suitable pieces of wood as levers. Clamp off the flexible brake hose leading to the caliper then connect a brake bleeding kit to the caliper bleed nipple. Open the bleed nipple as the piston is retracted, the surplus brake fluid will then be collected in the bleed kit vessel **(see illustration)**. Close the bleed nipple just before the caliper piston is pushed fully into the caliper. This should ensure no air enters the hydraulic system. **Note:** *The ABS unit contains hydraulic components that are very sensitive to impurities in the brake fluid. Even the smallest particles can cause the system to fail through blockage. The pad retraction method described here prevents any debris in the brake fluid expelled from the caliper from*

4.6 Measure the thickness of the pads friction material

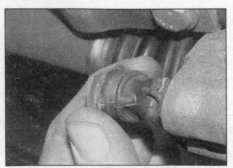

4.8 Check the condition of the guide pin rubbers

4.9 Open the bleed nipple and push the piston back (piston retraction tool shown)

4.10 Ensure the shims at the top and bottom of the caliper mounting bracket are correctly fitted

4.11 Refit the pads, with the chamfer (arrowed) at the top

4.12 Pivot the caliper down and over the pads, then fit and tighten the new caliper guide pin bolt

being passed back to the ABS hydraulic unit, as well as preventing any chance of damage to the master cylinder seals.

10 Check to make sure the shims at the top and bottom of the caliper bracket are correctly fitted **(see illustration)**.

11 Ensuring that the friction material of each pad is against the brake disc, fit the pads to the caliper mounting bracket. If the shims (where fitted) have become detached, ensure that they are correctly positioned on each pads backing plate. If the pads have a chamfer at one edge, fit the pads so that the chamfer is at the top **(see illustration)**.

12 Pivot the caliper down into position over the pads. If the threads of the new guide pin bolt are not already precoated with locking compound, apply a suitable thread-locking compound to them (Peugeot recommend Loctite Frenetanch – available

from your Peugeot dealer). Press the caliper into position, then install the guide pin bolt, tightening it to the specified torque setting **(see illustration)**.

13 Depress the brake pedal repeatedly, until the pads are pressed into firm contact with the brake disc, and normal (non-assisted) pedal pressure is restored.

14 Repeat the above procedure on the remaining front brake caliper.

15 Refit the roadwheels, then lower the vehicle to the ground and tighten the roadwheel bolts to the specified torque.

16 Check the hydraulic fluid level as described in *Weekly checks*.

Caution: New pads will not give full braking efficiency until they have bedded-in. Be prepared for this, and avoid hard braking as far as possible for the first hundred miles or so after pad renewal.

5 Rear brake pads – renewal

⚠️ *Warning: Renew both sets of rear brake pads at the same time – never renew the pads on only one wheel, as uneven braking may result. Note that the dust created by wear of the pads may contain asbestos, which is a health hazard. Never blow it out with compressed air, and don't inhale any of it. An approved filtering mask should be worn when working on the brakes. DO NOT use petrol or petroleum-based solvents to clean brake parts; use brake cleaner or methylated spirit only.*

Note: *New guide pin bolts must be fitted on reassembly.*

1 Chock the front wheels, slacken the rear roadwheel bolts, then jack up the rear of the vehicle and support it on axle stands (see *Jacking and vehicle support*). Remove the rear roadwheels.

2 Using a pair of pliers, release the handbrake cable from the caliper lever. Compress the clip and pull the cable from the support bracket **(see illustrations)**.

3 Slacken and remove the caliper lower guide pin bolt, and swing the caliper up, pivoting around the top guide pin bolt, and tie it in place **(see illustration)**.

4 Withdraw the inner and outer pads from the caliper bracket, and note the location of any shims fitted between the pads and caliper **(see illustrations)**.

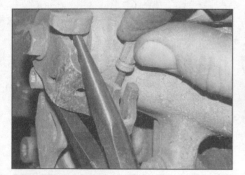

5.2a Disengage the handbrake cable from the caliper lever . . .

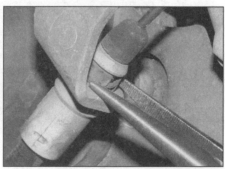

5.2b . . . then squeeze the clip and pull the outer cable from the support bracket

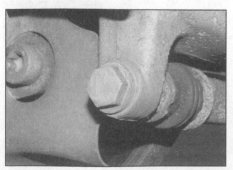

5.3 Remove the caliper lower guide pin bolt

5.4a Withdraw the inner . . .

5.4b . . . and outer pads

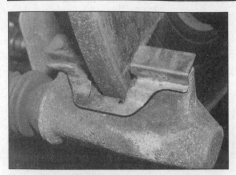

5.4c Note the fitted location of any shims fitted between the pads and caliper

5.8 Use a retraction tool to rotate the piston whilst pushing at the same time

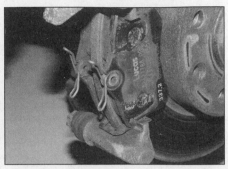

5.9 Ensure the pads are fitted with the friction material facing the brake disc

5 First measure the thickness of the friction material of each brake pad. If either pad is worn at any point to the specified minimum thickness or less, all four pads must be renewed. Also, the pads should be renewed if any are fouled with oil or grease; there is no satisfactory way of degreasing friction material, once contaminated. If any of the brake pads are worn unevenly, or fouled with oil or grease, trace and rectify the cause before reassembly. Examine the retaining pins for signs of wear and renew if necessary. New brake pads and retaining pin kits are available from Peugeot dealers.

6 If the brake pads are still serviceable, carefully clean them using a clean, fine wire brush or similar, paying particular attention to the sides and back of the metal backing. Clean out the grooves in the friction material, and pick out any large embedded particles of dirt or debris. Carefully clean the pad locations in the caliper body/mounting bracket.

7 Prior to fitting the pads, check that the guide sleeves are free to slide easily in the caliper body, and check that the rubber guide sleeve gaiters are undamaged. Brush the dust and dirt from the caliper and piston, but **do not** inhale it, as it is a health hazard. Inspect the dust seal around the piston for damage, and the piston for evidence of fluid leaks, corrosion or damage. If attention to any of these components is necessary, refer to Section 9.

8 If new brake pads are to be fitted, the caliper piston must be pushed back into the cylinder to make room for them. In order to retract the piston, the piston must be turned clockwise as it is pushed into the caliper. Peugeot tool No DF61 is available to retract the pistons, as are several available from good accessory/parts retailers **(see illustration)**. Clamp off the flexible brake hose leading to the caliper then connect a brake bleeding kit to the caliper bleed nipple. Open the bleed nipple as the piston is retracted, the surplus brake fluid will then be collected in the bleed kit vessel. Close the bleed nipple just before the caliper piston is pushed fully into the caliper. This should ensure no air enters the hydraulic system. **Note:** *The ABS unit contains hydraulic components that are very sensitive to impurities in the brake fluid. Even*

the smallest particles can cause the system to fail through blockage. The pad retraction method described here prevents any debris in the brake fluid expelled from the caliper from being passed back to the ABS hydraulic unit, as well as preventing any chance of damage to the master cylinder seals.

9 Slide the brake pads into position in the caliper, ensuring each pad's friction material is facing the brake disc. If the shims (where fitted) have become detached, ensure that they are correctly positioned on each pad's backing plate **(see illustration)**.

10 Untie the caliper and lower it into position. Insert the new caliper lower guide pin bolt, and tighten it to the specified torque.

11 Slide the handbrake cable into the support bracket and reconnect the cable end fitting.

12 Depress the brake pedal repeatedly until the pads are pressed into firm contact with the brake disc, and normal (non-assisted) pedal pressure is restored.

13 Repeat the above procedure on the remaining rear brake caliper.

14 Check the operation of the handbrake, and if necessary, carry out the adjustment procedure as described in Section 14.

15 Refit the roadwheels, then lower the vehicle to the ground and tighten the roadwheel bolts to the specified torque setting.

16 Check the hydraulic fluid level as described in *Weekly checks*.

Caution: New pads will not give full braking efficiency until they have bedded-in. Be

6.3 Use a micrometer to measure the disc thickness

prepared for this, and avoid hard braking as far as possible for the first hundred miles or so after pad renewal.

6 Front brake disc – inspection, removal and refitting

Note: *Before starting work, refer to the note at the beginning of Section 4 concerning the dangers of asbestos dust.*

Inspection

Note: *If either disc requires renewal, BOTH should be renewed at the same time, to ensure even and consistent braking. New brake pads should also be fitted.*

1 Apply the handbrake, slacken the front roadwheel bolts, then jack up the front of the car and support it on axle stands (see *Jacking and vehicle support*). Remove the appropriate front roadwheel.

2 Slowly rotate the brake disc so that the full area of both sides can be checked; remove the brake pads if better access is required to the inboard surface. Light scoring is normal in the area swept by the brake pads, but if heavy scoring or cracks are found, the disc must be renewed.

3 It is normal to find a lip of rust and brake dust around the disc's perimeter; this can be scraped off if required. If, however, a lip has formed due to excessive wear of the brake pad swept area, then the disc's thickness must be measured using a micrometer. Take measurements at several places around the disc, at the inside and outside of the pad swept area; if the disc has worn at any point to the specified minimum thickness or less, the disc must be renewed **(see illustration)**.

4 If the disc is thought to be warped, it can be checked for run-out. Either use a dial gauge mounted on any convenient fixed point, while the disc is slowly rotated, or use feeler blades to measure (at several points all around the disc) the clearance between the disc and a fixed point, such as the caliper mounting bracket **(see illustration)**. If the measurements obtained are at the specified maximum or beyond, the disc is excessively warped, and must be renewed; however, it is worth checking first that the hub bearing is in good condition (Chapter 1A or 1B). Also try the effect of removing the disc and turning it through 180°, to reposition it on the hub; if the run-out is still excessive, the disc must be renewed.

5 Check the disc for cracks, especially around the wheel bolt holes, and any other wear or damage, and renew if necessary.

Removal

6 Slacken and remove the two bolts securing the brake caliper mounting bracket to the hub carrier. Slide the assembly off the disc and tie it to the coil spring, using a piece of wire or string, to avoid placing any strain on the hydraulic brake hose.

7 Use chalk or paint to mark the relationship of the disc to the hub, then remove the screws securing the brake disc to the hub, and remove the disc (see illustration). If it is tight, lightly tap its rear face with a hide or plastic mallet.

Refitting

8 Refitting is the reverse of the removal procedure, noting the following points:
  a) Ensure that the mating surfaces of the disc and hub are clean and flat.
  b) Align (if applicable) the marks made on removal, and tighten the disc retaining screws to the specified torque setting.
  c) If a new disc has been fitted, use a suitable solvent to wipe any preservative coating from the disc, before refitting the caliper.
  d) Refit the roadwheel then lower the vehicle to the ground and tighten the wheel bolts to the specified torque. Apply the footbrake several times to force the pads back into contact with the disc before driving the vehicle.

7   Rear brake disc – inspection, removal and refitting

Note: Before starting work, refer to the note at the beginning of Section 5 concerning the dangers of asbestos dust.

Inspection

Note: If either disc requires renewal, BOTH

6.4 Check the disc run-out using a dial gauge

should be renewed at the same time, to ensure even and consistent braking. New brake pads should also be fitted.

1 Firmly chock the front wheels, slacken the appropriate rear roadwheel bolts, then jack up the rear of the car and support it on axle stands (see *Jacking and vehicle support*). Remove the relevant rear roadwheel.

2 Inspect the disc as described in Section 6.

Removal

3 Remove the brake pads as described in Section 5.

4 Slacken the two Torx bolts securing the caliper mounting bracket to the stub axle (see illustration).

5 Use chalk or paint to mark the relationship of the disc to the hub, then undo the screw(s) securing the disc to the hub. If necessary, gently tap the disc from behind and release it from the hub (see illustration).

Refitting

6 Refitting is the reverse of the removal procedure, noting the following points:
  a) Ensure that the mating surfaces of the disc and hub are clean and flat.
  b) Align (if applicable) the marks made on removal, and tighten the disc retaining screws to the specified torque.
  c) If a new disc has been fitted, use a suitable solvent to wipe any preservative coating from the disc, before refitting the caliper.
  d) Refit the roadwheel, then lower the vehicle to the ground and tighten the roadwheel bolts to the specified torque. Depress

7.5 Undo the Torx screws and remove the disc

6.7 Undo the two Torx screws, and remove the disc

the brake pedal several times to force the pads back into contact with the disc.

8   Front brake caliper – removal, overhaul and refitting

Caution: Ensure the ignition is switched off before disconnecting any braking system hydraulic union and do not switch it on until after the hydraulic system has been bled. Failure to do this could lead to air entering the regulator unit requiring the unit to be bled using special Peugeot test equipment (see Section 2).

Note: Before starting work, refer to the note at the beginning of Section 2 concerning the dangers of hydraulic fluid, and to the warning at the beginning of Section 4 concerning the dangers of asbestos dust.

Note: New caliper guide pin bolts and caliper mounting bracket bolts will be required on reassembly.

Removal

1 Apply the handbrake, slacken the relevant front roadwheel bolts, then jack up the front of the vehicle and support it on axle stands (see *Jacking and vehicle support*). Remove the appropriate roadwheel.

2 Minimise fluid loss by first removing the master cylinder reservoir cap, and then tightening it down onto a piece of polythene, to obtain an airtight seal. Alternatively, use a brake hose clamp, a G-clamp or a similar tool to clamp the flexible hose (see illustration).

8.2 To minimise fluid loss, fit a brake hose clamp to the flexible hose

7.4 Slacken the two caliper mounting bracket Torx screws (arrowed)

3 Clean the area around the caliper hose union, then loosen the union.

4 Slacken and remove the upper and lower caliper guide pin bolts **(see illustration 4.12)**. Discard the bolts, new ones must be used on refitting. Lift the caliper away from the brake disc, then unscrew the caliper from the end of the brake hose. Note that the brake pads need not be disturbed, and can be left in position in the caliper mounting bracket.

5 If required, the caliper mounting bracket can be unbolted from the hub carrier. Discard the bolts, new ones must be fitted.

Overhaul

Note: *Check the availability of repair kits for the caliper before dismantling.*

6 With the caliper on the bench, wipe away all traces of dust and dirt, but *avoid inhaling the dust, as it is a health hazard.*

7 Withdraw the partially ejected piston from the caliper body, and remove the dust seal.

> **HAYNES HiNT** *If the piston cannot be withdrawn by hand, it can be pushed out by applying compressed air to the brake hose union hole. Only low pressure should be required, such as is generated by a foot pump. As the piston is expelled, take great care not to trap your fingers between the piston and caliper.*

8 Using a small screwdriver, extract the piston hydraulic seal, taking great care not to damage the caliper bore.

9 Thoroughly clean all components, using only methylated spirit, isopropyl alcohol or clean hydraulic fluid as a cleaning medium. Never use mineral-based solvents such as petrol or paraffin, as they will attack the hydraulic system's rubber components. Dry the components immediately, using compressed air or a clean, lint-free cloth. Use compressed air to blow clear the fluid passages.

10 Check all components, and renew any that are worn or damaged. Check particularly the cylinder bore and piston; these should be renewed (note that this means the renewal of the complete body assembly) if they are scratched, worn or corroded in any way. Similarly check the condition of the guide pins and their gaiters; both pins should be undamaged and (when cleaned) a reasonably tight sliding fit in the caliper bracket. If there is any doubt about the condition of any component, renew it.

11 If the assembly is fit for further use, obtain the appropriate repair kit; the components should be available from Peugeot dealers in various combinations. All rubber seals should be renewed as a matter of course; these should never be re-used.

12 On reassembly, ensure that all components are clean and dry.

13 Soak the piston and the new piston (fluid) seal in clean brake fluid. Smear clean fluid on the cylinder bore surface.

14 Fit the new piston (fluid) seal, using only your fingers (no tools) to manipulate it into the cylinder bore groove.

15 Fit the new dust seal to the rear of the piston and seat the outer lip of the seal in the caliper body groove. Carefully ease the piston squarely into the cylinder bore using a twisting motion. Press the piston fully into position, and seat the inner lip of the dust seal in the piston groove.

16 If the guide pins are being renewed, lubricate the pin shafts with the special grease supplied in the repair kit, and fit the gaiters to the pin grooves. Insert the pins into the caliper bracket and seat the gaiters correctly in the bracket grooves.

Refitting

17 If previously removed, refit the caliper mounting bracket to the hub carrier, and tighten the new bolts to the specified torque.

18 Screw the caliper body fully onto the flexible hose union.

19 Ensure that the brake pads are correctly fitted in the caliper mounting bracket and refit the caliper (see Section 4).

20 If the threads of the new guide pin bolts are not already precoated with locking compound, apply a suitable locking compound to them (Peugeot recommend Loctite Frenetanch – available from your Peugeot dealer). Fit the new lower guide pin bolt, then press the caliper into position and fit the new upper guide pin bolt. Tighten both guide pin bolts to the specified torque.

21 Tighten the brake hose union nut to the specified torque, then remove the brake hose clamp or polythene (where fitted).

22 Bleed the hydraulic system as described in Section 2. Note that, providing the precautions described were taken to minimise brake fluid loss, it should only be necessary to bleed the relevant front brake.

23 Refit the roadwheel, then lower the vehicle to the ground and tighten the road-wheel bolts to the specified torque.

---

9 Rear brake caliper – removal, overhaul and refitting

Caution: *Ensure the ignition is switched off before disconnecting any braking system hydraulic union and do not switch it back on until after the hydraulic system has been bled. Failure to do this could lead to air entering the regulator unit requiring the unit to be bled using special Peugeot test equipment (see Section 2).*

Note: *Before starting work, refer to the note at the beginning of Section 2 concerning the dangers of hydraulic fluid, and to the warning at the beginning of Section 5 concerning the dangers of asbestos dust.*

Note: *New caliper mounting bracket bolts and guide pin bolts when be required on reassembly.*

Removal

1 Chock the front wheels, slacken the relevant rear roadwheel bolts, then jack up the rear of the vehicle and support on axle stands (see *Jacking and vehicle support*). Remove the relevant rear wheel.

2 Remove the brake pads (see Section 5).

3 Minimise fluid loss by first removing the master cylinder reservoir cap, and then tightening it down onto a piece of polythene, to obtain an airtight seal. Alternatively, use a brake hose clamp, a G-clamp or a similar tool to clamp the flexible hose at the nearest convenient point to the brake caliper.

4 Wipe away all traces of dirt around the brake hose union on the caliper. Unscrew the union nut and disconnect the brake pipe from the caliper **(see illustration)**. Plug the pipe and caliper unions to minimise fluid loss and prevent dirt entry.

5 Slacken and remove the guide pin bolt. Remove the caliper from the vehicle. If required, the caliper mounting bracket can be unbolted from the hub carrier. Discard the bolts, new ones must be fitted.

Overhaul

6 At the time of writing, no parts were available to recondition the rear caliper assembly, with the excepting of the guide pin bolts, guide pins and guide pin gaiters. Check the condition of the guide pins and their gaiters; both pins should be undamaged and (when cleaned) a reasonably tight sliding fit in the caliper bracket. If there is any doubt about the condition of any component, renew it.

Refitting

7 If previously removed, refit the caliper mounting bracket to the hub carrier, and tighten the new bolts to the specified torque.

8 Refit the caliper and insert the new guide pin bolts, tightening them to the specified torque settings.

9 Reconnect the brake pipe to the caliper, and tighten the brake hose union nut to the specified torque. Remove the brake hose clamp or polythene (where fitted).

10 Refit the brake pads as described in Section 5.

9.4 Unscrew the union nut (arrowed)

10.3a Undo the two bolts securing the upper reservoir . . .

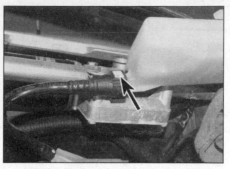

10.3b . . . then depress the button (arrowed) and disconnect the pipe

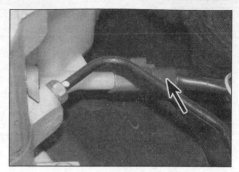

10.4 Disconnect the level sensor wiring plug (arrowed)

11 Bleed the hydraulic system as described in Section 2. Note that, providing the precautions described were taken to minimise brake fluid loss, it should only be necessary to bleed the relevant rear brake.

12 Refit the roadwheel, then lower the vehicle to the ground and tighten the road-wheel bolts to the specified torque.

10 Master cylinder –
removal, overhaul and refitting

Caution: Ensure the ignition is switched off before disconnecting any braking system hydraulic union and do not switch it back on until after the hydraulic system has been bled. Failure to do this could lead to air entering the regulator unit requiring the unit to be bled using special Peugeot test equipment (see Section 2).
Note: Before starting work, refer to the warning at the beginning of Section 2 concerning the dangers of hydraulic fluid.

Removal

1 Remove the battery and battery box as described in Chapter 5A.

2 Remove the master cylinder reservoir cap and filter, and syphon the hydraulic fluid from the reservoir. **Note:** Do not syphon the fluid by mouth, as it is poisonous; use a syringe or an old antifreeze tester. Alternatively, open any

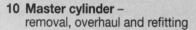

10.5 Brake master cylinder

1 Mounting nuts
2 Pipe union nuts
3 Clutch master cylinder fluid supply pipe

convenient bleed screw in the system, and gently pump the brake pedal to expel the fluid through a plastic tube connected to the screw until the reservoir is emptied (see Section 2).

3 Undo the two bolts and remove the upper reservoir, then depress the release button and disconnect the plastic pipe from the upper reservoir to the lower reservoir on the master cylinder **(see illustrations)**. Be prepared for fluid spillage.

4 Disconnect the wiring connector from the brake fluid level sender unit **(see illustration)**.

5 Empty the lower reservoir by disconnecting the clutch master cylinder fluid supply pipe and draining the fluid into a container **(see illustration)**. Plug the pipe opening to prevent dirt ingress.

6 Wipe clean the area around the brake pipe unions on the side of the master cylinder, and place absorbent rags beneath the pipe unions to catch any surplus fluid. Make a note of the correct fitted positions of the unions, then unscrew the union nuts and carefully withdraw the pipes. Plug or tape over the pipe ends and master cylinder orifices, to minimise the loss of brake fluid, and to prevent the entry of dirt into the system. Wash off any spilt fluid immediately with cold water.

7 Slacken and remove the two nuts securing the master cylinder to the vacuum servo unit, then withdraw the unit from the engine compartment. If the sealing ring fitted to the rear of the master cylinder shows signs of damage or deterioration, it must be renewed. If required, pull retaining lugs and separate the reservoir from the master cylinder **(see illustration)**.

Overhaul

8 The master cylinder may be overhauled after obtaining the relevant repair kit from a Peugeot dealer. Ensure that the correct repair kit is obtained for the master cylinder being worked on. Note the locations of all components to ensure correct refitting, and lubricate the new seals using clean brake fluid. Follow the assembly instructions supplied with the repair kit.

Refitting

9 Remove all traces of dirt from the master cylinder and servo unit mating surfaces and

ensure that the sealing ring is correctly fitted to the rear of the master cylinder.

10 Fit the master cylinder to the servo unit. Refit the master cylinder mounting nuts, and tighten them to the specified torque.

11 Wipe clean the brake pipe unions and refit them to the master cylinder ports, tightening them to the specified torque.

12 Press the mounting seals fully into the master cylinder ports then carefully ease the fluid reservoir into position. Slide the reservoir retaining pin into position and secure it in position, making sure the retaining clip is correctly located in the pin groove.

13 Reconnect the clutch master cylinder supply pipe, and level sensor wiring plug.

14 Refit the upper reservoir and tighten the retaining screws securely.

15 Refit any components removed to improve access then refill the master cylinder reservoir with new fluid. Bleed the complete hydraulic system as described in Section 2. **Note:** A hydraulic clutch shares its fluid reservoir with the braking system, and may also need to be bled (see Chapter 6).

11 Brake pedal –
removal and refitting

Removal

1 Prise up the centre pins, prise out the complete expanding plastic rivets, and remove the driver's side lower facia panel above the pedals.

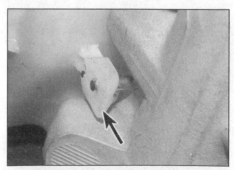

10.7 Pull the mounting lugs (arrowed) of the reservoir over the retaining pin

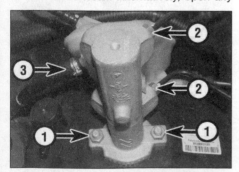

11.2 Slide off the clevis pin retaining clip (arrowed)

2 Slide off the retaining clip and withdraw the clevis pin securing the pedal crossover linkage pushrod to the pedal **(see illustration)**. Discard the clevis pin, a new one must be fitted.

3 Slacken and remove the pivot bolt and nut **(see illustration)**, and remove the brake pedal from the vehicle. Slide the spacer and washer (where fitted) out from the pedal pivot. Examine all components for signs of wear or damage, renewing them as necessary.

Refitting

4 Apply a smear of multi-purpose grease to the spacer and washer, and insert it into the pedal pivot bore.

5 Manoeuvre the pedal into position, making sure it is correctly engaged with the pushrod, and insert the pivot bolt. Refit the nut to the pivot bolt and tighten it securely.

6 Align the pedal with the pushrod and insert the new clevis pin, securing it in position with the retaining clip(s).

7 Refit the lower panel to the facia.

12 Vacuum servo unit – testing, removal and refitting

Testing

1 To test the operation of the servo unit, depress the footbrake several times to exhaust the vacuum, then start the engine whilst keeping the pedal firmly depressed. As the engine starts, there should be a noticeable

12.8 Rotate the clip (arrowed) then pull it from place

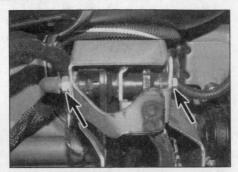

11.3 Slacken and remove the pivot bolt and nut (arrowed)

'give' in the brake pedal as the vacuum builds-up. Allow the engine to run for at least two minutes, then switch it off. If the brake pedal is now depressed it should feel normal, but further applications should result in the pedal feeling firmer, with the pedal stroke decreasing with each application.

2 If the servo does not operate as described, first inspect the servo unit check valve as described in Section 13. On diesel engine models, also check the operation of the vacuum pump as described in Section 21.

3 If the servo unit still fails to operate satisfactorily, the fault lies within the unit itself. Repairs to the unit are not possible – if faulty, the servo unit must be renewed.

Removal

4 Remove the master cylinder as described in Section 10.

5 Release the wiring harness adjacent to the servo from its retaining clips, and move it to one side.

6 Slacken or release the retaining clip (depending on type of securing clip), then disconnect the vacuum pipe from the servo unit check valve.

7 Working in the passenger's footwell, prise up the centre pins, lever out the complete plastic expanding rivets, and remove the trim beneath the passenger's glovebox.

8 Rotate the crossover shaft-to-servo pushrod clevis pin and remove it from the linkage **(see illustration)**. Discard the clevis pin, a new one must be fitted.

9 Slacken and remove the four nuts securing the housing to the bulkhead **(see illustration)**.

12.9 Undo the four servo mounting nuts (arrowed)

10 Depress the two retaining clips (one to the left of the servo gaiter, and one to the right), then ease the housing away from the bulkhead **(see illustration)**.

11 Manoeuvre the servo unit out of position, along with its gasket which is fitted between the servo and housing. Renew the gasket if it shows signs of damage.

Refitting

12 Refitting is the reverse of removal, noting the following points.

a) Prior to refitting, measure the distance from the end of the vacuum servo unit pushrod to the servo master cylinder mating surface. This should be 19.85 ± 0.3 mm; if not seek the advice of a Peugeot dealer before refitting the master cylinder.

b) Lubricate all crossover linkage pivot points with multi-purpose grease.

c) Tighten the servo unit and mounting bracket nuts and bolts to their specified torque settings.

d) Refit the master cylinder as described in Section 10 and bleed the complete hydraulic system as described in Section 2.

e) Always renew the crossover shaft clevis pins.

13 Vacuum servo unit check valve – removal, testing and refitting

Removal

1 Slacken or release the retaining clip (depending on type of securing clip), then disconnect the vacuum hose from the servo unit check valve.

2 Withdraw the valve from its rubber sealing grommet, using a pulling and twisting motion **(see illustration)**. Remove the grommet from the servo.

Testing

3 Examine the check valve for signs of damage, and renew if necessary. The valve may be tested by blowing through it in both directions. Air should flow through the valve in one direction only – when blown through

12.10 Release the servo retaining clips (left-hand one arrowed)

13.2 Servo unit check valve

14.2 Gently prise out the lower edge and remove the ashtray

14.4 Equaliser plate adjustment nut (arrowed)

from the servo unit end of the valve. Renew the valve if this is not the case.

4 Examine the rubber sealing grommet and flexible vacuum hose for signs of damage or deterioration, and renew as necessary.

Refitting

5 Fit the sealing grommet into position in the servo unit.

6 Carefully ease the check valve into position, taking great care not to displace or damage the grommet. Reconnect the vacuum hose to the valve and, where necessary, securely tighten its retaining clip.

7 On completion, start the engine and check for air leaks from the check valve-to-servo unit connection.

14 Handbrake – adjustment

1 To check the handbrake adjustment, applying normal moderate pressure, pull the handbrake lever to the fully-applied position, counting the number of clicks emitted from the handbrake ratchet mechanism. If adjustment is correct, there should be 2 clicks before the brakes begin to apply, and no more than 8 before the handbrake is fully applied. If this is not the case, adjust as follows.

2 Working at the rear of the centre console, pull open the lid, gently prise out the lower edge on each side and remove the ashtray **(see illustration)**.

15.5 Undo the handbrake lever nuts (arrowed)

3 Chock the front wheels, then jack up the rear of the vehicle and support it on axle stands (see *Jacking and vehicle support*).

4 Slacken the adjuster nut behind the equaliser plate on the rod from the lever **(see illustration)**.

5 Start the engine and depress the brake pedal approximately 40 times. Stop the engine.

6 Tighten the adjuster nut just enough to eliminate any free play in the cables.

7 Pull the handbrake lever on 10 times. On the last application, pull the lever up and stop after the second click is emitted.

8 Tighten the adjuster nut until the rear brake pads begin to make contact with the discs.

9 Release the lever and check by hand that the rear wheels rotate freely, then check that no more than eight clicks are emitted before the handbrake is fully applied.

10 Refit the ashtray, then lower the vehicle to the floor.

15 Handbrake lever – removal and refitting

Removal

1 Chock the front wheels then jack up the rear of the vehicle and support it on axle stands (see *Jacking and vehicle support*).

2 Referring to Section 14, release the handbrake lever and back off the adjuster nut to obtain maximum freeplay in the cable.

3 Remove the centre console as described in Chapter 11.

4 Peel back the gaiter (where necessary) and disconnect the wiring connector from the handbrake warning light switch.

5 Detach the handbrake cable from the lever then slacken and remove the lever retaining nuts, and remove the lever from the vehicle **(see illustration)**.

Refitting

6 Refitting is a reversal of removal. Tighten the lever retaining nuts to the specified torque, and adjust the handbrake (see Section 14).

16 Handbrake cables – removal and refitting

Removal

1 The handbrake cable consists of a left-hand section and a right-hand section connecting the rear brakes to the adjuster mechanism on the handbrake lever rod. The cables can be removed separately.

2 Firmly chock the front wheels, slacken the relevant rear roadwheel bolts, then jack up the rear of the vehicle and support it on axle stands (see *Jacking and vehicle support*).

3 Slacken the handbrake adjuster nut sufficiently to be able to disengage the relevant cable end fitting from the equaliser plate with reference to Section 14 **(see illustration)**.

4 Release the cable end fitting from the lever on the brake caliper, and remove the cable from the support bracket **(see illustration 5.2a)**.

5 Working underneath the vehicle, note its fitted location, then free the cable from the various retaining clips/brackets along its route, and pull the front end of the cable from the opening in the floor. Withdraw the cable from underneath the vehicle

Refitting

6 Refitting is a reversal of the removal pro-cedure, adjusting the handbrake as described in Section 14.

16.3 Disengage the cable end fitting from the equaliser plate

17.3 Rotate the stop-light switch 90° anti-clockwise, and pull it from the bracket

17 Stop-light switch –
removal, refitting and adjustment

1 The stop-light switch is located on the pedal crossover shaft bracket behind the passenger side of the facia. On models with automatic transmission or cruise control there are two switches fitted to the bracket – the stop-light switch is the left-hand of the two.

Removal

2 Working in the passenger's footwell, prise up the centre pins, lever out the complete plastic rivets, and remove the trim beneath the passenger's glovebox.
3 Disconnect the wiring, then rotate the switch 90 degrees anti-clockwise and remove it from the bracket **(see illustration)**.

Refitting and adjustment

4 Pull the switch plunger out to its full extent, then depress the brake pedal by hand.
5 Refit the switch back into position in the mounting bracket, then release the brake pedal, and pull it up as far as it will go. The switch should now be correctly positioned.
6 Reconnect the wiring connector, and check the operation of the stop-lights. Refit the glovebox.

18 Anti-lock braking system (ABS) –
general information

ABS is fitted to all models as standard, the system comprises a hydraulic regulator unit and the four roadwheel sensors. The regulator unit contains the electronic control unit (ECU), the hydraulic solenoid valves and the electrically-driven return pump. The purpose of the system is to prevent the wheel(s) locking during heavy braking. This is achieved by automatic release of the brake on the relevant wheel, followed by re-application of the brake.

The solenoid valves are controlled by the ECU, which itself receives signals from the four wheel sensors (front sensors are fitted to the hubs, and the rear sensors are fitted to the caliper mounting brackets), which monitor the speed of rotation of each wheel. By comparing these signals, the ECU can determine the speed at which the vehicle is travelling. It can then use this speed to determine when a wheel is decelerating at an abnormal rate, compared to the speed of the vehicle, and therefore predicts when a wheel is about to lock. During normal operation, the system functions in the same way as a non-ABS braking system.

If the ECU senses that a wheel is about to lock, it closes the relevant outlet solenoid valves in the hydraulic unit, which then isolates the relevant brake(s) on the wheel(s) which is/are about to lock from the master cylinder, effectively sealing-in the hydraulic pressure.

If the speed of rotation of the wheel continues to decrease at an abnormal rate, the ECU opens the inlet solenoid valves on the relevant brake(s), and operates the electrically-driven return pump which pumps the hydraulic fluid back into the master cylinder, releasing the brake. Once the speed of rotation of the wheel returns to an acceptable rate, the pump stops; the solenoid valves switch again, allowing the hydraulic master cylinder pressure to return to the caliper, which then re-applies the brake. This cycle can be carried out many times a second.

The action of the solenoid valves and return pump creates pulses in the hydraulic circuit. When the ABS system is functioning, these pulses can be felt through the brake pedal.

The operation of the ABS system is entirely dependent on electrical signals. To prevent the system responding to any inaccurate signals, a built-in safety circuit monitors all signals received by the ECU. If an inaccurate signal or low battery voltage is detected, the ABS system is automatically shut-down, and the warning light on the instrument panel is illuminated, to inform the driver that the ABS system is not operational. Normal braking should still be available, however.

The Peugeot 307 is also equipped with additional safety features built around the ABS system. These systems are EBFD (Electronic Brake Force Distribution), which automatically apportions braking effort between the front and rear wheels, EBA (Emergency Brake Assist) which guarantees full braking effort in the event of an emergency stop by monitoring

19.4 Lift the lever (arrowed) and disconnect the regulator wiring plug

the rate at which the brake pedal is depressed, and ESP (Electronic Stability Program) which monitors the vehicles cornering forces and steering wheel angle, then applies the braking force to the appropriate roadwheel to enhance the stability of the vehicle.

If a fault does develop in the any of these systems, the vehicle must be taken to a Peugeot dealer or suitably-equipped specialist for fault diagnosis and repair.

19 Anti-lock braking system (ABS) components –
removal and refitting

Regulator assembly

Caution: Disconnect the battery (see Chapter 5A) before disconnecting the regulator hydraulic unions, and do not reconnect the battery until after the hydraulic system has been bled. Also ensure that the unit is stored upright (in the same position as it is fitted to the vehicle) and is not tipped onto its side or upside down. Failure to do this could lead to air entering the regulator unit, requiring the unit to be bled using special Peugeot test equipment on refitting (see Section 2).
Note: *Before starting work, refer to the warning at the beginning of Section 2 concerning the dangers of hydraulic fluid.*

Removal

1 Disconnect the battery (see Chapter 5A).
2 The regulator assembly is located in the front left-hand corner of the engine compartment. Slacken the left-hand front roadwheel bolts, jack up the front of the vehicle and support it securely on axle stands (see *Jacking and vehicle support*).
3 Push in the centre pins a little, then prise out the complete plastic rivets and remove the left-hand front wheel arch liner.
4 Lift off the plastic cover and release the retaining clip and disconnect the main wiring connector from the regulator assembly **(see illustration)**. Where applicable, unscrew the retaining nut and disconnect the earth lead from the regulator.
5 Mark the locations of the hydraulic fluid pipes to ensure correct refitting, then unscrew the union nuts, and disconnect the pipes from the regulator assembly **(see illustration)**. Be prepared for fluid spillage, and plug the open ends of the pipes and the regulator to prevent dirt ingress and further fluid loss.
6 Slacken and remove the regulator mounting nuts and remove the regulator assembly from the engine compartment. If necessary, the mounting bracket can then be unbolted and removed from the vehicle. Renew the regulator mountings if they show signs of wear or damage.

Refitting

7 Manoeuvre the regulator into position and locate it in the mounting bracket. Refit

the mounting nuts and tighten them to the specified torque setting.

8 Reconnect the hydraulic pipes to the correct unions on the regulator and tighten the union nuts to the specified torque.

9 Reconnect the wiring connector to the regulator and connect the earth lead, tightening its retaining nut securely.

10 Bleed the complete hydraulic system as described in Section 2. Once the system is correctly bled, refit the wheels arch liner, roadwheel and reconnect the battery.

Electronic control unit (ECU)

11 The ECU is integral with the regulator assembly, and is not available separately.

Front wheel sensor

Removal

12 Ensure the ignition is turned off.

13 Apply the handbrake, slacken the appropriate front roadwheel bolts, then jack up the front of the vehicle and support securely on axle stands (see *Jacking and vehicle support*).

14 Trace the wiring back from the sensor, releasing it from all the relevant clips and ties whilst noting its correct routing, and disconnect the wiring connector.

15 Slacken and remove the retaining bolt and withdraw the sensor from the hub carrier (see illustration).

Refitting

16 Ensure that the mating faces of the sensor and the swivel hub are clean, and apply a little anti-seize grease to the swivel hub bore before refitting.

17 Make sure the sensor tip is clean and ease it into position in the swivel hub.

18 Clean the threads of the sensor bolt and apply a few drops of thread-locking compound (Peugeot recommend Loctite Frenetanch – available from your Peugeot dealer). Refit the retaining bolt and tighten it to the specified torque.

19 Work along the sensor wiring, making sure it is correctly routed, securing it in position with all the relevant clips and ties. Reconnect the wiring connector.

20 Lower the vehicle and tighten the wheel bolts to the specified torque.

Rear wheel sensor

Removal

21 Ensure the ignition is turned off.

22 Chock the front wheels, slacken the appropriate rear roadwheel bolts, then jack up the rear of the vehicle and support it on axle stands (see *Jacking and vehicle support*). Remove the appropriate roadwheel.

23 Trace the wiring back from the sensor, releasing it from all the relevant clips and ties whilst noting its correct routing, and disconnect the wiring connector.

24 Slacken and remove the retaining bolt and withdraw the sensor (see illustration).

19.5 Mark the location of the various brake pipes before disconnecting them from the regulator

19.24 Insert the tool (arrowed) through one of the roadwheel bolt holes to undo the speed sensor retaining bolt

Refitting

25 Ensure that the mating faces of the sensor and the hub are clean, and apply a little anti-seize grease to the hub bore before refitting.

26 Make sure the sensor tip is clean and ease it into position in the swivel hub.

27 Clean the threads of the sensor bolt and apply a few drops of thread-locking compound (Peugeot recommend Loctite Frenetanch – available from your Peugeot dealer). Refit the retaining bolt and tighten it to the specified torque.

28 Work along the sensor wiring, making sure it is correctly routed, securing it in position with all the relevant clips and ties. Reconnect the wiring connector, then lower the vehicle and (where necessary) tighten the wheel bolts to the specified torque.

20.3 Vacuum pump mounting bolts (arrowed) (1.4 litre models)

19.15 Undo the wheel speed sensor bolt (arrowed)

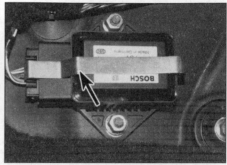

19.30 Release the clip (arrowed) and disconnect the Yaw rate sensor wiring plug

Yaw rate sensor

29 Remove the centre console as described in Chapter 11.

30 Release the clip then disconnect the wiring plug (see illustration).

31 Undo the two nuts and remove the sensor.

32 Refitting is a reversal of removal, ensuring the arrow on the top of the sensor points to the front of the vehicle.

---

20 Vacuum pump (diesel engine models) – removal and refitting

Removal

1 The pump is located at the left-hand end of the cylinder head. If necessary, to improve access to the vacuum pump, remove the air cleaner duct and air cleaner where applicable (see Chapter 4B), battery and battery box/tray (see Chapter 5A). **Note:** *On the 2.0 litre DOHC diesel engine, also disconnect the wiring from the coolant flow solenoid and remove the bracket and bolt directly over the vacuum pump.*

2 Depress the retaining clip button and disconnect the vacuum hose from the pump.

3 Slacken and remove the retaining bolts/nut (as applicable) securing the pump to the left-hand end of the cylinder head, then remove the pump (see illustration). Discard the sealing rings – new ones must be used on refitting.

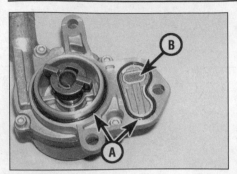

20.4a Vacuum pump O-ring seals location (A) and gauze filter (B) (2.0 litre models)

20.4b Ensure the pump drive dog engages with the slot in the end of the camshaft (arrowed)

Refitting

4 Fit new sealing ring(s) to the pump recess(es), then align the drive dog with the slot in the end of the camshaft, and refit the pump to the cylinder head, ensuring that the sealing ring(s) remain correctly seated **(see illustrations)**.

5 Refit the pump mounting bolts/nut (as applicable) and tighten them securely.

6 Reconnect the vacuum hose to the pump, ensuring its retaining clip engages correctly, and (where necessary) refit the air cleaner duct.

21 Vacuum pump (diesel engine models) – testing

1 The operation of the braking system vacuum pump can be checked using a vacuum gauge.

2 Disconnect the vacuum pipe from the pump, and connect the gauge to the pump union using a suitable length of hose.

3 Start the engine and allow it to idle, then measure the vacuum created by the pump. As a guide, after one minute, a minimum of approximately 500 mm Hg should be recorded. If the vacuum registered is significantly less than this, it is likely that the pump is faulty. However, seek the advice of a Peugeot dealer before condemning the pump.

4 Overhaul of the vacuum pump is not possible, since no components are available separately for it. If faulty, the complete pump assembly must be renewed.

Chapter 10
Suspension and steering

Contents

Degrees of difficulty

Easy, suitable for novice with little experience	Fairly easy, suitable for beginner with some experience	Fairly difficult, suitable for competent DIY mechanic	Difficult, suitable for experienced DIY mechanic	Very difficult, suitable for expert DIY or professional

Specifications

Wheel alignment and steering angles

Front wheel:

Toe setting	-0° 11' ± 4'
Camber.......................................	0° ± 30'
Castor (dependant on body style and tyre size).................	5° 00' ± 30' (nominal)
King pin inclination	11° 41' ± 30'

Rear wheel:

Toe setting:

Hatchback	0° 28' ± 4'
Estate	0° 30' ± 4'
Camber.......................................	1° 45' ± 30'

Roadwheels

Type	Pressed-steel or aluminium alloy (depending on model)
Tyre pressures	See end of *Weekly checks* on page 0•18

Torque wrench settings

	Nm	lbf ft
Front suspension		
Anti-roll bar:		
Connecting link nuts*....................................	36	27
Mounting clamp bolts....................................	104	77
Brake caliper mounting bracket bolts*..........................	105	77
Driveshaft retaining nut	325	240
Hub carrier to strut.......................................	90	66
Lower arm-to-subframe bolts	110	81
Lower balljoint:		
Balljoint to hub carrier	230	170
Retaining nut*.......................................	50	37
Subframe mounting bolts....................................	100	74
Suspension strut:		
Upper mounting plate nut...............................	69	51
Upper spring seat nut..................................	69	51

Torque wrench settings (continued)

	Nm	lbf ft
Rear suspension		
Caliper mounting bracket bolts*.	50	37
Hub nut*	210	155
Rear axle mounting bracket-to-body bolts	62	46
Rear axle-to-mounting bracket	76	56
Shock absorber:		
Lower mounting nut*	57	42
Upper mounting bolts.	62	46
Stub axle bolts	62	46
Steering		
Column-to-steering rack pinch-bolt.	22	16
Power steering pump mounting bolts:		
Lower mounting	17	13
Upper mounting	22	16
Steering column mounting bolts	22	16
Steering rack mounting nuts*.	80	59
Steering wheel bolt.	33	24
Track rod:		
Balljoint-to-hub carrier nut*	35	26
Balljoint locknut	40	30
Inner balljoint to steering rack	80	59
Roadwheels		
Wheel bolts.	90	66

*Do not re-use

1 General information

The independent front suspension is of the MacPherson strut type, incorporating coil springs and integral telescopic shock absorbers. The MacPherson struts are located by transverse lower suspension arms, which utilise rubber inner mounting bushes. The front hub carriers, which carry the wheel bearings, brake calipers and the hub/disc assemblies and lower balljoints, are bolted to the MacPherson struts, and connected to the lower arms via the balljoints. A front anti-roll bar is fitted to all models. The anti-roll bar is rubber-mounted onto the subframe, and is connected to the front suspension struts by link rods **(see illustration opposite)**.

The rear suspension has separate telescopic shock absorbers and coil springs fitted between the beam axle and the vehicle body. The rear beam axle has an integral anti-roll bar, and pivots around rubber bushes which are bolted to the front mounting brackets **(see illustration opposite)**.

The steering column has a universal joint fitted to its lower end, which is connected to the steering rack pinion by means of a clamp bolt.

The steering rack is mounted onto the front subframe, and is connected by two track rods, with balljoints at their outer ends, to the steering arms projecting rearwards from the hub carriers. The track rod ends are threaded, to facilitate adjustment. The hydraulic steering system is powered by an electrically operated pump, which is controlled by the engine management ECU.

A variable power steering system is fitted. The hydraulic pump alters the hydraulic pressure supplied to the steering rack to suit all conditions, ie, supplies high pressure when the vehicle is being driven slowly/parked and lower pressure when the vehicle is being driven at speed.

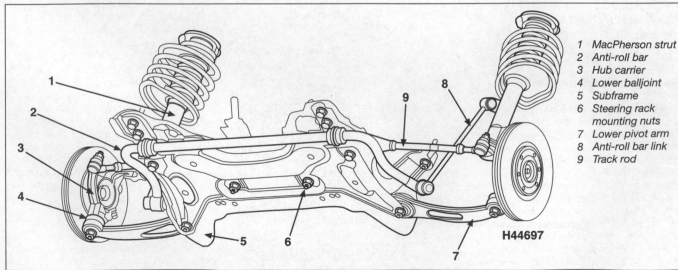

1 MacPherson strut
2 Anti-roll bar
3 Hub carrier
4 Lower balljoint
5 Subframe
6 Steering rack mounting nuts
7 Lower pivot arm
8 Anti-roll bar link
9 Track rod

H44697

1.1 Front suspension

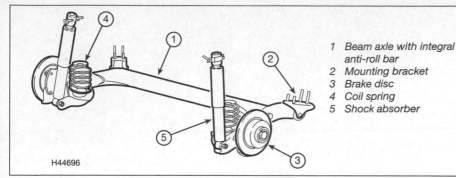

1 Beam axle with integral anti-roll bar
2 Mounting bracket
3 Brake disc
4 Coil spring
5 Shock absorber

1.2 Rear suspension

2.1 Prise out the R-clip (arrowed), remove the locking collar and slacken the driveshaft nut

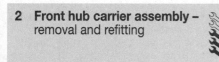

2 Front hub carrier assembly – removal and refitting

Note: *A new track rod balljoint nut, lower balljoint nut, brake caliper mounting bracket bolts, and strut-to-hub carrier nuts will be required on refitting.*

Removal

1 Remove the wheel trim/hub cap (as applicable) then withdraw the R-clip and remove the locking cap from the driveshaft retaining nut. Slacken the driveshaft nut with the vehicle resting on its wheels **(see illustration)**. Also slacken the wheel bolts.

2 Chock the rear wheels of the car, firmly apply the handbrake, then jack up the front of the car and support it on axle stands (see *Jacking and vehicle support*). Remove the appropriate front roadwheel.

3 Unbolt the wheel sensor and position it clear of the hub assembly (see Chapter 9). Note that there is no need to disconnect the wiring.

4 Slacken and remove the driveshaft retaining nut. If the nut was not slackened with the wheels on the ground (see paragraph 1), withdraw the R-clip and remove the locking cap. Refit at least two roadwheel bolts to the front hub, tightening them securely, then have an assistant firmly depress the brake pedal to prevent the front hub from rotating, whilst you slacken and remove the driveshaft retaining nut. Alternatively, a tool can be fabricated to hold the hub stationary (see Chapter 8, Section 2).

5 Slacken and remove the nut securing the steering rack track rod to the hub carrier then free the balljoint from the hub. If the balljoint is tight, use a universal balljoint separator to free it. Discard the nut, a new one should be used on refitting.

6 If the hub bearings are to be disturbed, remove the brake disc as described in Chapter 9. If not, unscrew the two bolts securing the brake caliper mounting bracket assembly to the hub carrier, and slide the caliper assembly off the disc. Using a piece of wire or string, tie the caliper to the front suspension coil spring, to avoid placing any strain on the hydraulic brake hose.

7 Slacken and remove the lower balljoint nut and free the balljoint shank from the lower arm, if necessary, using a universal balljoint separator **(see illustration)**. Use a Torx bit in the balljoint end to counterhold the nut. Discard the nut and lift off the protector plate (if loose).

8 Undo the nut and withdraw the hub carrier-to-suspension strut bolts, noting that the bolts are inserted from the front of the vehicle.

9 Free the hub carrier assembly from the end of the strut, then release it from the outer constant velocity joint splines, and remove it from the vehicle. Suspend the driveshaft by string from the suspension strut to prevent and damage to the constant velocity joints.

Refitting

10 Ensure that the driveshaft outer constant velocity joint and hub splines are clean, then slide the hub fully onto the driveshaft splines.

11 Slide the hub assembly fully into the suspension strut bracket. Inset the bolts from the front using new nuts, and tighten them to the specified torque.

12 Refit the protector plate (where removed) to the lower balljoint. Align the balljoint with the lower arm and fit the new retaining nut, tightening it to the specified torque.

13 Engage the track rod balljoint in the hub carrier, then fit the new retaining nut and tighten it to the specified torque.

14 Where necessary, refit the brake disc to the hub, referring to Chapter 9 for further information. Slide the caliper into position, making sure the pads pass either side of the disc, and tighten the new caliper bracket bolts to the specified torque setting.

2.7 Use a Torx bit (arrowed) in the balljoint end to counterhold the nut

15 Refit the wheel sensor as described in Chapter 9.

16 Lubricate the inner face and threads of the driveshaft retaining nut with clean engine oil, and refit it to the end of the driveshaft. Use the method employed on removal to prevent the hub from rotating (see paragraph 4), and tighten the driveshaft retaining nut to the specified torque. Check that the hub rotates freely then engage the locking cap with the driveshaft nut, so that one of its cut-outs is aligned with the driveshaft hole, and secure the cap in position with the R-clip. Alternatively, lightly tighten the nut at this stage and tighten it to the specified torque once the vehicle is resting on its wheels again.

17 Refit the roadwheel, then lower the vehicle to the ground and tighten the roadwheel bolts to the specified torque. If not already having done so, tighten the driveshaft retaining nut to the specified torque then refit the locking cap, aligning its cut-outs with the driveshaft hole, and secure it in position with the R-clip.

3 Front hub bearings – renewal

Note: *The bearing is a sealed, pre-adjusted and prelubricated, double-row roller type, and is intended to last the car's entire service life without maintenance or attention. Never overtighten the driveshaft nut beyond the specified torque wrench setting in an attempt to 'adjust' the bearing.*

Note: *A press will be required to dismantle and rebuild the assembly; if such a tool is not available, a large bench vice and spacers (such as large sockets) will serve as an adequate substitute. The bearing's inner races are an interference fit on the hub; if the inner race remains on the hub when it is pressed out of the hub carrier, a knife-edged bearing puller will be required to remove it. A new bearing retaining circlip must be used on refitting.*

1 Remove the hub carrier assembly as described in Section 2.

2 Support the hub carrier securely on blocks or in a vice. Using a tubular spacer which bears only on the inner end of the hub flange, press the hub flange out of the bearing **(see**

3.2 Press the hub flange from the bearing

3.3 Extract the circlip from the inner side of the hub carrier

3.7 Take great care not to damage the seal in the bearing (arrowed) – it contains the encoder for the wheel speed sensor

illustration). If the bearing's outboard inner race remains on the hub, remove it using a bearing puller (see note above).

3 Extract the bearing retaining circlip from the inner end of the hub carrier assembly **(see illustration)**.

4 Where necessary, refit the inner race back in position over the ball cage, and securely support the inner face of the hub carrier. Using a tubular spacer which bears only on the inner race, press the complete bearing assembly out of the hub carrier.

5 Thoroughly clean the hub and hub carrier, removing all traces of dirt and grease, and polish away any burrs or raised edges which might hinder reassembly. Check both for cracks or any other signs of wear or damage, and renew them if necessary. Renew the circlip, regardless of its apparent condition.

6 On reassembly, apply a light film of oil (Peugeot recommend Molykote 321R – available from your Peugeot dealer) to the bearing outer race and hub flange shaft, to aid installation of the bearing.

7 Securely support the hub carrier, and locate the bearing in the hub. Press the bearing fully into position, ensuring that it enters the hub squarely, using a tubular spacer which bears only on the bearing outer race. Note that the bearing is equipped with a magnetic encoder on its inboard face. When fitting the bearing ensure this face is inboard adjacent to the ABS wheel speed sensor **(see illustration)**. Take care not to damage this encoder, or place it adjacent to a magnetic source. Ensure the encoder face is clean.

8 Once the bearing is correctly seated, secure the bearing in position with the new

circlip, ensuring that it is correctly located in the groove in the hub carrier. **Note:** *Align the gap between the ends of the circlip with the gap for the ABS wheel speed sensor.*

9 Securely support the outer face of the hub flange, and locate the hub carrier bearing inner race over the end of the hub flange. Press the bearing onto the hub, using a tubular spacer which bears only on the inner race of the hub bearing, until it seats against the hub shoulder. Check that the hub flange rotates freely, and wipe off any excess oil or grease.

10 Refit the hub carrier assembly as described in Section 2.

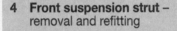

4 Front suspension strut –
removal and refitting

Note: *Always renew any self-locking nuts when working on the suspension/steering components.*

Removal

1 Chock the rear wheels, apply the handbrake, slacken the appropriate front roadwheel bolts, then jack up the front of the car and support on axle stands (see *Jacking and vehicle support*). Remove the appropriate roadwheel.

2 Unscrew the nut securing the anti-roll bar connecting link to the strut, and position the link clear of the strut; if necessary, retain the balljoint shank with a Torx bit to prevent rotation whilst the nut is slackened **(see illustration)**. Discard the nut, a new one should be used on refitting.

3 Undo the bolts and pull the hub carrier from the lower end of the strut, noting that the bolts fit from the front of the strut **(see illustration)**. To prevent the hub carrier assembly dropping whilst the strut is removed support the lower arm. Take care not to strain the brake hose and the wiring attached to the brake caliper and the hub carrier.

4 Remove both wiper arms as described in Chapter 12.

5 Remove the plastic scuttle trim from in front of the windscreen. The trim is secured by a plastic expanding rivet at each end. Push in the centre pins a little, then prise the complete rivets from place. Lift up the ends of the trim to release the trim, then pull it down to release it from the lower edge of the windscreen,

6 Working in the scuttle aperture, slacken and remove the strut upper mounting nut, counterholding the strut rod with an Allen key located in the end of the rod. Withdraw the strut from under the wheel arch **(see illustration)**. *Caution: As soon as the upper mounting nut is removed, the strut will be unsupported.*

Refitting

7 Manoeuvre the strut assembly into position, ensuring that the end of the strut rod is correctly located in the corresponding hole in the inner wing. Fit the upper mounting nut and tighten it to the specified torque.

8 Engage the lower end of the strut with the hub carrier, insert the bolts from the front and tighten them to the specified torque.

9 Refit the scuttle plastic trim, and the wiper arms.

10 Reconnect the anti-roll bar connecting link

4.2 Use a Torx bit to prevent rotation whilst the anti-roll bar link nut is undone

4.3 Note that the strut-to-hub carrier bolts are inserted from the front of the vehicle

4.6 Use an Allen key in the end of the rod to counterhold whilst slackening the strut nut

5.1 Fit the coil compressors to the springs

5.2 Slacken the top nut whilst retaining the rod with an Allen key

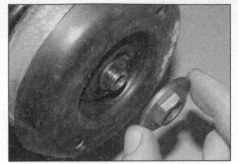

5.3a Remove the nut . . .

to the strut. Do not omit the wiring support bracket. Tighten the nut to the specified torque.
11 Refit the roadwheel, then lower the vehicle to the ground and tighten the road-wheel bolts to the specified torque.

5 Front suspension strut – overhaul

⚠ *Warning: Before attempting to dismantle the front suspension strut, a suitable tool to hold the coil spring in compression must be obtained. Adjustable coil spring compressors are readily-available, and are recommended for this operation. Any attempt to dismantle the strut without such a tool is likely to result in damage or personal injury.*
Note: *Always renew any self-locking nuts*

when working on the suspension/steering components.
1 With the strut removed from the car (as described in Section 4), clean away all external dirt, then mount it upright in a vice. Fit the spring compressor and compress the coil spring until tension is relieved from the spring seats **(see illustration)**.
2 Slacken and remove the upper spring seat nut whilst retaining the shock absorber piston with a suitable Allen key **(see illustration)**.
3 Remove the nut then lift off the thrust bearing followed by the spring seat **(see illustrations)**.
4 Lift off the coil spring and remove the cap, dust gaiter and rubber bump stop from the shock absorber piston **(see illustrations)**.
5 Examine the shock absorber for signs of fluid leakage. Check the piston for signs of pitting along its entire length, and check the shock body for signs of damage. While holding it in an upright position, test the operation of the

shock absorber by moving the piston through a full stroke, and then through short strokes of 50 to 100 mm. In both cases, the resistance felt should be smooth and continuous. If the resistance is jerky, or uneven, or if there is any visible sign of wear or damage to the shock absorber, renewal is necessary.
6 Inspect all other components for signs of damage or deterioration, and renew any that are suspect.
7 Slide the rubber bump stop onto the piston. Fit the dust gaiter and cap, making sure the lower end of gaiter is correctly positioned over the shock absorber end.
8 Refit the coil spring, making sure its lower end is correctly seated against the spring seat stop. Fit the upper spring seat, aligning its stop with the spring end, then the thrust bearing **(see illustration)**.
9 Fit the new nut. Retain the shock absorber piston and tighten the upper spring seat nut to the specified torque.

5.3b . . . the thrust bearing . . .

5.3c . . . the spring seat . . .

5.4a . . . followed by the cap . . .

5.4b . . . the dust gaiter . . .

5.4c . . . and the bump stop

5.8 Ensure the lower end of the spring locates correctly against the spring seat stop

6 Front suspension lower arm – removal, overhaul and refitting

Note: *Always renew any self-locking nuts when working on the suspension/steering components.*

Removal

1 Remove the relevant driveshaft as described in Chapter 8.
2 Slacken and remove the nut, then free the lower balljoint shank from the lower arm, if necessary, using a universal balljoint separator. Discard the nut and lift off the protector plate (if loose). Use a Torx bit in the end of the balljoint shank to counterhold the nut.
3 Slacken and remove the lower arm front pivot bolt and nut **(see illustration)**.
4 Slacken and remove the rear pivot bolt and nut **(see illustration)**.
5 Manoeuvre the lower arm assembly out from underneath the vehicle.

Overhaul

6 Thoroughly clean the lower arm and the area around the arm mountings, removing all traces of dirt and underseal if necessary, then check carefully for cracks, distortion or any other signs of wear or damage, paying particular attention to the pivot bushes, and renew components as necessary.
7 Renewal of the front pivot bush and rear mounting bracket will required the use of a hydraulic press, a bearing puller and several spacers and should therefore be entrusted to a Peugeot dealer or specialist with access to the necessary equipment.

7.2 Release the clips and remove the balljoint protector plate

7.3 Use a chisel or a punch to unstake the balljoint

6.3 Undo the lower arm front pivot bolt . . .

Refitting

8 Manoeuvre the lower arm assembly into position, and refit the front pivot bolt and nut, tightening it finger-tight only.
9 Refit the rear pivot bolt and nut, then tighten them to the specified torque.
10 Refit the protector plate (where removed) to the lower balljoint, then locate the balljoint shank in the lower arm. Fit the new retaining nut and tighten it to the specified torque.
11 Refit the driveshaft (see Chapter 8).
12 Refit the roadwheel, then lower the vehicle and tighten the roadwheel bolts to the specified torque. Rock the car to settle the disturbed components in position, then tighten the lower arm front pivot bolt to the specified torque.
13 Check and, if necessary, adjust the front wheel alignment as described in Section 26.

7 Front suspension lower balljoint – removal and refitting

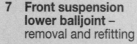

Removal

1 Remove the hub carrier assembly as described in Section 2.
2 Remove the protector plate from the balljoint and mount the assembly securely in a vice **(see illustration)**.
3 Using a hammer and pointed-nose chisel, tap up the staking securing the balljoint in position **(see illustration)**.
4 Fit a deep socket to the balljoint, then unscrew it and remove it from the hub carrier.

8.2 Use a Torx bit to counterhold the lower anti-roll bar link nut

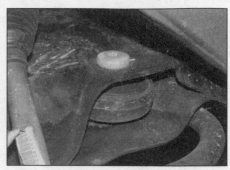

6.4 . . . and rear pivot bolt

Refitting

5 Screw the balljoint into the hub carrier assembly. Fit the special tool, taking care not to damage the balljoint gaiter, and tighten the balljoint to the specified torque. Secure the balljoint in position by firmly staking it into one of the hub carrier notches using a hammer and punch.
6 Fit the new protector plate to the balljoint and secure it in position by staking it into the one of the balljoint notches.
7 Refit the hub carrier (see Section 2).

8 Front suspension anti-roll bar – removal and refitting

Note: *Always renew any self-locking nuts when working on the suspension/steering components.*

Removal

1 Chock the rear wheels, firmly apply the handbrake, slacken the front roadwheel bolts, then jack up the front of the vehicle and support on axle stands (see *Jacking and vehicle support*). Remove both front roadwheels.
2 Slacken and remove the nuts securing the left- and right-hand connecting links to the anti-roll bar, and position the links clear of the bar; if necessary, retain the balljoint shank with a Torx bit to prevent rotation whilst the nut is slackened **(see illustration)**. Discard the nuts, new ones should be used on refitting.
3 Slacken the two anti-roll bar mounting clamp retaining bolts and nuts, and remove both clamps from the top of the subframe **(see illustration)**.

8.3 Undo the anti-roll bar clamp bolts (right-hand side arrowed)

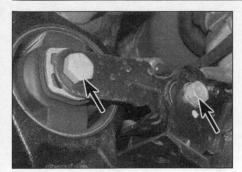

10.3 Undo the bolts (arrowed) securing the rear engine/transmission link rod

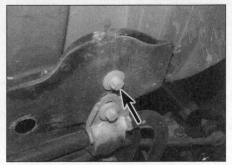

10.9a Undo the front subframe rear mounting bolts (arrowed) . . .

10.9b . . . and front mounting bolts (arrowed)

4 Manoeuvre the anti-roll bar out from underneath the vehicle, and remove the mounting bushes from the bar.
5 Carefully examine the anti-roll bar components for signs of wear, damage or deterioration, paying particular attention to the mounting bushes. Renew worn components as necessary.

Refitting

6 Fit the rubber mounting bushes to the anti-roll bar. Position each bush so that its flat surface is at the bottom and its internal flats are correctly engaged with the flats on the anti-roll bar; the bush split should be facing towards the rear.
7 Offer up the anti-roll bar, and manoeuvre it into position on the subframe. Refit the mounting clamps, ensuring that their ends are correctly located in the hooks on the subframe, and refit the retaining bolts and nuts. Engage the connecting links with the ends of the bar then tighten the mounting clamp retaining bolts to the specified torque.
8 Fit the new retaining nuts to the connecting links and tighten them to the specified torque setting.
9 Refit the roadwheels then lower the vehicle to the ground and tighten the wheel bolts to the specified torque.

9 Front suspension anti-roll bar connecting link – removal and refitting

Note: New connecting link nuts will be required on refitting.

Removal

1 Chock the rear wheels, firmly apply the handbrake, slacken the relevant roadwheel bolts, then jack up the front of the vehicle and support on axle stands (see Jacking and vehicle support). Remove the relevant roadwheel.
2 Slacken and remove the nuts securing the connecting link to the anti-roll bar and suspension strut and remove the link from the vehicle; if necessary, retain the balljoint shanks with a Torx bit to prevent rotation whilst each nut is slackened (see illustration 4.2).

3 Inspect the link for signs of wear or damage and renew if necessary.

Refitting

4 Refitting is the reverse of removal, using new nuts and tightening them to the specified torque setting.

10 Front suspension subframe – removal and refitting

Note: Always renew any self-locking nuts when working on the suspension/steering components.

Removal

1 Chock the rear wheels, firmly apply the handbrake, slacken the front roadwheel bolts, and then jack up the front of the vehicle and support it on axle stands (see Jacking and vehicle support). Remove both front roadwheels.
2 Remove the anti-roll bar as described in Section 8.
3 Slacken and remove the engine/transmission rear lower mounting bolt and nut, then undo the nut and bolt securing the link rod to the subframe and remove the link (see illustration).
4 Slacken and remove the left-hand lower balljoint nut and free the balljoint shank from the lower arm, if necessary, using a universal balljoint separator. Discard the nut. Repeat the procedure on the right-hand side.
5 Slacken and remove the steering rack mounting nuts and washers. Discard the nuts, new ones must be fitted.
6 Unclip the heat shield from the steering rack, then undo the bolt securing the power steering pipe bracket to the subframe.
7 Make a final check that all control cables/hoses that are attached to the subframe have been released and positioned clear so that they will not hinder the removal procedure.
8 Place a jack and a suitable block of wood under the subframe to support the subframe as it is lowered.
9 Slacken and remove the subframe mounting bolts then carefully lower the subframe assembly out of position and remove it from underneath the vehicle, taking great care to ensure that the subframe assembly does not

catch the power steering pipes as it is lowered out of position. Recover the washers between the steering rack and the subframe (see illustrations).

Refitting

10 Refitting is a reversal of the removal procedure, noting the following points:
 a) Use new connecting link and lower balljoint nuts, and steering rack nuts.
 b) Tighten all nuts and bolts to the specified torque settings (where given).
 c) On completion check and, if necessary, adjust the front wheel alignment as described in Section 26.

11 Rear hub assembly – removal and refitting

Note: Do not remove the hub assembly unless it is absolutely necessary. A puller will be required to draw the hub assembly off the stub axle, and the hub bearing will almost certainly be damaged by the removal procedure, necessitating renewal of the hub assembly. A new hub nut and centre cap must be used on refitting.

Removal

1 Remove the rear brake disc as described in Chapter 9.
2 Prise out the cap from the centre of the hub and discard; a new cap should be used on refitting (see illustration).
3 Using a hammer and punch, tap up the

11.2 Prise the cap from the hub

11.3 Unstake the retaining nut

11.5 Use a puller to remove the hub

11.10a Stake the new nut . . .

staking securing the hub retaining nut to the groove in the stub axle **(see illustration)**.

4 Using a socket and long bar, unscrew the rear hub nut and discard it; a new hub nut should be used on refitting.

5 Using a puller, draw the hub assembly off the stub axle, along with the outer bearing race **(see illustration)**. If necessary, with the hub removed, use the puller to draw the inner bearing race off the stub axle.

6 Check the hub bearing for signs of roughness. It is recommended that the hub bearing should be renewed as a matter of course, as it is likely to have been damaged during removal. This means that the complete hub assembly must be renewed, since it is not possible to obtain the bearing separately.

7 With the hub removed, examine the stub axle shaft for signs of wear or damage, and if necessary renew it (see Section 15).

Refitting

8 Ensure that the bearing is packed with grease and lubricate the stub axle shaft with clean engine oil.

9 Fit the new bearing assembly, tapping it fully onto the stub axle using a hammer and a tubular drift which bears only on the flat inside edge of the bearing inner race.

10 Fit the new hub nut and tighten it to the specified torque. Stake the nut firmly into the groove on the stub axle to secure it in position, then tap the new hub cap into place in the centre of the hub **(see illustrations)**.

11 Refit the rear brake disc as described in Chapter 9.

12 Rear hub bearings – renewal

The hub bearing is an integral part of the hub assembly and is not available separately. If the bearing is worn, renew the complete hub assembly as described in Section 11.

13 Rear suspension shock absorber – removal, testing and refitting

Note: *Always renew any self-locking nuts when working on the suspension/steering components.*

Removal

1 Chock the front wheels, slacken the relevant rear roadwheel bolts, then jack up the rear of the vehicle and support it on axle stands (see *Jacking and vehicle support*). Remove the relevant rear roadwheel.

2 Using a trolley jack positioned under the spring cup, raise the lower arm until the rear suspension coil spring is slightly compressed.

3 Working in the wheel arch, undo the two shock absorber upper mounting bolts **(see illustration)**.

4 Slacken and remove the lower mounting bolt and nut then manoeuvre the shock absorber out of position **(see illustration)**.

Testing

5 Examine the shock absorber for signs of fluid leakage or damage. Test the operation

of the shock absorber, while holding it in an upright position, by moving the piston through a full stroke and then through short strokes of 50 to 100 mm. In both cases, the resistance felt should be smooth and continuous. If the resistance is jerky, or uneven, or if there is any visible sign of wear or damage, renewal is necessary. Also check the rubber mountings for damage and deterioration. Renew worn components as necessary. Inspect the shank of the mounting bolt for signs of wear or damage, and renew as necessary. The self-locking nuts should be renewed as a matter of course.

Refitting

6 Prior to refitting the shock absorber, mount it upright in the vice, and operate it fully through several strokes in order to prime it. Apply a smear of multi-purpose grease to the lower mounting bolt and contact face of the new nut (Peugeot recommend Molykote G Rapide Plus – available from your Peugeot dealer).

7 Fully extend the piston and manoeuvre the assembly into position. Refit the upper mounting bolts, and tighten them to the specified torque.

8 Align the shock absorber lower mounting with the lower arm and refit the mounting bolt. Fit the new nut, tightening it lightly only at this stage.

9 Refit the rear roadwheel then lower the vehicle to the ground and tighten the wheel bolts to the specified torque. Rock the vehicle to settle the shock absorber in position then tighten the shock absorber lower mounting to the specified torque setting.

11.10b . . . then fit a new hub cap using a large socket

13.3 Undo the two shock absorber upper mounting bolts

13.4 Remove the lower shock absorber mounting bolt (arrowed)

14.9 Ensure the ends of the coil springs align correctly with the seats (arrowed)

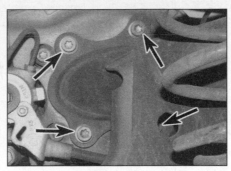

15.5 Undo the four bolts (arrowed) securing the stub axle to the lower arm

16.3 Undo the nut where the metal brake pipe joins the flexible pipe

14 Rear suspension coil spring – removal and refitting

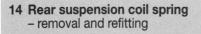

Note: *Always renew any self-locking nuts when working on the suspension/steering components.*

Removal

1 Chock the front wheels, slacken the rear roadwheel bolts, then jack up the rear of the vehicle and support it on axle stands (see *Jacking and vehicle support*). Remove the rear roadwheels.

2 Position a trolley jack underneath one of the lower arms' spring cup and raise the arm until the rear suspension coil spring on that side is slightly compressed.

3 Unscrew the shock absorber lower mounting bolt/nut and withdraw the bolt. Discard the nut; a new should be used on refitting.

4 Slowly lower the jack as far as the lower arm will go, then position the jack under the lower arm spring cup on the other side, and raise the arm until the coil spring on that side is slightly compressed.

5 Slacken and remove the shock absorber lower mounting bolt. Again, discard the nut a new one must be fitted.

6 Lower the jack until all tension in the springs is released, then remove the springs.

7 Inspect the coil spring and its seats for signs of wear or damage and renew if necessary.

Refitting

8 Fit the lower spring seat in position on the lower arm, and seat the upper seat on top of the coil spring. Lubricate the shanks of the shock absorber and lower arm bolts and the contact faces of the new nuts with multi-purpose grease (Peugeot recommend Molykote G Rapide Plus – available from your Peugeot dealer).

9 Manoeuvre the springs into position and carefully raise one lower arm with the jack, ensuring that the coil spring ends are correctly aligned with both seats, and point to the front of the vehicle **(see illustration)**.

10 Align the shock absorber with the lower arm and refit its mounting bolt. Fit the new

nut to the bolt, tightening it lightly only at this stage.

11 Remove the jack from underneath the lower arm, and position it under the lower arm spring cup on the remaining side.

12 Raise the jack and align the lower mounting of the shock absorber with the arm. Insert the bolt, and fit a new nut, tightening it lightly only at this stage.

13 Refit the rear roadwheel then lower the vehicle to the ground and tighten the wheel bolts to the specified torque. Rock the vehicle to settle the lower arm in position then tighten the shock absorber lower mounting bolts/nuts to their specified torque settings.

15 Rear suspension stub axle – removal, overhaul and refitting

Note: *Always renew any self-locking nuts when working on the suspension/steering components.*

Removal

1 Chock the front wheels, slacken the relevant rear roadwheel bolts, then jack up the rear of the vehicle and support it on axle stands (see *Jacking and vehicle support*). Remove the relevant roadwheel.

2 Unbolt the wheel sensor and position it clear of the stub axle (see Chapter 9). Note that there is no need to disconnect the wiring.

3 Remove the hub assembly as described in Section 11. **Note:** *If the stub axle is to be renewed, there is no need to remove the hub assembly, as the act of removal destroys the bearing necessitating its renewal.*

4 Undo the two rear brake caliper mounting bracket retaining bolts, and slide the caliper and bracket assembly from the disc. There is no need to disconnect the handbrake cable or caliper hose.

5 Undo the four bolts securing the stub axle to the lower arm and remove it, complete with disc backplate **(see illustration)**.

6 Inspect the stub axle for signs of wear or damage. If the stub axle shaft is worn or damaged then the assembly must be renewed.

Refitting

7 Obtain all the new nuts required and

lubricate the shanks of the pivot bolts and contact faces of the new nuts with multi-purpose grease (Peugeot recommend Molykote G Rapide Plus – available from your Peugeot dealer).

8 Offer up the stub axle and backplate, insert the bolts and tighten them to the specified torque.

9 Fit the new hub assembly as described in Section 11.

10 Refit the disc to the hub, and securely tighten the two disc retaining screws.

11 Slide the brake caliper and bracket assembly over the edge of the disc, and tighten the mounting bracket bolts to the specified torque.

12 Refit the wheel sensor to the stub axle (see Chapter 9).

13 Refit the rear roadwheel then lower the vehicle to the ground and tighten the wheel bolts to the specified torque.

16 Rear beam axle – removal, overhaul and refitting

Note: *Always renew any self-locking nuts when working on the suspension/steering components.*

Removal

1 Remove the coil springs as described in Section 14.

2 Trace the ABS wheel speed sensor wiring back to its connector, and unplug it. Free the sensor harness from any retaining clips on the axle.

3 Clamp the flexible brake hose, and undo the hose union where the flexible hose connects to the rigid hose **(see illustration)**. Plug the end of the hose/pipe to prevent dirt ingress. Repeat this procedure on the remaining side.

4 Release the handbrake cables from the retaining clips along the axle, then release the ends of the cables from the caliper levers and support brackets (see Chapter 9). Repeat the procedure on the remaining side.

5 Make alignment marks between the axle mounting brackets and the vehicle body to aid refitment. Undo the 4 bolts each side securing the mounting brackets to the vehicle body, and

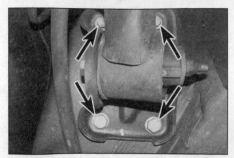

16.5 Undo the four bolts each side (arrowed) securing the axle brackets to the vehicle body

17.1 Lift the locking tab to disconnect the steering wheel lower wiring connector

17.3 Undo the steering wheel retaining bolt

lower the axle to the floor **(see illustration)**. If the axle is to be renewed, remove the brake caliper and disc (Chapter 9), and the stub axle (Section 15).

Overhaul

6 Thoroughly clean the axle and the area around the axle mountings, removing all traces of dirt and underseal if necessary, then check carefully for cracks, distortion or any other signs of wear or damage, paying particular attention to the pivot bushes.
7 Renewal of the pivot bushes will require the use of a hydraulic press and several spacers, and should therefore be entrusted to a Peugeot dealer or specialist with access to the necessary equipment.

Refitting

8 Lubricate the shanks of the axle mounting bracket bolts with multi-purpose grease (Peugeot recommend Molykote G Rapide Plus – available from your Peugeot dealer).
9 Offer up the axle and mounting brackets, aligning the previously made marks, and insert the retaining bolts. Tighten them to the specified torque.
10 Refit the handbrake cables to their retaining clips on the axle, and reconnect the cable ends to the caliper levers (see Chapter 9).
11 Reconnect the rear brake flexible hoses, tightening the hose/pipe unions securely. Remove the hose clamps.
12 Refit the coil spring with reference to Section 14. On completion bleed the brakes as described in Chapter 9.

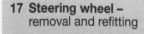

17 Steering wheel –
removing and refitting

Note: *All models are equipped with a driver's airbag.*

 Warning: Refer to the precautions given in Chapter 12 before proceeding.

Removal

1 Remove the airbag unit as described in Chapter 12. Disconnect the lower wiring connector **(see illustration)**.

2 Position the front wheels in the straight-ahead position and engage the steering lock.
3 Slacken and remove the steering wheel retaining bolt then mark the steering wheel and steering column shaft in relation to each other **(see illustration)**.
4 Lift the steering wheel off the column splines, feeding the airbag wires through the aperture in the steering wheel as it is withdrawn.

 If the wheel is tight, tap it up near the centre, using the palm of your hand, or twist it from side-to-side, whilst carefully pulling it upwards to release it from the shaft splines.

Refitting

5 Prior to refitting the steering wheel, ensure that the front wheels are still in the straight-ahead position.
6 Refitting is a reversal of removal, noting the following points:
a) *Prior to refitting, ensure that the indicator switch stem is in its central position. Failure to do this could lead to the steering wheel lug breaking the switch tab as the steering wheel is refitted.*
b) *On refitting, align the marks made on removal, taking great care not to damage the airbag unit wiring, then tighten the retaining bolt to the specified torque.*
c) *On completion, refit the airbag unit as described in Chapter 12.*

18 Steering column –
removal, inspection and refitting

Note: *As all models are equipped with a driver's airbag, refer to the precautions given in Chapter 12 before proceeding.*
Note: *A new pinch-bolt nut will be needed on refitting.*

Removal

1 Remove the steering wheel as described in Section 17.
2 Move the driver's seat as far back as possible.
3 Working in the driver's footwell, make alignment marks between the universal joint and the steering rack pinion, release the retaining clip, then undo and remove the pinch-bolt/nut from the joint at the base of the column **(see illustration)**.
4 Remove the combination switches from the top of the steering column as described in Chapter 12.
5 Release the retaining clips and remove the lower facia panel above the driver's pedals.
6 Trace the wiring back from the ignition switch and disconnect it at the wiring connectors.
7 Where applicable, undo the retaining bolt and free the wiring retaining bracket from the column. Note its fitted position, then release the wiring from its retaining clips and position it clear so that it does not hinder column removal.
8 Slacken and remove the four mounting bolts from the top of the column **(see illustration)**.

18.3 Release the retaining clip (arrowed) then remove the pinch-bolt/nut

18.8 Undo the steering column mounting bolts (arrowed)

19.3 Undo the lower shroud retaining screws (arrowed)

19.6 Lift the transponder ring clips (upper arrowed) and slide it from the ignition switch

19.9 Depress the peg (arrowed) and slide the switch from the steering column

Slide the column assembly upwards, and free from the steering rack pinion, and remove it from the vehicle.

Inspection

9 Before refitting the steering column, examine the column and mountings for signs of damage and deformation, and renew as necessary. Check the steering shaft for signs of free play in the column bushes, and check the universal joints for signs of damage or roughness in the joint bearings. If any damage or wear is found on the steering column universal joint or shaft bushes, the column must be renewed as an assembly.

Refitting

10 Align the marks made prior to removal and engage the column universal joint with the steering rack pinion.

11 Slide the column assembly into position making sure its mounting bracket is correctly engaged with the facia bracket. Refit the column mounting bolts and tighten them to the specified torque setting.

12 Refit the universal joint pinch-bolt and nut, tighten them to the specified torque setting, then refit the retaining clip.

13 The remainder of refitting is a reversal of the removal procedure, noting the following.

a) Ensure that all wiring is correctly routed and retained by all the necessary clips and ties.

b) Refit the steering wheel as described in Section 17.

19 Ignition switch/lock cylinder/ steering lock – removal and refitting

Ignition switch/steering lock

Removal

1 Disconnect the battery (see Chapter 5A).

2 Unclip and remove the facia panel below the steering column (see Chapter 11, Section 27).

3 Undo the retaining screws securing the steering column lower shroud in position, then lift the rear edge of the upper shroud, and release it from the two retaining clips at its front edge **(see illustration)**.

4 Release the ignition switch wiring harness from the retaining clip on the underside of the column.

5 Use a centre punch to mark the centre of the lock housing retaining screw then, using a drill and an extractor, remove the screw. Obviously, a new screw will be required.

6 Lift the two retaining clips and carefully pull the transponder immobiliser unit, to release it from the ignition switch housing **(see illustration)**. The transponder can then be put to one side, with its wiring still connected. Take care not to damage the transponder assembly.

7 Note its routing, then trace the wiring back from the ignition switch, and disconnect its wiring connectors from the main wiring harness.

8 Insert the key into the steering lock and turn it to the first position.

9 Use a small screwdriver to depress the locating peg and slide the assembly from the steering column housing **(see illustration)**.

10 Manoeuvre the ignition switch complete with the wiring block connectors out from the column.

Refitting

11 Refitting is a reversal of removal, noting the following points:

a) Ensure all wiring is correctly routed, and securely clipped back into its original positions.

b) Refit the steering lock housing with a new screw, tightening it until it shears.

Lock cylinder

12 At the time of writing, the lock cylinder

20.4 Steering rack mounting nuts (arrowed)

was not available separately from the ignition switch assembly.

20 Steering rack assembly – removal, overhaul and refitting

Note: Always renew any self-locking nuts when working on the suspension/steering components.

Removal

1 Firmly apply the handbrake, slacken the front roadwheel bolts, then jack up the front of the vehicle and support it on axle stands (see Jacking and vehicle support). Remove both front roadwheels.

2 Slacken and remove the nuts securing the steering rack track rod balljoints to the hub carriers. Release the balljoint tapered shanks using a universal balljoint separator. Discard the nuts, new ones will be needed on refitting.

3 Remove the plastic cover from the front right-hand corner of the engine compartment, and unscrew the power steering fluid reservoir cap.

4 Working underneath the vehicle, undo the remove the rack mounting nuts and studs. Recover the washers fitted between the rack and the subframe, noting their fitted positions **(see illustration)**. Discard the rack mounting studs and nuts, new ones must be fitted.

5 Unclip the heat shield from the steering rack, then undo the bolt securing the steering rack pipes bracket to the front of the subframe **(see illustration)**.

20.5 Steering rack pipes bracket (arrowed)

20.8 Undo the fluid pipes unions

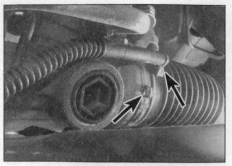

21.3 Rack gaiter breather pipe and inner clip (arrowed)

21.4 Rack gaiter outer retaining clip (arrowed)

6 Position a jack under the centre of the front subframe. Remove the four subframe mounting bolts **(see illustrations 10.9a and 10.9b)**. Note: *On diesel models, detach the exhaust rubber mountings from the subframe.*
7 Undo the bolt and detach the rear engine mounting link from the bracket on the rear of the cylinder block. Lower the subframe approximately 60 mm **(see illustration 10.3)**.
8 Clean the area around the rack pinion housing, then undo the nuts securing the fluid pipes to the rack pinion housing, release the pipes from the retaining clamp, and drain the fluid into a container **(see illustration)**. Turn the steering wheel from lock-to-lock to assist the draining process, remembering to recentre the steering wheel afterwards. Discard the pipes' O-ring seals, new ones must be fitted. Plug the ends of the pipes to prevent dirt ingress.
9 Working in the driver's footwell, using paint or a suitable marker pen, make alignment marks between the steering column universal joint and the steering rack pinion, then slacken and remove the universal joint pinch-bolt, and release the retaining clip **(see illustration 18.3)**.
10 Still in the driver's footwell, undo the two retaining nuts and remove the seal around the steering rack pinion.
11 Free the steering rack pinion from the column universal joint and manoeuvre it out through the driver's side wheel arch aperture.

Overhaul

12 Examine the steering rack assembly for signs of wear or damage, and check that the rack moves freely throughout the full length of its travel, with no signs of roughness or excessive free play between the steering rack pinion and rack. Inspect all the steering rack fluid unions for signs of leakage, and check that all union nuts are securely tightened.
13 It is possible to overhaul the steering rack assembly housing components, but this task should be entrusted to a Peugeot dealer or specialist. The only components which can be renewed easily by the home mechanic are the steering rack gaiters, the track rod balljoints and the track rods which are covered elsewhere in this Chapter.

Refitting

14 Manoeuvre the steering rack into position

and engage it with the column universal joint, aligning the marks made prior to removal.
15 Slide the washers into position between the subframe and steering rack. Insert the new mounting studs, and tighten the nuts to the specified torque.
16 The remainder of refitting is a reversal of removal, noting the following points:
a) *Top-up the fluid reservoir and bleed the hydraulic system as described in Section 22.*
b) *On completion check and, if necessary adjust the front wheel alignment as described in Section 26.*

21 Steering rack rubber gaiters – renewal

1 Remove the track rod balljoint as described in Section 24.
2 If renewing the left-hand side gaiter, remove the battery and battery box as described in Chapter 5A.
3 Disconnect the breather pipe from the gaiter **(see illustration)**.
4 Mark the correct fitted position of the gaiter on the track rod, then release the retaining clips and slide the gaiter off the steering rack housing and track rod end **(see illustration)**.
5 Thoroughly clean the track rod and the steering rack housing, using fine abrasive paper to polish off any corrosion, burrs or sharp edges, which might damage the new gaiter's sealing lips on installation. Scrape off all the grease from the old gaiter, and apply it to the track rod inner balljoint. (This assumes

23.2 Disconnect the fluid pipes (arrowed) from the pump

that grease has not been lost or contaminated as a result of damage to the old gaiter. Use fresh grease if in doubt.)
6 Carefully slide the new gaiter onto the track rod end, and locate it on the steering rack housing. Align the outer edge of the gaiter with the mark made on the track rod prior to removal, then secure it in position with new retaining clips (where fitted).
7 Reconnect the breather pipe to the gaiter.
8 Where applicable, refit the battery box and battery as described in Chapter 5A.
9 Refit the track rod balljoint as described in Section 24.

22 Power steering system – bleeding

1 This procedure will only be necessary when any of the hydraulic system has been disconnected.
2 Referring to *Weekly checks*, remove the fluid reservoir filler cap, and top-up with the new specified fluid to the upper level mark.
3 Start the engine and allow it to idle for 3 minutes without moving the steering wheel. Check the fluid level frequently during this period and top it up if necessary.
4 Slowly move the steering from lock-to-lock several times to purge out the trapped air, then top-up the level in the fluid reservoir. Repeat this procedure until the fluid level in the reservoir does not drop any further.
5 Turn the engine off and allow the system to cool. Once cool, check that fluid level is up to the upper mark on the power steering fluid reservoir, topping-up if necessary.

23 Power steering pump – removal and refitting

Removal

1 Remove the windscreen washer fluid reservoir from the right-hand front wheel arch as described in Chapter 12.
2 Release the retaining clips and disconnect the fluid pipes from the power steering pump **(see illustration)**. Be prepared for

23.4 Undo the upper and lower pump mounting bolt/nuts

24.4a Undo the balljoint nut . . .

24.4b . . . then use a balljoint separator to release the tapered shank

fluid spillage, and plug the pump and pipe openings to prevent dirt ingress.
Caution: Do not bend the rigid power steering pump fluid pipe.
3 Disconnect the power steering pump wiring plug(s).
4 Undo the upper and lower pump mounting bolt/nuts and remove the pump from the wheel arch **(see illustration)**.
5 If the power steering pump is faulty it must be renewed. The pump is a sealed unit and cannot be overhauled.

Refitting

6 Manoeuvre the pump into position, then refit its mounting bolts and tighten them to the specified torque.
7 Reconnect the feed pipe to the pump and securely tighten the union nut. Refit the supply pipe to the pump, and secure it with a new clip.
8 Refit the windscreen washer fluid reservoir as described in Chapter 12.
9 Refit the plastic cover to the right-hand side of the engine compartment.
10 On completion, bleed the hydraulic system as described in Section 22.

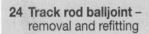

24 Track rod balljoint – removal and refitting

Note: *A new balljoint retaining nut will be required on refitting.*

Removal

1 Apply the handbrake, slacken the appropriate front roadwheel bolts, then jack up the front of the vehicle and support it on axle stands (see *Jacking and vehicle support*). Remove the appropriate front roadwheel.
2 If the balljoint is to be re-used, use a straight-edge and a scriber, or similar, to mark its relationship to the track rod.
3 Hold the track rod, and unscrew the balljoint locknut by a quarter of a turn. Do not move the locknut from this position, as it will serve as a handy reference mark on refitting.
4 Slacken and remove the nut securing the track rod balljoint to the hub carrier; discard the nut, a new one will be needed on

refitting. Release the balljoint tapered shank using a universal balljoint separator **(see illustrations)**.
5 Counting the **exact** number of turns necessary to do so, unscrew the balljoint from the track rod end.
6 Count the number of exposed threads between the end of the balljoint and the locknut, and record this figure. If a new balljoint is to be fitted, unscrew the locknut from the old balljoint.
7 Carefully clean the balljoint and the threads. Renew the balljoint if its movement is sloppy or too stiff, if excessively worn, or if damaged in any way; carefully check the stud taper and threads. If the balljoint gaiter is damaged, the complete balljoint assembly must be renewed; it is not possible to obtain the gaiter separately.

Refitting

8 If a new balljoint is to be fitted, screw the locknut onto its threads, and position it so that the same number of exposed threads are visible, as was noted prior to removal.
9 Screw the balljoint into the track rod by the number of turns noted on removal. This should bring the balljoint locknut to within a quarter of a turn of the alignment marks that were made on removal (if applicable).
10 Ensure that the protector plate is in position then locate the balljoint shank in the hub carrier. Fit a new retaining nut and tighten it to the specified torque.
11 Refit the roadwheel, then lower the vehicle to the ground and tighten the roadwheel bolts to the specified torque.
12 Check and, if necessary, adjust the front wheel alignment as described in Section 26, then securely tighten the balljoint locknut.

25 Track rod – removal and refitting

Note: *A special wrench (Peugeot number 0721-A) will be required to remove/refit the track rod inner balljoint from the end of the steering rack. Without the clamp damage to the assembly is likely. The special wrench engages with the balljoint housing allowing the track rod to be easily slackened/tightened without the risk of damage. Note that without access to the*

special tool, track rod removal will be difficult, especially without causing damage.
Note: *A new balljoint retaining nut will be required on refitting.*

Removal

1 Remove the relevant steering rack rubber gaiter as described in Section 21.
2 Using the special wrench (see note at the start of the Section), unscrew the track rod inner balljoint from the steering rack end. Take great care not to place excess strain on the rack as the joint is unscrewed, if necessary, prevent the steering rack from turning by holding it carefully with a pair of grips. Take great care not to mark the surfaces of the rack and balljoint. To eliminate the possibility of damage, a Peugeot special tool (0721-B) is available to prevent the rack from twisting.
3 Remove the track rod assembly. Examine the track rod inner balljoint for signs of slackness or tight spots, and check that the track rod itself is straight and free from damage. If necessary, renew the track rod; it is also recommended that the steering rack gaiter/dust cover is renewed.

Refitting

4 Screw the balljoint into the steering rack, and tighten it to the specified torque. If necessary, retain the steering rack with a pair of grips or the special Peugeot tool, again taking great care not to damage or mark the track rod balljoint or steering rack.
5 Carefully slide on the new gaiter, and locate it on the steering rack housing. Turn the steering fully from lock-to-lock, to check that the gaiter is correctly positioned on the track rod, then secure it in position with new retaining clips (where fitted).
6 Refit the track rod balljoint as described in Section 24.

26 Wheel alignment and steering angles – information, checking and adjustment

Definitions

1 A car's steering and suspension geometry is defined in four basic settings – all angles are expressed in degrees (toe settings are also

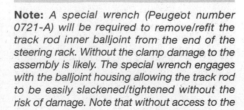

expressed as a measurement); the steering axis is defined as an imaginary line drawn through the axis of the suspension strut, extended where necessary to contact the ground.

2 Camber is the angle between each roadwheel and a vertical line drawn through its centre and tyre contact patch, when viewed from the front or rear of the car. Positive camber is when the roadwheels are tilted outwards from the vertical at the top; negative camber is when they are tilted inwards. The camber angle is not adjustable.

3 Castor is the angle between the steering axis and a vertical line drawn through each roadwheel's centre and tyre contact patch, when viewed from the side of the car. Positive castor is when the steering axis is tilted so that it contacts the ground ahead of the vertical; negative castor is when it contacts the ground behind the vertical. The castor angle is not adjustable.

4 Toe is the difference, viewed from above, between lines drawn through the roadwheel centres and the car's centre-line. 'Toe-in' is when the roadwheels point inwards, towards each other at the front, while 'toe-out' is when they splay outwards from each other at the front.

5 The front wheel toe setting is adjusted by screwing the track rod in or out of its balljoints, to alter the effective length of the track rod assembly.

6 Rear wheel toe setting is not adjustable.

Checking and adjustment

7 Due to the special measuring equipment necessary to check the wheel alignment and steering angles, and the skill required to use it properly, the checking and adjustment of these settings is best left to a Peugeot dealer or similar expert. Note that most tyre-fitting shops now possess sophisticated checking equipment. The following is provided as a guide, should the owner decide to carry out a DIY check.

Front wheel toe setting

8 The front wheel toe setting is checked by measuring the angle of the wheels in relation to the longitudinal axis of the vehicle. Proprietary toe measurement gauges are available from motor accessory shops. Adjustment is made by screwing the balljoints in or out of their track rods, to alter the effective length of the track rod assemblies.

9 For **accurate** checking, the vehicle **must** be at the reference height. This height is the distance between the lower edge of the reinforced sill seam of the jack support at the front of the sill (H1) and the rear of the sill (H2). These two reference heights (H1 and H2) are dependant on the tyre sizes:

Tyre size	H1	H2
195/65	157 mm	150 mm
205/55	152 mm	147 mm
205/50	160 mm	153 mm

These heights can be obtained by pulling the vehicle down by using clamps on a four poster vehicle ramp, although it may be possible to achieve the reference height by placing weights centrally within the vehicle. Consequently, checking the wheel alignment with gauges without the vehicle at reference height will only produce an approximate setting.

10 Before starting work, check first that the tyre sizes and types are as specified, then check the tyre pressures and tread wear, the roadwheel run-out, the condition of the hub bearings, the steering wheel free play, and the condition of the front suspension components (see *Weekly checks* and the relevant Part of Chapter 1). Correct any faults found.

11 Park the vehicle on level ground, check that the front roadwheels are in the straight-ahead position, then rock the rear and front ends to settle the suspension. Release the handbrake, and roll the vehicle backwards 1 metre, then forwards again, to relieve any stresses in the steering and suspension components. If possible, set the reference height of the vehicle as described in Paragraph 9.

12 Follow the tracking gauge manufacturer's instructions and measure the toe setting.

13 If adjustment is necessary, apply the handbrake, then jack up the front of the vehicle and support it securely on axle stands. Turn the steering wheel onto full-left lock, and record the number of exposed threads on the right-hand track rod end. Now turn the steering onto full-right lock, and record the number of threads on the left-hand side. If there are the same number of threads visible on both sides, then subsequent adjustment should be made equally on both sides. If there are more threads visible on one side than the other, it will be necessary to compensate for this during adjustment. **Note:** *It is most important that after adjustment, the same number of threads are visible on each track rod end.*

14 First clean the track rod threads; if they are corroded, apply penetrating fluid before starting adjustment. Release the rubber gaiter outboard clips (where necessary), and peel back the gaiters; apply a smear of grease to the inside of the gaiters, so that both are free, and will not be twisted or strained as their respective track rods are rotated.

15 Use a straight-edge and a scriber or similar to mark the relationship of each track rod to its balljoint then, holding each track rod in turn, unscrew its locknut fully.

16 Alter the length of the track rods, bearing in mind the note made in paragraph 13. Screw them into or out the balljoints, rotating the track rod using an open-ended spanner fitted to the flats provided on the track rod. Shortening the track rods (screwing them into their balljoints) will reduce toe-in/increase toe-out.

17 When the setting is correct, hold the track rods and tighten the balljoint locknuts to the specified torque setting. Check that the balljoints are seated correctly in their sockets, and count the exposed threads to check the length of both track rods. If they are not the same, then the adjustment has not been made equally, and problems will be encountered with tyre scrubbing in turns; also, the steering wheel spokes will no longer be horizontal when the wheels are in the straight-ahead position.

18 If the track rod lengths are the same, lower the vehicle to the ground and recheck the toe setting; re-adjust if necessary. When the setting is correct, tighten the track rod balljoint locknuts to the specified torque. Ensure that the rubber gaiters are seated correctly, and are not twisted or strained, and secure them in position with new retaining clips (where necessary).

Chapter 11
Bodywork and fittings

Contents

Degrees of difficulty

Easy, suitable for novice with little experience	**Fairly easy,** suitable for beginner with some experience	**Fairly difficult,** suitable for competent DIY mechanic 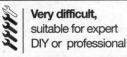	**Difficult,** suitable for experienced DIY mechanic 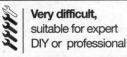	**Very difficult,** suitable for expert DIY or professional

Specifications

Torque wrench setting

	Nm	lbf ft
Seat belt mountings	30	22

---

1 General information

The bodyshell is made of pressed-steel sections, and is available in a three or five-door Hatchback version or five-door Estate. Most components are welded together, but some use is made of structural adhesives. The front wings are bolted on.

The bonnet, doors and some other vulnerable panels are made of zinc-coated metal, and are further protected by being coated with an anti-chip primer prior to being sprayed.

Extensive use is made of plastic materials, mainly in the interior, but also in exterior components. The front and rear bumpers and the front grille are injection-moulded from a synthetic material which is very strong, yet light. Plastic components such as wheel arch liners are fitted to the underside of the vehicle, to improve the body's resistance to corrosion.

2 Maintenance – bodywork and underframe

The general condition of a vehicle's bodywork is the one thing that significantly affects its value. Maintenance is easy, but needs to be regular. Neglect, particularly after minor damage, can lead quickly to further deterioration and costly repair bills. It is important also to keep watch on those parts of the vehicle not immediately visible, for instance the underside, inside all the wheel arches, and the lower part of the engine compartment.

The basic maintenance routine for the bodywork is washing – preferably with a lot of water, from a hose. This will remove all the loose solids which may have stuck to the vehicle. It is important to flush these off in such a way as to prevent grit from scratching the finish. The wheel arches and underframe need washing in the same way, to remove any accumulated mud which will retain moisture and tend to encourage rust. Paradoxically enough, the best time to clean the underframe and wheel arches is in wet weather, when the mud is thoroughly wet and soft. In very wet weather, the underframe is usually cleaned of large accumulations automatically, and this is a good time for inspection.

Periodically, except on vehicles with a wax-based underbody protective coating, it is a good idea to have the whole of the underframe of the vehicle steam-cleaned, engine compartment included, so that a thorough inspection can be carried out to see what minor repairs and renovations are necessary. Steam-cleaning is available at many garages, and is necessary for the removal of the accumulation of oily grime, which sometimes is allowed to become thick in certain areas. If steam-cleaning facilities are not available, there are one or two excellent grease solvents available, which can be brush-applied; the dirt can then be simply hosed off. Note that these methods should not be used on vehicles with wax-based underbody protective coating, or the coating will be removed. Such vehicles should be inspected annually, preferably just prior to winter, when the underbody should be washed down, and any damage to the wax coating repaired using underseal. Ideally, a completely fresh coat should be applied. It would also be worth considering the use of wax-based protection for injection into door panels, sills, box sections, etc, as an additional safeguard against rust damage, where such protection is not provided by the vehicle manufacturer.

After washing paintwork, wipe off with a chamois leather to give an unspotted clear finish. A coat of clear protective wax polish will give added protection against chemical pollutants in the air. If the paintwork sheen has dulled or oxidised, use a cleaner/ polisher combination to restore the brilliance of the shine. This requires a little effort, but such dulling is usually caused because regular washing has been neglected. Care needs to be taken with metallic paintwork, as a special non-abrasive cleaner/polisher is required to avoid damage to the finish. Always check that the door and ventilator opening drain holes and pipes are completely clear, so that water can be drained out. Brightwork should be treated in the same way as paintwork. Windscreens and windows can be kept clear of the smeary film which often appears, by the use of proprietary glass cleaner. Never use any form of wax or other body or chromium polish on glass.

3 Maintenance – upholstery and carpets

Mats and carpets should be brushed or vacuum-cleaned regularly, to keep them free of grit. If they are badly stained, remove them from the vehicle for scrubbing or sponging, and make quite sure they are dry before refitting. Seats and interior trim panels can be kept clean by wiping with a damp cloth and a proprietary upholstery cleaner. If they do become stained (which can be more apparent on light-coloured upholstery), use a little liquid detergent and a soft nail brush to scour the grime out of the grain of the material. Do not forget to keep the headlining clean in the same way as the upholstery. When using liquid cleaners inside the vehicle, do not over-wet the surfaces being cleaned. Excessive damp could get into the seams and padded interior, causing stains, offensive odours or even rot. If the inside of the vehicle gets wet accidentally, it is worthwhile taking some trouble to dry it out properly, particularly where carpets are involved.
Caution: Do not leave oil or electric heaters inside the vehicle for this purpose.

4 Minor body damage – repair

Scratches

If the scratch is very superficial, and does not penetrate to the metal of the bodywork, repair is very simple. Lightly rub the area of the scratch with a paintwork renovator, or a very fine cutting paste, to remove loose paint from the scratch, and to clear the surrounding bodywork of wax polish. Rinse the area with clean water.

Apply touch-up paint to the scratch using a fine paint brush; continue to apply fine layers of paint until the surface of the paint in the scratch is level with the surrounding paintwork. Allow the new paint at least two weeks to harden, then blend it into the surrounding paintwork by rubbing the scratch area with a paintwork renovator or a very fine cutting paste. Finally apply wax polish.

Where the scratch has penetrated right through to the metal of the bodywork, causing the metal to rust, a different repair technique is required. Remove any loose rust from the bottom of the scratch with a penknife, then apply rust-inhibiting paint, to prevent the formation of rust in the future. Using a rubber or nylon applicator, fill the scratch with bodystopper paste. If required, this paste can be mixed with cellulose thinners, to provide a very thin paste which is ideal for filling narrow scratches. Before the stopper-paste in the scratch hardens, wrap a piece of smooth cotton rag around the top of a finger. Dip the finger in cellulose thinners, and quickly sweep it across the surface of the stopper-paste in the scratch; this will ensure that the surface of the stopper-paste is slightly hollowed. The scratch can now be painted over as described earlier in this Section.

Dents

When deep denting of the vehicle's bodywork has taken place, the first task is to pull the dent out, until the affected bodywork almost attains its original shape. There is little point in trying to restore the original shape completely, as the metal in the damaged area will have stretched on impact, and cannot be reshaped fully to its original contour. It is better to bring the level of the dent up to a point which is about 3 mm below the level of the surrounding bodywork. In cases where the dent is very shallow anyway, it is not worth trying to pull it out at all. If the underside of the dent is accessible, it can be hammered out gently from behind, using a mallet with a wooden or plastic head. Whilst doing this, hold a suitable block of wood firmly against the outside of the panel, to absorb the impact from the hammer blows and thus prevent a large area of the bodywork from being 'belled-out'.

Should the dent be in a section of the bodywork which has a double skin, or some other factor making it inaccessible from behind, a different technique is called for. Drill several small holes through the metal inside the area – particularly in the deeper section. Then screw long self-tapping screws into the holes, just sufficiently for them to gain a good purchase in the metal. Now the dent can be pulled out by pulling on the protruding heads of the screws with a pair of pliers.

The next stage of the repair is the removal of the paint from the damaged area, and from an inch or so of the surrounding 'sound' bodywork. This is accomplished most easily by using a wire brush or abrasive pad on a power drill, although it can be done just as effectively by hand, using sheets of abrasive paper. To complete the preparation for filling, score the surface of the bare metal with a screwdriver or the tang of a file, or alternatively, drill small holes in the affected area. This will provide a really good 'key' for the filler paste.

To complete the repair, see the Section on filling and respraying.

Rust holes or gashes

Remove all paint from the affected area, and from an inch or so of the surrounding 'sound' bodywork, using an abrasive pad or a wire brush on a power drill. If these are not available, a few sheets of abrasive paper will do the job most effectively. With the paint removed, you will be able to judge the severity of the corrosion, and therefore decide whether to renew the whole panel (if this is possible) or to repair the affected area. New body panels are not as expensive as most people think, and it is often quicker and more satisfactory to fit a new panel than to attempt to repair large areas of corrosion.

Remove all fittings from the affected area, except those which will act as a guide to the original shape of the damaged bodywork (eg headlight shells etc). Then, using tin snips or a hacksaw blade, remove all loose metal and any other metal badly affected by corrosion. Hammer the edges of the hole inwards, in order to create a slight depression for the filler paste.

Wire-brush the affected area to remove the powdery rust from the surface of the remaining metal. Paint the affected area with rust-inhibiting paint; if the back of the rusted area is accessible, treat this also.

Before filling can take place, it will be necessary to block the hole in some way. This can be achieved by the use of aluminium or plastic mesh, or aluminium tape.

Aluminium or plastic mesh, or glass-fibre matting, is probably the best material to use for a large hole. Cut a piece to the approximate size and shape of the hole to be filled, then position it in the hole so that its edges are below the level of the surrounding bodywork. It can be retained in position by several blobs of filler paste around its periphery.

Aluminium tape should be used for small or very narrow holes. Pull a piece off the roll, trim it to the approximate size and shape required, then pull off the backing paper (if used) and stick the tape over the hole; it can be overlapped if the thickness of one piece is insufficient. Burnish down the edges of the tape with the handle of a screwdriver or similar, to ensure that the tape is securely attached to the metal underneath.

Filling and respraying

Before using this Section, see the Sections on dent, minor scratch, rust holes and gash repairs.

Many types of bodyfiller are available, but generally speaking, those proprietary kits which contain a tin of filler paste and a tube of resin hardener are best for this type of repair; some can be used directly from the tube. A wide, flexible plastic or nylon applicator will be found invaluable for imparting a smooth and well-contoured finish to the surface of the filler.

Mix up a little filler on a clean piece of card or board – measure the hardener carefully (follow the maker's instructions on the pack), otherwise the filler will set too rapidly or too slowly. Using the applicator, apply the filler paste to the prepared area; draw the applicator across the surface of the filler to achieve the correct contour and to level the surface. As soon as a contour that approximates to the correct one is achieved, stop working the paste – if you carry on too long, the paste will become sticky and begin to 'pick-up' on the applicator. Continue to add thin layers of filler paste at 20-minute intervals, until the level of the filler is just proud of the surrounding bodywork.

Once the filler has hardened, the excess can be removed using a metal plane or file. From then on, progressively-finer grades of abrasive paper should be used, starting with a 40-grade production paper, and finishing with a 400-grade wet-and-dry paper. Always wrap the abrasive paper around a flat rubber, cork, or wooden block – otherwise the surface of the filler will not be completely flat. During the smoothing of the filler surface, the wet-and-dry paper should be periodically rinsed in water. This will ensure that a very smooth finish is imparted to the filler at the final stage.

At this stage, the 'dent' should be surrounded by a ring of bare metal, which in turn should be encircled by the finely 'feathered' edge of the good paintwork. Rinse the repair area with clean water, until all of the dust produced by the rubbing-down operation has gone.

Spray the whole area with a light coat of primer – this will show up any imperfections in the surface of the filler. Repair these imperfections with fresh filler paste or bodystopper, and once more smooth the surface with abrasive paper. If bodystopper is used, it can be mixed with cellulose thinners, to form a really thin paste which is ideal for filling small holes. Repeat this spray-and-repair procedure until you are satisfied that the surface of the filler, and the feathered edge of the paintwork, are perfect. Clean the repair area with clean water, and allow to dry fully.

The repair area is now ready for final spraying. Paint spraying must be carried out in a warm, dry, windless and dust-free atmosphere. This condition can be created artificially if you have access to a large indoor working area, but if you are forced to work in the open, you will have to pick your day very carefully. If you are working indoors, dousing the floor in the work area with water will help to settle the dust which would otherwise be in the atmosphere. If the repair area is confined to one body panel, mask off the surrounding panels; this will help to minimise the effects of a slight mismatch in paint colours. Bodywork fittings (eg chrome strips, door handles etc) will also need to be masked off. Use genuine masking tape, and several thicknesses of newspaper, for the masking operations.

Before commencing to spray, agitate the aerosol can thoroughly, then spray a test area (an old tin, or similar) until the technique is mastered. Cover the repair area with a thick coat of primer; the thickness should be built up using several thin layers of paint, rather than one thick one. Using 400 grade wet-and-dry paper, rub down the surface of the primer until it is really smooth. While doing this, the work area should be thoroughly doused with water, and the wet-and-dry paper periodically rinsed in water. Allow to dry before spraying on more paint.

Spray on the top coat, again building up the thickness by using several thin layers of paint. Start spraying at the top of the repair area, and then, using a side-to-side motion, work downwards until the whole repair area and about 2 inches of the surrounding original paintwork is covered. Remove all masking material 10 to 15 minutes after spraying on the final coat of paint.

Allow the new paint at least two weeks to harden, then, using a paintwork renovator or a very fine cutting paste, blend the edges of the paint into the existing paintwork. Finally, apply wax polish.

Plastic components

With the use of more and more plastic body components by the vehicle manufacturers (eg bumpers, spoilers, and in some cases major body panels), rectification of more serious damage to such items has become a matter of either entrusting repair work to a specialist in this field, or renewing complete components. Repair of such damage by the DIY owner is not really feasible, owing to the cost of the equipment and materials required for effecting such repairs. The basic technique involves making a groove along the line of the crack in the plastic, using a rotary burr in a power drill. The damaged part is then welded back together, using a hot air gun to heat up and fuse a plastic filler rod into the groove. Any excess plastic is then removed, and the area rubbed down to a smooth finish. It is important that a filler rod of the correct plastic is used, as body components can be made of a variety of different types (eg polycarbonate, ABS, polypropylene).

Damage of a less serious nature (abrasions, minor cracks etc) can be repaired by the DIY owner using a two-part epoxy filler repair material. Once mixed in equal proportions, this is used in similar fashion to the bodywork filler used on metal panels. The filler is usually cured in twenty to thirty minutes, ready for sanding and painting.

If the owner is renewing a complete component himself, or if he has repaired it with epoxy filler, he will be left with the problem of finding a suitable paint for finishing which is compatible with the type of plastic used. At one time, the use of a universal paint was not possible, owing to the complex range of plastics encountered in body component applications. Standard paints, generally speaking, will not bond to plastic or rubber satisfactorily. However, it is now possible to obtain a plastic body parts finishing kit which consists of a pre-primer treatment, a primer and coloured top coat. Full instructions are normally supplied with a kit, but basically, the method of use is to first apply the pre-primer to the component concerned, and allow it to dry for up to 30 minutes. Then the primer is applied, and left to dry for about an hour before finally applying the special-coloured top coat. The result is a correctly-coloured component, where the paint will flex with the plastic or rubber, a property that standard paint does not normally posses.

5 Major body damage – repair

Where serious damage has occurred, or large areas need renewal due to neglect, it means that complete new panels will need welding-in, and this is best left to professionals. If the damage is due to impact, it will also be necessary to check completely the alignment of the bodyshell, and this can only be carried out accurately by a Peugeot dealer, or accident repair specialist, using special jigs. If the body is left misaligned, it is primarily dangerous, as the car will not handle properly, and secondly, uneven stresses will be imposed on the steering, suspension and possibly transmission, causing abnormal wear, or complete failure, particularly to such items as the tyres.

6.4 Undo the bumper-to-wing screws (arrowed)

6.5 Insert the rod into the slot alongside the clip, then twist the rod and pull down the clip

6.6a Prise up the centre pins, and lever out the expansion rivets

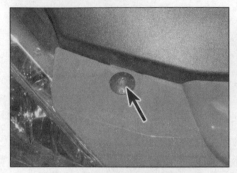

6.6b Undo the screws (arrowed)

6.7 Depress the levers to release the clips

6.11 Undo the bumper bar bolts (arrowed)

6 Front bumper – removal and refitting

Note: *The help of an assistant is useful to support the bumper during the removal and refitting procedure.*

Removal

1 Firmly apply the handbrake, then jack up the front of the vehicle and support it securely on axle stands (see *Jacking and vehicle support*). To improve access to the bumper fasteners, remove both front roadwheels.

2 Remove the headlamp washer jets, where fitted, as described in Chapter 12.

3 Push in the centre pins a little, then prise out the complete plastic expanding rivets securing bolt wheel arch liners to the body.

4 Remove the screws (one each side) securing the upper edge of the bumper to the underside of the wing **(see illustration)**.

5 Using a length of rod with a 10.00 mm 90° bend at the end, release the four clips (two each side) securing the bumper to the wing **(see illustration)**. Insert the rod along side the clip, then twist the rod 90° to pull the clips down and release the bumper.

6 The bumper is secured by four plastic expanding rivets along its top edge, and two screws adjacent to the headlamps. Prise up the centre pins a little, lever the complete rivets from place, then undo the screws **(see illustrations)**.

7 Depress the levers to release the two clips

on the underside of the bumper, and unscrew the three fasteners securing the engine undershield to the bumper **(see illustration)**.

8 With the help of an assistant, carefully pull the bumper forward. Take care no to damage the grille as it's manoeuvred over the bonnet lock assembly.

9 If required, the rubber bumper inserts can be carefully prised from place using a plastic spatula.

10 To remove the bumper bar, remove the washer fluid reservoir and headlamps as described in Chapter 12.

11 Undo the four bolts each side and remove the bumper bar **(see illustration)**. Tie the horn to one side, or disconnect the wiring plug and remove it from the vehicle.

Refitting

12 Refitting is a reversal of removal, ensuring

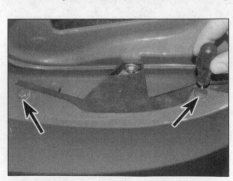

7.3 Remove the bolt and plastic rivet beneath the rear light aperture (arrowed)

that the bumper correctly engages with the retaining clips each side as it is located in position.

7 Rear bumper – removal and refitting

Note: *The help of an assistant is useful to support the bumper during the removal and refitting procedure.*

Removal

1 Chock the front wheels, then jack up the rear of the vehicle and support securely on axle stands (see *Jacking and vehicle support*).

Hatchback models

2 Remove the rear light cluster on both sides as described in Chapter 12.

3 Push down the centre pin, prise up the expanding plastic rivet, then undo the bolt beneath the rear light aperture **(see illustration)**. Repeat this procedure on the remaining side.

4 Undo the screw at the centre underside of the bumper **(see illustration)**.

5 At each end of the underside of the bumper, push in the centre pins, and prise out the plastic expanding rivets **(see illustration)**.

6 Push in the centre pin, prise out the expanding plastic rivet, then undo the nut and pull the rear section of the rear wheel arch liner forward **(see illustrations)**.

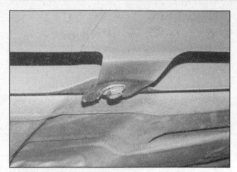

7.4 Undo the screw in the centre of the bumper underneath

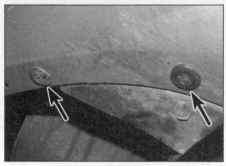

7.5 Push in the centre pins and prise out the plastic rivets (arrowed)

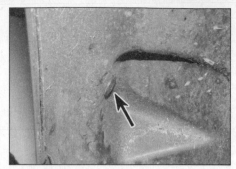

7.6a Push in the centre pin, prise out the plastic rivet (arrowed) . . .

7.6b . . . then undo the nut (arrowed) and pull the rear section of the wheel arch liner forward

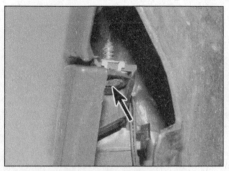

7.7 Undo the Torx screw (arrowed) at the front upper edge of the bumper

7.9 Undo the bumper bar bolts (left-hand side)

7 At the front upper edge of the bumper undo the Torx screw **(see illustration)**.

8 Disconnect the number plate lights as the bumper is withdrawn.

9 To remove the bumper bar, undo the three bolts on the left-hand side, and the four bolts on the right-hand side (lift the luggage compartment floor to access the inner bolt), and withdraw the bar from the vehicle **(see illustration)**.

10 If required, the rubber bumper inserts can be prised from place using a plastic spatula after the bumper cover has been removed.

Estate/SW models

11 Remove the rear light cluster on both sides as described in Chapter 12.

12 Undo the bolt each side under the light cluster aperture **(see illustration)**.

13 Push in the centre pins, prise out the complete rivets, undo the nuts and remove the wheel arch liner.

14 Undo the two screws each side securing the upper front corner of the bumper cover to the rear wing **(see illustration)**.

15 Push in the centre pins, and prise out the two complete plastic expanding rivets securing the under side of the bumper each side **(see illustration)**.

16 Undo the three screws underneath the centre of the rear bumper and manoeuvre the bumper from the vehicle.

17 If required, remove the bumper bar as described in Paragraph 9.

Refitting

18 Refitting is a reversal of removal.

8 Bonnet – removal, refitting and adjustment

Removal

1 Open the bonnet and have an assistant support it then, using a pencil or felt tip pen, mark the outline of each bonnet hinge relative to the bonnet, to use as a guide on refitting.

2 The bonnet insulation panel is secured by plastic expanding rivets. Prise up the centre pins a little, lever out the rivets, and remove the insulation panel **(see illustration)**.

3 Disconnect the washer jet tubing, and jet heater wiring (where fitted). Release the tubing and wiring from any retaining clips.

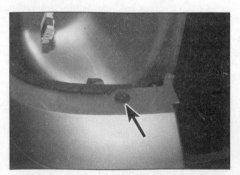

7.12 Undo the bolt under the rear light aperture (arrowed)

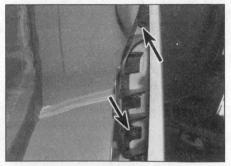

7.14 Two Torx screws secure the upper edge of the bumper (arrowed)

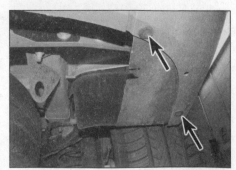

7.15 Push in the centre pins and prise out the two rivets each side (arrowed)

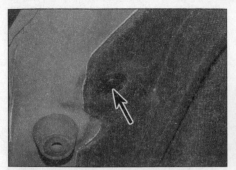

8.2 Prise up the centre pin then lever out the plastic rivet (arrowed)

8.4 Undo the two bonnet hinge bolts each side

4 Unscrew the bonnet-to-hinge retaining bolts each side **(see illustration)**. With the help of the assistant, carefully lift the bonnet from the vehicle. Store the bonnet out of the way in a safe place.

5 Inspect the bonnet hinges for signs of wear and free play at the pivots, and if necessary renew. Each hinge is secured to the body by two bolts, accessible after removing the scuttle grille panel as described in Section 22. On refitting, apply a smear of multi-purpose grease to the hinges.

Refitting and adjustment

6 With the aid of an assistant, offer up the bonnet, and engage the retaining bolts. Align the hinges with the marks made on removal, then tighten the retaining bolts securely.

7 Close the bonnet, and check for alignment with the adjacent panels. If necessary, slacken the hinge bolts and re-align the bonnet to suit.

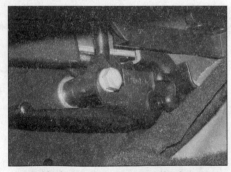

9.5 Undo the bolt securing the bonnet release handle

10.2 Bonnet lock retaining bolts (arrowed)

When correctly aligned, tighten the hinge bolts securely.

8 Once the bonnet is correctly aligned, check that the bonnet fastens and releases in a satisfactory manner. If adjustment is necessary, slacken the bonnet lock retaining bolts, and adjust the position of the lock to suit. Once the lock is operating correctly, securely tighten its retaining bolts.

9 Reconnect the washer jet tuning and wiring (where applicable), and refit the bonnet insulation panel

9 Bonnet release cable – removal and refitting

Removal

1 Remove the front bumper as described in Section 6.

2 Working in the engine compartment, disconnect the end of the cable from the lock lever. Work along the length of the cable in the engine compartment, note their fitted locations, and release the cable retaining clips.

3 Use a screwdriver to push the cable bulkhead grommet into the passenger cabin.

4 Remove the built-in systems interface/fusebox as described in Chapter 12.

5 Working under the facia on the left-hand side, unscrew the release lever bolt, and withdraw the lever assembly from its location **(see illustration)**.

6 Tie a length of string to the end of the cable in the engine compartment, note its routing, then carefully pull the cable through into the passenger compartment. Untie the string from the end of the cable, and leave it in position to aid refitting.

Refitting

7 Locate the cable in position in the passenger compartment.

8 Tie the end of the new cable to the string, and pull it through into the engine compartment.

9 Check that the bulkhead grommet is securely seated, then remove the string and connect the cable to the bonnet lock lever.

10 Secure the release lever in place, tightening its retaining bolt securely.

11 Secure the cable in place with its retaining clips. Check the lock operates satisfactorily before proceeding.

12 Refit the built-in systems interface/fusebox as described in Chapter 12.

13 Refit the front bumper as described in Section 6.

10 Bonnet lock – removal and refitting

Removal

1 Remove the front bumper as described in Section 6.

2 Unscrew the two bolts securing the lock assembly to the body upper crossmember **(see illustration)**.

3 Withdraw the lock and disconnect the bonnet release cable from the lock lever.

Refitting

4 Refitting is a reversal of removal. On completion, check the operation of the lock and, if necessary, adjust the position of the lock within the elongated bolt holes to achieve satisfactory operation prior to closing the bonnet.

11 Door – removal, refitting and adjustment

Front door

Removal

1 Using a small screwdriver, release the wiring harness guide retaining clips, and pull the harness and guide from the door pillar **(see illustration)**.

2 Prise up the locking catch and disconnect the door wiring connector **(see illustration)**.

3 Unscrew the securing bolt, and disconnect the door check strap from the door pillar **(see illustration)**.

4 Ensure that the door is adequately supported, slide out the hinge pin clips, then remove the upper and lower hinge pins. Carefully lift the door from the vehicle.

11.1 Prise out the wiring harness guide

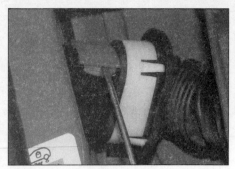

11.2 Lever up the locking catch and disconnect the wiring plug

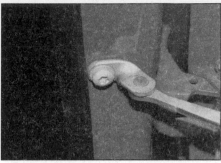

11.3 Undo the door check strap bolt

12.1a Undo the screw (arrowed) . . .

Refitting

5 Refitting is a reversal of removal.

Rear door

6 The procedure is as described for the front doors, but the hinge-to-body bolts are accessed for adjustment with the front door open.

---

12 Door inner trim panel –
removal and refitting

Front door

Removal

1 Undo the door handle switch retaining screw, and carefully prise up the switch/panel

assembly. Disconnect the switch wiring plug **(see illustrations)**.
2 Carefully pull the exterior mirror mounting cover from place **(see illustration)**.
3 Open the interior door release handle, insert a small screwdriver into the hole on the in the top of the recess trim. Release the retaining clip and withdraw the handle trim **(see illustration)**.
4 Undo the two screws located at the front edge of the door trim, and the single screw at its rear edge **(see illustrations)**.
5 Using a suitable forked tool, work around the edge of the trim panel, and release the securing clips **(see illustration)**.
6 Pull the panel outwards, lift it up and remove it from the door. Disconnect the speaker wiring plugs as the panel is withdrawn.

Refitting

7 Before refitting, check whether any of the trim panel retaining studs were broken on removal. Renew the panel retaining studs as necessary, then refit the panel using a reversal of removal.

Rear door

Removal

8 Open the interior door release handle, insert a small screwdriver in the hole in the top of the recess trim. Release the retaining clip and withdraw the handle trim **(see illustration 12.3)**. On Estate and SW models, the handle surround trim must first be carefully prised from place **(see illustration)**. Disconnect the window switch wiring plug (if applicable) as the trim is withdrawn.

12.1b . . . then lever up the switch/panel assembly

12.2 Pull the exterior mirror mounting cover from place

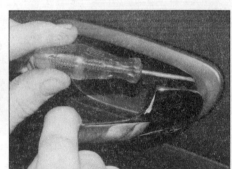

12.3 Insert a small screwdriver into the hole to release the retaining clip

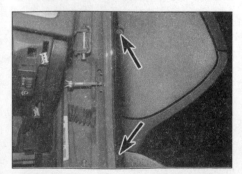

12.4a Undo the two screws (arrowed) at the front edge of the door trim . . .

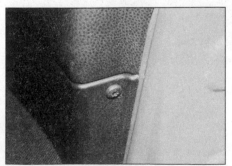

12.4b . . . and the one at the rear

12.5 Using a forked tool, release the retaining clips around the door trim

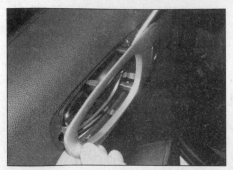

12.8 Carefully prise the handle surround trim from place (Estate/SW models)

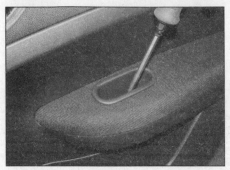

12.9b . . . and one in the handle recess

9 Undo the two panel retaining screws. One screw is located at the front edge of the panel, and the second is located in the recess of the door grab handle **(see illustrations)**.
10 On models with manual windows,

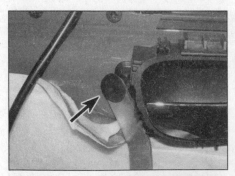

13.2 On front doors, prise out the interior door handle retaining clip (arrowed)

13.6a Prise off the circlip followed by the operating arm . . .

12.9a One screw (arrowed) is located at the front of the door trim . . .

12.10 Pull the manual window winder handle from the spindle

pull the winder handle off the spindle, and then remove the spindle trim plate **(see illustration)**.
11 Using a suitable forked tool, work around the lower and side edges of the trim panel,

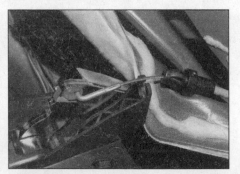

13.3 Unclip the connecting rod from the handle

13.6b . . . spring . . .

and release the securing clips **(see illustration 12.5)**.
12 Pull the panel upwards and outwards, and remove the panel from the door. Disconnect the speaker wiring plug as the panel is withdrawn.

Refitting

13 Refitting is a reversal of removal, after first renewing any broken panel retaining studs as necessary.

13 Door handle and lock components – removal and refitting

Interior door handle

Removal

1 Remove the door inner trim panel, as described in Section 12.
2 Release the handle from its location by prising out the retaining clip (front door only), then pulling it towards the front edge of the door **(see illustration)**.
3 Unclip the connecting rod from the handle **(see illustration)**.

Refitting

4 Refitting is a reversal of removal, but ensure that the link rod is correctly reconnected, and refit the inner trim panel (see Section 12).

Front door lock cylinder

Note 1: *A new door sealing sheet may be required on refitting.*
Note 2: *The exterior handle mounting bracket is riveted to the door. Ensure that new rivets of the correct size are available for refitting.*

Removal

5 Remove the exterior door handle support bracket as described in Paragraphs 18 to 23.
6 Prise off the circlip on the rear of the cylinder, and carefully remove the operating arm, spring and collar, noting their fitted positions **(see illustrations)**.
7 Insert the ignition key and pull the cylinder from place.

Refitting

8 Refitting is a reversal of removal, but ensure

13.6c . . . and collar

that the lock cylinder retaining clip is securely refitted.

Front door lock

Note: *A new door sealing sheet may be required on refitting.*

Removal

9 Remove the interior door handle as described previously.

10 Using a sharp knife, carefully release the plastic sealing sheet from the adhesive bead and remove the sheet from the area around the door lock. If care is taken, it may just be possible to remove the sheet in one piece and re-use it when refitting

11 Undo the two nuts securing the rear window guide channel, and move the channel towards the front of the door to access the lock **(see illustration)**.

12 Unclip the door lock link rod from the lever on the exterior handle and door lock **(see illustration)**.

13 Undo the three screws securing the lock assembly to the edge of the door **(see illustration)**.

14 Release the interior handle link cable from the guide clips on the door, then lower the lock assembly and manipulate it out through the door aperture.

15 Disconnect the central locking motor wiring plug and remove the lock assembly.

16 If required, the interior door handle cable can be unclipped from the lock assembly **(see illustrations)**.

Refitting

17 Refitting is a reversal of removal. Fit a new sealing sheet to the door if the original was damaged in any way during removal. On completion, refit the door inner trim panel as described in Section 12.

Front door exterior handle

Note 1: *A new door sealing sheet may be required for refitting.*
Note 2: *The exterior handle mounting bracket is riveted to the door. Ensure that new rivets of the correct size are available for refitting.*

Removal

18 Remove the interior door handle as described previously.

19 Using a sharp knife, carefully release the plastic sealing sheet from the adhesive bead and remove the sheet from the area around the door lock. If care is taken, it may just be possible to remove the sheet in one piece and re-use it when refitting

20 Undo the two nuts securing the rear window guide channel, and move the channel towards the front of the door to access the handle **(see illustration 13.11)**.

21 Slide the white plastic operating lever forward so that the locking clip engages in the groove, and the rear of the exterior handle no longer engages with it **(see illustration)**.

22 Pull the rear of the exterior handle outwards, and use a screwdriver to lever the

13.11 Undo the window rear guide channel retaining nuts (arrowed)

13.13 Three screws secure the lock to the edge of the door

13.16b ... then disconnect the cable inner

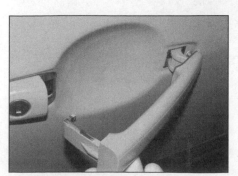

13.22 Pull out the rear of the handle and disengage the pin at the front

13.12 Unclip the link rod from the handle to the lock

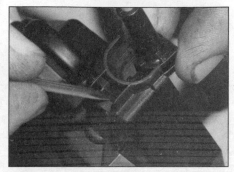

13.16a Depress the clip and slide out the cable outer ...

13.21 Slide the white lever forwards so the handle no longer engages with it

13.23 Prise off the cover to expose the two rear rivets

front of the handle from the front pivot pin **(see illustration)**. Manoeuvre the handle from the door.

23 If required, unclip the operating rod from the lock cylinder and operating arm, and the

plastic lock cylinder exterior cover. Then, using a 6.0 mm diameter drill bit, drill off the rivet heads from the outside, and remove the handle bracket from the door **(see illustration)**.

13.30a Undo the three lock screws . . .

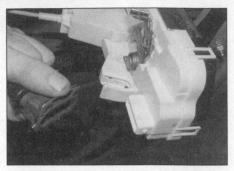

13.30b . . . disconnect the wiring plug as the lock is withdrawn

14 Door window glass, regulator and quarter light – removal and refitting

Refitting

24 Refitting is a reversal of removal, using new pop rivets to secure the handle. Fit a new sealing sheet to the door if the original was damaged in any way during removal. On completion, refit the inner trim panel as described in Section 12.

Rear door lock

Note: *A new door sealing sheet may be required on refitting.*

Removal

25 Remove the interior door handle as described previously.
26 Using a sharp knife, carefully release the plastic sealing sheet from the adhesive bead and remove the sheet from the door in the area of the lock. If care is taken, it may just be possible to remove the sheet in one piece and re-use it when refitting.
27 Free the interior handle link cable from the guide clips on the door.
28 Release the wiring harness clip from the door frame.
29 Disengage the exterior handle link rod from the lever on the door lock.
30 Undo the three screws securing the lock assembly to the edge of the door, then manipulate the unit out through the door aperture **(see illustrations)**. Disconnect the lock wiring plug as it is withdrawn.

Refitting

31 Refitting is a reversal of removal. Fit a new sealing sheet to the door if the original was damaged in any way during removal. On

completion, refit the door inner trim panel as described in Section 12.

Rear door exterior handle

Note 1: *A new door sealing sheet may be required for refitting.*
Note 2: *The exterior handle bracket is riveted to the door. Ensure that new rivets of the correct size are available for refitting.*

Removal

32 Remove the interior door handle as previously described.
33 Using a sharp knife, carefully release the plastic sealing sheet from the adhesive bead and remove the sheet from the door. If care is taken, it may just be possible to remove the sheet in one piece and re-use it when refitting.
34 Slide the white plastic operating lever forward so that the locking clip engages in the groove, and the rear of the exterior handle no longer engages with it **(see illustration 13.21)**.
35 Pull the rear of the exterior handle outwards, and use a screwdriver to lever the front of the handle from the front pivot pin **(see illustration 13.22)**. Manoeuvre the handle from the door.
36 If required, remove the plastic exterior cover, then using a 6.0 mm diameter drill bit, drill off the rivet heads from the outside, and remove the handle bracket from the door.

Refitting

37 Refitting is a reversal of removal. Fit a new sealing sheet to the door if the original was damaged in any way during removal. On completion, refit the inner trim panel as described in Section 12.

Front door window glass

Note: *A new door sealing sheet may be required on refitting.*
1 Fully lower the window, and carefully remove the interior and exterior waist seal from the window aperture **(see illustration)**. Raise the window approximately one-third of the way up.
2 Remove the door inner trim panel as described in Section 12.
3 Drill out the rivets securing the door trim panel support bracket **(see illustration)**.
4 Using a sharp knife, carefully release the plastic sealing sheet from the adhesive bead and remove the sheet from the door. If care is taken, it may just be possible to remove the sheet in one piece and re-use it when refitting.
5 Undo the two window clamp screws, and remove the window up through the aperture, and out of the door **(see illustration)**.
6 Refitting is a reversal of removal, but fit a new sealing sheet to the door if the original was damaged in any way during removal. On completion, refit the inner trim panel as described in Section 12.

Front door window regulator

7 Position the window approximately one-third of the way up.
8 Remove the door inner trim panel as described in Section 12.
9 Drill out the rivets securing the door trim panel support bracket to the door frame **(see illustration 14.3)**.
10 Using a sharp knife, carefully release the plastic sealing sheet from the adhesive bead and remove the sheet from the door. If care is taken, it may just be possible to remove the sheet in one piece and re-use it when refitting.
11 Undo the two window clamp bolts **(see illustration 14.5)**.
12 Slide the window up to the fully closed position and secure it in this position with masking tape over the top of the door frame. Temporarily reconnect the window switch and fully lower the mechanism.

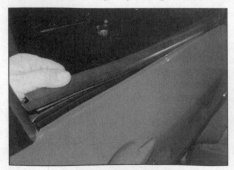

14.1 Carefully prise up the door waist seals

14.3 Drill out the door trim panel support bracket rivets

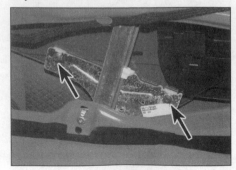

14.5 Undo the two window clamp screws (arrowed)

14.13 Undo the three Torx screws (arrowed) and remove the window motor

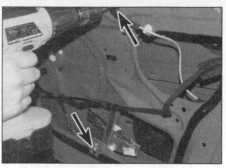

14.14 Drill out the two rivets (arrowed) . . .

14.15 . . . and release the clips

13 Undo the three Torx screws and remove the electric motor from the regulator **(see illustration)**. Disconnect the motor wiring plug.

14 Drill out the two rivets securing the regulator assembly to the door frame **(see illustration)**.

15 Release the three clips securing the regulator assembly to the door panel **(see illustration)**.

16 Lower the regulator, and manoeuvre it from the door.

17 Refitting is a reversal of removal.

Rear door window glass

Note: *A new door sealing sheet may be required on refitting.*

18 Remove the interior door handle as described in Section 13.

19 Drill out the rivet securing the door trim support bracket to the door frame, then lift the bracket upwards and remove it.

20 Using a sharp knife, carefully release the plastic sealing sheet from the adhesive bead and remove the sheet from the door. If care is taken, it may just be possible to remove the sheet in one piece and re-use it when refitting.

21 Prise the door interior waistline rubber seal from the door frame **(see illustration)**.

5-door Hatchback models

22 Temporarily reconnect the window switch/ regulator handle, and raise the window until the window clamp screws are visible through the opening in the door frame. Undo the two window clamp screws **(see illustration)**.

Estate/SW models

23 Carefully prise of the triangular plastic trim from the rear lower corner of the window outer aperture. The trim is retained by two push-on clips **(see illustration)**.

24 Prise up and remove the exterior waist seal from the window aperture.

All models

25 Beginning in the rear lower corner carefully remove the window aperture channel seal from the door frame.

26 Undo the two nuts at the rear of the door frame securing the window guide channel, and withdraw the guide channel **(see illustration)**.

27 Slide the window up to the fully closed position and secure it in this position with masking tape over the top of the door frame.

28 Using the switch/regulator handle, fully lower the regulator mechanism.

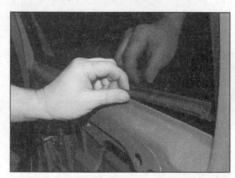

14.21 Prise the interior waistline seal from the door

29 Fully lower the window, then lift the rear of the window glass upwards and remove it from the outside of the door **(see illustration)**. Take care not to damage the paintwork on the door.

30 Refitting is a reversal of removal, but fit a new sealing sheet to the door if the original was damaged in any way during removal. On completion, refit the interior door handle as described in Section 13.

Rear door window regulator

Note: *A new door sealing sheet may be required on refitting.*

31 Remove the interior door handle as described in Section 13.

32 Drill out the rivet securing the door trim support bracket to the door frame, then lift the bracket upwards and remove it.

33 Using a sharp knife, carefully release the plastic sealing sheet from the adhesive bead and remove the sheet from the door. If care

14.22 Undo the two window clamp screws (arrowed)

14.23 On Estate/SW models, prise the triangular shaped trim from the door exterior

14.26 Undo the two nuts securing the window guide channel

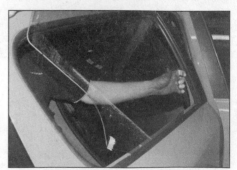

14.29 Lift up the rear end and manoeuvre the window from the door

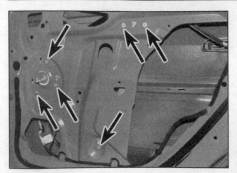

14.37 Drill out the rivets (arrowed) and remove the regulator assembly

14.41 Undo the quarter light frame retaining screw (arrowed)

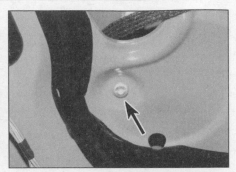

14.43 Drill out the front window guide rivet (arrowed)

is taken, it may just be possible to remove the sheet in one piece and re-use it when refitting.

34 Temporarily reconnect the window switch or refit the regulator handle, and position the window so the attachment to the lifting channel is accessible through the door aperture. Release the clamping screws on the lifting channel bracket **(see illustration 14.22).**

35 Slide the window glass upwards by hand, and tape it to the top of the door frame to secure it in the raised position.

36 Fully lower the window regulator mechanism using the switch or handle.

37 Drill out the rivets, or undo the bolts securing the regulator assembly to the door frame, and manoeuvre it from the door **(see illustration).**

38 Refitting is a reversal of removal, but fit a new sealing sheet to the door if the original was damaged in any way during removal. On completion, refit the interior door handle as described in Section 13.

Front door quarter light

39 Remove the front door window glass as described earlier in this Section.

40 Prise the window guide rubber from the window aperture adjacent to the quarter light pillar.

41 Unscrew the quarter light retaining screw **(see illustration).**

42 Undo the three Torx screws and remove the exterior mirror.

43 Drill out the rivet securing the lower end of the front window guide **(see illustration).**

44 Pull up the exterior weather seal, then pull

15.9 Prise out the clip and pull the strut from the balljoint

the top of the quarter light pillar to the rear, and manoeuvre the quarter light from the door.

45 Refitting is a reversal of removal.

15 Tailgate and support struts – removal and refitting

Tailgate

Removal

1 Remove the tailgate trim panels as described in Section 25.

2 Disconnect the wiring harness connectors at the tailgate internal components, referring to the relevant procedures contained in Chapter 12. Release the grommet from the tailgate and withdraw the wiring harness.

3 Remove the high-level brake light as described in Chapter 12.

4 With the aid of an assistant, suitably support the tailgate, then prise out the support strut spring clips, and pull the struts from the balljoints on the tailgate.

5 Unscrew the two bolts each side securing the hinges to the tailgate, and carefully lift the tailgate from the vehicle.

Refitting

6 If a new tailgate is to be fitted, transfer all serviceable components (lock mechanism, wiper motor, etc) to it, with reference to the relevant procedures in this Chapter, and in Chapter 12.

7 Refitting is a reversal of removal, bearing in mind the following points:

a) If necessary, adjust the rubber buffers to obtain a good fit when the tailgate is shut.

b) If necessary, adjust the position of the tailgate lock and/or hinge bolts within their elongated holes to achieve satisfactory lock operation.

Support struts

Removal

8 Support the tailgate in the open position, with the help of an assistant, or using a stout piece of wood.

9 Using a small screwdriver, release the spring clip, and pull the support strut from its balljoint on the body **(see illustration).**

10 Similarly, release the strut from the balljoint on the tailgate, and withdraw the strut from the vehicle.

Refitting

11 Refitting is a reversal of removal, but ensure the spring clips are correctly engaged.

16 Tailgate lock components – removal and refitting

Tailgate lock

1 Remove the tailgate lower trim panel as described in Section 25.

2 Disconnect the wiring connector.

3 Undo the two lock retaining screws and withdraw the lock **(see illustration).**

4 Refitting is a reversal of removal, but adjust the tailgate lock striker as necessary to obtain satisfactory closure.

Tailgate lock striker

5 Undo the screws and remove the tailgate aperture lower panel (see Section 25) for access to the striker plate retaining bolts.

6 Mark the position of the striker on the body, for use when refitting. Unscrew the two securing bolts, and remove the striker from the body **(see illustration).**

7 Refitting is a reversal of removal. Before tightening the securing bolts, the position of the striker should be altered (the securing bolt holes are elongated) until satisfactory lock operation is obtained. Use the marks made prior to removal, if appropriate.

16.3 Undo the two bolts and remove the lock

16.6 Undo the two bolts and remove the lock striker (arrowed)

16.9 Disconnect the handle wiring plug (Hatchback models)

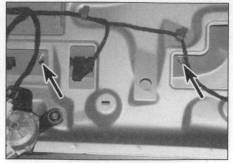

16.11a Undo the four nuts (two left-hand ones arrowed) . . .

Tailgate exterior handle

8 Removal the tailgate lower trim panel as described in Section 25.
9 Disconnect the handle wiring plug **(see illustration)**.

Hatchback models

10 Undo the two handle retaining nuts, and remove the handle assembly complete with seal.

Estate/SW models

11 Undo the four nuts, release the two retaining clips and remove the handle housing/ number plate light cowling from the exterior of the tailgate **(see illustrations)**.
12 Release the two retaining clips, and slide the handle out **(see illustration)**.

All models

13 Refitting is a reversal of removal.

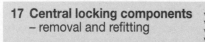

16.11b . . . then release the retaining clips

16.12 Release the clips and slide the handle out

17 Central locking components
– removal and refitting

Control unit

1 The central locking system is controlled by the Built-in Systems Interface (BSI) which is the vehicle central computer controlling the main body electrical system functions. The unit is located under the facia adjacent to the steering column. Refer to Chapter 12 for further information.
2 Should any problems be experienced with the operation of the central locking system or any of the other functions controlled by the BSI, the vehicle should be taken to a Peugeot dealer for diagnostic investigation.

Door lock motor

3 The motor is integral with the door lock assembly. Removal and refitting of the lock assembly is described in Section 13.

Tailgate lock motor

4 Removal of the tailgate lock motor is described as part of the tailgate lock removal and refitting procedure described in Section 16.

Remote control transmitter

Battery renewal

5 When the remote control transmitter battery is nearing the end of its life, an audible signal will be emitted from within the vehicle, accompanied by a message on the instrument panel multi-function screen. The battery should then be renewed with a type CR 2016 (3 volt) battery.
6 Using a small screwdriver, undo the screw, carefully prise the two halves of the transmitter apart, and remove the battery .
7 Fit the new battery and reassemble the transmitter.

Initialisation

8 To initialise the unit after renewing the battery, switch off the ignition, then switch on the ignition and immediately press the locking button. Switch off the ignition and remove the key from the ignition lock.

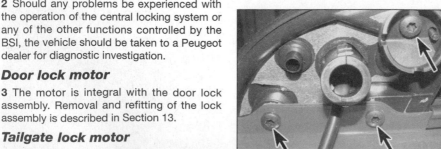

18.4 Undo the three screws (arrowed) and remove the mirror from the door frame

18 Mirrors and mirror glass –
removal and refitting

Exterior mirror assembly

1 Ensure the ignition is turned off.
2 Remove the door inner trim panel as described in Section 12.
3 Disconnect the mirror wiring plugs.
4 Undo the three retaining screws and remove the mirror from the door frame **(see illustration)**.
5 Refitting is a reversal of removal.

Exterior mirror glass

6 Working through the gap at the inner edge of the mirror glass, using a screwdriver, release the ends of the spring clip which secures the glass to the mirror body **(see illustrations)**.

18.6a Insert a screwdriver at the inner edge of the mirror glass . . .

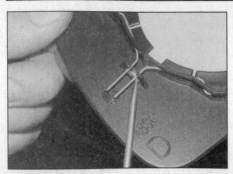

18.6b . . . to release the retaining clip

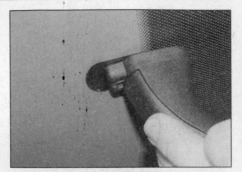

18.10 Slide the mirror up from the base

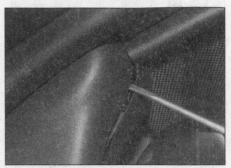

18.11 Prise apart the plastic cover over the mirror

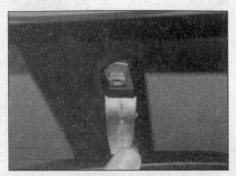

18.12a Push the mirror housing down to release it . . .

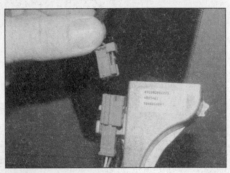

18.12b . . . then disconnect the wiring plug

7 Withdraw the glass, and disconnect the wiring connector (where fitted).

8 Refit the ends of the spring clip to the rear of the mirror glass, ensuring the clip is correctly located in the slots in the rear of the mirror glass.

9 Push the mirror glass into the mirror until the spring clip locks into position in the mirror adjuster groove.

Interior mirror

Basic mirror

10 Slide the mirror up from the base on the windscreen **(see illustration)**.

Anti-dazzle mirror

11 Using a small flat-bladed screwdriver, carefully prise apart the two plastic covers over the mirror base housing, then release the clips and detach the right-hand cover from the housing **(see illustration)**.

12 Push the mirror base housing sharply downwards to release it from the base bonded to the windscreen. Disconnect the wiring plug as the mirror is withdrawn **(see illustrations)**.

All mirrors

13 Refitting is a reversal of removal.

---

19 Windscreen, tailgate and fixed/hinged side window glass – general information

These areas of glass are secured by the tight fit of the weatherstrip in the body aperture, and are bonded in position with a special adhesive. Renewal of such fixed glass is a difficult, messy and time-consuming task, which is considered beyond the scope of the home mechanic. It is difficult, unless

one has plenty of practice, to obtain a secure, waterproof fit. Furthermore, the task carries a high risk of breakage; this applies especially to the laminated glass windscreen. In view of this, owners are strongly advised to have this sort of work carried out by one of the many specialist windscreen fitters.

Note that the rear side hinged windows on the 3-door models is also bonded in at the front edge, and therefore replacement should be entrusted to a specialist.

Rear side window hinge

3-door Hatchback models

1 Remove the C-pillar trim as described in Section 25.

2 Carefully prise the cap from place, then undo the retaining nut at the window end of the hinge **(see illustration)**.

3 Drill out the rivets securing the hinge to the C-pillar **(see illustration)**.

4 Refitting is a reversal of removal.

---

20 Sunroof – general information

The factory-fitted sunroof is of the electric tilt/slide type.

Due to the complexity of the sunroof mechanism, considerable expertise is required to repair, renew or adjust the sunroof components successfully. Removal of the roof first requires the headlining to be removed, which is a tedious operation, and not a task to be undertaken lightly. Any problems with the sunroof should be referred to a Peugeot dealer.

---

21 Body exterior fittings – removal and refitting

Wheel arch liners/mud shields

1 The wheel arch liners are secured by expanding plastic rivets. To remove the liners, push in the centre pins a little, then prise the complete rivet from place. With all the rivets removed, manoeuvre the liner from the wheel

19.2 Prise off the cap and undo the hinge nut (arrowed)

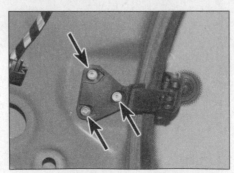

19.3 Drill out the three rivets (arrowed)

21.1a Push in the centre pins a little then prise out the plastic rivets

21.1b The rear liners are also secured by two nuts (arrowed)

22.3 Undo the two screws securing the master cylinder upper reservoir (arrowed)

22.4 Push in the centre pins and prise out the plastic rivet at each end of the scuttle panel trim

22.5 Prise up the centre pins, and lever out the rivets securing the sound insulation material

22.6 Undo the bolt at each end securing the plastic scuttle crossmember

arch. Note that the rear liners are also secured by two nuts each side (see illustrations)

Body trim strips and badges

2 The various body trim strips and badges are held in position with a special adhesive membrane. Removal requires the trim/badge to be heated, to soften the adhesive, and then cut away from the surface. Due to the high risk of damage to the vehicle paintwork during this operation, it is recommended that this task should be entrusted to a Peugeot dealer.

22 Scuttle grille panel –
removal and refitting

Removal

1 Open the bonnet and support it in the highest position.
2 Remove the windscreen wiper arms as described in Chapter 12.
3 Undo the two screws securing the brake/clutch master cylinder reservoir to the crossmember, and move it to one side. There is no need to disconnect the reservoir hose (see illustration).
4 Push in the centre pins a little, then prise up the complete plastic expanding rivet at each end of the panel (see illustration).
5 Prise up the centre pins, then prise out the complete plastic rivets securing the sound insulation material to the scuttle crossmember (see illustration).
6 Undo the bolt at each end securing the

scuttle crossmember, and remove it (see illustration).
7 Pull the scuttle panel up at each end to release it from the windscreen clips, then downwards and forwards to release it from the lower centre windscreen clip.

Refitting

8 Refitting is a reversal of removal.

23 Seats –
removal and refitting

Front seats

⚠ Warning: The front seats are equipped with side airbags built into the outer sides of the seats. Refer to Chapter 12 for the precautions which should be observed when dealing

23.5 Undo the two bolts at the front of the seal rails (arrowed)

with an airbag system. Do not tamper with the airbag unit in any way, and do not attempt to test any airbag system components. Note that the airbag is triggered if the mechanism is supplied with an electrical current (including via an ohmmeter), or if the assembly is subjected to a temperature of greater than 100°C.

1 De-activate the airbag system (see Chapter 12) before attempting to remove the seat.
2 Move the seat fully forwards.
3 Remove the bolts (one on each side) securing the rear of the seat rails to the vehicle floor.
4 Move the seat fully rearwards.
5 Remove the bolts (one bolt on each side) securing the front of the seat frame to the floor (see illustration).
6 Disconnect the seat wiring plugs and remove it from the passenger cabin (see illustration).

23.6 Disconnect the seat wiring plug(s)

23.9 Undo the hinge nut in the centre

23.13 Undo the two bolts and remove the catch from the seat

23.14 Release the clip (arrowed) and lift the seat from place

7 Refitting is a reversal of removal, but observe the following precautions before reconnecting the battery.

  a) *Ensure that there are no occupants in the vehicle, and that there are no loose objects around the vicinity of the seats.*

  b) *Ensure that the ignition is switched off then reconnect the airbag ECM and the battery.*

  c) *Open the driver's door and switch on the ignition. Check that the airbag warning light illuminates briefly then extinguishes.*

  d) *Switch off the ignition.*

  e) *If the airbag warning light does not operate as described in paragraph c), consult a Peugeot dealer before driving the vehicle.*

Rear seats

Hatchback/Estate models seat cushion

8 Lift the front edge first, followed by the rear edge, then push the stays to the side and remove the seat from the vehicle.

Hatchback/Estate models seat backs

9 With the seat cushions folded forward, undo the hinge nut in the centre **(see illustration)**.

10 Fold the seat back forward and undo the bolt securing the hinge to the vehicle floor.

11 Lift the seat back up at the hinge, disengage the outer hinge, and remove it from the vehicle.

12 To remove the rear seat back catch, unclip the inner lower and side edges of the seat cover **(see illustrations 24.13a and 24.13b)**.

13 Undo the two bolts and manoeuvre the catch from the seat back **(see illustration)**.

SW models

14 Fold the seat back forward, followed by the seat base. Release the retaining clip and lift the seat from the passenger cabin **(see illustration)**.

All models

15 Refitting is a reversal of removal, tightening the hinge bolts securely.

---

24 Seat belt components – removal and refitting

Note: *Record the positions of the washers and spacers on the seat belt anchors, and ensure they are refitted in their original positions.*

Front seat belt

⚠️ **Warning: The front seat belt inertia reels are equipped with a pyrotechnic pretensioner mech-anism. Refer to the airbag system precautions contained in Chapter 12 which apply equally to the seat belt pretensioners. Do not tamper with the inertia reel pretensioner unit in any way, and do not attempt to test the unit. Note that the unit is triggered if the mechanism is supplied with an electrical current (including via an ohmmeter), or if the assembly is subjected to a temperature of greater than 100°C.**

1 De-activate the airbag system (which will also de-activate the pyrotechnic pretensioner mechanism) as described in Chapter 12 before attempting to remove the seat belt.

2 If desired, to improve access, remove the relevant front seat as described in Section 23.

3 Remove the B-pillar trim panels as described in Section 25.

4 Disconnect the wiring connector from the inertia reel pretensioner unit.

5 Undo the seat belt lower anchor bolt and the inertia reel anchor bolt, and recover the washers **(see illustration)**.

6 Undo the seat belt upper anchor bolt and withdraw the inertia reel from the door pillar **(see illustration)**. Remove the seat belt assembly from the vehicle.

7 Refitting is a reversal of removal, but observe the following precautions before reconnecting the battery.

  a) *Ensure that there are no occupants in the vehicle, and that there are no loose objects around the vicinity of the seats.*

  b) *Ensure that the ignition is switched off then reconnect the battery.*

  c) *Open the driver's door and switch on the ignition. Check that the airbag warning light illuminates briefly then extinguishes.*

  d) *Switch off the ignition.*

  e) *If the airbag warning light does not operate as described in paragraph c), consult a Peugeot dealer before driving the vehicle.*

  f) *Tighten the seat belt mountings to the specified torque.*

24.5a Undo the seat belt lower anchor bolt (arrowed)

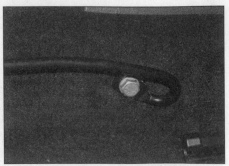

24.5b Prise off the rubber cap and undo the anchor bolt (3-door model)

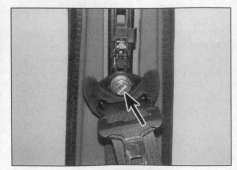

24.6 Seat belt upper anchor bolt (arrowed)

24.9 Undo the seat belt reel nut (arrowed)

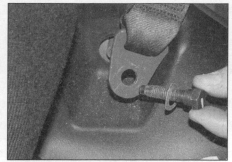

24.10 Undo the seat belt anchor bolt

24.11 Rear seat belt stalk bolt

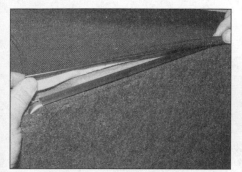

24.13a Unclip the lower . . .

24.13b . . . and side edges of the seat back cover . . .

24.13c . . . to expose the centre seat belt inertia reel

Rear seat belts

Hatchback and Estate models

8 Remove the C-pillar trim as described in Section 25.

9 Undo the nut securing the seat belt inertia reel to the vehicle body (see illustration).

10 Undo the bolt securing the seat belt anchor to the vehicle body (see illustration).

11 To remove the seat belt stalk, fold forward the rear seat cushions, and undo the bolt securing the seat belt stalk to the vehicle body (see illustration).

12 To remove the centre seat belt inertia reel, the seat back cover must be partially removed. Remove the seat back as described in Section 23.

13 Unclip the inner lower and side edges of the seat cover to expose the inertia reel retaining nut (see illustrations).

14 Use a screwdriver to release the seat belt webbing trim piece from the top of the seat, then undo the nut and remove the inertia reel and belt assembly (see illustration).

SW models

15 Remove the luggage compartment side trim as described in Section 25.

16 Undo the bolts securing the upper anchorage points to the C- or D-pillar trims (see illustration).

17 Undo the bolts securing the inertia seat belt reels (see illustrations).

18 To remove the central seat belt inertia reel, pull out the belt a little, then undo the Torx screw at the front of the trim (see illustration).

19 Pull the trim down to release it from the retaining clips at the rear.

20 Undo the bolt securing the inertia reel to the vehicle (see illustration).

21 To remove the seat belt stalks, fold the rear seat backs and cushions forward, then undo the screw securing the trim over the stalk (see illustration).

22 Pull out the base of the trim, then slide it up.

24.14 Unclip the seat belt webbing trim piece

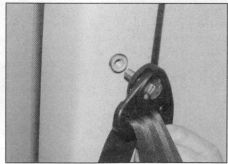

24.16 Undo the seat belt upper anchorage bolt

24.17a Rear seat belt inertia reel bolt (arrowed) . . .

24.17b . . . and middle row seat belt inertia reel bolt (arrowed)

24.18 Undo the Torx screw at the front of the trim (arrowed)

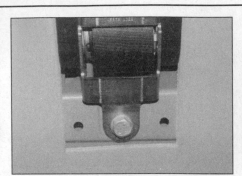

24.20 Rear central inertia reel bolt

24.21 Undo the seat belt stalk trim cover screw (arrowed)

24.23 Undo the seat belt stalk bolt

23 Undo the bolt securing the seat belt stalk (see illustration).

All models

24 Refitting is a reversal of removal. Tighten the mounting bolts to the specified torque.

25.3 Unclip the trim from the A-pillar

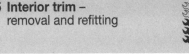

25 Interior trim – removal and refitting

Door inner trim

1 Refer to Section 12.

A-pillar trim

2 Prise the weatherstrip from the front door aperture in the vicinity of the pillar trim.
3 Carefully prise the trim away from the pillar starting at the middle, then pull the top edge from behind the headlining (see illustration).
4 Lift the trim up to disengage the lower locating lugs and remove it from the vehicle.
5 Refitting is a reversal of removal, but ensure that all retaining clips are fully engaged and that the weatherstrip is fully seated.

25.6 Pull the door sill trim up from its clips

Lower B-pillar trim

5-door Hatchback and Estate/SW models

6 Carefully pull the front sill trim upwards to release its retaining clips (see illustration). Release the front edge of the rear sill trim from its retaining clips.
7 Pull the lower end of the trim from its retaining clips, then pull it down to disengage it from the locating lugs at the top (see illustration).

Upper B-pillar trim

3-door Hatchback models

8 Remove the rear side trim panel as described in this Section.
9 Undo the bolt securing the lower seat belt anchor rail to the vehicle.
10 Release the clip at is base, then pull the trim towards the centre of the vehicle, and release it from the retaining clips (see illustration). Feed the seat belt through as the trim is removed.
11 Refitting is a reversal of removal, but ensure that all retaining clips are fully engaged.

5-door Hatchback and Estate/SW models

12 Remove the lower pillar trim as previously described. Undo the seat belt lower anchor bolt, and recover any washer/spacers, noting the fitted positions.
13 Undo the screw/clip securing the lower edge of the trim (see illustration).
14 Pull the trim towards the centre of the

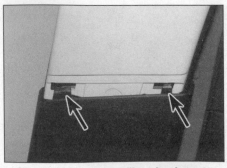

25.7 Pull the centre pillar trim down to disengage the lugs at the top (arrowed)

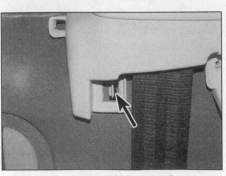

25.10 Release the clip (arrowed) and pull the trim from place

25.13 Undo the screw and clip at the lower edge of the trim (arrowed)

vehicle, and release it from the retaining clips. Feed the seat belt through as the trim is withdrawn **(see illustration)**.

15 Refitting is a reversal of removal, but ensure that all retaining clips are fully engaged.

C-pillar trim

5-door Hatchback models

16 Remove the parcel shelf support as described below.

17 Undo the screw securing the lower edge of the C-pillar/rear door sill trim panel, then carefully pull the pillar trim from the vehicle body to release its retaining clips **(see illustrations)**.

18 Refitting is a reversal of removal.

3-door Hatchback models

19 Remove the parcel shelf support and side trim panel as described below.

20 Carefully pull the trim from the pillar, releasing the push-on retaining clips.

Estate/SW models

21 Remove the parcel shelf support panel as described below.

22 Prise off the plastic cap, then undo the bolt securing the seat belt upper bracket.

23 Undo the screw at the base of the trim, release the retaining clip and carefully pull the trim from the vehicle **(see illustration)**.

All models

24 Refitting is a reversal of removal.

D-pillar trim

Estate/SW models

25 Pull away the rubber weatherstrip from the tailgate aperture adjacent to the D-pillar trim.

26 Carefully pull the D-pillar trim away, releasing the retaining clips as it is removed **(see illustration)**.

27 Refitting is a reversal of removal.

Parcel shelf support panel

Hatchback models

28 Fold the relevant rear seat back forward.

29 Undo the screw and nut securing the parcel shelf support to the body sidemember **(see illustration)**.

30 Disconnect the wiring connectors from the accessories socket and interior light (as applicable) as the support is removed..

Estate/SW models

31 Remove the D-pillar trim as described in this Section. Lift the luggage compartment cover/crossmember from the vehicle.

32 On SW models, prise up the centre pin a little, then lever out the complete plastic expanding rivet at the front of the panel **(see illustration)**.

33 Prise out the air grille at the top of the panel, and undo the two Torx screws in the grille aperture **(see illustration)**.

34 Undo the two screws, release the retaining clips and remove the support panel **(see illustration)**. Disconnect the accessory

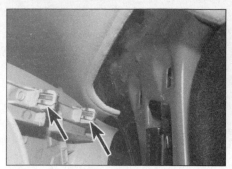

25.14 Release the clips (arrowed) at the upper edge of the trim

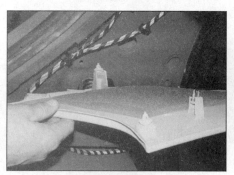

25.17b ... then pull the pillar trim from the retaining clips

socket wiring plug (where fitted) as the panel is withdrawn

All models

35 Refitting is a reversal of removal, but

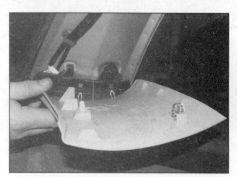

25.26 Pull the trim away from the pillar to release the clips

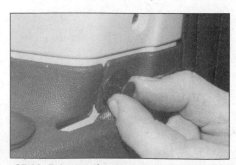

25.32 Prise up the centre pin a little, then prise out the complete expanding plastic rivet

25.17a Undo the screw at the lower edge of the pillar trim . . .

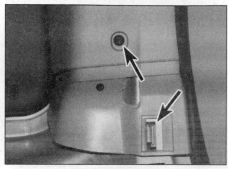

25.23 Undo the screw and release the clip (arrowed)

ensure that all retaining clips are fully engaged, that the seat belt is correctly located in the slot in the support, and the luggage compartment light wiring is correctly routed (where applicable).

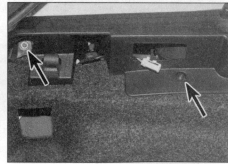

25.29 The parcel shelf is secured by a screw and nut (arrowed)

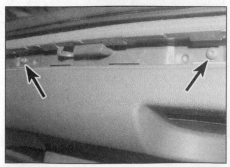

25.33 Prise out the grille and undo the two Torx screws (arrowed)

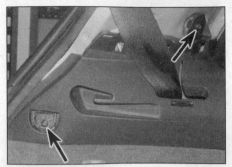

25.34 Undo the two screws (arrowed) and remove the parcel shelf support panel

25.39 Remove the expanding rivet at the lower edge of the trim

25.43 Unclip the lower C-pillar/rear door sill plastic trim

Luggage area lower side trim

36 Remove the parcel shelf support bracket as described previously.

Hatchback models

37 Prise the weatherstrip from the bottom of the tailgate aperture, then undo the screws and remove the tailgate sill trim panel as described in paragraphs 73 to 75.

38 If working on the left-hand side, on vehicles with a satellite navigation system, remove the storage bin cover. Undo the three bolts securing the navigation unit to the body sidemember. Withdraw the unit and disconnect the wiring connectors.

39 Prise up the centre pin, then lever up the complete expanding plastic rivet(s) at the lower edge of the trim **(see illustration)**.

40 Undo the screw securing the upper edge of the lower C-pillar/rear door sill trim panel **(see illustration 25.17a)**. Pull the top edge

of the panel out and manoeuvre the luggage area lower side trim from the vehicle.

Estate models

41 Remove the rear seat back on the relevant side, as described in Section 23.

42 Undo the four Torx screws and remove the lower tailgate aperture trim **(see illustration 25.76)**.

43 Undo the seat belt lower anchorage point, then unclip the rear door sill/lower C-pillar plastic trim **(see illustration)**.

44 Starting at the front of the unit, prise out the luggage compartment light and disconnect the wiring plug.

45 Prise up the centre pins a little, then lever out the two plastic rivets at the front of the side trim, and the one at the rear **(see illustrations)**.

46 Carefully prise the storage compartment trim surround from place **(see illustration)**.

47 Lift the luggage compartment carpet adjacent to the side trim and prise up the centre pins a little, then lever out the two plastic rivets at the base of the side trim **(see illustration)**.

48 Manoeuvre the side trim from the vehicle.

SW models

49 Pull up the fabric cover from the top of the wheel arch to release its retaining clips. Undo the two Torx screws and remove the plastic grab handle from the top of the wheel arch **(see illustration)**.

50 Undo the four Torx screws and remove the lower tailgate aperture trim **(see illustration 25.76)**.

51 Reach behind the side trim and disconnect the luggage compartment light wiring plug.

52 Undo the bolt securing the seat belt lower anchorage point at the front of side trim.

53 Carefully pull the rear of the door sill plastic trim towards the centre of the vehicle to release it from the retaining clip.

54 Lever up the centre pins a little, then prise out the two plastic rivets at the front lower edge of the side trim, and manoeuvre the trim from the vehicle **(see illustration)**.

All models

55 Refitting is a reversal of removal, but ensure that all retaining clips are fully engaged.

Rear side trim panel

3-door models

56 Remove the rear seats as described in Section 23.

25.45a Remove the two plastic expanding rivets at the front of the trim . . .

25.45b . . . and the one at the rear

25.46 Remove the storage compartment trim surround

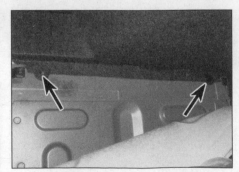

25.47 Lift the carpet and remove the plastic rivets (arrowed)

25.49 Undo the two screws (arrowed) and remove the grab handle

25.54 Remove the two plastic rivets (arrowed) at the front of the side trim

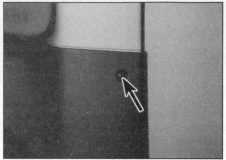

25.58a Undo the screw (arrowed) at the front . . .

25.58b . . . and rear (arrowed) of the side trim

57 Undo the rear seat belt lower anchor bolt.

58 Undo the screw at front and rear of the trim (see illustrations).

59 Open the side hinged rear window, and pull up the weatherstrip adjacent to the trim.

60 Carefully pull the panel from the vehicle body to release the clips at the front and rear edges of the trim, and manoeuvre it from place.

61 Refitting is a reversal of removal, tightening the seat belt mounting bolt to the specified torque.

Tailgate trim

Lower trim – Hatchback models

62 Undo the two screws in the handle recesses (see illustration).

63 Carefully pull the panel away from the tailgate, releasing the retaining clips.

Lower trim – Estate/SW models

64 Remove the upper and side trims.

65 Push in the centre pins a little, then prise out the plastic expansion rivets adjacent to the tailgate lock (see illustration).

66 Carefully pull the panel away from the tailgate, releasing the retaining clips.

Upper trim

67 Open the tailgate and unhook the parcel shelf straps.

68 Pull the panel away from the tailgate at the top corners to release the retaining clips, then remove the panel from the tailgate (see illustration).

Side trims – Hatchback models

69 Remove the upper trim and lower trim as previously described.

70 Undo the two screws (one for each trim) and unclip the panel (see illustration).

Side trims – Estate/SW models

71 Remove the upper trim.

72 Carefully prise the two halves of the side trims from place (see illustration).

Sill trim – Hatchback models

73 Lift the luggage compartment floor panel.

74 Prise up the centre pins, then remove the complete expanding plastic rivets (see illustration).

75 Pull the sill trim panel straight upwards to release the retaining clips, and remove the panel.

Sill trim – Estate models

76 The trim is secured by four Torx screws, two on each side. Undo the screws and remove the trim (see illustration).

25.62 Remove the screw in the handle recess each side

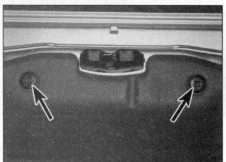

25.65 Push in the centre pins a little, then prise out the plastic rivets (arrowed)

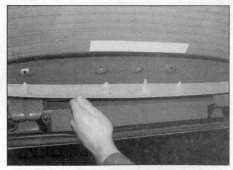

25.68 Pull the upper trim from place to release the clips

25.70 Remove the side trim screw (arrowed)

25.72 Unclip the two halves of the tailgate side trims

25.74 Remove the plastic rivet at each end of the tailgate sill trim (Hatchback models)

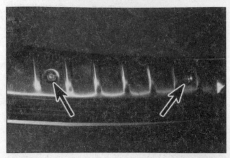

25.76 On Estate/SW models, the tailgate sill trim is secured by two screws each side (arrowed)

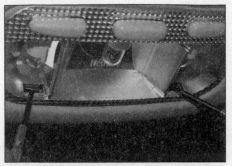

25.80 Lever back the two clips and remove the light unit

25.81 Release the two clips and pull the front of the console down

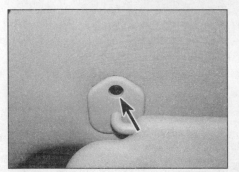

25.83 The sunvisor is secured by a single screw (arrowed)

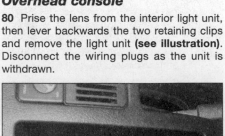

25.88 Undo the screw at each end of the grab handle

All models

77 Refitting is a reversal of removal, but ensure that all retaining clips are fully engaged.

Headling

Note: *Headlining removal requires considerable skill and experience if it is to be carried out without damage, and is therefore best entrusted to a Peugeot dealer or bodywork specialist. A general overview of the procedure is given below for those with the expertise to attempt the operation on a DIY basis.*

78 The headlining is clipped and glued to the roof, and can be withdrawn only once all fittings such as the grab handles, courtesy lights, sun visors, sunroof (if fitted), pillar trim panels, and associated additional panels have been removed. The door, tailgate and sunroof aperture weatherstrips

will also have to be prised clear and any additional screws and clips removed. Once the headlining attachments are released, the adhesive bonding in the centre panels must be broken using a hot air gun and spatula, starting at the front and working rearwards.

79 When refitting, a coat of neoprene adhesive (available from Peugeot dealers) must be applied to the centre panels in the locations noted during removal. Position the headlining carefully and refit all components disturbed during removal. Clean the headlining with soap and water or white spirit on completion.

Overhead console

80 Prise the lens from the interior light unit, then lever backwards the two retaining clips and remove the light unit **(see illustration)**. Disconnect the wiring plugs as the unit is withdrawn.

81 Release the two retaining clips and pull the front of the console down, then pull it forward to disengage the locating lug at the rear **(see illustration)**. Disconnect any wiring plugs as the console is removed.

82 Refitting is a reversal of removal.

Sunvisor

83 The sunvisor is retained by a single screw **(see illustration)**. Prior to removing the sunvisor, remove the interior light unit as described in Paragraph 80, and disconnect the wiring plugs.

84 Remove the sunvisor retaining screw and unclip the mounting from the headlining. Identify the sunvisor vanity light wiring plug at the overhead console, and tie a length of string to it. Withdrawn the sunvisor, pulling the string through the interior light aperture. When the string emerges at the sunvisor mount aperture, untie it from the wiring plug.

85 Tie the length of string to the visor wiring, and pull it through to the interior light aperture. Reconnect the wiring plug.

86 Refit the sunvisor mount to the headlining, and tighten the retaining screw securely.

Grab handle

87 Levering at the top and bottom edges, prise the plastic covers from the front and rear ends of the grab handle.

88 Undo the retaining screws and remove the handle **(see illustration)**.

89 Refitting is a reversal of removal.

26 Centre console – removal and refitting

Removal

1 Remove the facia lower centre panel as described in the next Section.

2 Pull up and remove the storage tray/cup holder from the centre console in front of the handbrake lever **(see illustration)**.

3 Lift up the rubber base from the storage compartment at the rear of the console and undo the retaining screw **(see illustration)**.

4 Prise up and disconnect the passenger's airbag disarming switch **(see illustration)**.

26.2 Pull up the storage tray/cup holder from in front of the handbrake lever

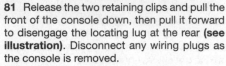

26.3 Undo the screw in the base of the storage compartment

26.4 Prise up and disconnect the airbag disarming switch

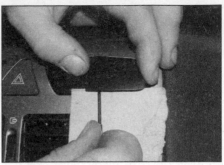

27.2 Carefully prise out the outer switches/blanks above the air vents

27.3 Undo the two screws (arrowed)

5 Raise the front of the console, reach under and disconnect the 12V power socket wiring plug.

6 Lift the console over the handbrake lever, and rearwards out of the vehicle.

Refitting

7 Refitting is a reversal of removal.

27 Facia panel components – removal and refitting

Upper centre panel

Removal

1 Remove the lower centre panel as described in this Section.

2 Carefully prise out the two outer switches (or switch blanks) from the upper edge of the panel, above the centre air vents **(see illustration)**.

3 Undo the two screws from the switch/blank aperture, and the two screws at the lower edge of the panel **(see illustration)**.

4 Carefully pull the panel back and disconnect the various wiring plugs, having first noted their fitted positions.

Refitting

5 Refitting is a reversal of removal.

Lower centre panel

Removal

6 Disconnect the battery as described in Chapter 5A.

7 Remove the radio/cassette/CD player as described in Chapter 12.

8 Remove the ashtray from the panel by pulling it open and depressing the retaining clip **(see illustration)**.

9 Undo the two screws from the ashtray aperture **(see illustration)**.

10 Remove the rubber trim from the storage tray.

11 On models with manual transmission, carefully unclip the gear lever gaiter from the panel. On models with automatic transmission, carefully prise up the selector lever position display trim **(see illustrations)**.

12 Prise the upper section of the panel from place **(see illustration)**.

Refitting

13 Refitting is a reversal of removal, ensuring that the lug at the rear of the panel engages with the locating slot in the centre console **(see illustration)**.

27.8 Press down the retaining clip (arrowed) and remove the ashtray

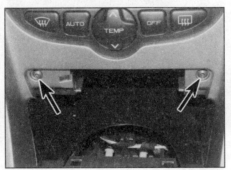

27.9 Undo the two screws (arrowed) above the ashtray aperture

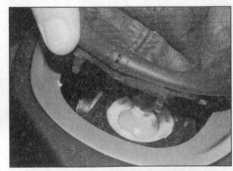

27.11a On manual transmission models, prise up the gear lever gaiter . . .

27.11b . . . or prise up the selector lever position display trim on automatic transmission models

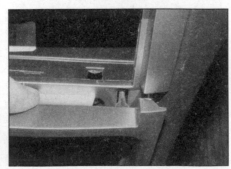

27.12 Starting at the top, prise the panel from place

27.13 Ensure the lug at the rear of the centre panel (arrowed) engages correctly

27.14a Two screws (arrowed) secure the steering column lower shroud

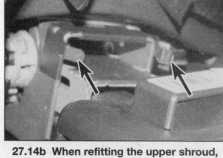

27.14b When refitting the upper shroud, ensure the guide lugs (arrowed) engage correctly

27.16a The trim panel below the steering column is clipped into place . . .

27.16b . . . and the adjacent panel is secured by a screw-type fastener and push-on clips

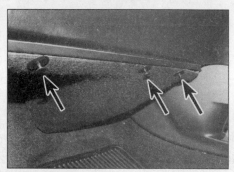

27.17 Footwell trims are retained by plastic expanding rivets (arrowed)

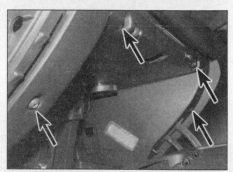

27.21a Open the glovebox and remove the 4 upper screws (arrowed) . . .

Steering column shrouds

Removal

14 Unscrew the two lower steering column shroud securing screws. Unclip and lift off the upper shroud, then remove the lower shroud (see illustrations).

Refitting

15 Refitting is a reversal of removal.

Lower facia panels

Removal

16 The trim panel on the driver's side below the steering column shrouds is clipped into place, and the adjacent panel is removed after undoing the screw fastener a quarter of a turn and pulling it free from the clips. Upon refitting ensure the metal clips are refitted to the panel (see illustrations).

17 The trim panels above the driver's pedals and passenger footwell are secured by expanding plastic rivets. Prise the centre pins up a little, then lever the complete rivets from place (see illustration). When refitting, ensure the front edge of the panel engages with the support bracket.

Refitting

18 Refitting is a reversal of removal.

Instrument panel

19 Refer to Chapter 12.

Passenger side glovebox

Removal

20 Release the three clips, and remove the trim beneath the facia (see illustration 27.17).
21 Open the glovebox, and undo the 7 screws securing the glovebox to the facia and

withdraw it. Disconnect the light wiring plug as the glovebox is withdrawn (see illustrations).
22 If required, the glovebox lock cylinder can be removed by inserting a flat-bladed tool between the lock catch and the glovebox lid, then pressing down on the catch to release the retaining clips (see illustrations). Refit the lock cylinder by pushing it into place.

Refitting

23 Refitting is a reversal of removal.

Multi-function display

Removal

24 Ensure the ignition is switched off.
25 Carefully pull up on the rear edge of the surround, and release it from the facia (see illustration).
26 Disconnect the wiring plug as the unit is withdrawn.

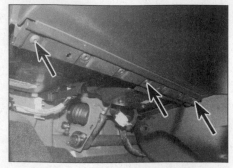

27.21b . . . and the 3 lower screws (arrowed)

27.22a Insert a flat-bladed tool between the lock catch and the glovebox lid . . .

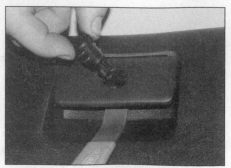

27.22b . . . then press the catch down to release the cylinder

27.25 Pull up the rear of the unit to release the clips (arrowed)

27.34 Press the clip (arrowed) to release interior temperature sensor

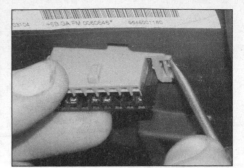

27.39 Depress the clip and push the diagnostic connector in

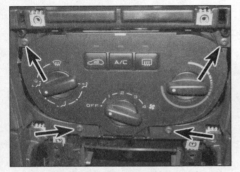

27.40 Undo the 4 screws (arrowed) and push the control panel into the facia

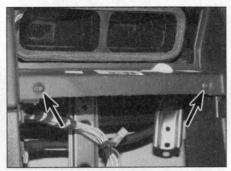

27.41 Undo the two screws (arrowed) in the audio unit aperture

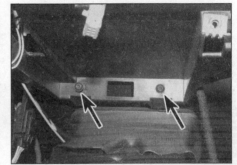

27.44 Undo the two screws (arrowed) at the centre lower section of the facia

27 Refitting is a reversal of removal.

Complete facia assembly

Note: *This is an involved operation entailing the removal of numerous components and assemblies, and the disconnection of a multitude of wiring connectors. Make notes of the location of all disconnected wiring, or attach labels to the connectors, to avoid confusion when refitting.*

Removal

28 Disconnect the battery (see Chapter 5A).
29 Move the front seats as far back as possible. Set the steering wheel in the straight-ahead position, and engage the steering lock.
30 Remove the centre console as described in Section 26.
31 Extract the stud-type plastic clips, using a forked type tool, and remove the lower trim panel from the footwell on both sides.
32 Remove the steering wheel as described in Chapter 10.
33 Remove the following facia panels as described previously in this Section:

a) Facia upper centre panel.
b) Facia lower centre panel.
c) Facia lower panels.
d) Instrument panel.
e) Multi-function display
f) Passenger side glovebox

34 On models fitted automatic climate control, working in the centre air vent aperture, unclip and remove the interior temperature sensor.

Disconnect the wiring plug as it is withdrawn **(see illustration)**.
35 On models fitted with automatic headlights-on function, reach through the multi-function display aperture, and push the light sensor upwards to unclip it. Disconnect the wiring plug.
36 Remove the steering column combination switches as described in Chapter 12.
37 Remove the built-in systems interface (BSI) unit from the facia as described in Chapter 12.
38 Carefully prise out the driver's and passenger's side air vents, then reach through the apertures, and release the facia end cover retaining clip. Carefully pull the end panels from the facia, releasing the retaining clips as the panel is withdrawn.
39 Prise out and disconnect the headlamp height adjustment control, then depress the

27.46 Facia screw (arrowed) in the multi-function display aperture

retaining clips and press in the diagnostic connector **(see illustration)**. Release their wiring loom retaining clip adjacent to the connector aperture.
40 Undo the four screws surrounding the heater control panel trim, release the two retaining clips and push the control panel forward 'into' the facia **(see illustration)**.
41 Working in the audio unit aperture, undo the two screws securing the facia to the heater/air conditioner housing **(see illustration)**.
42 Undo the two screws, release the retaining stud, and remove the footwell central kick panels from the driver's and passenger's side.
43 Disconnect the two rear air ducts from the heater housing.
44 Undo the two screws at the centre lower section of the facia **(see illustration)**.
45 Working as described in Chapter 10, undo the steering column upper mounting nuts and lower mounting bolts and lower the column from its location. Note that it is not necessary to disconnect the steering column universal joint.
46 Undo the Torx screw visible thought the multi-function display aperture **(see illustration)**.
47 Undo the bolt securing the facia bracket to the floor centre section on the passenger's side, and the bolt accessible through the instrument panel aperture **(see illustration)**.
48 Working through the apertures at each end of the facia, unscrew the two bolts each side securing the facia crossmember.

27.47 Facia screw (arrowed) in the instrument panel aperture

49 Note their fitted positions and harness routing, then disconnect the facia wiring plugs. Take note of the location of the various wiring harness retaining clips, to aid refitment.
50 With the help of an assistant, lift the facia from place, and remove it from the vehicle.

Refitting

51 Refitting is a reversal of removal ensuring that all wiring is correctly reconnected and all mountings securely tightened.

Chapter 12
Body electrical systems

Contents

Degrees of difficulty

Easy, suitable for novice with little experience	**Fairly easy,** suitable for beginner with some experience	**Fairly difficult,** suitable for competent DIY mechanic	**Difficult,** suitable for experienced DIY mechanic 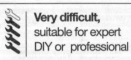	**Very difficult,** suitable for expert DIY or professional

Specifications

General

System type .... 12 volt negative earth

Bulbs

	Type	Wattage
Direction indicator light	Bayonet	21
Direction indicator side repeater	Push-fit	5
Front ashtray light......................................	Push-fit	1.2
Front foglight	H1	55
Front sidelights...	Push-fit	5
Glovebox light	Push-fit	5
Headlights:		
Main beam bulbs	H1	55
Dip beam bulbs	H7	55
High-level stop-light.....................................	Push-fit	5
Interior/courtesy lights	Push-fit	5
Luggage compartment light...............................	Push-fit	5
Number plate light	Push-fit	5
Rear foglight...	Bayonet	21
Reversing light	Bayonet	21
Stop-light	Bayonet	21
Tail light...	Bayonet	5
Vanity lights	Festoon	3

Torque wrench setting	**Nm**	**lbf ft**
Airbag control unit retaining nuts..........................	8	6

1 General information

Warning: Before carrying out any work on the electrical system, read through the precautions given in 'Safety first!' at the beginning of this manual, and in Chapter 5A.

The electrical system is of 12 volt negative earth type. Power for the lights and all electrical accessories is supplied by a lead-acid type battery, which is charged by the alternator.

Many of the body electrical systems are controlled by individual electronic control units (ECUs) and these are in turn controlled by a main ECU known as a Built-in Systems Interface (BSI). The various ECUs and the BSI exchange data with each other via a multiplex network. The multiplex network is a two-wire system linking the BSI with the system ECUs and is termed by Peugeot as CAN (controlled area network) and VAN (vehicle area network). Essentially this means that the BSI and the ECUs controlling the 'comfort' systems, safety systems, security systems, and entertainment systems in the vehicle, are all inter-connected via Vehicle Area Networks **(see illustration)**.

An ECU connected to the multiplex network only receives some of the data needed for it to operate directly, with the remaining data being supplied by the other ECUs on the network. Because the ECUs share information via the network, several ECUs can control the operation of the same system. Also, one ECU can control several systems in an autonomous manner. The BSI is the manager of this information interchange as well as also being responsible for the control of certain vehicle systems itself. The BSI has a full diagnostic capability whereby any fault in any of the ECUs on the multiplex network can be traced using diagnostic equipment connected to the vehicle diagnostic connector. Should any fault develop with a system on the network, have the self-diagnosis facility interrogated by a Peugeot dealer or suitably-equipped specialist.

This Chapter covers repair and service procedures for the various electrical components not associated with the engine. Information on the battery, alternator and starter motor can be found in Chapter 5A.

It should be noted that, prior to working on any component in the electrical system, the battery should first be disconnected, to prevent the possibility of electrical short-circuits (see Chapter 5A).

2 Electrical fault finding – general information

Note: *Refer to the precautions given in 'Safety first!' and in Chapter 5A before starting work. The following tests relate to testing of the main electrical circuits, and should not be used to test delicate electronic circuits (such as anti-lock braking systems), particularly where an electronic control unit (ECU) or multiplexing is used (see Section 1).*

General

1 A typical electrical circuit consists of an electrical component, any switches, relays, motors, fuses, fusible links or circuit breakers related to that component, and the wiring and connectors which link the component to both the battery and the chassis. To help to pinpoint a problem in an electrical circuit, wiring diagrams are included at the end of this Chapter.

2 Before attempting to diagnose an electrical fault, first study the appropriate wiring diagram, to obtain a more complete understanding of the components included in the particular circuit concerned. The possible sources of a fault can be narrowed down by noting whether other components related to the circuit are operating properly. If several components or circuits fail at one time, the problem is likely to be related to a shared fuse or earth connection.

3 Electrical problems usually stem from simple causes, such as loose or corroded connections, a faulty earth connection, a blown fuse, a melted fusible link, or a faulty relay (refer to Section 3 for details of testing relays). Visually inspect the condition of all fuses, wires and connections in a problem circuit before testing the components. Use the wiring diagrams to determine which terminal connections will need to be checked, in order to pinpoint the trouble-spot.

4 The basic tools required for electrical fault finding include a circuit tester or voltmeter; an ohmmeter (to measure resistance); a battery and set of test leads; and a jumper wire, preferably with a circuit breaker or fuse incorporated, which can be used to bypass suspect wires or electrical components. Before attempting to locate a problem with test instruments, use the wiring diagram to determine where to make the connections.

5 To find the source of an intermittent wiring fault (usually due to a poor or dirty connection, or damaged wiring insulation), a 'wiggle' test can be performed on the wiring. This involves wiggling the wiring by hand, to see if the fault occurs as the wiring is moved. It should be possible to narrow down the source of the fault to a particular section of wiring. This method of testing can be used in conjunction with any of the tests described in the following sub-Sections.

6 Apart from problems due to poor connect-

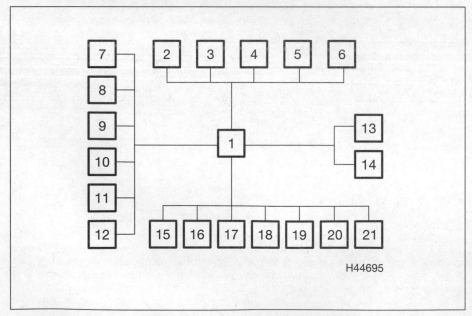

1.1 Multiplexing – Vehicle Area Network (VAN)

1 Built-in Systems Interface (BSI)	*11 ESP control unit*
2 Electric windows	*12 Automatic transmission ECU*
3 Fuel additive ECU (2.0 litre diesel with particulate filter)	*13 Airbag ECU*
4 Anti-theft alarm	*14 Fusebox*
5 Central locking transmitter	*15 Air conditioning ECU*
6 Sunroof motor	*16 Instrument cluster*
7 Power steering pump	*17 CD player*
8 Engine management ECU	*18 Multi-function display*
9 Steering column combination switches	*19 Parking aid ECU*
10 ABS control unit	*20 Radio*
	21 Radio/telephone ECU

H44695

2.20a Earth connection adjacent to the left-hand gearbox mounting . . .

2.20b . . . in front of the engine compartment fuse/relay box . . .

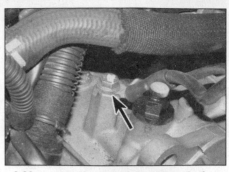

2.20c . . . on the top of the transmission (arrowed)

ions, two basic types of fault can occur in an electrical circuit – open-circuit, or short-circuit.

7 Open-circuit faults are caused by a break somewhere in the circuit, which prevents current from flowing. An open-circuit fault will prevent a component from working, but will not cause the relevant circuit fuse to blow.

8 Short-circuit faults are caused by a 'short' somewhere in the circuit, which allows the current flowing in the circuit to 'escape' along an alternative route, usually to earth. Short-circuit faults are normally caused by a breakdown in wiring insulation, which allows a feed wire to touch either another wire, or an earthed component such as the bodyshell. A short-circuit fault will normally cause the relevant circuit fuse to blow. **Note:** *As an aid to economy and to prevent battery discharge, certain functions of the electrical system can only be used for 30 minutes after the engine has been stopped. Bear this in mind when tracing power supply faults on these systems.*

  Functions affected:
  Windscreen wipers.
  Electric windows.
  Sunroof.
  Courtesy lights.
  Audio equipment.

After this period the BSI (Built-in Systems Interface) cuts the power to these circuits. To restore power, start the engine.

It is also possible for the BSI to turn off certain functions (heater blower, heated rear window) depending on the state of charge of the battery. When tracing a fault, ensure the battery is in a good state of charge.

Finding an open-circuit

9 To check for an open-circuit, connect one lead of a voltmeter to either the negative battery terminal or a known good earth.

10 Connect the other lead to a connector in the circuit being tested, preferably nearest to the battery or fuse.

11 Switch on the circuit, bearing in mind that some circuits are live only when the ignition switch is moved to a particular position.

12 If voltage is present (indicated either by the tester bulb lighting or a voltmeter reading, as applicable), this means that the section of the circuit between the relevant connector and the battery is problem-free.

13 Continue to check the remainder of the circuit in the same fashion.

14 When a point is reached at which no voltage is present, the problem must lie between that point and the previous test point with voltage. Most problems can be traced to a broken, corroded or loose connection.

Finding a short-circuit

15 To check for a short-circuit, first disconnect the load(s) from the circuit (loads are the components which draw current from a circuit, such as bulbs, motors, heating elements, etc).

16 Remove the relevant fuse from the circuit, and connect a circuit tester or voltmeter to the fuse connections.

17 Switch on the circuit, bearing in mind that some circuits are live only when the ignition switch is moved to a particular position.

18 If voltage is present (indicated either by the tester bulb lighting or a voltmeter reading, as applicable), this means that there is a short-circuit.

19 If no voltage is present, but the fuse still blows with the load(s) connected, this indicates an internal fault in the load(s).

Finding an earth fault

20 The battery negative terminal is connected to 'earth' – the metal of the engine/transmission and the car body – and most systems are wired so that they only receive a positive feed, the current returning via the metal of the car body. This means that the component mounting and the body form part of that circuit. Loose or corroded mountings can therefore cause a range of electrical faults, ranging from total failure of a circuit, to a puzzling partial fault. In particular, lights may shine dimly (especially when another circuit sharing the same earth point is in operation), motors (eg, wiper motors or the radiator cooling fan motor) may run slowly, and the operation of one circuit may have an apparently-unrelated effect on another. Note that on many vehicles, earth straps are used between certain components, such as the engine/transmission and the body, usually where there is no metal-to-metal contact between components, due to flexible rubber mountings, etc **(see illustrations).**

21 To check whether a component is properly earthed, disconnect the battery, and connect one lead of an ohmmeter to a known good earth point. Connect the other lead to the wire or earth connection being tested. The resistance reading should be zero; if not, check the connection as follows.

22 If an earth connection is thought to be faulty, dismantle the connection, and clean back to bare metal both the bodyshell and the wire terminal or the component earth connection mating surface. Be careful to remove all traces of dirt and corrosion, then use a knife to trim away any paint, so that a clean metal-to-metal joint is made. On reassembly, tighten the joint fasteners securely; if a wire terminal is being refitted, use serrated washers between the terminal and the bodyshell, to ensure a clean and secure connection. When the connection is remade, prevent the onset of corrosion in the future by applying a coat of petroleum jelly or silicone-based grease, or by spraying on (at regular intervals) a proprietary ignition sealer or water-dispersant lubricant.

3 Fuses and relays – general information

Fuses

1 Fuses are designed to break a circuit when a predetermined current is reached, in order to protect the components and wiring which could be damaged by excessive current flow. Any excessive current flow will be due to a fault in the circuit, usually a short-circuit (see Section 2).

2 The majority of fuses are located behind the glovebox lid on the passenger's side of the facia. Additional fuses (including the larger, higher-rated fuses) are located in the fuse/relay box on the left-hand side of the engine compartment.

3 To gain access to the facia fuses, open the glovebox, rotate the cover fastener through 90 degrees then remove the cover from the facia **(see illustrations).** To gain access to the fuses in the engine compartment, simply unclip the cover from the fuse/relay box.

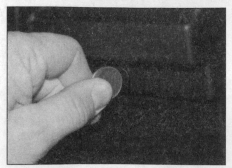

3.3a Rotate the fastener 90° . . .

3.3b . . . and pull down the cover . . .

3.3c . . . to access the main fusebox

3.5 Pull the fuse from its socket

3.8 The cooling fan relays are located in the front panel

4 A list of circuits each fuse protects is given on the fusebox cover.

5 To remove a fuse, first switch off the circuit concerned (or the ignition), then pull the fuse out of its terminals **(see illustration)**. The wire within the fuse should be visible; if the fuse has blown it will be broken or melted.

6 Always renew a fuse with one of the correct rating, never use a fuse with a different rating from that specified. The fuse rating is stamped on the top of the fuse, the fuses are also colour-coded as follows. Refer to the wiring diagrams for details of the fuse ratings and the circuits protected.

Colour	Rating
Orange	5A
Red	10A
Blue	15A
Yellow	20A
Clear or white	25A
Green	30A

4.5a Slacken the switch assembly retaining clamp bolt . . .

7 Never renew a fuse more than once without tracing the source of the trouble. If the new fuse blows immediately, find the cause before renewing it again; a short to earth as a result of faulty insulation is most likely. Where a fuse protects more than one circuit, try to isolate the fault by switching on each circuit in turn (where possible) until the fuse blows again. Always carry a supply of spare fuses of each relevant rating on the vehicle; a spare of each rating should be clipped into the fusebox.

Relays

8 The majority of relay functions are incorporated into the built-in system interface (BSI) unit (see Section 23). Other relays are located in the fuse/relay box in the engine compartment and the cooling fan relay(s) is/are located in front panel **(see illustration)**.

9 If a circuit or system controlled by a relay

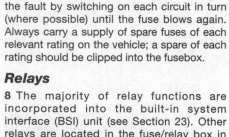

4.5b . . . then carefully lift the retaining catches

develops a fault and the relay is suspect, operate the system. If the relay is functioning, it should be possible to hear it 'click' as it is energised. If this is the case, the fault lies with the components or wiring of the system. If the relay is not being energised, then either the relay is not receiving a main supply or a switching voltage, or the relay itself is faulty. Testing is by the substitution of a known good unit, but be careful – while some relays are identical in appearance and in operation, others look similar but perform different functions.

10 To remove a relay, first ensure that the relevant circuit is switched off. The relay can then simply be pulled out from the socket, and pushed back into position.

---

4 Switches –
removal and refitting

Note: *Disconnect the battery before removing any switch, and reconnect the lead after refitting the switch (see Chapter 5A).*

Ignition switch

1 Refer to Chapter 10.

Steering column switches

2 Remove the driver's airbag as described in Section 22.

3 Remove the steering wheel as described in Chapter 10.

4 Remove the steering column lower and upper shrouds as described in Section 27 of Chapter 11.

5 If the switch assembly is to be refitted, immobilise the airbag rotary contact disc with adhesive tape. Note that as long as the wheels are in the straight-ahead position, the contact disc should lock in position. Slacken the switch assembly retaining clamp, then using a small screwdriver, carefully prise the retaining catches away from the column and lift the switch assembly from place **(see illustrations)**. Disconnect the wiring plugs as the assembly is withdrawn.

Caution: Take great care not damage the switch assembly retaining catches.

6 If required, the cruise control switch and

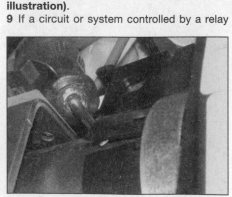

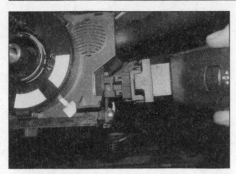

4.6 Unclip and slide out the cruise control/ radio remote switch

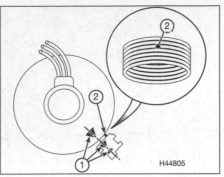

4.11 Align the three triangles (1), with the contact needle in the third groove (2)

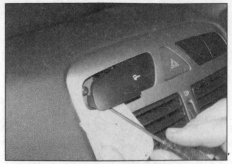

4.15a Working at the top and bottom edges, carefully prise the switch from the panel

remote radio control switch can be unclipped from the combination switch assembly **(see illustration)**.

7 Although refitting is a reversal of removal, the airbag contact unit built into the switch assembly must be set in the correct position as follows:

8 Ensure the wheels are in the straight-ahead position.

8 If refitting the existing switch assembly, simply remove the adhesive tape applied during removal.

10 If the new switch assemblies are manufactured by Delphi a setting-up procedure must be carried out. Units supplied by other manufacturers are supplied with the contact ring immobilised in the correct position by a self-adhesive label, which should be removed just prior to steering wheel refitment.

11 The following procedure applies to new or used Delphi units. Press in the centre collar of the rotary contact unit, then gently rotate the collar clockwise until it comes to a stop. Turn the collar 2.5 revolutions anti-clockwise until the three triangles are in line, and the contact needle is in the third groove **(see illustration)**. If the steering wheel is not to be fitted immediately, immobilise the contact in this position with adhesive tape.

Caution! Do not turn the collar anti-clockwise until the 'stop' has been reached – the unit will be irreparably damaged.

Note: *If a new switch assembly if fitted to a vehicle with ESP (Electronic Stability Programme) the unit must be initialised using dedicated test equipment. Entrust this task to a Peugeot dealer or suitably-equipped specialist.*

Audio unit control stalk/ cruise control

12 Undo the two screws securing the steering column lower shroud in place, then lift the rear edge of the upper shroud and disengage the lugs at the front edge (see Section 27 of Chapter 11).

13 Release the clips and slide the switch from position, disconnecting the wiring plug(s) as the unit is withdrawn **(see illustration 4.6)**.

14 Refitting is the reversal of removal.

Facia-mounted switches

15 The facia-mounted switches for the central locking, alarm and ESP, are located above the central air vents. To remove one of these switches, using a plastic or wooden spatula, working at the top and lower edges, gently prise the switch from the panel, disconnecting the wiring plug as the switch is withdrawn. The headlight height control switch is prised from place after first pulling away the covering trim panel **(see illustrations)**. Take care not to mark the surrounding trim.

16 To remove the hazard-warning switch, remove the facia upper centre panel as described in Section 27 of Chapter 11. Prise out the switch/blanking plate either side of the hazard switch, release the retaining clips and remove the switch **(see illustration)**.

17 Refitting is the reverse of removal.

4.15b Undo the screw, pull the panel away . . .

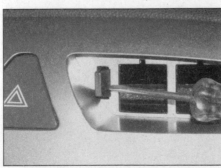

4.16 To remove the hazard light switch, release the retaining clip each side

Heating/ventilation control

18 The switches are an integral part of the heater/ventilation control panel, and cannot be renewed separately. If any switch is faulty, the complete control panel must be renewed – refer to Chapter 3 for details.

Stop-light switch

19 Refer to Chapter 9.

Handbrake warning light switch

20 Remove the centre console as described in Chapter 11.

21 Disconnect the switch wiring connector, the push the switch to the rear, and lift up the front edge. Remove the switch **(see illustration)**.

22 Refitting is the reverse of removal.

4.15c . . . and prise the headlight levelling switch out

4.21 Handbrake warning switch

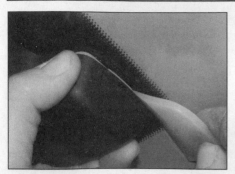

4.29 Squeeze the plastic cover, and prise it off at the same time

4.31 Prise the retaining clips open to the 45° position

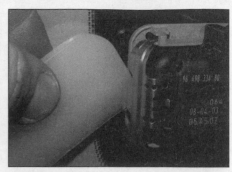

4.32 Carefully lever the sensor from place

Courtesy light switch

23 The courtesy light switches are an integral part of the door lock assemblies. Refer to Chapter 11 for door lock removal and refitting details.

Luggage compartment light switch

24 The luggage compartment light switch function is integral with the tailgate lock assembly. For tailgate lock removal, refer to Chapter 11.

Windscreen wiper rain sensor

Models without brightness sensor

25 Disconnect the wiring plug from the sensor, located on the windscreen.
26 Disconnect the wiring connector then carefully release the side retaining clips and remove the rain sensor from the windscreen.
Caution: Do not touch the rain sensor lens or the windscreen glass in the area of the sensor. These areas must be kept spotlessly clean if the sensor is to function correctly.
27 Refitting is the reverse of removal, ensuring the sensor is securely retained by its securing the clips in the following order:
a) *Fit the clip opposite the connector.*
b) *Engage the clip on the right-hand side (by the chamfer).*
c) *Fully clip-in the left-hand clip.*
d) *Fully clip-in the right-hand clip.*
If a new sensor is being fitted, it will be necessary to remove the protective film from the sensor prior to installation. On completion, check the sensor operation by spraying the

screen with water (wiper stalk in the auto position).

Models with brightness sensor

28 Ensure the ignition is switch off. Remove the interior mirror as described in Chapter 11.
29 Clamp the sensor protector between fingers and thumb, then slide a plastic spatula between the protector and the windscreen. Remove the protector **(see illustration)**.
30 Unplug the sensor connector.
31 Using a small screwdriver, carefully prise away the spring clip from the ends of the sensor assembly to the 45 degrees position **(see illustration)**.
32 Levering (from the side in the centre) between the sensor and the base, lever the sensor until the assembly detaches from the windscreen **(see illustration)**.
Caution: Do not touch the rain sensor lens or the windscreen glass in the area of the sensor. These areas must be kept spotlessly clean if the sensor is to function correctly. Take great care not to damage the sensor 'cushion'.
33 Refitting is a reversal of removal. If a new sensor is being fitted, it will be necessary to remove the protective film from the sensor prior to installation. make sure there are no air bubbles between the sensor and the windscreen. On completion, check the sensor operation by spraying the screen with water (wiper stalk in the auto position).

Glovebox illumination switch

34 The switch is integral with the light. Remove the light as described in Section 6.

Sunroof switch

35 Prise out the lower edge of the interior light lens, from the overhead console. Remove the light, disconnecting the wiring plug as the unit is withdrawn. Disconnect the sunvisor wiring plug.
36 Working through the light aperture, release the two retaining clips, and slide the console downwards to release it.
37 Remove the switch from the console assembly.
38 Refitting is a reversal of removal.

5 Bulbs (exterior lights) – renewal

General

1 Whenever a bulb is renewed, note the following points:
a) *Remember that, if the light has just been in use, the bulb may be extremely hot.*
b) *Always check the bulb contacts and holder, ensuring that there is clean metal-to-metal contact between the bulb and its live(s) and earth. Clean off any corrosion or dirt before fitting a new bulb.*
c) *Wherever bayonet-type bulbs are fitted (see Specifications), ensure that the live contact(s) bear firmly against the bulb contact.*
d) *Always ensure that the new bulb is of the correct rating, and that it is completely clean before fitting it; this applies particularly to headlight/foglight bulbs (see below).*

Headlight

2 To improve access to the right-hand headlight, remove the plastic cover from the washer fluid reservoir. The cover is secured by two expanding plastic rivets. Push in the centre pins a little, then prise the complete rivet from place **(see illustration)**.
3 The main beam and dipped beam bulbs are separate from each other. Reach behind the headlamp, and turn the relevant beam's protective cover 90 degrees anti-clockwise and remove it **(see illustration)**.

5.2 The cover over the reservoirs is retained by two plastic rivets (arrowed)

5.3 Turn the headlight bulb protective cover 90° anti-clockwise

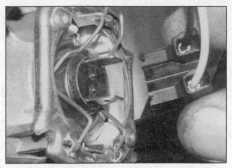

5.4 Disconnect the headlight bulb wiring plug

5.5a Release the retaining clip . . .

5.5b . . . and remove the bulb

5.11a Squeeze together the retaining clips (arrowed), pull the bulbholder to the rear . . .

5.11b . . . and pull the bulb from the holder

4 Disconnect the wiring plug from the bulb **(see illustration)**.

5 Release the bulb retaining clip, and withdraw the bulb **(see illustrations)**.

6 When handling the new bulb, use a tissue or clean cloth to avoid touching the glass with the fingers; moisture and grease from the skin can cause blackening and rapid failure of this type of bulb. If the glass is accidentally touched, wipe it clean using methylated spirit.

7 Install the new bulb, ensuring that its locating tabs are correctly seated in the light cut-outs, and secure it in position with the retaining clip.

8 Reconnect the wiring plug, and refit the protective cover with the arrow upwards, then rotate it 90 degrees clockwise.

9 Refit the plastic cover over the washer fluid reservoir.

Front sidelight

10 To improve access to the right-hand headlight, remove the plastic cover from the

washer fluid reservoir. The cover is secured by two expanding plastic rivets. Push in the centre pins a little, then prise the complete rivets from place **(see illustration 5.2)**.

11 Reach behind the headlight and rotate the inner protective cover 90 degrees anti-clockwise, Squeeze together the retaining clips and pull the bulbholder to the rear. The bulb is of the capless (push-fit) type, and can be removed by simply pulling it out of the holder **(see illustrations)**.

12 Refitting is the reverse of the removal procedure, ensuring that the bulbholder seal is in good condition.

Front foglight

Early models

13 To improve access to the right-hand head-light, remove the plastic cover from the washer fluid reservoir. The cover is secured by two expanding plastic rivets. Push in the centre pins a little, then prise the complete

rivets from place and release the side clip **(see illustration 5.2)**.

14 Rotate the cover anti-clockwise and remove it **(see illustration 5.3)**.

15 Disconnect the wiring connector from the foglight bulb.

16 Unhook the end of the bulb retaining clip and release it from the rear of the foglight unit **(see illustration)**. Withdraw the bulb.

17 When handling the new bulb, use a tissue or clean cloth to avoid touching the glass with the fingers; moisture and grease from the skin can cause blackening and rapid failure of this type of bulb. If the glass is accidentally touched, wipe it clean using methylated spirit.

18 Install the new bulb, ensuring that its locating tabs are correctly seated in the light cut-outs. Secure the bulb in position with the retaining clip then reconnect the wiring connector.

19 Ensure the seal is in good condition then securely refit the cover to the rear of the light unit. Where necessary, refit the washer fluid reservoir plastic cover.

Later models

20 On later models, the front foglights are located in the front bumper. Chock the rear wheels then jack up the front of the vehicle and support it on axle stands (see *Jacking and vehicle support*). Remove the engine undershield. For access to the right-hand foglight, it is necessary to release the front of the wheelarch liner by removing the fasteners.

21 Reach up under the front bumper and disconnect the wiring from the foglight bulbholder.

22 Turn the bulbholder 90° anticlockwise and withdraw it from the rear of the foglight, then remove the bulb **(see illustration)**.

23 When handling the new bulb, use a tissue or clean cloth to avoid touching the glass with the fingers; moisture and grease from the skin can cause blackening and rapid failure of this type of bulb. If the glass is accidentally touched, wipe it clean using methylated spirit.

24 Fit the new bulb using a reversal of the removal procedure.

Front direction indicator

25 To improve access to the right-hand headlight, remove the plastic cover from the washer fluid reservoir. The cover is secured by two plastic expanding rivets. Push in the

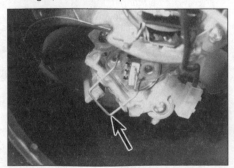

5.16 Release the foglight bulb retaining clip (arrowed)

5.22 Removing the bulbholder from the foglight

5.26a Rotate the bulbholder anti-clockwise . . .

5.26b . . . then press in the bulb and rotate it anti-clockwise to remove it

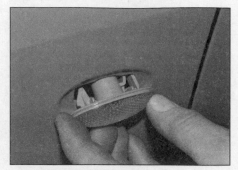

5.28 Push the side repeater to the rear, and ease it out of the wing

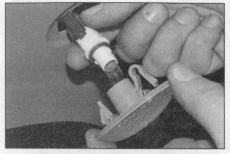

5.29a Rotate the bulbholder anti-clockwise and pull it from the light . . .

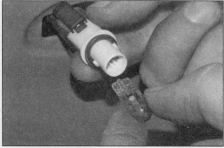

5.29b . . . then pull the capless bulb out

centre pins a little, then prise the complete rivets from place (see illustration 5.2).

26 Rotate the bulbholder anti-clockwise, and free it from the rear of the headlight unit. The bulb is a bayonet-fit in the holder, and can be removed by pressing it in and rotating it anti-clockwise (see illustrations).

27 Refitting is the reverse of the removal procedure, ensuring that the bulbholder seal is in good condition.

Side repeater

28 Push the light unit to the rear to free its front retaining clip, then ease it out from the front wing (see illustration).

29 Rotate the bulbholder anti-clockwise and free it from the rear of the light. The bulb is of the capless (push-fit) type, and can be removed by simply pulling it out of the holder (see illustrations).

30 Refitting is a reversal of the removal procedure.

Rear light cluster

Hatchback models

31 Lift up the luggage compartment carpet in the area of the tailgate sill. Push in the centre pins a little, then prise out the complete rivets and lift the tailgate sill trim panel upwards (see illustration).

32 Move the side trim panel to one side to access the bulbholder.

Estate/SW models

33 Remove the relevant rear light unit as described in Section 7.

All models

34 Squeeze together the retaining tabs and remove the bulbholder assembly (see illustration).

35 All the bulbs have bayonet fittings. The relevant bulb can be removed by pressing it in and rotating it anti-clockwise (see illustration).

36 Refitting is the reverse of removal, ensuring the light unit and bulbholder seals are in good condition.

High-level stop-light

37 Remove the light unit (see Section 7).

38 Release the retaining clips and detach the light unit from the bulbholder (Hatchback models) or rotate the bulbholders 90 degrees anti-

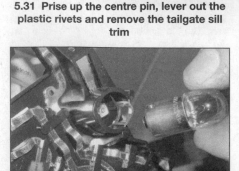

5.31 Prise up the centre pin, lever out the plastic rivets and remove the tailgate sill trim

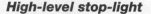

5.34 Squeeze together the tabs (arrowed) and remove the bulbholder assembly

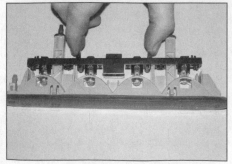

5.35 Press in and rotate the bulb anti-clockwise to remove

5.38a On Hatchback models, squeeze together the retaining clips . . .

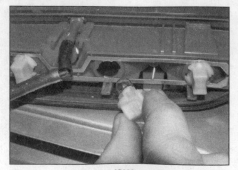

5.38b . . . on Estate/SW models rotate the bulbholder anti-clockwise

5.40 Carefully prise the light lens from place

5.42 Prise the side of the lens out to release it from the clip

3 Carefully prise the lens from the light. The bulb is of the capless (push-fit) type, and can be removed by simply pulling it out of the bulbholder **(see illustrations)**.
4 Refitting is the reverse of the removal procedure

Instrument panel lights

5 The instrument panel and warning lights are illuminated by integral LEDs. It is not possible to renew them independently of the panel. Instrument panel renewal is described in Section 9.

Heating/ventilation control illumination

6 Remove the heater control panel as described in Chapter 3.
7 Rotate the bulbholder anti-clockwise and remove it. The capless bulb simply pulls from the bulbholder **(see illustration)**.

Multi-function display illumination

8 Remove the multi-function display as described in Section 10.
9 Rotate the bulbholders anti-clockwise and remove them. The capless bulbs simply pull from the bulbholder **(see illustration)**.

Ashtray illumination

10 Unclip the ashtray and remove it from the centre console.
11 Free the bulbholder from the console and pull the bulb out from its holder **(see illustration)**.

clockwise. Each bulb is of the capless (push-fit) type, and can be removed by simply pulling it out of the bulbholder **(see illustrations)**.
39 Refitting is the reverse of removal. Do not overtighten the light unit retaining nuts on Hatchback models, as the plastic is easily broken.

Number plate light

Hatchback models

40 Using a small flat-bladed screwdriver, carefully prise the end of the lens downwards, and remove it. The bulb is of the capless (push-fit) type, and can be removed by simply pulling it out of the light unit **(see illustration)**.
41 Refitting is the reverse of the removal procedure, ensuring that the lens is securely clipped in position.

Estate/SW models

42 Carefully prise the side of the lens out and

remove it from the light unit. The bulb is of the capless (push-fit) type, and can be removed by simply pulling it out of the light unit **(see illustration)**.
43 Refitting is a reversal of removal procedure, ensuring the lens is securely clipped in position.

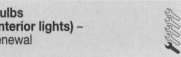

6   Bulbs (interior lights) – renewal

General

1 Refer to Section 5, paragraph 1.

Passenger compartment lights

2 Using a flat bladed-screwdriver, carefully ease the light unit out of position and disconnect it from the wiring connector **(see illustration)**.

6.2 Prise the light unit from place (luggage compartment light)

6.3a Prise the lens from the light . . .

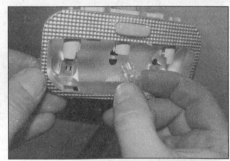

6.3b . . . and pull the bulb from the holder

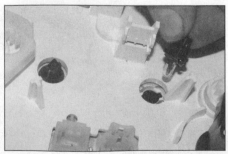

6.7 Rotate the bulbholder anti-clockwise and remove it from the rear of the heater control panel

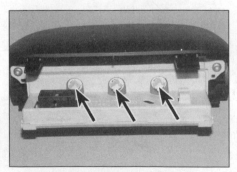

6.9 The multi-function display unit bulbholders (arrowed)

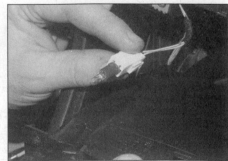

6.11 Pull the bulbholder from the rear of the ashtray

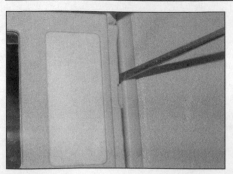

6.16 Carefully prise the lens and mirror from place . . .

12 Securely fit the new bulb to its holder then clip the holder back into position on the console. Refit the ashtray.

Switch illumination

13 All of the switches that are illuminated, are done so by LEDs. These LEDs are an integral part of the switch and cannot be renewed separately. Renewal will therefore require renewal of the complete switch assembly (see Section 4).

Glovebox illumination

14 Open the glovebox, and carefully prise the front end of the lens from place. Remove the light unit, and disconnect the wiring plug as it is withdrawn. Note that the switch is integral with the light.
15 The capless bulb simply pulls from the bulbholder.

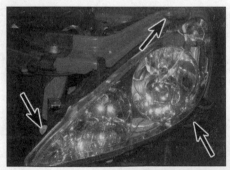

7.4a Undo the three headlamp mounting bolts (arrowed) . . .

7.6 Rotate the headlight levelling motor anti-clockwise

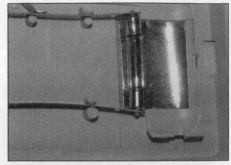

6.17 . . . then lever out the festoon bulb

Vanity mirror illumination

16 Carefully prise the lens and mirror from the sunvisor (see illustration).
17 Prise the festoon bulb(s) from place (see illustration).

7 Exterior light units – removal and refitting

Headlight

1 Remove the front bumper (see Chapter 11).
2 If removing the left-hand headlight, prise out the two clips and detach the air intake ducting adjacent to the headlight.
3 Unclip the washer jet from the headlight lens (where fitted).
4 Slacken and remove the three mounting

7.4b . . . then slide up the locking latch and disconnect the wiring plug

7.7 Carefully prise the adjuster upwards, and remove the motor

bolts and free the headlight unit from its mounting. Slide up the locking latch and disconnect the wiring connectors from the headlight unit, then manoeuvre the unit out of position (see illustrations).
5 To remove the headlight levelling motor, rotate the inner protective cap anti-clockwise. Disconnect the motor wiring plug.
6 Rotate the motor anti-clockwise and, using a flat-bladed screwdriver, disengage the motor balljoint (see illustration).
7 Carefully prise the adjuster upwards and withdraw the motor from the headlamp (see illustration).
8 Prior to refitting, ensure the levelling system motor (where fitted) is correctly installed.
9 Offer up the headlight unit and securely reconnect its wiring connectors.
10 Position the headlight in its aperture.
11 Refit and tighten the headlight mounting bolts.
12 Check the operation of the headlight, then refit the front bumper. If the left-hand side headlight was removed, refit the air intake ducting and retaining clips prior to refitting the bumper.
13 Check the headlight beam alignment using the information given in Section 8.

Headlight luminosity sensor

14 Remove the multi-function display as described in Chapter 11, Section 27.
15 Reach through the exposed aperture, and push the sensor upwards, and out of the facia. Disconnect the sensor wiring plug as it is withdrawn.

Front indicator side repeater

16 Push the light unit forward, to free its retaining clips, then ease it out from the wing panel (see illustration 5.28).
17 Disconnect the wiring connector and remove the light unit from the vehicle.
18 Refitting is a reversal of the removal procedure.

Rear light unit

Hatchback models

19 Pull back the trim panel behind the light unit, and undo the two nuts securing the light unit (see illustration).
20 Disconnect the wiring connector from the

7.19 Undo the two rear light unit nuts (arrowed)

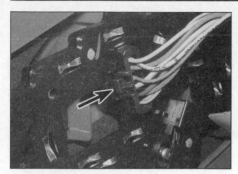

7.20 Release the clip (arrowed) and disconnect the light unit wiring plug

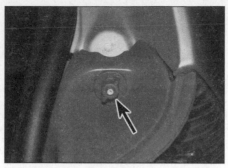

7.22 Undo the nut (arrowed) at the top of the light . . .

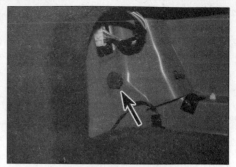

7.23 . . . and the nut (arrowed) at the base

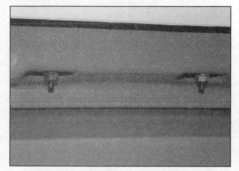

7.26 High-level stop-light retaining nuts (Hatchback models)

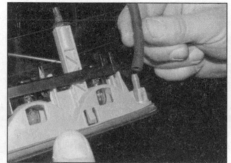

7.27 Disconnect the tailgate screen washer tube

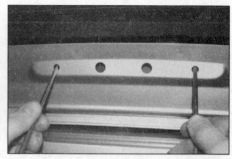

7.31 Use two screwdrivers to release the high-level stop-light clips (Estate/SW models)

light unit then remove the light unit from the vehicle **(see illustration)**.

21 Refitting is the reverse of removal, ensuring the light unit seal is in good condition.

Estate/SW models

22 Open the tailgate, and undo the fastener at the top of the relevant light unit **(see illustration)**.

23 Pull away the plastic trim behind the light unit and undo the nut at the base of the unit **(see illustration)**.

24 Disconnect the wiring plug and manoeuvre the unit from the vehicle.

25 Refitting is a reversal of removal.

High-level stop-light

Hatchback

26 Open the tailgate then unscrew the nuts securing the light unit to the tailgate **(see**

illustration). Carefully push on the light unit studs to ease the unit out.

27 Disconnect the wiring connector and washer tube, then remove the light unit from the tailgate **(see illustration)**.

28 Refitting is the reverse of removal. Do not overtighten the light unit retaining nuts as the plastic is easily broken.

Estate/SW models

29 Using a forked type tool, extract the stud-type clips from the periphery of the tailgate interior upper trim.

30 Pull the panel away from the tailgate at the top corners to release the retaining clips, then remove the panel from the tailgate.

31 Using two flat-bladed screwdrivers, push through the access holes, releasing the two retaining clips and remove the light unit. Disconnect the wiring connector as the unit is withdrawn **(see illustration)**.

32 Refitting is a reversal of removal.

Number plate light

Hatchback models

33 Remove the rear bumper (see Chapter 11).

34 Disconnect the wiring plug as the light is withdrawn.

35 Carefully push the relevant light unit clip to one side, and ease it from place **(see illustration)**.

36 Refitting is a reversal of removal.

Estate/SW models

37 Remove the tailgate lower trim panel as described in Chapter 11, Section 25.

38 Undo the four retaining nuts, release the retaining clips, and remove the exterior trim from above the number plate lights **(see illustrations)**.

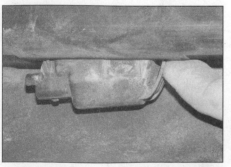

7.35 Compress the clip and remove the number plate light (Hatchback models)

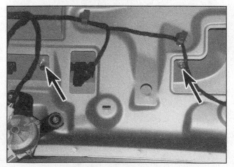

7.38a Undo the exterior trim nuts (left-hand ones arrowed)

7.38b . . . and release the retaining clips (arrowed)

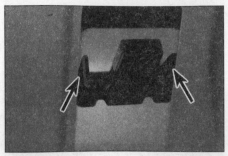

7.39 Squeeze together the clips (arrowed) and remove the number plate light (Estate/SW models)

7.43a Undo the mounting screws . . .

7.43b . . . and remove the foglight from the front bumper

8.2a Vertical headlight adjuster (arrowed) . . .

8.2b . . . and horizontal adjuster (arrowed)

39 Squeeze together the retaining clips then push the relevant light unit out from the tailgate. Disconnect the wiring connector and remove the light unit **(see illustration)**.
40 Refitting is the reverse of removal.

Front foglights (later models)

41 Chock the rear wheels then jack up the front of the vehicle and support it on axle stands (see *Jacking and vehicle support*). Remove the engine undershield. For access to the right-hand foglight, it is necessary to release the front of the wheelarch liner by removing the fasteners.
42 Reach up under the front bumper and disconnect the wiring from the foglight bulbholder.
43 Undo the mounting screws and remove the foglight from the front bumper **(see illustrations)**.
44 Refitting is a reversal of removal.

8 Headlight beam alignment – general information

1 Accurate adjustment of the headlight beam is only possible using optical beam-setting equipment, and this work should therefore be carried out by a Peugeot dealer or suitably-equipped workshop.
2 For reference, the vertical alignment of the headlights can be adjusted using a suitable-sized Allen key to rotate the adjuster assemblies accessible from the top of the headlight casing, whilst the horizontal alignment is adjusted by removing the cover from the dip beam bulb, and rotating the adjuster with a screwdriver **(see illustrations)**.
3 On models equipped with headlight levelling, ensure the adjuster switch is set to position 0 before the headlights are adjusted.

9 Instrument panel – removal and refitting

Removal

1 Disconnect the battery as described in Chapter 5A.
2 Insert two pins as shown, to release the panel retaining clips **(see illustration)**. **Note:** *If required, instrument panel removal pins (No -.1212) are available from Peugeot dealers.*
3 With the clips released, pull on the pins/tools and remove the panel. Disconnect the panel wiring plug(s) as the unit is withdrawn. Should the instrument panel develop a fault, have the vehicle's self-diagnosis facility interrogated by a Peugeot dealer or suitably-equipped specialist. With the exception of the panel 'glass', no parts are available separately for the instrument panel, if faulty, the complete assembly must be renewed **(see illustration)**.

Refitting

4 Refitting is a reversal of removal, ensuring that the upper locating lugs of the panel engage correctly.

10 Clock/multi-function unit – removal and refitting

Removal

1 Ensure the ignition is switched off.
2 Carefully pull up on the rear edge of the

9.2 Insert two pins to release the retaining clips

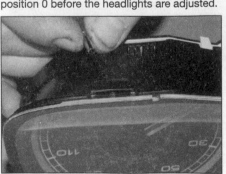

9.3 Release the clips to remove the panel 'glass'

10.2 Pull up the rear of the unit to release the clips (arrowed)

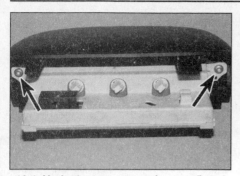

10.4 Undo the two screws (arrowed) and remove the unit from the cowling

surround, and release it from the facia **(see illustration)**.

3 Disconnect the wiring plug as the unit is withdrawn.

4 Undo the two screws and remove the display from the cowling **(see illustration)**.

Refitting

5 Refitting is a reversal of removal.

11 Cigarette lighter/ accessory socket – removal and refitting

Removal

1 Remove the centre console as described in Chapter 11.

2 Carefully release the retaining clips and slide the illumination light assembly off the base of the lighter, taking great care not to break its electrical contacts.

3 Pull out the lighter element then release the tangs and push out the metal insert/accessory socket. The plastic outer section can then be removed from the console.

Refitting

4 Align the plastic outer section tab with the cut-out then insert it into the console.

5 Align the bulbholder contact on the metal insert with the holder tangs on the plastic outer then clip the insert into position.

6 Slide the illumination light assembly onto the metal insert and clip it securely onto the plastic outer.

13.1 Wiper blade alignment mark (arrowed)

12.3 Undo the mounting nut and remove the horn

7 Ensure the cigarette lighter is correctly assembled then refit the centre console.

12 Horn – removal and refitting

Removal

1 The horn is located behind the front bumper, on the left-hand side.

2 Remove the front bumper as described in Chapter 11.

3 Disconnect the wiring connector(s) then slacken the mounting nut and remove the horn from the vehicle **(see illustration)**.

4 To remove the horn push, remove the driver's airbag as described in Section 22, then undo the three screws and carefully remove the push ring assembly **(see illustration)**.

Refitting

5 Refitting is a reversal of removal.

13 Wiper arm – removal and refitting

Note: *The wiper arms are a very tight fit on their spindles and it is likely that a puller will be needed to remove them safely and without damage.*

Removal

1 Operate the wiper motor, then switch it off

13.2 Lift up the cover and undo the wiper spindle nut

12.4 Undo the three screws (arrowed) and remove the horn push

so that the wiper arm returns to the at-rest position. Stick tape to the screen alongside the wiper blade to ensure correct refitment. There is also an alignment mark provided on the windscreen **(see illustration)**.

2 Lift up the wiper arm spindle nut cover (where fitted) then slacken and remove the spindle nut **(see illustration)**.

3 Lift the blade off the glass, and pull the wiper arm off its spindle. If the arm is very tight, free it from the spindle using a suitable puller **(see illustration)**.

Refitting

4 Ensure that the wiper arm and spindle splines are clean and dry, then refit the arm to the spindle, aligning the wiper blade with the tape fitted on removal, or the alignment marks provided.

5 Refit the spindle nut, tightening it securely, and clip the nut cover (where fitted) back into position.

14 Windscreen wiper motor and linkage – removal and refitting

Removal

1 Jack up the front of the vehicle and support it on axle stands (see *Jacking and vehicle support*). Undo the screws and remove the engine undershield (where fitted).

2 Remove the wiper arms (see Section 13).

3 Remove the battery and battery box as described in Chapter 5A.

13.3 If the wiper arm is tight on the spindle, use a puller

14.8 The scuttle trim panel is secured by a plastic rivet at each end

14.11 Prise up the centre pins a little, lever up and remove the plastic rivets securing the sound insulation material

4 Undo the two screws and move the brake fluid upper reservoir to one side. There is no need to disconnect the supply hose, but be prepared for fluid spillage.

5 Remove the engine compartment fusebox lid, and the plastic cover from above the washer fluid reservoir. The cover is secured by two plastic expanding rivets. Push the centre pins in a little, then prise the complete rivet from place, and release the side clip.

6 On 2.0 litre engines, undo the fasteners and remove the plastic cover from the top of the engine. On 1.4 litre diesel engines, the cover simply pulls up from place.

7 Remove the air cleaner housing to inlet manifold intake duct to improve access (see Chapter 4A or 4B). On 1.4 and 1.6 litre petrol models, remove the throttle body as described in Chapter 4A.

8 Remove the plastic panel from the scuttle. The panel is secured by an expanding plastic rivet at each end. Push the centre pins in a little, then prise the complete rivets from place. Lift the outer edges of the trim, then pull the centre area downwards to unclip it from the base of the windscreen **(see illustration)**.

9 Position a jack under the transmission casing, and take the weight of the transmission.

10 Undo the central retaining nut from the transmission mounting at the left-hand side of the engine compartment (see the relevant Part of Chapter 2). Lower the transmission slightly to facilitate removing the wiper motor and linkage.

11 Release the clips and remove the scuttle soundproofing **(see illustration)**.

12 Undo the two retaining bolts, and remove scuttle crossmember **(see illustration)**.

13 Release the wiring harness retaining

clips, then unscrew the retaining clips and remove the soundproofing from over the wiper motor.

14 Using a screwdriver, prise the connecting rod from the left-hand wiper spindle linkage **(see illustration)**. Disconnect the wiper motor wiring plug.

15 The wiper linkage assembly is secured by a bolt each side and a central nut. Undo the bolts/nut, lift the assembly from the locating pin. Press down at the centre of the linkage assembly and lift the left-hand end over the strut upper mounting, then manoeuvre the assembly from the engine compartment **(see illustrations)**. **Note:** *Access to the wiper linkage assembly is very poor – dexterity and patience will be required to manoeuvre the linkage from place. Take great care not to damage the windscreen or the vehicle paintwork.*

16 At the time of writing, it would appear that the motor is not available separately from the linkage assembly. Check availability with your Peugeot dealer.

Refitting

17 Refitting is a reversal of removal, ensuring all fasteners are securely tightened. Note that before tightening the linkage mounting nut/bolts, ensure the assembly is correctly fitted over the locating dowels. It's impossible to see the dowels with the linkage in place, so use your fingers to check.

15 Tailgate window wiper motor – removal and refitting

Note: *A pop rivet gun and suitable rivets will be required on refitting.*

Removal

1 Ensure the ignition is turned off.

2 Remove the wiper arm (see Section 13).

3 Remove the tailgate lower trim panel as described in Chapter 11, Section 25.

4 Using a 7.5 mm drill, carefully drill the heads off the pop rivets securing the wiper motor

14.12 The plastic crossmember is secured by one bolt at each end

14.14 Prise the connecting rod from the left-hand spindle linkage

14.15a Wiper linkage right-hand bolt (arrowed) . . .

14.15b . . . left-hand bolt . . .

14.15c . . . and central nut (arrowed)

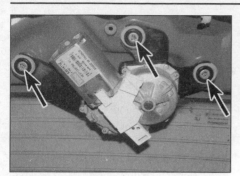

15.4 Drill out the three rivets (arrowed)

16.2 Push in the centre pins, then prise up the complete expanding rivet

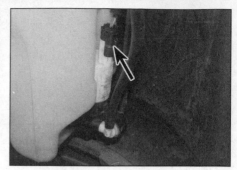

16.7 Disconnect the washer pump wiring plug

bracket to the tailgate **(see illustration)**. To prevent the rivets falling into the tailgate, position a cloth on either side of the motor.
Caution: Take care not to damage the motor and tailgate when drilling out the rivets.

5 With the three rivets removed, disconnect the wiring connector and remove the wiper motor from the tailgate. Take care not to lose the collars from the motor mounting rubbers.

6 Remove the wiper motor sealing grommet from the tailgate glass.

7 Remove the cloths and recover the remnants of each rivet from the motor bracket/tailgate. Ensure all traces of rivet are removed.

8 The wiper motor is not available separately. If faulty renew the assembly as a whole.

Refitting

9 Prior to refitting check the sealing grommet and rubber mountings for signs of damage or deterioration and renew as necessary.

10 Ensure the rubber grommet is correctly fitted to the tailgate glass, and the rubber mountings and collars are correctly fitted to the motor mounting bracket.

11 Manoeuvre the wiper motor into position and secure it in position with new pop rivets.

12 Reconnect the wiring connector to the motor then refit the trim panel to the tailgate. Turn on the ignition, then operate the wiper and allow it to stop in the park position.

13 Refit the wiper arm as described in Section 13.

16 Washer system components – removal and refitting

1 The washer reservoir is located behind the right-hand front wing and supplies both the windscreen and tailgate washers via the same pump. On models equipped with headlight washers, the reservoir also supplies the headlight washer jets via an additional pump.

Washer fluid reservoir

2 Working in the engine compartment, remove the plastic cover from above the washer fluid reservoir. The cover is secured by two expanding plastic rivets. Push the centre pins in a little, then prise the complete rivets from place **(see illustration)**.

3 Slacken the right-hand front roadwheel bolts. Jack up the front of the vehicle, and support it securely on axle stands (see *Jacking and vehicle support*). Remove the right-hand roadwheel.

4 Remove the front right-hand wheel arch liner. The liner is secured by several expanding plastic rivets. Push the centre pins a little, then prise the complete rivets from place, and manoeuvre the front section of the liner out from underneath the wing.

5 Pull the reservoir filler neck upwards from the reservoir.

6 Note the correct fitted location of the washer hoses (if necessary, mark them for

identification purposes) then disconnect the hoses from the washer pump(s).

7 Disconnect the wiring connector(s) from the washer pump(s) **(see illustration)**.

8 Slacken and remove the retaining nut then move the reservoir to the rear, and free it from the body. Manoeuvre it out from underneath the wing **(see illustrations)**.

9 Refitting is the reverse of removal, ensuring that the hoses are securely reconnected. Refill the reservoir and check for leaks.

Washer pump

10 Proceed as described in paragraphs 3 to 7 and disconnect the hose(s) and wiring connector from the pump.

11 Position a container beneath the reservoir to catch the washer fluid as the pump is removed.

12 Carefully ease the pump out from the reservoir, and recover its sealing grommet **(see illustration)**. Wash off any spilt fluid with cold water.

13 Refitting is the reverse of removal, using a new sealing grommet if the original shows signs of damage or deterioration. Refill the reservoir and check the pump grommet for leaks on completion.

Windscreen washer jet

14 Open the bonnet. Prise up the centre pins a little, lever out the complete plastic expanding rivets, and remove the bonnet insulation panel to gain access to the base

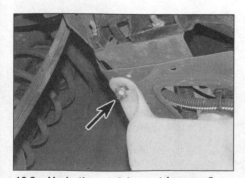

16.8a Undo the retaining nut (arrowed) . . .

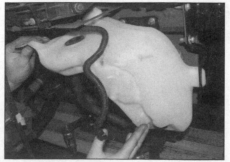

16.8b . . . then move the reservoir backwards

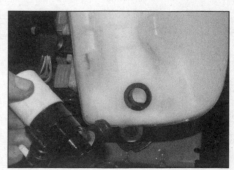

16.12 Ease the washer pump from the reservoir

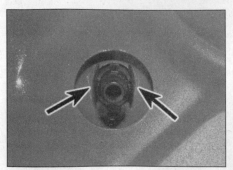

16.14 Squeeze together the clips (arrowed) and ease the jet from the bonnet

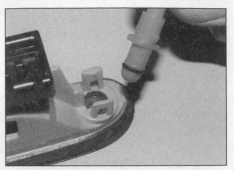

16.18 Release the clips and remove the washer jet

of the windscreen washer jets. Disconnect the washer hose(s) from the relevant jet, then depress the retaining clips and ease the jet out of position **(see illustration)**.

15 On refitting, clip the jet into the bonnet and reconnect the hose. The aim of the washer jets is not adjustable.

Tailgate washer jet

16 Remove the high-level stop-light unit as described in Section 7.

17 On Hatchback models, release the retaining clips and detach the light unit from the bulbholder **(see illustration 5.33a)**.

18 Disconnect the washer hose from the jet then free the jet from the light unit, by releasing the two retaining clips **(see illustration)**. Recover the jet O-ring.

19 Refitting is the reverse of removal. Do

not overtighten the light unit retaining nuts on Hatchback models, as the plastic is easily broken. The washer jet is not adjustable.

Headlight washer jet

20 Carefully prise the jet cover from the bumper, and pull the assembly out to its full extent.

21 Have an assistant grip the washer jet tube with a pair or grips, then depress the two retaining clips and pull the jet from the tube .

22 To remove the washer cylinders, remove the front bumper as described in Chapter 11, then disconnect the washer tubing, and unclip the cylinders.

23 Refitting is the reverse of removal.

17 Audio unit – removal and refitting

Note: *The following procedure is for the range of equipment fitted by Peugeot.*

Removal

1 Ensure the audio unit and ignition is switched off.

2 Insert a small screwdriver/punch into the hole on each side of the unit and pushing it in until the clip releases **(see illustration)**.

3 Once both retaining clips have been released, slide the audio unit out of position. Disconnect the wiring connections and aerial

lead (where applicable) and remove the unit from the vehicle.

Refitting

4 Prior to refitting, reset the unit retaining clips.

5 Securely reconnect the aerial lead (where applicable) and wiring connectors then slide the unit back into position, taking care not to trap the wiring.

18 Loudspeakers – removal and refitting

Removal
Front door speaker

1 Remove the door inner trim panel as described in Chapter 11.

2 Slacken and remove the retaining screws then remove the speaker from the door, disconnecting the wiring connector as it becomes accessible **(see illustration)**.

Front tweeter

3 Carefully prise the tweeter cover from the facia and remove it along with the tweeter **(see illustration)**. Disconnect the wiring plug as it is withdrawn.

4 Rotate the tweeter speaker clockwise to free it from the cover.

Rear speaker – 5-door models

5 Remove the door inner trim panel as described in Chapter 11.

6 Undo the screws and remove the speaker from the door, disconnecting the wiring plug as it becomes accessible.

Rear speaker – 3-door models

7 Remove the rear side trim panel as described in Chapter 11, Section 25.

8 Pull the foam surround from place then slacken and remove the retaining screws then remove the speaker from the body, disconnecting the wiring connector as it becomes accessible **(see illustration)**.

Refitting

9 Refitting is a reversal of removal. Ensure the trim panels are clipped securely in position and are correctly located behind the edges of the sealing strips.

17.2 Insert two pins into each side of the audio unit to release the clips, then pull the unit from place

18.2 Undo the screws (arrowed) and remove the speaker

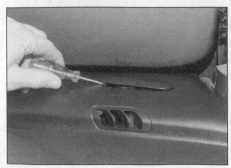

18.3 Carefully prise the tweeter cover from the facia

18.8 Rear speaker retaining screws (arrowed) (3-door Hatchback)

19 Radio aerial –
removal and refitting

Removal

1 The aerial is a screw-fit in its base and is easily removed.

2 To remove the complete aerial on models where the aerial is mounted on the rear of the roof, open the tailgate then free the tailgate sealing strip from the top of its aperture. Undo the two screw fixings and carefully lower the rear of the headlining to gain access to the aerial nut.

3 Disconnect the wiring plug, undo the nut and remove the aerial.

Refitting

4 Refitting is the reverse of removal.

20 Engine immobiliser and anti-theft alarm system –
general information

Note: *This information is applicable only to the systems fitted by Peugeot as standard equipment.*

Engine immobiliser

1 An engine immobiliser system is fitted as standard to all models and the system is operated automatically every time the ignition key is inserted/removed.

2 The immobiliser system ensures the vehicle can only be started using the original Peugeot ignition key. The key contains an electronic chip (transponder) which is programmed with a code. When the key is inserted into the ignition switch it uses the current present in the sensor ring (which is fitted to the ignition switch housing) to send a signal to the immobiliser electronic control unit (ECU). The ECU is incorporated into the built-in systems interface (BSI) unit (see Section 23). The ECU checks this code every time the ignition is switched on. If the key code does not match the ECU code, the ECU will disable the starter, fuel and ignition (as applicable) to prevent the engine being started.

3 When the vehicle is new, a confidential security card is supplied along with the other vehicle documentation. This card contains the security code which your Peugeot dealer requires when carrying out any work on the immobiliser system. Keep this card in a safe place at home; never store it in the vehicle. If the ignition key is lost, a new one can be obtained from a Peugeot dealer. Take the confidential security card and all the existing keys along to your Peugeot dealer who will supply a new key and reprogram all the keys with a new security code; this will render the lost key useless.

Caution: Without the confidential security card, it will not be possible to have the keys and immobiliser system reprogrammed.

 If you have purchased the vehicle second-hand, as a precaution have all the keys and the immobiliser system reprogrammed with a new security code. This will ensure the keys in your possession are the only ones able to start the vehicle and render all other keys useless.

4 Any problems with the engine immobiliser system should be referred to a Peugeot dealer.

Anti-theft alarm system

5 Most models covered in this were also equipped with an anti-theft alarm system as standard equipment. The system was available as a option on all other models. The alarm is automatically armed when the deadlocking is set using the remote central locking transmitter and is disarmed when the doors are unlocked using the remote transmitter. The alarm system has switches on the bonnet, tailgate and each of the doors and also has ultrasonic sensing, which detects movement inside the vehicle, via sensors mounted on either side of the vehicle interior.

6 When the system is activated, the direction indicators will flash continuously for two seconds and the indicator light on the alarm switch, fitted to the rear section of the centre console, will flash continuously. **Note:** *If the bonnet, tailgate or one of the doors are not properly closed when the alarm is set, the siren will sound briefly. If the bonnet/tailgate/ door (as applicable) is properly closed within 45 seconds the alarm will be armed. If not the alarm will remain disarmed.*

7 If for some reason the remote central locking transmitter fails whilst the alarm is armed, the alarm can be disarmed using the key. To do this, open the door with the key, then enter the vehicle, noting that the alarm will sound as the door is opened. Insert the key and switch on the ignition, the immobiliser will recognise the key and will switch off the alarm.

8 If required, the ultrasonic sensing facility of the alarm can be switched off, whilst retaining the switched side of the system. To switch off the ultrasonic sensing, with the ignition switched off, depress the alarm switch (mounted on the facia above the centre air vents) until the alarm indicator light on the switch is continuously lit. Get out of the vehicle and operate the deadlocking function using the remote transmitter to arm the alarm. The direction indicators will flash as normal but only the switched (door, tailgate and bonnet) side of the alarm system will be operational. This facility is useful, as it allows you to leave the windows/sunroof open, and still arm the alarm. If the windows/sunroof are left open with the ultrasonic sensing not switched off, the alarm may be falsely triggered by a gust of wind.

9 Prior to disconnecting the battery, the alarm system should be disabled; this will prevent the alarm sounding when the battery is disconnected/reconnected. To do this, switch on the ignition then immediately depress and hold the alarm switch for two seconds; the indicator light on the switch should then flash rapidly for approximately three seconds indicating the alarm has been disabled. Switch off the ignition and disconnect the battery.

10 Once the battery has been reconnected, operate the deadlocking with the remote transmitter then unlock the vehicle. The alarm will be set as normal, the next time the deadlocking is set.

11 Should the alarm system become faulty, the vehicle should be taken to a Peugeot dealer for examination.

21 Airbag system –
general information and precautions

1 All models in the range are fitted with a driver's airbag, passenger's airbag, side-front airbags, and side curtain airbags.

2 The airbag system is triggered in the event of a heavy frontal impact above a predetermined force, depending on the point of impact. The airbag is then inflated within milliseconds, and forms a safety cushion between the cabin occupants and the vehicle interior. This prevents contact between the upper body and vehicle interior, and therefore greatly reduces the risk of injury. The airbag then deflates almost immediately. The control unit also operates the front seat belt tensioner mechanisms at the same time (see Chapter 11).

3 The side airbags are fitted to the seat back of each front seat. Each airbag unit has its own lateral acceleration sensor which is mounted onto the vehicle body on the outside of each front seat. The side airbags are not linked in anyway and operate individually.

4 The curtain airbags are fitted behind the windscreen pillars and headlining on each side of the passenger cabin.

5 Every time the ignition is switched on, the airbag control unit performs a self-test. The self-test takes approximately six seconds and during this time the warning light in the instrument panel will be illuminated. After the self-test is complete, the warning light will go out (unless the passenger airbag unit has been deactivated – see paragraph 6). If the warning light fails to come on, remains illuminated after the self-test period, or comes on at any time when the vehicle is being driven, there is a fault in the airbag system. The vehicle should be taken to a Peugeot dealer for examination at the earliest possible opportunity.

6 Most vehicles with a passenger airbag are equipped with a disabling switch fitted to the centre console. The switch is operated using the ignition key and switches off the passenger airbag (it is not possible to disable the driver's or side/curtain airbags) to enable a rear-facing child seat to be installed in the passenger seat. Whilst the passenger airbag is disabled, the airbag warning light on the instrument panel will remain illuminated all the time.

Warning: *Before carrying out any operations on the airbag system, disconnect the battery (see Chapter 5A) and wait at least two minutes. Remove the centre console (see Chapter 11) then release the retaining clip and disconnect the wiring connector(s) from the airbag control unit. When the operations are complete, securely reconnect the control unit then refit the centre console (see Chapter 11). Make sure no one is inside the vehicle when the battery is reconnected then, with the driver's door open, switch the ignition on from outside vehicle and check the operation of the airbag warning light.*

Warning: *Do not subject the area of the body around the control unit to any form of shock which could trigger the system.*

Warning: *Note that the airbags must not be subjected to temperatures in excess of 100ºC. When the airbag is removed, ensure that it is stored the correct way up to prevent possible inflation.*

Warning: *Do not allow any solvents or cleaning agents to contact the airbag assemblies. They must be cleaned using only a damp cloth.*

Warning: *The airbags and control unit are both sensitive to impact. If either is dropped or damaged they should be renewed.*

Warning: *Disconnect the airbag control unit wiring connector prior to using arc welding equipment on the vehicle.*

Warning: *Never fit a rear-facing child seat to the front passenger seat unless the passenger airbag has been disabled (paragraph 6).*

Warning: *Peugeot recommend that the airbag units be renewed every ten years.*

22 Airbag system components – removal and refitting

 Warning: *Refer to the precautions given in Section 21 before carrying out the following operations.*

Driver's airbag

Removal

1 Disconnect the battery (see Chapter 5A) and wait at least two minutes. Remove the centre console (see Chapter 11) then release the retaining clip and disconnect the wiring connector(s) from the airbag control unit **(see illustration 22.15)**. If necessary, remove the facia bracket lower mounting bolt to gain the clearance necessary to disconnect the connector.
2 With the wheel in the straight-ahead position and the steering lock engaged, insert thin flat-bladed screwdriver into the holes

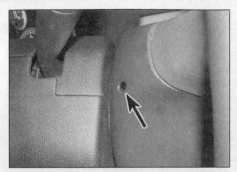

22.2a Insert a thin screwdriver into the hole (arrowed) each side of the steering wheel . . .

22.3a Disconnect the airbag wiring connectors (arrowed) . . .

in the side of the steering wheel boss, and release the retaining clips **(see illustrations)**.
3 Carefully lift the airbag unit away from the wheel, disconnecting the wiring connectors as they become accessible **(see illus-trations)**.

 Warning: *Do not knock or drop the airbag unit and store it the correct way up with its padded surface uppermost.*

Refitting

4 Securely reconnect the wiring connectors then seat the airbag unit in the steering wheel, ensuring the wiring does not become trapped. Note that the main connectors are colour-coded to correspond with their respective sockets.
5 Fit the airbag unit, press it into place until the retaining clips engage.
6 Securely reconnect the airbag control unit wiring connector(s). Refit the centre console (see Chapter 11). Make sure no one is inside

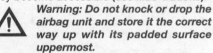

22.9a The facia covering trim is secured by numerous fasteners along its lower edge (arrowed) . . .

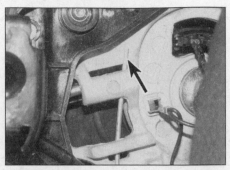

22.2b . . . and push the clip (arrowed) to release it

22.3b . . . by lifting the locking clip and sliding them from place

the vehicle then reconnect the battery. With the driver's door open, switch the ignition on from outside vehicle and check the operation of the warning light.

Passenger airbag

Removal

7 Disconnect the battery and wait at least two minutes. Remove the centre console (see Chapter 11) then release the retaining clip and disconnect the wiring connector(s) from the airbag control unit **(see illustration 22.15)**.
8 Remove the facia as described in Chapter 11.
9 The facia covering trim is secured by numerous fasteners along its lower edge and ends. It's also secured by fasteners accessible through the instrument panel aperture, and multi-function display aperture **(see illustrations)**. Remove the fasteners.

22.9b . . . its ends (arrowed) . . .

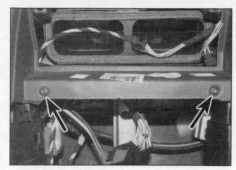

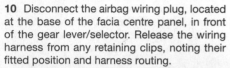

22.9c . . . centre section (arrowed) . . .

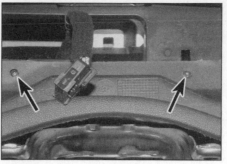

22.9d . . . and instrument cluster aperture (arrowed)

22.12 Undo the two airbag retaining nuts (arrowed)

10 Disconnect the airbag wiring plug, located at the base of the facia centre panel, in front of the gear lever/selector. Release the wiring harness from any retaining clips, noting their fitted position and harness routing.

11 Lift up the rear edge of the facia covering trim, and release the remaining retaining clips. Remove the trim along with the airbag.

12 Undo the two nuts, and remove the airbag **(see illustration)**.

Refitting

13 Fit the airbag unit and panel to the facia trim, ensuring the wiring is correctly routed, and the nuts are securely tightened.

14 The remainder of refitting is the reverse of removal. On completion, securely reconnect the airbag control unit wiring connector(s). Refit the centre console (see Chapter 11). Make sure no one is inside the vehicle then reconnect the battery. With the driver's door open, switch the ignition on from outside vehicle and check the operation of the warning light.

Airbag control unit

Removal

15 Disconnect the battery (see Chapter 5A) and wait at least two minutes. Remove the centre console (see Chapter 11) then release the retaining clip and disconnect the wiring connector(s) from the airbag control unit **(see illustration)**.

16 Unscrew the retaining nuts then remove the control unit from the vehicle.

Refitting

17 Refit the control unit, making sure the arrow on the top of the unit is pointing towards the front of the vehicle. Refit the control unit retaining nuts and tighten them to the specified torque.

18 Securely reconnect the airbag control unit wiring connector(s).

19 Refit the centre console (see Chapter 11). Make sure no one is inside the vehicle then reconnect the battery. With the driver's door open, switch the ignition on from outside vehicle and check the operation of the warning light.

Side airbag

20 Removal and refitting of the side airbag units should be entrusted to a Peugeot dealer. The seat must be dismantled to enable the airbag unit to removed/refitted.

Side airbag acceleration sensor

Removal

21 Remove the relevant front seat as described in Chapter 11.

22 Referring to Section 25 of Chapter 11, on three-door models remove the rear side trim panel, and on five-door models remove the B-pillar upper and lower trim panels.

23 On all models, remove the sill trim.

24 Peel back the carpet to gain access to the side airbag control unit.

25 Disconnect the wiring connector then undo the retaining bolt and remove the control unit from the vehicle.

Refitting

26 Refitting is the reverse of removal, tightening the acceleration sensor bolt securely.

Curtain airbag

27 Removal and refitting of the curtain airbag units should be entrusted to a Peugeot dealer. The headlining must be partially removed to enable the airbag unit to removed/refitted.

23 Built-in systems interface (BSI) unit/fusebox –
general, removal and refitting

General information

1 The built-in systems interface (BSI) unit is an electronic control unit which controls a variety of functions, normally controlled by individual control units and relays. The BSI unit is located behind the lower cover on the passenger's side of the facia where it is situated directly beneath the fusebox. The BSI unit controls the following functions (not all functions are fitted to all models).

a) Direction indicator/hazard warning lights.
b) Windscreen/tailgate wiper motors.
c) Rear screen heating element.
d) Immobiliser system.
e) Anti-theft alarm system.
f) Lights-on/ignition key warning buzzer.
g) Central locking/deadlocking, including the remote central locking receiver.
h) Door open indicator.
i) Courtesy light delay timer.
j) Automatic transmission audible warning system.

2 Should any of the above functions become faulty, first check the condition of the fuses. If this fails to locate the problem, take the vehicle to a Peugeot dealer for testing. The only satisfactory way to test the BSI unit is by substitution with another unit which is known to be functioning correctly.

Removal

3 Disconnect the battery (see Chapter 5A).

4 Remove the passenger side glovebox as described in Section 27 of Chapter 11.

5 Rotate the two white plastic fasteners 90 degrees anti-clockwise, and prise the fusebox outwards slightly **(see illustration)**.

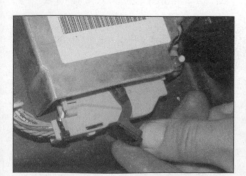

22.15 Lift the locking catch and disconnect the airbag ECU wiring plug

23.5 Rotate the fasteners 90° anti-clockwise

23.6 The rear of the BSI unit locates in the retaining clips (arrowed)

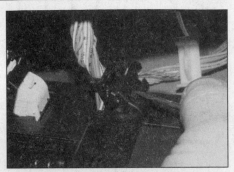

23.7 Some of the BSI connectors are retained by clips and locking catches

6 Lower the rear edge of the unit, then lift up the front edge and slide it from place **(see illustration)**.

7 Note their fitted positions, then release the retaining clips then disconnect all the wiring connectors and remove the BSI unit from the vehicle. Note that there are several different designs of locking catches for the various connectors. Take your time to study the wiring connectors, and release them without using excessive force as they are easily damaged **(see illustration)**.

Refitting

8 Refitting is the reverse of removal, ensuring the wiring connectors are all securely reconnected. Note that the connector colours are listed adjacent to their respective sockets on the BSI.

24 Satellite navigation system – general information

1 A satellite navigation system was offered as an optional extra on some models. The navigation unit and remote control are located in the glovebox. Refer to the manufacturer's handbook supplied with the vehicle for operating instructions. Any problems with the system must be referred to a Peugeot dealer.

PEUGEOT 307 wiring diagrams

Diagram 1

Key to symbols

Bulb	
Switch	
Fuse/fusible link and current rating	F5 30A
Resistor	
Variable resistor	
Connecting wires	
Item no.	2
Pump/motor	M
Earth point and location	E12
Gauge/meter	
Diode	
Wire joint	
Solenoid actuator	
Light emitting diode (LED)	
Screened cable	

Dashed outline denotes part of a larger item, containing in this case an electronic or solid state device.
Pin types:
2   - Unspecified colour connector, pin 2.
2Br 1 - Brown two pin connector, pin 1.

The prime method of wire identification is by using the terminal pin numbers (moulded into each component or connector and shown in the diagrams) together with the number code printed on each wire. To relate each diagram to the vehicle wiring, locate the relevant component or connector illustrated and find the wire(s) connected to the terminal pin(s) as shown in the diagram.

Caution: While a number (indicating the function of that wire) may be printed on each wire, this is not always the case, and in such instances, this is reflected by the absence of such wire numbering on our diagrams. Similarly, numbering of the connector/component terminal pins is not always available from the manufacturers' source information and may also be missing from our diagrams. In these cases, it may be necessary to refer to your local dealer for further information.

Note that the conventional method of using colour coding does not apply – whilst the wires on the vehicle will be coloured, the wire colour has no relevance. Accordingly, the wires on our diagrams all appear in black.

Earth points

E1	Main engine earth	E8	LH transmission tunnel
E2	Battery earth	E9	LH footwell
E3	LH footwell	E10	RH front wing
E4	LH engine compartment	E11	RH centre console
E5	Lower centre of console	E12	LH front wing
E6	Rear upper pillar	E13	LH engine bulkhead
E7	RH rear of centre console		

Key to circuits

Diagram 1	Information for wiring diagrams
Diagram 2	Starting and charging, built-in system interface supply, radio with CD player, dual tone horn, heated rear window, cigarette lighter and 12V socket
Diagram 3	Airbag, ABS and sunroof
Diagram 4	Electric windows, power steering, power and heated mirrors
Diagram 5	Air conditioning, wash/wipe, brake lights, headlights, side lights and tail lights
Diagram 6	Direction indicator lights, hazard warning, foglights, reversing lights, interior lights and diagnostic connector
Diagram 7	Central locking, instrument module
Diagram 8	Petrol and diesel engine cooling

Typical fuse table
(see vehicle handbook for specific allocation)

Main fuse box

Fuses	Rating	Circuit protected
MF1	30A	Fan
MF2	30A	ABS pump motor
MF3	30A	ABS solenoid valves
MF4	60A	Built-in systems interface
MF5	70A	Built-in systems interface
MF6	-	Not used
MF7	30A	Ignition switch
MF8	70A	Power steering
F1	10A	Reversing light switch, vehicle speed sensor, water in diesel sensor
F2	15A	Fuel pump, canister solenoid valve
F3	10A	ABS, power steering pump
F4	10A	Engine control module, heater control, automatic transmission, fan relays
F5	15A	Emmision filter control unit
F6	15A	Front fog lights
F7	-	Not used
F8	20A	Fan relays, engine control module, diesel injection pump
F9	15A	LH dipped beam
F10	15A	RH dipped beam
F11	10A	RH main beam
F12	10A	LH main beam
F13	15A	Horn
F14	10A	Wash/wipe
F15	30A	Engine control module, EGR valve, fuel injectors, diesel pressure regulator, air flow sensor, fuel heater, pre-heat control module
F16	40A	Engine air pump (automatic transmission)
F17	30A	Windscreen wiper
F18	40A	Air conditioning

Built-in system interface

Fuses	Rating	Circuit protected
F1	10A	Rear fog light
F2	15A	Rear screen wiper
F3	-	Not used
F4	15A	Front electric windows, sunroof
F5	15A	LH brake light
F6	-	Not used
F7	20A	Interior lights, cigarette lighter
F8	-	Not used
F9	30A	Electric windows, sunroof
F10	15A	12V rear socket, diagnostic connector
F11	15A	Radio, multi-function display, steering wheel controls, automatic transmission
F12	10A	RH side lights, licence plate light, instrument lights, cigarette lighter, headlight leveling
F13	-	Not used
F14	30A	Central locking
F15	30A	Rear electric windows
F16	5A	Main fuse box, alarm, air bags, steering wheel controls, emmision filter
F17	10A	RH brake light, high level brake light
F18	10A	Diagnostic connector, steering wheel controls, brake switches, clutch switch, coolant level switch
F19	30A	PARC shunt
F20	-	Not used
F21	-	Not used
F22	10A	LH side lights, licence plate light
F23	15A	Alarm
F24	15A	Radio, instrument module, parking aid, air conditioning, multi-function display
F25	-	Not used
F26	30A	Heated rear window

H32824/a

Connector colours

Bl	Blue	**Or**	Orange
Br	Brown	**Ro**	Red
Ge	Yellow	**Sw**	Black
Gr	Grey	**Ws**	White
Gn	Green		
Mc	Multicolored		

Key to items

1 Battery
2 Ignition switch
3 Main fuse box
4 Alternator
5 Starter motor
6 Built-in System Interface
7 Engine control module
8 Horn relay
9 Low tone horn
10 High tone horn
11 Instrument module
12 Aerial
13 Radio
14 CD player
15 LH front tweeter
16 RH front tweeter
17 LH front speaker
18 RH front speaker
19 LH rear speaker
20 RH rear speaker
21 Cigarette lighter
22 Rear 12V socket
23 Heated rear window
24 Heated rear window relay

Diagram 2

MTS
H32825

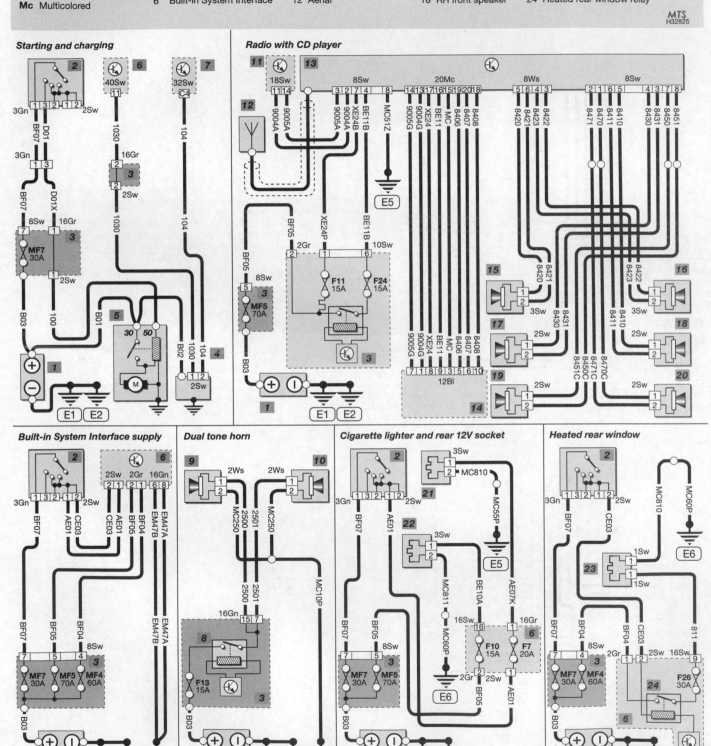

Starting and charging

Radio with CD player

Built-in System Interface supply

Dual tone horn

Cigarette lighter and rear 12V socket

Heated rear window

Connector colours

Bl	Blue	**Or**	Orange
Br	Brown	**Ro**	Red
Ge	Yellow	**Sw**	Black
Gr	Grey	**Ws**	White
Gn	Green		
Mc	Multicolored		

Key to items

1 Battery
2 Ignition switch
3 Main fuse box
6 Built-in System Interface
25 Airbag control module
26 Passenger's airbag
27 Driver's airbag
28 Steering wheel switches
29 Driver's seatbelt
    pre-tensionner
30 Passenger's seatbelt
    pre-tensionner
31 RH airbag screen module
32 RH bottom side airbag
33 LH airbag screen module
34 LH bottom side airbag

35 LH bottom airbag sensor
36 LH side airbag screen module
37 RH bottom airbag sensor
38 RH side airbag screen module
39 Driver's remote module
40 Passenger's remote module
41 Passenger's airbag
    disable switch

42 ABS control unit
43 Diagnostic socket
44 Brake fluid level switch
45 LH front wheel sensor
46 LH rear wheel sensor
47 RH rear wheel sensor
48 RH front wheel sensor
49 Sunroof motor module
50 Sunroof switch

Diagram 3

MTS
H32826

Airbag

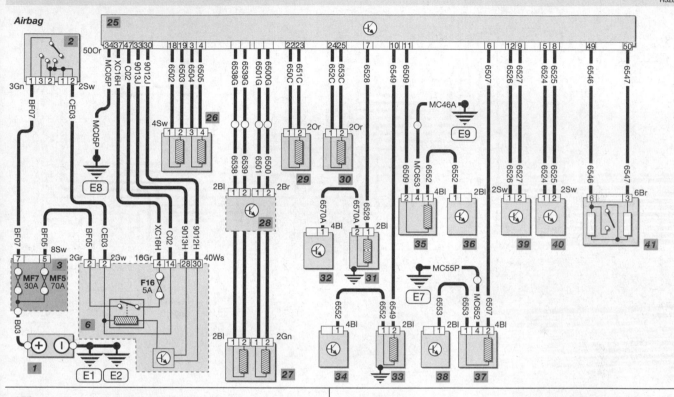

ABS

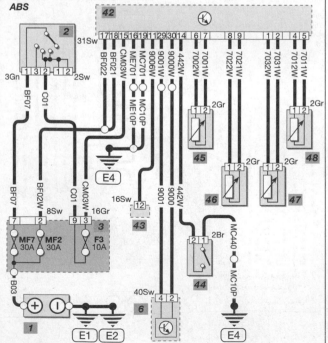

Sunroof

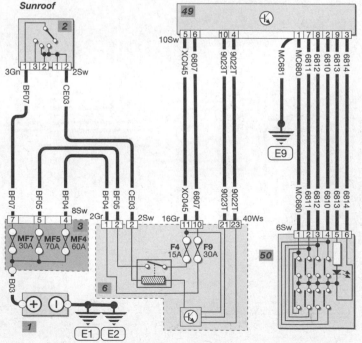

Connector colours

Bl	Blue	**Or**	Orange
Br	Brown	**Ro**	Red
Ge	Yellow	**Sw**	Black
Gr	Grey	**Ws**	White
Gn	Green		
Mc	Multicolored		

Key to items

1 Battery
2 Ignition switch
3 Main fuse box
6 Built-in System Interface
28 Steering wheel switches
42 ABS control unit
43 Diagnostic socket

51 Driver's one-touch motor & control module
52 Passenger's one-touch motor & control module
53 Driver's door mounted switch module
54 RH rear window switch

55 LH rear window switch
56 RH rear window motor module
57 LH rear window motor module
58 Passenger window switch
59 Passenger window motor

60 Driver's rear view mirror
61 Passenger's rear view mirror
62 Power steering pump

Diagram 4

MTS
H32827

Electric windows

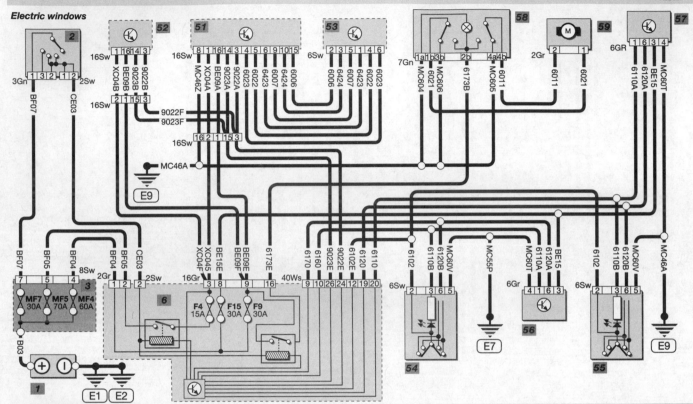

Power and heated mirrors

Power steering

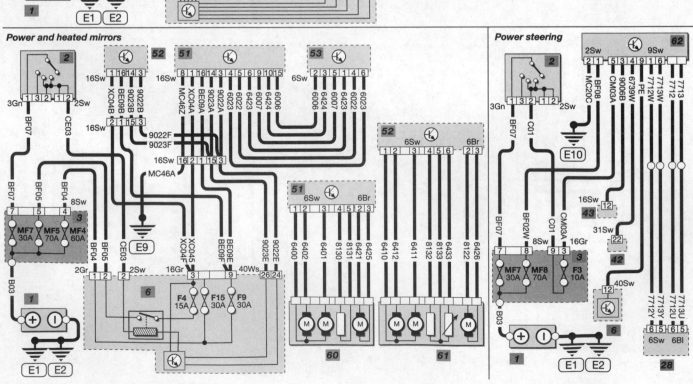

Connector colours

Bl	Blue	**Or**	Orange
Br	Brown	**Ro**	Red
Ge	Yellow	**Sw**	Black
Gr	Grey	**Ws**	White
Gn	Green		
Mc	Multicolored		

★ If separate

Key to items

1 Battery
2 Ignition switch
3 Main fuse box
6 Built-in System Interface
7 Engine control module
11 Instrument module
63 Heater panel
64 Air inlet reduction flap
65 Blower motor resistor
66 Heater blower motor
67 Pressostat
68 A/C compressor
69 Evaporator thermistor
70 Headlight washer
71 Front/rear screen washer
72 Windscreen wiper motor
73 Rear screen wiper motor
74 Rain sensor
75 Light sensor
76 Headlight leveling module
77 LH headlight unit
a) main beam
b) dipped beam
c) side light
d) leveling motor
78 RH headlight unit
(as 77)
79 LH tail light unit
a) tail light
b) brake light
80 RH tail light unit
(as 79)
81 LH licence plate light
82 RH licence plate light
83 High level brake light
84 Brake light switch

Diagram 5

MTS
H32828

Air conditioning (without climate control)

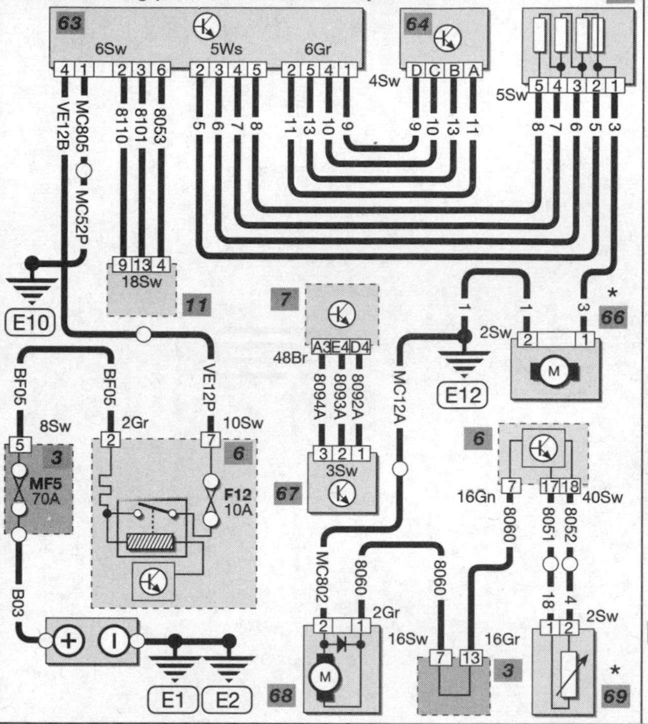

Wash/Wipe

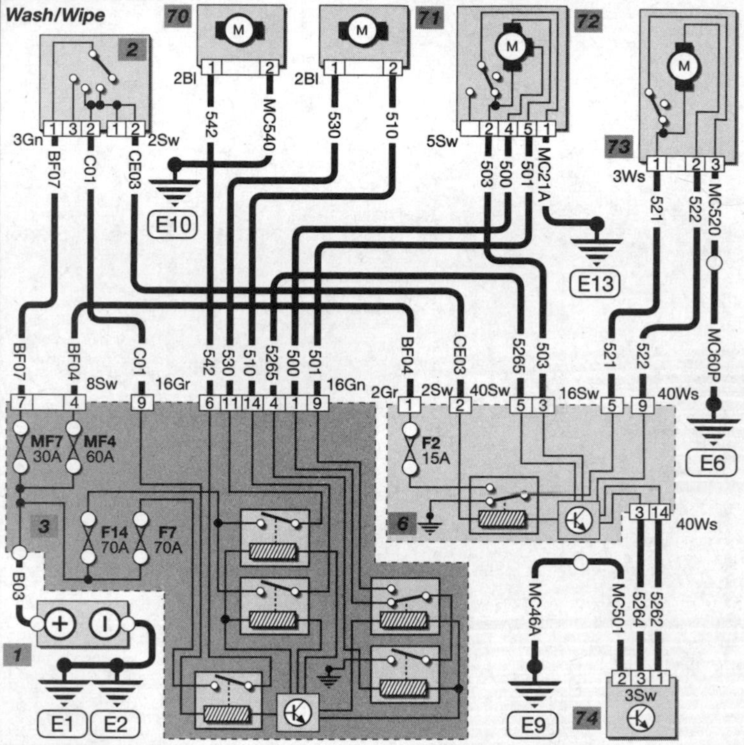

Headlights, side lights and tail lights

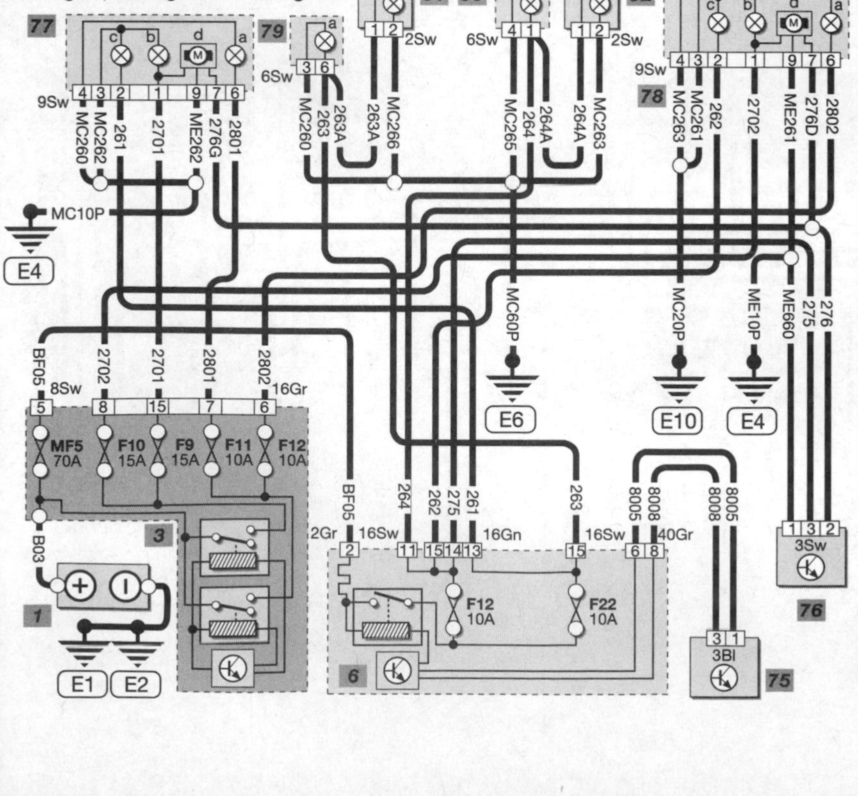

Brake lights

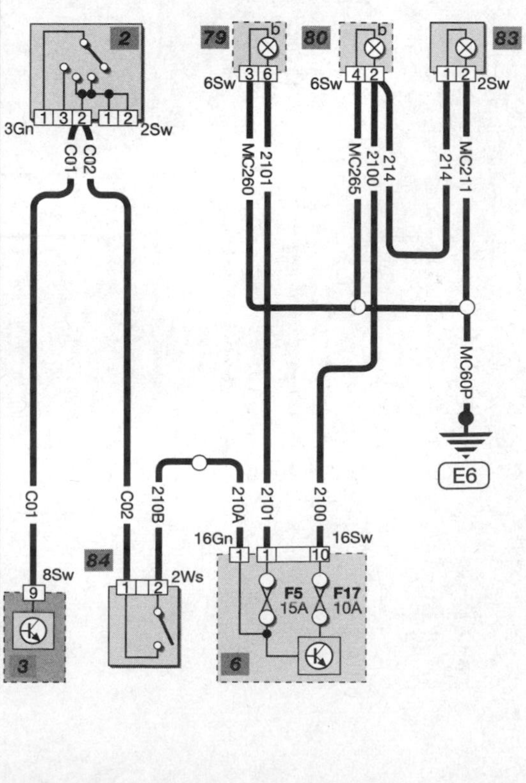

Connector colours

Bl	Blue	Or	Orange
Br	Brown	Ro	Red
Ge	Yellow	Sw	Black
Gr	Grey	Ws	White
Gn	Green		
Mc	Multicolored		

Key to items

1 Battery
2 Ignition switch
3 Main fuse box
6 Built-in System Interface
7 Engine control module
11 Instrument module
28 Steering wheel switches
43 Diagnostic connector
77 LH headlight unit
  e) direction indicator
  f) fog light
78 RH headlight unit
  (as 77)
79 LH tail light unit
  c) direction indicator
  d) reversing light
  e) fog light
80 RH tail light unit
  c) direction indicator
  d) reversing light
85 Hazard light switch
86 LH side repeater
87 RH side repeater
88 Reverse light switch
89 Glove box light
90 Rear courtesy light
91 Luggage compartment
  light switch and lock motor
92 Luggage compartment light
93 Front courtesy light switch
94 LH front courtesy light
95 RH front courtesy light
96 Passenger's front door lock
97 Drivers front door lock

Diagram 6

MTS
H32829

Direction indicator and hazard lights

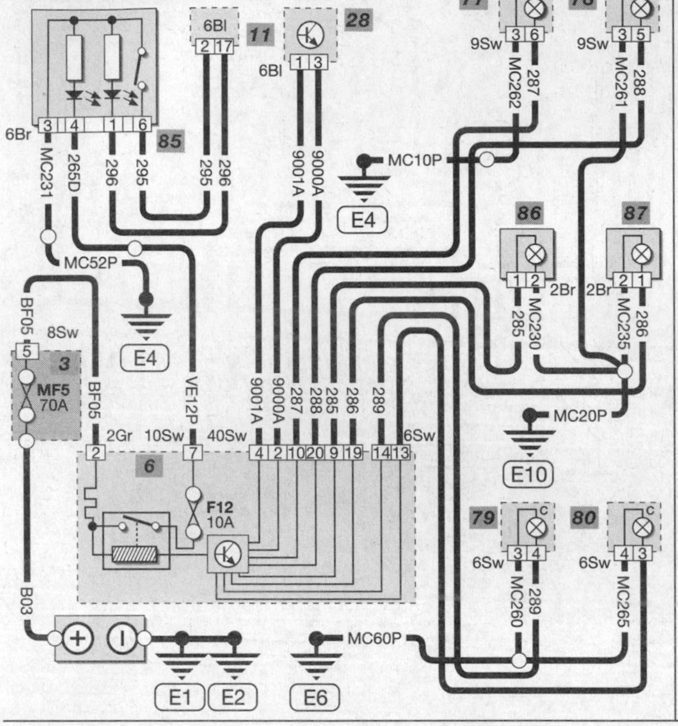

Reversing lights

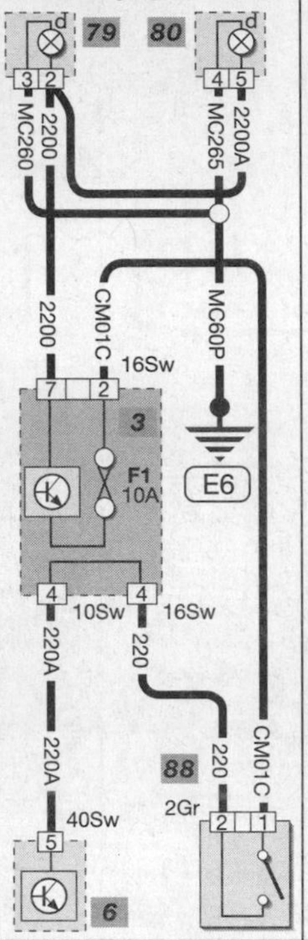

Fog lights

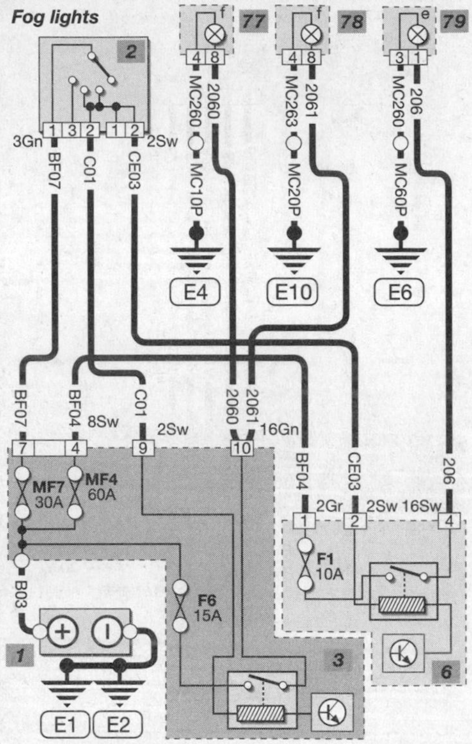

Interior lights

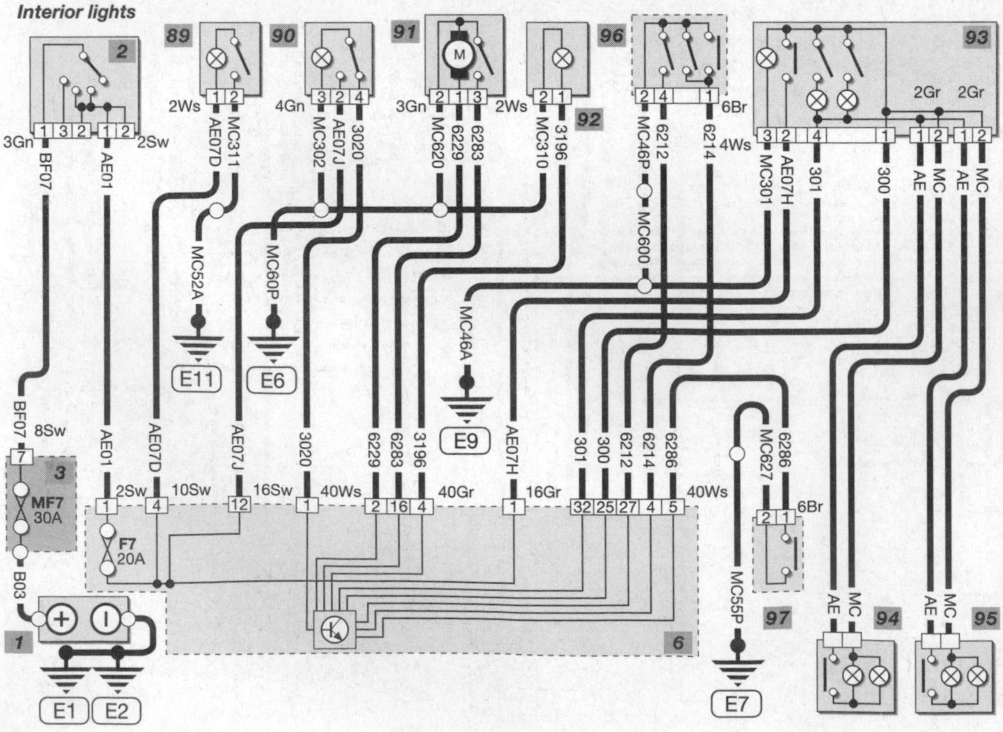

Diagnostic connector

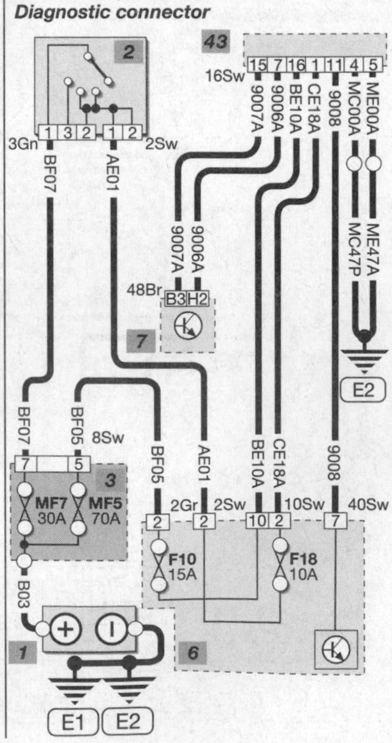

MTS
H32830

Connector colours

Bl Blue
Br Brown
Ge Yellow
Gr Grey
Gn Green
Mc Multicolored

Or Orange
Ro Red
Sw Black
Ws White

Key to items

1 Battery
2 Ignition switch
3 Main fuse box
6 Built-in System Interface
7 Engine control module
11 Instrument module
91 Luggage compartment light switch and lock motor
96 Passenger's front door lock
97 Drivers front door lock
98 LH rear door lock
99 RH rear door lock
100 Luggage compartment unlocking switch
101 Door locking switch
102 Oil pressure switch
103 Fuel pump and gauge
104 Handbrake switch
105 Passenger's seatbelt switch
106 Driver's seatbelt switch
107 Multifunction display
108 Engine temperature heat switch
109 Coolant temperature switch
110 Engine speed sensor

Diagram 7

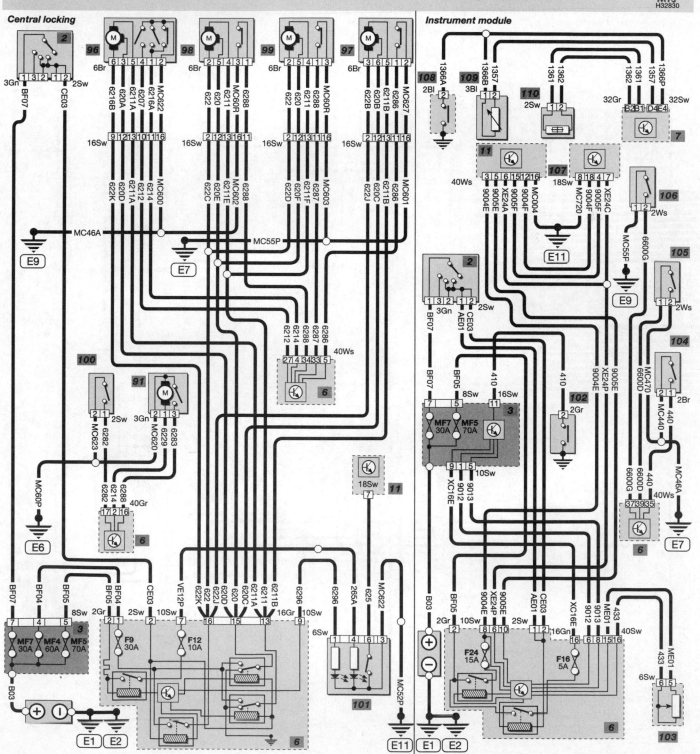

Connector colours

Bl	Blue	**Or**	Orange
Br	Brown	**Ro**	Red
Ge	Yellow	**Sw**	Black
Gr	Grey	**Ws**	White
Gn	Green		
Mc	Multicolored		

Key to items

1 Battery
2 Ignition switch
3 Main fuse box
6 Built-in System Interface
7 Engine control module
108 Engine temperature heat switch
109 Coolant temperature switch
110 Engine speed sensor
111 Pressostat
112 High speed fan relay
113 Low speed fan relay
114 Two speed cooling fan resistor
115 Cooling fan
116 Cooling fan fuse
117 Engine coolant level switch

Diagram 8

* RFN only
** KFW & NFU only

MTS
H32831

Petrol engine cooling

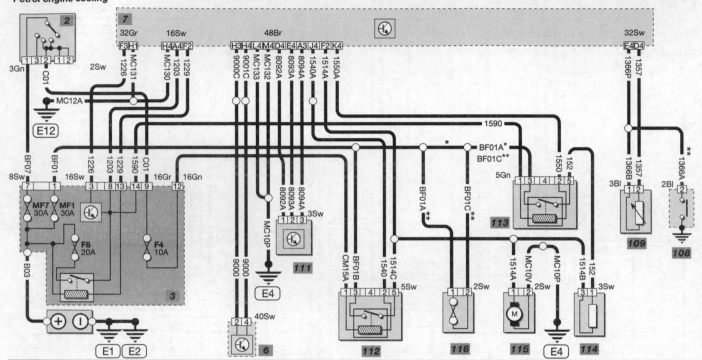

Diesel engine cooling

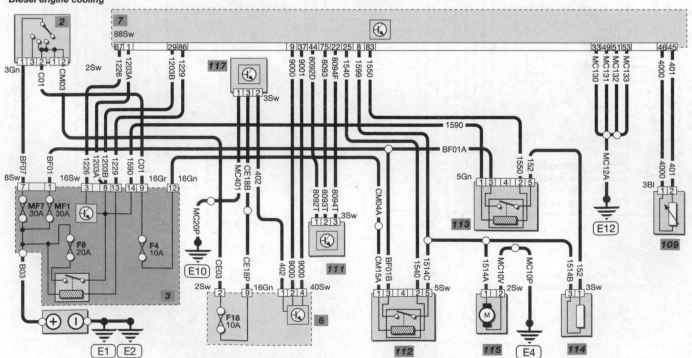

Dimensions and weights

Note: *All figures are approximate, and may vary according to model. Refer to manufacturer's data for exact figures.*

Dimensions

	Hatchback	Estate
Overall length	4212 mm	4428 mm
Overall width (excluding mirrors)	1762 mm	1762 mm
Overall height (unladen)	1530 mm	1580 mm
Wheelbase	2608 mm	2708 mm

Weights

Kerb weight:
Petrol engine models:
1.4 litre engine	1234 kg
1.6 litre engine	1268 kg
2.0 litre engine	1313 kg

Diesel engine models:
1.4 litre engine	1271 kg
1.6 litre engine	1325 kg
2.0 litre engine	1335 kg

Maximum gross vehicle weight*:
Petrol engine models:
1.4 litre engine	1659 kg
1.6 litre engine	1693 kg
2.0 litre engine	1719 kg

Diesel engine models:
1.4 litre engine	1696 kg
1.6 litre engine	1770 kg
2.0 litre engine:	
SOHC	1760 kg
DOHC	1850 kg

Maximum gross train (vehicle and trailer) weight*:
Petrol engine models:
1.4 litre engine	2659 kg
1.6 litre engine	2893 kg
2.0 litre engine	3019 kg

Diesel engine models:
1.4 litre engine	2836 kg
1.6 litre engine	3130 kg
2.0 litre engine:	
SOHC	3060 kg
DOHC	3450 kg

Maximum towing weight**:
Unbraked trailer:
1.4 litre petrol engine model	590 kg
1.6 litre petrol engine model	610 kg
2.0 litre petrol engine model	625 kg
1.4 litre diesel engine model	635 kg
1.6 litre engine	655 kg
2.0 litre engine:	
SOHC	655 kg
DOHC	715 kg

Braked trailer:
1.4 and 1.6 litre petrol engine models	1200 kg
1.4 litre diesel engine model	1140 kg
1.6 litre engine	1360 kg
2.0 litre engine:	
SOHC	1300 kg
DOHC	1600 kg

*Refer to the Vehicle Identification Plate for the exact figures for your vehicle – see 'Vehicle identification numbers'
**Ensure the combined weight of the trailer and vehicle never exceeds the gross train weight when towing.

Conversion factors

Length (distance)

Inches (in)	x 25.4	= Millimetres (mm)	x 0.0394	= Inches (in)
Feet (ft)	x 0.305	= Metres (m)	x 3.281	= Feet (ft)
Miles	x 1.609	= Kilometres (km)	x 0.621	= Miles

Volume (capacity)

Cubic inches (cu in; in³)	x 16.387	= Cubic centimetres (cc; cm³)	x 0.061	= Cubic inches (cu in; in³)
Imperial pints (Imp pt)	x 0.568	= Litres (l)	x 1.76	= Imperial pints (Imp pt)
Imperial quarts (Imp qt)	x 1.137	= Litres (l)	x 0.88	= Imperial quarts (Imp qt)
Imperial quarts (Imp qt)	x 1.201	= US quarts (US qt)	x 0.833	= Imperial quarts (Imp qt)
US quarts (US qt)	x 0.946	= Litres (l)	x 1.057	= US quarts (US qt)
Imperial gallons (Imp gal)	x 4.546	= Litres (l)	x 0.22	= Imperial gallons (Imp gal)
Imperial gallons (Imp gal)	x 1.201	= US gallons (US gal)	x 0.833	= Imperial gallons (Imp gal)
US gallons (US gal)	x 3.785	= Litres (l)	x 0.264	= US gallons (US gal)

Mass (weight)

Ounces (oz)	x 28.35	= Grams (g)	x 0.035	= Ounces (oz)
Pounds (lb)	x 0.454	= Kilograms (kg)	x 2.205	= Pounds (lb)

Force

Ounces-force (ozf; oz)	x 0.278	= Newtons (N)	x 3.6	= Ounces-force (ozf; oz)
Pounds-force (lbf; lb)	x 4.448	= Newtons (N)	x 0.225	= Pounds-force (lbf; lb)
Newtons (N)	x 0.1	= Kilograms-force (kgf; kg)	x 9.81	= Newtons (N)

Pressure

Pounds-force per square inch (psi; lbf/in²; lb/in²)	x 0.070	= Kilograms-force per square centimetre (kgf/cm²; kg/cm²)	x 14.223	= Pounds-force per square inch (psi; lbf/in²; lb/in²)
Pounds-force per square inch (psi; lbf/in²; lb/in²)	x 0.068	= Atmospheres (atm)	x 14.696	= Pounds-force per square inch (psi; lbf/in²; lb/in²)
Pounds-force per square inch (psi; lbf/in²; lb/in²)	x 0.069	= Bars	x 14.5	= Pounds-force per square inch (psi; lbf/in²; lb/in²)
Pounds-force per square inch (psi; lbf/in²; lb/in²)	x 6.895	= Kilopascals (kPa)	x 0.145	= Pounds-force per square inch (psi; lbf/in²; lb/in²)
Kilopascals (kPa)	x 0.01	= Kilograms-force per square centimetre (kgf/cm²; kg/cm²)	x 98.1	= Kilopascals (kPa)
Millibar (mbar)	x 100	= Pascals (Pa)	x 0.01	= Millibar (mbar)
Millibar (mbar)	x 0.0145	= Pounds-force per square inch (psi; lbf/in²; lb/in²)	x 68.947	= Millibar (mbar)
Millibar (mbar)	x 0.75	= Millimetres of mercury (mmHg)	x 1.333	= Millibar (mbar)
Millibar (mbar)	x 0.401	= Inches of water (inH₂O)	x 2.491	= Millibar (mbar)
Millimetres of mercury (mmHg)	x 0.535	= Inches of water (inH₂O)	x 1.868	= Millimetres of mercury (mmHg)
Inches of water (inH₂O)	x 0.036	= Pounds-force per square inch (psi; lbf/in²; lb/in²)	x 27.68	= Inches of water (inH₂O)

Torque (moment of force)

Pounds-force inches (lbf in; lb in)	x 1.152	= Kilograms-force centimetre (kgf cm; kg cm)	x 0.868	= Pounds-force inches (lbf in; lb in)
Pounds-force inches (lbf in; lb in)	x 0.113	= Newton metres (Nm)	x 8.85	= Pounds-force inches (lbf in; lb in)
Pounds-force inches (lbf in; lb in)	x 0.083	= Pounds-force feet (lbf ft; lb ft)	x 12	= Pounds-force inches (lbf in; lb in)
Pounds-force feet (lbf ft; lb ft)	x 0.138	= Kilograms-force metres (kgf m; kg m)	x 7.233	= Pounds-force feet (lbf ft; lb ft)
Pounds-force feet (lbf ft; lb ft)	x 1.356	= Newton metres (Nm)	x 0.738	= Pounds-force feet (lbf ft; lb ft)
Newton metres (Nm)	x 0.102	= Kilograms-force metres (kgf m; kg m)	x 9.804	= Newton metres (Nm)

Power

Horsepower (hp)	x 745.7	= Watts (W)	x 0.0013	= Horsepower (hp)

Velocity (speed)

Miles per hour (miles/hr; mph)	x 1.609	= Kilometres per hour (km/hr; kph)	x 0.621	= Miles per hour (miles/hr; mph)

Fuel consumption*

Miles per gallon, Imperial (mpg)	x 0.354	= Kilometres per litre (km/l)	x 2.825	= Miles per gallon, Imperial (mpg)
Miles per gallon, US (mpg)	x 0.425	= Kilometres per litre (km/l)	x 2.352	= Miles per gallon, US (mpg)

Temperature

Degrees Fahrenheit = (°C x 1.8) + 32   Degrees Celsius (Degrees Centigrade; °C) = (°F - 32) x 0.56

It is common practice to convert from miles per gallon (mpg) to litres/100 kilometres (l/100km), where mpg x l/100 km = 282

Spare parts are available from many sources, including maker's appointed garages, accessory shops, and motor factors. To be sure of obtaining the correct parts, it may sometimes be necessary to quote the vehicle identification number. If possible, it can also be useful to take the old parts along for positive identification. Items such as starter motors and alternators maybe available under a service exchange scheme – any parts returned should be clean.

Our advice regarding spare part sources is:

Officially-appointed garages

This is the best source of parts which are peculiar to your car, and are not otherwise generally available (eg, badges, interior trim, certain body panels, etc). It is also the only place at which you should buy parts if the vehicle is still under warranty.

Accessory shops

These are very good places to buy materials and components needed for the maintenance of your car (oil, air and fuel filters, spark plugs, light bulbs, drivebelts, oils and greases, brake pads, touch-up paint, etc). Components of this nature sold by a reputable shop are of the same standard as those used by the car manufacturer.

Besides components, these shops will also sell tools and general accessories, usually have convenient opening hours, charge lower prices, and can often be found close to home. Some accessory shops also have parts counters where components needed for almost any repair job can be purchased or ordered.

Motor factors

Good factors will stock all the more important components which wear out comparatively quickly and can sometimes supply individual components needed for the overhaul of a larger assembly. They may also handle work such as cylinder block reboring, crankshaft regrinding and balancing, etc.

Tyre and exhaust specialists

These outlets may be independent or members of a local or national chain. They frequently offer competitive prices when compared with a main dealer or local garage, but it will pay to obtain several quotes before making a decision. Also ask what 'extras' may be added to the quote – for instance, fitting a new valve and balancing the wheel are both often charged on top of the price of a new tyre.

Other sources

Beware of parts or materials obtained from market stalls, car boot sales or similar outlets. Such items are not invariably sub-standard, but there is little chance of compensation if they do prove unsatisfactory. In the case of safety-critical components such as brake pads there is the risk not only of financial loss but also of an accident causing injury or death.

Vehicle identification numbers

Modifications are a continuing and unpublicised process in vehicle manufacture, quite apart from major model changes. Spare parts manuals and lists are compiled upon a numerical basis, the individual vehicle identification numbers being essential for correct identification of the part concerned.

When ordering spare parts, always give as much information as possible. Quote the car model, year of manufacture, body and engine numbers, but most importantly, the 4-digit production code (sometimes referred to as the 'spares number').

The *vehicle production code* is stamped or painted onto the driver's door pillar, adjacent to the door hinges **(see illustration)**. The code provides Peugeot dealers with details of the exact build date and model. The vehicle paint code is also given here.

The *vehicle identification number (VIN) plate* is riveted onto right-hand chassis rail, in the engine compartment. The plate carries the vehicle identification number (VIN) and vehicle weight information **(see illustration)**.

The *vehicle identification number (VIN)* is stamped onto a plate visible through the base of the windscreen **(see illustration)**.

The engine number is situated on the front face of the cylinder block, and can be found in the following locations:

a) On petrol engines the engine number is located on the left-hand side of the cylinder block. The number is either stamped directly onto the block or is stamped onto a plate which is riveted to the block.

b) On diesel engines the engine number is stamped on the base of the cylinder block on the flat surface located on the left- (2.0 litre engines) or right- (1.4 and 1.6 litre engines) hand side of the oil filter/cooler.

Note: *The first part of the engine number gives the engine code, eg KFW.*

The vehicle production and paint codes are located on the driver's door pillar

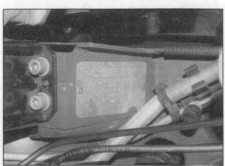
The vehicle identification plate is fixed to the right-hand chassis in the engine compartment

The VIN is also visible through the windscreen

Whenever servicing, repair or overhaul work is carried out on the car or its components, observe the following procedures and instructions. This will assist in carrying out the operation efficiently and to a professional standard of workmanship.

Joint mating faces and gaskets

When separating components at their mating faces, never insert screwdrivers or similar implements into the joint between the faces in order to prise them apart. This can cause severe damage which results in oil leaks, coolant leaks, etc upon reassembly. Separation is usually achieved by tapping along the joint with a soft-faced hammer in order to break the seal. However, note that this method may not be suitable where dowels are used for component location.

Where a gasket is used between the mating faces of two components, a new one must be fitted on reassembly; fit it dry unless otherwise stated in the repair procedure. Make sure that the mating faces are clean and dry, with all traces of old gasket removed. When cleaning a joint face, use a tool which is unlikely to score or damage the face, and remove any burrs or nicks with an oilstone or fine file.

Make sure that tapped holes are cleaned with a pipe cleaner, and keep them free of jointing compound, if this is being used, unless specifically instructed otherwise.

Ensure that all orifices, channels or pipes are clear, and blow through them, preferably using compressed air.

Oil seals

Oil seals can be removed by levering them out with a wide flat-bladed screwdriver or similar implement. Alternatively, a number of self-tapping screws may be screwed into the seal, and these used as a purchase for pliers or some similar device in order to pull the seal free.

Whenever an oil seal is removed from its working location, either individually or as part of an assembly, it should be renewed.

The very fine sealing lip of the seal is easily damaged, and will not seal if the surface it contacts is not completely clean and free from scratches, nicks or grooves. If the original sealing surface of the component cannot be restored, and the manufacturer has not made provision for slight relocation of the seal relative to the sealing surface, the component should be renewed.

Protect the lips of the seal from any surface which may damage them in the course of fitting. Use tape or a conical sleeve where possible. Lubricate the seal lips with oil before fitting and, on dual-lipped seals, fill the space between the lips with grease.

Unless otherwise stated, oil seals must be fitted with their sealing lips toward the lubricant to be sealed.

Use a tubular drift or block of wood of the appropriate size to install the seal and, if the seal housing is shouldered, drive the seal down to the shoulder. If the seal housing is unshouldered, the seal should be fitted with its face flush with the housing top face (unless otherwise instructed).

Screw threads and fastenings

Seized nuts, bolts and screws are quite a common occurrence where corrosion has set in, and the use of penetrating oil or releasing fluid will often overcome this problem if the offending item is soaked for a while before attempting to release it. The use of an impact driver may also provide a means of releasing such stubborn fastening devices, when used in conjunction with the appropriate screwdriver bit or socket. If none of these methods works, it may be necessary to resort to the careful application of heat, or the use of a hacksaw or nut splitter device.

Studs are usually removed by locking two nuts together on the threaded part, and then using a spanner on the lower nut to unscrew the stud. Studs or bolts which have broken off below the surface of the component in which they are mounted can sometimes be removed using a stud extractor. Always ensure that a blind tapped hole is completely free from oil, grease, water or other fluid before installing the bolt or stud. Failure to do this could cause the housing to crack due to the hydraulic action of the bolt or stud as it is screwed in.

When tightening a castellated nut to accept a split pin, tighten the nut to the specified torque, where applicable, and then tighten further to the next split pin hole. Never slacken the nut to align the split pin hole, unless stated in the repair procedure.

When checking or retightening a nut or bolt to a specified torque setting, slacken the nut or bolt by a quarter of a turn, and then retighten to the specified setting. However, this should not be attempted where angular tightening has been used.

For some screw fastenings, notably cylinder head bolts or nuts, torque wrench settings are no longer specified for the latter stages of tightening, "angle-tightening" being called up instead. Typically, a fairly low torque wrench setting will be applied to the bolts/nuts in the correct sequence, followed by one or more stages of tightening through specified angles.

Locknuts, locktabs and washers

Any fastening which will rotate against a component or housing during tightening should always have a washer between it and the relevant component or housing.

Spring or split washers should always be renewed when they are used to lock a critical component such as a big-end bearing retaining bolt or nut. Locktabs which are folded over to retain a nut or bolt should always be renewed.

Self-locking nuts can be re-used in non-critical areas, providing resistance can be felt when the locking portion passes over the bolt or stud thread. However, it should be noted that self-locking stiffnuts tend to lose their effectiveness after long periods of use, and should then be renewed as a matter of course.

Split pins must always be replaced with new ones of the correct size for the hole.

When thread-locking compound is found on the threads of a fastener which is to be re-used, it should be cleaned off with a wire brush and solvent, and fresh compound applied on reassembly.

Special tools

Some repair procedures in this manual entail the use of special tools such as a press, two or three-legged pullers, spring compressors, etc. Wherever possible, suitable readily-available alternatives to the manufacturer's special tools are described, and are shown in use. In some instances, where no alternative is possible, it has been necessary to resort to the use of a manufacturer's tool, and this has been done for reasons of safety as well as the efficient completion of the repair operation. Unless you are highly-skilled and have a thorough understanding of the procedures described, never attempt to bypass the use of any special tool when the procedure described specifies its use. Not only is there a very great risk of personal injury, but expensive damage could be caused to the components involved.

Environmental considerations

When disposing of used engine oil, brake fluid, antifreeze, etc, give due consideration to any detrimental environmental effects. Do not, for instance, pour any of the above liquids down drains into the general sewage system, or onto the ground to soak away. Many local council refuse tips provide a facility for waste oil disposal, as do some garages. If none of these facilities are available, consult your local Environmental Health Department, or the National Rivers Authority, for further advice.

With the universal tightening-up of legislation regarding the emission of environmentally-harmful substances from motor vehicles, most vehicles have tamperproof devices fitted to the main adjustment points of the fuel system. These devices are primarily designed to prevent unqualified persons from adjusting the fuel/air mixture, with the chance of a consequent increase in toxic emissions. If such devices are found during servicing or overhaul, they should, wherever possible, be renewed or refitted in accordance with the manufacturer's requirements or current legislation.

OIL CARE
FOLLOW THE CODE

OIL BANK LINE
0800 66 33 66
www.oilbankline.org.uk

Note: It is antisocial and illegal to dump oil down the drain. To find the location of your local oil recycling bank, call this number free.

The jack supplied with the vehicle should only be used for changing the roadwheels – see *Wheel changing* at the front of this manual. When carrying out any other kind of work, raise the vehicle using a hydraulic (or 'trolley') jack, and always supplement the jack with axle stands at the vehicle jacking points.

When using a hydraulic jack or axle stands, always position the jack head or axle stand head under one of the relevant jacking points; the jacking point is the area in below the cut-out on the sill **(see illustration)**. Use a block of wood between the jack or axle stand and the sill – the block of wood should have a groove cut into it, into which the welded flange of the sill will locate.

Do not attempt to jack the vehicle under the front crossmember, the sump, or any of the suspension components.

The jack supplied with the vehicle locates in the jacking points on the underside of the sills – see *Wheel changing*. Ensure that the jack head is correctly engaged before attempting to raise the vehicle.

Never work under, around, or near a raised vehicle, unless it is adequately supported in at least two places.

The jacking point is below the cut-out in the sill

Introduction

A selection of good tools is a fundamental requirement for anyone contemplating the maintenance and repair of a motor vehicle. For the owner who does not possess any, their purchase will prove a considerable expense, offsetting some of the savings made by doing-it-yourself. However, provided that the tools purchased meet the relevant national safety standards and are of good quality, they will last for many years and prove an extremely worthwhile investment.

To help the average owner to decide which tools are needed to carry out the various tasks detailed in this manual, we have compiled three lists of tools under the following headings: *Maintenance and minor repair, Repair and overhaul,* and *Special.* Newcomers to practical mechanics should start off with the *Maintenance and minor repair* tool kit, and confine themselves to the simpler jobs around the vehicle. Then, as confidence and experience grow, more difficult tasks can be undertaken, with extra tools being purchased as, and when, they are needed. In this way, a *Maintenance and minor repair* tool kit can be built up into a *Repair and overhaul* tool kit over a considerable period of time, without any major cash outlays. The experienced do-it-yourselfer will have a tool kit good enough for most repair and overhaul procedures, and will add tools from the *Special* category when it is felt that the expense is justified by the amount of use to which these tools will be put.

Maintenance and minor repair tool kit

The tools given in this list should be considered as a minimum requirement if routine maintenance, servicing and minor repair operations are to be undertaken. We recommend the purchase of combination spanners (ring one end, open-ended the other); although more expensive than open-ended ones, they do give the advantages of both types of spanner.

- ☐ *Combination spanners:*
  Metric - 8 to 19 mm inclusive
- ☐ *Adjustable spanner - 35 mm jaw (approx.)*
- ☐ *Spark plug spanner (with rubber insert) - petrol models*
- ☐ *Spark plug gap adjustment tool - petrol models*
- ☐ *Set of feeler gauges*
- ☐ *Brake bleed nipple spanner*
- ☐ *Screwdrivers:*
  Flat blade - 100 mm long x 6 mm dia
  Cross blade - 100 mm long x 6 mm dia
  Torx - various sizes (not all vehicles)
- ☐ *Combination pliers*
- ☐ *Hacksaw (junior)*
- ☐ *Tyre pump*
- ☐ *Tyre pressure gauge*
- ☐ *Oil can*
- ☐ *Oil filter removal tool*
- ☐ *Fine emery cloth*
- ☐ *Wire brush (small)*
- ☐ *Funnel (medium size)*
- ☐ *Sump drain plug key (not all vehicles)*

Repair and overhaul tool kit

These tools are virtually essential for anyone undertaking any major repairs to a motor vehicle, and are additional to those given in the *Maintenance and minor repair* list. Included in this list is a comprehensive set of sockets. Although these are expensive, they will be found invaluable as they are so versatile - particularly if various drives are included in the set. We recommend the half-inch square-drive type, as this can be used with most proprietary torque wrenches.

The tools in this list will sometimes need to be supplemented by tools from the *Special* list:

- ☐ *Sockets (or box spanners) to cover range in previous list (including Torx sockets)*
- ☐ *Reversible ratchet drive (for use with sockets)*
- ☐ *Extension piece, 250 mm (for use with sockets)*
- ☐ *Universal joint (for use with sockets)*
- ☐ *Flexible handle or sliding T "breaker bar" (for use with sockets)*
- ☐ *Torque wrench (for use with sockets)*
- ☐ *Self-locking grips*
- ☐ *Ball pein hammer*
- ☐ *Soft-faced mallet (plastic or rubber)*
- ☐ *Screwdrivers:*
  Flat blade - long & sturdy, short (chubby), and narrow (electrician's) types
  Cross blade – long & sturdy, and short (chubby) types
- ☐ *Pliers:*
  Long-nosed
  Side cutters (electrician's)
  Circlip (internal and external)
- ☐ *Cold chisel - 25 mm*
- ☐ *Scriber*
- ☐ *Scraper*
- ☐ *Centre-punch*
- ☐ *Pin punch*
- ☐ *Hacksaw*
- ☐ *Brake hose clamp*
- ☐ *Brake/clutch bleeding kit*
- ☐ *Selection of twist drills*
- ☐ *Steel rule/straight-edge*
- ☐ *Allen keys (inc. splined/Torx type)*
- ☐ *Selection of files*
- ☐ *Wire brush*
- ☐ *Axle stands*
- ☐ *Jack (strong trolley or hydraulic type)*
- ☐ *Light with extension lead*
- ☐ *Universal electrical multi-meter*

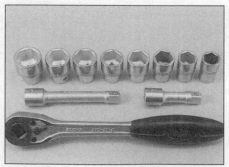

Sockets and reversible ratchet drive

Brake bleeding kit

Torx key, socket and bit

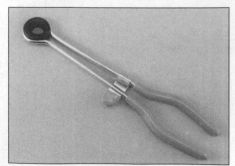

Hose clamp

Angular-tightening gauge

Special tools

The tools in this list are those which are not used regularly, are expensive to buy, or which need to be used in accordance with their manufacturers' instructions. Unless relatively difficult mechanical jobs are undertaken frequently, it will not be economic to buy many of these tools. Where this is the case, you could consider clubbing together with friends (or joining a motorists' club) to make a joint purchase, or borrowing the tools against a deposit from a local garage or tool hire specialist. It is worth noting that many of the larger DIY superstores now carry a large range of special tools for hire at modest rates.

The following list contains only those tools and instruments freely available to the public, and not those special tools produced by the vehicle manufacturer specifically for its dealer network. You will find occasional references to these manufacturers' special tools in the text of this manual. Generally, an alternative method of doing the job without the vehicle manufacturers' special tool is given. However, sometimes there is no alternative to using them. Where this is the case and the relevant tool cannot be bought or borrowed, you will have to entrust the work to a dealer.

- ☐ Angular-tightening gauge
- ☐ Valve spring compressor
- ☐ Valve grinding tool
- ☐ Piston ring compressor
- ☐ Piston ring removal/installation tool
- ☐ Cylinder bore hone
- ☐ Balljoint separator
- ☐ Coil spring compressors (where applicable)
- ☐ Two/three-legged hub and bearing puller
- ☐ Impact screwdriver
- ☐ Micrometer and/or vernier calipers
- ☐ Dial gauge
- ☐ Stroboscopic timing light
- ☐ Dwell angle meter/tachometer
- ☐ Fault code reader
- ☐ Cylinder compression gauge
- ☐ Hand-operated vacuum pump and gauge
- ☐ Clutch plate alignment set
- ☐ Brake shoe steady spring cup removal tool
- ☐ Bush and bearing removal/installation set
- ☐ Stud extractors
- ☐ Tap and die set
- ☐ Lifting tackle
- ☐ Trolley jack

Buying tools

Reputable motor accessory shops and superstores often offer excellent quality tools at discount prices, so it pays to shop around.

Remember, you don't have to buy the most expensive items on the shelf, but it is always advisable to steer clear of the very cheap tools. Beware of 'bargains' offered on market stalls or at car boot sales. There are plenty of good tools around at reasonable prices, but always aim to purchase items which meet the relevant national safety standards. If in doubt, ask the proprietor or manager of the shop for advice before making a purchase.

Care and maintenance of tools

Having purchased a reasonable tool kit, it is necessary to keep the tools in a clean and serviceable condition. After use, always wipe off any dirt, grease and metal particles using a clean, dry cloth, before putting the tools away. Never leave them lying around after they have been used. A simple tool rack on the garage or workshop wall for items such as screwdrivers and pliers is a good idea. Store all normal spanners and sockets in a metal box. Any measuring instruments, gauges, meters, etc, must be carefully stored where they cannot be damaged or become rusty.

Take a little care when tools are used. Hammer heads inevitably become marked, and screwdrivers lose the keen edge on their blades from time to time. A little timely attention with emery cloth or a file will soon restore items like this to a good finish.

Working facilities

Not to be forgotten when discussing tools is the workshop itself. If anything more than routine maintenance is to be carried out, a suitable working area becomes essential.

It is appreciated that many an owner-mechanic is forced by circumstances to remove an engine or similar item without the benefit of a garage or workshop. Having done this, any repairs should always be done under the cover of a roof.

Wherever possible, any dismantling should be done on a clean, flat workbench or table at a suitable working height.

Any workbench needs a vice; one with a jaw opening of 100 mm is suitable for most jobs. As mentioned previously, some clean dry storage space is also required for tools, as well as for any lubricants, cleaning fluids, touch-up paints etc, which become necessary.

Another item which may be required, and which has a much more general usage, is an electric drill with a chuck capacity of at least 8 mm. This, together with a good range of twist drills, is virtually essential for fitting accessories.

Last, but not least, always keep a supply of old newspapers and clean, lint-free rags available, and try to keep any working area as clean as possible.

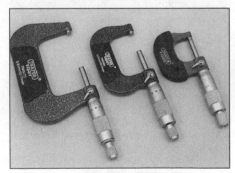
Micrometers

Dial test indicator ("dial gauge")

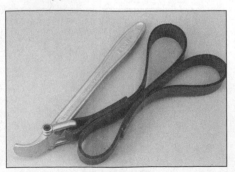
Strap wrench

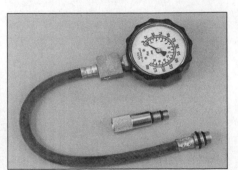
Compression tester

Fault code reader

This is a guide to getting your vehicle through the MOT test. Obviously it will not be possible to examine the vehicle to the same standard as the professional MOT tester. However, working through the following checks will enable you to identify any problem areas before submitting the vehicle for the test.

It has only been possible to summarise the test requirements here, based on the regulations in force at the time of printing. Test standards are becoming increasingly stringent, although there are some exemptions for older vehicles.

An assistant will be needed to help carry out some of these checks.

The checks have been sub-divided into four categories, as follows:

1 Checks carried out **FROM THE DRIVER'S SEAT**

2 Checks carried out **WITH THE VEHICLE ON THE GROUND**

3 Checks carried out **WITH THE VEHICLE RAISED AND THE WHEELS FREE TO TURN**

4 Checks carried out on **YOUR VEHICLE'S EXHAUST EMISSION SYSTEM**

---

1 Checks carried out **FROM THE DRIVER'S SEAT**

Handbrake

☐ Test the operation of the handbrake. Excessive travel (too many clicks) indicates incorrect brake or cable adjustment.
☐ Check that the handbrake cannot be released by tapping the lever sideways. Check the security of the lever mountings.

Footbrake

☐ Depress the brake pedal and check that it does not creep down to the floor, indicating a master cylinder fault. Release the pedal, wait a few seconds, then depress it again. If the pedal travels nearly to the floor before firm resistance is felt, brake adjustment or repair is necessary. If the pedal feels spongy, there is air in the hydraulic system which must be removed by bleeding.

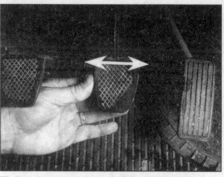

☐ Check that the brake pedal is secure and in good condition. Check also for signs of fluid leaks on the pedal, floor or carpets, which would indicate failed seals in the brake master cylinder.
☐ Check the servo unit (when applicable) by operating the brake pedal several times, then keeping the pedal depressed and starting the engine. As the engine starts, the pedal will move down slightly. If not, the vacuum hose or the servo itself may be faulty.

Steering wheel and column

☐ Examine the steering wheel for fractures or looseness of the hub, spokes or rim.
☐ Move the steering wheel from side to side and then up and down. Check that the steering wheel is not loose on the column, indicating wear or a loose retaining nut. Continue moving the steering wheel as before, but also turn it slightly from left to right.
☐ Check that the steering wheel is not loose on the column, and that there is no abnormal

movement of the steering wheel, indicating wear in the column support bearings or couplings.

Windscreen, mirrors and sunvisor

☐ The windscreen must be free of cracks or other significant damage within the driver's field of view. (Small stone chips are acceptable.) Rear view mirrors must be secure, intact, and capable of being adjusted.

☐ The driver's sunvisor must be capable of being stored in the "up" position.

Seat belts and seats

Note: *The following checks are applicable to all seat belts, front and rear.*

☐ Examine the webbing of all the belts (including rear belts if fitted) for cuts, serious fraying or deterioration. Fasten and unfasten each belt to check the buckles. If applicable, check the retracting mechanism. Check the security of all seat belt mountings accessible from inside the vehicle.

☐ Seat belts with pre-tensioners, once activated, have a "flag" or similar showing on the seat belt stalk. This, in itself, is not a reason for test failure.

☐ The front seats themselves must be securely attached and the backrests must lock in the upright position.

Doors

☐ Both front doors must be able to be opened and closed from outside and inside, and must latch securely when closed.

2 Checks carried out WITH THE VEHICLE ON THE GROUND

Vehicle identification

☐ Number plates must be in good condition, secure and legible, with letters and numbers correctly spaced – spacing at (A) should be at least twice that at (B).

☐ The VIN plate and/or homologation plate must be legible.

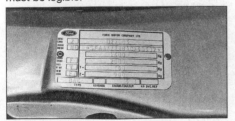

Electrical equipment

☐ Switch on the ignition and check the operation of the horn.

☐ Check the windscreen washers and wipers, examining the wiper blades; renew damaged or perished blades. Also check the operation of the stop-lights.

☐ Check the operation of the sidelights and number plate lights. The lenses and reflectors must be secure, clean and undamaged.

☐ Check the operation and alignment of the headlights. The headlight reflectors must not be tarnished and the lenses must be undamaged.

☐ Switch on the ignition and check the operation of the direction indicators (including the instrument panel tell-tale) and the hazard warning lights. Operation of the sidelights and stop-lights must not affect the indicators - if it does, the cause is usually a bad earth at the rear light cluster.

☐ Check the operation of the rear foglight(s), including the warning light on the instrument panel or in the switch.

☐ The ABS warning light must illuminate in accordance with the manufacturers' design. For most vehicles, the ABS warning light should illuminate when the ignition is switched on, and (if the system is operating properly) extinguish after a few seconds. Refer to the owner's handbook.

Footbrake

☐ Examine the master cylinder, brake pipes and servo unit for leaks, loose mountings, corrosion or other damage.

☐ The fluid reservoir must be secure and the fluid level must be between the upper (**A**) and lower (**B**) markings.

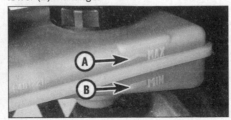

☐ Inspect both front brake flexible hoses for cracks or deterioration of the rubber. Turn the steering from lock to lock, and ensure that the hoses do not contact the wheel, tyre, or any part of the steering or suspension mechanism. With the brake pedal firmly depressed, check the hoses for bulges or leaks under pressure.

Steering and suspension

☐ Have your assistant turn the steering wheel from side to side slightly, up to the point where the steering gear just begins to transmit this movement to the roadwheels. Check for excessive free play between the steering wheel and the steering gear, indicating wear or insecurity of the steering column joints, the column-to-steering gear coupling, or the steering gear itself.

☐ Have your assistant turn the steering wheel more vigorously in each direction, so that the roadwheels just begin to turn. As this is done, examine all the steering joints, linkages, fittings and attachments. Renew any component that shows signs of wear or damage. On vehicles with power steering, check the security and condition of the steering pump, drivebelt and hoses.

☐ Check that the vehicle is standing level, and at approximately the correct ride height.

Shock absorbers

☐ Depress each corner of the vehicle in turn, then release it. The vehicle should rise and then settle in its normal position. If the vehicle continues to rise and fall, the shock absorber is defective. A shock absorber which has seized will also cause the vehicle to fail.

Exhaust system

☐ Start the engine. With your assistant holding a rag over the tailpipe, check the entire system for leaks. Repair or renew leaking sections.

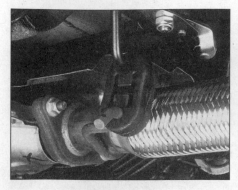

3 Checks carried out **WITH THE VEHICLE RAISED AND THE WHEELS FREE TO TURN**

Jack up the front and rear of the vehicle, and securely support it on axle stands. Position the stands clear of the suspension assemblies. Ensure that the wheels are clear of the ground and that the steering can be turned from lock to lock.

Steering mechanism

☐ Have your assistant turn the steering from lock to lock. Check that the steering turns smoothly, and that no part of the steering mechanism, including a wheel or tyre, fouls any brake hose or pipe or any part of the body structure.

☐ Examine the steering rack rubber gaiters for damage or insecurity of the retaining clips. If power steering is fitted, check for signs of damage or leakage of the fluid hoses, pipes or connections. Also check for excessive stiffness or binding of the steering, a missing split pin or locking device, or severe corrosion of the body structure within 30 cm of any steering component attachment point.

Front and rear suspension and wheel bearings

☐ Starting at the front right-hand side, grasp the roadwheel at the 3 o'clock and 9 o'clock positions and rock gently but firmly. Check for free play or insecurity at the wheel bearings, suspension balljoints, or suspension mountings, pivots and attachments.

☐ Now grasp the wheel at the 12 o'clock and 6 o'clock positions and repeat the previous inspection. Spin the wheel, and check for roughness or tightness of the front wheel bearing.

☐ If excess free play is suspected at a component pivot point, this can be confirmed by using a large screwdriver or similar tool and levering between the mounting and the component attachment. This will confirm whether the wear is in the pivot bush, its retaining bolt, or in the mounting itself (the bolt holes can often become elongated).

☐ Carry out all the above checks at the other front wheel, and then at both rear wheels.

Springs and shock absorbers

☐ Examine the suspension struts (when applicable) for serious fluid leakage, corrosion, or damage to the casing. Also check the security of the mounting points.

☐ If coil springs are fitted, check that the spring ends locate in their seats, and that the spring is not corroded, cracked or broken.

☐ If leaf springs are fitted, check that all leaves are intact, that the axle is securely attached to each spring, and that there is no deterioration of the spring eye mountings, bushes, and shackles.

☐ The same general checks apply to vehicles fitted with other suspension types, such as torsion bars, hydraulic displacer units, etc. Ensure that all mountings and attachments are secure, that there are no signs of excessive wear, corrosion or damage, and (on hydraulic types) that there are no fluid leaks or damaged pipes.

☐ Inspect the shock absorbers for signs of serious fluid leakage. Check for wear of the mounting bushes or attachments, or damage to the body of the unit.

Driveshafts (fwd vehicles only)

☐ Rotate each front wheel in turn and inspect the constant velocity joint gaiters for splits or damage. Also check that each driveshaft is straight and undamaged.

Braking system

☐ If possible without dismantling, check brake pad wear and disc condition. Ensure that the friction lining material has not worn excessively, (A) and that the discs are not fractured, pitted, scored or badly worn (B).

☐ Examine all the rigid brake pipes underneath the vehicle, and the flexible hose(s) at the rear. Look for corrosion, chafing or insecurity of the pipes, and for signs of bulging under pressure, chafing, splits or deterioration of the flexible hoses.

☐ Look for signs of fluid leaks at the brake calipers or on the brake backplates. Repair or renew leaking components.

☐ Slowly spin each wheel, while your assistant depresses and releases the footbrake. Ensure that each brake is operating and does not bind when the pedal is released.

☐ Examine the handbrake mechanism, checking for frayed or broken cables, excessive corrosion, or wear or insecurity of the linkage. Check that the mechanism works on each relevant wheel, and releases fully, without binding.

☐ It is not possible to test brake efficiency without special equipment, but a road test can be carried out later to check that the vehicle pulls up in a straight line.

Fuel and exhaust systems

☐ Inspect the fuel tank (including the filler cap), fuel pipes, hoses and unions. All components must be secure and free from leaks.

☐ Examine the exhaust system over its entire length, checking for any damaged, broken or missing mountings, security of the retaining clamps and rust or corrosion.

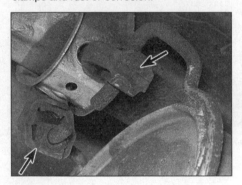

Wheels and tyres

☐ Examine the sidewalls and tread area of each tyre in turn. Check for cuts, tears, lumps, bulges, separation of the tread, and exposure of the ply or cord due to wear or damage. Check that the tyre bead is correctly seated on the wheel rim, that the valve is sound and properly seated, and that the wheel is not distorted or damaged.

☐ Check that the tyres are of the correct size for the vehicle, that they are of the same size

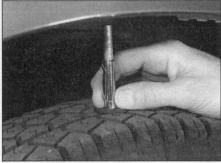

and type on each axle, and that the pressures are correct.

☐ Check the tyre tread depth. The legal minimum at the time of writing is 1.6 mm over at least three-quarters of the tread width. Abnormal tread wear may indicate incorrect front wheel alignment.

Body corrosion

☐ Check the condition of the entire vehicle structure for signs of corrosion in load-bearing areas. (These include chassis box sections, side sills, cross-members, pillars, and all suspension, steering, braking system and seat belt mountings and anchorages.) Any corrosion which has seriously reduced the thickness of a load-bearing area is likely to cause the vehicle to fail. In this case professional repairs are likely to be needed.

☐ Damage or corrosion which causes sharp or otherwise dangerous edges to be exposed will also cause the vehicle to fail.

4 Checks carried out on YOUR VEHICLE'S EXHAUST EMISSION SYSTEM

Petrol models

☐ The engine should be warmed up, and running well (ignition system in good order, air filter element clean, etc).

☐ Before testing, run the engine at around 2500 rpm for 20 seconds. Let the engine drop to idle, and watch for smoke from the exhaust. If the idle speed is too high, or if dense blue or black smoke emerges for more than 5 seconds, the vehicle will fail. Typically, blue smoke signifies oil burning (engine wear); black smoke means unburnt fuel (dirty air cleaner element, or other fuel system fault).

☐ An exhaust gas analyser for measuring carbon monoxide (CO) and hydrocarbons (HC) is now needed. If one cannot be hired or borrowed, have a local garage perform the check.

CO emissions (mixture)

☐ The MOT tester has access to the CO limits for all vehicles. The CO level is measured at idle speed, and at 'fast idle' (2500 to 3000 rpm). The following limits are given as a general guide:

At idle speed – Less than 0.5% CO
At 'fast idle' – Less than 0.3% CO
Lambda reading – 0.97 to 1.03

☐ If the CO level is too high, this may point to poor maintenance, a fuel injection system problem, faulty lambda (oxygen) sensor or catalytic converter. Try an injector cleaning treatment, and check the vehicle's ECU for fault codes.

HC emissions

☐ The MOT tester has access to HC limits for all vehicles. The HC level is measured at 'fast idle' (2500 to 3000 rpm). The following limits are given as a general guide:

At 'fast idle' – Less then 200 ppm

☐ Excessive HC emissions are typically caused by oil being burnt (worn engine), or by a blocked crankcase ventilation system ('breather'). If the engine oil is old and thin, an oil change may help. If the engine is running badly, check the vehicle's ECU for fault codes.

Diesel models

☐ The only emission test for diesel engines is measuring exhaust smoke density, using a calibrated smoke meter. The test involves accelerating the engine at least 3 times to its maximum unloaded speed.

Note: *On engines with a timing belt, it is VITAL that the belt is in good condition before the test is carried out.*

☐ With the engine warmed up, it is first purged by running at around 2500 rpm for 20 seconds. A governor check is then carried out, by slowly accelerating the engine to its maximum speed. After this, the smoke meter is connected, and the engine is accelerated quickly to maximum speed three times. If the smoke density is less than the limits given below, the vehicle will pass:

Non-turbo vehicles: 2.5m-1
Turbocharged vehicles: 3.0m-1

☐ If excess smoke is produced, try fitting a new air cleaner element, or using an injector cleaning treatment. If the engine is running badly, where applicable, check the vehicle's ECU for fault codes. Also check the vehicle's EGR system, where applicable. At high mileages, the injectors may require professional attention.

Engine

- ☐ Engine fails to rotate when attempting to start
- ☐ Engine rotates, but will not start
- ☐ Engine difficult to start when cold
- ☐ Engine difficult to start when hot
- ☐ Starter motor noisy or excessively-rough in engagement
- ☐ Engine starts, but stops immediately
- ☐ Engine idles erratically
- ☐ Engine misfires at idle speed
- ☐ Engine misfires throughout the driving speed range
- ☐ Engine hesitates on acceleration
- ☐ Engine stalls
- ☐ Engine lacks power
- ☐ Engine backfires
- ☐ Oil pressure warning light on with engine running
- ☐ Engine runs-on after switching off
- ☐ Engine noises

Cooling system

- ☐ Overheating
- ☐ Overcooling
- ☐ External coolant leakage
- ☐ Internal coolant leakage
- ☐ Corrosion

Fuel and exhaust systems

- ☐ Excessive fuel consumption
- ☐ Fuel leakage and/or fuel odour
- ☐ Excessive noise or fumes from exhaust system

Clutch

- ☐ Pedal travels to floor – no pressure or very little resistance
- ☐ Clutch fails to disengage (unable to select gears)
- ☐ Clutch slips (engine speed rises, with no increase in vehicle speed)
- ☐ Judder as clutch is engaged
- ☐ Noise when depressing or releasing clutch pedal

Manual transmission

- ☐ Noisy in neutral with engine running
- ☐ Noisy in one particular gear
- ☐ Difficulty engaging gears
- ☐ Jumps out of gear
- ☐ Vibration
- ☐ Lubricant leaks

Automatic transmission

- ☐ Fluid leakage
- ☐ Transmission fluid brown, or has burned smell
- ☐ General gear selection problems
- ☐ Transmission will not downshift (kickdown) on full throttle
- ☐ Engine won't start in any gear, or starts in gears other than P or N
- ☐ Transmission slips, shifts roughly, is noisy, or has no drive in forward or reverse gears

Driveshafts

- ☐ Clicking or knocking noise on turns (at slow speed on full-lock)
- ☐ Vibration when accelerating or decelerating

Braking system

- ☐ Vehicle pulls to one side under braking
- ☐ Noise (grinding or high-pitched squeal) when brakes applied
- ☐ Excessive brake pedal travel
- ☐ Brake pedal feels spongy when depressed
- ☐ Excessive brake pedal effort required to stop vehicle
- ☐ Judder felt through brake pedal or steering wheel when braking
- ☐ Brakes binding
- ☐ Rear wheels locking under normal braking

Suspension and steering systems

- ☐ Vehicle pulls to one side
- ☐ Wheel wobble and vibration
- ☐ Excessive pitching and/or rolling around corners, or during braking
- ☐ Wandering or general instability
- ☐ Excessively-stiff steering
- ☐ Excessive play in steering
- ☐ Lack of power assistance
- ☐ Tyre wear excessive

Electrical system

- ☐ Battery will not hold a charge for more than a few days
- ☐ Ignition/no-charge warning light stays on with engine running
- ☐ Ignition/no-charge warning light fails to come on
- ☐ Lights inoperative
- ☐ Instrument readings inaccurate or erratic
- ☐ Horn inoperative, or unsatisfactory in operation
- ☐ Windscreen/tailgate wipers failed, or unsatisfactory in operation
- ☐ Windscreen/tailgate washers failed, or unsatisfactory in operation
- ☐ Electric windows inoperative, or unsatisfactory in operation
- ☐ Central locking system inoperative, or unsatisfactory in operation

Introduction

The vehicle owner who does his or her own maintenance according to the recommended service schedules should not have to use this section of the manual very often. Modern component reliability is such that, provided those items subject to wear or deterioration are inspected or renewed at the specified intervals, sudden failure is comparatively rare. Faults do not usually just happen as a result of sudden failure, but develop over a period of time. Major mechanical failures in particular are usually preceded by characteristic symptoms over hundreds or even thousands of miles. Those components which do occasionally fail without warning are often small and easily carried in the vehicle.

With any fault-finding, the first step is to decide where to begin investigations.

Sometimes this is obvious, but on other occasions, a little detective work will be necessary. The owner who makes half a dozen haphazard adjustments or replacements may be successful in curing a fault (or its symptoms), but will be none the wiser if the fault recurs, and ultimately may have spent more time and money than was necessary. A calm and logical approach will be found to be more satisfactory in the long run. Always take into account any warning signs or abnormalities that may have been noticed in the period preceding the fault – power loss, high or low gauge readings, unusual smells, etc – and remember that failure of components such as fuses or spark plugs may only be pointers to some underlying fault.

The pages which follow provide an easy-

reference guide to the more common problems which may occur during the operation of the vehicle. These problems and their possible causes are grouped under headings denoting various components or systems, such as Engine, Cooling system, etc. The general Chapter which deals with the problem is also shown in brackets; refer to the relevant part of that Chapter for system-specific information. Whatever the fault, certain basic principles apply. These are as follows:

Verify the fault. This is simply a matter of being sure that you know what the symptoms are before starting work. This is particularly important if you are investigating a fault for someone else, who may not have described it very accurately.

Don't overlook the obvious. For example, if

the vehicle won't start, is there fuel in the tank? (Don't take anyone else's word on this particular point, and don't trust the fuel gauge either!) If an electrical fault is indicated, look for loose or broken wires before digging out the test gear.

Cure the disease, not the symptom. Substituting a flat battery with a fully-charged one will get you off the hard shoulder, but if the underlying cause is not attended to, the new battery will go the same way. Similarly, changing oil-fouled spark plugs (petrol models) for a new set will get you moving again, but remember that the reason for the fouling (if it wasn't simply an incorrect grade of plug) will have to be found and corrected.

Don't take anything for granted. Particularly, don't forget that a 'new' component may itself be defective (especially if it's been rattling around in the boot for months), and don't leave components out of a fault diagnosis sequence just because they are new or recently-fitted. When you do finally diagnose a difficult fault, you'll probably realise that all the evidence was there from the start.

Engine

Engine fails to rotate when attempting to start

☐ Battery terminal connections loose or corroded (*Weekly checks*).
☐ Battery discharged or faulty (Chapter 5A).
☐ Broken, loose or disconnected wiring in the starting circuit (Chapter 5A).
☐ Defective starter motor (Chapter 5A).
☐ Starter pinion or flywheel/driveplate ring gear teeth loose or broken (Chapter 2A , 2B, 2C, 2D or 2E and 5A).
☐ Engine earth strap broken or disconnected (Chapter 5A).

Engine rotates, but will not start

☐ Fuel tank empty.
☐ Battery discharged (engine rotates slowly) (Chapter 5A).
☐ Battery terminal connections loose or corroded (*Weekly checks*).
☐ Worn, faulty or incorrectly-gapped spark plugs – petrol models (Chapter 1A).
☐ Preheating system faulty – diesel models (Chapter 5C).
☐ Engine management system fault – petrol models (Chapter 4A).
☐ Air in fuel system – diesel models (Chapter 4B).
☐ Fuel injector/injection pump fault – diesel models (Chapter 4B).
☐ Low cylinder compressions (Chapter 2A, 2B, 2C, 2D or 2E).
☐ Major mechanical failure (eg camshaft drive) (Chapter 2A, 2B, 2D or 2E).

Engine difficult to start when cold

☐ Battery discharged (Chapter 5A).
☐ Battery terminal connections loose or corroded (*Weekly checks*).
☐ Worn, faulty or incorrectly-gapped spark plugs – petrol models (Chapter 1A).
☐ Preheating system faulty – diesel models (Chapter 5C).
☐ Engine management system fault – petrol models (Chapter 4A).
☐ Fuel injector/injection pump fault – diesel models (Chapter 4B).

Engine difficult to start when hot

☐ Engine management system fault – petrol models (Chapter 4A).
☐ Fuel injector/injection pump fault – diesel models (Chapter 4B).
☐ Low cylinder compressions (Chapter 2A, 2B, 2C, 2D or 2E).

Starter motor noisy or excessively-rough in engagement

☐ Starter pinion or flywheel/driveplate ring gear teeth loose or broken (Chapters 2A, 2B, 2C, 2D or 2E and 5A).
☐ Starter motor mounting bolts loose or missing (Chapter 5A).
☐ Defective starter motor (Chapter 5A).

Engine starts, but stops immediately

☐ Vacuum leak at the throttle housing/inlet manifold – petrol models (Chapter 4A).
☐ Engine management system fault – petrol models (Chapter 4A).
☐ Air in fuel system – diesel models (Chapter 4B).
☐ Fuel injector/injection pump fault – diesel models (Chapter 4B).

Engine idles erratically

☐ Vacuum leak at the throttle housing/inlet manifold – petrol models (Chapter 4A).
☐ Worn, faulty or incorrectly-gapped spark plugs – petrol models (Chapter 1A).
☐ Engine management system fault – petrol models (Chapter 4A).
☐ Air in fuel system – diesel models (Chapter 4B).
☐ Fuel injector/injection pump fault – diesel models (Chapter 4B).
☐ Uneven or low cylinder compressions (Chapter 2A, 2B, 2C, 2D or 2E).
☐ Camshaft lobes worn (Chapter 2A, 2B, 2C, 2D or 2E).
☐ Timing belt incorrectly fitted (Chapter 2A, 2B, 2C, 2D or 2E).

Engine misfires at idle speed

☐ Worn, faulty or incorrectly-gapped spark plugs – petrol models (Chapter 1A).
☐ Vacuum leak at the throttle housing/inlet manifold – petrol models (Chapter 4A).
☐ Engine management system fault – petrol models (Chapter 4A).
☐ Faulty injector(s) – diesel models (Chapter 4B).
☐ Uneven or low cylinder compressions (Chapter 2A, 2B, 2C, 2D or 2E).
☐ Disconnected, leaking, or perished crankcase ventilation hoses (Chapter 4C).

Engine misfires throughout the driving speed range

☐ Fuel filter blocked (Chapter 1A or 1B).
☐ Fuel pump faulty (Chapter 4A or 4B).
☐ Fuel tank vent blocked, or fuel pipes restricted (Chapter 4A or 4B).
☐ Worn, faulty or incorrectly-gapped spark plugs – petrol models (Chapter 1A).
☐ Vacuum leak at the throttle housing/inlet manifold – petrol models (Chapter 4A).
☐ Engine management system fault – petrol models (Chapter 4A).
☐ Fuel injector/injection pump fault – diesel models (Chapter 4B).
☐ Faulty ignition HT coil – petrol models (Chapter 5B).
☐ Uneven or low cylinder compressions (Chapter 2A, 2B, 2C, 2D or 2E).

Engine hesitates on acceleration

☐ Worn, faulty or incorrectly-gapped spark plugs – petrol models (Chapter 1A).
☐ Vacuum leak at the throttle housing/inlet manifold – petrol models (Chapter 4A).
☐ Engine management system fault – petrol models (Chapter 4A).
☐ Fuel injector/injection pump fault – diesel models (Chapter 4B).

Engine stalls

☐ Fuel filter blocked (Chapter 1A or 1B).
☐ Fuel pump faulty (Chapter 4A or 4B).
☐ Fuel tank vent blocked, or fuel pipes restricted (Chapter 4A or 4B).
☐ Worn, faulty or incorrectly-gapped spark plugs – petrol models (Chapter 1A).
☐ Vacuum leak at the throttle housing/inlet manifold – petrol models (Chapter 4A).
☐ Engine management system fault – petrol models (Chapter 4A).
☐ Fuel injector/injection pump fault – diesel models (Chapter 4B).

Engine (continued)

Engine lacks power

- [ ] Timing belt incorrectly fitted (Chapter 2A, 2B, 2C, 2D or 2E).
- [ ] Fuel filter blocked (Chapter 1A or 1B).
- [ ] Fuel pump faulty (Chapter 4A or 4B).
- [ ] Uneven or low cylinder compressions (Chapter 2A, 2B, 2C, 2D or 2E).
- [ ] Worn, faulty or incorrectly-gapped spark plugs – petrol models (Chapter 1A).
- [ ] Vacuum leak at the throttle housing/inlet manifold – petrol models (Chapter 4A).
- [ ] Engine management system fault – petrol models (Chapter 4A).
- [ ] Fuel injector/injection pump fault – diesel models (Chapter 4B).
- [ ] Brakes binding (Chapters 1A or 1B and 9).
- [ ] Clutch slipping (Chapter 6).

Engine backfires

- [ ] Timing belt incorrectly fitted (Chapter 2A, 2B, 2C, 2D or 2E).
- [ ] Vacuum leak at the throttle housing/inlet manifold – petrol models (Chapter 4A).
- [ ] Engine management system fault – petrol models (Chapter 4A).

Oil pressure warning light on with engine running

- [ ] Low oil level, or incorrect oil grade (*Weekly checks*).
- [ ] Faulty oil pressure warning light switch (Chapter 5A).
- [ ] Worn engine bearings and/or oil pump (Chapter 2F).
- [ ] High engine operating temperature (Chapter 3).
- [ ] Oil pressure relief valve defective (Chapter 2A, 2B, 2C, 2D or 2E).
- [ ] Oil pick-up strainer clogged (Chapter 2A, 2B, 2C, 2D or 2E).

Engine runs-on after switching off

- [ ] Excessive carbon build-up in engine (Chapter 2F).
- [ ] High engine operating temperature (Chapter 3).
- [ ] Engine management system fault – petrol models (Chapter 4A).
- [ ] Fuel injection pump fault – diesel models (Chapter 4B).

Engine noises

Pre-ignition (pinking) or knocking during acceleration or under load

- [ ] Engine management system fault – petrol models (Chapter 4A).
- [ ] Incorrect grade of spark plug – petrol models (Chapter 1A).
- [ ] Incorrect grade of fuel – petrol models (Chapter 4A).
- [ ] Vacuum leak at the throttle housing/inlet manifold – petrol models (Chapter 4A).
- [ ] Excessive carbon build-up in engine (Chapter 2F).

Whistling or wheezing noises

- [ ] Leaking inlet manifold or throttle housing gasket – petrol models (Chapter 4A).
- [ ] Leaking vacuum hose (Chapters 4A or 4B and 9).
- [ ] Blowing cylinder head gasket (Chapter 2A, 2B, 2C, 2D or 2E).

Tapping or rattling noises

- [ ] Worn valve gear or camshaft (Chapter 2A, 2B, 2C, 2D or 2E).
- [ ] Ancillary component fault (coolant pump, alternator, etc) (Chapters 3, 5A, etc).

Knocking or thumping noises

- [ ] Worn big-end bearings (regular heavy knocking, perhaps less under load) (Chapter 2F).
- [ ] Worn main bearings (rumbling and knocking, perhaps worsening under load) (Chapter 2F).
- [ ] Piston slap (most noticeable when cold) (Chapter 2F).
- [ ] Ancillary component fault (coolant pump, alternator, etc) (Chapters 3, 5A, etc).

Cooling system

Overheating

- [ ] Insufficient coolant in system (*Weekly checks*).
- [ ] Thermostat faulty (stuck closed) (Chapter 3).
- [ ] Radiator core blocked, or grille restricted (Chapter 3).
- [ ] Electric cooling fan or sensor faulty (Chapter 3).
- [ ] Pressure cap faulty (Chapter 3).
- [ ] Inaccurate temperature gauge/sensor (Chapter 3).
- [ ] Airlock in cooling system (Chapter 1A or 1B).
- [ ] Engine management system fault (Chapter 4).

Overcooling

- [ ] Thermostat faulty (stuck open) (Chapter 3).
- [ ] Inaccurate temperature gauge/sensor (Chapter 3).

External coolant leakage

- [ ] Deteriorated or damaged hoses or hose clips (Chapter 1A or 1B).

- [ ] Radiator core or heater matrix leaking (Chapter 3).
- [ ] Pressure cap faulty (Chapter 3).
- [ ] Coolant pump leaking (Chapter 3).
- [ ] Boiling due to overheating (Chapter 3).
- [ ] Core plug leaking (Chapter 2F).

Internal coolant leakage

- [ ] Leaking cylinder head gasket (Chapter 2A, 2B, 2C, 2D or 2E).
- [ ] Cracked cylinder head or cylinder bore (Chapter 2A, 2B, 2C, 2D, 2E or 2F).

Corrosion

- [ ] Infrequent draining and flushing (Chapter 1A or 1B).
- [ ] Incorrect coolant mixture or inappropriate coolant type (Chapter 1A or 1B).

Fuel and exhaust systems

Excessive fuel consumption

- [ ] Air filter element dirty or clogged (Chapter 1A or 1B).
- [ ] Engine management system fault (Chapter 4).
- [ ] Faulty injector(s) (Chapter 4).
- [ ] Tyres under-inflated (*Weekly checks*).
- [ ] Brakes binding (Chapters 1A or 1B and 9).

Fuel leakage and/or fuel odour

- [ ] Damaged or corroded fuel tank, pipes or connections (Chapter 4A or 4B).

Excessive noise or fumes from exhaust system

- [ ] Leaking exhaust system or manifold joints (Chapters 1A or 1B and 4A or 4B).
- [ ] Leaking, corroded or damaged silencers or pipe (Chapters 1A or 1B and 4A or 4B).
- [ ] Broken mountings causing body or suspension contact (Chapters 1A or 1B and 4A or 4B).

Clutch

Pedal travels to floor – no pressure or very little resistance

☐ Air in hydraulic system/faulty master or slave cylinder (Chapter 6).
☐ Broken clutch release bearing or fork (Chapter 6).
☐ Broken diaphragm spring in clutch pressure plate (Chapter 6).

Clutch fails to disengage (unable to select gears)

☐ Air in hydraulic system/faulty master or slave cylinder (Chapter 6).
☐ Clutch disc sticking on gearbox input shaft splines (Chapter 6).
☐ Clutch disc sticking to flywheel or pressure plate (Chapter 6).
☐ Faulty pressure plate assembly (Chapter 6).
☐ Clutch release mechanism worn or incorrectly assembled (Chapter 6).

Clutch slips (engine speed rises, with no increase in vehicle speed)

☐ Faulty hydraulic release system (Chapter 6).

☐ Clutch disc linings excessively worn (Chapter 6).
☐ Clutch disc linings contaminated with oil or grease (Chapter 6).
☐ Faulty pressure plate or weak diaphragm spring (Chapter 6).

Judder as clutch is engaged

☐ Clutch disc linings contaminated with oil or grease (Chapter 6).
☐ Clutch disc linings excessively worn (Chapter 6).
☐ Faulty or distorted pressure plate or diaphragm spring (Chapter 6).
☐ Worn or loose engine or gearbox mountings (Chapter 2A or 2B).
☐ Clutch disc hub or gearbox input shaft splines worn (Chapter 6).

Noise when depressing or releasing clutch pedal

☐ Worn clutch release bearing (Chapter 6).
☐ Worn or dry clutch pedal bushes (Chapter 6).
☐ Faulty pressure plate assembly (Chapter 6).
☐ Pressure plate diaphragm spring broken (Chapter 6).
☐ Broken clutch disc cushioning springs (Chapter 6).

Manual transmission

Noisy in neutral with engine running

☐ Input shaft bearings worn (noise apparent with clutch pedal released, but not when depressed) (Chapter 7A).*
☐ Clutch release bearing worn (noise apparent with clutch pedal depressed, possibly less when released) (Chapter 6).

Noisy in one particular gear

☐ Worn, damaged or chipped gear teeth (Chapter 7A).*

Difficulty engaging gears

☐ Clutch fault (Chapter 6).
☐ Worn or damaged gear selection cables (Chapter 7A).
☐ Worn synchroniser units (Chapter 7A).*

Jumps out of gear

☐ Worn or damaged gear selection cables (Chapter 7A).
☐ Worn synchroniser units (Chapter 7A).*
☐ Worn selector forks (Chapter 7A).*

Vibration

☐ Lack of oil (Chapters 1 and 7A).
☐ Worn bearings (Chapter 7A).*

Lubricant leaks

☐ Leaking differential output oil seal (Chapter 7A).
☐ Leaking housing joint (Chapter 7A).*
☐ Leaking input shaft oil seal (Chapter 7A).

Although the corrective action necessary to remedy the symptoms described is beyond the scope of the home mechanic, the above information should be helpful in isolating the cause of the condition, so that the owner can communicate clearly with a professional mechanic.

Automatic transmission

Note: *Due to the complexity of the automatic transmission, it is difficult for the home mechanic to properly diagnose and service this unit. For problems other than the following, the vehicle should be taken to a Peugeot dealer service department or suitably equipped specialist.*

Fluid leakage

☐ Automatic transmission fluid is usually dark in colour. Fluid leaks should not be confused with engine oil, which can easily be blown onto the transmission by airflow.
☐ To determine the source of a leak, first remove all built-up dirt and grime from the transmission housing and surrounding areas using a degreasing agent, or by steam-cleaning. Drive the vehicle at low speed, so airflow will not blow the leak far from its source. Raise and support the vehicle, and determine where the leak is coming from.

Transmission fluid brown, or has burned smell

☐ Transmission fluid level low, or fluid in need of renewal (Chapter 1A and 7B).

General gear selection problems

☐ Chapter 7B deals with checking and adjusting the selector cable on automatic transmissions. The following are common problems which may be caused by a poorly-adjusted cable:

a) Engine starting in gears other than Park or Neutral.
b) Indicator panel showing a gear other than that being used.
c) Vehicle moves when in Park or Neutral.
d) Poor gear shift quality or erratic gear changes.
☐ Refer to Chapter 7B for the selector cable adjustment procedure.

Transmission will not downshift (kickdown) at full throttle

☐ Low transmission fluid level (Chapter 1A).
☐ Incorrect selector cable adjustment (Chapter 7B).

Engine won't start in any gear, or starts in gears other than Park or Neutral

☐ Incorrect multi-function switch adjustment (Chapter 7B).
☐ Incorrect selector cable adjustment (Chapter 7B).

Transmission slips, shifts roughly, is noisy, or has no drive in forward or reverse gears

☐ There are many probable causes for the above problems, but the home mechanic should be concerned with only one possibility – fluid level. Before taking the vehicle to a dealer or transmission specialist, check the fluid level as described in Chapter 1A. Correct the fluid level as necessary, or change the fluid. If the problem persists, professional help will be necessary.

Driveshafts

Clicking or knocking noise on turns (at slow speed on full-lock)

- ☐ Lack of constant velocity joint lubricant, possibly due to damaged gaiter (Chapter 8).
- ☐ Worn outer constant velocity joint (Chapter 8).

Vibration when accelerating or decelerating

- ☐ Worn inner constant velocity joint (Chapter 8).
- ☐ Bent or distorted driveshaft (Chapter 8).
- ☐ Worn intermediate bearing (Chapter 8).

Braking system

Note: *Before assuming that a brake problem exists, make sure that the tyres are in good condition and correctly inflated, that the front wheel alignment is correct, and that the vehicle is not loaded with weight in an unequal manner. Apart from checking the condition of all pipe and hose connections, any faults occurring on the anti-lock braking system should be referred to a Peugeot dealer for diagnosis.*

Vehicle pulls to one side under braking

- ☐ Worn, defective, damaged or contaminated brake pads on one side (Chapter 9).
- ☐ Seized or partially-seized front brake caliper (Chapter 9).
- ☐ A mixture of brake pad materials fitted between sides (Chapter 9).
- ☐ Brake caliper mounting bolts loose (Chapter 9).
- ☐ Worn or damaged steering or suspension components (Chapters 1A or 1B and 10).

Noise (grinding or high-pitched squeal) when brakes applied

- ☐ Brake pad material worn down to metal backing (Chapters 1A or 1B and 9).
- ☐ Excessive corrosion of brake disc. May be apparent after the vehicle has been standing for some time (Chapter 9).
- ☐ Foreign object (stone chipping, etc) trapped between brake disc and shield (Chapter 9).

Excessive brake pedal travel

- ☐ Faulty master cylinder (Chapter 9).
- ☐ Air in hydraulic system (Chapter 9).
- ☐ Faulty vacuum servo unit (Chapter 9).

Brake pedal feels spongy when depressed

- ☐ Air in hydraulic system (Chapter 9).
- ☐ Deteriorated flexible rubber brake hoses (Chapters 1A or 1B and 9).
- ☐ Master cylinder mounting nuts loose (Chapter 9).
- ☐ Faulty master cylinder (Chapter 9).

Excessive brake pedal effort required to stop vehicle

- ☐ Faulty vacuum servo unit (Chapter 9).
- ☐ Disconnected, damaged or insecure brake servo vacuum hose (Chapter 9).
- ☐ Primary or secondary hydraulic circuit failure (Chapter 9).
- ☐ Seized brake caliper (Chapter 9).
- ☐ Brake pads incorrectly fitted (Chapter 9).
- ☐ Incorrect grade of brake pads fitted (Chapter 9).
- ☐ Brake pads contaminated (Chapter 9).

Judder felt through brake pedal or steering wheel when braking

- ☐ Excessive run-out or distortion of discs (Chapters 9).
- ☐ Brake pads worn (Chapters 1A or 1B and 9).
- ☐ Brake caliper mounting bolts loose (Chapter 9).
- ☐ Wear in suspension or steering components or mountings (Chapters 1A or 1B and 10).

Brakes binding

- ☐ Seized brake caliper (Chapter 9).
- ☐ Incorrectly-adjusted handbrake mechanism (Chapter 9).
- ☐ Faulty master cylinder (Chapter 9).

Rear wheels locking under normal braking

- ☐ Rear brake pads contaminated (Chapters 1A or 1B and 9).
- ☐ ABS system fault (Chapter 9).

Suspension and steering

Note: *Before diagnosing suspension or steering faults, be sure that the trouble is not due to incorrect tyre pressures, mixtures of tyre types, or binding brakes.*

Vehicle pulls to one side

- ☐ Defective tyre (*Weekly checks*).
- ☐ Excessive wear in suspension or steering components (Chapters 1A or 1B and 10).
- ☐ Incorrect front wheel alignment (Chapter 10).
- ☐ Damage to steering or suspension components (Chapter 1A or 1B).

Wheel wobble and vibration

- ☐ Front roadwheels out of balance (vibration felt mainly through the steering wheel) (Chapters 1A or 1B and 10).
- ☐ Rear roadwheels out of balance (vibration felt throughout the vehicle) (Chapters 1A or 1B and 10).
- ☐ Roadwheels damaged or distorted (Chapters 1A or 1B and 10).
- ☐ Faulty or damaged tyre (*Weekly checks*).
- ☐ Worn steering or suspension joints, bushes or components (Chapters 1A or 1B and 10).
- ☐ Wheel bolts loose (Chapters 1A or 1B and 10).

Suspension and steering (continued)

Excessive pitching and/or rolling around corners, or during braking

- ☐ Defective shock absorbers (Chapters 1A or 1B and 10).
- ☐ Broken or weak spring and/or suspension part (Chapters 1A or 1B and 10).
- ☐ Worn or damaged anti-roll bar or mountings (Chapter 10).

Wandering or general instability

- ☐ Incorrect front wheel alignment (Chapter 10).
- ☐ Worn steering or suspension joints, bushes or components (Chapters 1A or 1B and 10).
- ☐ Roadwheels out of balance (Chapters 1A or 1B and 10).
- ☐ Faulty or damaged tyre (Weekly checks).
- ☐ Wheel bolts loose (Chapters 1A or 1B and 10).
- ☐ Defective shock absorbers (Chapters 1A or 1B and 10).

Excessively-stiff steering

- ☐ Lack of power steering fluid (Chapter 10).
- ☐ Seized track rod end balljoint or suspension balljoint (Chapters 1A or 1B and 10).
- ☐ Incorrect front wheel alignment (Chapter 10).
- ☐ Steering rack or column bent or damaged (Chapter 10).
- ☐ Power steering pump fault (Chapter 10).

Excessive play in steering

- ☐ Worn steering column universal joint (Chapter 10).
- ☐ Worn steering track rod end balljoints (Chapters 1A or 1B and 10).
- ☐ Worn steering rack (Chapter 10).
- ☐ Worn steering or suspension joints, bushes or components (Chapters 1A or 1B and 10).

Lack of power assistance

- ☐ Incorrect power steering fluid level (Weekly checks).
- ☐ Restriction in power steering fluid hoses (Chapter 1A or 1B).
- ☐ Faulty power steering pump (Chapter 10).
- ☐ Faulty steering rack (Chapter 10).

Tyre wear excessive

Tyre treads exhibit feathered edges

- ☐ Incorrect toe setting (Chapter 10).

Tyres worn in centre of tread

- ☐ Tyres over-inflated (Weekly checks).

Tyres worn on inside and outside edges

- ☐ Tyres under-inflated (Weekly checks).

Tyres worn on inside or outside edges

- ☐ Incorrect camber/castor angles (wear on one edge only) (Chapter 10).
- ☐ Worn steering or suspension joints, bushes or components (Chapters 1A or 1B and 10).
- ☐ Excessively-hard cornering.
- ☐ Accident damage.

Tyres worn unevenly

- ☐ Tyres/wheels out of balance (Weekly checks).
- ☐ Excessive wheel or tyre run-out (Chapter 1A or 1B).
- ☐ Worn shock absorbers (Chapters 1A or 1B and 10).
- ☐ Faulty tyre (Weekly checks).

Electrical system

Note: For problems associated with the starting system, refer to the faults listed under 'Engine' earlier in this Section.

Battery won't hold a charge for more than a few days

- ☐ Battery defective internally (Chapter 5A).
- ☐ Battery terminal connections loose or corroded (Weekly checks).
- ☐ Auxiliary drivebelt broken, worn or incorrectly adjusted (Chapter 1A or 1B).
- ☐ Alternator not charging at correct output (Chapter 5A).
- ☐ Alternator or voltage regulator faulty (Chapter 5A).
- ☐ Short-circuit causing continual battery drain (Chapters 5A and 12).

Ignition/no-charge warning light stays on with engine running

- ☐ Auxiliary drivebelt broken, worn, or incorrectly adjusted (Chapter 1A or 1B).
- ☐ Internal fault in alternator or voltage regulator (Chapter 5A).
- ☐ Broken, disconnected, or loose wiring in charging circuit (Chapter 5A).

Ignition/no-charge warning light fails to come on

- ☐ Warning light bulb blown (Chapter 12).
- ☐ Broken, disconnected, or loose wiring in warning light circuit (Chapter 12).
- ☐ Alternator faulty (Chapter 5A).

Lights inoperative

- ☐ Bulb blown (Chapter 12).
- ☐ Corrosion of bulb or bulbholder contacts (Chapter 12).
- ☐ Blown fuse (Chapter 12).
- ☐ Faulty relay (Chapter 12).

- ☐ Broken, loose, or disconnected wiring (Chapter 12).
- ☐ Faulty switch (Chapter 12).

Instrument readings inaccurate or erratic

Fuel or temperature gauges give no reading

- ☐ Faulty gauge sensor unit (Chapter 3 or 4).
- ☐ Wiring open-circuit (Chapter 12).
- ☐ Faulty gauge (Chapter 12).

Fuel or temperature gauges give continuous maximum reading

- ☐ Faulty gauge sensor unit (Chapter 3 or 4).
- ☐ Wiring short-circuit (Chapter 12).
- ☐ Faulty gauge (Chapter 12).

Horn inoperative, or unsatisfactory in operation

Horn operates all the time

- ☐ Horn push either earthed or stuck down (Chapter 12).
- ☐ Horn cable-to-horn push earthed (Chapter 12).

Horn fails to operate

- ☐ Blown fuse (Chapter 12).
- ☐ Cable or cable connections loose, broken or disconnected (Chapter 12).
- ☐ Faulty horn (Chapter 12).

Horn emits intermittent or unsatisfactory sound

- ☐ Cable connections loose (Chapter 12).
- ☐ Horn mountings loose (Chapter 12).
- ☐ Faulty horn (Chapter 12).

Electrical system (continued)

Windscreen/tailgate wipers failed, or unsatisfactory in operation

Wipers fail to operate, or operate very slowly

- [ ] Wiper blades stuck to screen, or linkage seized or binding (Chapters 1A or 1B and 12).
- [ ] Blown fuse (Chapter 12).
- [ ] Cable or cable connections loose, broken or disconnected (Chapter 12).
- [ ] Faulty built-in system interface (BSI) unit (Chapter 12).
- [ ] Faulty wiper motor (Chapter 12).

Wiper blades sweep over too large or too small an area of the glass

- [ ] Wiper arms incorrectly positioned on spindles (Chapter 12).
- [ ] Excessive wear of wiper linkage (Chapter 12).
- [ ] Wiper motor or linkage mountings loose or insecure (Chapter 12).

Wiper blades fail to clean the glass effectively

- [ ] Wiper blade rubbers worn or perished (*Weekly checks*).
- [ ] Wiper arm tension springs broken, or arm pivots seized (Chapter 12).
- [ ] Insufficient windscreen washer additive to adequately remove road film (*Weekly checks*).

Windscreen/tailgate washers failed, or unsatisfactory in operation

One or more washer jets inoperative

- [ ] Blocked washer jet (*Weekly checks*).
- [ ] Disconnected, kinked or restricted fluid hose (Chapter 12).
- [ ] Insufficient fluid in washer reservoir (*Weekly checks*).

Washer pump fails to operate

- [ ] Broken or disconnected wiring or connections (Chapter 12).
- [ ] Blown fuse (Chapter 12).
- [ ] Faulty washer switch (Chapter 12).
- [ ] Faulty washer pump (Chapter 12).

Electric windows inoperative, or unsatisfactory in operation

Window glass will only move in one direction

- [ ] Faulty switch (Chapter 12).

Window glass slow to move

- [ ] Regulator seized or damaged, or in need of lubricant (Chapter 11).
- [ ] Door internal components or trim fouling regulator (Chapter 11).
- [ ] Faulty motor (Chapter 11).

Window glass fails to move

- [ ] Blown fuse (Chapter 12).
- [ ] Broken or disconnected wiring or connections (Chapter 12).
- [ ] Faulty motor (Chapter 11).
- [ ] Faulty built-in systems interface (BSI) unit (Chapter 12).

Central locking system inoperative, or unsatisfactory in operation

Complete system failure

- [ ] Blown fuse (Chapter 12).
- [ ] Broken or disconnected wiring or connections (Chapter 12).
- [ ] Faulty built-in system interface (BSI) unit (Chapter 12).

Door/tailgate locks but will not unlock, or unlocks but will not lock

- [ ] Broken or disconnected link rod(s) (Chapter 11).
- [ ] Faulty lock motor (Chapter 11).

One lock fails to operate

- [ ] Broken or disconnected wiring or connections (Chapter 12).
- [ ] Faulty lock motor (Chapter 11).
- [ ] Broken, binding or disconnected link rod(s) (Chapter 11).

Note: *References throughout this index are in the form "Chapter number" • "Page number"*

Haynes Manuals – The Complete **UK Car** List

Title	Book No.
ALFA ROMEO Alfasud/Sprint (74 - 88) up to F *	0292
Alfa Romeo Alfetta (73 - 87) up to E *	0531
AUDI 80, 90 & Coupe Petrol (79 - Nov 88) up to F	0605
Audi 80, 90 & Coupe Petrol (Oct 86 - 90) D to H	1491
Audi 100 & 200 Petrol (Oct 82 - 90) up to H	0907
Audi 100 & A6 Petrol & Diesel (May 91 - May 97) H to P	3504
Audi A3 Petrol & Diesel (96 - May 03) P to 03	4253
Audi A4 Petrol & Diesel (95 - 00) M to X	3575
Audi A4 Petrol & Diesel (01 - 04) X to 54	4609
AUSTIN A35 & A40 (56 - 67) up to F *	0118
Austin/MG/Rover Maestro 1.3 & 1.6 Petrol (83 - 95) up to M	0922
Austin/MG Metro (80 - May 90) up to G	0718
Austin/Rover Montego 1.3 & 1.6 Petrol (84 - 94) A to L	1066
Austin/MG/Rover Montego 2.0 Petrol (84 - 95) A to M	1067
Mini (59 - 69) up to H *	0527
Mini (69 - 01) up to X	0646
Austin/Rover 2.0 litre Diesel Engine (86 - 93) C to L	1857
Austin Healey 100/6 & 3000 (56 - 68) up to G *	0049
BEDFORD CF Petrol (69 - 87) up to E	0163
Bedford/Vauxhall Rascal & Suzuki Supercarry (86 - Oct 94) C to M	3015
BMW 316, 320 & 320i (4-cyl) (75 - Feb 83) up to Y *	0276
BMW 320, 320i, 323i & 325i (6-cyl) (Oct 77 - Sept 87) up to E	0815
BMW 3- & 5-Series Petrol (81 - 91) up to J	1948
BMW 3-Series Petrol (Apr 91 - 99) H to V	3210
BMW 3-Series Petrol (Sept 98 - 03) S to 53	4067
BMW 520i & 525e (Oct 81 - June 88) up to E	1560
BMW 525, 528 & 528i (73 - Sept 81) up to X *	0632
BMW 5-Series 6-cyl Petrol (April 96 - Aug 03) N to 03	4151
BMW 1500, 1502, 1600, 1602, 2000 & 2002 (59 - 77) up to S *	0240
CHRYSLER PT Cruiser Petrol (00 - 03) W to 53	4058
CITROËN 2CV, Ami & Dyane (67 - 90) up to H	0196
Citroën AX Petrol & Diesel (87 - 97) D to P	3014
Citroën Berlingo & Peugeot Partner Petrol & Diesel (96 - 05) P to 55	4281
Citroën BX Petrol (83 - 94) A to L	0908
Citroën C15 Van Petrol & Diesel (89 - Oct 98) F to S	3509
Citroën C3 Petrol & Diesel (02 - 05) 51 to 05	4197
Citroen C5 Petrol & Diesel (01-08) Y to 08	4745
Citroën CX Petrol (75 - 88) up to F	0528
Citroën Saxo Petrol & Diesel (96 - 04) N to 54	3506
Citroën Visa Petrol (79 - 88) up to F	0620
Citroën Xantia Petrol & Diesel (93 - 01) K to Y	3082
Citroën XM Petrol & Diesel (89 - 00) G to X	3451
Citroën Xsara Petrol & Diesel (97 - Sept 00) R to W	3751
Citroën Xsara Picasso Petrol & Diesel (00 - 02) W to 52	3944
Citroën Xsara Picasso (03-08)	4784
Citroën ZX Diesel (91 - 98) J to S	1922
Citroen ZX Petrol (91 - 98) H to S	1881
Citroën 1.7 & 1.9 litre Diesel Engine (84 - 96) A to N	1379
FIAT 126 (73 - 87) up to E *	0305
Fiat 500 (57 - 73) up to M *	0090
Fiat Bravo & Brava Petrol (95 - 00) N to W	3572
Fiat Cinquecento (93 - 98) K to R	3501
Fiat Panda (81 - 95) up to M	0793
Fiat Punto Petrol & Diesel (94 - Oct 99) L to V	3251
Fiat Punto Petrol (Oct 99 - July 03) V to 03	4066
Fiat Punto Petrol (03-07) 03 to 07	4746
Fiat Regata Petrol (84 - 88) A to F	1167
Fiat Tipo Petrol (88 - 91) E to J	1625
Fiat Uno Petrol (83 - 95) up to M	0923
Fiat X1/9 (74 - 89) up to G *	0273
FORD Anglia (59 - 68) up to G *	0001

Title	Book No.
Ford Capri II (& III) 1.6 & 2.0 (74 - 87) up to E *	0283
Ford Capri II (& III) 2.8 & 3.0 V6 (74 - 87) up to E	1309
Ford Cortina Mk I & Corsair 1500 ('62 - '66) up to D*	0214
Ford Cortina Mk III 1300 & 1600 (70 - 76) up to P *	0070
Ford Escort Mk I 1100 & 1300 (68 - 74) up to N *	0171
Ford Escort Mk I Mexico, RS 1600 & RS 2000 (70 - 74) up to N *	0139
Ford Escort Mk II Mexico, RS 1800 & RS 2000 (75 - 80) up to W *	0735
Ford Escort (75 - Aug 80) up to V *	0280
Ford Escort Petrol (Sept 80 - Sept 90) up to H	0686
Ford Escort & Orion Petrol (Sept 90 - 00) H to X	1737
Ford Escort & Orion Diesel (Sept 90 - 00) H to X	4081
Ford Fiesta (76 - Aug 83) up to Y	0334
Ford Fiesta Petrol (Aug 83 - Feb 89) A to F	1030
Ford Fiesta Petrol (Feb 89 - Oct 95) F to N	1595
Ford Fiesta Petrol & Diesel (Oct 95 - Mar 02) N to 02	3397
Ford Fiesta Petrol & Diesel (Apr 02 - 07) 02 to 57	4170
Ford Focus Petrol & Diesel (98 - 01) S to Y	3759
Ford Focus Petrol & Diesel (Oct 01 - 05) 51 to 05	4167
Ford Galaxy Petrol & Diesel (95 - Aug 00) M to W	3984
Ford Granada Petrol (Sept 77 - Feb 85) up to B *	0481
Ford Granada & Scorpio Petrol (Mar 85 - 94) B to M	1245
Ford Ka (96 - 02) P to 52	3570
Ford Mondeo Petrol (93 - Sept 00) K to X	1923
Ford Mondeo Petrol & Diesel (Oct 00 - Jul 03) X to 03	3990
Ford Mondeo Petrol & Diesel (July 03 - 07) 03 to 56	4619
Ford Mondeo Diesel (93 - 96) L to N	3465
Ford Orion Petrol (83 - Sept 90) up to H	1009
Ford Sierra 4-cyl Petrol (82 - 93) up to K	0903
Ford Sierra V6 Petrol (82 - 91) up to J	0904
Ford Transit Petrol (Mk 2) (78 - Jan 86) up to C	0719
Ford Transit Petrol (Mk 3) (Feb 86 - 89) C to G	1468
Ford Transit Diesel (Feb 86 - 99) C to T	3019
Ford Transit Diesel (00-06)	4775
Ford 1.6 & 1.8 litre Diesel Engine (84 - 96) A to N	1172
Ford 2.1, 2.3 & 2.5 litre Diesel Engine (77 - 90) up to H	1606
FREIGHT ROVER Sherpa Petrol (74 - 87) up to E	0463
HILLMAN Avenger (70 - 82) up to Y	0037
Hillman Imp (63 - 76) up to R *	0022
HONDA Civic (Feb 84 - Oct 87) A to E	1226
Honda Civic (Nov 91 - 96) J to N	3199
Honda Civic Petrol (Mar 95 - 00) M to X	4050
Honda Civic Petrol & Diesel (01 - 05) X to 55	4611
Honda CR-V Petrol & Diesel (01-06)	4747
Honda Jazz (01 - Feb 08) 51 - 57	4735
HYUNDAI Pony (85 - 94) C to M	3398
JAGUAR E Type (61 - 72) up to L *	0140
Jaguar Mkl & II, 240 & 340 (55 - 69) up to H *	0098
Jaguar XJ6, XJ & Sovereign; Daimler Sovereign (68 - Oct 86) up to D	0242
Jaguar XJ6 & Sovereign (Oct 86 - Sept 94) D to M	3261
Jaguar XJ12, XJS & Sovereign; Daimler Double Six (72 - 88) up to F	0478
JEEP Cherokee Petrol (93 - 96) K to N	1943
LADA 1200, 1300, 1500 & 1600 (74 - 91) up to J	0413
Lada Samara (87 - 91) D to J	1610
LAND ROVER 90, 110 & Defender Diesel (83 - 07) up to 56	3017
Land Rover Discovery Petrol & Diesel (89 - 98) G to S	3016
Land Rover Discovery Diesel (Nov 98 - Jul 04) S to 04	4606
Land Rover Freelander Petrol & Diesel (97 - Sept 03) R to 53	3929
Land Rover Freelander Petrol & Diesel (Oct 03 - Oct 06) 53 to 56	4623

Title	Book No.
Land Rover Series IIA & III Diesel (58 - 85) up to C	0529
Land Rover Series II, IIA & III 4-cyl Petrol (58 - 85) up to C	0314
MAZDA 323 (Mar 81 - Oct 89) up to G	1608
Mazda 323 (Oct 89 - 98) G to R	3455
Mazda 626 (May 83 - Sept 87) up to E	0929
Mazda B1600, B1800 & B2000 Pick-up Petrol (72 - 88) up to F	0267
Mazda RX-7 (79 - 85) up to C *	0460
MERCEDES-BENZ 190, 190E & 190D Petrol & Diesel (83 - 93) A to L	3450
Mercedes-Benz 200D, 240D, 240TD, 300D & 300TD 123 Series Diesel (Oct 76 - 85)	1114
Mercedes-Benz 250 & 280 (68 - 72) up to L *	0346
Mercedes-Benz 250 & 280 123 Series Petrol (Oct 76 - 84) up to B *	0677
Mercedes-Benz 124 Series Petrol & Diesel (85 - Aug 93) C to K	3253
Mercedes-Benz A-Class Petrol & Diesel (98-04) S to 54	4748
Mercedes-Benz C-Class Petrol & Diesel (93 - Aug 00) L to W	3511
Mercedes-Benz C-Class (00-06)	4780
MGA (55 - 62) *	0475
MGB (62 - 80) up to W	0111
MG Midget & Austin-Healey Sprite (58 - 80) up to W *	0265
MINI Petrol (July 01 - 05) Y to 05	4273
MITSUBISHI Shogun & L200 Pick-Ups Petrol (83 - 94) up to M	1944
MORRIS Ital 1.3 (80 - 84) up to B	0705
Morris Minor 1000 (56 - 71) up to K	0024
NISSAN Almera Petrol (95 - Feb 00) N to V	4053
Nissan Almera & Tino Petrol (Feb 00 - 07) V to 56	4612
Nissan Bluebird (May 84 - Mar 86) A to C	1223
Nissan Bluebird Petrol (Mar 86 - 90) C to H	1473
Nissan Cherry (Sept 82 - 86) up to D	1031
Nissan Micra (83 - Jan 93) up to K	0931
Nissan Micra (93 - 02) K to 52	3254
Nissan Micra Petrol (03-07) 52 to 57	4734
Nissan Primera Petrol (90 - Aug 99) H to T	1851
Nissan Stanza (82 - 86) up to D	0824
Nissan Sunny Petrol (May 82 - Oct 86) up to D	0895
Nissan Sunny Petrol (Oct 86 - Mar 91) D to H	1378
Nissan Sunny Petrol (Apr 91 - 95) H to N	3219
OPEL Ascona & Manta (B Series) (Sept 75 - 88) up to F *	0316
Opel Ascona Petrol (81 - 88)	3215
Opel Astra Petrol (Oct 91 - Feb 98)	3156
Opel Corsa Petrol (83 - Mar 93)	3160
Opel Corsa Petrol (Mar 93 - 97)	3159
Opel Kadett Petrol (Nov 79 - Oct 84) up to B	0634
Opel Kadett Petrol (Oct 84 - Oct 91)	3196
Opel Omega & Senator Petrol (Nov 86 - 94)	3157
Opel Rekord Petrol (Feb 78 - Oct 86) up to D	0543
Opel Vectra Petrol (Oct 88 - Oct 95)	3158
PEUGEOT 106 Petrol & Diesel (91 - 04) J to 53	1882
Peugeot 205 Petrol (83 - 97) A to P	0932
Peugeot 206 Petrol & Diesel (98 - 01) S to X	3757
Peugeot 206 Petrol & Diesel (02 - 06) 51 to 06	4613
Peugeot 306 Petrol & Diesel (93 - 02) K to 02	3073
Peugeot 307 Petrol & Diesel (01 - 04) Y to 54	4147
Peugeot 309 Petrol (86 - 93) C to K	1266
Peugeot 405 Petrol (88 - 97) E to P	1559
Peugeot 405 Diesel (88 - 97) E to P	3198
Peugeot 406 Petrol & Diesel (96 - Mar 99) N to T	3394
Peugeot 406 Petrol & Diesel (Mar 99 - 02) T to 52	3982

* Classic reprint

Title	Book No.
Peugeot 505 Petrol (79 - 89) up to G	0762
Peugeot 1.7/1.8 & 1.9 litre Diesel Engine (82 - 96) up to N	0950
Peugeot 2.0, 2.1, 2.3 & 2.5 litre Diesel Engines (74 - 90) up to H	1607
PORSCHE 911 (65 - 85) up to C	0264
Porsche 924 & 924 Turbo (76 - 85) up to C	0397
PROTON (89 - 97) F to P	3255
RANGE ROVER V8 Petrol (70 - Oct 92) up to K	0606
RELIANT Robin & Kitten (73 - 83) up to A *	0436
RENAULT 4 (61 - 86) up to D *	0072
Renault 5 Petrol (Feb 85 - 96) B to N	1219
Renault 9 & 11 Petrol (82 - 89) up to F	0822
Renault 18 Petrol (79 - 86) up to D	0598
Renault 19 Petrol (89 - 96) F to N	1646
Renault 19 Diesel (89 - 96) F to N	1946
Renault 21 Petrol (86 - 94) C to M	1397
Renault 25 Petrol & Diesel (84 - 92) B to K	1228
Renault Clio Petrol (91 - May 98) H to R	1853
Renault Clio Diesel (91 - June 96) H to N	3031
Renault Clio Petrol & Diesel (May 98 - May 01) R to Y	3906
Renault Clio Petrol & Diesel (June '01 - '05) Y to 55	4168
Renault Espace Petrol & Diesel (85 - 96) C to N	3197
Renault Laguna Petrol & Diesel (94 - 00) L to W	3252
Renault Laguna Petrol & Diesel (Feb 01 - Feb 05) X to 54	4283
Renault Mégane & Scénic Petrol & Diesel (96 - 99) N to T	3395
Renault Mégane & Scénic Petrol & Diesel (Apr 99 - 02) T to 52	3916
Renault Megane Petrol & Diesel (Oct 02 - 05) 52 to 55	4284
Renault Scenic Petrol & Diesel (Sept 03 - 06) 53 to 06	4297
ROVER 213 & 216 (84 - 89) A to G	1116
Rover 214 & 414 Petrol (89 - 96) G to N	1689
Rover 216 & 416 Petrol (89 - 96) G to N	1830
Rover 211, 214, 216, 218 & 220 Petrol & Diesel (Dec 95 - 99) N to V	3399
Rover 25 & MG ZR Petrol & Diesel (Oct 99 - 04) V to 54	4145
Rover 414, 416 & 420 Petrol & Diesel (May 95 - 98) M to R	3453
Rover 45 / MG ZS Petrol & Diesel (99 - 05) V to 55	4384
Rover 618, 620 & 623 Petrol (93 - 97) K to P	3257
Rover 75 / MG ZT Petrol & Diesel (99 - 06) S to 06	4292
Rover 820, 825 & 827 Petrol (86 - 95) D to N	1380
Rover 3500 (76 - 87) up to E *	0365
Rover Metro, 111 & 114 Petrol (May 90 - 98) G to S	1711
SAAB 95 & 96 (66 - 76) up to R *	0198
Saab 90, 99 & 900 (79 - Oct 93) up to L	0765
Saab 900 (Oct 93 - 98) L to R	3512
Saab 9000 (4-cyl) (85 - 98) C to S	1686
Saab 9-3 Petrol & Diesel (98 - Aug 02) R to 02	4614
Saab 9-3 Petrol & Diesel (02-07) 52 to 57	4749
Saab 9-5 4-cyl Petrol (97 - 04) R to 54	4156
SEAT Ibiza & Cordoba Petrol & Diesel (Oct 93 - Oct 99) L to V	3571
Seat Ibiza & Malaga Petrol (85 - 92) B to K	1609
SKODA Estelle (77 - 89) up to G	0604
Skoda Fabia Petrol & Diesel (00 - 06) W to 06	4376
Skoda Favorit (89 - 96) F to N	1801
Skoda Felicia Petrol & Diesel (95 - 01) M to X	3505
Skoda Octavia Petrol & Diesel (98 - Apr 04) R to 04	4285
SUBARU 1600 & 1800 (Nov 79 - 90) up to H *	0995

Title	Book No.
SUNBEAM Alpine, Rapier & H120 (67 - 74) up to N *	0051
SUZUKI SJ Series, Samurai & Vitara (4-cyl) Petrol (82 - 97) up to P	1942
Suzuki Supercarry & Bedford/Vauxhall Rascal (86 - Oct 94) C to M	3015
TALBOT Alpine, Solara, Minx & Rapier (75 - 86) up to D	0337
Talbot Horizon Petrol (78 - 86) up to D	0473
Talbot Samba (82 - 86) up to D	0823
TOYOTA Avensis Petrol (98 - Jan 03) R to 52	4264
Toyota Carina E Petrol (May 92 - 97) J to P	3256
Toyota Corolla (80 - 85) up to C	0683
Toyota Corolla (Sept 83 - Sept 87) A to E	1024
Toyota Corolla (Sept 87 - Aug 92) E to K	1683
Toyota Corolla Petrol (Aug 92 - 97) K to P	3259
Toyota Corolla Petrol (July 97 - Feb 02) P to 51	4286
Toyota Hi-Ace & Hi-Lux Petrol (69 - Oct 83) up to A	0304
Toyota RAV4 Petrol & Diesel (94-06) L to 55	4750
Toyota Yaris Petrol (99 - 05) T to 05	4265
TRIUMPH GT6 & Vitesse (62 - 74) up to N *	0112
Triumph Herald (59 - 71) up to K *	0010
Triumph Spitfire (62 - 81) up to X	0113
Triumph Stag (70 - 78) up to T *	0441
Triumph TR2, TR3, TR3A, TR4 & TR4A (52 - 67) up to F *	0028
Triumph TR5 & 6 (67 - 75) up to P *	0031
Triumph TR7 (75 - 82) up to Y *	0322
VAUXHALL Astra Petrol (80 - Oct 84) up to B	0635
Vauxhall Astra & Belmont Petrol (Oct 84 - Oct 91) B to J	1136
Vauxhall Astra Petrol (Oct 91 - Feb 98) J to R	1832
Vauxhall/Opel Astra & Zafira Petrol (Feb 98 - Apr 04) R to 04	3758
Vauxhall/Opel Astra & Zafira Diesel (Feb 98 - Apr 04) R to 04	3797
Vauxhall/Opel Astra Petrol (04 - 08)	4732
Vauxhall/Opel Astra Diesel (04 - 08)	4733
Vauxhall/Opel Calibra (90 - 98) G to S	3502
Vauxhall Carlton Petrol (Oct 78 - Oct 86) up to D	0480
Vauxhall Carlton & Senator Petrol (Nov 86 - 94) D to L	1469
Vauxhall Cavalier Petrol (81 - Oct 88) up to F	0812
Vauxhall Cavalier Petrol (Oct 88 - 95) F to N	1570
Vauxhall Chevette (75 - 84) up to B	0285
Vauxhall/Opel Corsa Diesel (Mar 93 - Oct 00) K to X	4087
Vauxhall Corsa Petrol (Mar 93 - 97) K to R	1985
Vauxhall/Opel Corsa Petrol (Apr 97 - Oct 00) P to X	3921
Vauxhall/Opel Corsa Petrol & Diesel (Oct 00 - Sept 03) X to 53	4079
Vauxhall/Opel Corsa Petrol & Diesel (Oct 03 - Aug 06) 53 to 06	4617
Vauxhall/Opel Frontera Petrol & Diesel (91 - Sept 98) J to S	3454
Vauxhall Nova Petrol (83 - 93) up to K	0909
Vauxhall/Opel Omega Petrol (94 - 99) L to T	3510
Vauxhall/Opel Vectra Petrol & Diesel (95 - Feb 99) N to S	3396
Vauxhall/Opel Vectra Petrol & Diesel (Mar 99 - May 02) T to 02	3930
Vauxhall/Opel Vectra Petrol & Diesel (June 02 - Sept 05) 02 to 55	4618
Vauxhall/Opel 1.5, 1.6 & 1.7 litre Diesel Engine (82 - 96) up to N	1222
VW 411 & 412 (68 - 75) up to P *	0091
VW Beetle 1200 (54 - 77) up to S	0036
VW Beetle 1300 & 1500 (65 - 75) up to P	0039

Title	Book No.
VW 1302 & 1302S (70 - 72) up to L *	0110
VW Beetle 1303, 1303S & GT (72 - 75) up to P	0159
VW Beetle Petrol & Diesel (Apr 99 - 07) T to 57	3798
VW Golf & Jetta Mk 1 Petrol 1.1 & 1.3 (74 - 84) up to A	0716
VW Golf, Jetta & Scirocco Mk 1 Petrol 1.5, 1.6 & 1.8 (74 - 84) up to A	0726
VW Golf & Jetta Mk 1 Diesel (78 - 84) up to A	0451
VW Golf & Jetta Mk 2 Petrol (Mar 84 - Feb 92) A to J	1081
VW Golf & Vento Petrol & Diesel (Feb 92 - Mar 98) J to R	3097
VW Golf & Bora Petrol & Diesel (April 98 - 00) R to X	3727
VW Golf & Bora 4-cyl Petrol & Diesel (01 - 03) X to 53	4169
VW Golf & Jetta Petrol & Diesel (04 - 07) 53 to 07	4610
VW LT Petrol Vans & Light Trucks (76 - 87) up to E	0637
VW Passat & Santana Petrol (Sept 81 - May 88) up to E	0814
VW Passat 4-cyl Petrol & Diesel (May 88 - 96) E to P	3498
VW Passat 4-cyl Petrol & Diesel (Dec 96 - Nov 00) P to X	3917
VW Passat Petrol & Diesel (Dec 00 - May 05) X to 05	4279
VW Polo & Derby (76 - Jan 82) up to X	0335
VW Polo (82 - Oct 90) up to H	0813
VW Polo Petrol (Nov 90 - Aug 94) H to L	3245
VW Polo Hatchback Petrol & Diesel (94 - 99) M to S	3500
VW Polo Hatchback Petrol (00 - Jan 02) V to 51	4150
VW Polo Petrol & Diesel (02 - May 05) 51 to 05	4608
VW Scirocco (82 - 90) up to H *	1224
VW Transporter 1600 (68 - 79) up to V	0082
VW Transporter 1700, 1800 & 2000 (72 - 79) up to V *	0226
VW Transporter (air-cooled) Petrol (79 - 82) up to Y *	0638
VW Transporter (water-cooled) Petrol (82 - 90) up to H	3452
VW Type 3 (63 - 73) up to M *	0084
VOLVO 120 & 130 Series (& P1800) (61 - 73) up to M *	0203
Volvo 142, 144 & 145 (66 - 74) up to N *	0129
Volvo 240 Series Petrol (74 - 93) up to K	0270
Volvo 262, 264 & 260/265 (75 - 85) up to C *	0400
Volvo 340, 343, 345 & 360 (76 - 91) up to J	0715
Volvo 440, 460 & 480 Petrol (87 - 97) D to P	1691
Volvo 740 & 760 Petrol (82 - 91) up to J	1258
Volvo 850 Petrol (92 - 96) J to P	3260
Volvo 940 petrol (90 - 98) H to R	3249
Volvo S40 & V40 Petrol (96 - Mar 04) N to 04	3569
Volvo S40 & V50 Petrol & Diesel (Mar 04 - Jun 07) 04 to 07	4731
Volvo S60 Petrol & Diesel (01-08)	4793
Volvo S70, V70 & C70 Petrol (96 - 99) P to V	3573
Volvo V70 / S80 Petrol & Diesel (98 - 05) S to 55	4263

DIY MANUAL SERIES

Title	Book No.
The Haynes Air Conditioning Manual	4192
The Haynes Car Electrical Systems Manual	4251
The Haynes Manual on Bodywork	4198
The Haynes Manual on Brakes	4178
The Haynes Manual on Carburettors	4177
The Haynes Manual on Diesel Engines	4174
The Haynes Manual on Engine Management	4199
The Haynes Manual on Fault Codes	4175
The Haynes Manual on Practical Electrical Systems	4267
The Haynes Manual on Small Engines	4250
The Haynes Manual on Welding	4176

* Classic reprint

Preserving Our Motoring Heritage

< The Model J Duesenberg Derham Tourster. Only eight of these magnificent cars were ever built – this is the only example to be found outside the United States of America

Almost every car you've ever loved, loathed or desired is gathered under one roof at the Haynes Motor Museum. Over 300 immaculately presented cars and motorbikes represent every aspect of our motoring heritage, from elegant reminders of bygone days, such as the superb Model J Duesenberg to curiosities like the bug-eyed BMW Isetta. There are also many old friends and flames. Perhaps you remember the 1959 Ford Popular that you did your courting in? The magnificent 'Red Collection' is a spectacle of classic sports cars including AC, Alfa Romeo, Austin Healey, Ferrari, Lamborghini, Maserati, MG, Riley, Porsche and Triumph.

A Perfect Day Out

Each and every vehicle at the Haynes Motor Museum has played its part in the history and culture of Motoring. Today, they make a wonderful spectacle and a great day out for all the family. Bring the kids, bring Mum and Dad, but above all bring your camera to capture those golden memories for ever. You will also find an impressive array of motoring memorabilia, a comfortable 70 seat video cinema and one of the most extensive transport book shops in Britain. The Pit Stop Cafe serves everything from a cup of tea to wholesome, home-made meals or, if you prefer, you can enjoy the large picnic area nestled in the beautiful rural surroundings of Somerset.

John Haynes O.B.E., Founder and Chairman of the museum at the wheel of a Haynes Light 12. >

< Graham Hill's Lola Cosworth Formula 1 car next to a 1934 Riley Sports.

The Museum is situated on the A359 Yeovil to Frome road at Sparkford, just off the A303 in Somerset. It is about 40 miles south of Bristol, and 25 minutes drive from the M5 intersection at Taunton.
Open 9.30am - 5.30pm (10.00am - 4.00pm Winter) 7 days a week, *except Christmas Day, Boxing Day and New Years Day*
Special rates available for schools, coach parties and outings Charitable Trust No. 292048